World Religions

A Historical Approach

World Religions

A Historical Approach

Third Edition

S. A. Nigosian
University of Toronto, Victoria College

Bedford/St. Martin's
Boston ◆ New York

For Bedford/St. Martin's

Developmental Editor: Jane B. Smith
Senior Editor, Publishing Services: Douglas Bell
Production Supervisor: Cheryl Mamaril
Project Management: Books By Design, Inc.
Marketing Manager: Karen Melton
Text Design: Books By Design, Inc.
Cover Design: Lucy Krikorian
Cover Photo: Tony Stone Images/Don Lowe
Composition: Thompson Type
Printing and Binding: Haddon Craftsman,
          an R. R. Donnelley & Sons Company

President: Charles H. Christensen
Editorial Director: Joan E. Feinberg
Editor in Chief: Nancy Perry
Director of Editing, Design, and Production: Marcia Cohen
Manager, Publishing Services: Emily Berleth

Library of Congress Catalog Card Number: 99-62275

For information, write: Bedford/St. Martin's, 75 Arlington Street, Boston, MA 02116   (617-426-7440)

ISBN: 0-312-15268-X   (paperback)
      0-312-22757-4   (hardcover)

Published and distributed outside North America by:
MACMILLAN PRESS LTD
Houndmills, Basingstoke, Hampshire RG21 6XS and London.
Companies and representatives throughout the world.

ISBN: 0-333-72722-3

A catalog record for this book is available from the British Library.

This volume is dedicated to
my family
not out of sentimentality
but with a deep sense of gratitude and affection.

Foreword

This third edition of *World Religions: A Historical Approach* provides an opportunity to ask why the demand for it continues. Basically, of course, it is its clear presentation of the substance of each faith under similar headings such as Background, Founders, Scriptures, Teachings, Observances, and so on. But there are other attractive features: The presentation of the history of a whole spectrum of faith, ancient and modern, is presented succinctly and with a genuine attempt at fairness; also included are more recent faiths, such as Baha'i; concerns of current interest, such as the changing position of women; descriptions of festivals and Holy Days; and with our new interest in ecology we are led to appreciate aboriginal attitudes to Nature in both North and South America.

Here you find yourself watching the moving stage of the human drama through the great systems of faith, thought, and action that have won the allegiance of millions.

And finally, by showing how different faiths in the past influenced each other in their development, we are led to question what may be the result of a mutual sharing of insights in the shaping of today's "global village."

Kingsley J. Joblin
Emeritus Professor of Religion
University of Toronto, Canada

Preface

This book had its genesis in 1990. Since then, the subject matter has been recast and appropriate modifications and additions have been made. This third edition, under the new title, *World Religions: A Historical Approach*, is a revision of the second edition of *World Faiths*. The change in title clarifies the approach and purpose of our study. But its essential character remains intact: namely, that of a general survey of the religious traditions of the world, both living and extinct. As such, it provides a clear, straightforward account of the development, doctrines, scriptures, and practices of the more influential religions of the world. This means that each chapter includes the origin of a religion, followed by its historical development, division of groups, sacred writings, principal teachings, and major observances and festivals. Traditional viewpoints as well as scholarly opinions are presented in a balanced and accurate manner.

Additional features in each chapter include study aids such as maps, timelines, photographs, study questions, and a list of suggested reading. Seventeen maps (six of which are new to this edition) illustrate the distribution of religions as well as provide a sense of geographical reality to the historical discussions presented. The timelines (which have been redesigned and simplified) recapitulate the historical development of each religious tradition. The narrative captions accompanying the photographs (one-third of which are new) offer an insight into the characteristics of each tradition. Study questions (which have been added to every chapter) are a mix of those that require students to summarize what they have learned from the chapter and those that require deeper analysis and interpretation. The latter may often provide natural springboards for class discussion, or may serve as topics for short papers.

In prior editions, an extensive bibliography was provided at the end of the book. This has been replaced by a list of suggested reading for further study or research placed at the end of every chapter. As before, there is a glossary at the end of the book, which provides brief explanations of technical terms.

INSTRUCTOR'S MANUAL

An eighty-page instructor's manual has been prepared for this third edition. Its purpose is to provide instructors with a source book (or file) for selecting essay topics, discussion questions, term tests, and final examinations. The order of chapters in the manual follows the textbook. Instructors who wish to receive a copy should write to Bedford/St. Martin's, Faculty Services, 33 Irving Place, New York, NY 10003, or contact your Bedford/St. Martin's Sales Representative. You may also fax your request to the attention of Faculty Services (212) 995-5003.

ACKNOWLEDGMENTS

No project of this magnitude can be accomplished without the help of others. A word of thanks is therefore in order. I want to acknowledge once again my debt of gratitude to all those who were involved with the success of the first two editions. Next, I want to offer special thanks to all those who were directly concerned with this third edition. To the following reviewers for their helpful suggestions: Stephen W. Angell, Florida A&M University; Robert Gnuse, Loyola University; Steven R. Johnson, California State University-Fullerton; Garrett C. Kenny, Eastern Washington University; J. E. Llewellyn, Southwest Missouri State; Aruna Mathur, University of Western Ontario, Huron College; Preston L. McKever-Floyd, Coastal Carolina University; Robert J. Miller, Midway College; Craig Payne, Indian Hills Community College; and Laeron A. (Tony) Roberts, Tarrant County Junior College—Northwest. To the staff of Bedford/St. Martin's, particularly to Jane Smith for her indefatigable support in seeing this edition into production and to Doug Bell for his guidance thereafter; to Debbie van Eeken for her tireless labors; and last, but not least, to my wife, for her magnificent support.

S. A. Nigosian

Contents

Foreword   vii

Preface   ix

Maps and Timelines   xvii

About the Author   xix

1   Understanding Religion   1

    An Intellectual Inquiry   1
    The Study of Religion   2
    The Origin of Religion   4
    Definitions of Religion   5
    Approaches and Goals   7
    Study Questions   9
    Suggested Reading   9
    Notes   10

2   Prehistoric Religion   11

    Human Skulls   11
    Bear Skulls   12
    Corpses   14
    Works of Art   15
    Stone Structures   17
    Study Questions   19
    Suggested Reading   19

3   Hinduism   20

    Origins   20
    Hindu Social Structure   22
    Hindu Sacred Texts   27
    Hindu Teachings   29

Hindu Reform Movements   46
Popular Hinduism   49
Hindu Observances   51
Study Questions   55
Suggested Reading   56
Notes   57

4 Jainism   **58**

Mahavira   58
The Twelve Vows of Jainism   61
Jain Groups   62
Jain Sacred Texts   63
Jain Teachings   64
Jain Observances   66
Study Questions   67
Suggested Reading   67
Notes   67

5 Buddhism   **68**

The Buddha   68
The Spread of Buddhism   74
Buddhist Sacred Texts   80
Buddhist Teachings   80
Buddhist Groups   86
Buddhist Observances   92
Study Questions   99
Suggested Reading   100
Notes   101

6 Taoism and Confucianism   **102**

Early Chinese Religion   104
Taoism   112
Confucianism   119
Chinese Observances   131
Study Questions   134
Suggested Reading   135
Note   136

7   Shinto   137

    Defining Shinto   137
    Ancient Records   140
    The Development of Shinto   141
    Shinto Observances   158
    Study Questions   161
    Suggested Reading   161
    Note   162

8   Egyptian Religion   163

    Egyptian Civilization   163
    Egyptian Religious Thought   164
    Egyptian Mythology   171
    Egyptian Observances   172
    Study Questions   174
    Suggested Reading   175
    Notes   175

9   Mesopotamian Religion   177

    Mesopotamian Civilization   177
    Mesopotamian Religious Thought   180
    Mesopotamian Mythology   181
    Mesopotamian Observances   182
    Study Questions   185
    Suggested Reading   185
    Notes   185

10 Greek Religion   186

    Early Greek Religion   187
    Intellectual Views   190
    Popular Religion   192
    Mystery Religions   195
    Festivals   197
    Hellenistic Syncretism   199
    Study Questions   199
    Suggested Reading   200
    Notes   201

11   Roman Religion   **202**

Roman Religion   203
Foreign Accretions   207
Festivals   213
Study Questions   214
Suggested Reading   214

12   Zoroastrianism   **216**

Zoroaster   216
The Spread of Zoroastrianism   220
Zoroastrian Sacred Texts   221
Zoroastrian Teachings   222
Zoroastrian Observances   228
Study Questions   233
Suggested Reading   234

13   Judaism   **235**

Biblical Tradition   237
The Rise and Development of Judaism   243
Jews under Christian and Muslim Rule   249
Jewish Groups in the Middle Ages   252
Modern Jewish Groups   253
The Bible   254
The Talmud and the Midrash   257
Jewish Teachings   258
Jewish Observances   262
Study Questions   267
Suggested Reading   268
Note   269

14   Christianity   **270**

The Roman Empire   270
Jesus Christ   272
Teachings Attributed to Jesus   275
Paul   279
Early Christianity   281
Christianity in the Middle Ages   288

Christianity in Modern Times   293
The Bible   298
Christian Teachings   300
Christian Observances   303
Study Questions   307
Suggested Reading   308
Notes   309

15   Islam   310

Understanding Islam   310
Muhammad, Messenger of God   311
Islamic Empires   315
Islam in Modern Times   322
Islamic Groups   325
The Qur'an   327
Islamic Law and Jurisprudence   330
Articles of Faith   333
The Pillars of Islam   336
Holy War (Jihad)   339
Islamic Observances   340
Study Questions   341
Suggested Reading   342

16   Sikhism   344

Guru Nanak   345
The Development of Sikhism   347
Sikh Sacred Text   349
Sikh Teachings   350
Sikh Groups   352
Sikh Observances   353
Study Questions   355
Suggested Reading   355
Notes   355

17   African Traditions   356

Historical Overview of Africa   356
African Traditional Religions   362

2

Basic Common Views   366
Religious Activities   371
Study Questions   375
Suggested Reading   376
Note   377

18 American Indian Traditions   378

Ancient Civilizations   378
Modern American Indians   386
Basic Common Views   387
Ceremonials   393
Study Questions   396
Suggested Reading   397
Notes   398

19 Baha'i   399

The Origin and Development of Baha'i   399
Sacred Writings   403
Baha'i Teachings   403
Baha'i Observances   407
Study Questions   409
Suggested Reading   410
Notes   410

20 Religions: A Comparison   411

Unity or Diversity   413
Comparison of Paths   414
Comparison of Goals   416
East-West Comparison   417
Study Questions   419
Suggested Reading   419
Notes   420

Glossary   423

Index   433

Maps and Time Lines

Maps

Distribution of the Major
  Religions of the World   *inside front cover*
Prehistoric Sites   13
Hinduism   22
Jain Centers   63
Spread of Buddhism   75
China and Japan   105
Japan   142
Ancient Egypt   168
Ancient Mesopotamia   179
Ancient Greece   189
The Roman Empire   207
Zoroastrian Centers   221
Jewish Population of the Diaspora   241
Christianity at the Time of the Schism, 1054   287
Early Islam   316
African Peoples   360
American Indian Traditions   388

Time Lines

Prehistoric Religion   12
Hinduism   21
Jainism   59
Buddhism   69
Taoism and Confucianism   103
Shinto   138
Egyptian Religion   164
Mesopotamian Religion   178
Greek Religion   187

Roman Religion   203
Zoroastrianism   217
Judaism   236
Christianity   271
Islam   311
Sikhism   345
African Traditions   357
American Indian Traditions   379
Baha'i   400

About the Author

Solomon Alexander Nigosian is Research Associate at the University
of Toronto, Victoria College, where he teaches World Religions and
Hebrew Bible/Old Testament. His numerous books include *Judaism:
The Way of Holiness*, *Islam: The Way of Submission*, and *The Zoroastrian
Faith: Tradition and Modern Research*. Dr. Nigosian received the Excel-
lence in Teaching Award from the University of Toronto, School of Continuing Studies.

1 Understanding Religion

The historical, critical, and comparative study of the religions of the world as an object of intellectual inquiry dates from the last decades of the nineteenth century, although its roots are much older.[1] In 1870, the expatriate German philologist Friedrich Max Müller wrote what is generally considered the foundation document of comparative religion in the English speaking world. According to Müller, who spoke at the Royal Institution in London on February 19, 1870,

> A Science of Religion, based on an impartial and truly scientific comparison of all, or at all events, of the most important, religions of mankind, is now only a question of time. It is demanded by those whose voice cannot be disregarded.[2]

At the turn of the twentieth century, Louis Henry Jordan produced the first lengthy handbook of the study of comparative religion, in which he defined the emergent discipline in these words:

> Comparative Religion is that Science which compares the origin, structure, and characteristics of the various Religions of the world, with the view of determining their genuine agreements and differences, the measure of relation in which they stand one to another, and their relative superiority and inferiority when regarded as types.[3]

More than a hundred years separate us from the world that produced scholars who claimed that the study of religion belonged among the sciences and that their field of inquiry should be called the *science of religion.* No such "science" appears to exist. Instead, the term *religious studies* has been in use, and it is significant to note that the terms *history*

1

of religion and *comparative religion* have not been altogether abandoned. In fact, in the world of scholarship, the study of world religions implies the serious, critical examination of material drawn from the diverse religious traditions of the world. We use that method to summarize the results of critical investigations that have engaged the attention of scholars past and present. But first, let us deal with four basic issues: (1) the study of religion, (2) the origin of religion, (3) definitions of religion, and (4) approaches and goals.

THE STUDY OF RELIGION

The study of religion, like almost all academic disciplines, has no one method of inquiry or approach accepted by all scholars. Instead, there are many approaches and many methods, and a single specialist cannot pretend to possess more than a general acquaintance with all the agendas that form part of the study of world religions.

Interest in the study of world religions is not peculiar to the twentieth century, although it has been evident primarily in Western rather than Eastern cultures. On the whole, approaches to understanding other religions grew out of attempts to defend, to criticize, or to interpret religious faiths in harmony with the development of knowledge.

The rise and spread of Christianity provided the early Church Fathers with a standard by which to understand and assess the various religious movements and philosophical systems that flourished in the vast Greco-Roman world. That standard not only helped them to confirm the overall skeptical attitude of ancient Greek and Roman philosophers toward religion, it also provided them with a rationale for dismissing divergent beliefs as irrelevant to the worship of the one true God.

In the thirteenth century, European travelers (such as Marco Polo, an Italian) came in contact with Asian peoples and returned with knowledge of Asian religions. Their reports opened the way for an inductive (fact-based) treatment of those religions. The ongoing interest in the systematic documentation of religions around the world, made possible by the explorations of lands hitherto unknown to Europeans in the sixteenth, seventeenth, and eighteenth centuries, prepared the way for the development of modern analytical methods for the study of world religions.

The growth of various academic disciplines (such as history, archaeology, philology, philosophy, anthropology, sociology, and psychology) in the latter half of the nineteenth century compelled scholars to develop improved scientific procedures for an objective, analytical approach to the study of world religions. At least five basic methodologies can be distinguished: philosophical, sociological, psychological, phenomenological, and historical. These five approaches represent the application of modern critical techniques to the study of world religions, and each of the five is in some way invaluable to the study of world religions.

Philosophy of Religion

For many years, the study of religion was principally the province of theologians and philosophers. Consequently, matters of faith and belief, of truth and falsehood, and of revelation and reason often served as both the starting point and the principal focus of inquiry. Three main trends currently are discernible in the scope of the philosophy of religion: (1) an analysis of religious language, (2) an analysis of the nature of religion in the general framework of a world view, and (3) a philosophical justification or rejection of various religious positions. Thus, theological arguments, metaphysical systems, moral and ethical issues, and many other similar matters arising from philosophical discussions have come under critical examination by all those who apply the tools of philosophy.

Sociology of Religion

The basic unit of study among sociologists is not the individual personality but the network of relationships that bind people in cohesive groups called *societies.* Somewhat related to sociologists are social anthropologists, who have made important contributions to the study of religion, particularly through studies of primitive and tribal peoples. The sociological method is applied to crucial issues such as how religion contributes to social integration and what function religion serves in the social complex of which it is a part. Thus, both sociologists and anthropologists emphasize the importance of religion through its cultural symbols and expressions.

Psychology of Religion

The study of religious psychology involves, among other things, the collection and classification of psychological data, the investigation of religious responses as correlated with various personality types, the testing of various psychological explanations, the examination of the religious symbols and practices that aid or impede individuals in working out personal problems, and the bearing of religious issues on the integration of personality. Some researchers also conduct empirical investigations into the effects of mystical and meditative experiences and drug-induced states of consciousness.

Phenomenology of Religion

Phenomenologists believe that every human activity is relevant to the study of whatever "phenomenon" on which they are focusing. To the phenomenologist who focuses on religion, music, painting, sculpture, labor, and any other product of human endeavor must be observed and analyzed in terms of its potential to illuminate and explain the phenomenon of religious faith. Thus, the phenomenological approach to religion is to identify a general pattern and define its essential elements. Significant contributions have been made by this method, especially in the comparison of one religious form with another.

History of Religion

Historians of religion study religious behavior through the sequences of events or series of transformations that characterize the evolution of various religious traditions into their current forms or up to the points at which they vanished. Historians consider religions as specific traditions that encompass fundamental beliefs, important practices, and institutionalized systems, all of which have gone through complex courses of development and transformation. Unraveling the process of religious development requires special skill and scientific knowledge. The contributions made in the last few centuries by historians, archaeologists, philologists, classicists, and Orientalists, among others, are invaluable to scholars who apply the historical method to understand religion. Because of the profound impact of religion on the course of human civilization, we use the historical model in this text.

THE ORIGIN OF RELIGION

At the beginning of the modern era, several attempts were made to explain the origin of religion in terms of its supposedly universal characteristics. Chief among those objective analyses were philological, sociological, and psychological theories proposed in the late nineteenth and early twentieth centuries.

Perhaps the most influential philologically based theory was proposed by Friedrich Max Müller (1823–1900), who suggested that religion arose out of the myths and cults based on original personification of natural phenomena. Rejecting that view in favor of a sociological perspective, Herbert L. Spencer (1820–1903) located the origin of religion in early experiences of ghosts (later identified as spirits and later yet as gods), who were thought to be the heroic ancestors of a particular tribe or group. Spencer said that, because a person's first reaction to the experience of ghosts is fear, emotion is the fundamental cause of all religion. Enlarging on Spencer's views, Edward B. Tylor (1832–1917) suggested belief in souls as the origin of religion, and James G. Frazer (1854–1941) pointed to totemic rites designed to promote the social solidarity or well-being of a group or tribe. It remained for Karl Marx (1818–1883) to offer the most sweeping sociological theory, that religion is "the sigh of the oppressed creature . . . the opiate of the people."[4]

Psychologically motivated theories of the origin of religion grew out of the works of Sigmund Freud (1856–1939). In Freud's estimation, religion arose from humanity's infantile wish to defend itself from the forces and terrors of life. In that sense, religion represents the rationalization of human delusions and deceptions — the insistent but unrealistic wishes of humanity. Following Freud, others suggested that religion arose as a result of the appearance in dreams of deceased members of the tribe, which led to the belief in the existence of spirits.

Although all those theorists made significant contributions in other ways to the study of religion, their attempts to explain the origin of religion have long been discredited. One weakness of such theories is that they were based on speculation about prehistoric times and therefore impossible to verify. The origins of religion, like those of many other human activities, are lost in humanity's unrecorded past.

DEFINITIONS OF RELIGION

No matter when or how human beings developed, from the time they became human, the irresistible urge to worship has created — and still creates — endless forms of religious behavior. Indeed, so powerful is that force in humans that it has produced a mosaic of beliefs, attitudes, and practices. Wherever people are found, from the great metropolitan cities to the smallest villages, one can find temples, shrines, and other monuments as expressions of religious life. In fact, religious ideas and practices orient billions of people everywhere at all times. Myths, doctrines, rituals, narratives, tales, legends, art, music, and dance all offer meaning and guidance to religious life. A very basic question, therefore, is this: What is religion?

The Christian theologian Augustine (354–430) once said, "If you do not ask me what time is, I know; if you ask me, I do not know."[5] The same point applies to the terms *religion* and *religious*. At first sight, the terms appear to be self-evident or self-explanatory, yet they defy precise definition because they carry different meanings for different people.

Etymological Definitions

The term *religion* is derived from the Latin term *religio,* the etymology of which is disputed. Some scholars have tried to connect *religio* with other Latin terms, such as *relegere* (to reread), *relinquere* (to relinquish), and *religare* (to relegate, to unite, to bind together). The root word *religare,* particularly when applied in the sense of persons being bound to God or to superior powers, has been the most common, or classical, understanding. But is it satisfactory?

Proposed Definitions

Most definitions of religion are satisfactory, up to a point. Most explain religion in terms of worship, belief, feeling, attitude, and conduct. In other words, some definitions emphasize the intellectual function; some stress the emotional function; others express the worship function; still others relate religion to individual experience or emphasize the social or psychological function. Whoever estimated that there are ten thousand definitions of religion probably understated the case. It is impossible, of course, to examine all ten thousand definitions, but it is useful to analyze a few.

To say that one is religious only through belief in God is to restrict the meaning of religion to intellectual activity, thus excluding all those who, like the Buddhists, act and behave very much like conventional religious believers but do not believe in a god. Similarly, to say that one is religious only when one feels an experience is to restrict the meaning to emotional activity. Human beings possess multiple capacities: we think, feel, and act inwardly as well as outwardly. Hence, the concept of religion cannot be tied solely to either the concept of God or that of feeling.

Equally inadequate is any definition of *religion* and *religious* in terms of participation in a particular faith, which thereby excludes all those outside that faith. It is also misleading to define religion as a code of ethics or of morals, since people can reject all religions yet maintain high moral and ethical standards. Belief in a religion or loyalty to a particular faith is no guarantee of moral or ethical behavior. The pages of human history are filled with accounts of "religious" people who committed immoral acts in the name of religion.

To say that religion is awe or wonder or love is to say nothing at all, because a flash of lightning or a flight of birds can inspire awe or wonder, and love is as often equated with self-indulgence or self-gratification as it is with self-sacrifice. Awe, wonder, and love are only aspects of religion.

The preceding definitions generally fall into one of two categories: those that seek to define religion in terms of human attitudes and relationships and those that seek to define it in terms of the human motivation underlying those attitudes. In other words, one category of definition seeks to explain *what* religion is by analyzing human attitudes and behavior, whereas the other seeks to explain *why* religion is a factor in human affairs by analyzing the motives behind human attitudes and behavior.

No one, for instance, can study themes of art or forms of architecture without some reference to the impetus provided by religion. Similarly, one cannot learn about music and poetry without somehow mentioning the influence of religious inspiration. History, sociology, and anthropology cannot be taught or interpreted without consideration of religious customs and practices. To discuss psychology without reference to religion as a force that motivates, regulates, influences, and even directs the behavior of many individuals is almost impossible. What is true of those disciplines is also true, to a greater or lesser degree, of politics, economics, philosophy, and medicine.

An important point is that the term *religion* has little, if any, significance to non-Western people. The national Japanese "religion" (to use the Western label) is Shinto, meaning the "way of the gods"; Buddhism is described as the "Noble Eightfold Path"; Confucius called his teaching "the Way"; and the term Taoism derives from Tao, which also means "the Way."

The terms *religion* and *the Way* can be considered two different explanations of a worldwide phenomenon. To non-Western people, "the Way" means a process, a concept that implies direction and therefore relation to a goal or purpose. Western people, on the other hand, are more concerned with the concept of a person, which implies a relationship between (let us say) God and human beings.

Founders of Faith

Those two distinctive ways of understanding religion are best reflected in the lives of the world's religious leaders who created the faiths that have endured for centuries.

Certain individuals possess a unique, uncommon, or rarefied quality of the mind. They see and hear in the "mind's eye and ear" that which is hidden from the sight and hearing of ordinary people. Their vision takes the shape of an extraordinary revelation (a Western notion) or a profound insight (an Eastern notion). So powerful is this mode of thinking that the thinker's mind soars in time and space, moves beyond reason, visualizes and generates ideas, alters the course of events, and creates or invents another order of existence or reality beyond this life.

Such individuals are possessed and haunted by fixed and besetting images that are ascribed either to an internal source known as insight, awareness, or consciousness (an Eastern notion) or to an external source known as revelation (a Western notion). This imaginative experience is immediately translated as "Ultimate Reality" or "Absolute Truth." Finally, through the labor of the individual and usually of several supporters or disciples, the image takes organic form and body; it is realized in actions, customs, and laws and imposes itself on millions of people.

In that way, organized religion — with its elaborate temples, shrines, mosques, and churches; its complex systems of rituals related to the stages of life; its sacred festivals and solemn observances; its hymns, prayers, and occult activities; its formulations of moral and ethical codes; its legacy of holy books, sacred narratives, and basic beliefs— originates in the imaginative projection of a religious innovator.

Often, it is difficult to fully understand and appreciate the nature or behavior of religious innovators. Statements made by their disciples affirm the paradoxical (i.e., natural-supernatural or human-divine) character of these religious masters. Some followers regard them as incarnations of a divine being or a cosmic principle; others consider them to be infallible individuals, possessing the power of dissimulation, transmigration, or resurrection.

Whatever ambiguities they exhibit in behavior or character, religious geniuses initiate radical and massive changes in civilization because their religious perception appeals to large segments of society. Such geniuses help shape the course of human history, instituting actions by which whole governments and societies are organized. They break with custom, with accepted values, with tribal and societal loyalties, with time-honored traditions, with fixed patterns. They strongly react against established religious systems, openly challenge ancient beliefs, and courageously threaten prescribed rituals. They set their own norms and lead people to yet another vision of truth or reality. They express their experiences in terms of the inconceivable. They make demands that are difficult and at times unintelligible. Their influence begins at once —that is, during their lifetimes—because they actively proclaim their religious perceptions and experiences as eternal truths. That becomes intelligible only in the light of knowledge about the history of world religions.

APPROACHES AND GOALS

The goal of this text is to introduce the reader to the study of world religions, for which purpose the historical model offers the most advantages. Consequently, we examine certain basic religious features from the point of view of history and the historical interactions of religions.

TABLE 1.1   RELIGIONS OF THE WORLD

Name of Religion	Country of Origin	Name and Date of Founder	Distribution in the Modern World
Hinduism	India		India and throughout the world.
Jainism	India	Mahavira (c. 599–527 BCE)[a]	India.
Buddhism	India	Gautama (Buddha) (c. 563–483 BCE)	Adherents found all over the world.
Taoism	China	Li-Poh Yang/ Lao-Tzu (?) (? 6th cent. BCE)	Far East, including China and Japan.
Confucianism	China	K'ung-Fu-Tzu (c. 551–479 BCE)	Far East, including China and Japan.
Shinto	Japan		Japan.
Zoroastrianism	Persia (Iran)	Zarathustra (c. 628–551 BCE)	Iran, India. Adherents also found in Britain, Europe, USA, and Canada.
Judaism	Palestine (Israel)	Moses (? 13th cent. BCE)	Israel and throughout the world.
Christianity	Palestine (Israel)	Jesus (Christ) (4 BCE–29 CE)[b]	Adherents found all over the world.
Islam	Arabia	Muhammad (c. 571 CE–632 CE)	Adherents found all over the world.
Sikhism	India	Nanak (1469–1539 CE)	India. Adherents also found throughout the world.
Baha'i	Iran	Baha'u'llah (1817–1892 CE)	Adherents found all over the world.

[a]Before the Common Era.
[b]Common Era.

This choice of method, in turn, dictates the selection of world religions. Obviously we must choose from the hundreds of religious traditions and systems, past and present, historical and prehistorical. Many were once active but have since disappeared. Others are still as active and viable today as they were centuries ago. In modern times, new religious groups are proliferating on a global scale.

Our attempt, then, is to describe in a historical context the following religions, stretching from prehistoric to modern times: Prehistoric religion, Hinduism, Jainism, Buddhism, Taoism and Confucianism, Shinto,

Egyptian religion, Mesopotamian religion, Greek religion, Roman religion, Zoroastrianism, Judaism, Christianity, Islam, Sikhism, modern African traditions, modern American Indian traditions, and Baha'i. Each chapter deals with the traditional viewpoint as well as the latest scholarly opinion on the subject under discussion. The discussion includes an analysis of the following:

- origin of religious tradition
- growth and spread
- sacred texts or literature
- central concepts and philosophical views
- important practices and ceremonies

This book will help the reader understand the values that individual religions give to their followers and how people in different times and under different circumstances thought, felt, and acted.

STUDY QUESTIONS

1. Which of the five methodologies for the study of religion do you consider to be most valuable? State your reasons.
2. Name several major theories of the origin of religion.
3. What would you consider to be the most inclusive definition of the term *religion*?
4. How does an object of intellectual inquiry differ from a creed to be followed?
5. What do you expect to learn from the study of world religions?

Suggested Reading

Bowker, John W. *The Sense of God: Sociological, Anthropological and Psychological Approaches to the Origin of the Sense of God.* Oxford: Clarendon Press, 1973.

Carter, Robert E. (ed.). *God, The Self, and Nothingness — Reflections: Eastern and Western.* New York: Paragon House, 1990.

Eliade, Mircea. *The Sacred and the Profane: The Nature of Religion.* New York: Harper & Row, 1961.

Livingston, James C. *Anatomy of the Sacred: An Introduction to Religion.* New York: Macmillan, 1989.

Roberts, John Morris. *History of the World.* New York: Oxford University Press, 1993.

Smith, Wilfred Cantwell. *The Meaning and End of Religion.* New York: Mentor Books, 1962.

Thomas, Hugh. *An Unfinished History of the World,* rev. ed. London: Papermac, 1995.

Wulff, David M. *Psychology of Religion: Classic and Contemporary Views.* New York: John Wiley & Sons, 1991.

Notes

1. One of the first books to trace the history of the subject in great detail is E. J. Sharpe, *Comparative Religion: A History* (New York: Charles Scribner's Sons, 1975).

2. F. M. Müller, *Introduction to the Science of Religion* (London: Longmans, Green, and Co., 1873), p. 34f.

3. L. H. Jordan, *Comparative Religion: Its Genesis and Growth* (Edinburgh: T. & T. Clark, 1905), p. 63.

4. Karl Marx, "Contribution to the Critique of Hegel's Philosophy of Law," *Marx, Engels on Religion* (Moscow: Progress Publishers, 1957), p. 39.

5. Augustine, *The Confessions of St Augustine,* trans. E. B. Pusey (London: J. M. Dent & Sons, 1957), p. 262.

2 Prehistoric Religion

Religion is virtually as old as the human scene itself. No matter when or how human beings developed, from the time they became human, religious ideas and practices have been part of humanity's experience. Even in prehistoric civilizations, the discovery of sculptures, paintings, engravings, and cult objects all point to the religious nature of human beings.

Our knowledge of the religious practices of prehistoric people comes from archeologists and anthropologists who painstakingly uncover, catalog, and interpret artifacts and cultural remains. Yet, precisely when, where, and how religion originally emerged are matters of conjecture. Discoveries by archeologists are the principal source of data, but the difficulty lies in the fact that for the most part the data are confined strictly to discoveries or finds that have escaped the destructive forces of time: human and animal skeletal remains, stone tools, cult objects, sculptures, paintings, and engravings. The best type of archaeological evidence relating to prehistoric religion is skeletal remains. The treatment of the human corpse—its disposal, its position, the objects placed by it, and the types of graves used—provides the most valuable information for reconstructing the religion of early human beings.

HUMAN SKULLS

Several reliable finds dating from the prehistoric period at various sites in Germany (Mauer and Steinheim), England (Swanscombe), France (Fontéchevade), Italy (Monte Circeo), Croatia, China (Dragon-bone Hill, near Choukoutien), and elsewhere seem to offer some proof of cultic or religious customs. From those sites, skeletal remains of several human beings, quantities of animal bones, a few hearths, human skull fragments, and heaps of cherry pits have been identified. No mat-

Prehistoric Religion

BCE

c. 600,000 Cult of human skulls
c. 100,000 Cult of bear skulls; cult of the dead
 c. 30,000 Works of art
  c. 5000 Rise of civilizations in ancient Near East
  c. 3000 Invention of writing in ancient Near East; beginning of recorded history

ter how one tries to explain the discoveries, two elements are worth noting. First, the skeletal remains appear to have been scattered about indiscriminately, just like the animal bones. Second, the human skulls, as well as a number of animal bones, show signs of injuries or of having been split open. In fact, most of the human and animal bones are greatly damaged and partially burned.

Those facts have led many scientists to conclude one or more of the following theories about early human beings:

- They practiced cannibalism and considered the human brain and marrow delicacies.
- They practiced cannibalism of a ritual nature connected with some belief in magic properties of the human brain and marrow.
- They preserved human skulls or scalps as trophies, family relics, or souvenirs.
- They assigned human skulls and other bones some special role in human settlements, though what that role was cannot be established with any degree of certainty.
- They carried about skulls of dead persons as expressions of fidelity and pious remembrance.
- They venerated human skulls and bones as the indestructible relics of the dead and as possessing magico-religious powers and potency.

No matter how ingenious or intriguing such theories are, one thing is certain: the ideas and religious conceptions bound up with the cult of the skulls are not immediately discernible.

BEAR SKULLS

Animal remains from the prehistoric period also are available from numerous sites and illuminate an interesting aspect of the religious sphere of early humans. One of the most contended possessions of early humans was the skull of the enormous cave bear, and Alpine caves present the most fascinating bear cult practices.

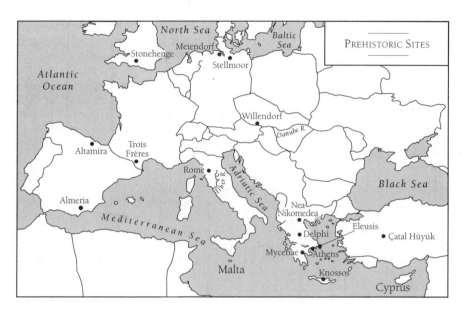

Source: David S. Noss and John B. Noss, *A History of the World's Religions*, 9th ed. (New York: Macmillan, 1994). Reprinted by permission of Prentice-Hall/Pearson Higher Education.

The richest finds come from the Swiss Alps (Drachenloch and Wildenmannlishloch caves), the southern German Alps (Petershohle cave), and the Austrian Alps (Salzofen cave). Partly intact, bear skulls were found arranged in groups, and in most cases the first of two cervical vertebrae were distinguishable. According to scientists, only human hands could have performed the decapitation. At any rate, the two most remarkable finds in the caves of the Swiss Alps were seven well-preserved cave bear skulls in a stone-made chest and fifteen cave bear skulls set in niches on the wall of the cave. The latter skulls lay on stone slabs bordered by other slabs and covered by a protective slab.

As for the finds in the foothills of the southern German Alps, excavators discovered a tremendous collection of bear skulls and bones in niches or on stone platforms along the walls of the remotest part of Petershohle cave. The cave was also rich with charcoal deposits. In the Austrian Alps, cave bear skulls also were found in nichelike hollows in the innermost cave wall and covered with thick charcoal. Near each skull some bear limb bones lay in orderly arrangement and orientated from east to west.

Remarkable finds like those are not confined to the Alps. In Mornova cave in Slovenia, a bear skull with its lower jaw missing was found in a niche. Directly above the skull and across it lay several unimpaired limb bones. In Furtins cave in France, seven cave bear skulls arranged in a distinctive concentric pattern on a stone slab were uncovered.

From such discoveries, we know that early humans displayed cave bear skulls and limb bones with unmistakably pious care in the remotest and darkest parts of caves. But what were the religious concepts underlying those rituals? Interpretations vary from the purely secular to the highly religious. According to one theory, the finds are evidence of an ancient supply depot, or a kind of storage cellar. Another theory holds that the discoveries point to the practice of storing brains and marrow either as delicacies or as tanning agents for skin treatment. Still another theory explains the discoveries as hunting trophies. A theory that favors a religious interpretation explains the remains partly in terms of an animal cult and magic and partly in terms of sacrifice to a superior power.

Undoubtedly, there is something here more than mere disposal of bear skulls. It seems that the humans who placed the skulls in the caves sought, for one reason or another, to guard them from damage and desecration. While it may be impossible to know the precise rubrics connected with the skull ceremonies or the beliefs associated with them, it must be admitted that early humans performed some sort of cave bear skull ritual.

CORPSES

More important than the cult of bear or human skulls is the cult of corpses. Numerous prehistoric graves discovered in Asia, Europe, and other areas indicate the attitudes of early humans toward death. For instance, two skeletons found in the Kiik-Koba cave on the Crimean Peninsula were those of a man and a male baby. The man's skeleton lay on its right side, with legs slightly contracted, in a trench dug in the cave floor. The infant's skeleton lay on its left side, with the left hand placed under the left knee, only a few feet away from the man. The skeleton of a woman, lying on its back and with the lower jaw of a man nearby, was found in Et-Tabun cave in Israel. Ten skeletal remains—five men, two women, and three children—were discovered in Es-Sukhul cave in Israel. In all cases, the legs were completely contracted, but the positions and the directions the skeletons faced varied considerably. In Teshik-Tash cave in Uzbekistan, the damaged skeleton of a child encircled by ibex horns was found.

Excavations in Europe have yielded various interesting burial sites. In France, the skeleton of a youth lying on its right side, with legs slightly bent and head supported by a pillow of flint flakes resting on the right arm, was discovered at Le Moustier. Next to the skeleton were animal bones, a flint scraper, and a hand axe. In a cave at La Chapelle-aux-Saints, a male skeleton was found lying in a trench with animal bones, flint tools, and lumps of red ochre beside it. At the entrance of the cave was a hearth containing charred bones and their ashes. In a cave at La Ferrassie, the skeletal remains of a woman, a man, and four children were discovered. Much like the other sites, near the corpses were flint tools, quantities of animal bones and ashes, and a limestone slab marked with cup-shaped depressions. All the skeletons, with the exception of the woman's, were oriented east to west in the direction of the setting sun.

All those finds clearly indicate concern over and special treatment of human corpses. But what were the beliefs underlying such attitudes? Many scholars consider the care bestowed on the disposal and ornamentation of human corpses evidence of a cult of the dead with a belief in an afterlife. That inference is based on several pieces of evidence.

First, the implements left next to the corpses seem intentional and appear to indicate the equipment necessary for the departed to obtain provisions in the afterlife. If that assumption is correct, then life in the world beyond was conceived to be virtually identical to life on earth. Yet there is no way of knowing whether the world beyond was in any way associated with the idea of a god or divine being or with the idea of just rewards and punishments.

Second, the flexed positions of the skeletons are assumed to be either an imitation of sleep and rest, symbolic of the fetal position (presupposing prehistoric humans' knowledge of prenatal forms), or an attempt to prevent the dead from returning and molesting survivors. The ashes also are regarded as a magical covering that no corpse could breach, keeping it confined to its grave.

Third, the deposits of red ochre are thought to be associated with a life-giving principle and therefore security for a renewal of life in the hereafter. As for the vast numbers of animal bones, it is generally assumed that the survivors held funerary feasts, either in memory of the deceased ancestors or as sacrificial meals. In the latter case, it is impossible to determine whether the offerings were made to solicit good fortune, protection, or any other favors.

Of course, any theories are hypothetical. Yet the positioning of the corpses, the implements placed beside them, the numerous animal bones, the ashes, and the red ochre all seem to describe some sort of religious practice or cult of the dead.

WORKS OF ART

One of the most remarkable achievements of early humans is their artwork. Precisely where and when humans started to create works of art and what prompted them to do so are, admittedly, difficult to discern. Nevertheless, numerous paintings and sculptures indicate the use of artwork as part of magical rituals.

Some of the earliest works of art date earlier than 10,000 BCE and are found on rock surfaces inside the darkest recesses of caves in Europe. Images of animals, such as bison, deer, horses, wild boars, reindeer, cave bears, and mammoths, are incised, painted, and sculpted on the walls and ceilings of caves and rock shelters. Because the images are hidden away in almost inaccessible places, as if to protect them from the casual intruder, it is often supposed that they served a purpose far more serious than public display or mere decoration. In fact, there is little doubt that they were produced as part of a magic ritual to ensure a successful hunt.

The magical use of the works of art of early humans is also suggested in several other clear examples. A vivid mural in the cave of Les Trois

Prehistoric painting of the "Dancing Sorcerer" from the cave of Les Trois Frères at Ariège, France. The image depicts a shaman (or possibly a "spirit" engaged in a hunting dance) wearing a costume made of reindeer antlers, the ears of a stag, the eyes of an owl, the beard and feet of a man, the paws of a bear, the tail of a horse, and a patchwork of animal skins.

Courtesy of the American Museum of Natural History.

Frères at Ariège, France, shows an image that is part human, part animal. The image has the antlers of a reindeer, the ears of a stag, the eyes of an owl, the beard and feet of a human, the front paws of a bear, and the tail of a horse. Modern experts believe the representation to be that of a sorcerer or shaman engaged in a magical hunting ritual.

Similarly, the cave of Niaux at Ariège has the image of an engraved and painted bison whose body is punctured with spears and darts. The image indicates one magical assumption of early humans: like produces like. The walls of the caves of Addaura in Sicily have incised drawings of animal and human figures in dancelike poses, representing some sort of magical ritual.

Another category of prehistoric artwork comprises sculptures and carvings in stone, bone, and horn. Early humans saw in those materials certain representational qualities that rendered them magical. Numerous tiny sculptures of nude female figures dating before 10,000 BCE have been discovered all over Europe and Asia. In most of the figurines, like the famous "Venus" found at Willendorf, Austria, the head generally is blank and represented as a mere knob, while the breasts, abdomen, and buttocks are extremely large. It is believed that such figurines were symbols of maternity or female fertility and may have been used as charms or in fertility rituals. A mural painting in the rock shelter of Cogul, Spain, also attests to the existence of prehistoric fertility rituals. Nine women are depicted surrounding a nude male, who seems to be the leader in a ritual connected with fertility magic.

Carved and modeled animal figurines have also been discovered in central Europe and southern Russia. Carved ivory representations of mammoths and lions and clay models of rhinoceroses, tigers, wolves, reindeer, and other animals all seem to indicate that the religion of early humans was based on magic for hunting or for reproductive processes.

A group of sculpted human skulls discovered in Jericho, Jordan, dating from 10,000 to 7000 BCE also indicates the use of magic rituals. Faces

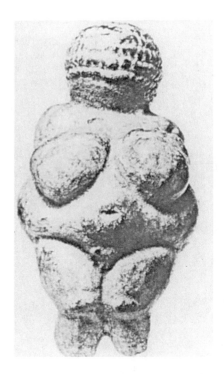

The Great Goddess, or the so-called Venus of Willendorf. The exaggerated breasts, hips, and abdomen suggest that this image was connected with fertility or mother-goddess rituals.

Courtesy of the American Museum of Natural History.

modeled in plaster with seashells for eyes were added to existing skulls. In the view of some scholars, the heads were not intended to "create" life but to perpetuate it beyond death. Apparently, the sculpted faces were "spirit traps," designed to keep the spirits or souls of the departed in their original place (the head) to ensure their beneficent presence over the fortunes of later generations. That theory is based on the circumstances in which the sculpted skulls were discovered: they were above ground, while the rest of the corpse was buried.

STONE STRUCTURES

Other discoveries dating from 7000 to 3000 BCE include various collective tombs and sacred monuments in Europe. Structurally, the tombs consist of two types: those in which the grave room or chamber is approached by a long passage and those in which there is a single chamber, sometimes with a small antechamber. The tombs with long passages have walls made from dry stone or large rocks or are walled and roofed by megalithic (i.e., large stone) slabs.

Although the tombs are quite impressive, other structures that are, in some respects, of greater interest are the remarkable "sacred" monuments of megalithic construction found in France and Great Britain. Those monumental structures consist of huge blocks or boulders placed on each other without mortar. Some, known as *menhirs*, are single stones on end. Others, known as *dolmens*, are two upright stones bridged by a

A close view of Stonehenge, Britain's prehistoric monument dating from about
2200–1300 BCE, situated on Salisbury Plain in the county of Wiltshire in southern
England. Stonehenge consists of a circular earthwork about 200 feet in diameter,
within which is a ring of fifty-six small pits, at the center of which is the circle of standing
stones seen in this photograph. The heaviest stone on the site weighs fifty tons.
Courtesy of the British Travel Association, British Consulate-General, Toronto, Canada.

single giant slab for a roof. Still others, known as *cromlechs,* form a circular structure. Then there are the alignments, or rows of stones, that
extend over several miles, like the one in Carnac, France.

The function of such megalithic monuments has often been debated,
but many scholars insist that the impressive structures were in some way
connected with religious observances. For instance, the structure at
Stonehenge, in England, is a huge circular enclosure consisting of evenly
spaced upright stones supporting horizontal slabs. Two inner circles are
similarly formed, with an altarlike stone at the center. The entire monument apparently is oriented toward the exact point of sunrise on the day
of the summer solstice (about June 22), thereby leading to one conclusion—that Stonehenge was a sacred spot for sun-worshiping rituals.

STUDY QUESTIONS

1. Describe the principal sources of data for understanding prehistoric religion.
2. Discuss the theories proposed by scientists regarding discoveries of human skulls.
3. Identify the religious interpretations that explain the discoveries of cave bear skulls.
4. What evidence clearly indicates the practice or cult of the dead?
5. Explain the discoveries that signify the belief of magical rituals.
6. Identify the massive structures and monuments that suggest religious ceremonies.
7. Examine the theories proposed by modern scholars for the origin of religion.

Suggested Reading

Biaggi, Cristina. *Habitations of the Great Goddess.* Manchester, Ct.: Knowledge, Ideas and Trends, 1994.

Burl, Aubrey. *The Stonehenge People.* London: Barrie & Jenkins, 1989.

Castleden, Rodney. *The Making of Stonehenge.* London/New York: Routledge, 1993.

Dickson, D. Bruce. *The Dawn of Belief: Religion in the Upper Paleolithic of Southwestern Europe.* Tucson: University of Arizona Press, 1990.

Gimbutas, Marija Alseikaite. *The Language of the Goddess: Unearthing the Hidden Symbols of Western Civilization.* San Francisco: Harper & Row, 1989.

Jacobsen, Esther. *The Deer Goddess of Ancient Siberia: A Study in the Ecology of Belief,* vol. 55 of *Studies in the History of Religions.* Leiden, The Netherlands: E. J. Brill, 1993.

Maringer, Johannes. *The Gods of Prehistoric Man.* New York: Alfred A. Knopf, 1960.

North, John David. *Stonehenge: Neolithic Man and the Cosmos.* London: HarperCollins, 1996.

Souden, David. *Stonehenge Revealed.* London: Collins & Brown, 1997.

Pager, Harald L. *Stone Age Myth and Magic as Documented in the Rock Paintings of South Africa.* Graz, Austria: Akademische Druck, u. Verlagsanstalt, 1975.

Pfeiffer, John E. *The Creative Explosion: An Inquiry into the Origins of Art and Religion.* Ithaca, N.Y.: Cornell University Press, 1985, c1982.

Wainwright, Geoffrey. *The Henge Monuments: Ceremony and Society in Prehistoric Britain.* London: Thames & Hudson, 1990.

3 Hinduism

Hinduism, one of the oldest surviving religions, is practiced by millions of people in the vast subcontinent of India. Unlike most other religions of the world, Hinduism has no identifiable founder. There have been many great teachers in its history, but no one individual is considered by all Hindus as the founder of Hinduism. Instead, the earliest scriptures of the Aryans, the *Vedas,* have always been acknowledged to embody the primordial truths on which Hinduism bases itself.

The chief concern of Hindu religious conviction is not the existence or nonexistence of God or whether there is one God or many gods. Hindus can choose to be monotheists, polytheists, pantheists, atheists, agnostics, dualists, monists, or pluralists. They may or may not follow strict standards of moral conduct, spend time on everyday religious rituals, or attend a temple. Magic, fetishism, animal worship, and belief in demons coexist, supplement, and accompany profound theological doctrines, asceticism, mysticism, and esoteric beliefs. Religious truth, according to Hinduism, is not conceived necessarily in dogmatic terms, because truth transcends all verbal definitions. Consequently, Hinduism represents an astonishingly complex conglomeration of doctrines, cults, rituals, practices, observances, and institutions.

ORIGINS

The Aryans

India, like the Middle East, has given birth to several religious movements. Excavations from two ancient sites, Harappa and Mohenjo-daro, in the area of the Indus Valley (modern northwest Pakistan), indicate that a civilization flourished there about 2500 BCE. Modern scholars think that sometime between 2000 and 1500 BCE, migrating bands of people invaded the area of the Indus Valley and for the next thousand years extended their influence all over India. Those wandering, warlike

Hinduism

BCE

c. 2500 Evidence of Indus Valley civilization
c. 1500 Aryan invasion of northern India
c. 800   Creation and development of the Vedas
c. 600   Composition of the Upanishads; appearance of Hindu caste system
c. 200   Compilation of Code of Manu
c. 100   Composition of Bhagavad Gita

CE

c. 200   Beginning of Vedanta system of thought
c. 788   Birth of Shankara (d. 820)
c. 800   Teaching of Advaita Vedanta philosophy by Shankara
1017   Birth of Ramanuja (d. 1137)
c. 1100 Defense of Vaisnava tradition by Ramanuja
c. 1200 Beginning of Muslim domination of India
c. 1500s Introduction of Christianity
1526   Founding of Mogul Empire by Babar (1526–1707)
1653   Completion of Taj Mahal in India
1757   Beginning of British domination of India (ended 1947)
1828   Founding of Brahmo Samaj
1869   Birth of Mohandas Gandhi (d. 1948)
1875   Founding of Arya Samaj
1905   Founding of anti-British, nationalist societies in Bengal
1947   Independence of India; establishment of Pakistan as separate Muslim state; partition of Punjab
1948   Assassination of Mohandas Gandhi
1950   India becomes a republic
1984   Assassination of Indira Gandhi by Sikh extremists
1992   Destruction of Muslim mosque at Ayodhya, India, by Hindu militants

invaders called themselves Aryans (meaning "noblemen" or "landlords") and their religion *ārya-dharma* (meaning "Aryan law" or "Aryan way of life"). Today, Hindus consider the Aryans and their religion their source and inspiration, even though many aspects of Hinduism may well have been inspired by the Indus Valley civilization and regional tribal cultures of India.

The Term *Hindu*

The term *Hindu* is a corruption of the word *Sindhu*, the Sanskrit name for the Indus River (now mainly in Pakistan). The Persians, who found it difficult to pronounce an initial *s*, called it *Hindu*. From Persia, the word passed to Greece (and later to the West), and the corruption of the word engendered other words like *Hinduism, Indus,* and *India*.

HINDUISM

○ City	∴ Indus Valley city
● Hindu pilgrimage sites	⋯⋯ Early Vedic Culture
➤ Probable route of Aryan invaders	– – – Late Vedic Culture
⦓ Mountain pass	

Today, the word *Hindu* usually is applied only to members of the Hindu religion, and many Hindus have appropriated the designation to distinguish themselves from the followers of other religious traditions, such as Buddhists, Muslims, and Christians. Some Hindus, however, prefer to define their religion in a more restricted fashion, that is, by their particular caste or community. But the most common description that Hindus give to their religion is *sanatana dharma,* meaning "eternal law."

HINDU SOCIAL STRUCTURE

Caste

The characteristic that most distinguishes the Hindu religion from other religions is its system of social stratification, called *varna* (literally "color"). This Hindu system of *caste,* or *jati* (literally "birth"), has no historical counterpart in terms of persistence, continuity, and pervasive consequences long after the circumstances that gave it credence in tradition had been forgotten. Scholars can only speculate as to its origins. Some maintain that the caste system developed out of the multiracial nature of Indian society, although it is not clear whether that development predated or postdated the arrival of the Aryans. Others explain caste as a discriminatory system of color differentiation imposed by the lighter-skinned Aryan conquerors on the darker-skinned Dravidians. For whatever reasons, the class system grew and expanded, eventually evolving into a highly complex system comprising some three thousand distinct groups.

In theory, there are four major classes: the *brahmana* or *brahmin,* the *kshatriya,* the *vaisya,* and the *sudra.* The division into only four classes in all probability is theoretical, because references to a much more complicated structure date back to the earliest times. Nevertheless, analysis of the four main social classes adequately serves to describe the caste system, which represented a division of labor based on accidents of birth and which was justified by moral and religious concepts.

The traditional duties or obligations of the four groups were ranked as follows. In the first rank were the *brahmins,* who occupied the central place of power in Hindu society. The *brahmins* were priests, the spiritual and intellectual leaders of society. They devoted their time to studying, teaching, performing sacrifices, and officiating at religious services. Second came the *kshatriyas,* who as rulers, warriors, and nobles protected, administered, and promoted the material welfare of society. Third in rank were the *vaisyas,* who as farmers, merchants, and traders contributed to the economic well-being of the society. Fourth were the *sudras,* who as laborers and servants supplied the manual labor or service needed by the first three groups.

Eventually, a fifth category emerged, the *chandalas,* or "untouchables," whose status was so low that they belonged to no class at all and were excluded from communal ritual. In some parts of India, *chandalas* were forbidden access to certain public roads and bazaars. They often were required to identify themselves as untouchables as they walked, so members of higher castes could avoid them. They were not allowed entrance to certain temples and were not permitted to draw water from public wells except those designated for their use.

Linked with and justifying such social stratification was the religious justification of *karma* (action) and *samsara* (reincarnation): social status as determined by birth. Each individual's birth into a particular class was considered to be determined by the past *karma* of that person. Birth into a *brahmin* class, for example, was a consequence of good *karma* accumulated in previous existences. Status as a *sudra* or any lower form of life (i.e., an animal or a plant) implied *karma* in previous existences that merited no better status. The following quotation from the Hindu scriptures makes the point quite clearly:

> Those whose conduct here [on earth] has been good will quickly attain some good birth—birth as a brahmin, birth as a kshatriya, or birth as a vaisya. But those whose conduct here has been evil will quickly attain some evil birth—birth as a dog, birth as a pig, or birth as a chandala. (Chandogya Upanishad 5.10.7)

In that view, birth determined class, which in turn defined an individual's social and religious status, the duties and obligations that such status required, and the restrictions that applied to all aspects of everyday life (food, clothing, occupation, marriage, social intercourse, civil rights, and religious duties). In time, each class made its own rules and established its own customs and values.

The Role of Women

The various Hindu codes of law that developed over the centuries prescribed the different duties of castes and defined the role of women in society. The views proposed in the Code of Manu concerning women are explicit. From birth to death, a woman is to be protected by — that is, under the control of — her father, husband, or son. Here is how it is stated:

> In childhood a female must be subject to her father; in youth, to her husband; when her lord [husband] is dead, to her sons. A woman must never be independent. She must not seek to separate from her father, husband or sons. (Manu 5.148–149)

In no way, then, are women considered to be equal to men or even to be free members of the family or caste. The Code lists the various disciplines that men are to impose on women to guarantee "proper behavior" by the latter. The assumption is that uncontrolled women tend to be emotional, sensual, violent, and potentially destructive to social order.

Proper behavior for a woman means an arranged marriage by her father at the proper time, usually soon after puberty (in some localities, child marriage is still a common practice). Monogamy is the rule, but polygamy is customary in many communities. The next proper duty of a woman is to respect, obey, and worship her husband, even if he is unfaithful, virtueless, and devoid of good qualities.

> Him to whom her father may give her, or her brother with the father's permission, she shall obey as long as she lives. Though destitute of virtue, or seeking pleasure elsewhere, or devoid of good qualities, a husband must be constantly worshiped as a god by a faithful wife. (Manu 5.151–154)

The ideal couple in Hindu thought is represented by the epic story of Rama and his wife, Sita, in the Ramayana. Rama represents the concern, sensitivity, and tenderness of a male lover, whereas Sita's pleas, tears, and utter devotion reflect the behavior appropriate to women. Although Rama boasts that none can guard Sita better than he in the perilous forest, she is stolen away by the demon Ravana, only to be rescued by Rama's friend, the monkey god Hanuman. Even so, the onus is on Sita, the victim, to prove her fidelity.

Thus, a husband's duty is to protect his wife from threats inherent both in society and in a woman's nature. That ensures the purity and virtue of their offspring. Besides fulfilling her proper obligations to her husband and occupying herself with household duties, a bride is expected to become a member of her husband's family. That means, as a rule, the subjugation of every wife to the will of her mother-in-law.

After her husband's death, a woman of whatever age, be it fifteen or sixty-five, may not remarry. She is to live quietly, patiently, and chastely until death:

> She must never mention the name of another man after her husband has died. Until death let her be patient, self-controlled, chaste and strive to fulfill that most excellent duty which is prescribed for wives who have one husband only. (Manu 5.157–158)

If she lacks sons to protect her, a widow is expected to fast, sleep on floors, and live as an ascetic dressed in "widow's weeds." Should she violate that duty, she "brings on herself disgrace in this world, and loses her place with her husband in heaven" (Manu 5.160–161).

Traditionally, a widow was expected to accompany the corpse of her husband to the funeral pyre and be burned alive by his side *(sati)* on the assumption that a woman who outlived her husband had caused his death by her evil *karma*. How widespread the practice of *sati* was and is in India is uncertain, but attempts have been made in modern times to eradicate it.

Although the role and the status of women in Hindu society are, from the point of view of Western life, unenviable, conditions are gradually improving since Prime Minister Indira Gandhi's tenure in office. Exemptions from caste and other social constraints are being worked out. Women are able to pursue certain careers, and religious restraints on their civil liberties are being re-evaluated. Despite opposition to the introduction of Western influences, ancient traditions are slowly changing, particularly among upper-class and well-educated Hindus.

The Stages of Life

Another social structure that is closely connected to the caste system is the Hindu observance of *ashrama* (stage of life), which dates from about 500 BCE. Just as birth determines a Hindu's status, *ashrama* prescribes a specific set of duties and responsibilities for each of the four stages in the lives of male Hindus in the three upper castes, who often are known as "twice-born." The four stages, corresponding to youth, adulthood, middle age, and old age, are termed *brahmacarin, grihashta, vanaprastha,* and *sannyasin.*

The stage of the *brahmacarin,* or student, starts after a boy undergoes a ceremony between the ages of eight and twelve in which he becomes a full-fledged member of his caste. From that point until the boy reaches the age of twenty to twenty-four, he is disciplined and instructed by his *guru* (teacher), whom he obeys and serves with absolute humility.

The second stage, that of the *grihashta,* or householder, is the longest of the *ashramas,* lasting until middle age. During this period, the Hindu is supposed to lead an active married life and apply with particular rigor the three ideals of social living associated with this stage in life: the observance of accepted religious duties, the accumulation of wealth, and the enjoyment of pleasure (including sensual pleasures).

A *sadhu* (wandering holy man) who has broken ties with the world and its ordinary social duties to enter the fourth stage of life as a *sannyasin* (renouncer). The typical garb of a *sadhu* is rags, and he carries a begging-bowl, a water pot, a staff, and a few other meager possessions. The *sadhu* is treated with great respect by young and old alike.

From the private collection of the author.

The stage of the *vanaprastha*, or forest dweller, starts when the householder's hair begins to turn grey or when his first grandson is born. Accompanied by his wife (if she so wishes), he leaves home and retires into the forest to lead a life of reflection and meditation. There, as a hermit, he is expected to concentrate on developing a complete detachment from everything in the world to which he was previously attached.

In the fourth and last stage, a pious Hindu becomes the *sannyasin*, or renouncer. This stage begins when the forest dweller feels spiritually ready to leave the forest life and begin the life of a wandering ascetic. Renouncing all former ties (including his wife, if she has been with him in the forest), the *sannyasin* becomes a homeless nomad released from material desires, attachments, and possessions. His goal is to attain liberation from rebirth or reincarnation (see p. 34–36).

The four stages of life largely remain doctrine rather than practice. The last two stages are honored more in spirit than in observance, except among a few *brahmins*, who often live apart in a small cottage or in a room in their home compound.

HINDU SACRED TEXTS

The Hindu attitude toward Hinduism's sacred writings is eclectic. Although hundreds of sacred texts are considered authoritative, there is no equivalent of the Christian Bible or the Muslim Qur'an, that is, no single, definitive text. Instead, Hindu scriptures are classified into two categories: *shruti* and *smriti.*

Shruti

Shruti means "hearing" and applies to a group of writings that represent eternal, sacred knowledge. They were revealed to *rishis,* or seers, and transmitted orally for generations by *brahmins.* The *Vedas,* the *Brahmanas,* the *Aranyakas,* and the *Upanishads* are among the most important of the *shruti.*

The Vedas. The *Vedas* (bodies of knowledge), composed between 1500 and 800 BCE, consist of four collections known as the Rig-Veda, the Sama-Veda, the Yajur-Veda, and the Atharva-Veda. The Rig-Veda is a collection of about one thousand hymns, mostly prayer and praise, to either a single deity or a group of deities. The Sama-Veda consists mainly of rhythmic chants borrowed from the Rig-Veda. The Yajur-Veda contains, in addition to verses taken from the Rig-Veda, many original prose passages dealing with sacrificial ritual. The Atharva-Veda, a special class of texts, deals with charms, magical spells, incantations, and kingly duties.

The Brahmanas. The *Brahmanas* are a voluminous body of writings that describe in exhaustive detail ritual observances and sacrifices and discuss the mystical meanings of various rites. Each of the four Vedas is supplemented by its own Brahmana or Brahmanas, which probably were written between 800 and 300 BCE.

The Aranyakas. The *Aranyakas,* or Forest Books, which supplement the Brahmanas, were written mainly for the religious aesthete who chooses to retire to the isolation of the forest and thus is unable to perform ritual sacrifices. They are esoteric in content and are concerned with the innermost nature of humankind and the universe.

The Upanishads. The *Upanishads,* a large group of writings attached to the end of the Aranyakas, contain the basic philosophic framework of Hinduism. They are viewed as the "culmination of sacred knowledge" (Vedanta), and their importance to those who seek a nonritualistic type of religion and insight into the oneness of things through self-consciousness can scarcely be exaggerated. As a collection of speculative texts composed by many authors, the Upanishads do not attempt to present a logical, coherent view of reality. They probably were composed over a period of three to four centuries, from 800 to 500 BCE.

Smriti

Smriti means "memory" and identifies writings that represent tradition: knowledge remembered and transmitted from generation to generation. The Epics, the Code of Manu, and the Puranas are significant examples of *smriti.*

The Epics. The Epics consist of two great literary works, the Mahabharata and the Ramayana. The Mahabharata, the longer of the two, is the longest epic in world literature, over seven times the combined length of the Iliad and the Odyssey. (Strictly speaking, the Mahabarata is not entirely epic, since more than half of it deals with politics, law, religion, and other topics.) The entire work probably was completed by the second or third century CE. Within the Mahabharata are three famous stories greatly loved by Hindus, including the Bhagavad-Gita (Song of the Lord). That immortal poem, produced about the second century BCE, is written in the form of a dialog between a warrior and the Blessed Lord Krishna, disguised as the warrior's charioteer, and emphasizes the Path of Devotion as the way of liberation from rebirth. A number of Hindu movements base their teachings on the Bhagavad-Gita.

The Ramayana recounts the story of a prince called Rama who is exiled to the forest for fourteen years because of a rival half-brother and the intrigues of a jealous mother. In the meantime, Sita, Rama's ever-faithful wife, is abducted by a wicked demon. Unable to find her, Rama is aided by his friend Hanuman, the monkey, who succeeds in restoring Sita to her husband. Rama, Sita, and Hanuman have long since been deified, and they remain objects of worship for millions of Hindus.

The Code of Manu. The Code of Manu, compiled some time before the second century CE, is accepted by most branches of Hinduism as the most complete expression of Hindu sacred law. Manu is traditionally acknowledged as the father of humankind (somewhat like Adam) and of the social and moral orders. The book includes marriage laws, dietary regulations, the duties of various castes, civil and criminal laws, and daily rites and sacrifices, as well as statements on a variety of ethical subjects. Although many practices and rules no longer are followed in rigid detail, the laws still exert an enormous cultural influence on Hindus.

The Puranas. The Puranas are a collection of ancient lore, mythological data (on the genealogy of gods, sages, and kings), and descriptions of the creation, destruction, and re-creation of the universe. The texts, eighteen of which are generally held to be authoritative, represent the product of theistic developments during the fourth to the eighth centuries CE. Closely linked with the Epics in origin, the Puranas are the scriptures of the common folk, because they are accessible to everybody, including women (whose status in Hinduism is lower than that of men) and the lowest members of the society.

Yoga Sutras

The Yoga Sutras represent ascetic techniques and meditational exercises that aim to free an individual from the continuous change of the material world in order to recapture one's original spiritual purity. Although the Yoga Sutras may not have been compiled before the second century CE, it is clear that the techniques and exercises they describe are much more ancient.

HINDU TEACHINGS

The central beliefs of Hinduism cluster around three concepts: Absolute Reality, Rebirth, and Liberation.

Absolute Reality

Generally, Hindu thought represents Absolute Reality as male-female. The female aspect is represented as energetic, violent, emotional, and potentially destructive; the male aspect is cool, dispassionate, and serene. The goddess Kali is one of the most dramatic representations of the feminine aspect of Absolute Reality, but Hindu theology often juxtaposes opposites to heighten the transcendent quality of male-female reality. Inconsistency and contradiction are not issues in Hindu thought, as long as one understands the ineffability of infinity. Hindu epics blend theology, romance, poetry, dramatic stories, and models of human behavior to suggest the oneness of all opposites, including divine-human and male-female.

Vedic Deities. The gods and goddesses of early Hinduism (also known as Vedic religion) can be derived from its sacred texts, especially the Vedas. In that work, numerous deities, called *devas,* are identified with powers and functions associated with natural phenomena: celestial, atmospheric, and terrestrial.

The most important celestial deities are Varuna, Mitra, and Vishnu. Varuna, the sky god, maintains cosmic order and protects moral action. Conceived of as the creator of the universe, he rules by the standard of rite, that is, an ordered form of procedure or the proper course of things. Mitra, the sun god (corresponding to the Iranian god Mithra), stimulates life and brings prosperity to humans, animals, and vegetation. He is infinitely benevolent and omnipresent, the chief assistant to Varuna, and the benefactor of humanity. Vishnu, the third in the triumvirate of celestial divinities, is distinguished by his "three strides," which encompass earth, atmosphere, and paradise. Another of Vishnu's distinguishing attributes is his ability to appear in this world in various incarnations, or *avatars,* the most famous of which is his *avatar* as the divine-human Lord Krishna.

The most important atmospheric deity is Indra, the thunder god. As the model and champion of the Aryan warrior, he is appealed to for help in waging successful warfare against the human enemies of the Aryans. Other deities in the atmospheric pantheon are Vayu, the wind god; Parjanya, the rain cloud god; a troop of storm gods called Maruts; and Kudra, the father of the Maruts. Rudra, the god of violence, destruction, disease, and death, defines and controls the limits of atmospheric catastrophes. Those who invoke Rudra's name do so in the expectation that he will prescribe healing remedies that will protect them from his anger and destruction.

Among the terrestrial group of deities are Agni, the fire god, and Soma, the god of libation. Agni is identified with the sacrificial fire (called *agni*), the most important symbol of Hindu worship. Consequently, he is the progenitor of humankind, the lord of good fortune, and the first *hotar* (sacrificial priest). Agni is viewed as the divine agent who acts on behalf of humanity and mediates between the universe and, on the one hand, the public, official cult of the temple and, on the other, everyday life and the private, domestic cult of the home. He is the primordial element that sustains all creation and is omnipresent, even in water, since rain accompanies lightning, another manifestation of fire.

The list of major deities is filled out by numerous female divinities, including Surva, the sun goddess; Dhishana, the fertility goddess; and Sarasvati, the patron goddess of language, literature, and knowledge.

Supplementing the functions of the major figures are "helper" deities, responsible for, among other things, creating prosperity and happiness, healing sickness, contracting marriages, protecting roads and pastures, and getting people out of bed each morning. The helper god whose importance and popularity has survived to the present day is Shiva, thought of as the "lord of creatures" and depicted as the great ascetic, with an erect penis, his symbol. Shiva's animal companion is Nandi, the bull on which he rides.

No less popular than Shiva are his numerous consorts. One of them, Kali (also called Durga), is particularly revered. A more terrible divinity than Shiva, Kali is frequently depicted as drinking blood, tearing away the flesh of sacrificial animals, and wearing a necklace of human skulls. Hindu mythology also connects her with the founding of Calcutta.

The Vedic religion evolved over time into a ritualistic cult, a complex system of sacrifices, an elaborate class of priests to officiate at a host of esoteric rites, and ecstatic ascetics who became known for transcending the limits of the physical body. Various ceremonies in which spells, incantations, and occult practices were emphasized occupied the center of the Hindu religious stage. Eventually, the ritual of sacrifice by fire came to dominate Hindu religious life. Agni, the god of fire, became the sacrificial fire itself, the medium by which Hindus related to the other deities. In fact, the deities themselves were said to have performed sacrifices to attain divine status. Sacrifice was (and still is) not regarded merely as a ceremony offered to the deities or as a symbolic gesture representing reality but as reality itself. Through sacrifice, the adherent learns of reality, or truth.

The One. As the various sacrificial rites developed, spoken formulas, called *mantras,* came to be considered as formulations of truth in sound: in other words, *mantras* were thought to embody in their sounds truth, or reality. *Mantras* were not viewed as the only means of expressing truth, however. Thought, which was defined as internalized speech, offered yet another aspect of truth. And if words and thoughts designated different aspects of truth, or reality, there had to be an underlying unity behind all phenomena. That unity, or the One, constituted hidden and unmanifested reality. Belief in the One meant that the deities no longer could be considered creators of the universe but only components of it, divine expressions of the entire cosmic order. Who or what, then, was the creator or origin of the multiple forms and appearances of truth?

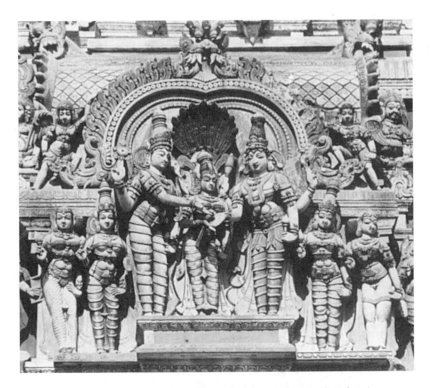

Carvings and decorative details of Hindu temples are superb examples of ancient Indian art. Reliefs such as those depicted at Meenakshi Temple in Madurai show scenes from the lives of gods and goddesses.
Courtesy of Government of India Tourist Office, Toronto.

One answer to that question was that the universe originated in a cosmic human sacrifice. In that view, *Purusha,* the original cosmic Man, produced gods from himself, who in turn made a sacrifice of Purusha:

> Purusha alone is all this universe, what has been, and what is yet to be. . . . All creatures are one-fourth of Him; three-quarters are the immortal heaven. . . . When the gods performed the sacrifice with Purusha, Spring was melted butter, Summer the fuel, and Autumn the oblation. The gods, the celestial beings, and the seers performed the sacrifice with Him. (Rig-Veda 10.90)

The basic significance of this quotation is clear: creation is a sacrifice, and all celestial beings, as well as the universe and everything in it, are Purusha. That conclusion had such an impact that eventually sacrifices came to be regarded as a cosmic ritual. In other words, the sacrificial ritual performed by the priests came to be regarded as a creative act. But that view was only one among several that were being shaped.

Other profound thinkers were questioning the nature of the universe and the role of the deities vis-à-vis the universe and human beings. Their search for a unity in the totality of things led them to belief in a nameless, all-originative One.

They call it Indra, Mitra, Varuna, Agni; or it is the heavenly Sun-bird. That which is One, the seers speak of in various terms. (Rig-Veda 1.164)

Most arresting was the emergence of the view that before anything was created, before the universe existed or the deities had come into being, there was a great, unnamed cosmic reality, a neutral principle or activity, simply referred to as *Tad Ekam,* or That One.

Then was not nonexistent nor existent; there was no realm of air, no sky beyond it. What covered in, where and what gave shelter? Was water there, unfathomed depth of water? Death was not then, nor was there aught immortal; no sign was there, the day's and night's divider. That One breathed without breath by its own nature; apart from it was nothing else whatsoever. Darkness there was; at first hidden by darkness, this All was indiscriminate chaos. All that existed then was void and formless: by the great power of warmth That One was born. Who truly knows and who can here declare it, whence it was born and whence came this creation? The gods are later than this world's production. Who knows, then, whence it first came into being? He, the first origin of this creation, whether he formed it all or did not form it, Whose eye controls this world in highest heaven. He verily knows it, or perhaps he knows not. (Rig-Veda 10.129)

The imagery is unambiguous. Before anything existed or did not exist, before there was any realm of air or sky, before there was any death or deathlessness, before there was light or darkness, day or night, there was only That One. From the void, formless, and indiscriminate chaos emanated That One, the generative principle and impelling force behind all creation.

Out of such philosophical speculations grew the idea that knowledge alone, without recourse to ritual observances, might reveal cosmic unity — the unmanifested reality, the ultimate truth. In other words, it was believed that all ritual sounds and actions could be performed in the mind and that mental performance would yield the same results as external ritualistic performance. An individual, then, could meditate on and search for the hidden meaning of sacrifice, that is, reality. In their search for inner connections between the cosmic principle of creation, the universe, and human beings, Hindu thinkers discovered equivalents or identities everywhere.

Brahman-Atman.   The ancient, ritualistic Vedic religion, with its elaborate sacrifices, gradually gave way to the idea of Brahman-Atman, a concept that is difficult to grasp, because it attempts to define the undefinable and transcendent. *Brahman* is Absolute Reality, which transcends time, space, and causality. Brahman pervades the entire universe and yet remains beyond it. Moreover, Brahman is all that is objective as well as subjective. In other words, Brahman is the whole external world, as well as the whole inner being—the self, or soul—of an individual, a beast, a bird, a fish, or a rock. That innermost and unseen force, or self, of a human, animate, or inanimate object is called *Atman*. And Atman is Brahman.

These concepts are expressed most fully—and most beautifully—in the Upanishads. Consider this verse:

> Verily in the beginning this was Brahman; that Brahman knew its
> Atman only, saying, "I am Brahman." From it all this sprang. . . .
> Now also he who thus knows that he is Brahman becomes all this.
> (Brihadaranyaka Upanishad 1.4.1)

The most significant contribution of the Upanishads to the Hindu religion is the idea of the utter oneness of Brahman-Atman. The identification of the individual self with the universal Self in a mystical experience establishes the existence of a reality that is infinite, unlimited, directly perceived, and spiritual. Neither philosophical speculation nor any kind of reasoning can penetrate deeper than this metaphysical reality: the nonduality of existence. Hence, Hindus do not believe that a person is created in the image of God; rather, they believe that a person is God, or divine. The universe, with everything in it, including human beings, is not to be considered as something apart and distinct from the Absolute Being; it *is* the Absolute Being. There is no subject-object, no "I"and no "you." The Absolute is not "up there" or "beyond," but within. The First Principle of things must not be sought in the external, but rather in one's innermost self. Thus, the true self of a person and the Absolute Universal Self are one; they are identical. That identity is most emphatically expressed in a famous formula: *tat tvam asi*, which means "That art thou."

Hindu religious literature attempts to explain the concept of identity by analogy and illustration. For example, just as honey is the nectar of different flowers, so Brahman is the Atman of every living and nonliving being.

> "As bees, my dear," explains the father to his son, "make honey by
> collecting the juices of trees located at different places, and reduce them
> to one form; and as these juices have no discrimination (so as to be able
> to say): 'I am the juice of this tree,' or 'I am the juice of that tree'—even
> so, indeed, my dear, all these creatures, though they reach Pure Being,
> do not know they have reached Pure Being. . . . Now that which is the
> subtle essence—in it all that exists has its self. That is the True. That is
> the Self. That art thou." (Chandogya Upanishad 6.9.1–2)

Again, just as a river originates from the sea as moisture and precipitation, only to merge once more with the sea, so does the individual Atman emerge from Brahman and return to a source or origin that is substantially one.

> "Please, venerable Sir, give me further instruction," says the son. "So be
> it, my dear," Uddalaka replies. "These rivers, my dear, flow—the east-
> ern towards the east, and the western towards the west. They arise from
> the sea and flow into the sea. Just as these rivers, while they are in the
> sea, do not know: 'I am this river' or 'I am that river,' even so, my dear,
> all these creatures even though they have come from Pure Being, do not

know that they have come from Pure Being. . . . Now, that which is subtle essence—in it all that exists has its self. That is the True. That is the Self. That art thou." (Chandogya Upanishad 6.10.1–3)

Brahman-Atman is, therefore, Absolute Reality. There is no subject-object, no creator and creature, no "I" and "you," no "I" and the "universe"—there is simply the identity of everything. The Absolute Reality pervades everything.

> "Place this salt in water and then come to me in the morning." The son does as he is told. Uddalaka says to him: "My son, bring me the salt which you placed in the water last night." Looking for it, the son does not find it, for it is completely dissolved. The father says: "My son, take a sip of water from the surface. How is it?"
> "It is salt."
> "Take a sip from the middle. How is it?"
> "It is salt."
> "Take a sip from the bottom. How is it?"
> "It is salt."
> "Throw it away and come to me."
> The son does as he is told, saying, "The salt was there all the time."
> Then the father says, "Here also, my dear, in this body, verily, you do not perceive Being; but It is indeed there." (Chandogya Upanishad 6.13.2)

It is interesting to note that the analogies of the bees and the rivers stress the loss of individuality, the merging of the individual self into the universal Self. The analogy of the salt on the other hand illustrates the pervasive quality of Being. The Absolute Being—That One, Brahman, God, whatever the appropriate label may be—is present in everything that exists. In other words, in the Hindu religion there is no Creator above and creatures below, no duality; there is only One. Brahman-Atman is ultimately One; the human soul, or self, is the Absolute. Ignorance of that truth—or, rather, the inability to grasp Absolute Reality—leads to a continuous chain of rebirths, or reincarnations.

Rebirth

What is known about the origin and the development of the concepts of *samsara* (rebirth or reincarnation) and *karma* (action or work) basically is limited to teachings in Hindu literature that are attributed to two sages: Uddalaka Aruni, for *samsara,* and Yajnavalka, for *karma.* Both teachings may predate the sages, who simply may have recorded beliefs and ideas that originated among small groups of ascetics. The sages probably kept those concepts secret from the public, fearing the orthodox priests. Whatever their precise origins, *samsara* and *karma* eventually became parts of established belief associated with the concept of Brahman-Atman.

Samsara, the whole process of rebirth, or reincarnation, is based on the assumption that every living form is subject to an indefinite series of lives or existences that culminates when the form becomes at death indistinguishable from Brahman. *Samsara* is beginningless and, in most cases, endless. It is neither a process of purification nor a cycle of progress but a perpetual sequence of rebirth in one form or another. The endless series of births and deaths may occur on earth in any of the forms of life—human, animal, or vegetable—or in any of the series of heavens or hells.

What determines the outcome of each successive birth? One's future existence is determined by the law of *karma,* which literally means "action"—whether it be good or bad, religious or secular. Under the law of *karma,* everything one does in this life in thought, word, or deed ordains one's destiny in future existences. Hindus believe that because actions invariably produce good and evil fruits, their future lives are determined by their *karma* in the present; to put it differently, a Hindu's present life is the result of accrued past *karma.* Consequently, pain, suffering, and any sort of misfortune are regarded by Hindus not as afflictions imposed externally by a divine being or by the actions of an individual, but as the result of the person's evil *karma* in a past existence or existences.

Thus, Hindus, like adherents of many other religions, do not think of life as an end in itself. The end of one life simply signals the beginning of another, which represents the inevitable consequences of *karma.* In the chain or cycle of rebirths, to which all living things are inescapably bound, reincarnation may occur at either a higher or a lower level than the status of life in the present or in any past existence. What determines the nature of the next rebirth is the law of *karma,* a law considered as implacable and impersonal as a law of nature. Accordingly, inequalities of birth are explained and even justified by the theory of *karma* and *samsara.*

That central concept of *karma-samsara* evolved from a question that has preoccupied the human mind from time immemorial: What happens after death? Not only do different religions offer different answers, but within each religion the answers seem to change with the passage of time. Why? Perhaps because what happens after death is, to the rational mind, a mere matter of conjecture; each successive age develops a more plausible theory. Such evolution of ideas is also true of Hinduism.

Early Hindu scriptures, such as the Rig-Veda, describe how the soul of a good person who has died is carried up on high by Agni (the fire god who consumes the body at cremation). When the soul arrives on high, there is eating and drinking, various other enjoyments, reunion with loved ones, and perfect, carefree bliss. In the heavenly world there are neither rich nor poor, neither powerful nor oppressed; sickness and old age do not detract from joys a hundred times greater than the greatest bliss on earth. For evildoers, there is an "abyss," a place that is "black-darkness."

The idea of a postmortem judgment evolved during the later Brahmanic period. It was an idea that, during the same period, was prominent in the Iranian tradition of Zoroastrianism. One's deeds, it was thought, were weighed in the balance after death and rewarded or punished according to their good or evil nature. But to certain profound thinkers that theory seemed questionable and difficult to accept, so once again the element of doubt played a significant role in shaping a new concept.

"Who can demonstrate the experiences of the hereafter?" ask Upan-
ishadic thinkers. "There is doubt about a man when he is dead," says
an inquirer to Yama (the Death-deity). "Some say that he exists; others,
that he does not. This I should like to know, taught by you. . . ." (Katha
Upanishad 1.1.20). Yama, the God of Death, replies by first illustrating
the indestructibility of the "soul."

> The knowing Self [or Soul] is not born; It does not die. It has not sprung
> from anything; nothing has sprung from It. Birthless, eternal, everlast-
> ing, and ancient, It is not killed when the body is killed. If the killer
> thinks he kills and if the killed man thinks he is killed, neither of these
> apprehends aright. The Self kills not, nor is It killed. (Katha Upanishad
> 1.2.18-19)

Yama then goes on to state the doctrine of rebirth:

> Well then . . . I shall tell you about this profound and eternal Brahman,
> and also about what happens to the Atman [soul] after meeting death.
> Some [souls] enter the womb for the purpose of re-embodiment, and
> some enter into stationary objects—according to their work [karma] and
> according to their knowledge. If a man is able to realize Brahman here,
> before the falling asunder of his body, then he is liberated; if not, he is
> embodied again in the created worlds. (Katha Upanishad 2.2.6–7; 3.4)

Two similes vividly describe the cycle of rebirth:

> Just as a leech moving on a blade of grass reaches its end, takes hold of
> another, and draws itself together towards it, so does the "self," after
> throwing off this body, that is to say, after making it unconscious, take
> hold of another support and draw itself together towards it. Just as a
> goldsmith takes a small quantity of gold and fashions [out of it] another
> —a newer and better form—so does the self, after throwing off this
> body, that is to say, after making it unconscious, fashion another—a
> newer and better form—suited to the manes [dead and deified ances-
> tors] or the gandharvas [demigods] or the gods, . . . or other beings. (Bri-
> hadarenyaka Upanishad 4.4.3–4)

The concept of karma-samsara finally became the central concept in
all Hindu thought. If living souls are subject to an indefinite series of
lives or existences, how can one be released or liberated (moksha is the
Indian word for such liberation) from the cycle of rebirths? True, if one
could only reach the point at which one experienced a total identification of one's individual self with the universal Self (Brahman-Atman),
then one would attain moksha. But how can one attain that transcendent
experience? The Hindu masses, with their socioreligious caste system,
were far from attaining such a blissful state.

Liberation

From a very early period, Hinduism recognized four basic needs of
human life (or lives). The first two, pleasure and wealth, are referred to
as the "path of desire"; the last two, moral duty and liberation, as the
"path of renunciation." Hindus do not criticize those who pursue personal pleasure, nor do they blame those who wish to accumulate great

possessions. Nevertheless, it is thoroughly understood that neither of those needs represents the highest goals and that sooner or later in this or in some future existence (as a member of a lower caste, as an animal, or as a thing) the individual must come to terms with that fact. Hindus recognize the satisfaction of performing their duty, but ultimate satisfaction can be found only in *moksha,* liberation from the cycles of rebirth.

Although there is a difference of opinion among the Hindus about the path *(marga)* to final emancipation *(moksha),* orthodox Hindus now recognize three paths: *karma marga, jnana marga,* and *bhakti marga.* These paths are valued differently by different adherents, but all three are respected.

Karma Marga (Path of Duties). This path represents the methodical fulfillment of rites, ceremonies, and social obligations, including sacrificing to the deities and to one's ancestors, reverencing and saluting the sun, keeping the hearth fire alight, performing the appropriate rites and ceremonies that mark the important events in life (birth, naming, the first ingestion of solid food, the first haircut, initiation, marriage, and death), and strictly observing all the social regulations and dietary laws of one's caste.

The Code of Manu prescribes for each separate caste a list of dietary laws, social regulations, domestic rites, public ceremonies, and religious duties. The Code also stipulates the honors due to the guardian deities of the household. For example, the head of the house must see to it that the deities are properly worshiped each day and that portions of prepared food are presented to them before each meal. An important domestic rite is the *shraddha* rite, the rite to ancestral spirits. The *shraddha* rite consists of periodic offerings of portions of food and memorial prayers. The most important food offering is the *pinda,* little balls of rice pressed into a firm cake.

High ethical values are also a characteristic feature associated with the practice of the *karma marga.*

> Against an angry man let him not in return show anger; let him bless when he is cursed; and let him not utter speech devoid of truth. (Manu 6.48)

Although many Hindus still observe the Code in minute detail, modern conditions have forced certain changes in its ancient customs and rites. To an outsider, the path of duties may seem an exacting way of life, but to the faithful Hindu, it is an action-filled way of fulfillment and ultimately a means to liberation.

> He who thus recognizes the Self through the self in all created beings, becomes equal minded towards all, and enters the highest state, Brahman. (Manu 12.125)

Jnana Marga (Path of Knowledge). For those spiritual aspirants who have a strong intellectual bent, Hinduism prescribes *jnana marga,* or the path of knowledge. Its purpose is to enable the aspirant to attain ultimate bliss through the perception of the illusory nature of names and forms and the realization of the sole reality of Brahman-Atman. Naturally, only those who are of a philosophical temperament can develop a keen power of reasoning by which they can distinguish the real from the unreal, the changing from the changeless. Aspirants must cultivate control over their minds and their senses, which leads to inner calm, forbearance, and concentration. By reasoning and uninterrupted contemplation, their ignorance gives way to the realization that the entire universe and all beings are one and the same Brahman. But to reach that ultimate realization requires long preparation and self-discipline.

Through the centuries (from about 500 BCE to CE 1500), a great number of systems of philosophy, or *darshana,* developed. Hindus have pointed out that most of them cover the same ground as any of six recognized systems. Thus, Hindu scholars have arranged those six systems in their logical rather than chronological order.

The Nyaya System. Based on a text ascribed to a philosopher called Gautama (not Gautama the Buddha), the Nyaya system attempts a complete analysis of correct reasoning. It asserts that true or real knowledge is based on four processes of knowing: sense-perception, inference, comparison of fact, and trustworthy testimony. False notions give rise to activities that have evil consequences in successive rebirths; hence, all misery arises from false notions. Liberation depends on sound or true knowledge.

The Vaisheshika System. This system, founded by Kanada, applies logical methods to the study of the external world. The external world is regarded as a self-existent reality, formed by eternal and indivisible atoms eternally combining and recombining. Later thinkers declared that the process is not purely mechanistic but takes place by the power of Advishta, the divine "unseen force." All agree that alongside the eternal atoms and individual selves is an eternal Self, the source of all selves. Hence, both atoms and selves are eternally indestructible.

The Sankhya System. The Sankhya system is dualistic, in sharp contrast to the doctrine expressed in the Upanishads that only one Being (Brahman-Atman) exists. It maintains that there are only two real eternal categories of being: *prakriti* ("matter") and *purusha* ("self"). Individual selves are not the product of an eternal Self but are regarded as eternal, independent, and infinite. Why these selves *(purushas)* are associated with a body and a mind *(prakriti)* in one existence or life after another is an insoluble mystery associated, in some way, with *karma.* The self needs to be liberated from its association with matter. But the self cannot achieve that state. It is in the realm of matter that the "higher intelligence" *(budhi)* realizes in its moment of insights the true character, or being, of the *purusha.* The insight destroys not only ignorance or illusion but also matter. Hence, it enables the self to realize its freedom of eternal and unearthly existence.

The Yoga System. The term *yoga* ("discipline") is used in two distinct senses. The meaning most familiar to the West is the physical, mental, and psychic discipline or technique practiced for either purely spiritual purposes or to attain maximum physical and mental, as well as spiritual, well-being. The word also is used to denote one of the six philosophical systems.

The greatest appeal of the Yoga system lies in its physiological and psychological measures to control the mind in an effort to concentrate. It consists largely of special postures, controlled breathing, and rhythmical repetition of the proper thought formulas. The claim of the Yoga system is that through controlled breathing one can control the senses. By controlling the senses, one gradually can control mental processes. By controlling the activity of the mind, one can pass through a succession of stages in which the activities of the mind become more and more restricted: first to an area of concentration, then to a restricted concentration on a single object of thought, and finally to a state of uninterrupted contemplation in which there is no distinction between the mind and its object of thought. In that final state, which is devoid of all mental activity, there is only pure undistracted consciousness.

Mentioned first in the Upanishads, the Yoga system was given its classical form by Patanjali, a yogin who probably dates from the second century CE. Influenced partly by the Sankhya system, Patanjali defined the Yoga system as "the suppression of the modifications of the mind." Its goal is the attainment of a state of pure consciousness, undisturbed by psychic or mental processes or by any object of awareness. That state is known as *samadhi,* a state of trance in which the mind, "emptied of all content and no longer aware of either object or subject, is absorbed into the Ultimate and is one with the One."

The means to attain that goal is the eightfold yoga, or discipline, described in the Yoga Sutras. The first two steps deal mainly with ethical disciplines, such as nonviolence, truthfulness, study, and prayer. The next two describe the correct postures and controlled breathing that, in turn, help in the practice of the final four steps, which are associated with concentration and meditation.

Another form of yoga associated with esoteric and magical aspects is known as *Tantrism,* which dates back to about the fourth century CE or earlier. The term *tantra* derives from the root meaning "to expand" or "to extend," that is, knowledge. Hence, Tantrism is based on mystic speculations concerning divine *shakti,* creative feminine energy. Opinions differ, however, as to what Tantrism is. Followers of Tantrism assume that the macrocosm (the universe) and the microcosm (the individual) are closely connected. The initiate has to perform certain physical rites to transform the chaotic state of the body into a normal "cosmos." By yoga and ritual means, in part magical and in part orgiastic, adherents attempt to master transcendent powers to realize oneness with the highest Principle. They describe physiological processes with cosmological terminology and define states of consciousness with sensual or erotic language.

Some followers of Tantrism seek emancipation from rebirth by awakening the "female nature-energy" (representing the *shakti*), which is said to be dormant and coiled like a serpent, or *kundalini.* That energy is awakened and made to rise through the six centers of the body. Other followers, like the Hatha Yoga and the Mantra Yoga, apply yoga practices of abstinence, bodily postures, breath control, concentration, contemplation, and muscular contractions. Hatha Yoga involves some form of self-torture and internal purification, such as an emetic flushing of the bowels. The entire process is intended to control the "gross" body in order to free the "subtle" body.

Among some *shakti* cults, the experience of transcending space and time and of realizing the identity and unity of the divine in all things is also expressed through the ritual satisfaction of lust as means of release from the cycle of rebirth. In that context, ritual copulation becomes (for males only) a sacred rite in experiencing and participating in cosmic and divine processes. The very mystery of *shakti* cults (Shaktism) is the realization of the identity of God and his creative energy. Sexual relationships, therefore, help to transcend all opposites—but only among initiates, since participation in such rites is conditional on the capacity of merging one's mind with the Supreme Being.

The characteristic feature of yoga in any of its forms is the discipline of the whole body to aid the suppression of the activities of the mind. The result is a state of pure ecstasy, of complete freedom of the true self from earthly bonds.

The Purva-Mimansa System. Founded by Jaimini, this system is considered to be the least philosophical of the six systems. Followers of the Purva-Mimansa system are known as literalists because they cling to the literal inspiration of the Vedas. So highly did Jaimini regard the truth of the Vedas that he asserted that they never had an author, that they were uncreated and eternal, and written in the language of Being Itself. Hence, the Vedas have a magical power that prevails even over the deities.

The Vedas—and, for that matter, the Brahmanas—prescribe the whole duty of a person. By determining the literal meaning of the Vedas and the Brahmanas and carrying out their rites and ceremonies, one could attain liberation. Although that position essentially has not changed, followers of the Purva-Mimansa system declare that the duties of a person prescribed in the Vedas and the Brahmanas should be studied and practiced as an offering to a "Supreme God" who waits to liberate his followers as a reward for their faithfulness.

The Vedanta System. The name of this system derives from the Upanishads, also commonly called Vedanta, which means "the concluding portions of the Vedas." Although an attempt was made in the first century BCE by Badarayana to set forth the monistic teaching (the doctrine that only one Being exists) of the Upanishads in a systematic philosophical structure, it was not until centuries later that three different systems of Vedanta philosophy were founded: by Sankara, in the ninth century CE; by Ramanuja, in the twelfth century CE; and by Madhva in the thirteenth century CE.

Sankara's system of thought (called *advaita*, or nondualism) holds that the world, the individual self, and Brahman, while not absolutely one, do not really exist separately and are, in reality, "not different." Brahman is eternal, undecaying, indescribable, and impersonal. Besides Brahman, all else is transient, impure, and unsubstantial, in short, a product of "illusion" *(maya)*. To regard the physical world and the individual self as realities (as is the common experience) is to exist in the

Temple of Lord Krishna in Mathura, Uttar Pradesh, considered to be the birthplace of the Lord Krishna. Large temples, rivers, and the junctions of rivers attract huge numbers of pilgrims. Hindu temples have developed rest houses for travelers and provisions for feeding pilgrims who travel great distances from one part of the country to another to arrive at renowned sacred sites. Hindu pilgrims consider bathing in sacred waters, especially at specific times, as a most auspicious act.
Courtesy of Government of India Tourist Office, Toronto.

world of illusion. There is only one reality, which is spaceless, timeless, and solely existent, in short, Brahman-Atman. Liberation from the cycle of rebirths comes when the "veil of ignorance" is lifted and one realizes the identity of Brahman-Atman.

Three hundred years later, Ramanuja suggested a diametrically opposed interpretation of the Upanishads (Vedanta). He asserted that the physical world, individual selves, and Ultimate Reality are not illusions but real, though nondivisible, because the physical world and individual selves make up the "body" of the Ultimate Reality. In other words, the physical world and individual selves are the forms through which the Ultimate Reality is manifested. The Ultimate Reality is a personal being (not, as Sankara stated, an impersonal being) named Vishnu. Vishnu is endowed with every desirable quality; he is all-knowing, all-powerful, and all-loving and manifests himself in many ways. The ideal goal of humans is not absorption in an impersonal reality but going to "heaven to enjoy Vishnu's presence in full consciousness."

A third interpretative version of the Upanishads came through Madhva. He maintained that the individual self is neither to be identified with nor one with the Ultimate Reality. Furthermore, liberated selves will enjoy bliss in the presence of the Supreme Self, Vishnu. Non-liberated selves are doomed to spend eternity in hell or in endless re-births. The self is liberated through Vayu, the Wind-god, son of Vishnu. Vayu is the "vehicle of the grace of God," a sort of "holy spirit" who "breathes his life-giving power into those whom he liberates." That version of the Upanishads echoes Christian and Muslim views, which were known in India by Madhva's time.

Bhakti Marga (Path of Devotion). Many people cannot be inspired by pure reasoning or rationality, but they can rise to heights of spiritual elevation through the path of devotion, *bhakti marga*. Often, such experiences assume the form of a passionate love of a deity, whether a god or a goddess. The most characteristic features of such experiences are the surrender of self to the deity or divine being, private acts of devotion, and temple worship.

The first important literary record of *bhakti marga* as a true way of liberation is found in one of the great classics of religious literature, the Bhagavad-Gita, which means "Song of the Blessed One." Its author is unknown, and the date of its composition may fall anywhere from 200 BCE to 200 CE.

The Bhagavad-Gita is a poem in the form of a dialogue between the warrior Arjuna and his charioteer Krishna, who is none other than the manifestation of the Supreme Deity, Vishnu, in human form. Their conversation takes place just before a battle. Arjuna sees in the ranks of the opposing army a large number of his friends and kinsmen. Horror stricken at the thought of fighting against them, he quickly lays down his weapons, preferring to be killed than to kill. Krishna, however, justifies the fight on the grounds that a person's real soul is immortal and independent of the body; it neither kills nor is killed.

> These bodies come to an end.
> It is declared, of the eternal embodied [soul],
> Which is indestructible and unfathomable.
> Therefore fight, son of Bharata!
> Who believes him a slayer,
> And who thinks him slain,
> Both these understand not
> He slays not, is not slain.
> He is not born, nor does he ever die;
> Nor, having come to be, will he ever come not to be.
> Unborn, eternal, everlasting, this ancient one
> Is not slain when the body is slain. (Bhagavad-Gita 2.18–20)

In front of Shiva temples one usually finds the statue or image of *nandi,* a bull, quite often of huge proportions. This particular one is found outside the temple of Chamundi Hills in Mysore. From time immemorial, the bull has been considered the carrier of Lord Shiva.
Courtesy of Trans World Airlines.

In the course of eighteen chapters, the Bhagavad-Gita sets forth many religious viewpoints. While it expounds *karma marga* and *jnana marga,* it emphasizes *bhakti marga,* the path of devotion. It grants that both the path of knowledge and the path of duties lead to liberation:

> In this world, aspirants may find enlightenment by two different paths: for the contemplative, the path of knowledge; for the active, the path of duties. (Bhagavad-Gita 3.3)

Nevertheless, the highest secret of all and the supreme message of the Bhagavad-Gita is devotion:

> I am the same to all beings;
> no one is hateful or dear to me;
> those who revere me with devotion
> are in me and I in them. . . .
> No devotee of mine perishes.
> For those who take refuge in me,
> though they may be born of base origin—
> women, *vaisyas* or *sudras*—
> all attain the highest goal.
> Fix your mind on me,
> be devoted to me,
> worship me, adore me,
> and to me you will come.
> (Bhagavad-Gita 9.29–34)

Thus, the path of devotion assumes passionate devotion and absolute surrender to a particular deity, either a god or a goddess. Neither the path of duties, which is largely traditional, nor the path of knowledge, which is highly intellectual, can satisfy the profound religious need of millions of Hindus to the same degree as the path of devotion. For most Hindus, unconditional, selfless love and faith in a deity are the highest ideals in attaining emancipation. To adore a personal god or goddess with every element of one's being is the ultimate goal of this path. Devotees are expected to adore the deity not out of a sense of fear or punishment, much less from expectations of reward, but for love's sake alone. Needless to say, *bhakti marga* is the most popular of the three paths.

Among the thousands of deities adored and worshiped by millions of Hindus, three command the highest respect: Shiva, Vishnu, and Brahma. Those divinities make up the *trimurti*, the three figures who represent Absolute Reality.

The most popular of the three gods is Shiva, who is known as the Destroyer. His followers, called Shaivites, give him the title *Mahadeva,* which means "Great God." His character is a complex amalgam of contrasting attributes. He is the god of death, destruction, and disease, but he is also the god of the dance and reproduction. He is both terrible and mild, "ceaselessly active and eternally restful." The seemingly contradictory aspects of his character generally are accepted as representing two sides of one nature. That is also true of his consort, the goddess Kali, who is represented in a great many forms, both benign and malicious. In her benevolent aspects, Kali protects and nourishes her devotees and the world. In her malevolent appearance, she is terrifying and loathsome, forcing her devotees to turn away from the world toward their eternal destiny of liberation from embodied existence with its inevitable sorrows.

The origins of Shaivites and the cult of Shiva may lie in pre-Aryan times. Most, though not all, groups associated with Shiva represent manifestations of local folk worship combined with various pan-Hindu religious ideologies. The reproductive and sexual energy identified with Shiva is represented, to one group of his worshipers, by the human re-

Devotees of Shiva worship the *lingam* and *yoni* emblems (the male and female sex organs), representing Shiva's universal male energy in everlasting union with his female counterpart.

Courtesy of John Capana.

productive organs — the erect penis *(lingam)* and the vagina *(yoni)*. To another group, the mystery of Shiva's creative force is characterized by a miniature phallic symbol worn around the neck. To yet another group, Shiva is worshiped as the Skull Bearer, an image represented by a necklace of beads shaped like miniature human skulls.

In contrast to Shiva, Vishnu is known as the Preserver. He is the god of love and benevolence and the preserver of values associated with such attributes. His chief characteristic is his concern for humanity, which he expresses by appearing on earth at different times and in various forms, or *avatars*. According to tradition, Vishnu so far has made nine appearances on earth as various animals and creatures associated with functions that help to preserve and restore humanity. He also has appeared in human form as Krishna and as Gautama, the Buddha, and he is expected to appear on earth once more to close this era and bring the world to an end. Vishnu's consort is the goddess Lakshmi, who is associated with wealth, luck, fertility, well-being, political power, and royalty. Today, she is considered to be the most popular Hindu goddess throughout India.

Faith in Vishnu is essentially monotheistic, whether the object of worship is Vishnu himself or one of his alternative forms, and the doctrine of corporeal appearances, or *avatars*, is a powerful integrating force in Hinduism. It is based on the belief that whenever the world degenerates, Vishnu, the Protector and Preserver, manifests himself by assuming an earthly form to destroy evil and guard goodness.

Of the three gods with mass appeal in the contemporary era, Brahma, the Creator, is perhaps the oldest and the least worshiped. Even

though he is accorded deep respect as one of the *trimurti,* his importance is gradually declining. Few Hindus describe themselves as devotees of Brahma, and very few temples are dedicated to him. Both nature
and society derive from Brahma. In art, he is represented with four faces
and is often shown riding on a white swan or goose. His consort is the
goddess Sarasvati, who is associated with wisdom, knowledge, and culture. Her most typical places of worship are in artistic and scholastic
institutions.

HINDU REFORM MOVEMENTS

The Impact of Islam

In the seventh century CE, a new and vital religion sprang unheralded,
with the force of a coiled spring suddenly released, from the deserts of
Arabia. That new religion, under the name of Islam, spread rapidly
across the entire Middle East and, a century later, penetrated into India.
Northwestern India was conquered by the Muslim Mahmud al-Ghazni
in 1021, and during the twelfth and thirteenth centuries, all of northern
and central India came under Islamic rule from a single administrative
center in Delhi. Several centuries later, the Islamic conquest of India
was completed by the Mughals (Mongol rulers). The advent of Islam
meant the end of universal royal patronage of Hinduism in India. The
attitude of Muslim rulers toward Hinduism varied. Some tolerated their
Hindu subjects, whereas others persecuted them. More fanatical rulers
destroyed numerous Hindu temples.

Muslim occupation of India, though it brought Hinduism into close
contact with a different, more aggressive religion, did little to inhibit
the continued development of new forms of Hindu devotional sects,
popular folk religion, and philosophical systems. Hindu-Muslim influences also inspired spiritual leaders such as Kabir (1440–1518), whose
teaching was essentially a simplified form of Hinduism blended with
Islamic mysticism. Later, Nanak (1469–1539), one of Kabir's disciples,
became the founder of a new religion, Sikhism, which in its final form
represented elements from both Hinduism and Islam.

Hindu-Muslim syncretism reached its zenith in the reign of Akbar
(1556–1605), who tried to establish a single, all-embracing religion for
his empire. Although his efforts failed, his influence persisted for half
a century, until, during the reign of Aurangzeb (1659–1707), orthodox
Muslim teachers did all in their power to discourage the growth of
syncretic tendencies. The advent of British domination in the nineteenth century virtually brought Hindu-Muslim syncretic movements
to an end.

The Impact of Christianity

According to tradition, Christianity came to southern India in the first
century CE. Its impact on Hinduism was minimal, however, until the arrival of the Portuguese in the sixteenth century, followed by the Dutch,
the British, and the French. Both Roman Catholic and Protestant mis-

sionaries made converts, although the masses were—and still are—largely unaffected.

The spread of Christian ideas by missionaries influenced a number of Hindus who, in turn, launched Hindu reform movements. One such movement was the Brahmo Samaj, founded in 1828 by Ram Mohun Roy. From his perspective, the precepts of Jesus were "the guide to peace and happiness." Ram Mohun Roy denounced all forms of polytheism and advocated a purge of Hinduism, to strip from it all elements of idolatry and polytheism. In religious services, the worship of the Brahmo Samaj was patterned after Protestantism: hymns, scripture readings, and sermons. Another reformer, Dayananda Sarasvati, founded the Arya Samaj group in 1875. Sarasvati believed that the religion documented in the Vedas was the oldest and purest of all faiths, because the Vedas represented a direct revelation from the one God.

The most important, because it was the most widespread, Hindu adaptation of the Christian tradition was proposed by Sri Ramakrishna (1836–1886), founder of the Ramakrishna movement. A mystic and a devotee of the goddess Kali, he came to the conclusion that "all religions were different paths to God; nevertheless, the religion of a person's own time and place is the best expression of God." After Ramakrishna's death, his successor, Vivekananda, established Ramakrishna centers in India, Europe, and the Americas.

Many other Hindu teachers and thinkers were attracted to the Western intellectual tradition and Christian ideals. Among them were the Bengali poet Rabindranath Tagore (1861–1941); Swami Sivananda (1862–1902), who organized the Divine Life Society; Sri Aurobindo Ghose (1872–1950); Sarvepalli Radhakrishnan (1888–1975); and Mohandas Gandhi (1869–1948), who preached the doctrine of *satyagraha*, or passive resistance to British rule.

Other Hindus resisted—and still resist—Christian missionary teaching as inimical to their time-honored institutions. Since India achieved independence in 1947, conversion to Christianity has been viewed with disfavor by many influential Hindus, who advocate in Hinduism the same characteristics that prompted other Hindus to accept Christianity (e.g., incantation, faith in and devotion to one deity, the pursuit of ultimate bliss). Serious efforts are being made to reconvert Indian Christians to Hinduism. Some Indian Christians have even formed groups analogous to castes, but those are exceptions rather than the rule. In general, the Hindu masses tolerate Christian converts, even though the latter ignore time-honored Hindu customs and traditions.

Krishna Consciousness. Although modern forms of Hinduism seem barely to maintain a tenuous existence in Christian lands, new manifestations are more than likely to develop in the future. The most recent manifestation of the Hindu-Christian encounter is the Hare Krishna movement (officially known as the International Society of Krishna Consciousness), founded by Swami Prabhupada in 1965. Its purpose is to spread Hindu religious beliefs in the Western world, a process that began in the eighteenth century with the first English translation of the Bhagavad-Gita.

Gandhi

Mohandas Gandhi, popularly known as Mahatma (a title of reverence) Gandhi (1869–1948), was an outstanding figure in modern India and a famous religious personality who was loved throughout the world. Born on October 2, 1869, in Porbandar, a small coastal town in Gujarat in western India, Gandhi (usually called "Gandhiji" or "Bapu" by Indians) was the son of an important minister of a princely state. After he completed his primary and secondary education in India, he left for England at the age of nineteen to study law and soon became a barrister.

A legal case sent him to South Africa at the age of twenty-four. He lived there for the next twenty years and experienced firsthand the prejudice of "white-skinned" European settlers against "dark-skinned" people (Africans and Indians). That attitude and the treatment that accompanied it persuaded Gandhi to stay in South Africa and fight for the rights of Africans and Indians. But the method he used for fighting prejudice and discrimination was novel and significant.

Gandhi believed that violence is too great a price to pay even for fair treatment and justice. Violence, he said, always leads to more violence. There is only one way to fight injustice: through nonviolence. Hence, if Gandhi decided that a certain law was unfair or unjust, he considered it his duty to disregard it, cheerfully accepting the consequences without hatred and without retaliation. "Truth" and "nonviolence" were the two basic values of life to which Gandhi always adhered.

Gandhi returned to India during World War I, only to find that the same situation and attitudes he had resisted in South Africa existed between the ruling British officials and the Indian public. After the war, Gandhi and a few Indian national leaders challenged Indians to oppose British rule and what they considered was British injustice. Hundreds of thousands of men and women accepted Gandhi's call, among them a future prime minister of India, Jawaharlal Nehru.

Gandhi wanted Indians to fight for their freedom, but he wanted them to achieve their goals in such a way that Britons and Indians could reach new levels of understanding and become better people. To him, achieving the goals was far less important than how they were achieved. In a world full of violence and hatred, Gandhi was profoundly convinced that all national and international problems could be solved through nonviolence.

On August 14, 1947, India (excluding Pakistan) finally won freedom by virtue of Gandhi's two principles. Less than six months later, the "apostle of nonviolence and angel of peace" died at the hands of an assassin. Three pistol shots struck Gandhi as he knelt for prayers on the evening of January 30, 1948. With his hands folded in prayer, he uttered the words, "*Ram, Ram,*" (the name of God) and fell.

Gandhi was murdered before he could achieve all his objectives. He preached religious tolerance in an attempt to alleviate frictions between India's warring Hindu and Muslim factions. In addition, in his fight against all practices he thought unjust, Gandhi attempted to reform India's socioreligious tradition of caste, even going so far as to champion the rights of the *chandalas,* or untouchables.

Social and National Reform

Other far-reaching changes in Hindu culture have been made in modern times. Attempts to abolish stratified class distinctions, especially the restrictions imposed on untouchables, gradually are succeeding, although the process is still far from complete. In 1948, India's Constituent Assembly abolished untouchability, and although social integration has lagged far behind legislation, the process of modern industrialization gradually is eroding the justification for time-honored traditions of class. In addition, various Hindu religious leaders have formed new sects in which all converts are regarded as equals, no matter what their previous castes; they are free to visit, eat, mix, and intermarry with other members of their sect. The nationalistic desire to preserve Hindu unity and to prevent the development of national minority religious groups has led to a struggle for self-determination. Leading minds of India have established two important objectives: national self-determination for Hindu India and unyielding ideals in matters of religious principles. Many orthodox Hindus advocate making India an official Hindu state. Whether or not that dream is ever realized, a quotation that seems particularly fitting as a concluding statement comes from a great Hindu philosopher and a former president of the Republic of India, Sarvepalli Radhakrishnan:

> There has been no such thing as a uniform, stationary, unalterable Hinduism whether in point of belief or practice. Hinduism is a movement, not a position; a process, not a result; a growing tradition, not a fixed revelation.[1]

POPULAR HINDUISM

Occult Practices

The main motive of religious practices for millions of Hindus is the fear of malevolent and benevolent deities, who are omniscient and perpetual observers of day-to-day events in every person's life. Each god must be appropriately propitiated to forestall disaster or guarantee security. The lower castes often confine themselves to manipulating the deities or spirits that dwell in trees, stones, water, and other natural elements. To counteract plagues, diseases, curses, witchcraft, and evil, most villagers—which is to say, most Hindus—and millions of urban workers resort to divination, astrology, and various occult practices. To millions of Hindus, ritual purifications, time-honored rites and customs, charms, and amulets are of greater importance than the doctrine of Brahman-Atman.

Scholars generally find it difficult to distinguish popular folk Hinduism from Indian tribal religion, because the beliefs and practices are closely allied. Practices based on ritual nudity, black magic, and the worship of snakes are as prevalent as ever. Exorcists and mediums claim to be possessed by divine powers and submit themselves to self-torture. One of the striking features of folk Hinduism is the propitiation of female deities associated with local village communities. The goddesses, like the tutelary deities of ancient Near Eastern cities, have no relation to the universe nor any jurisdiction beyond the life of a particular village. They are usually represented by sticks, stone pillars, clay figurines, or, on occasion, a small shrine.

The beliefs and customs of the masses are much the same today as they were in the past. To obtain rain, fertility, or children, many Hindu women worship stone figures of snakes. The snake goddess Manasa is believed to live in a plant or a stone carving bearing her name, and a special day is devoted to her worship.

Many Hindus adopt and enshrine a single god or goddess as their household patron. The number of these deities is, according to Hindu tradition, "thirty-three *cores*" — some 330 million! Hindus also go from temple to temple as needs arise. For good fortune and luck, they may worship Ganesha, the elephant-headed son of Shiva. For physical health and bodily strength, they may turn to Hanuman, the monkey god. In times of sorrow and anguish, they may call on Rama. Above all, the average Hindu villager has two spiritual or religious ambitions: to go to some holy place of pilgrimage and to attend temple festivals.

Sacred places for pilgrims are plentiful throughout India. Mountains, caverns, rivers, and the sites of mythological occurrences (such as theophanies) have become sacred or holy spots. Temples or shrines are erected on or beside these locations, and pilgrims long to go to one or more of them. Sites such as Hardwar in the Himalayas, the Bay of Bengal, and Varanasi (Benares) are considered hallowed territories. Pilgrims come from all over India and are often overcome with joy at the sight of the temples that identify the significance of holy places. The Ganges is the holiest river of all; also sacred are the Jumna and Saraswati rivers, to which millions of pilgrims go for religious festivals.

Cow Veneration

Another feature of Hinduism is the veneration of cows, which receive the same honor as deities. Garlands are placed around their necks, and water is poured at their feet and oil on their foreheads. The deep and sincere feelings of numerous Hindus toward cows (also oxen and bulls) were best expressed by M. Monier-Williams:

> The cow is of all animals the most sacred. Every part of its body is inhabited by some deity or other. Every hair on its body is inviolable. All its excreta are hallowed. Not a particle ought to be thrown away as impure. On the contrary, the water it ejects ought to be preserved as the best of all holy waters—a sin-destroying liquid which sanctifies everything it touches, while nothing purifies like cow-dung. Any spot which a cow has condescended to honor with the sacred deposit of her excrement is forever afterwards consecrated ground.[2]

Among most Hindus today, cows are believed to be extremely sacred. The removal of serious types of impurities may involve the use of cow milk, urine, and dung. Such products are considered extremely purifying elements for cleansing a person or a house from pollution or impurity. A common practice found in most villages today is the sprinkling of dried, powdered cow dung in those areas of the house where lower castes have visited or stayed. Cow dung is also used as fuel, disinfectant, and medicine. In the words of Mahatma Gandhi, the cow "is the mother to millions of Indian mankind. Protection of the cow means protection of the whole dumb creation of God."

HINDU OBSERVANCES

Devotional Obligations

Hindu religion lays great emphasis on the performance of numerous rituals, all observed during any of the successive stages of a Hindu's life. These rituals at one time numbered more than three hundred, but they gradually have been reduced to fewer than twenty. Today, most Hindus observe one or more devotional obligations, which may be performed either privately in daily rituals in the home or communally in a temple.

There are countless forms of devotional service. Ideally, a Hindu should make five offerings daily, to gods, to ancestors, to seers, to animals, and to the poor. Many, however, perform their ritual once or, at most, three times a day. Private devotions also consist of tending the sacred household fire, recitation of texts, repetition of *mantras,* meditation, and yoga exercises.

In modern times, especially in Westernized cities, many Hindus find it difficult, if not impossible, to give the necessary time for private traditional religious requirements. For that reason, they tend to go at least once a week to their temple, where there is usually an image of a deity in whose honor regular ceremonies are conducted. Rites include the ceremonial awakening and bathing of the deity and an invocation of the name of the deity, followed by a formal adoration and salutation in which the deity is presented with garlands and water. As an act of homage, worshipers circumambulate the image and then offer a gift, generally consisting of rice, grain, *ghee* (melted butter), spices, incense, and aromatic vapors. Next, a lighted lamp is waved before the deity as *mantras* are chanted. Then follows supplication for personal requests. Finally, the deity is dismissed, and the ceremonies close with the chanting of appropriate *mantras.*

On special occasions, such as festive days, the deity is entertained by dancing girls and fanned by a retinue of farmers, as well as bathed, garlanded, and robed. Whenever possible, the deity is taken into procession around the temple or on the streets.

Ritual Purification

Ritual purification plays a vital part in Hindu religious observances and is closely related to the concepts of cleanliness and contamination. Hindu scriptures declare that only those who practice cleanliness are qualified to witness Brahman.

Purity is of several kinds and can be achieved by various means. Physical purity has two aspects, external and internal, and can be achieved either through the natural functions of the body or through external cleansing, including washing and bathing. Internal purity is accomplished by esoteric techniques that include the intoning of prescribed formulas, yogic postures, and certain purificatory acts. Those acts or rites are designed to remove all traces of contamination that may have come from infringing some caste regulation or neglecting to discharge certain obligatory acts.

Pilgrimage

Visiting holy places is one of the main sacred duties of all Hindu devotees who want to please the deity, accumulate religious merit, and secure bliss in the hereafter. There are thousands of holy places in India; some are especially sacred to followers of Shiva, others to followers of Vishnu, but a Hindu need not be limited to a sectarian shrine for purposes of pilgrimage.

All pious Hindus, even those who do not live in India, attempt to visit one of the holy places at least once in their lifetimes. Many devout Hindus hope to die in the precincts of Varanasi (Benares), since that ensures advancement at the time of rebirth. The merit of a pilgrimage is further enhanced if pilgrims add self-inflicted hardships to the normal rigors of the journey (for example, by making the journey hopping on one foot or going on their knees). Today, of course, the time spent on pilgrimage has been shortened considerably by the conveniences of modern travel.

Festivals

No religion has a longer calendar of holy days than does Hinduism. Hundreds of sacred occasions are celebrated by festive observances. Many festivals are seasonal. Others commemorate the birth, inauguration, or victory of a god or a hero. A number are celebrated in honor of deities: Krishna, Vishnu, Shiva, Parvati, Kama, Devi, Ganesha, Rama, Gayatri, Lakshmi, Saravati, Chitragupta, and so on. Many festivals are held in honor of snakes, cows, buffaloes, rivers, hills, plants, coconuts, ancestors, and spirits. Still other festivals are dedicated to important days, to famous incidents in mythology, to phases of the moon, and to eclipses, solstices, equinoxes, and the stars.

A festival may be observed in different ways: with acts of worship, fasting vigils, bathing, recitation of chants, taking of vows, lighting of lamps, fairs, games, drinking, gambling, and the offering of gifts to *brahmins*. Certain days are considered more auspicious than others. The merit resulting from virtuous deeds is believed to be augmented and intensified if they are performed on a particularly auspicious day.

Hindu religious ceremonies and festivals represent nothing more than imaginative symbols of the infinite aspects of Cosmic Reality. In fact, the festive occasion itself, rather than the deity who is honored, takes precedence. The most important attribute of a festivity is that it be celebrated.

Hindus attempt to make a pilgrimage at least once in a lifetime to the holy city of Varanasi (Benares), where they take a holy bath in the waters of the Ganges. Umbrellas provide shade, and the special platforms offer places for meditation and rest. Cremation of the dead takes place at various *ghats* (steps), and the ashes are strewn on the waters. Spires and pavillions of temples are seen in the background.
Courtesy of Government of India Tourist Office, Toronto.

The Hindu masses continue to practice their traditional religious beliefs today as they did centuries ago, even as the religion continues to evolve and form new branches or systems. Not only do millions of people worship in the method they best understand, numerous individuals also try to interpret the complexities of particular religious thoughts according to a modern way of thinking.

To provide a complete list of all Hindu festivals would be difficult, since many are linked to local legends and myths. Only the most important festivals are discussed here.

Divali or Dipavali (Cluster of Lights). This festival is celebrated in October or November. In northern India, Divali lasts for four days and is a New Year festival. In other parts of the country, Divali comprises many festivals and lasts for five days.

In general, the first day is dedicated to Parvati and Lakshmi, the goddesses of wealth and prosperity. Homes are lighted with clay oil lamps, and windows are kept open to welcome the goddesses into the house. The second day is devoted to gambling, especially with dice, to celebrate the reconciliation of the deity Shiva with the consort Parvati. The third day commemorates the victory of the deity Vishnu over the demon king Bali (or Naraka). Also on the third day, which is called Lakshmi-puja, the goddess Lakshmi is worshiped in the evening, after an all-day fast. (Among Bengali Hindus, the goddess Kali is the object of worship.) The fourth day is Divali proper, when little earthen bowls filled with oil are lighted and set up in extended rows both inside and outside homes. The fifth day commemorates an occasion when the deity Yama dined with his sister Yamuna and commanded everyone to do likewise. Consequently, every Hindu male must dine in the house of a sister, cousin, or other female relative and give her presents.

Holi or Hutashami. This festival starts about ten days before the full moon in either February or March but is generally observed only during the last three or four days before the full moon. The Holi festival commemorates either the frolics of the youthful deity Krishna, the death of the female demon Puthana, the burning of the female demoness Holika, or the destruction of Kama by Shiva. The ceremonies are somewhat like a carnival. Bonfires are lit, and evil influences (represented by effigies of demons) are symbolically burned. A pole is erected, and people walk around it in ritual fashion, while a great din from horns, drums, and cymbals accompanies dancing and shouting. The distinguishing feature of the Holi festival is the throwing of colored powders and the sprinkling of colored liquids on people.

Celebrations Associated with Deities. Such celebrations are considered quite important. The thirteenth day in the dark half of each month is sacred to Shiva. The celebrations occurring during January-February and February-March are regarded as exceedingly auspicious. A day of strict fasting precedes the days of a festival, and a vigil is kept all night, during which the phallic symbol of Shiva is worshiped and various rites performed.

The birthday of Ganesha, the elephant-headed god of good luck, is celebrated in August or September. Clay figures of Ganesha are made and worshiped for a period ranging from two to ten days. Lights are waved before the image, *mantras* chanted, and coconuts broken. At the end of the festival, the image is thrown into water and left to sink.

Numerous celebrations revolve around Krishna. The festival that commemorates the birth of Krishna (called Janmashtami or Gokulashtami) is celebrated in August-September. Preceding the festival is a day of fasting, which terminates at midnight, the time Krishna is said to have been born. Another popular festival commemorates the occasion on which Krishna lifted a hill of cow dung called Govardhana. Krishna taught the cowherds to pay homage to the hill instead of to the god Indra, his rival. Angered by that act, Indra sent a deluge to wash away the hill and its inhabitants. Krishna reacted by lifting the Govardhana

The local dieties at a festival in Kulu (Valley of the Gods), high in
the Himalayas. The festival is the *Dussehra*, ten days of merriment
and feasting. Observed throughout India each fall, the celebration
honors the triumph of good over evil, and each region of the
country has its own special way of marking the holiday.
Courtesy of Government of India Tourist Office, Toronto.

hill on his little finger and holding it like a canopy for seven days, until
Indra was thwarted in his design and departed in frustration.

Anniversaries Associated with Religious Leaders. Pious followers also consider anniversaries of religious leaders to be important. For instance,
the birthday of Swami Vivekananda is celebrated in January, the birthday of Sri Ramakrishna in February, and the birthday of Swami Prabhupada in September. Such occasions are marked by elaborate preparations, devotional worship, and rejoicing.

STUDY QUESTIONS

1. State the significance of the Aryan invasion of India.
2. List the four major castes and their traditional duties.
3. Describe the role of women in Hinduism.
4. Explain the specific duties prescribed for the observance of
   ashrama.

5. Distinguish between the *shruti* and *smriti* categories of scripture.

6. Identify the most important Vedic deities.

7. Discuss the development of the view of Brahman-Atman.

8. Explain the theory of *karma-samsara*.

9. Recount the major paths of emancipation, or *moksha,* from rebirth.

10. Describe any two of the six philosophical systems that lead to liberation.

11. Distinguish between the different forms of yoga.

12. Compare the theories proposed by Sankara, Ramanuja, and Madhva.

13. What are the attributes of the *trimurti*?

14. Relate the reforms generated by the Muslim and the Christian occupations of India.

15. List the characteristic features of popular Hinduism.

16. Describe the performance of several rituals.

17. What are the more popular festivals?

18. Examine the role and meaning of pilgrimage in Hindu tradition.

19. What private devotional obligations are performed by Hindus?

20. Did Mahatma Gandhi reform Hinduism?

Suggested Reading

Baird, Robert D. *Religions and Law in Independent India.* New Delhi: Manohar, 1993.

Brockington, John L. *The Sacred Thread: Hinduism in its Continuity and Diversity.* Edinburgh: Edinburgh University Press, 1981.

Bronkhorst, Johannes. *The Two Sources of Indian Asceticism.* Schweizer Asiatische Studien. Bd 13. Bern: P. Lang, 1993.

Bumiller, Elizabeth. *May You Be the Mother of a Hundred Sons.* New York: Random House, 1990.

Coward, Harold G. *Hindu Ethics: Purity, Abortion, and Euthanasia.* Albany, N.Y.: SUNY, 1989.

Eck, Diana L. *Darsan, Seeing the Divine Image in India.* 2nd ed. New York: Columbia University Press, 1996.

Erndl, Kathleen M. *Victory to the Mother: The Hindu Goddess of Northwest India in Myth, Ritual, and Symbol.* New York: Oxford University Press, 1993.

Feldhaus, Anne. *Water and Womanhood: Religious Meanings of Rivers in Maharashtra.* New York: Oxford University Press, 1995.

Gatwood, Lynn E. *Devi and the Spouse Goddess: Women, Sexuality, and Marriages in India.* Riverdale, Md.: Riverdale, 1985.

Hawley, John S., and Donna M. Wulff. *Devi: Goddesses of India.* Berkeley: University of California Press, 1996.

Hiriyana, Mysore. *The Essentials of Indian Philosophy.* London: Allen & Unwin, 1985.

Jordens, Joseph Teresa Florent. *Gandhi's Religion: A Homespun Shawl.* New York: St. Martin's Press, 1998.

Kinsley, David R. *Hindu Goddesses: Visions of the Divine Feminine in the Hindu Religious Tradition.* Berkeley: University of California Press, 1986.

_____. *Hinduism: A Cultural Perspective,* 2nd ed. Englewood Cliffs, N.J.: Prentice-Hall, 1993.

Klostermaier, Klaus K. *A Survey of Hinduism,* 2nd ed. Albany, N.Y.: SUNY, 1994.

Maw, Geoffrey Waring. *Pilgrims in Hindu Holy Land: Sacred Shrines of the Indian Himalayas.* York, England: Sessions Book Trust, 1997.

Panikkar, Raimundo. *The Vedic Experience.* London: Dartman, Longman & Todd, 1977.

Pintchman, Tracy. *The Rise of the Goddess in the Hindu Tradition.* Albany, N.Y.: SUNY, 1994.

Sharma, Arvind. *Hinduism for Our Times.* Delhi and New York: Oxford University Press, 1996.

Sinclair-Brull, Wendy. *Female Ascetics: Hierarchy and Purity in an Indian Religious Movement.* Richmond, Surrey, England: Curzon, 1997.

Notes

1. S. Radhakrishnan, *The Hindu View of Life* (New York: Macmillan, 1927), p. 91.
2. M. Monier-Williams, *Brahmanism and Hinduism* (London: Murray, 1891), p. 381.

4 Jainism

Jainism originated in India in the sixth century BCE, during a period of reaction against the prevailing Hindu priestly class, which was seeking to extend its dominant power through prescribed rituals, sacrifices, and yoga exercises, as well as in other ways. Dissatisfied with that trend, several thinkers sought a more coherent and intellectual system of religion. Some attempted to undermine the control of priestly power, others developed philosophical ideas, and still others sought to explore the nature of Ultimate Reality. One of the foremost dissident thinkers was Siddhartha Gautama (described in Chapter 5), the other was Nataputta Vardhamana.

MAHAVIRA

Traditional Account

Mahavira (meaning "Great Hero") is the accepted title of Nataputta Vardhamana, traditionally identified as the founder of Jainism.[1] According to Jain tradition, twenty-three *Tirthankaras* (makers of a *tirtha*, or ford — a crossing place) had preceded Mahavira in the present degenerating cosmic age. In the next cosmic age, which will represent an ascending order of happiness, another twenty-four Tirthankaras will appear. Modern scholarship credits only the last two Tirthankaras, Parshva and Mahavira, as historical figures.[2] The alleged dates and life spans of other Tirthankaras are too impractical (and incredible) to make their earthly existence plausible. Jains, however, worship all twenty-four Tirthankaras.

Tradition states that Mahavira was born in Vaisali (modern Bihar) in 599 BCE and died at the age of seventy-two, in 527 BCE. Scholars have

Jainism

BCE

c. 800s Parshva, the twenty-third *Tirthankara*

 c. 599 Birth of Mahavira (d. 527 BCE)

 c. 300s Compilation of Jain sacred texts

CE

    80 Split of Svetambara and Digambara groups

  800s Composition of *Adi purana* by Jinasena

 1600s Beginning of Sthanakvasi, subgroup of Svetambara

 1700s Beginning of Terapanth, subgroup of Svetambara

 1970s Migration of Jains to the West

debated the traditional date of his birth, suggesting a date of some sixty years later. The question is academic in the context of Jain tradition, which does not identify the beginning of Mahavira's life with his physical birth. Rather, Jains recognize several incarnations as god, king, and priest that antedate Mahavira's birth.

The uncertain state of the records, written by one of the Jain sects some nine hundred years after Mahavira's death, make the task of authenticating historical facts almost impossible. In spite of that difficulty, scholars have been able to reconstruct the following story.

Mahavira was the second son of a wealthy Indian ruler, or rajah. As members of the *kshatriya* caste, his parents probably adhered to the established religious patterns of the Hinduism of the time, although some scholars think that they may have belonged to Parshva's group. Mahavira married and had a daughter, but he found his status and wealth a burden to endure rather than a privilege to enjoy. Conforming to tradition, however, he waited until his parents died before renouncing his family and his status. At the age of thirty, he joined a band of wandering *ascetics* who followed the rule of Parshva.

Before long, Mahavira grew disillusioned with his companions, who did not practice extreme asceticism. In Mahavira's opinion, one had to apply two principles to liberate oneself from the cycles of birth or existence: extreme asceticism and *ahimsa* ("noninjury") of all living things. Consequently, he tore at his hair and beard, stripped off his loincloth, and walked nude through the villages and plains of central India during the hottest and coldest seasons. On rainy days he stayed off the roads to avoid stepping inadvertently on insects, and in dry weather he swept the road before him for the same reason. He always strained his drinking water through a cloth to reduce the risk of extinguishing the life of any creature.

Tradition states that for some years Mahavira wandered about with Goshala Makkhali, another naked mendicant who was the head of an ascetic sect, the Ajivakas. Whatever the association of the two men may have been, Mahavira and Goshala apparently disagreed on the issue of *karma*, and Mahavira went off on his own. He refrained from speaking to or greeting anyone, lest he form agreeable attachments that might bind him to the world and its pleasures. As an ascetic, he felt he should give up all worldly attachments, including clothes. Thus, he conquered his senses, including the sense of shame.

After twelve years of wandering from place to place and applying his principles of severe asceticism and *ahimsa*, Mahavira claimed to have attained *moksha* (release from the bonds of rebirth) and turned his attention to searching for people who might be capable of learning from him. He considered himself a *jina* (conqueror) who had achieved *kevala* (pure omniscient consciousness).

Challenge of Hindu Tradition

Mahavira challenged the traditional societal caste system of the Hindu faith. As disciples and followers converted to the Jain religion, they dropped their caste distinctions. Much later, however, the pervasive and established dominance of Hindu tradition influenced Jains to resume some caste distinctions.

Mahavira also spoke out against the deities of Hinduism. In his view, it was useless to pray to or to seek the aid of any deity. He stated that an individual needed no friend or being beyond himself or herself, on earth or anywhere else. In fact, Mahavira may be said to have been an atheist, because he rejected any justification for a supreme being or a creator of the universe. He insisted, further, that no special authority was vested in priestly castes; that the Hindu scriptures, the Vedas, were not sacred; and that no one should place any trust in external aids to liberation, the only path to which lay through one's self. Ironically, in spite of such teachings, his followers later considered him to be a divine incarnation.

Mahavira also modified the Hindu doctrine of *karma*. Contrary to Hindu thought of the time, Mahavira insisted that both matter and mind (or soul) are separate and eternal existences. He identified that dualistic ultimate reality as *jiva* ("soul" or "living things") and *ajiva* ("matter" or "lifeless things"). The purpose of life, according to Mahavira, is to liberate *jiva* from *ajiva*, the soul from matter. He taught that gods, prayers, worship, and rituals are profitless. Because *karma* encrusts the soul with matter, one simply must act as little as possible. The mere accumulation of *karma*, far from being a medium of liberation, is an obstacle to release from successive rebirth. The most rewarding alternative, then, is severe asceticism.

For thirty years, Mahavira went about preaching and teaching his form of severe asceticism. His followers were deeply impressed by his perceptive, ethical teachings and believed that he was omniscient and an incarnation of the divine. Accounts of Mahavira's death vary greatly; one states that he died practicing starvation, whereas another records his peaceful death after a lecture.

The Five Great Vows

Mahavira's asceticism is summed up in what came to be called the Five Great Vows. Some modern critics speculate that the vows were derived from Mahavira's association with the religious movement of Parshva. Others insist that they represent Mahavira's independent thinking. Whatever the case, they distinguish Jains from other religious devotees and concern, in order, *ahimsa*, truth, stealing, sex, and attachment.

1. To renounce killing and to deny the right of others to kill.
2. To renounce all vices associated with lies arising from greed, fear, laughter, or anger and to repudiate indifference to the lies of others.
3. To renounce all forms of stealing, whether the object is great or small, animate or inanimate, and to refuse to accept anything that is not freely given.
4. To renounce all sexual pleasures in favor of chastity and not to consent to sensuality in others. (Mahavira renounced not only sexual pleasures but also women in general. He is said to have declared that "women are the greatest temptation in the world.")
5. To renounce all forms of attachment that cause pleasure or pain and love or hate and to forbid consent to others to do so. (It was precisely because of the Fifth Vow that Mahavira renounced his family and possessions and refused to stay in any place more than five days.)

The Five Great Vows constituted the ground rules for the ascetic followers of Mahavira. In time, a less severe moral system of twelve vows was developed for disciples unable to match the rigors of the original five vows.

THE TWELVE VOWS OF JAINISM

Mahavira's ascetic rigor for monks was too severe a doctrine for any except the most disciplined followers. Consequently, a modified rule of life, consisting of twelve vows, was prescribed for ordinary people:

1. Maintain *ahimsa* at all times. Never take the life of a sentient creature.
2. Never lie.
3. Never steal nor take what is not given.
4. Never be unchaste.
5. Check greed by limiting wealth and giving away any excess.
6. Avoid temptation by refraining from excessive travel.

7. Lead a simple life by limiting material needs.

8. Guard against evils that can be avoided.

9. Meditate at stated periods.

10. Observe special periods of self-denial.

11. Spend time occasionally as a monk, to devote all your energies to a higher order of human behavior.

12. Give alms generously, especially to monks and ascetics.

Of the twelve vows, the first has had the most important social and economic effects in India. Jain adherents avoid all occupations—such as farming, fishing, butchering, brewing, and the sale or manufacture of arms, instruments, and intoxicants—that threaten life. Instead, they turn to business and professional careers, such as banking, merchandising, landowning, the law, and teaching. Along with the status of Jains as professionals, their observance of the other eleven vows, which place moral restraints on their behavior, has earned them a level of social respect that has contributed to their survival in India.

JAIN GROUPS

During the Middle Ages, several castes emerged within the Jain laity, although not among the monks. Social differentiations in Jainism are not as marked as those in Hinduism, although certain features (mainly occupational) are common to both.

The contributions of Jains to public welfare and culture in India have been extraordinary. Jains have founded such welfare institutions as public dispensaries, public lodging, and boarding institutions for the poor and the helpless. Their cultural contributions also have been numerous—not only in religion and philosophy, but in other fields as well.

Jainism, with its emphasis on asceticism, may have been popular at one time in India, but today fewer than two million people follow its tenets. Various schisms gradually led to two principal sects: the Svetambaras, the "white-clad" group, who allowed the wearing of at least one garment and admitted women, and the Digambaras, the "sky-clad" group, who insisted on total nudity and the exclusion of women from temples and monasteries, on the assumption that women could not attain liberation until they were reborn as men. The Svetambaras are dominant in Kathiawar, Gujarat, and Rajasthan (in northwestern India, near the Pakistan border); the Digambaras prevail in southern India, in Hyderabad and Mysore. The two groups are further divided into subsects.

Proscriptions against clothing and veneration of the Tirthankaras became the two critical issues dividing the followers of Mahavira. The eminence of Mahavira was gradually reduced by the veneration accorded the twenty-three Tirthankaras who were thought to have preceded him. Shrines and temples were erected to honor, for instance, Rishabha, the first of the Tirthankaras; Nemi, the twenty-second Tirthankara; and Parshva, the twenty-third Tirthankara.

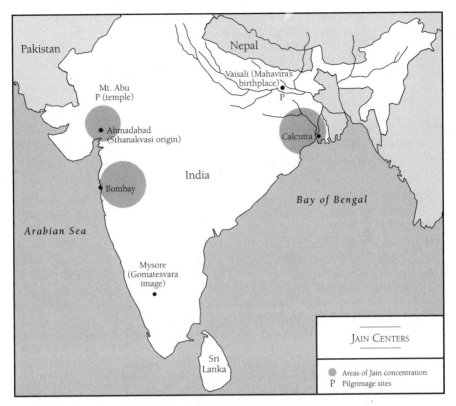

Source: David S. Noss and John B. Noss, *A History of the World's Religions*, 9th ed. (New York: Macmillan, 1994). Reprinted by permission of Prentice-Hall/Pearson Higher Education.

JAIN SACRED TEXTS

Jain scriptures do not belong to a single period, nor are the texts free from later revisions and additions. Tradition states that a sacred piece of literature, the Purvas, was preserved orally for three hundred years from Mahavira's time until the death of Bhadrabahu (c. 300 BCE), the last person to have memorized it. A council was called after the death of that venerable person to reconstruct and systematize a sacred canon. However, the Svetambaras and the Digambaras could not agree on the compilation of sources. The Digambaras declared that the Purvas were hopelessly lost and began to compose new texts. Later, two more councils were called, one in the third century CE and the other in the fifth century, to commit the current oral texts to writing. By that time, some texts had been lost, some had been corrupted, and some new material had been added. Despite those difficulties, the Jain scriptures finally were formulated and, according to scholars, seem to contain some of Mahavira's basic teachings.

The Svetambara scripture consists of forty-five Agamas, or texts, which deal with matters such as *cosmogony* (an account of the origin of the universe), astronomy, geography, divisions of time, doctrines, views on Hindu and Buddhist heresies, rules on ascetic life, and death by voluntary starvation. The Digambara canon consists of two major works that address the doctrines of *karma* and passions, such as attachment and aversion, that defile and bind the *jiva*. Digambaras and Svetambaras also value other works that deal with logic, epistemology, ethics, and so on.

JAIN TEACHINGS

Jainism is fundamentally an ethical religion, and its chief concern is the moral life of an individual. To be sure, Jainism has developed a set of beliefs, yet strictly speaking, those beliefs relate not to theology but to a philosophy of life.

Time and the Universe

Time, for the Jains, is eternal and formless. The universe is infinite, beginningless, and endless. There is no god, no creator, no ultimate being. The universe operates in accordance with its own inherent principles. It was never created. Its constituent elements are soul, matter, time, space, and the principles of motion and rest. Those elements change constantly, but they are indestructible and eternal.

Jains perceive time as a wheel with twelve spokes, called ages, which are divided into two cycles. Six ages make an ascending cycle, during which humans progress in age, stature, knowledge, and happiness. The other six ages make a descending cycle, during which there is a gradual deterioration in the state of everything. Joined together, the two cycles make one rotation of the wheel of time.

Dualism

Jains conceive of ultimate reality as being dualistic. As already noted, the two separate eternal entities of *jiva* and *ajiva* constitute reality. *Jiva* is the life principle. Its essential characteristic is consciousness, or mental function. In its pure state, *jiva* possesses the qualities of limitless knowledge, endless perception, infinite power, and eternal bliss. It is formless and cannot be perceived by the senses. By expansion or contraction, it can occupy various proportions of state. *Ajiva* is the lifeless principle, or matter. Its essential characteristic is lack of consciousness. In its pure state, it possesses the characteristics of touch, taste, smell, and color. *Ajiva* clusters into any shape or form, such as earth, water, wind, and sentient beings.

Jiva is divisible into five groups, depending on the number of sense organs possessed. The highest group has the five senses of touch, smell, taste, hearing, and sight; included in this group are animals, humans, deities, and demons. Next comes the group that possesses four senses, such as bees, flies, and the larger insects. The three-sense group includes the smaller insects, such as moths, and the two-sense group includes leeches, worms, and shellfish. The final, single-sense group includes vegetables, trees, seeds, and the animated four elements of earth, water, air, and fire.

Interior view of one of the many Jain marble temples on top of Mount Abu, Rajasthan, India. The statue of a Tirthankara sits in meditative repose surrounded by exquisite figurative carvings in marble. Built in the eleventh century CE, these Jain temples at Mount Abu command a magnificent view of the surrounding countryside in Rajasthan.
Courtesy of Government of India Tourist Office, Toronto.

Liberation from Rebirth

Jains conceive of *karma* rather materialistically, as formation of subtle matter around the soul. Because every event has a definite cause behind it, all phenomena are linked in a universal chain of cause and effect. The influx of *karma* adheres to the soul like a sticky substance and affects the course of rebirth. At the end of each substance, the soul carries with it the *karma* matter that vitiates its purity, causing the soul's rebirth in a form appropriate to its moral condition. If the soul has only a little *karma* matter, it will be light enough to rise on the scale of transcendental embodiments. If, however, the soul carries a heavy *karma* matter, it will sink into lower levels of existence.

To release oneself from *karma* matter, one must be embodied in a human form and live the life of an ascetic monk (or an ascetic nun, in some groups). To arrest further accretion of *karma* matter, one must follow all the ascetic practices designed for monks. Of the three main steps leading to the path of liberation, the first is faith in the twenty-four Tirthankaras. Next, one must obtain right knowledge by studying the teachings of those omniscient masters. Finally, that essential knowledge must be realized by practicing right conduct, which involves the control of thoughts, words, actions, emotions, and senses in light of the Five Great Vows.

Observance of the three principles of faith, knowledge, and right practices prevents the formation of further *karma*. But how can one rid oneself of the *karma* already accumulated? The remedy is to practice severe asceticism, such as prolonged endurance of thirst, hunger, pain, heat, and cold. Confession, penance, the study of scriptures, and meditations also are important, but a prolonged period of severe austerity will annihilate more *karma* matter than will meditation and scripture reading combined. When all *karma* matter is completely annihilated, the soul attains liberation.

Because the attainment of liberation is difficult, Jains believe that many souls will never succeed in liberating themselves but will migrate from one form to another all through eternity. The few who attain liberation—freedom from *karma* matter—also shed their physical bodies, and their souls ascend in a straight line to the top of the universe, where all the released souls, called *siddhas*, dwell. In that pristine, blissful state, the *siddhas* have no individuality and are invisible and intangible. Moreover, all *siddhas* are identical and possess a spiritual quality of omniscience, an absolute blissful state. Because of their spiritual feat in the conquest of *karma*, *siddhas* are called *jinas*, or conquerors. Thus Jainism, the religion of conquerors, involves the heroic feat of self-liberation.

JAIN OBSERVANCES

Jains observe the Hindu domestic rites of birth, marriage, and death. Hindu rites of worship such as prayers and offerings to the gods (*puja*) also have been adopted, together with Hindu gods and goddesses, although the latter occupy a position greatly subordinate to the Tirthankaras. Despite the fact that the Tirthankaras in their released state have no concern for human beings, devout Jains offer prayers to them daily. In the temple, the central image is a Tirthankara. The favorites are the first Tirthankara, Rishabha, and the last three: Nemi, Parshva, and Mahavira. There are also a few temples to the other Tirthankaras. The Digambaras' images are naked, but the Svetambaras' images are clothed and wear ornaments and crowns. Every twelve years, the Digambaras in Mysore stage a great celebration to bathe the fifty-seven-foot image of Gomatesvara, one of the Tirthankaras, with *ghee* ("melted butter").

STUDY QUESTIONS

1. Relate the traditional account of Mahavira.
2. What are the ideological differences between Mahavira and the Hindu faith?
3. List the Jain vows adopted by ascetics and those followed by ordinary people.
4. Summarize the disagreements between the two principal Jain sects.
5. What do scholars know about the Jain sacred texts?
6. Discuss Jain teachings on time, universe, and dualism.
7. Describe the heroic feat of self-liberation.

Suggested Reading

Babb, Lawrence A. *Absent Lord: Ascetics and Kings in a Jain Ritual Culture*. Comparative Studies in Religion and Society, 8. Berkeley: University of California Press, 1996.

Dundas, Paul. *The Jains. Library of Religious Beliefs and Practices*. London and New York: Routledge, 1992.

Jaini, Padmanabh S. *The Jaina Path of Purification*. Berkeley: University of California Press, 1979.

Laidlaw, James. *Riches and Renunciation: Religion, Economy, and Society among the Jains*. Clarendon, England, and New York: Oxford University Press, 1995.

Roy, Ashim Kumar. *A History of the Jainas*. New Delhi: Gitanjali Publishing House, 1984.

Sangave, Vilas Adinath. *Jaina Community: A Social Survey*, 2nd ed. Bombay: Popular Prakashan, 1980.

Notes

1. Jain or Jaina is derived from *jina,* an Indian term meaning "conqueror" and applied as an honorific title to the ascetic teachers of the Jain tradition.
2. Parshva is said to have lived around the eighth century BCE (some two centuries before Mahavira) and is often depicted in iconography in the posture of meditation with hooded serpents over his head.

5 Buddhism

Buddhism, like Christianity and Islam, is a worldwide religion. It covers a huge part of Asia and the Far East: India, Sri Lanka (Ceylon), Thailand, Mongolia, Manchuria, Tibet, China, Korea, and Japan. It also has many followers in Europe, Britain, Canada, and the United States.

Buddhism takes its name from the title *Buddha* ("Enlightened One"), by which the first and most famous Buddhist leader, Siddhartha Gautama was known. The traditional story of his life and his teachings were transmitted orally for over four centuries before being documented some time between the first century BCE and the first century CE. The biography given here is based on several Buddhist scriptures.

THE BUDDHA

Traditional Account

Siddhartha Gautama (c. 563–483 BCE), commonly known as the Buddha, was born in the ancient kingdom of the Sakyas (modern Nepal).[1] His father was an Indian chieftain of the Sakya clan and thus a member of the Hindu *kshatriya* (warrior) caste. According to the traditional account of the life of Siddhartha, one night before he was born his mother dreamed that a white elephant entered her womb through her side. Hindu priests called in to interpret the dream predicted the birth of a son who would become either a universal monarch or a universal teacher.

Ten lunar months after his conception, Siddhartha's mother set out to visit her parents in a neighboring village. On her way, she passed through a park called Lumbini, where she went into labor and gave

Buddhism

BCE

c. 563   Birth of Buddha (d. 483 BCE)
c. 395   Second council of Vesali (Vaisali)
272–232   Asoka, Buddhist ruler of India
c. 225   Theravada Buddhism introduced in Sri Lanka (Ceylon)

CE

c. 65   Earliest evidence of a Buddhist community in China
c. 180   Development of Mahayana Buddhism
c. 200   Nagarjuna established the Madhyamika school of philosophy
399   Introduction of Buddhism in Korea
470   Birth of Bodhidharma, founder of Ch'an
c. 500s   Introduction of Chinese Buddhism in Japan
538   Birth of Chih-i, founder of T'ien-t'ai/Tendai (d. 597)
594   Buddhism established as the state religion of Japan
749   First Buddhist monastery in Tibet
c. 800   Tendai and Shingon Buddhism founded in Japan
845   Persecution of Buddhists in China
900s   Revival of Lamaism in Tibet
1000s   Revival of Theravada tradition in Sri Lanka and Burma
1200s   Decline of Buddhism in northern India
1222   Birth of Nichiren (d. 1282)
1360   Buddhism established as state religion in Thailand
1400s   Decline of Buddhism in southern India
1598   Control of Buddhism by Tokugawa shogunate in Japan (ended 1868)
c. 1617   Tibet ruled by a series of Dalai Lamas (ended 1959)
1900s   Beginning of Buddhist missionary activities in the West
1920s   Buddhism attacked in Mongolia by Soviet Communists
1949   Beginning of Chinese Communist attack on Buddhism
1952   Formation of World Fellowship of Buddhists
1959   Chinese takeover of Tibet with destruction of temples and monasteries; Dalai Lama and several Tibetans forced to flee to India

birth to a son. The site, now called Rummindei, lies in Nepal, and a pillar raised by King Asoka in the third century BCE stands there still in commemoration of the event.

Details associated with the infancy of Siddhartha are fragmentary. According to tradition, the Hindu sage Asita (also called Kala Devala) recognized auspicious signs on the child's body at the time of his birth and concluded that the child would be a universal teacher, or Buddha.[2] That augury was partly confirmed five days after the child's birth, when Hindu priests predicted during the name-giving ceremony that if the child remained at home he would become a universal monarch and that if he did not he would become a Buddha. On the seventh day after the child's birth, his mother died and he was placed in the care of his mother's sister.

Accounts of Siddhartha's boyhood are no better documented than are details concerning his infancy. Part of the traditional record refers to an incident that presaged the young boy's eventual career. One day, the little boy Siddhartha was taken to a local public festival in which both his father and the local farmers took part. The nurses attending Siddhartha were so attracted by the festivities that they left the boy alone in the tent. When they returned, they found him seated cross-legged in the posture of a *yogin* (one who practices a self-controlled, meditative position prescribed by yoga), absorbed in a trance.

Siddhartha was brought up in great luxury and comfort. At the age of sixteen (or, according to another account, nineteen), he married a cousin, who also was sixteen years old. Although the birth of a son followed the union, Siddhartha was dissatisfied with a life limited to family and social obligations. His concerns transcended such limitations.

The Four Sights

Tradition states that the turning point in Siddhartha's life came at the age of twenty-nine, when his awareness of human suffering became the motivating force behind his quest for truth. Four sights, or perceptions, are usually cited as the instigation of his religious crisis. The first sight associated with Siddhartha's heightened perception was that of a decrepit old man leaning on his staff as he walked. The second was that of a sick man, suffering in pain and soiled by incontinence brought on by his enfeebled condition. The third was that of a human corpse being carried to a funeral pyre and the fourth that of a calm, ascetic monk with a clean-shaven head and wearing a yellow robe. The sum of those images struck Siddhartha with the force of a revelation: all humans are subject to suffering. Transformed by the insight, he decided to leave home in search of a solution to the problem of human suffering. Thus began what is known as the "Great Renunciation": Siddhartha's abdication of a princely life in favor of one as a wandering ascetic in selfless denial of material possessions.

The Quest for Truth

For the next six years, Siddhartha struggled to find an answer to human misery. His first recourse was to Alara Kalama, a famous Hindu sage, who gladly taught him to achieve the "realm of nothingness." Siddhartha quickly matched his teacher's mastery of the mystical state of nothingness, but he found the consequences to be disappointing. He then consulted another great Hindu teacher, who taught him to attain the "realm of neither perception nor nonperception." That higher mystical state proved no more satisfying than previous solutions that Siddhartha had tested and rejected. He thereupon turned from Hindu

philosophic meditation to severe bodily austerity in his search for absolute truth.

After a short period of wandering, Siddhartha reached a village near
Uruvela (modern Gaya in India), where he was joined by a group of
five ascetics. According to tradition, one of those ascetics was the Hindu
priest who had predicted during the name-giving ceremony that the
child Siddhartha one day would become a Buddha. In the company of
that group, Siddhartha subjected himself to a regimen of extreme austerity that is vividly described in sacred texts (Buddhacarita XII.90–106).
It is said that, among other things, he sat on a couch of thorns, ate all
sorts of nauseous foods, and let filth accumulate on his body. As a result of such self-mortification, Siddhartha's health deteriorated to the
point where his friends thought he had died. In the course of a slow re-
cuperation, Siddhartha came to the conclusion that a regimen of austerity and self-mortification was no more effective a path to the identification of absolute truth than asceticism and philosophic meditation had
been. As a prerequisite to a new approach, he decided to restore his
health by eating and drinking properly once again. His five Hindu companions, outraged by what they interpreted as his surrender to self-
indulgence, left him in disgust.

The Temptations of the Buddha

Having regained his health, Siddhartha set out once more by himself to
follow his own quest for truth. At some point he turned off the road to
sit cross-legged at the foot of a tree (now known as a *bodhi* tree, or tree
of knowledge), determined not to rise before he had attained enlightenment. According to the earliest canonical texts, Siddhartha's first encounter or experience was with the personification of evil, the tempter
Mara, whose mission it was to confound and frustrate Siddhartha's
search.

Mara's three temptations are graphically described in the texts (Buddhacarita XIII.1–6, 71–72). First, Mara tried to convince Siddhartha that
a cousin and a former archenemy had revolted at home, taken his wife,
and imprisoned his father. Siddhartha sat unmoved. Next, Mara pa-
raded three voluptuous "daughters," or goddesses, accompanied by a
group of sensuous dancers, around Siddhartha's tree with instructions
to seduce him by any means they might devise. Siddhartha ignored
them. Finally, Mara summoned a host of demons to terrify Siddhartha
with their deadly missiles. Siddhartha reacted by touching the ground
with the fingers of his right hand. The contact produced a great thun-
dering sound, at which Mara and his host of demons fled in confusion.[3]

The Enlightenment of the Buddha

Having defeated Mara, Siddhartha spent the night under the tree in
deep meditation. As he passed through deeper and deeper states of consciousness, he was transported by visions of his former existences. With
the insights born of that knowledge, he suddenly understood the cause
and the cycle of rebirth. He had solved the riddle of human suffering

and discovered a way of eliminating it. Thus, at the age of thirty-five, Siddhartha attained enlightenment and became the supreme Buddha (Buddhacarita XIV.1–9, 47–51, 83–108).

Buddhist texts describe the cosmic portents that accompanied Buddha's enlightenment: the earth swelled, fruit and blossoms fell, and the sky shone bright. Buddha, however, spent the next several weeks (five or seven, according to different accounts) meditating on the various aspects of the truth he had realized and debating with himself the wisdom of communicating his discovery to others. He resolved the conflict by means of an analogy to a lotus pond, in which some lotuses remain under water, some float on the surface, and some rise above it. In a similar way, Buddha decided, humans differ in their capacity to comprehend the cosmic truth, or *dharma*, he had discovered. To those to whom it was given to understand, he would communicate his discovery.

The First Disciples of the Buddha

Buddha's next concern was to identify those capable of receiving *dharma*. His two former Hindu teachers were dead, and his five ascetic Hindu companions had deserted him. Nevertheless, because he had been close to them, Buddha decided to find those five companions, who were now in Benares (modern Varanasi, a city halfway between Delhi and Calcutta). When he finally caught up with them, Buddha described his "enlightened" state and offered to share his newly found insight into *dharma* with them, but to no avail. His former companions accused him again of abandoning austerity in favor of self-indulgence and of forfeiting any prospect of enlightenment. When Buddha asked them only for a fair hearing, they reiterated their disappointment and disgust. He appealed to them yet once more, and for the third time, they demonstrated their bitterness and resentment. Buddha is said to have challenged them with this brief question: "Do you admit, O monks, that I have never spoken like this before?" Struck by his sincerity and persistence, the Buddha's five former friends answered, "Lord, you have not." The Buddha then delivered his first discourse, whereupon the five ascetic companions became his first disciples and founding members of the *sangha*, or monastic order.

Buddha now devoted his time to preaching his new doctrine. His father, his stepmother, and his former wife converted, followed by many others. Some converts, as might be expected, were from either his own societal caste (the *kshatriya*) or lower castes, but many Hindu priests of the *brahmin* caste also joined the *sangha*. Hindu caste distinctions, so sharply defined in Indian society, ceased to apply once an individual joined the *sangha*.

So compelling was the attraction of the new movement that soon Buddha had sixty *arhats*, or "perfected" disciples who had attained liberation and enlightenment. Buddha commissioned them to travel all over India and into the world beyond to spread his message of peace, truth, and compassion. He remained in India and converted leading ascetics and leaders of influence, including several rulers. As the number of his followers increased, monasteries were built for Buddha and his

Gautama Buddha delivering his first discourse. Beneath him, his disciples are shown surrounding a wheel, a symbol of early Buddhist iconography. This sculpted sandstone, Gupta style, dates from the fifth century BCE and is presently at Sarnath Museum.

Courtesy of Government of India Tourist Office, Toronto.

sangha in virtually every important city in India, including monasteries in Savatthi and Jetanana.

The *sanghas* were institutions dominated by men. Ananda, Buddha's cousin and later his chief and constant disciple, pleaded with him on behalf of women. After some hesitation, Buddha agreed to the institution of an order of nuns. His aunt and some of her friends were the first women to enter the order.

Devadatta, another cousin of Buddha, was a convert with ulterior motives. First, he plotted to succeed the aging Buddha as leader of the *sangha*. When no one would take him seriously, Devadatta made three unsuccessful attempts on the life of Buddha. Finally, he tried to induce a schism in the *sangha* by establishing a separate order; that was short-lived, however, and Devadatta's supporters soon returned to Buddha. Nine months after he had seen his hopes dashed for the third time, Devadatta died.

Death of the Buddha

Never seriously threatened by rivals such as Devadatta, Buddha's mission lasted for forty-five years. He taught and trained a large group of well-disciplined followers until, at the age of eighty, he succumbed to a serious illness. His last words to his disciples were, "And now, O monks, I take leave of you; transient are all conditioned things; try to accomplish your aim with diligence." A week later, his body was cremated by his clansmen in Kusinara (modern Kasia, in Uttar Pradesh). In spite of Buddha's dying injunction to be aware of the transience of "conditioned things" (actions, thoughts, and the like dictated by societal norms or natural instinct), his family and followers quarreled over the disposition of his relics. Finally, by common consent, the relics were divided into eight portions, satisfying the wishes of all disputants.

The portrait of Buddha that emerges from ancient texts is one of great wisdom and great compassion. The spectacle of human suffering made him seek a rational system of thought that would free humanity from its fetters. His unique reputation rests less on his intellectual power and his abilities as a leader than it does on his record as a great teacher.

THE SPREAD OF BUDDHISM

Early Councils

Little is known about the spread of Buddhism immediately after the death of Buddha (483 BCE). Buddhist tradition maintains that a council was called immediately after his death, but many scholars have questioned whether such a council was ever convened. According to tradition, at the council five hundred monks formulated an authorized canon and rules governing early Buddhist monasteries.

Scholars more or less have accepted that a council was held a century later. That council resulted in a schism over doctrinal issues and disciplinary rules, principally between a group called the Mahasanghika ("Great Sangha"), which interpreted doctrine and discipline liberally, and a group called the Theravadins ("Adherents of the Teaching of the Elders"), which represented orthodoxy and conservatism. Other groups, or schools (the traditional number is eighteen), also emerged from the council.

Tradition refers to a third council, held in the third century BCE. At that gathering, according to some accounts, the Buddhist canon, the *Tripitaka,* was completed, and longstanding sectarian controversies led to additional splits and divisions.

A fourth council, dealing with the composition of commentaries, is believed to have been held sometime during the first century CE, although the absence of several Buddhist groups has led scholars to conclude that it was simply a sectarian synod, not an ecumenical council. That conclusion is based partly on subsequent events within the Buddhist community, which eventually split into several formal sects.

Asoka's Conversion

Sometime during the third century BCE, Asoka, a ruler of the Mauryan empire of northern India embraced the Buddhist faith. Asoka was the grandson of an army officer who defeated the forces of Alexander the

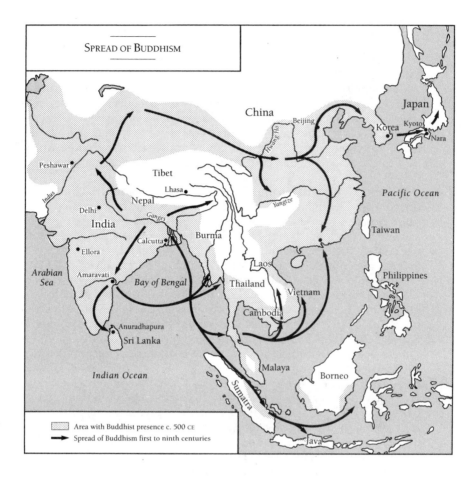

SPREAD OF BUDDHISM

China

Beijing

Japan

Korea

Kyoto

Nara

Peshawar

Tibet

Lhasa

Pacific Ocean

Nepal

Yangtze

Delhi

India

Ganges

Taiwan

Calcutta

Burma

Arabian
Sea

Amaravati

Laos

Philippines

Bay of Bengal

Thailand

Vietnam

Cambodia

Anuradhapura

Sri Lanka

Malaya

Borneo

Indian Ocean

Sumatra

Java

Area with Buddhist presence c. 500 CE
Spread of Buddhism first to ninth centuries

Great. Like his father and his grandfather, Asoka continued to expand
his imperial territory through conquest until he was attracted to the
teachings of Buddhism. Upon publicly accepting Buddhism, he for-
swore warfare and sought to foster the spread of Buddhism throughout
his empire. Archaeologists are still finding traces of the temples he built
and other legacies of his conversion. Asoka is best remembered, however, for the missionary work he sponsored. He sent Buddhist missionaries not only to all parts of India but also westward to the Hellenized
kingdoms of Asia, Africa, and Europe, southward to Sri Lanka (Ceylon), and eastward to Burma.

Buddhist Expansion Eastward

China. By the beginning of the first century CE, the two main branches
of Buddhism, Theravada and Mahayana, were moving through central
Asia into China. Ruling China at that time was the Han dynasty (206
BCE–220 CE), a power in the East that matched the Roman Empire in
the West. The Han regime dominated eastern Asia from Korea to
Turkistan and from the Gobi Desert to Vietnam. By the time Buddhist

missionaries arrived, the national creed was Confucianism, which emphasized social rankings according to intellectual status, a rigid family structure, and a moral code based on humanity and the practice of perfect virtue for its own sake.

Tradition has it that the White Horse Temple, reputedly the first Chinese Buddhist monastery, was founded as a consequence of a manifestation of Buddha, in the form of a golden deity, in a dream of Emperor Ming (58–76 CE). The earliest historical reference to a Chinese Buddhist community dates from 65 CE, and by the middle of the second century, Buddha was being worshiped in the imperial palace, along with other deities.

Incursions by Turkish and Tibetan tribes into northern China produced a social climate ripe for Buddhism, because by becoming Buddhist monks, Chinese adherents could avoid military and labor service, as well as taxation. Also, the invaders of the northern territories came to embrace the Buddhist faith in order to consolidate their conquests and ensure continued prosperity. Meanwhile, social uncertainty and frustration in southern China favored the growth of metaphysical speculation. Taoists, predecessors of Confucians, considered "inactivity" virtue and "nonbeing" the origin of all things. Those beliefs seemed to mirror the basic Buddhist ideal of *nirvana,* and a sympathetic dialogue developed between Buddhist monks and the Taoist literati, whose influence enabled Buddhism to gain converts among royalty and the rich.

A few eminent monks laid the philosophical foundation of Chinese Buddhism during the fourth century, a period in which cave temples were carved out of hills to serve Buddhist traveling monks and native believers. The cave temples were centers of devotion and pilgrimage for the next thousand years and serve as repositories of Buddhist art to this day.

Two great events marked the turn of the fifth century. In 399, Fa-hsien became the first Chinese Buddhist monk to complete his pilgrimage to India, during which he survived great hardships to reach sacred Buddhist sites along the Ganges and to study Buddhist teachings at the source. After visiting Ceylon (now Sri Lanka), he returned to China in 414. In 401, the Buddhist monk Kumarajiva, captured by a Chinese raiding force, traveled from Kucha in northwestern India to the Chinese capital of Ch'ang-an, where he remained for the rest of his life. Under Kumarajiva's direction, approximately three hundred scholars rendered into Chinese some of the most important Mahayana scriptures.

By the early fifth century, northern China had been unified by a Turkic tribe whose emperors identified themselves with Buddha. The emperors encouraged the erection of Buddhist images and temples and invited Buddhist monks to be their advisors. In 446, however, one of the potentates issued a draconian edict that called for the destruction of all Buddhist temples, shrines, paintings, and scriptures and the summary execution of all monks. The storm was brief: eight years later, the destroyer's successor pronounced himself to be the reincarnation of Buddha and restored Buddhism to his realm.

A second persecution of Buddhists occurred in 574, when Emperor Wu sought to advance Confucianism by charging Buddhism with fostering disloyalty and breaking down filial piety. Before Emperor Wu died in 578, the imperial family and the aristocracy had appropriated tens of thousands of temples and defrocked more than one million monks and nuns.

Those reverses in China were mirrored to an aggravated degree in India, where invading Huns, a nomadic Asian people, destroyed numerous Buddhist monasteries. That invasion presaged the decline of Buddhism in India. Scholars are not satisfied that they have yet established all the factors that contributed to the disappearance of Buddhism from India, but some maintain that the tolerance of Buddhism for other faiths doomed it to reabsorption by the dominant Hindu tradition.

Buddhism survived sporadic persecution in China until the Sui dynasty, founded by Emperor Wen in 581, ushered in the golden age of Chinese Buddhism. Calling himself a disciple of Buddha, Emperor Wen used Buddhism as a binding influence in the reunification of northern and southern China. His fame attracted envoys from Japan and Korea who came to receive Buddhist teaching. For the next two and a half centuries, Buddhism spread throughout China, Korea, and Japan. Then, in 845, Buddhist hegemony in China came to an abrupt end amid a third great wave of persecution. Thousands of temples and shrines were demolished, hundreds of thousands of monks and nuns were defrocked, hundreds of acres of temple land were confiscated, and an untold number of gold, silver, bronze, and iron images were melted down. Although the emperor responsible for such punitive measures died only one year after implementing them—and with his death, Buddhism was restored— the golden age of Chinese Buddhism had ended.

Pilgrims and worshipers visit and pay homage to the revered image of the Buddha (Daibutsu) in Kamakura, Japan. The statue, fifty feet tall and made of bronze, was crafted in 1252.
Courtesy of British Airways (BOAC), Toronto.

Japan. Buddhism was introduced to Japan from Korea in the sixth century. At first, the new religion was regarded only as a talisman for the protection of the country. During the Nara period (710–794), however, Buddhism became a state religion, and a great statue of Buddha, called Daibutsu, was erected in the capital city of Nara, which became a national cult center. In time, various Buddhist groups found acceptance among the Japanese people, who in turn developed their own sectarian variants.

Buddhism proved no less vulnerable to sporadic persecution in Japan than it had in China. The most recent occurred during the Meiji period (1868–1912), when Japan's ruling class sought to promote Shinto as the state religion. The result was the confiscation of temple properties and the defrocking of thousands of Buddhist priests. In spite of those comparatively recent depredations, no other Buddhist country in the world can match the number and diversity of Buddhist sects that characterize Japan in modern times.

Tibet. Although Buddhism had spread into Tibet as early as the seventh century, it was not until the eighth century that Buddhism overshadowed Bon, the native shamanistic cult. The Tibetans followed Indian rather than Chinese forms of Buddhism and eventually formulated the curious mixture of Bon, Indian Buddhism, and *Tantrism* (an esoteric practice and doctrine; see Chapter 3), currently known as *Lamaism.* After initially receiving active encouragement from Tibetan rulers, Buddhism was subjected in the ninth century to persecution so severe and protracted that it took two centuries for it to become re-established. By that time, two distinctive groups of Lamaists, the Dalai Lamas and the Panchen Lamas, along with numerous Buddhist sects based mainly on Indian teachings, had evolved.

By the fourteenth century, the Tibetans had translated all the Buddhist literature they could obtain and had produced their own canon. Separate orders of Buddhist monks also developed, and as the various monasteries acquired power, rivalries grew intense. The political struggle for dominance was ultimately resolved in the seventeenth century by the Mongol chieftain Guuhri Khan, who awarded Tibet to the Dalai Lama, who became both spiritual and temporal leader.

The history of Tibetan Buddhism is characterized by political intrigue motivated by a lust for power. Rivalry among Buddhist factions was exacerbated by the territorial claims of various military forces and, in this century, of various governments, including the Nationalist Chinese, the British, and the Chinese Communists. The Chinese Communists finally took over Tibet in 1959 and sent the Dalai Lama into exile.

Buddhism: A Worldwide Religion

The strength of Buddhism in Asian cultures is difficult to assess, because a religion cannot be measured solely in terms of the numbers of its members or institutions. Buddhist virtues and ideals still play a dominant role in Asia, and new Buddhist movements serve to give laypeople a deeper sense of commitment to religious activities and goals. Buddhism still survives in Nepal, where its founder was born. It also flourishes in Bhutan, Burma, Thailand, Laos, Vietnam, and Indonesia. The Indian heritage is clearly evident in most of these places.

In addition, several Buddhist groups have shown a new interest in Buddhist missions in Europe and the Americas. In fact, some scholars maintain that the increasing interest in Buddhist teachings shown by Western societies represents more than academic curiosity, that it may represent a sincere acceptance of the teachings of Buddha and an application of spiritual energy. For many Western people, the Buddhist faith meets their needs and contributes to peace on earth.

An ancient Buddhist prophecy foretold that after 2500 years Buddhism would either fade away or enjoy a renaissance. Some Buddhist historians speculate that the critical period anticipated by that ancient prophecy began with the rise to power of the Chinese Communist Party (CCP) in 1949, which was accompanied by draconian measures against Buddhists reminiscent of those of the early emperors.

The Communist government promptly confiscated monastery lands and revenues, forced monks and nuns to work in fields and factories, and shipped young men off as "volunteers" in the Korean War. Chinese Buddhist scholars were carefully screened for political "reliability." U Nu, prime minister of neighboring Burma, convinced that it was futile to challenge the Chinese government with arms alone, sponsored a meeting of the Sixth World Buddhist Council in Rangoon in 1954–1956, the first meeting of its kind in more than five hundred years. Thousands of monks and devout Buddhists from all over southeastern Asia gathered in an attempt to build a Buddhist ideological front. Many, however, knew that Communism had won the day, in China at least, and that no strategy was likely to modify the attitude of the Communist regime in China to Buddhism. The Communists themselves were quick to point out apparent similarities between Buddhism and Marxism, such as a commitment in both ideologies to a classless society.

Buddhism has survived greater and more sustained depredation than has been its lot in China since 1949, and it still maintains its prominence in Japan and southeastern Asia. In fact, some observers see a Buddhist renaissance and a vindication of positive prophetic vision in the active growth of popular expressions of Mahayana Buddhism. They point out that Buddhist religious life is still practiced in many temples and homes and that Buddhism is highly compatible with modern science and psychological studies.

Whatever the future may hold, it is undeniable that in the twentieth century Buddhism has become a worldwide religion. Buddhist groups and temples can be found not only in Asian countries but also in most of the major cities in Africa, Europe, and the Americas. Asian Buddhists are sending missionaries to the West to win their allegiance, and Western converts are proclaiming Buddha's teachings through books, pamphlets, films, and meditation centers. The Indian Buddha is now honored by millions of adherents all over the world.

BUDDHIST SACRED TEXTS

Buddhism does not require orthodoxy of belief. Consequently, although Buddhist texts include canonical treatises, there is no closed canon of sacred writings. As Buddhism developed through the centuries, numerous important works attained the status of scripture. The bulk of Buddhist sacred books is truly enormous, amounting to hundreds of volumes. Today, different groups and subgroups emphasize one or more works, according to how they understand and interpret Buddha's teaching. For instance, one sect adheres to the Pali canon of 45 volumes, exclusive of commentaries, whereas the Tibetans include no fewer than 325 volumes. Of the hundreds of Buddhist texts in Pali, Sanskrit, Chinese, and Tibetan considered to be sacred, only a small number have been translated into English.

The most basic and possibly the earliest body of sacred writings is the *Tripitaka* (the Three Baskets), so-called because it consists of three "baskets," or collections, of disciplines: the Vinayana Pitaka, which lists the rules of the Buddhist order; the Sutta Pitaka, which describes dialogues between Buddha and his disciples on Buddhist teachings; and the Abhidhamma Pitaka, which consists of metaphysical instruction.

Texts written in Pali that are considered to be reliable sources of early Buddhism include the Dhammapada, the Intivuttaka, the Udana, the Sutta Nipata, the Theratherigatha, and a few others.

Sacred collections written in Sanskrit and used primarily by Mahayanists include the Mahavastu, the Lalita Vistara (which emphasizes Buddha's divinity), the Prajnaparamitas, the Samadhiraja, the Lankavatara, the Saddharmapundarika, and the Amitayurdhyana.

Tibetan and Chinese sources retain their independent value and are too numerous to be listed here. For instance, a collection of stories known as the *Jataka* (Birth Tales) relates popular beliefs about the 550 previous births of Buddha.

BUDDHIST TEACHINGS

Buddha wrote nothing. Like most religious leaders, he talked with his disciples on various topics and on many different occasions. The teachings attributed to him were transmitted orally for centuries by his disciples before several different Buddhist groups finally committed them to writing. Allowing for factors such as oral distortions and differences of opinions and interpretation, scholars more or less agree on several essentials of Buddha's teachings: denial of the existence of a creator god, denial of the individual soul, the Four Noble Truths, the Middle Way, the Noble Eightfold Path, and *nirvana*.

Denial of the Existence of a Creator God

Fundamental to Buddhism is the belief that at the basis of all created and manifested existence is an underlying unitary reality, the source of all things seen and unseen. This reality is beyond the reach of finite intelligence and is conceived of in impersonal or, rather, suprapersonal terms. Yet there is recognition that the life-principle, which permeates the whole of nature, including human nature, fundamentally is one with reality. By penetrating the depths of one's own nature, one can arrive at an intuitive recognition of this reality.

Although Buddhism, especially the Mahayana of China and Japan, philosophically denies the existence of a creator god that controls both nature and human destiny, in popular religion Buddhism is incurably polytheistic. Homage and worship are given to a whole hierarchy of spiritual beings—gods, Buddhas, deified persons, and animals—at the head of which is a Supreme Deity endowed with personality, will, intelligence, and love. Strictly speaking, these heavenly beings are not "gods" in any absolute sense. To be sure, they inhabit the heavenly sphere and are invisible to mortals. But they are not eternal and are subject, like all other sentient beings, to the law of rebirth. Undoubtedly, in discussions of Buddhism, it is incorrect to use the term "God," with its Christian, Jewish, and Islamic connotations.

Denial of the Individual Soul

Buddha maintained that an individual soul or ego does not exist. In his view, no individual, permanent entity exists, let alone passes from one existence to another. Nothing within a person, Buddha claimed, is metaphysically real. Human beings are made up of five *skandhas,* or components: body, feelings, perceptions, dispositions, and consciousness. Humans are caught in a cycle of rebirth because of the mechanism by which human beings evolve—the chain of causation called the law of dependent origination. According to that law, every mode of being is caused by another immediately preceding mode and in turn causes a subsequent mode. Stated differently, one condition arises out of another, which, in turn, arose out of prior conditions.

The original condition in the chain of causes and effects is ignorance, which gives rise to the following series of causes and effects: predispositions, or karmic agents; consciousness; name and form (or individuality); the five sense organs and the mind; other objects (selves or things); sensation; self-desire *(tanha);* attachment to existence; the process of becoming; progressive states of being (each unlike preceding states); and human suffering *(dukkha).*

The Four Noble Truths

Buddha reduced the many ideas that Hindus associated with rebirth to one concept: the flow of becoming. That *dharma* (cosmic truth) is summed up in the Four Noble Truths propounded in Buddha's first discourse, "Setting in Motion the Wheel of Truth." Since that epochal address, the wheel has been the symbol of Buddhism and the Four Noble Truths the foundation of Buddhist teaching.

The First Truth is that all composite things (existing phenomena) are, by their very nature, in a state of *dukkha.* There is no precise English equivalent for that term, which encompasses dissatisfaction, anxiety, frustration, suffering, pain, and misery. All events and features in life are characterized by *dukkha:* birth, sickness, old age, death, failure to fulfill ambitions or desires, separation from loved ones, marriage, association with people one dislikes, and so on. Such experiences as happiness and enjoyment, which are characteristic of most lives, merely presuppose their opposites. Consequently, life, or existence, is characterized not only by *dukkha* but also by *anicca* (impermanence) and *anatta* (no self). Everything in the universe is in an endless process of impermanence, change, and decay. Life is transitory; nothing about it is permanent. If there is no permanent reality inside or outside the individual (except the reality of the ceaseless state of becoming) and all forms are ever changing, then there is no permanent self or ego, let alone an immortal soul.

The Second Truth is that this unsatisfactory state of affairs is a consequence of *tanha*. *Tanha* is a desire or craving for sentient material possessions or intellectual gratification induced by clinging to things without realizing their impermanent, insubstantial, and unsatisfactory nature. Most people delude themselves into thinking that possessions, attachments, and relationships represent the essence of a happy, civilized life, whereas in reality they are simply the cause of *dukkha*.

The Third Truth is self-evident: escape from *tanha* is a prerequisite to inner peace and tranquility. By eliminating all desire and selfish craving, one eliminates *dukkha*. To put it differently, freedom from *dukkha* is possible only by severing the chain of *tanha*.

The Fourth Truth concerns the path, or way, that leads to that freedom—the Middle Way, the life of calm detachment through which the wise person avoids the extremes of asceticism and self-indulgence.

The Middle Way

Anyone searching for truth should avoid the two extremes of self-indulgence and self-mortification. Self-indulgence is degrading, sensual, vulgar, unworthy, and useless. Self-mortification is painful, degrading, and useless. By avoiding those extremes, one gains the enlightenment of the Middle Way, which leads to insight, knowledge, calmness, awakening, and—finally—*nirvana* (which means, literally, "extinction").

The practical techniques to be followed in the Middle Way fall into eight categories, known collectively as the Noble Eightfold Path. The categories do not represent stages or steps that must be followed in sequence; rather, they are characteristics of day-to-day living that must be practiced and realized simultaneously.

The Noble Eightfold Path

The Noble Eightfold Path consists of right understanding, right intention, right speech, right conduct, right occupation, right endeavor, right contemplation, and right concentration. The key to this concept is the word *right* and consists of the following eight points:

- *Right understanding.* Having a right understanding means perceiving and believing the Four Noble Truths.
- *Right intention.* Once one has perceived and believed the Four Noble Truths, one must renounce worldly life, accept the "homeless" state, and follow the Noble Eightfold Path.

- *Right speech.* One must act with compassion and consideration of others and abstain from lies, slander, abuse, and idle talk.
- *Right conduct.* Right conduct or behavior means abstaining from killing, stealing, lying, committing adultery, and using intoxicants.
- *Right occupation.* One must never accept a means of livelihood that may be considered questionable.
- *Right endeavor.* One must always strive after all that is good and make a strong effort to keep away from all that is evil or wicked.
- *Right contemplation.* One must always learn to control the mind in peaceful contemplation so that joy, sorrow, or any other emotion is not allowed to disturb one's calm.
- *Right concentration.* When all the other principles have been followed, one can reach the stage where the mind is completely subject to one's will. One can develop the mind to heights beyond reasoning, indeed, to *nirvana.*

Nirvana

Buddha taught that those who follow the Noble Eightfold Path, will ultimately break the bonds that tie them to life and to their craving for existence. They alone will achieve release from the cycle of rebirth. Only

Reclining figures of the Buddha always represent his *parinirvana,* the final moment of dissolution of the physical components of his mortal life. This giant stone figure at Gal Vihara, in Sri Lanka (Ceylon), is forty-four feet long.
From the private collection of Mr. and Mrs. G. Brooks.

the extinction of *tanha,* like the extinction of a candle flame after it has passed from candle to candle, can free a person from the cycle of rebirth and, consequently, from *dukkha,* or misery. That extinction—that "going out"—is the state of *nirvana.*

Nirvana is difficult, if not impossible, to define, because it is not an intellectual goal. The term literally means "extinction," as the flame of a candle is said to be extinguished. Hence, *nirvana* is the extinction of all *tanha. Nirvana* is not, however, a state of total annihilation; on the contrary, it is a state in which a person, having been freed from all *tanha,* is liberated from the cycle of rebirth and, hence, from *dukkha.* In the words of Buddha, "There is, O monks, a condition where there is neither earth, nor water, nor fire, nor air, nor the sphere of infinite consciousness, nor the sphere of the void. . . . That condition, O monks, do I call . . . nirvana."[4] *Nirvana,* accordingly, is the end of all transitory states: the final, peaceful bliss, the ultimate goal of each individual.

Here is how Buddha's discourse is recorded:

> There are two extremes, O monks, that should not be practiced by one who has assumed that homeless life. And what are these two? That devoted to passions and luxury—which is low, vulgar, unworthy and useless; and that devoted to self-mortification—which is painful, unworthy and useless. By avoiding these two extremes, the *Tathagata* ["one who has discovered the truth," referring to the Buddha] has gained the enlightenment of that Middle Path, which gives insight of knowledge; which leads to calmness, to higher knowledge and enlightenment—*Nirvana.*
>
> And what, O monks, is the Middle Path, which gives insight of knowledge, which leads to calmness, to higher knowledge and enlightenment—*Nirvana?* Truly it is the Noble Eightfold Way: right understanding, right intention, right speech, right conduct, right occupation, right endeavor, right contemplation, and right concentration. This, O monks, is the Middle Path, which gives insight and knowledge, which leads to calmness, to higher knowledge and enlightenment—*Nirvana.*
>
> Now this, O monks, is the noble truth of *dukkha* ["suffering"]: birth is *dukkha;* old age is *dukkha;* sickness is *dukkha;* death is *dukkha;* sorrow, lamentation, anguish, and despair are *dukkha;* contact with unpleasant factors is *dukkha;* not acquiring what one desires is *dukkha.* In short, the five *skandhas* ["one's constituents"] are *dukkha.* Now this, O monks, is the noble truth of the cause of *dukkha; tanha* ["selfish craving, desire"] which leads to rebirth . . . *tanha* for passions; *tanha* for existence; *tanha* for nonexistence.
>
> Now this, O monks, is the noble truth for the cessation of *dukkha;* the cessation without a residue of *tanha:* abandonment; forsaking; release; nonattachment.
>
> Now this, O monks, is the noble truth of the way that leads to the cessation of *dukkha.*
>
> The Noble Eightfold Way: right understanding, right intention, right speech, right conduct, right occupation, right endeavor, right contemplation, and right concentration. (Vinayana Pitaka)

To put his imaginative vision in its simplest form, Buddha saw life as a stream of countless individuals going through an endless cycle of rebirth, within which the form of every new life is dictated by former lives and every fate is the effect of former good or evil deeds. Within the cycle of rebirth, suffering is inevitable. Liberation from suffering is conditional on a break from the cycle and the attainment of *nirvana,* an inscrutable state of absolute transcendence.

Buddha's final message to his disciples was:

> Be ye lamps unto yourselves; rely on yourselves; and do not rely on any external help! Hold fast to the Truth [the Four Noble Truths] as a lamp! Seek salvation alone in the Truth. Look not for assistance to any one besides yourselves!
>
> Be earnest then . . . be steadfast in resolve. Keep watch over your own hearts. Who wearies not, but holds fast to his Truth, shall cross this ocean of life—shall cease *dukkha!* (Mahaparinibbana Suttanta)

A short but interesting narrative recorded in the Buddhist scripture illustrates the significance of those important principles.

> Once, Gotami, an Indian woman, came to the Buddha crying, "O Exalted One, my only son has died. I went to everyone and asked, 'Is there no medicine to bring my son back to life?' And they replied, 'There is no medicine; but go to the Exalted One, he may be able to help you.' Can you, O Exalted One, give me medicine to bring my only son back to life?"
>
> Looking at her compassionately, the Buddha replied, "You did well, Gotami, in coming here for medicine. Go, and bring me for medicine some tiny grains of mustard seed from every house where no one—neither parent, child, relative, nor servant—has died."
>
> Gotami, delighted in her heart, went away to fetch as many tiny grains of mustard seed as she could find. From one house to the other, she moved frantically all day long, as each time she was told, "Alas! Gotami, great is the count of the dead in this house."
>
> Overcome with exhaustion, she finally went to the burning-ground outside the city with her dead son in her arms. "My dear little boy," said she, "I thought you alone had been overtaken by this thing which men call death. But now I see that you are not the only one, for this is a law common to all mankind." And so saying, she cast the little corpse into the fire. Then she sang:
>
>> No village law, no law of market town,
>> No law of a single house is this [death],
>> Of all the world, and all the worlds of gods,
>> This only is law: All things are *anicca.*
>
> When she returned to the Buddha, she was greeted by him. "Gotami, did you get the tiny grains of mustard seed for medicine?" "Done, O Exalted One, is the business of the mustard seed! Only give me refuge."

All that exists is *anicca* and is subject to the changes that occur through the cycle of birth, growth, decay, and death. To crave or desire life *(tanha)* is to go through that process, and that process is *dukkha.* Even death, the Buddhists believe, is only one point in the cycle of change: it does not mark the end of existence. Nothing is permanent, unchanging, eternal, or immortal.

BUDDHIST GROUPS

From the time of the second council, Buddhism has been divided into two main branches: Theravada and Mahayana. During the first centuries after the death of Buddha, the Buddhist community, according to the ancient records, consisted of eighteen different groups. In fact, the number of Buddhist sects probably was legion, but scholars tend to group them under one or the other of the two main branches. A few of the more important and popular groups are briefly examined here.

Theravada

The Theravadins, the "orthodox" wing of the movement, represent the earliest group or school of Buddhism. This group covers southern India, Sri Lanka (formerly Ceylon), Burma, Thailand (formerly Siam), and Cambodia. It sometimes is called the Southern School, to distinguish it from the Northern or Mahayana School, which covers Tibet, Mongolia, China, Korea, and Japan. Until recently, the Theravada group was known in the West by its generic name of Hinayana, meaning "Small (or Lesser) Vehicle of Salvation)," but that term of reproach, originally coined by the followers of Mahayana (meaning "Great Vehicle of Salvation"), has been dropped in favor of the more accurate and less discourteous name of Theravada ("Way of the Elders").

The central figure in Theravada Buddhism is the monk, whose ideal is to attain *nirvana*. Hence, monastic discipline and solitary meditation are the rule. With shaven head and yellow robe, a monk rises at daybreak, washes himself, lights a candle before the image of Buddha, and chants and meditates before leaving the monastery. Outside, his begging bowl in hand, he makes his silent rounds, stopping quietly at every door to receive whatever food is offered. He returns to the monastery to eat breakfast, after which he joins other monks in the assembly hall for prayers, instruction, and meditation. The main and last meal of the day follows between 11:00 and 11:30 A.M. in a communal dining room. The afternoon is devoted to scripture reading and meditation. Before retiring to bed, monks gather in one final assembly at sunset. By following this daily routine, monks acquire merit toward their liberation.

All Buddhists revere Buddha as the great Master and living embodiment of the religious ideal they seek to realize. But when Theravada Buddhists speak of their Master, they are referring to the human Buddha of flesh and blood, not the manifestation in human form of an eternal essence, the abstraction that represents the way in which Mahayana Buddhists think of their Master. In other words, Theravada Buddhists regard Buddha as the great enlightened man—but still only a man. By practicing detachment, Buddha simply pioneered and fulfilled his quest

It is customary to beat the drum during the chanting of the Buddhist scriptures, as here at a Japanese Buddhist Pure Land sect, in Toronto, Canada.

From the private collection of the author.

for *nirvana*, and anyone can follow his lead. By accepting the homeless state, each individual can attain the same liberation through effort and self-discipline.

Naturally, not everyone can justify setting aside the obligations and responsibilities of everyday life in favor of the homeless state, but it is the Theravadins' only recourse. To attain *nirvana*, every individual must, sooner or later, renounce worldly pursuits and enter the homeless state of a monk. The alternative is consignment to an eternal cycle of rebirth.

The scriptures of Theravada Buddhism consist of the three collections written in Pali that are known as the Tripitaka. In contrast, Mahayana Buddhism acknowledges numerous canonical texts in various local dialects. The Pali texts of Theravada Buddhism contain some early ideas on which the Mahayanists later elaborated: for instance, that other Buddhas had preceded Gautama and that the latter was a divine being who, through countless rebirths, lived a perfect life.

Over the centuries, various divisions developed within Theravada Buddhism on the basis of doctrinal matters, the acceptance or rejection of certain canonical texts, and disputes over disciplinary rules and the observance of ethical precepts. Basically, though, Theravada Buddhism was—and remains—restricted to monastic orders.

Mahayana

Although the character and the nature of Mahayana Buddhism vary a great deal from sect to sect, most, if not all, Mahayana Buddhists regard Buddha as an incarnation of an eternal Buddha essence that has existed in all ages and in innumerable worlds for the liberation of all sentient beings. His manifestation on earth in human form, they believe, came about out of compassion for others. Buddha, they claim, willingly postponed his entrance into *nirvana* in order to help others attain it, too.

Mahayana Buddhists, in contrast to Theravadins, believe that an individual can aspire to *nirvana* without accepting the homeless state of a monk. This liberal attitude contributed to the gradual development of many sects and many versions of Buddhist belief. For instance, the idea that the eternal Buddha essence was incarnate in Siddhartha prompted some Mahayana Buddhists to deify and worship Siddhartha. Similarly, the special significance of the *bodhisattva* (one who, out of compassion for the welfare of others, delays his entry into *nirvana*) created a vast number of "saviors" who became objects of faith, worship, and devotion. In turn, images were introduced to help many Buddhists worship *bodhisattvas,* and vivid portrayals of heaven and hell, which appealed to the public at large because they gave substance to vague abstractions, were invented. Of the innumerable schools of thought and independent sects in Mahayana Buddhism, a few of the more important are described here: Madhyamika, T'ien-t'ai (or Tendai), the Pure Land sect, Ch'an (or Zen), and Tantrism.

Madhyamika. This important philosophical school of Buddhism was founded by the Indian Nagarjuna in about the second or third century CE and later spread to China and Japan. Nagarjuna taught the necessity of taking the middle position between two opposites: being and nonbeing, existence and nonexistence, affirmation and negation, and so forth. With rigorous logic, he demonstrated the absurdity of philosophical positions that advocated or were postulated on extremes. To Nagarjuna, any opposites or contradictions were proof of error. In his words,

> Nothing comes into being, nor does anything disappear.
> Nothing is eternal, nor has anything an end.
> Nothing is identical, nor is anything differentiated.
> Nothing moves here, nor does anything move there.[5]

Such pairs of opposites, Nagarjuna argued, are empty of meaning or, at best, are relative; the truth lies somewhere in the middle or, more correctly, "above opposites." The middle position is beyond thought and words and devoid of name and character.

Although Madhyamika never gained wide appeal, its teachings were quite influential. They provided the basis of logical and philosophical thought among groups of intellectuals whose numbers never justified the formation of an independent sect.

T'ien-t'ai (Tendai). T'ien-t'ai is associated with Chinese Buddhism; Tendai is its Japanese counterpart. Tradition states that Chih-i (538–597 CE) established a monastery on Mount T'ien-t'ai in China and became the founder of the school identified by the same name. His teachings were markedly syncretistic, incorporating various forms of Buddhism. Central to his doctrine was the "threefold truth":

1. Emptiness: All things are void, without substantial reality.

2. Temporary existence: All things have only a passing life.

3. Middle state: All things are empty and temporary at the same time, thus constituting the mean or middle state.

Those three truths are mutually inclusive and exist in harmonious unity, with the middle state being equivalent to Absolute Reality.

The T'ien-t'ai religious philosophy never became widely acceptable to the masses, although a few Buddhists still adhere to its tenets.

Pure Land Sect. The Pure Land sect is one of the most popular Buddhist groups in China and Japan. Its enchanting picture of a Pure and Happy Land presided over by *Amitabha* (the Buddha of Infinite Light), who responds to anyone meditating on or calling his name in good faith, has been particularly appealing to ordinary working people. The main proponents of this view were Tao-cho (562–645 CE) and his disciple Shan-tao (613–681). Those two teachers promoted various devotional practices, including uttering the name of Amitabha with an undivided mind, to ensure rebirth in the "Western Paradise"; chanting *sutras* (scriptural texts); worshiping images; and meditating on and singing praises to the Buddha. They also painted vivid images of heaven and hell, the latter replete with horrors of torture and violence. In the twelfth century CE, a Japanese convert introduced the Pure Land sect to Japan, where it is now known as the Jodo school.

The emphasis of this school is on salvation by faith in Amitabha (O-mi-to in Chinese; Amida in Japanese). Traditionally, O-mi-to was a king who renounced his title, became a monk, and later took the vow of a *bodhisattva*. Out of his infinite compassion and by the power of his accumulated merit, O-mi-to called into existence the domain called Sukhavati, the "Western Paradise," or, as it is generally known, "the Pure Land." According to the Pure Land sect, all who are ensnared by desire *(tanha)* or ignorance but who sincerely invoke the name of O-mi-to are reborn in the Western Paradise, where they can continue the process of liberation under happier and more encouraging conditions than they can in this existence. The Pure Land, then, is not the goal but a stepping-stone to the goal; it is simply a place where one can receive, under favorable conditions, liberation from the cycle of bodily existence.

A devotee who merely repeats the sacred name of O-mi-to endlessly is assured of reaching the Pure Land: "Namu O-mi-to Fo" (Chinese version), "Namu Amida Butsu" (Japanese version), "Hail Amitabha Buddha" (English version).

Ch'an (Zen). The most important Buddhist sect originating in China is the Ch'an group, whose Japanese parallel is called Zen. Ch'an and Zen represent intuitive meditation accompanied by strict discipline, through which one's Buddha nature can be revealed.

According to tradition, this school was introduced by Bodhidharma (470–543 CE), an Indian Buddhist who came to China by crossing the Yangtze River on a reed branch. Legend also has it that the Chinese emperor sent for Bodhidharma and, during their interview, asked him, "How much merit would I accumulate if I were to donate to the Buddhist Order and encourage the translation of the sacred books?"

"No merit at all!" was the blunt reply. "No merit is accumulated from good works; reading scriptures is useless and worthless; only inward meditation is the path to enlightenment." To demonstrate to the skeptical emperor what he meant, Bodhidharma is said to have gone to Mount Su and to have sat in meditation, facing a wall, for the next nine years.

Whatever this sect's origin and historicity, that story illustrates the emphasis Ch'an and Zen place on inner enlightenment, to the exclusion of words, images, temples, and scriptures. Ch'an Buddhism has no set pattern and no institutions. Its adherents absolutely reject deification of Buddha. A frequently quoted expression of this sect is, "If you meet the Buddha, kill him." The quotation implies that the Buddha was a man, not a god, and that he never wished to be worshiped; it also implies that a meditative awareness is greater than Buddhahood.

In the ninth century, an argument among adherents over how enlightenment *(satori)* can be gained split Ch'an into two major schools: Rinzai and Soto.

The Rinzai (in Chinese: Lin-chi) School was founded by the Chinese Buddhist Lin Chi or I-hsüan (d. 867 CE) and introduced into Japan by Eisai (1141–1215). It distinguished itself from Soto by advocating the idea that intuitive wisdom and enlightenment come suddenly. It also employed unorthodox means to attain sudden enlightenment: striking and shouting, the use of nonsensical language and paradox, and exercises in riddle solving *(koan)*. It flourished in the Kamakura period, and its huge temples became centers of great cultural and artistic achievements.

The Soto (in Chinese, Ts'ao-tung) School was founded by two Chinese Buddhists, Tung-shan (807–869) and Ts'ao-shan (840–901), and introduced into Japan by Dogen (1200–1253). It insisted on gradual enlightenment. Training, which concentrated on sitting cross-legged in meditation *(zazen)*, followed a system of five stages (the Five Relationships), leading from recognition of a "real" or "higher" self, overshadowing the "seeming" self, up to the realization of complete oneness with Absolute Reality. Thus, enlightenment came through gradual silent illumination. Modern Soto tends toward quietism and is somewhat less popular than Rinzai.

Besides these two major schools of Zen, a third and smaller sect called Obaku, the Japanese name for the Chinese Buddhist Huang-po (d. 850), was introduced to Japan in 1654 by Ingen (1592–1673). Obaku combined the teachings of Soto and Rinzai. Sudden enlightenment, it claimed, was for the highly gifted; a more gradual way was open for those with less talent. The most useful means for sudden enlightenment was *zazen* and the practice of *koan*. For the gradual way of enlightenment, the use of calling on the name of the Buddha *(nembutsu)* was the best method.

Ch'an and Zen masters today differ in their approaches to teaching. Some enjoin meditation and silence; others advocate instruction in a question-and-answer format; still others apply enigmatic sounds, gestures, or acts, which may include such extreme measures as scolding and beating. Whatever their techniques, they all consider words a poor medium and logic self-defeating. Everyone, they believe, possesses a Buddha nature; one simply has to awaken it. The result is a sudden flash of insight encompassing enlightenment and the unity of all existence.

To achieve *satori* (enlightenment), one must practice *zazen* (sitting in meditation). The technique of the *koan* is employed to promote the experience of *satori*. The *koan* is a riddle or problem that cannot be solved by the intellect. Zen masters propose *koans* to students in an effort to heighten and develop students' intuitive faculty, thus forcing them to reach beyond reasoning and attain *satori*.

There are hundreds of different *koans*, each designed to probe beyond the grasp of reasoning. A favorite *koan* introduced to new disciples is "What was your original face before your parents begot you?" Others are "All things return to the one; what does the one return to?" and "If clapping two hands produces a sound, what is the sound of one hand clapping?"

There is no logical answer to a *koan*. The purpose of the exercise is to realize one's own Buddha nature, to accept the limitations of human reasoning, and to probe beyond the barriers of rational thinking to insight. If a learner persists in reasoning by asking further questions, the Zen Master may kick him, slap him, or even throw him down. Such treatment is justified by the necessity of breaking the learner's hold on reason.

Tantrism. The precise origin and development of Tantrism (also called Vajrayana and Mantrayana) are difficult to ascertain, because its doctrine is mysterious or esoteric and its practices are unorthodox. Many of its practices were taken over from popular indigenous Indian or Hindu Tantrism. Its basic aim was infinitely enhanced psychic experience here and now rather than the distant goal of *nirvana* after countless rebirths. Like Hindu Tantrism, Buddhist Tantrism entailed greater concern with the occult and with magical transformations and miracles. Today, this school of Buddhism has gained prominence in India, China, Tibet, and Japan.

Buddhist Tantrism is fundamentally nonspeculative: aspirants must experience numerous yoga stages before achieving enlightenment. *Nirvana* is seen as one side of a polarity. The other side is *karuna* (compassion) emanating from the *bodhisattvas*, whose help is solicited through appropriate rituals. Those rituals fall under three *M* groups:

- *mudra*, various symbolic gestures made by the hands and fingers
- *mantra*, formulas of an esoteric nature based on scientific knowledge of the occult power of sound
- *mandala*, visual aids, such as picture charts, diagrams, and magical circles, designed to help the devotee acquire a mystical union with a particular *bodhisattva*

Before they are allowed to share the more important secrets of the sect, devotees go through a preliminary training period, which consists of thousands of prostrations, breathing exercises, repetitions of mystical formulas in precise sound patterns, and preparations of symbolic sacrifices. Each *bodhisattva* is represented by certain symbols and formulas peculiar to that *bodhisattva*. By performing specific rituals, the devotee is gradually able to identify and become one with a particular *bodhisattva*. Some of the mystical rites consist of elaborate rituals performed to the accompaniment of music. Secret formulas, symbols, and visualizations are all interpreted gradually to the disciples as their insight into the mystical nature of the *bodhisattva* grows deeper.

Enlightenment is achieved when one realizes experientially, not cognitively, that seeming opposites are in truth one and the same. In other words, Tantrism maintains that all things are of one nature: *sunyata* (emptiness or void). Physical and mental processes are, therefore, equal means for enlightenment.

Experts in Tantrism teach that an individual's body is the entire cosmos and that in this age of degeneration (i.e., human existence) one must achieve enlightenment through one's own body. However, only a Master who has been thoroughly initiated into the mysteries of Tantrism can teach an aspirant how to use the body's processes correctly to achieve identification with the void, which is enlightenment.

After undertaking several yogic exercises that help to produce mental and physical experiences, the Master leads the initiate to further stages of spiritual growth. This process of advancement involves leading the initiate to identify with deities that represent various cosmic forces. The purpose of the procedure is to help the initiate discover that each identification is *sunyata,* or void; the outcome is to endow the initiate with a "diamondlike" body representing a condition beyond all duality.

BUDDHIST OBSERVANCES

Monasticism

During Buddha's lifetime, he and his followers gathered annually during the rainy season. After his death, his followers continued having yearly "rain retreats," which gradually turned into permanent monastic settlements. Those settlements, in turn, developed into great monasteries serving as centers of Buddhist learning and missionary enterprise. From the monasteries, Buddhist missionaries were sent to propagate the faith in China, Japan, Tibet, and southeastern Asia.

Naturally, monks who lived closely together in permanent monasteries required disciplinary rules and a degree of hierarchical organization. The first such rules, according to tradition, were handed down by the first council. Soon the abbot became the head of the administrative hierarchy and was vested with almost unlimited powers over monastic affairs.

Eventually, Buddhist monastic orders developed different character-istics according to the country and the branch of Buddhism to which they belonged. Today, some orders permit lay participation in monastic affairs, whereas others are strictly authoritarian. Entry to a monastic order, however, has always been an individual affair, one that depends on the commitment of either the applicant or the applicant's family.

The life of a Buddhist monk was originally one of poverty, celibacy, and wandering mendicancy. Over time, however, these early features were modified or changed. For instance, begging has become merely a symbolic gesture to teach humility, and the growth of large monaster-ies, made possible through large endowments from wealthy donors, often has led to compromises on the rule of poverty. In Japan during the tenth to thirteenth centuries, Buddhist monasteries even recruited large armies of mercenaries and monks to fight rival religious groups as well as temporal wars. Celibacy and strict sexual abstinence, once the rule in all Buddhist monastic orders, have been relaxed. The Shin sect of Japan encouraged the abolition of monastic celibacy, and some groups have allowed sexual intercourse as symbolic of enlightenment.

Buddhist Nuns

The role of women in Buddhist history has been characterized by ten-sion between their perceived roles as seductresses and as domestic paragons. On the one hand, women have been associated with sensual indulgence of lust, carnal desire, and seduction. Buddhist monks have perceived women as bestial and evil purveyors of sexuality and hence a potential threat to their spiritual welfare. Pain, suffering, mental an-guish, and ritual impurity, according to the monks, result from attach-ment to women. Consequently, women have been viewed as biologi-cally and mentally weaker than men, more vulnerable to ignorance, somewhat defective, and spiritually handicapped. On the other hand, married women have been respected as paragons of motherhood through their procreative role and function.

That tension and inconsistency have remained the basic Buddhist at-titude to this day. Even the idealized domestic function is seen as pre-venting women from active involvement in religious institutions in that it keeps them from pursuing the Buddhist goal of detachment. When women do decide to leave their homes and familial responsibilities to join monastic orders, they are accused of causing the disintegration of the family structure, which in turn is viewed as potentially disruptive to the stability of society.

Nonetheless, Buddhist nuns have lived and worked in their separate convents from the time of Buddha's death. A large number of female disciples, particularly among the Theravada group, have pioneered much of what is now known in the West as social service; they also are noted for their learning, piety, and austere life-style. They either live in separate convents or share the same monastic settlement with male monks but live in their own quarters. Female monks shave their heads and wear precisely the same clothing as their male counterparts do. In each principal convent or monastery is an abbess, whose tutorial, leadership, and meditative abilities are considered to be unmatched, even though each differs in her techniques for achieving the common Buddhist goal.

Relics of the Buddha

Since the death of Buddha, relics of his body, including his teeth, hair, and collarbone, have been preserved and enshrined in *stupas* or *pagodas* (domed or towerlike shrines), both in major cities and in the countryside throughout the Far East. Every temple has a *stupa*, some small and some enormous. When devotees enter the temple precincts, they first walk around the *stupa* three times and then worship it kneeling, prostrate, or standing. This observance is believed to bring great merit. Laypersons as well as monks flock to the shrines to make offerings of food and flowers and to meditate on Buddha's teachings. Such acts also acquire merit that leads to rebirth in a better life. In fact, building a *stupa* or contributing to building one in itself brings great merit.

Images of the Buddha

Image worship occupies a central place in the devotional life of Buddhists. In earlier ages, there were no images of Buddha, who was represented by symbols: his footprint, the seat on which he sat, or the eight-spoked wheel. Later, Buddha was represented by images carved on rocks or made of stone or metal. Most Buddhist temples and private homes possess images of Buddha. Usually a corner in a home is set aside as a shrine for images, which are believed to be a source of magical protection or blessing. Images of Buddha show him in one of three postures: standing, seated, or reclining.

Many Buddhists have in their homes pictures and images of the Buddha in front of which candles and incense are burnt, and other spirits may be venerated as well. Other Buddhists have a household *butsudan* (Buddha shelf, or altar), an often elaborate shrine in which the central figure of Buddha is surrounded by decorations, utensils, flowers, and oil lamps.

Buddhist worshipers offer flowers, incense, food, and drink. Offerings of light, such as candlelight or the light of oil lamps, are believed to bring rich stores of lasting merit. Prayers accompany the oblations, because any sort of offering is considered meritorious.

Devotional Acts

Every act of worship begins with the recital of the following formula: "Homage to Him, the Blessed One, the Exalted One, the fully Enlightened One." Next comes the recitation of the Three Refuges, known as the *tri-ratna* ("three gems"). A devout Buddhist recites several times daily the following Three Refuges invocation:

> I go to the Buddha as my Refuge;
> I go to the Dharma [Law, Doctrine] as my Refuge;
> I go to the Sangha [Brotherhood of Monks] as my Refuge.

Interior of the Wat Benchamabopit Temple, also known as Marble Temple, in Bangkok,
Thailand. Worshipers gather to pay homage to the revered golden image of the Buddha.
Flowers, incense, and prayers are usually offered.

Courtesy of British Airways (BOAC), Tourist Information Center, Toronto.

Immediately after that recitation, the following resolutions—or Five
Precepts, as they are commonly known—are renewed:

> I undertake to abstain from destroying life.
> I undertake to abstain from taking things not given.
> I undertake to abstain from sexual misconduct.
> I undertake to abstain from false speech.
> I undertake to abstain from intoxicants.

Monks, who renounce the world, repeat an additional Five Precepts:

> I undertake to abstain from eating at forbidden times.
> I undertake to abstain from dancing, singing, and shows.
> I undertake to abstain from adorning or beautifying myself
>   by the use of garlands, scents, unguents, ornaments, and
>   finery.
> I undertake to abstain from using a high or large couch or bed.
> I undertake to abstain from accepting gold or silver.

Rosaries are widely used, small ones by the laity, larger ones by
monks. The larger ones have 108 beads, with one large bead in the
middle representing Buddha. Generally, the rosary is carried on the

A pilgrim at Temple of Shikoku in Japan, famous for its eighty-eight temples related to the Buddhist prelate Kukai (Kobo Daishi, 774–835), founder of the Japanese version of the Chinese Shingon school. Some half-million pilgrims come to visit the temple. They wear white garments and usually make the trip on foot, a journey that may take forty-five to sixty days.

Courtesy of Japan Information Center, Consulate General of Japan, Toronto.

left wrist in daily life and encircles the two hands when clasped together for prayer. Worshipers perform individual or congregational acts of devotion.

In modern times, especially in Western societies, worshipers gather every Sunday (because it is the most convenient day) for congregational meetings, and *dharma* schools are provided for children, after the Western model (Sunday schools). Other groups prefer to hold regular sessions one or more evenings during the week.

Pilgrimage

Pilgrimages to sacred sites (holy places) are considered to be meritorious deeds, and the more pilgrimages an individual completes, the greater the merit. The birthplace of Buddha, the site of his enlightenment, the park where he preached his first discourse, and the place where he died are the four most sacred destinations of any Buddhist pilgrimage. Millions of pilgrims through the ages—monks, nuns, and laypeople from all over the Far East—have made and continue to make the long journey to those four remote places, often on foot, frequently braving many dangers, and seldom undergoing the experience without hardship.

Todaiji Temple in Nara, Japan, was founded in 745 CE and is well known for its Daibutsu, a colossal image of the Buddha (160 feet high, 187 feet long, and 166 feet wide) in the act of preaching a sermon.

Courtesy of Japan Information Center, Consulate General of Japan, Toronto.

Festivals and Ceremonies

Many festivals and ceremonies observed in Buddhism commemorate historical and religious events in the life of Buddha, as well as in the lives of numerous *bodhisattvas* and founders of various groups. In addition, there are seasonal festivals and regional festivals that are celebrated differently by Japanese and Chinese Buddhists.

The major festivals can be divided into two types: festivals observed by all Buddhists, whether Theravada or Mahayana, although the dates may differ according to each tradition, and festivals observed by either Japanese Buddhists or Chinese Buddhists only. For the second type, there also are two types of festivals: those observed by all sects and those observed by only some sects.

Three important festivals are observed by all Buddhists the world over: Hanamatsuri/Vesak, Bodhi Day, and Nirvana Day. Two festivals observed by all Japanese Buddhist sects are Ohigan and Obon. Brief descriptions of these five and a few other ceremonies observed by different groups follow.

Hanamatsuri (Flower Festival). Mahayana Buddhists observe Hanamat-suri on April 8 to celebrate the birthday of Buddha. According to Mahayana tradition, Buddha was born on that day in 563 BCE in Lumbini Gardens (present-day Nepal) in the midst of flower blossoms. On this occasion, a flower shrine is set up in front of the main shrine in the worship hall of Buddhist temples; enshrined in the flowers is a statuette of the infant Buddha. According to Theravada tradition, Buddha was born on Vesak (Wesak), or Full Moon Day (corresponding to April–May), in 623 BCE. Theravada Buddhists celebrate this day not simply as the birthday of Buddha but also in memory of his enlightenment and his entry into *nirvana.*

Bodhi Day. Mahayana Buddhists celebrate Bodhi Day on December 8 to commemorate the historic event of Buddha's enlightenment. To them, this event took place as the first faint light of day began to glow in the eastern sky while Buddha was sitting in meditation under a tree.

Nirvana Day. Mahayana Buddhists commemorate Buddha's death and entry into *nirvana* on February 15. Some Buddhists also reserve this day for a memorial service for deceased family members.

Ohigan or Higan ("Other Shore"). All Japanese Buddhists celebrate Ohigan twice a year, during the spring and autumn equinoxes. The celebrations generally last for a week, during which faithful Buddhists gather in their temples to express to Buddha their thankfulness for his great compassion and to offer flowers and various foods of the season to Buddha. More important, Buddhists recall and devote themselves to the fulfillment of the Six Perfections — charity, morality, endurance, endeavor, meditation, and wisdom — which are considered to be the gates through which one enters and crosses to the "other shore," the Pure Land of the Amitabha Buddha.

Obon or Bon. This festival is essentially an ancestral memorial rite held on either July 15 (according to the solar calendar) or August 15 (according to the lunar calendar). A festive mood pervades the entire gathering, even though there is a solemn sense of loss of loved ones. Buddhists celebrate this traditional festival by lighting candles or lanterns to guide the spirits of departed ancestors on their annual visit to the family home. Delicacies are offered to the spirits, and the festival ends with a circular folk dance.

Dharma-Chakka. Theravada Buddhists celebrate this festival on the day of the full moon in July to commemorate the first proclamation of the *dharma* by Buddha to the five ascetics in the Deer Park in Varanasi (Benares).

Dharma-Vijaya or Poson. Theravada Buddhists celebrate Dharma-Vijaya at the full moon in June. This festival commemorates the beginning of the preaching of the *dharma* to foreign countries, especially to Sri Lanka (Ceylon), under the reign of Emperor Asoka of India.

A family grave. Families in Japan maintain grave plots containing ashes of deceased family members on the grounds of Buddhist temples near their homes.
Courtesy of Japan Information Center, Consulate General of Japan, Toronto.

Besides the special days mentioned here, each Buddhist group or sect observes its particular festival or ceremony. In many cases, traditional customs have been intermingled with Buddhist celebrations. Nevertheless, all these festivals bring a special religious fervor into the life of Buddhists everywhere.

STUDY QUESTIONS

1. Recount the traditional story of Siddhartha.
2. What is the significance of the four sights usually cited as the sum of Siddhartha's quest?
3. Describe the three temptations experienced by Siddhartha.
4. Identify the cosmic truth or *dharma* that Siddhartha discovered.
5. Discuss the introduction of Buddhism into China and Japan.
6. What important Buddhist works have attained the status of scripture?
7. Explain the Buddhist view of no-self or no-ego.

8. Describe the notion of the Four Noble Truths.

9. Discuss the concept of the Noble Eightfold Path.

10. What are the basic differences between the Theravada and the Mahayana groups?

11. Explain Nagarjuna's philosophy of the "middle position."

12. What is the central threefold philosophy of T'ien-t'ai (Tendai)?

13. State the characteristics of the Pure Land sect.

14. Trace the origin and development of Ch'an (Zen) Buddhism.

15. Describe the techniques of *satori* and *zazen*.

16. Explain the concept of *sunyata*.

17. Identify the "unorthodox" practices of Tantrism.

18. What are the three *M* yogic rituals?

19. Describe the origin and development of monastic orders.

20. Discuss the role of women in Buddhist history.

Suggested Reading

Austin, James H. *Zen and the Brain: Toward an Understanding of Meditation and Consciousness.* Cambridge: MIT Press, 1998.

Blackstone, Kathryn R. *Women in the Footsteps of Buddha: Struggle for Liberation in the Therigatha.* Surrey, Eng.: Curzon, 1998.

Carrithers, Michael. *The Buddha.* Oxford and New York: Oxford University Press, 1983.

Clifford, Patricia Hart. *Sitting Still.* New York: Paulist Press, 1994.

Cole, R. Alan. *Mothers and Sons in Chinese Buddhism.* Stanford, Calif.: Stanford University Press, 1998.

Enomiya-Lasalle, Hugo M. *The Practice of Zen Meditation.* London and San Francisco: Aquarian, 1992.

Gethin, Rupert. *The Foundations of Buddhism.* Oxford and New York: Oxford University Press, 1998.

Gombrich, Richard Francis. *Theravada Buddhism: A Social History from Ancient Benares to Modern Colombo.* London and New York: Routledge & Kegan Paul, 1988.

Gross, Rita M. *Buddhism after Patriarchy: A Feminist History, Analysis, and Reconstruction of Buddhism.* Albany, N.Y.: SUNY, 1993.

Harvey, B. Peter. *An Introduction to Buddhism: Teaching, History and Practices.* Cambridge: Cambridge University Press, 1990.

Johnston, William. *Christian Zen,* 3rd ed. New York: Fordham University Press, 1997.

Kalupahana, David J. *A History of Buddhist Philosophy.* Honolulu: University of Hawaii Press, 1992.

Lester, Robert C. *Buddhism.* Hagerstown, Md.: Torch Publishing Group, 1987.

Nukariya, Kaiten. *The Religion of the Samurai: A Study of Zen Philosophy and Discipline in China and Japan.* London: Luzac, 1973.

Paul, Diana Mary. *Women in Buddhism: Images of the Feminine in Mahayana Tradition,* 2nd ed. Berkeley: University of California Press, 1985.

Simpkins, Annellen M. *Zen around the World: A 2500-Year Journey from the Buddha to You.* Boston: Charles E. Tuttle, 1997.

Tucci, Giuseppe. *The Religions of Tibet.* Berkeley: University of California Press, 1980.

Tuck, Donald R. *Buddhist Churches of America.* Lewiston, N.Y.: Edwin Mellen Press, 1987.

Suzuki, Daisetz Teitaro. *Zen and Japanese Culture.* Princeton, N.J.: Princeton University Press, 1970.

Williams, Paul. *Mahayana Buddhism: The Doctrinal Foundations.* London and New York: Routledge, 1989.

Notes

1. The dates given for Buddha's life vary from one Buddhist group to another. According to one Theravada group, the correct dates are 623–543 BCE; for another Theravada group, the dates are 624–544 BCE. The Mahayana group and most modern scholars prefer the dates c. 566–486 BCE or 563–483 BCE. Note that all the dates give a life span of eighty years.

2. Asita's prediction has been compared with the episode of Simeon and the baby Jesus in Luke 2:8–20, 25–35.

3. Compare Buddha's temptation to that of Jesus (Luke 4:1–13).

4. Cited in E. A. Burtt, ed., *The Teachings of the Compassionate Buddha* (New York: Mentor, 1955), pp. 113ff.

5. From "Examination of Causality," cited in E. A. Burtt, ed., *The Teachings of the Compassionate Buddha* (New York: Mentor, 1955), pp. 170–172.

6 Taoism and Confucianism

More than one-fifth of the world's five billion people live in eastern Asia—a tremendously diversified cultural area, with many different ethnic and linguistic groups. People there find it difficult to accept the rigid exclusiveness of the monotheistic religions of Judaism, Christianity, and Islam. Rather, their attitude toward religion is eclectic. Some adhere to one particular religious group, but many actively participate in several. The following story illustrates that syncretistic tendency.

Around the sixth century CE, a famous Chinese scholar was asked by the emperor if he was a Buddhist. The scholar pointed to his Taoist cap. Asked if he was a Taoist, the scholar raised the skirt of his robe to reveal his Confucian shoes. "Are you then a Confucian?" asked the puzzled emperor, whereupon the scholar tugged at the Buddhist scarf he wore.

Thus, it is possible for east Asians to belong to more than one religion without feeling guilty or confused about priorities. Buddhist priests often are in charge of Taoist temples, and many Taoists worship Confucius as their ancestral deity. All religions are mutually inclusive and fulfill complementary needs in the lives of east Asians.

The unifying principle in Chinese religion is harmony. Harmony is manifested in the cosmos, in nature, in human relationships, and in one's interior life or being. It is also represented in the earliest forms of Chinese religion, in Taoism, and in Confucianism.

Ancient Chinese religion consisted of a regional form of nature worship, presupposing a universal order that manifested itself in the sky, the ruling powers, nature, living creatures, earthly spirits, subterranean beings, and planetary, regional, and clan deities. Early Chinese cosmology distinguished between two interacting but complementary cosmic forces: *yin* and *yang*. The harmonious complementarity of opposites provided the religious, ethical, and social basis of Chinese society. In

Taoism and Confucianism

BCE

c. 3000 Beginning of early Chinese civilization

c. 1500 Shang era (ended 1125 BCE); evidence of oracle-bone inscriptions

c. 1125 Chou era (ended 221 BCE)

c. 1000 First use of I Ching

c. 551 Birth of Confucius (d. 479 BCE)

481 Start of the Warring States period (ended 221 BCE)

c. 470 Birth of Mo-tzu (d. 391 BCE)

c. 390 Birth of Meng Tzu (Mencius, d. 305 BCE)

c. 365 Birth of Chuang Tzu (d. 290 BCE)

c. 340 Birth of Hsün Tzu (d. 245 BCE)

c. 250 Compilation of *Tao Te Ching*

221 Ch'in dynasty (ended 206 BCE)

c. 213 Persecution of Confucian scholars and burning of the Classics

c. 206 Han dynasty (ended 220 CE)

124 The Five Classics made the basis of examinations in the imperial college

CE

142 Taoist Heavenly Masters group founded by Chang-Ling (Chang Tao-Ling)

215 Official imperial recognition of the Heavenly Masters group

589 Sui dynasty (ended 618)

618 T'ang dynasty (ended 907)

960 Sung dynasty (ended 1127)

1368 Ming dynasty (ended 1644)

1644 Emergence of Neo-Confucianism as China's state religion (ended 1911)

1851 Nanjing, China, established as capital of T'ai-p'ing rebellion (until 1865)

1893 Birth of Mao Tse-tung (d. 1976)

1905 Confucian civil service examination abolished

1911 Chinese revolution

1919 Antitraditionalist May Fourth movement in China

1949 Proclamation of People's Republic of China

1966 Chinese Cultural Revolution attacks all forms of religion

1973 Anti-Confucius campaign in the People's Republic of China

1989 Religious freedom limited by Chinese government

addition, Chinese religion stressed (and still does) the importance of divination and ancestral rites.

The search for alternative political, social, and philosophical solutions gave rise to diverse groups, two of which shaped and maintained the structure of Chinese society: Taoism and Confucianism. Taoism was a vision of "natural simplicity" or "harmonious living," which meant an individual could cultivate an interior harmony or unity with Tao, the frictionless or actionless flow of being by moving along, not pushing against, the course of life. The teachings of Confucius, on the other hand, stressed the principle of propriety *(li)* as a means to inner harmony and balanced governance. In time, each tradition developed its own assumption and contributed to the eclectic nature of Chinese society. With the introduction of Buddhism in the first century CE, the fortunes of the three traditions fluctuated with changing imperial patronages, until they all succumbed to the Communist revolution and the establishment of Chinese nationalism.

EARLY CHINESE RELIGION

Historical Background

Ideograms scratched on bones, together with human remains and cultural artifacts excavated in the valley of the Hwang (Yellow) River, place the beginnings of Chinese history with the rule of the Shang dynasty, some time around 1500 BCE. (Early Chinese writers refer to an earlier kingdom, the Hsia dynasty, but no archaeological evidence supporting the historicity of such a dynasty has yet been discovered.) During the Shang dynasty (c. 1500–1125 BCE), the cult of the royal ancestor was practiced and a priestly calendar adopted for religious and agricultural activities. The period also was characterized by two particularly significant inventions: ideographic writing and the two-wheeled chariot.

The Shang dynasty fell to the Chou warriors, whose dynasty ruled for almost a thousand years (1125–221 BCE). The founders of the Chou dynasty introduced the concept of the virtuous ruler, whose chief duty was the welfare of his subjects. During that period, the first Chinese literary records appeared, providing the earliest evidence of Chinese ethical ideas and religious beliefs, practices, and observances.

The latter half of the Chou dynasty rule, commonly called the Classical period (722–221 BCE), was also one of gradual decay and feudal conflict, which resulted in the impoverishment of many of the old noble families and the enrichment and political ascendancy of a new middle class of farmers and merchants. In addition, the inability of the Chou emperors during the Classical era to protect the country from invading Asian hordes encouraged local warlords to raise private armies to defend their own territories. Agricultural serfs seized the opportunity offered by the declining power of landlords to free themselves from the system that had denied them possession of property and to become owners of their own fields. The decay of the feudal system culminated in violent civil disorders called the Warring States period (481–221 BCE), which lasted some two hundred years. The result was the disappearance of feudal states and kingdoms, the collapse of royal families, and the reunification of China in 221 BCE under Emperor Shih Huang Ti.

That conflict, transition, and change stimulated a search for political and philosophical solutions and alternatives to chaos. Some schools of thought, such as the Legalists, attacked the feudal system and did what

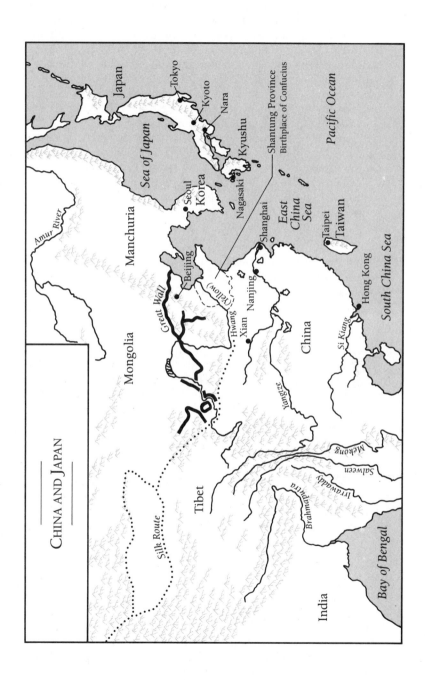

CHINA AND JAPAN

they could to discredit and demolish it. A few, such as the Mohists (or Motseans), advocated the return of "old-time religion" and universal benevolence. Others, such as the Confucians, wanted the feudal system restored but in a more rationalized or idealized form. Still others, such as the Taoists, refused to have anything to do with a political system that required structure and conformity. According to Chinese tradition, the age witnessed the flowering of a "hundred philosophers." From among the host of contenders, Taoism and Confucianism overshadowed all others. Those two religions, along with Buddhism, shaped and maintained the structure of a durable society.

This chapter examines the basic features of early Chinese religion, the lives and thoughts of Lao Tzu and Confucius, and the consequences of their teachings for the religion and the history of east Asian people. Lao Tzu lived in the Yangtze River region, which was characterized by a population that opposed the thousand-year feudal stranglehold of the Chou dynasty. Confucius lived in the Hwang River region, which was dominated by Chou culture.

Folk Religion

The character of folk religion in early Chinese history is obscure. The available evidence indicates that the following important deities and spirits were worshiped.

The highest of all deities was Shang Ti, the Supreme Ruler. His status in heaven was analogous to that of the emperor on earth; his petitioners were occult practitioners, rather than court officials, continuously intent on anticipating his demands. Later, during the Chou dynasty, a deity appeared called *T'ien*. That impersonal designation meant "the abode of the great spirits," that is, the sky or heaven. T'ien was identified with Shang Ti and was worshiped as the reigning universal power, the ultimate regulator of human affairs.

Also worshiped were the messengers of Shang Ti: the deities of wind, cloud, sun, and moon; the gods of the four cardinal points of the compass; and deities of the mountains and the rivers. In different regions, different deities were the objects of consistent worship. Every village had a mound of soil, called *She*, that symbolized fertility. The mounds were the focal points of an agricultural cult, the purpose of which was to ensure the growth of crops. In addition to deities related to agriculture, each home was guarded by a group of household deities, who were propitiated to guarantee the prosperity and security of the family. They included those of the outer and inner doors of the house, the hearth, the well, and the cupboard.

From the earliest times, then, the Chinese believed that the universe was alive with spirits, in heaven as well as on earth. Not all deities or spirits were considered beneficent. One category of spirits, the *kuei*, was associated with malevolent agents of destruction. A second category, the *shen*, came to represent benevolent forces. *Shen* spirits were believed to animate seas, mountains, rivers, trees, and stones, as well as the sun, moon, stars, wind, and thunder. Whereas *shen* spirits animated nature, *kuei* spirits lurked in its shadows. They haunted the lonely places—the

desolation of mountain rock and desert, the dark forest path, the unin-
habited stretch of road — and infested crops. There were also demons,
gigantic devils, and vampires. Fear of *kuei* spirits and demons so dominated the lives of Chinese villagers that they spent much of their time
keeping the evil spirits at a distance with bonfires, torches, candles, and
lanterns. Conversely, all *shen* spirits were kept firmly on the villagers'
side with appropriate talismans, taboos, gestures, and gifts.

Yin-Yang

Perhaps as early as 1000 BCE, Chinese thinkers established a distinction
between two interacting cosmic forces that they attributed to every natural phenomenon. Those forces were identified by the ideogram of *yin-
yang*. *Yin* represented the passive, cold, wet, feminine, evil, and negative principle or force; *yang* the active, warm, dry, masculine, good, and
positive principle. The two concepts were viewed not as mutually exclusive, which would imply a cosmos of diametrically conflicting opposites, but as complementary and necessary opposites, implying a cosmos in equilibrium.

According to that philosophical theory, *yin-yang* is an attribute of
everything and every person. Although *yin* is the higher principle and
yang the lower, *yin-yang* represents a union of elemental principles essential to creative interaction in the ceaseless, dynamic movement of
the universe. Nature and humanity operate through the interplay of
yin-yang until death, at which time an individual's *yang* component is
received into heaven, where it influences surviving descendants for
good. The *yin* component of a person accompanies the corpse to the
grave and must be propitiated through sacrifices performed by surviving relatives and succeeding generations, to inhibit unwelcome meta-
morphoses of *yin* into hostile spirits. Thus, gods were essentially *yang*
spirits (*shen* in Chinese), and demons or malignant beings were *yin* spirits (*kuei* in Chinese).

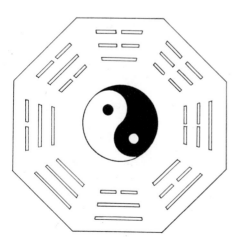

The *yin-yang* symbol surrounded by the *pa kua* (eight trigrams), arranged within an octagon. A black spot appears within the light-colored *yang*, symbolic of the embryonic *yin*; and a light spot appears within the dark-colored *yin*, symbolic of the embryonic *yang*.

Divination

One of the major practices of Chinese religion during the Classical period was *divination:* determination of the most auspicious period for any undertaking and of the predilection of the appropriate deity. The media for those messages—apart from Fu Hsi's closed and broken lines, described in the I Ching (discussed later in this chapter)—were ox bones and tortoise shells, although occasionally sheep bones were used. Tortoise shells were preferred as sources of information, because their structure was thought to resemble the shape of the universe. Other methods of divination included signs and portents revealed by the seasons, astrology, dreams, coins, and the *pa kua,* or eight trigrams. Eventually, one of the Five Classics, the I Ching, became the principal manual for providing clues concerning one's actions.

The status of diviners, popularly known as *wu,* was sometimes second only to that of the emperor. The *wu* were charged not only with divination but also with rainmaking, ridding the community and individuals of pestilence and plague and securing them against disaster, offering sacrifices, fortune-telling, and performing exorcisms and various forms of magic.

Emperor Rites

Chinese religion stressed the importance of imperial authority and the grave responsibilities attached to it. According to Chinese religion, the growth of crops in the fields and the maintenance of law and order in society depend on the sacrifices the emperor performed. As a monarch, he surpassed all others in *te,* an attribute of inherent power and virtue invested in his office; accordingly, he was the individual capable of reaping the greatest advantage from any sacrifice. The emperor's unique contribution to society, aside from the day-to-day administration of the country, lay in the performance of appropriate rituals dedicated to a pantheon of cosmic powers and spirits.

Those emperors who regularly worshiped the spirits and took seriously the welfare of society, for which they acted as supreme advocates of last resort, were highly revered and thought of as fulfilling the duty of the mandate of heaven. Any failure to live by that celestial mandate was a threat to cosmic prosperity and might result in crop failure and social revolt. Thus, the emperor played a pivotal role in maintaining harmony in the cosmic process.

At no time were the emperors considered divine; on the contrary, it was their duty to pay the utmost reverence to the spirit *tablets* of heaven and earth, the great powers of the universe. Emperors sacrificed—without humbling themselves—to the subsidiary powers of nature: the sun, the moon, heavenly bodies, mountains, and rivers. Emperors also owed imperial ancestors their due: burial rites appropriate to their stations in life and spirit tablets raised in their memory in the ancestral hall alongside the spirit tablets of heaven and earth. The association of imperial ancestral tablets with spirit tablets of heaven and earth was the symbolic expression of the belief that the ancestors of the emperors dwelt with the Supreme Ruler in heaven, where they presumably could exert

A worshiper divines with blocks inside a Chinese temple in Taiwan. Worshipers come either with a specific purpose or periodically to sacrifice to the spirits.
Courtesy of Jordan Paper.

influence. Consequently, emperors often consulted their ancestors and offered sacrifices to them.

According to surviving bone inscriptions, some emperors of the Shang and Chou dynasties were buried with bronze vessels, hunting weapons, animals, and human victims, all provided to accommodate the emperor in the next world. The practice of animal and human sacrifice continued late into Chou times, when funerary substitutes—first pottery, later paper—gradually replaced live victims in imperial tombs.

Ancestor Rites

Although it was introduced by members of the royal family during the Shang period, the cult of ancestor worship soon spread to court officials and beyond them to the general populace. Every family reserved a special spot in the home for an ancestral shrine, which became a repository of wooden tablets inscribed with the names of family ancestors. Later, local *clans* maintained family temples, often elaborately furnished, containing the spirit tablets of their ancestors.

Both the clan temple and the domestic shrine became focal points for propitiatory offerings of food and drink and the performance of religious rituals. There, in the presence of their ancestors, family members announced plans for enterprises such as business ventures, journeys, and marriages and delivered formal decisions of all kinds to receive ancestral endorsement. Spring and autumn were occasions for special pilgrimages to ancestral graves, where sacrifices and offerings were performed. According to cult tradition, anyone who abandoned or betrayed the ancestral rites was doomed to suffer the vengeance of ancestral spirits and to wander in death as an unlucky, lonely, hungry ghost lacking a living descendant to sustain memorial rites and sacrifices.

Similarly, the absence of a male heir was a heinous offense against ancestral spirits because without one the ancestral rites could not be continued. In such cases, a substitute son was found either by adopting one or by making the son of a concubine the heir. In families in which there was more than one son, the eldest assumed the responsibility for performing ancestral rites at the death of his father.

Ancestral rites played an indispensable role in Chinese religion from the beginning. They implied continuous contact between the dead and the living and an affirmation of life after death in some form or other. By virtue of their close association with the Supreme Ruler in heaven, which gave them the power to intercede on behalf of their living descendants, ancestors were seen as possessing influence that was denied the living. Ancestors were, in a sense, deified. Their relationship with their living descendants was one of mutual dependence: protection in exchange for filial sacrifices.

Aside from religious rites, the frequent recall of names and accomplishments recorded in genealogical accounts gave people a sense of being rooted in established traditions. Some lineages stretched in unbroken succession through many generations, often to the remotest past. The presence of ancestors was a pervasive and comforting element of daily family activity. Today, the observance of ancestral rites is still prevalent in parts of Asia.

The Five Classics

The classical literature of Chinese religion consists of a set of texts called the Five Classics. A sixth text, the Book of Music, has been lost, but its existence is implied in Confucian tradition. The texts of the Five Classics were edited during the Chou dynasty to conform to the official philosophy of the period, destroyed in the Ch'in era (221–206 BCE), and reconstructed during the Han dynasty (206 BCE–220 CE). The authenticity of the reconstructed texts has been a subject of dispute, but it is generally agreed that, although much of the material is of late derivation, it preserves the outlines of older religious ideas. The Five Classics are

- Shu Ching (Book of History or Historical Documents)
- Shih Ching (Book of Poems)
- I Ching (Book of Changes)
- Chun Chiu (Spring and Autumn Annals)
- Li Chi (Records of Ceremonies or Ritual)

Altar inside a house in Taiwan, showing the eclectic nature of Chinese religion. On the left is a family shrine, and in the middle is the shrine dedicated to Kuan-Yan, goddess of mercy. Daily burning of incense and periodic sacrifices take place at the altar.
Courtesy of Jordan Paper.

The Shu Ching is the primary source for the "legendary" history of China. It also contains moralizing speeches by emperors and noblemen.

The Shih Ching is a collection of 305 folk songs covering a period of more than one thousand years, beginning with the Shang dynasty. According to tradition, at one time it consisted of 3000 poems, of which Confucius selected the best 305 dealing with love, piety, and war.

The I Ching, perhaps the most important of the five texts, presents a system of divination based on the symbolic interpretation of trigrams and hexagrams. The system of hexagrams, traditionally attributed to an ancient hero, Fu Hsi, comprises varying combinations of unbroken lines *(yang)* and broken lines *(yin)*. The complicated method of combining broken and unbroken lines gave diviners the evidence, data, or signs they needed to fulfill a petitioner's request for prophecy or advice. Later, it provided the basis for much philosophical and mystical speculation.

The Chun Chiu, traditionally ascribed to Confucius, is a history of the kingdom of Lu (722–484 BCE), Confucius's native country. It is considered to be one of the first accurate historical texts of China.

The Li Chi contains rules for dancing, music, ancestor worship, and imperial sacrifices and represents the work of later Confucian generations.

TAOISM

Both Chinese scholars and Western sinologists distinguish between philosophical (mystical) and religious (popular) Taoism. The former is viewed as a philosophy of life or a form of mysticism, the first evidence of which is found in texts dating from the sixth to the third centuries BCE. In that form, Taoism has represented, throughout Chinese history, the spiritual goal of the educated few. Religious Taoism, on the other hand, is a highly organized system with ceremonials, temples, and a hereditary priesthood, the earliest evidence of which dates from the second century CE. As such, it is a popular folk religion that attracts all ranks and classes of Chinese people.

Although in theory the two views of Taoism are distinct, in actual fact they are interrelated, sharing many linguistic and conceptual features. A Taoist may participate in both the ceremonial aspects of organized religion and the realm of solitary, mystical abstraction. An earlier view that religious Taoism represents a debasement of philosophical Taoism no longer is considered valid by some modern scholars, who argue that any distinction between the two types of Taoism should be made simply for the sake of descriptive convenience.

Lao Tzu

Who was Lao Tzu? Was he a legendary figure or a historical individual? The question has not been answered with certainty. The first mention of Lao Tzu (meaning "Old Master") was made in an early Chinese classic book called Chuang Tzu, written probably around the fourth or third century BCE. In the book, Lao Tzu is described as the teacher of Chuang Tzu, the author of the book. Parts of the text are even attributed to Lao Tzu, who is represented as a renowned Taoist Master who earned his living working as a curator of the archives at the courts of the Chou dynasty. The book also asserts that Lao Tzu met Confucius and, as the senior of the two, confounded Confucius with his Taoist teachings. The sole account of Lao Tzu's death occurs in the Chuang Tzu.

A biographical account of Lao Tzu written after the Classical period is incorporated into the Shih-chi (Historical Records), China's first historical record, authored around the second century BCE by Ssu-ma Ch'ien. According to the Shih-chi, Lao Tzu's given name was Erh, and his family name was Li. The biography also records that Lao Tzu worked at the Chou court as an archivist and that he left the court as the result of disenchantment with the declining Chou dynasty. He is said to have written, at the request of the guardian of the frontier gate where he made his exit from China, his treatise on Tao and its power, better known as Tao Te Ching. The biography also states that Lao Tzu instructed Confucius on points of ceremony before he left China for good. It does not say what became of him.

Most modern scholars question the credibility of these two accounts and attribute references concerning Lao Tzu to legend. Some even argue that the Lao Tzu of tradition is nothing more than a fictitious figure invented by Taoists to establish their historical primacy over Confucianism. A few scholars dissent from that assessment. Based on certain Confucian evidence, they accept the traditions associated with Lao Tzu as historical, although disagreeing among themselves on the precise dates of Lao Tzu's life. According to some, the midpoint of his career came around 570 BCE; according to others, it may have fallen closer to 604 BCE. All scholars do agree, however, that nothing for certain is known about Lao Tzu.

Origin and Development

Behind all forms of Taoism stands the figure of Lao Tzu, traditionally considered the founder of Taoism and the author of the Tao Te Ching. Modern scholarship discredits both claims, although it generally is agreed that the first evidence of philosophical Taoism occurs in the Tao Te Ching.

Taoism in the Ch'in (221–206 BCE) and Han (206 BCE–220 CE) periods is associated, at least among scholars, with official or imperial patronage. Representatives of different religious traditions met at the imperial court not only to exchange ideas but to compete for official favor. Their activities were recorded by court officials, who often were active participants in the events they described. Taoists were among the various thaumaturgic (wonder-working) individuals who visited the courts of the Ch'in and Han dynasties.

By the third century BCE, Taoist masters were expounding the teachings of Lao Tzu, which spread from court officials to various learned individuals throughout the country. Their teachings about ideal government and immortality evoked considerable interest, especially among Han statesmen. The officials applied Taoist principles of nonaction to the function of government—an early example of laissez-faire statesmanship.

During the first and second centuries CE, several messianic revolts broke out, some of them led by *charismatic* (gifted or divinely empowered) Taoist leaders, one of whom claimed to be the reincarnation of Lao Tzu. Other would-be messiahs included Taoist ideological elements in revolutionary religious movements that somehow reconciled action and nonaction as two elements of the same indivisible concept. The sporadic revolutionary manifestations of messianism eventually were defeated by imperial forces.

Official Recognition

It is generally thought that religious Taoism was developed in the province of Szechwan by a certain Chang Ling (Chang Tao-Ling) in 142 CE. Chang Ling is said to have received a revelation from the Most High Lord Lao Tzu, who instructed him to replace the degenerated and demonic religious practices of the people with Lao Tzu's "orthodox and sole doctrine of the authority of the covenant." Later, according to tradition, Chang Ling ascended to heaven and received the title of Heavenly Master. His successors, also called Heavenly Masters, established an independent organization to continue his work and to instruct the faithful in the revealed work of the Most High Lord Lao Tzu. Their fundamental teachings concerned right actions and good works, which, in turn, ensured immunity from disease.

In 215, Chang Lu, grandson of Chang Ling, pledged himself to the Wei dynasty of northern China. That act of submission and fealty resulted in official imperial recognition of the group as an organized religion. The Heavenly Masters were authorized to act as intermediaries between the responsible ruler and the public; as their influence grew, they sometimes assumed secular power when a ruler proved weak or ineffective.

The Taoist group was so readily accepted that in less than a century it counted among its adherents most of the powerful families in northern China. By the beginning of the fourth century, the religious Taoism of the Heavenly Masters had penetrated into southeastern China, where nonaction was complemented by coercion. After war had been waged against indigenous cults, sorcerers, and mediums, the entire region was converted to the religion of the Heavenly Masters.

In time, each Heavenly Master represented a different aspect of religious Taoism. Detailed liturgies replaced the older, simpler rites of the earlier Heavenly Masters. Certain observances, featuring countless formulas and practices, were developed in the expectation that they would restore vital life forces and thus increase longevity. Various hygienic and respiratory techniques also were developed to maintain a continuous circulatory process of all energies in the body. Some Taoist priests performed exorcisms and increasingly complex rituals. Other eminent Taoists searched, edited, or annotated revealed texts. Some were recipients of revelations from the heavenly immortals.

The founders of the T'ang (618–907) and Ming (1368–1644) dynasties routinely resorted to Taoist prophecies and occult practices to ensure and maintain public support. The most spectacular success of religious Taoism came during the T'ang dynasty, whose founder, Li Yuan, claimed to be a descendant of Lao Tzu. Taoists accepted him as the long-awaited fulfillment of messianic prophecy, and that conviction became the ideology of the state. The wide diffusion of Taoism throughout the vast T'ang empire is evident from contacts of Taoists with Buddhists, Christians, Eastern Nestorians, and Manicheans. In the seventh century, Taoism reached Japan, where adherents can be found to this day.

That wide dissemination encouraged the development, to impressive dimensions, of a number of new Taoist sects, some of which have survived to the present. Other Taoist sects formed religious communities and established monasteries to facilitate the daily observance of Taoist meditation, liturgy, hygiene, and other characteristics of the contemplative life. It must be emphasized, however, that religious Taoism never established a permanent central authority. No institutional cohesion existed among the sects. Each sect looked back to its founder, adhered independently to its scriptures, and observed its ritualistic ceremonies.

In contrast, the essential and distinctive element of philosophical Taoism was to gain and preserve the vital force through a realization of *Tao* (the Way). The quest to be in harmony with Tao—with the universal rhythm or mechanism behind all perceptible and imperceptible

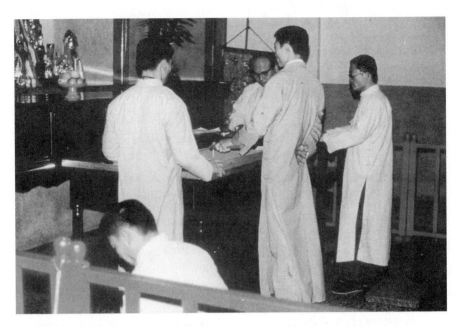

Inside a private temple, a Taoist possessed by a spirit is in a trance.
Courtesy of Julian Pas.

existence — was the essential preoccupation with one's vital force. In that regard, Taoist mystics were neither theologians in the Christian sense nor philosophers in the Buddhist sense, but poets who expressed the individual need of harmony with Tao.

Taoist Sacred Texts

Tao Te Ching. The Tao Te Ching is at once a short anthology of paradoxical statements on the nature of Tao and a handbook of maxims for the ruler-sage. Nothing is known for certain about its date of origin, which scholars have placed some time between the sixth and fourth centuries BCE, or about its author(s). Tradition holds that Lao Tzu was its author, but modern critics speculate that the Tao Te Ching is an anthology of works from a variety of sources that were collected in an effort to preserve them for posterity.

The Tao Te Ching is written so cryptically that understanding may escape the casual reader of this deceptively short book. Behind its brevity, ambiguity, and paradoxical style is a mystical philosophy centered on five fundamental principles: Tao, Relativity, Nonaction, Return, and Government. In spite of its enigmatic language, the Tao Te Ching remains the fundamental text for both philosophical and religious Taoism.

Chuang Tzu. The Chuang Tzu, named after its author, probably was written in the fourth and third centuries BCE. Along with valuable documentary material and passages that reflect the philosophical trends and religious practices of the Warring States period (481–221 BCE), it includes descriptions of "spirit journeys," practices of ecstatic religion, accounts of Taoist Masters and disciples, and techniques of meditation, breath control, sexual activity, gymnastics, and diets.

Tao is represented as indescribable. One can only attain identity with Tao—complete identification or fusion with the "rhythm" of the forces of nature. That identity is totally indistinguishable from the rhythm of nature and shares its infinity, beyond the cycle of life and death. In other words, identity with Tao is identity with the power and rhythm behind the forces of all nature, existence, and the universe.

Other Sacred Texts. A vast body of Taoist sacred texts is of special significance to popular, or religious, Taoism, in contrast to philosophical Taoism. Those sacred texts are reserved for and restricted to priests, to help them communicate with the deities, ward off demons, learn esoteric secrets, perform liturgies for burial, chart spiritual maps, and check the lists or names of spirits. The use or even the perusal of a proscribed text by the uninitiated—and, therefore, the unauthorized—is regarded as sacrilegious.

The 1120 volumes of the Tao Tsang (Storehouse of Tao) were not published in their entirety until some time during the Ming dynasty (1368–1644). The collection consists of several sections, each representing the teachings of a separate Taoist sect, in addition to the teachings of other groups. Each section includes basic doctrines, vows, and rituals for initiates, collections of magical rites, hymns and melodies, cures and incantations, memorials and biographies of famous Taoists, and miscellaneous documents.

Two other important texts associated with Taoism are the T'ai-p'ing Ching (Classic of the Great Peace) and the Pao P'u Tzu (Master Embracing Simplicity), both written during the third and fourth centuries CE. The latter work includes Confucian teachings, but its main theme is the quest for immortality through alchemic elixirs, special diets, and certain sexual activities. In fact, the major concern of most Taoist sacred texts is with gaining superhuman, immortal power by engaging in special exercises.

Taoist Teachings

Tao. The most fundamental concept in Chinese thought is Tao. In common usage, it means "the way" and, by extension, a code of behavior. Tao also means *the Way*, the cosmic force behind all phenomena. In religious Taoism, Tao identifies the magical feat of bringing supernatural powers into communication with humans. In philosophical Taoism, Tao is understood as the ecstatic integral fusion of a person with the principle behind cosmic order and disorder.

The Tao Te Ching defines (or attempts to define) the undefinable: the various meanings of Tao, which is imperceptible, indiscernible, formless, and nameless. All categories in heaven and earth arise from Tao, but Tao lies outside all categories. Nothing can be predicated about Tao, yet it latently embodies the forms, categories, entities, and forces behind and within all phenomena. Tao even defies description as nonbeing. Tao and nonbeing are not identical. Being and nonbeing, which grow out of one another and are interdependent, are two aspects of Tao. Nonbeing does not mean nothingness, but emptiness—the void, the absence of perceptible qualities. Tao, then, is the primordial, undivided state underlying both being and nonbeing. In short, Tao is the inherent, purposeless, impersonal, amoral Cosmic Principle. The Tao Te Ching[1] (Chapter 2) "describes" Tao this way:

> Look, it cannot be seen—it is beyond form.
> Listen, it cannot be heard—it is beyond sound.
> Grasp, it cannot be held—it is intangible.
> From above it is not bright;
> From below it is not dark:
> An unbroken thread beyond description.
> It returns to nothingness.
> The form of the formless,
> The image of the imageless,
> It is called indefinable and beyond imagination.
> Stand before it and there is no beginning.
> Follow it and there is no end.
> Stay with the ancient Tao,
> Move with the present.
> Knowing the ancient beginning is the essence of Tao.

Nonaction. Tao is usually expressed by its aspects, one of which is *wu-wei*, or nonaction. The term does not imply anti-action or deliberate intervention (such as passive resistance). On the contrary, nonaction is nonstriving; it represents the natural course of things, the harmonious, cyclical order of change and reversal, of active-passive (i.e., *yang-yin*) complementary energies. One need only look at nature to understand natural action or nonaction. Nature functions quietly and through nonaction (or the natural course of things) accomplishes its purposes of creating, sustaining, and destroying. The concept of nonaction excludes efforts to fight for or against the course of events. Nature does not support or resist the cosmic rhythm; it simply lets things happen naturally. According to the Tao Te Ching (Chapters 48 and 73),

> The Tao of heaven does not strive, and yet it overcomes.
> It does not speak, and yet is answered.
> It does not ask, yet is supplied with all its needs.
> In the pursuit of Tao, every day something is dropped.
> Less and less is done until non-action is achieved.
> When nothing is done, nothing is left undone.
> The world is ruled by non-action, not by action.

Relativity. Another aspect of Tao is *chiao*, or the relativity of everything. According to the concept of *chiao*, good and evil, right and wrong, beauty and ugliness, strength and weakness, glory and humiliation are not polar opposites but standards of value that are relative to time and place.

Judgments of what is right or wrong are relative to one's personal stance, situation, and needs. What is considered cold weather for people living in southern regions, for example, is welcomed as warm by those living in northern territories. Water is precious for travelers in the desert but a constant hazard for people in lowlands.

Nothing—not water, not climate, not morality, not anything—has any intrinsic or absolute value or specific purpose. Value and purpose arise only in relation to something else. This is how *chiao* is expressed in the Tao Te Ching (Chapter 2):

> Under heaven all can see beauty as beauty only because
>   there is ugliness.
> All can know good as good only because there is evil.
> Therefore having and not having arise together.
> Difficult and easy complement each other.

Identity of Opposites. The concept of relativity was further developed by Chuang Tzu, who argued that, because truth is relative to one's need and situation, opposites are identical. All dualities—like and dislike, large and small, short and long, life and death, beginning and end, knowledge and ignorance, finite and infinite—are not really opposites but identical aspects of one and the same reality. Tao transcends distinction.

Chuang Tzu's view is best expressed by his "wake-dream" reality. After dreaming that he was a butterfly, Chuang Tzu woke and pondered: "I do not know whether I dreamt that I was a butterfly, or I am a butterfly now dreaming that I am Chuang Tzu!" The reality (or Tao) that characterizes waking and dreaming has no opposites, only identical aspects. A prerequisite to the attainment of a real state of identity is to discard all concepts of opposites and distinctions. When the duality of aspects is dissolved, all things become the One, or Tao.

Return. The invariable law of nature is *fu,* or return. The phenomenon of reversal, the process by which all things are ordained to return to their original state, is yet another aspect of Tao. The law of Tao, as it relates to natural order, means the continuous reversion of everything to its starting point. Anything that develops a certain quality invariably will revert to the opposite quality. Because everything issues out of Tao, everything inevitably returns to Tao. The One becomes the all, and the all returns to the One. From nonbeing comes being, from which comes nonbeing. That is the eternal, endless law of Tao. Consider this passage from the Tao Te Ching (Chapter 16):

> The ten thousand things rise and fall while the Self watches
>   their return.
> They grow and flourish and then return to the source.
> Returning to the source is stillness, which is the way of nature.

Transformation. Chuang Tzu saw the invariable law of nature not as *fu,* or return, but as *hua,* or transformation. For him, life was an eternal transformation from one form to another. Chuang Tzu did not believe in a "soul" that transmigrated from one form to another, nor did he understand the transformation as a moral cause-and-effect relationship. On the contrary, Chuang Tzu conceived of life in terms of an infinite

Taoist priests perform a funeral ceremony at the home of the deceased. Mourners wear hemp cloth and prostrate themselves during the ceremony.
Courtesy of Julian Pas.

process of change, or transformation, that involved ceaseless mutations with no absolute end. It is precisely that process, which is the function of the Tao, that makes humans, like the universe, immortal.

To let oneself follow the natural process of transformation results, according to Chuang Tzu, in a sense of peace and tranquillity that transcends description. Only those who experience it are aware of the reality beyond duality. That reality is nothing less than an identity with Tao.

CONFUCIANISM

Confucius

The world into which Confucius was born is considered by scholars to have been one of the most intellectually creative periods in Chinese history, yet it was characterized by political and cultural anarchy. Petty rulers attempted to extend their authority at the expense of the royal house of the Chou dynasty, which was then in decline. Boundaries between states were in a constant state of flux. Feudal rulers, who reigned by virtue of their noble ancestry, were so corrupt that society suffered economic and moral deterioration. Nevertheless, the eastern Chou period (771–255 BCE) was one of intense social, political, and intellectual activity that provoked fundamental changes in most established conventions and institutions.

This is the age commonly referred to as the Classical period and as the Age of a Hundred Philosophers. Contending vigorously for solutions to the pressing social and political problems of the period, the "hundred philosophers" eventually were classified into six schools: Confucianism, Taoism, Mohism, the School of Yin-Yang, the Dialecticians, and Legalism. In the second century BCE, Confucianism was elevated to the status of a state cult at the expense of the other schools.

Debate on the question of whether Confucianism is a religion or a philosophical system implies a characteristic ambiguity. Those who tend to see Confucianism as a system of philosophy argue that it has no religious structure or sanction; rather, it represents a body of noble ethical teachings and important political ideologies. They point out that proponents of the claim that Confucianism is a religion have difficulty explaining the absence of any reference to immortality or life beyond death — a concept fundamental to most, if not all, religions. Those who are inclined to see Confucianism as a religion justify their views in terms of the religious characteristics embraced by Confucianism: reverence toward heaven, ancestor worship, ceremonial and sacrificial practices, and temples. True, Confucian temples are memorial monuments rather than religious institutions. Nevertheless, the Chinese consider Confucianism more than a creed to be professed or rejected. To them, Confucianism is Chinese life in all its political, social, moral, and religious aspects. After all, Confucius taught that the principle of morality should govern political and social relations.

Traditional Account. No accurate account of the life of Confucius is likely to be found, because his biographies were written centuries after his death, by which time he had been elevated to a semidivine status. His given name was Chiu, meaning "small hill," a reference to a noticeable bulge on his head. His family name was Kung. The name Confucius is a Latinized form of K'ung Fu Tzu, or Master Kung.

Confucius was born in 551 BCE in the state of Lu, the present Ch'u Fu, in the northern province of Shantung. His father, Shu Ho (Shu-Liang-Ho), was a distinguished soldier, and his mother was from the Yen family. Both his parents died when he was a child.

Confucius married at the age of nineteen, although nothing is known about his wife, and had a son and a daughter. His son, Po-Yu, later became one of his early disciples but died before his father. Nothing is known of his daughter.

Government Service. Confucius's first occupation was as a clerk in the Memorial Temple of the Duke Chou, where he was expected to attend and participate in all ceremonies. Later, he was a leader of ceremonies in a village temple. His love for learning prompted him to study the ceremonial rituals of the local community from the well-informed elders of the village school. He became the local prodigy, a boy wonder who went on to read the Shu Ching (Book of History or Historical Documents) and the Shih Ching (Book of Poems) with the village music master. Even in his callow youth, Confucius acquired a reputation as an expert in ancient ritual.

According to tradition, Confucius attempted to pass the qualifying examination for a government post several times, failing each time. Frustrated but not embittered, he withdrew from the competitive scramble for prestigious government preferment and began to teach, not as a tutor for aristocrats' children, but as a mentor of anyone, poor and rich alike, who matched his capacity and will to learn. In short, he was demanding; he selected only the cream of the crop.

Tradition states that after countless attempts, Confucius finally passed the civil service examination at the age of fifty. Accordingly, he became the chief magistrate of Cheng-tu, an outlying town west of the Lu capital, where he was able to apply his political ideologies. The following year, he was a delegate in the retinue of the imperial ambassador appointed to head a peace conference in Outer Mongolia. An assignment as deputy minister of justice, one of the six highest-ranking imperial offices achieved by commoners, followed. His wisdom, though widely praised, was not always heeded. Disillusioned with the state of affairs, he resigned his post.

Western scholars have found little, if any, historical evidence to confirm that traditional account. They argue that if Confucius had occupied a commanding position of authority in imperial service, it surely would be mentioned in the definitive collection of Confucian quotations, the Analects. Far from documenting any such record in the corridors of power, the Analects reflects Confucius's concern, self-doubt, and speculation about whether he possessed the qualities that would enable him to hold important office. Perhaps, critics have said, Confucius held office in minor roles in the court of Lu in later life, but his resignation may have been prompted by boredom, the inconsequential nature of the work, or simply the fact that the court was corrupt, weak, and increasingly impotent.

His Later Years. Accompanied by a few disciples, Confucius spent the next ten or more years traveling and visiting vassals of the imperial court, regional governors, and warlords in the hope of putting his philosophy into practice. He first went north to the state of Chi and almost immediately became a victim of the lawlessness that prevailed outside the bastions of government authority: he was mistaken for someone else and almost lost his life. The setback did not dampen his enthusiasm for recommending his vision of government to those in power. After completing his mission in the north, he traveled south to the state of Sung, then to the state of Wei, and then to the rest of the states in China.

Traditional accounts of his odyssey imply that Confucius was well received, especially when he advised rulers on government policy, but the effect of such encouragement must have been tempered by the reluctance of any potentate to take him on staff. Confucius offered to justify his teachings and policies in terms of concrete results within a year and to apply his total program of governmental reform within three years, but no one ever took him up on this offer. Disappointed and disheartened, Confucius returned to his hometown in the state of Lu.

For the next five years, Confucius devoted himself to teaching and editing the Five Classics while his disciples reaped the benefits of their teacher's former proselytizing zeal. Some were appointed to important posts in different states. Others established schools and taught Confucius's ideas. Confucius himself died in 479 BCE, at the age of seventy-two, convinced that he had failed to achieve his mission.

What kind of man was Confucius? Invariably, his manner is described in traditional accounts as informal and cheerful. The keystone of his teaching was sincerity, a characteristic that bordered on uncompromising frankness. Although he had many friends and admirers, his sincerity may have weakened his prospects of achieving his political ambitions. He also had a sense of humor and approved of pleasure in moderation.

Although he may have viewed himself as a failed politician, Confucius never lost his keen appetite for learning and teaching, which may have been his primary vocation. He demanded two qualities from his students: intelligence and the willingness to work hard. That earned him the well-deserved title of Master. His humility was always evident in his capacity to listen to his disciples and to compromise or admit error. He was totally dedicated to the improvement of government in the interest of and to the advantage of the governed—a goal that escaped him, at least during his lifetime.

Disciples of Confucius

Confucius lived in an era of great political and social unrest dominated by warlords more interested in their own comfort than anyone else's, and his ideas of reform had little, if any, impact during his lifetime. Nevertheless, a select number of enthusiastic disciples combined forces in what they called the Ju school to maintain Confucian ideals in the face of competition from rival ideologies during the Warring States period (481–221 BCE). They perpetuated the study of the ancient classics, which their Master had esteemed so highly, and preserved and transmitted the many oral traditions that were associated with Confucius.

Meng Tzu (Mencius). The next major Confucian thinker, Meng Tzu, also known as Mencius (390–305 BCE), appeared at the end of the fourth century BCE. The book that bears his name describes how he, like Confucius before him, traveled throughout China and beyond to persuade rulers that he had an alternative to the endless wars between states. Two of his theories are worth noting. First, he emphasized government by compassion and virtue instead of by guile and reliance on force. He maintained that if a ruler was sincere and righteous, he would so win the hearts of neighboring populations, as well as his own, that people would flock to his standard, abandoning leaders who suffered by comparison. Second, Meng Tzu insisted on the innate goodness of human nature—an issue that has occupied Confucian thinkers for centuries. He based that view on his personal observations, which had persuaded him that humans are naturally disposed to sympathetic responses. Evil, he believed, is a consequence of the corruption of that innate sympathetic disposition.

Hsün Tzu. Hsün Tzu (340–245 BCE) strongly opposed Meng Tzu's doctrine of the innate goodness of human nature. In Hsün Tzu's view, humans are born with desires; because the means of satisfying those desires are limited, conflicts are inevitable unless some kind of order or conformity can be imposed on society from above. An orthodox Confucian, he propagated the concept of a universal moral order, embodied in the teachings and institutions of the ancient sages.

State Recognition of Confucianism

The Classical period of intellectual creativity came to an end with the rise of the Ch'in dynasty. During the short-lived but important political period of that dynasty (221–206 BCE), writing was standardized, the Great Wall of China was built, and the totalitarian principles of the Legalists (who believed that people should be nothing more than organs of the state, having no personal thoughts or feelings) were adopted. The Confucian school opposed many of those principles and consequently suffered. In 213 BCE, a deliberate attempt was made to kill all Confucian scholars, and orders were given for the burning of the Classics.

Fortunately, the Ch'in dynasty did not last long. Under its successor, the Han dynasty (206 BCE–220 CE), there was a resurgence of Confucianism. According to tradition, the first Han emperor demonstrated his respect for Confucius by attending the family's ancestral temple in Shantung in 195 BCE. However, imperial patronage did not shield Confucianism from competition with other doctrines, such as Taoism

The Great Wall of China, symbol of the unification of China during the Ch'in dynasty.
From the private collection of the author.

and Legalism. Confucianism did not supplant competing ideologies until, in the reign of Emperor Wu (140–87 BCE), it became the orthodox ideology of the state and the basis of education for official positions. As a result, posthumous titles were conferred on Confucius, special honors accorded to his descendants, and sacrifices at the ancestral temple of the Kung family officially sponsored.

Eclipse of Confucianism

The second century CE was a time of deepening crisis, as power passed from the Han court into the hands of military leaders. During this period of disunity, which lasted for over three and a half centuries (221–589), Confucianism fell somewhat into disrepute. Although it remained the foundation of all literate culture and the model for political life, various brands of Taoism and the new, foreign religion of Buddhism pushed Confucianism into the background.

The period of unrest ended with the rise of the Sui dynasty (589–618), which was followed by the T'ang dynasty (618–907). During those three centuries, Confucianism regained some measure of influence, but it never approached its former status as the leading intellectual force. Buddhism provided the unifying element in the Sui dynasty and reached the zenith of its power and prestige during the T'ang dynasty. Taoism also had a particular appeal to the T'ang emperors, who claimed to be the descendants of Lao Tzu.

The arrival and spread of Buddhism in China put Confucianism to a severe test. Many intellectuals were attracted by the novelty and the freshness of Buddhism, which they compared unfavorably to the formal, traditional, lifeless, and prescriptive character that Confucianism had assumed as the ideology of an educated elite. Taoists scoffed at Confucians and circulated derogatory stories about Confucius and his movement. Nevertheless, Confucians maintained their distinctive character. As long as the Imperial Academy and several other educational institutions drilled their students in the Analects and the Five Classics, Confucians felt themselves safe from rival religions. Indeed, their persistence finally gave rise to another Confucian revival.

Neo-Confucianism

From the time of the Sung dynasty (960–1127) until the establishment of the Republic of China in 1912, Confucianism was the dominant intellectual force in Chinese history. A revived Confucianism, or Neo-Confucianism, absorbed certain metaphysical and mystical elements from Taoism and Buddhism in response to the needs of the age. Throughout that long period, no radically new school of thought or rival religion threatened Confucian hegemony in China, except for minor incursions by Islam and Christianity, neither of which was ever fully accepted into Chinese life and culture.

In promoting traditional Confucian morality, which emphasized loyalty, filial piety, self-cultivation, and involvement in society, Confucians succeeded in turning the public's view outward toward relations with others and away from the inner contemplative or mystical life advocated by Buddhists and Taoists. Not that Confucian thinkers neglected human nature; on the contrary, self-cultivation meant for some not the study of texts but introspection designed to bring out what was present in one's inner world. In accord with that line of thought, Wang Yang-ming (or Wang Shou-jen, 1472–1529) identified the individual mind with the Universal Mind and maintained that the way to moral perfection lay in discovering one's innate "good knowledge." That innate principle, he insisted, was constantly in danger of being obscured by rationalizations and selfish desires.

Neo-Confucianism also spread to Japan and Korea, where it evolved into a peculiarly rigid form and nearly extinguished Buddhism. In China, during the rule of the Mongols (1279–1368), the Confucian curriculum was at first proscribed but then reinstated as a means of recruiting officials.

The disruptive influences of Western culture since the nineteenth century have had only a superficial effect on Chinese scholars, who remain immersed in the Confucian tradition. In fact, Confucian tradition for centuries has provided the thread linking all Chinese people, despite the many changes Chinese culture has undergone.

In 1905, the examination system for civil service, which was based on Confucianism, was abolished. Even more important, the Nationalist Revolution in 1911 swept away the imperial system and, with it, institutional Confucianism. In the early years of the ensuing republic, Confucian traditionalists attempted to perpetuate the state's former commitment to sponsor sacrifices to Confucius. Their efforts were nullified or countered after 1916 with the emergence of the New Culture movement, whose proponents saw Confucianism as an obstacle in the

Temple of Heaven in Beijing (Peking), an Imperial Temple in which Chinese priests and the Emperor performed sacrificial rites.

From the private collection of the author.

path of modernization. Although many traditional characteristics of Chinese civilization survived ideological pogroms launched in the name of reform, the currents of social change gradually eroded what was left of Confucian ideology.

The Status of Women

Confucian teaching, Communist detractors pointed out, gave no credence to the concept that women were individuals. The code of conduct for women was defined in terms of three stages of dependence: when a female is young, she is dependent on her father; when she marries, she is dependent on her husband; and when she is old, she is dependent on her son. Each stage represented a link in an unbroken chain of dependence in the life of women. And along with acknowledging their dependent status, women were obliged to accept four Confucian criteria for virtuous female conduct: (1) a woman has to know her proper place in the home; (2) she must not speak unless she is spoken to; (3) she has to be pretty; and (4) she must be able to fulfill traditional female tasks, such as taking care of the family, cooking, and sewing.

Confucian teachings on the subject of correct behavior and ritual protocol *(li)*, which largely shaped the status of women in China through the centuries, was based on five superior-inferior relationships: (1) ruler-subject, (2) elders-juniors, (3) father-son, (4) husband-wife, and (5) eldest son-younger sons. The relationship of husband and wife established or codified the inferior role and position of women and girls. No daughter could perform ancestral rites for her parents; only sons had that right. The dire poverty of many periods in Chinese history forced many poor couples to get rid of their baby daughters, either by selling them to wealthy people or by infanticide. An alternative method of disposal was the "rearing marriage," a custom that allowed parents to place the custody and care of a baby daughter in the hands of her future in-laws. In the last resort, females were expendable.

Moreover, to ensure family stability and purity of lineage, Confucianism demanded premarital chastity and marital fidelity for females. At times, that rule was applied so rigidly that it led to absolute sexual segregation until couples were formally married. Because women were regarded primarily as sources of sons, few females were educated. All land inheritance was divided solely among sons. Daughters were simply possessions, first of the father, then of their husbands and mothers-in-law.

In spite of the cultural denials of any sense of female autonomy, many women managed to transcend cultural limitations by force of character, but they were the exception rather than the rule. Others sought refuge in the Buddhist female order of the *sangha* as an alternative to marriage. Overall, Confucian ethics hardened social norms and forced women into greater seclusion.

The Impact of Communism

The victory of Communism in 1949 and the impact of the Cultural Revolution in 1966 may have brought down the final curtain on Confucianism. According to the Communists, Confucianism had divided society into two basic classes: the aristocrats, who possessed wealth, enjoyed leisure, were the privileged recipients of education, and were the undeserving beneficiaries of hereditary status; and the masses, who lived in utter ignorance and squalor. Communists justified their point of view, for instance, by arguing that one legacy of Confucianism was the subjugation of women, a conclusion implied by a direct quote from the Analects: "Women and small people [those who are not gentlemen] are difficult to keep" (Analects XVII.23).

The revolution headed by Mao Tse-tung and the establishment of a Communist regime in China in 1949 brought about a radical change in the position of women. The old Confucian system of clan oppression, male dominance, bigamy, concubinage, child betrothal, and dowries was swept aside in favor of free choice of a marital partner, monogamy, equal divorce rights for both sexes, equal rights to child custody, the right of widows to remarry, and the right to own land regardless of sex. Also in line with Communist ideology, the new regime established regulations associated with paid maternity leave, day-care centers, assignments to nursing mothers, and assistance to older women. Nonetheless, disparities persist between women in urban and rural communities and among old and new generations. But if some old stereotypes and ancient prejudices remain, the age-old Confucian order is dead.

The cultural influence of Confucianism remains potent, however. Communist vilification of Confucianism as an outdated, repressive, and retrograde ideology irrelevant to a modern, progressive, proletarian society may have compromised the status of Confucianism as a uniquely Chinese ideology but not as a wellspring of Chinese culture.

The same may be said of Taoism and Buddhism in mainland China, because Marxist categories and Communist policies discourage religious affiliations of any kind. Drastic changes and suppressive measures certainly have changed the forms of Chinese religion, but whether such measures will extinguish the religious aspirations of the Chinese people remains doubtful.

Confucian Sacred Texts

The Analects. The aphorisms, discourses, and sayings attributed to Confucius provide the subject matter of Lun Yu (meaning Conversations), more commonly identified in the Western world as the Analects, a term derived from the Greek word *analekta* ("things gathered"). The text, which comprises some twenty sections (12,700 Chinese characters), is a collection of notes and journals of the Master's discourses, conversations, and travels, ostensibly recorded for posterity by his disciples. Although rival versions existed at one time, the present form dates from about the first century CE.

The Analects is considered to be the earliest and most reliable single source on the life and teachings of Confucius, and it is the most widely read of all the Chinese classics. Even though it is unsystematic, repetitive, and sometimes historically inaccurate, it contains practically all the basic concepts of Confucius and Confucianism.

The Confucian Canon. The heart of the Confucian canonical texts, or scriptures, is a massive, heterogeneous collection of material that occupied the minds of all educated Chinese from the second century BCE to the mid-twentieth century. Those who mastered the contents of the Confucian canon became the literati—the elite, or learned, who by virtue of their learning were eligible to be appointed as officials in the imperial government.

An imperial university was founded in the capital around 124 BCE, during the early Han period (206 BCE–9 CE), for the teaching of the Confucian canon. The importance of the institution can be judged from its enrollment, which is said to have reached some 30,000 students.

The contents of the Confucian canon were never fixed permanently. During the early Han period, the Confucian canon included nine works: the Five Classics (Shu Ching, Shih Ching, I Ching, Chun Chiu, and Li Chi) and the Four Books, which are Lun-Yu, Meng Tzu (Mencius), Hsiao Ching, and Erh Ya. An additional Book of Music is said to have been lost in Han times.

In T'ang times (618–907), the Confucian canon comprised thirteen works: the Five Classics, the Four Books, plus the Chung Yung, Ta Hsueh, I Li, and Chou Li. In the Sung period (960–1280), Confucian philosophers edited a revised version of the canon that consisted of the Five Classics and the Four Books. The Five Classics were the same as in the early Han period, but the Four Books were Lun-Yu, Chung Yung, Ta Hsueh, and Meng Tzu. The Sung version remains to this day the "orthodox" Confucian canon.

The antiquity of those works and the traditional claim that Confucius himself compiled or edited them give them a status unequaled by other sacred literature. But modern Western scholars have seriously questioned the authorship and authenticity of the works. The burning of the Five Classics during the short-lived Ch'in dynasty (221–206 BCE) is known to have created immense problems for the Han scholars, who tried to restore the original texts from the different versions they were able to retrieve. Modern research indicates that the restored originals show evidence not only of editorial liberties assumed by Han scholars but also of outright forgery. In addition, four of the Five Classics antedate Confucius, even though tradition credits Confucius with having collected or edited all of them. Nevertheless, all five constitute the common literary heritage of all educated Chinese, both ancient and modern.

Confucian Teachings

Good Government. Confucius has often been accused of merely seeking to revive the past or the ways of antiquity. Actually, he was a selective traditionalist, that is, he affirmed certain traditional concepts and rituals that were significant to him, but he was also an innovator. Two of his fundamental principles were revolutionary in the Chinese culture of the time: (1) those who govern should be chosen not on the basis of heredity but on demonstrable characteristics of virtue and ability, and (2) the true end of government is the total welfare and happiness of the people.

In accord with those ideas, Confucius maintained that the state should be a totally cooperative enterprise. His view was in direct opposition to those of the existing regime. Confucius openly challenged the idea that aristocrats were descended from divine ancestors and ruled by virtue of the latter's authority. In his view, the right to govern depended on the individual ruler's moral character and ability to make his subjects happy.

Good government could be established, Confucius argued, only by governors schooled in virtue and cultivated in character as well as in competence. The essence of Confucian doctrine was the negation of punishment and rigid law in favor of a positive example of virtue based on *li* and proper conduct exemplified by the criterion of *shu* (reciprocity)—the capacity to deal with others as we would have them deal with us. In the famous words of Confucius, "Do not do to others what you would not desire yourself" (Analects XV.24; see also XII.2 and V.11; cf. Matthew 7:12 and Luke 6:31). Putting the case more positively, he said, "You yourself desire rank and standing; then help others attain rank and standing" (Analects VII.28).

Confucius did not advocate revolution, but he challenged established principles of government based on feudal states parceled out like private properties among those wealthy or ruthless enough to exercise the power of life and death over those they ruled. The nobles and aristocratic families waged war, levied ruinous taxes, and oppressed their

Every year a memorial celebration of the birthday of Confucius is held on September 28 in the Confucian temple in Taipei, Taiwan. The celebration is a family affair because the man without the head-covering (extreme right) is a descendant of Confucius.
Courtesy of Jordan Paper.

subjects with forced labor; Confucius disparaged warfare as a solution to any problem, urged that taxes be reduced, and pleaded for measures to mitigate the severity of punishment for even minor infractions of the law. He challenged the very foundations of authoritarian government by insisting on the right of all individuals to make basic decisions for themselves, and he did what he could to mitigate aristocracy's monopoly on education by accepting the poorest students, provided they were intelligent, hardworking, and unpretentious.

The Superior Man.   According to Confucius, the characteristics that distinguish the superior man (*chun-tzu*, literally "prince-son") from the inferior man are qualities such as *li* (the code of moral, social conduct), *jen* (virtue, compassion, human heartedness, love), *yi* (righteousness), and *te* (virtue). In the words of Confucius, "The superior man is concerned with virtue, the inferior man with land; the superior man understands what is right, the inferior man what is profitable" (Analects IV.11).

Confucius acknowledged that individuals vary in inherent virtues and abilities, but he believed that an appropriate education could nurture and cultivate the inherent moral characteristics that are prerequisites for the creation of the superior man. His curriculum for developing ability, skill, and strength of character stressed music, poetry, and ritual. Poetry, in his view, stimulates the emotions, heightens powers of observation, increases sympathy, and moderates resentment of injustice. Music, Confucius claimed, expresses the inward, heavenly aspect of the universe; rituals express the outward, earthly aspect. A harmonious relationship among all three is necessary for perfect order: "All three arts — music, poetry and ritual — rise from the human soul and are integral in understanding proper human conduct" (Analects VIII.8).

With the components of art and nature blended in harmony, the superior man feels neither fear nor anxiety but is always calm and at peace. The inferior man, in contrast, is always worried and full of anxiety.

A consequence of inner harmony is *li*, an outward manifestation of moral and social conduct that affects every contact with fellow beings, both within the family and within society. From a practical point of view, that means a husband is considerate of his wife and a wife subservient to her husband; a father is kind to his son and a son obedient to his father; an elder brother is helpful to his younger brother and a younger brother respectful of his elder brother.

Extending that principle to society, Confucius urged that a senior friend help a junior friend and a junior friend respect his senior, and that a ruler act beneficently to his subjects and the subjects obey their ruler. Those obligations and duties, which characterize Confucian teaching, came to be known as the Five Relationships.

An individual's conduct should reflect in private, social, or government life the obligations of the role he plays. Confucius identified the correspondence between conduct and role as the true "meaning of names," or, in the Master's words, *cheng ming*. That is to say, one must fulfill the proper functions of a father (an elder brother, a senior friend, a ruler) before one can be truly called a father (a brother, a friend, a ruler).

In terms of morality and ethics, Confucius was more concerned with honesty and conduct than with theological speculation. He himself prayed, fasted, attended sacrifices, offered to ancestors, and respected those who venerated heaven and performed religious ritual aesthetically. At the same time, however, he severely condemned a large part of the religious activities of his day as sheer superstition (Analects VI.22). Confucius remained silent about spirits and supernatural forces. The closest he came to expressing an opinion on the topic was his statement that it was more productive to establish the purpose of life on earth than to waste energy on fruitless speculation about life after death. In his opinion, no one was qualified to speak of serving the spirits without first learning how to serve humanity (Analects XI.11).

Obedience and trust in Heaven *(T'ien)* gave Confucius courage and a sense of mission, and he recommended the "way of Heaven" as the model by which sages, rulers, and nobles should conduct their lives (Analects XV.28, XVI.2). A ruler, according to Confucius, rules by the authority vested in *T'ien*, or the Mandate of Heaven; if he is unworthy, that authority should be transferred to others. "There are three things of which the superior man stands in awe," Confucius is reported to have told his disciples. "He stands in awe of the ordinances of Heaven. He stands in awe of noblemen. He stands in awe of the words of the sages" (Analects XVI.8).

Confucius accepted the importance of ritual, but he stressed that the inner attitude of the worshiper, not the outward display, made a ritual meaningful. He therefore condemned pompous ceremony and was critical of those who took part in rituals and sacrifices without reverence or inner feeling. For Confucius, sincerity and reverence in ritual were absolutely essential; otherwise, ritual was meaningless. What determined the value of ritual, in other words, was the motive of the worshiper.

CHINESE OBSERVANCES

Millions of rural Chinese, as well as emigrants residing in other parts of Asia, have preserved the major currents of Chinese religion. The most obvious religious activities are the construction of new temples, birthday celebrations of gods and goddesses, reenactment of ancient rituals, and a series of annual festivals. An almanac, or religious calendar for festivals, lists the festival days for each year. Tradition prescribes how the festivals are to be celebrated, but customs vary from region to region.

Devotional Acts

Most Chinese cities and towns enshrine a tutelary god, who protects and watches over all municipal projects and businesses. The same function is fulfilled in homes by the guardian hearth or kitchen god, Tsao Chun or Tsai Wang, who is dispatched to heaven on New Year's Eve to report on the behavior of each family to the Jade Emperor Yu Huang, the deified personification of Tao. Women pray to various goddesses for conception, for a safe delivery at childbirth, and for the resolution of family problems. Farmers invoke the agricultural god, carpenters call on the god of carpentry, and each trade has a patron deity.

The services of a particular deity are dictated by the need of the moment. To seek the blessings of a certain god or goddess on one day and the aid of another deity the next day is quite appropriate in Chinese religion. That does not mean the other gods and goddesses are dishonored or rejected—only that some deities are better equipped or more effective than others in responding to specific requests.

Worshipers make offerings to the temple if the resident god or goddess has answered their requests; thus, the maintenance of a temple is a measure of the deity's performance. A public crisis such as crop failure, famine, plague, or similar disaster may revive interest, renew confidence, or inspire hope in the power of a long-neglected deity. The deity's temple is then quickly restored, and worshipers return to submit their prayers and offerings.

Among the numerous gods and goddesses invoked by Chinese worshipers, two have gained popular respect and devotion: the god Kuan Kung (also called Kuan Yü) and the goddess Matsu T'ien Hou. Kuan Kung is a mighty warrior and a god of war, but he is also worshiped by the common people as a beneficent healer. Merchants, professionals, and businesspeople worship him as a god of avowal in sealing or affirming business contracts and as a god of wealth. Soldiers recognize him as their patron god. Local communities, social organizations, fraternities, and secret societies look to him for protection and to supervise the operation of mutual interest and justice among fraternal ties.

Matsu, the Queen of Heaven, is particularly revered in Taiwan, and pilgrims come from all over the island to her central shrine at Peikang. There, devotees worship Matsu with warm and enthusiastic devotion, often parading in the streets for hours in her honor.

Ceremonies and Festivals

Several annual ceremonies and festivals are celebrated by the entire Chinese people, regardless of social group or religious orientation. No festival is more popular throughout the Chinese world than the celebration of the autumn Harvest Moon, which is celebrated in China on the fifteenth night of the eighth month. People feast out of doors late at night to enjoy the glorious moon and exchange gifts, traditionally circular "moon cakes."

The second major popular celebration is the Dragon Boat Festival, celebrated on the fifth day of the fifth month. The Dragon Boat Festival may represent the search for the drowned poet Ch'u Yuan, who committed suicide because his advice was spurned by his lord. The theme, however, is a traditional Chinese one—the fighting of dragons in the skies. Whatever its true origin, the festival is a purely secular observance.

The third of the most popular and universally celebrated Chinese festivals is the Ch'ing Ming (Clear and Bright Festival), observed on the third day of the third month in memory of ancestors. On that date, people visit ancestral tombs, renovate them if necessary, and offer sacri-

Graveside offerings from all the members of the family during the
Ch'ing Ming Festival. Food offered to the deceased is later taken
back home to be eaten by the family members.
Courtesy of Jordan Paper.

fices to their ancestors. The Ch'ing Ming is the most important of the
three special occasions of the year reserved for visiting ancestral tombs.
The second remembrance observance takes place during the entire seventh month, when family members take special measures to placate
ghosts and spirits and avert the harm those ghosts and spirits could
bring on the souls of departed ancestors. Measures include elaborate
ceremonies and generous offerings to temples and shrines. The third
annual ancestral observance is held on the first day of the tenth month.
It differs from similar visits to ancestral tombs in that families leave
mock paper money and paper effigies of clothes and articles that are
thought to be necessary in life beyond the grave.

The celebration of the New Year is undoubtedly the most important
and the most elaborate of all Chinese festivals. In the past, all government offices throughout China remained closed for a whole month,
starting ten days before the end of the old year. Nowadays, the period
of celebration varies from region to region. Nevertheless, a week before
the New Year—that is, on the twenty-third day of the twelfth month—

every home sends Tsao Chun (the guardian kitchen god) off on his annual duty to report to the Jade Emperor. Tsao Chun ordinarily is represented by a printed image pasted on the wall above the stove, a strategic location from which to hear and keep a daily record of the words and deeds of the family before he is sent to the ethereal realm by burning. On New Year's Eve, a new picture of Tsao Chun is pasted up over the stove as a sign of his return to the home.

The rituals connected with New Year's Eve include the worship of the tutelary deities of the home, of Heaven and Earth, and of ancestors. Then comes the family feast, attended by as many family members as possible (but not "foreign" guests). At midnight, all attending family members approach the eldest family couple and in order of precedence prostrate themselves by touching the floor with their foreheads. The next few days of the New Year (in some places, as long as a week) are spent visiting family members and friends. Several other symbolic observances mark the hope for a healthy and prosperous year.

Numerous other observances and celebrations mark agricultural occasions, natural forces, and the birthdays of hundreds of deities. Traditional forms of Chinese ceremonies vary from region to region, depending on the social and political climate. Nevertheless, an indestructible element in the Chinese psyche operates to permit society to adapt to new developments with only a slight effort of adjustment. The evidence lies in the demonstrated ability of the Chinese to handle the incredible diversity of beliefs and practices that surround them.

STUDY QUESTIONS

1. Discuss the Chinese attitude toward religion.
2. Consider the historical background of early China.
3. What are the characteristics of folk religion in early Chinese history?
4. Discuss the importance of ancestor rites.
5. What do the texts of the Five Classics contain?
6. Examine the figure of Lao Tzu according to both tradition and modern research.
7. Give a brief survey of the history of Taoism.
8. Describe the contents of the Tao Te Ching.
9. Discuss the Taoist notion of nonaction and relativity.
10. How did Chuang Tzu's conception differ from the Tao Te Ching?
11. Give the traditional account of Confucius's life.
12. Discuss the theories proposed by both Meng Tzu and Hsün Tzu.
13. Give a brief account of the rise and fall of Confucianism.
14. Describe the role and the status of women during Imperial China.

15. Describe the history and contents of the Confucian canon.

16. Analyze the Confucian teachings on good government and the superior man.

17. Describe the important devotional acts that most Chinese observe.

18. What are the four most popular celebrations observed by almost all Chinese people?

Suggested Reading

Chinese Religions

Birrell, Anne. *Chinese Mythology: An Introduction.* Baltimore: Johns Hopkins University Press, 1993.

Ching, Julia. *Chinese Religions.* London: Macmillan, 1993.

Johnson, Kay Ann. *Women, the Family, and Peasant Revolution in China.* Chicago: Chicago University Press, 1985.

Weller, Robert Paul. *Unities and Diversities in Chinese Religion.* Seattle: University of Washington Press, 1987.

Overmyer, Daniel L. *Religions of China.* San Francisco: Harper & Row, 1986.

Taoism

Cooper, Jean C. *Taoism: The Way of the Mystic.* Wellingborough, Eng.: Aquarian Press, 1990.

Creel, Herrlee Glessner. *What Is Taoism?* Chicago: University of Chicago Press, 1970.

Dean, Kenneth. *Taoist Ritual and Popular Cults of Southeast China.* Princeton, N.J.: Princeton University Press, 1993.

Hoff, Benjamin. *The Tao of Pooh.* London and New York: Penguin Books, 1982.

——. *The Te of Piglet.* New York: Dutton, 1992.

Girardot, Norman J. *Myth and Meaning in Early Taoism: The Theme of Chaos (Hun-tun).* Berkeley: University of California Press, 1983.

Kaltenmark, Max. *Lao Tzu and Taoism.* Stanford, Calif.: Stanford University Press, 1969.

Lagerwey, John. *Taoist Ritual in Chinese Society and History.* New York: Macmillan, 1987.

Robinet, Isabelle. *Taoism: Growth of a Religion.* Stanford, Calif.: Stanford University Press, 1997.

Saso, Michael R. *The Gold Pavilion: Taoist Ways to Peace, Healing, and Long Life.* Boston: Charles E. Tuttle, 1995.

Schipper, Kristofer Marinus. *The Taoist Body.* Berkeley, Calif.: University of California Press, 1993.

Welch, Holmes. *Taoism. The Parting of the Way.* Boston: Beacon Press, 1966.

Confucianism

Berthrong, John H. *Transformations of the Confucian Way.* Boulder, Colo.: Westview Press, 1998.

Creel, Herrlee Glessner. *Confucius and the Chinese Way.* New York: Harper & Row, 1960.

De Bary, William Theodore. *The Trouble with Confucianism.* Cambridge: Harvard University Press, 1991.

Eber, I., ed. *Confucianism: The Dynamics of Tradition.* New York: Macmillan, 1986.

Ebrey, Patricia Buckley. *Confucianism and Family Rituals in Imperial China: A Social History of Writing about Rites.* Princeton, N.J.: Princeton University Press, 1991.

Fingarette, Herbert. *Confucius: The Secular As Sacred.* New York: Harper & Row, 1972.

Jensen, Lionel M. *Manufacturing Confucianism: Chinese Traditions and Universal Civilization.* Durham, N.C.: Duke University Press, 1997.

Louie, Kam. *Critiques of Confucius in Contemporary China.* New York: St. Martin's Press, 1980.

Nivison, David S. *The Ways of Confucianism: Investigations in Chinese Philosophy.* Chicago: Open Court, 1996.

Taylor, Rodney Leon. *The Religious Dimensions of Confucianism.* Albany, N.Y.: SUNY, 1990.

Note

1. All translations of the Tao Te Ching are from the *Tao Te Ching,* trans. by Gia-Fu Feng and Jane English (New York: Vintage Books, 1972).

7 Shinto

Shinto is the Japanese national religion, and because it is closely associated with the Japanese value system, it is better assessed in terms of the social behavior and personal motivation of the Japanese people than in terms of formal beliefs or a codified doctrine. Ancient religious practices, concepts of patriotism, and social attitudes that have been established by long historical precedent are all equated with the term *Shinto*.

DEFINING SHINTO

Shinto represents various indigenous Japanese religious beliefs and practices, as well as a Japanese pattern of social conventions, that have persisted for centuries without necessarily being consciously regarded as a religion. *Shinto* is a collective term that refers to a multitude of varying Japanese religious and national practices, including folklore, magic, ancestral spirits, ritualism, and nationalism. As a result, the word *Shinto*, unless it is qualified in some way, may refer to an animistic cult, a healing group, or a political ideology.

The term *Shinto* was not officially coined until the sixth century CE and then only to distinguish the native Japanese religious systems from systems introduced from abroad, such as Buddhism and Confucianism. The word derives from the Chinese term *Shen-tao,* which, roughly translated, means "the way *(tao)* of the gods/spirits *(shen)*." The Japanese use the term *kami-no-michi,* which also means the way *(no-michi)* of the gods/spirits *(kami)*.

Kami

Although *kami* is usually translated as "gods" or "spirits," the term is more inclusive. Certainly, *kami* refers to the deities of heaven and earth, but it also refers to the spirit of human beings and to spirits in the

Shinto

BCE

1000s Evidence of human presence on Japanese islands

CE

300s Rise of Yamato clan

500s Introduction of Chinese Buddhism in Japan

594 Buddhism established as state religion in Japan

710 Nara era (ended 794)

712 Publication of *Kojiki*

720 Publication of *Nihongi*

800s Tendai and Shingon Buddhism introduced in Japan

927 Publication of *Engishiki*

1222 Birth of Nichiren, founder of Nichiren Buddhism (d. 1282)

1542 Introduction of Christianity in Japan

1814 Kurozumi-kyo founded by Kurozumi Munetada (1780–1850)

1837 Tenri-kyo founded by Nakayama Miki (1798–1887)

1859 Konko-kyo founded by Kawade (1814–1883)

1868 Meiji period (ended 1912); Shinto established as state religion (until 1945)

1930 Seicho no Ie founded by Taniguchi Masaharu (1893–1985)

1937 Soka Gakkai founded by Tsunesaburo Makiguchi (1871–1944)

1945 State Shinto disestablished

universe—in animals, plants, seas, mountains, and so on. Anyone, anything, or any force that possesses "superior power" is considered a *kami*.

As a religion, then, Shinto is concerned with a variety of *kami*, from heavenly gods, deified ancestors, heroes, and emperors to the forces or spirits of trees, rocks, mountains, rivers, and animals. In other words, the concept of *kami* does not refer to an Absolute Being who stands apart from the world but rather to a quality in the universe, in persons, in animals, in things, and in forces that evokes a sense of awe, wonder, fear, attraction, or repulsion. Ceremonies and festivals centered around the *kami* are closely related to community and national traditions that are rooted in the indigenous beliefs and practices of the ancient Japanese. A peculiar awareness of *kami* is one basis of Shinto belief.

On

The second basis of Shinto belief is awareness of the productive goodness of nature. That awareness, which is implicit in the Shinto interpretation of life, has significant philosophical and ethical implications. Central to the ethical outlook of Shinto is the recognition of *on*, the obligation individuals have to their benefactors and the expression of

The annual Jidai Matsuri festival performed on October 23 by Shinto devotees. The ark represents the presence of the *kami* and is carried through the streets.
Courtesy of Japan Information Center, Consulate General of Japan, Toronto.

gratitude. Concepts of purity and pollution are closely related to that awareness of productivity and life.

Commitment and Loyalty

Another important theme in Shinto is the principle of *saisei-itchi,* according to which the religious and political dimensions of life are essentially one. This concept forms the basis of national consciousness. Commitment to the nation is the ultimate commitment, because the emperor is the leader of the nation and the priest who serves the nation's *kami.* The principle of *saisei-itchi* was set aside after World War II as a result of the separation of church and state, but many Japanese remain convinced that the ideal human society can be realized only when both mundane and divine activities are completely and harmoniously integrated.

It is worth reiterating that according to Shinto the most important determinant of life here and in the hereafter is the observance of rituals and taboos, not ethical conduct. Keeping out of trouble by fulfilling obligations is more important than doing good to others. One's thoughts, words, and actions should demonstrate loyalty to and fulfill the duties and expectations of one's family, ancestors, emperor, country, and Shinto rites.

Hara-kiri

No Shinto tradition better illustrates the preoccupation with conduct than the ritual of *hara-kiri* (literally, "belly cutting"), the act of honorable self-execution or ritual suicide. When an individual believes he has failed the standard of conduct prescribed by tradition and wishes to prove continuing loyalty and to redeem whatever honor has been lost, he performs *hara-kiri. Hara-kiri* was not mere suicide. It was a legal and ceremonial institution invented about the twelfth century and carried out with great ceremony by warriors and nobles, usually in the presence of witnesses and with a relative or special friend in attendance. Women, in a similar action, cut their jugular veins by a method called *jigai.* The ritual was still practiced in World War II. Disloyalty, not disbelief, is the greatest shortcoming for a Shinto adherent.

ANCIENT RECORDS

Kojiki and Nihongi

Shinto has no accepted or official scriptures and no fixed system of doctrine or ethics. Consequently, no binding moral code or list of commandments has ever evolved from Shinto. In fact, Shinto adherents are not at home with ethical codes or moral laws, believing that the actions of individuals depend on circumstances and situations. The realm of human experience is more important to Shintoists than the sphere of ethical codes. Nonetheless, a number of valuable records exist, two of which are considered to be the most ancient and important of all surviving documents: the Kojiki (Records of Ancient Matters) and the Nihongi or Nihon-shoki (Chronicles of Japan), written in Chinese script and completed in 712 and 720 CE, respectively.

Other Collections

Two other works produced in the eighth century are the Kogoshui (a historical account of early Japan) and the Manyoshu (a collection of ancient poems). Two valuable documents for understanding early Shinto are the Shinsen Shojiroku (a compilation of the register of families), which dates from 815, and the Engishiki or Yangi-shiki (Codes of the Engi Era), written around 927 but containing materials predating the era.

Those four works contain legends, chronicles, ballads, and poems thematically centered on the divine origin and the early history of the islands of Japan. They also prescribe prayers for various ceremonial occasions, as well as patterns of behavior and action. In general the concepts of major catastrophes and tragic themes as well as the idea of fear-inducing divinities are absent. Ritual is devoted mainly to acts of praise; if the need arises, it also may serve to placate or reconcile the *kami.*

Creation of the World

The main Shinto sources of information for the beginnings of the world are the two ancient books of history, the Kojiki and the Nihongi. "The deity who originally founded this country," says one legend, "is the deity who descended from heaven and established this state in the period when heaven and earth became separated, and when the trees and herbs could speak" (Nihongi i.64 and ii.77).

According to tradition, heaven and earth are in the beginning not separate but an incohate mass containing the life principle. Then, something, in form like a reed-shoot, springs up between heaven and earth. This reed-shoot becomes transformed into a god *(kami)*, and is referred to as "the one who established the eternal land." Six generations later, by spontaneous creation, came the primal couple: *Izanagi* (the male principal), and *Izanami* (the female principal). One day, two of the original *kami,* Izanagi (male) and Izanami (female), were on the bridge of heaven when Izanagi lowered his celestial spear into the ocean of chaos beneath. As he raised his spear, the drops of water that fell from the shaft coagulated in the sea and formed the Japanese islands. These two *kami* descended on the islands, married, and gave birth to numerous *kami* offspring that are popularly worshiped in Shinto.

Divine Origin

Besides their natural offspring, Izanagi produced the sun goddess, Amaterasu, and the moon god, Tsukiyomi-no-Mikoto, by an act of purification. Years later, Amaterasu, who was dissatisfied with the disorder prevalent among the islands, commissioned her grandson Ninigi to descend and rule them. Ninigi obeyed, and later his great-grandson, the first human emperor, succeeded as ruler. Meanwhile, other *kami* who had settled on the islands produced the leading families of Japan (the *samurai*) and, indeed, the entire Japanese people.

The implication of the story is obvious: the islands of Japan, as well as the Japanese people, have a divine origin. Every emperor from that day until after World War II was considered a direct descendant, in an unbroken line, of the sun goddess Amaterasu.

THE DEVELOPMENT OF SHINTO

The Early Period

The little that is known about early Japanese history and religion is the fruit of speculation based on archaeological discoveries, racial characteristics, and ancient legends. The historical evidence suggests a human presence on the Japanese islands after, rather than during or before, the Paleolithic Age. Whenever they came, there is no doubt that many autonomous clans, each competing for control of territory, lived in prehistoric Japan. The identity of the earliest inhabitants of Japan has been the subject of scholarly debate, particularly over a group called the Ainu, who have no written language of their own but who have preserved their oral tradition for centuries. In the opinion of some historians, settlers in Japan represented three racial strains: one indigenous and the other two from the Chinese mainland and the islands of southeastern Asia. The cultural, linguistic, and religious fusion of the different strands resulted in what is generally referred to today as early Shinto.

The religion of the early Japanese was an unorganized, animist worship of various *kami* that included all natural phenomena. The reaction of the early Japanese to the strange, the unknown, and the inexplicable

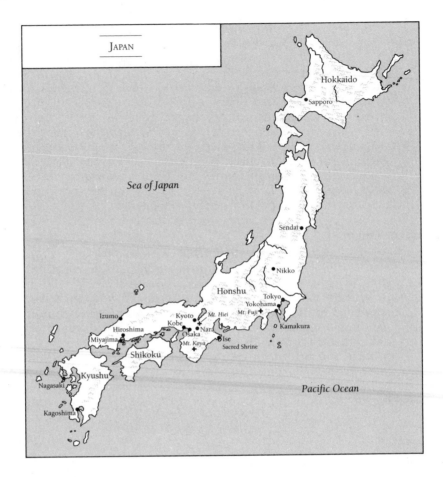

was characterized by a mysterious feeling of awe and a keen sense of the presence of superior forces. Such traits encouraged the development of occult practices carried out by both males and females who were thought to possess the requisite powers to perform various religious rites, usually in the form of ceremonial purification or lustration to guard against evil, pollution, and decay by means of magic and divination.

Adherents of early Shinto made little or no distinction between the superior forces of heaven and those of earth, the world of the living and that of the dead, or animate and inanimate objects. Gods, animals, and all natural and unnatural objects were believed to be in communion with humans. As a result, the roles of the deities in the Shinto pantheon were so ill defined and their powers so nebulous that religion, social conventions, magic, politics, and other aspects of daily life were combined in the early Shinto religion. Two major harvest festivals, one in the spring and the other in the autumn, were held to celebrate and honor the appropriate *kami*. That tradition led to the erection of appropriate *kami* shrines.

Patterns of belief and worship were rooted in the life of an agricultural people settled in tightly knit communities with local legends and customs. Eventually, local beliefs with universal appeal coalesced into acceptance of the supremacy of Amaterasu, the sun goddess, who was adored as the protectress of agriculture and revered as the ancestress of the ruling family. How did that come about?

As stated earlier, ancient Japan was divided among numerous autonomous clans. Religious rites, which basically consisted of ceremonial purifications and agricultural rituals, were performed either by clan chieftains or by members of the community who were respected agents of occult powers (a magical attribute that is recognized as Folk Shinto in modern Japan). Each autonomous clan dominated its own territory and prescribed the *kami* that should serve as local gods. Religious observances in each autonomous enclave gradually centered around the local clan's tribal site, where the tutelary *kami* of the clan resided and eventually was enshrined.

The Yamato Clan

Some time around the third or fourth century CE, one dominant group, the Yamato clan, established its authority over the other clans through conquest and consolidation. Although regional traditions and practices at local shrines continued with few or no changes, the Yamatos imposed their traditions and their tutelary *kami,* Amaterasu, the sun goddess, on the other clans and established the authority of their chieftain to perform certain religious rites on behalf of all the people. Successive chieftains of the Yamato clan gradually came to be recognized as the rulers and chief priests of the nation. In time, their legends and deities dominated popular belief, which included dogmas associated with the divine origin of the chief national leader and the country of Japan and the superiority of the Japanese race.

As it evolved, the Shinto pantheon of gods came to encompass both human and nonhuman personalities and elements. For instance, early Shinto characterized both human beings and animals as gods and attributed the power of speech to plants and rocks, among other objects, a belief that persists among some modern adherents. Shinto always has recognized no firm dividing line between the mortal and the immortal, the human and the divine, the spiritual and the material. Gods, spirits, humans, animals, principalities, and powers operate on both sides of the line that separates the spiritual from the material, moving across it at will, depending on the force of their influence.

The Impact of Chinese Religions

Between the third and sixth centuries, the Japanese, through minor expeditions associated with war and trade, came into contact with Chinese culture and religion, which seemed far superior to Japanese standards. The ruling Yamato dynasty sent envoys to China to study Chinese civilization as a prerequisite to social and cultural reform at home. One effect of the admiration of Chinese models was that Yamato

The Grand Shrine of Ise on the Shima peninsula of Nagoya, dedicated to the worship of Amaterasu, the sun goddess. The sacred precincts are secluded behind one outer and two inner fences. The buildings, which conform to ancient Japanese architecture, are made of unpainted cypress wood. The shrine (at left) has been rebuilt every twenty years since the day of Emperor Temmu in the seventh century CE.
Courtesy of Japan Information Center, Consulate General of Japan, Toronto.

chieftains, although retaining their role as high priests, assumed the title of emperor in the Chinese sense and tradition. The aristocratic governing elite learned to read and write China's monosyllabic language, and soon efforts were made to use Chinese script to express the Japanese polysyllabic language. Inevitably, many Japanese were particularly attracted to Confucian ethics and/or the Buddhist religion.

In a very short time, elements of Chinese superstition, the cult of ancestor worship, and Taoist philosophical concepts were incorporated into Shinto. It was Confucianism, however, that gave the Japanese the model they were looking for to further their religious and national development. Although Confucian ethics came to govern Japanese morality, Confucianism's greatest influence was on the development of Japanese legal and educational institutions. Confucianism, unlike Buddhism, was a pragmatic religion—a system of practical ethics, with little or no room for creed and dogma. In the spheres of family and ruler-subject relationships, Confucian concepts quickly took hold in Japanese life.

The syncretistic character of Shinto also facilitated the introduction of Buddhism into Japan in the sixth century. Buddhism was particularly influential in promoting higher ideals and in encouraging the arts, the

The Miyajima Itsukushima Shrine, situated off the shore of Miyajima Island, is dedicated to the goddess Itsukushima-Hima, daughter of Susanowo, the storm god. Except for the tame deer and during unpreventable events, no person or animal is allowed to be born or to die on the sacred island. In the background, the Torii (the sacred gateway) extends into the sea with the rest of the sacred buildings.
Courtesy of Japan Information Center, Consulate General of Japan, Toronto.

sciences, and literature. Within a century, Buddhism had become the religion of the upper classes; its artistic and ceremonial forms, its organizational structures, and its highly developed doctrine and philosophical outlook had few if any counterparts in the Shinto customs and traditions that prevailed among the common people.

Surprisingly, the advent of Chinese culture and religion in Japan did not eclipse the old forms. Although Buddhism and Confucianism prospered under the patronage of the imperial court and dominated the intellectual outlook of government officials, Shinto's solar deity, Amaterasu, proved a convenient vehicle through which to assert the divine origin of the imperial ruler of the people and of the land. In that way, Shinto remained part of the political machinery of the court. Amaterasu was elevated to the status of a national deity, and a great national shrine to honor her was established at Ise, where virgin imperial princesses conducted appropriate ceremonies. Meanwhile, large Buddhist temples were built and dedicated under the auspices of priests conducting

Shinto ceremonies. Many Buddhist temples in Japan still include protective Shinto shrines erected to house guardian spirits.

Buddhism and Shinto became most closely integrated during the classical Heian period (794–1192), which was characterized by peaceful coexistence and the intermingling of the two religions. During the Heian period, two new Buddhist movements, the Tendai and the Shingon, were introduced from China. The Shingon school stressed ritual and the use of art objects. Even as Buddhism gradually attained an overpowering dominance, Shinto's oral traditions, legends, and myths were documented for the first time in the form of Shinto "scriptures." Buddhism was modified to accommodate the numerous *kami* of Shinto as manifestations of the Buddhist pantheon of preexistent Buddhas; in turn, Shinto added to its pantheon the Buddhist deities introduced from China.

The merging of Shinto deities with those of the Buddhist pantheon resulted in the rapid spread of Buddhism among the general population. Buddhist priests took charge of Shinto shrines, Shinto priests were relegated to minor roles in the officiating of ceremonies, and Shinto shrines and celebrations took on a decidedly Buddhist flavor. However, neither amalgamation of the two religions nor eradication of Shinto ensued. What did develop was a division of labor. Ecclesiastical organization, preaching, dogma, and funeral services became the responsibility of Buddhist priests; the celebration of births, marriages, and seasonal festivals and national victories was assumed by Shinto priests. Exorcism and divination were shared responsibilities, as were rituals associated with ancestor worship, which, under Confucian influence, had become a national practice.

Gradually, Shinto became—to ordinary people at least—almost indistinguishable from Buddhism. During the twelfth and thirteenth centuries, the new cults of Amida, Zen, and Nichiren, which represented Japanese adaptations of Buddhism, enlisted such a groundswell of popular support that, despite official government persecution, they eventually became the most important Buddhist groups in Japan. Attempts by Shinto priests to reverse the order of primacy in Japanese religious life were of no avail, and Buddhism continued to dominate the political and religious life of the nation.

Confucianism, which never achieved the status of an independent religion in Japan, provided the ideological framework of the governing feudal regime, complementing in secular affairs Shinto's role as the official religion of government. Ancestor worship was a key Confucian contribution to Japanese society, as was a system of ethics that became the basis for Japanese social conduct. During the eighteenth and nineteenth centuries, Confucianism abetted the rise of the loyalist movement, the restoration of imperial rule, and the reestablishment of Shinto as a national cult preeminent over all other religions.

Of course, efforts to revive Shinto had never been abandoned. Successive Shinto apologists, imbued with a fervent nationalistic spirit, had attempted to purge Shinto of all "foreign" influences. For those thinkers, the simplicity and unsophisticated traditions of Shinto represented the apex of religious thought and the ideal for which they should strive. They considered Buddhist philosophy and metaphysics as corrupting and irrelevant influences on a people of divine origin who were descended from the *kami*. Not surprisingly, advocates of a return to Shinto basics cited the prerogative of the divine emperor to rule the country to justify their arguments. Over the centuries, various local Shinto sects developed around certain personalities, particular traditions, and specific shrines. Finally, in the nineteenth century, a political upheaval enabled Shinto nationalism to triumph. Meanwhile, another foreign religion, Christianity, sought to establish roots in Japanese soil.

The Impact of Christianity

Japanese contact with the West dates from 1542, when Portuguese explorers landed in Japan. Seven years later, Francis Xavier and two other Spanish Jesuits came to spread Christianity among the Japanese. Soon they were followed by other Catholic missionaries, both Jesuits and Franciscans, whose efforts met with considerable success, especially in southern Japan. No doubt, because of the tolerant attitude of Buddhist and Shinto leaders, Christianity at first enjoyed the favor of the political authorities as well as the public.

It was not long, however, before the imperial court, as well as Shinto and Buddhist leaders, recognized in Christianity a dangerous rival. What provoked their enmity and contributed to a rising tide of anti-Christian sentiment was the arrogant assumption of Christian missionaries that all religions were inferior to their own and that their mission was to convert the nation. Another contributing cause of irritation was the Christian doctrine that all converts owed allegiance to the pope in Rome. In addition, the rivalry between the Jesuits and the Franciscans for converts and control convinced the imperial court that Christian missionaries were the harbingers of Western political intrigue and aggression.

As a result, Japanese authorities undertook a series of campaigns, mounted between 1587 and 1638, to suppress Christianity. First, all Christian missionaries were banned from Japan. Next, warnings and mild persecutions were directed against Japanese Christian converts. Initially, only those who clung to the Christian faith with tenacity were put to death. The disclosure of pockets of resolute Christian resistance, where even missionaries could find shelter, soon led to wholesale persecution. As the wave of persecution gathered force, leading to the torture, imprisonment, and death of Christian converts and missionaries, Japanese authorities severed all relationships with the West and, eventually, eradicated all overt signs of Christianity in Japan. For the next two hundred years, Japan remained isolated from the West, and Christianity survived only among clandestine groups operating underground in certain parts of the country.

The propagation of Christianity continued covertly until the 1880s, when Japanese authorities realized that their nation's isolation had caused it to lag behind Western civilization. A renewal of contact with Western nations and a government policy calculated to exploit international trade and technology eased the strictures imposed on Christians in Japan. Meanwhile, the government officially sponsored a national Shinto cult for the purpose of inculcating loyalty and obedience. No efforts were spared to establish a theocratic state based on Shinto.

State Shinto

An immediate effort was made by the young Emperor Meiji, who ascended to the throne in 1868, to dissociate Shinto from Buddhism. Under Meiji's rule, Shinto was designated the national religion, and most shrines and priests were brought under government control. Persecution of Buddhists inevitably followed: temples were closed, estates appropriated, and priests dispossessed and dispersed. Buddhism, however, proved too deeply rooted in the culture and tradition to be easily exterminated. Despite official disfavor and occasional periods of suppression, Buddhism gradually recovered much of its lost prestige, although it never regained its former stature.

In 1882, the Meiji government recognized three religious organizations: Buddhist, Christian, and Shinto. All religious institutions and organizations not associated with Buddhism or Christianity were classified as Shinto, which itself was divided into two categories or groups: Jinja, or Shrine Shinto, and Kyoha, or Sectarian Shinto. As a national obligation, the government required all Japanese, whatever their religious inclinations, to participate in the rites conducted at the State Shinto shrines. Such rituals were considered patriotic expressions and sentiments of respect owed to the divine imperial personage. In addition, the government promoted Shinto ancestral traditions through systematic instruction in all schools and assumed responsibility for the administration and supervision of religious organizations, the priesthood, and religious ceremonies.

From 1868 to 1945, the government promoted Shinto as the national religion of Japan. The test of loyalty to the government was acceptance of State Shinto. Other religions, such as Buddhism and Christianity, were able to maintain a presence in Japan so long as they were willing to accommodate themselves to the government's views on State Shinto, which included belief in a land divinely created, a succession of emperors descended in an unbroken line from Amaterasu, and a people of divine origin. Under the sanction of religious belief, the government maintained absolute political and military power.

Belief in the emperor as the living incarnation of the sun goddess, Amaterasu, was based on long-standing traditions predating the twelfth century, but in the nineteenth century that belief was enshrined in dogma. Accordingly, the emperor was considered sacred, inviolable, and a manifestation of the Absolute. At its most extreme, the dogma incorporated the belief that the emperor was a god in human form who deserved the worship and devotion of his people. In addition, some believed that the emperor was not only the head of the Japanese nation but also the ruler of the entire universe. By extension and another leap of faith, they also believed that the Japanese nation was destined to rule the world.

That edifice of state religion endured until December 15, 1945, when the supreme commander of the Allied forces of occupation ordered the emperor and the Japanese government to disestablish State Shinto, to relegate rites performed by the imperial family to the status of private religious ceremonies, and to place all existing religions, including Shrine Shinto and Sectarian Shinto, on the same footing, with equal entitlement to support and protection. On January 1, 1946, the emperor publicly denounced the "false conception that the emperor is divine and that the Japanese people are superior to other races and fated to rule the world."[1]

The impact, in both practical and theoretical terms, of the sudden reversal of Shinto hegemony was too widespread to document here. A few examples will have to suffice. Imperial portraits, which had been kept in sacred repositories in schools, were removed. The imperial chrysanthemum crest, which had identified all court buildings, was obliterated and banned from future issues of postage stamps and currency. Some 110,000 State Shinto shrines, which had depended on and been supported by the national government, suddenly found themselves thrown back on their own resources and on the generosity of voluntary contributors. Fundamental Shinto doctrines and ideologies that had advocated ritual suicide as an honorable act of expiation suddenly were declared "myths, legends, and false conceptions." The emperor, who once had been venerated as divine, was now regarded as a mere mortal.

Today, religion and state in Japan are completely separate. There is no compulsory national religion, religious instruction in public schools is prohibited, and freedom of religion is guaranteed to all. According to the postwar constitution, the emperor is considered "the symbol of the state and of the unity of the people." His function as the high priest of Shinto is restricted to officiating at traditional ceremonies in one of three shrines on the imperial palace grounds. State Shinto is—at least for the present—dead.

Shrine Shinto

The Meiji government, in its attempt to make Shinto the official state religion, had sponsored and partly supported Shrine Shinto. Nationalistic sentiment was particularly associated with certain shrines, especially those that were closely linked to emperor worship. The shrine at Ise, for example, came to be known as the Grand Shrine of Amaterasu, the sun goddess.

Under State Shinto, the government administered the shrines and designated some of them as centers for the worship of Amaterasu and the emperor. In that way, shrines, which for centuries had been identified with and maintained by particular families, became subject to bureaucratic control. Political and military friends of government officials often were made priests. All rites, ceremonies, and festivals were prepared by the government and centered around loyalty to and worship of the emperor and Amaterasu.

Today, Shrine Shinto is Japan's indigenous religion. Its religious practices are perpetuated in rites related to numerous shrines found in every

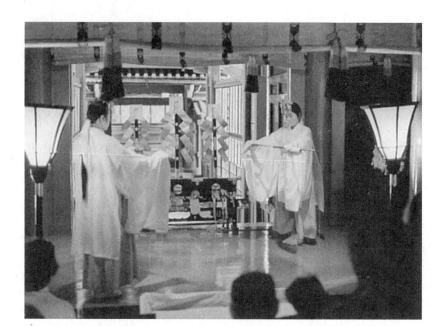

Novitiate temple girls performing the annual celebration of the sacred sword dance
during the Yayoi festival in March in the Futaarasan shrine, in Nikko, Japan.
Courtesy of British Airways (BOAC), Toronto.

locality of Japan. Like all other Shinto groups, Shrine Shinto originated
in the worship of nature and spirit. Shrines were rare in early prehistoric times, when trees, mountains, rivers, rocks, lightning, and so forth
were worshiped directly, but in the course of time worshipers built
shrines to house gods or the objects of worship. Today, shrines include
a variety of structures, from simple, modest shelters to elaborate buildings. Many are nothing more than worship halls; others are sacred en-
closures identified by a fence or even a straw rope hung with paper
cutouts surrounding the object to be worshiped. Currently, there are
about 110,000 shrines throughout Japan.

Shinto shrines depend entirely on public contributions. The priests,
who are no longer government officials, are not bound to invoke the
aid of particular deities. Some shrines are devoted exclusively to historical emperors, such as Meiji, Omi, and Hideyoshi, while others are dedicated to deities. The most common objects of worship are mirrors,
swords, stones, trees, mountains, caves, pigeons, snakes, and foxes.

No clear distinction is made between the *kami* of human beings and
those of natural phenomena. Humans have the potential to become *kami*.
Because human nature is regarded as essentially good, human defile-
ments and impurities can easily be purified by very simple ceremonies.

Shrine Shinto is characterized by ritual rather than doctrine and by
the absence of any legalistic code of ethics, systematic statement of
creed, or collection of sacred writings. Instead of indulging in specula-

tive abstractions about another world, Shrine Shinto emphasizes the physical, material world and respect and veneration for traditional values and forms. Its primary aim is to promote human health and happiness, not in a future blissful realm, but here and now, in this world.

Sectarian Shinto

Sectarian Shinto encompasses thirteen heterogeneous Shinto sects that the Meiji government arbitrarily grouped in 1882 as an administrative convenience designed to foster government control. As a condition of government approval to function as religious sects, they were required to fulfill certain obligations. Any group not specifically identified under government regulations had no choice except to seek affiliation with a group that was.

For a while, the Meiji government managed to maintain administrative control over all the religious sects, but gradually a few were permitted to become independent. Since the end of World War II and the disestablishment of State Shinto, all restrictions have been removed, and many Shinto groups that were nominally affiliated with the thirteen established sects have become independent. However, the purely arbitrary classification of thirteen Shinto sects that was established by government fiat still survives. The thirteen sects are classified into five groups:

- Pure Shinto (three sects)
- Confucian Shinto (two sects)
- Mountain Shinto (three sects)
- Purification Shinto (two sects)
- Redemptive Shinto (three sects)

Estimates of the number of subsects range as high as six hundred, although the exact total is not known. Unlike Shrine Shinto, Sectarian Shinto is characterized by large congregations that meet regularly for religious services and that incorporate elaborate rituals and modern sermons. Some sects lay claim to a historical founder, an organized membership, a canonized scripture, a codified doctrine, and a prescribed ritual. Other sects are centered around ancient traditional practices and imperialistic loyalism. Many actively promote and publicize their doctrines and practices with missionary fervor. Brief descriptions of the five groups follow.

Pure Shinto. The three sects in this category are Tai-kyo, Shinri-kyo, and Taisha-kyo. In the tradition of early Shinto, none acknowledges an authentic historical founder, and all three claim to represent the embodiment of "pure" Shinto as practiced in prehistoric times and seek to perpetuate ancient beliefs and practices and foster national patriotism. The group's name implies the absence of all contaminating foreign influences. The teachings of the Pure Shinto sects are based on the classical myths, with special emphasis on gratitude to ancestors and loyalty to emperors. The predominant deities in all three sects are the two parent deities of the Japanese people, Izanagi and Izanami, and the sun goddess, Amaterasu. Loyalty to the state, anonymous charity, moral virtue, and purification through appropriate rites are among the basic aims of the three sects.

Confucian Shinto. This group comprises two sects: Shusei-ha and Taisei-kyo. Their main purpose is to emphasize the ethical principles of Confucianism along with the fundamentals of Shinto; accordingly, they exalt patriotism and are considered to be the most nationalistic Shinto sects. They embrace divination, fortune-telling, and astrology, and adherents rely on prayer and meditation to gain inner tranquility.

Mountain Shinto. The three sects that associate mountains with the dwelling place of the *kami* are Jikko-kyo, Fuso-kyo, and Mitake-kyo. Mountain worship is an ancient tradition whose origins are lost in Japanese antiquity. The custom is to erect small shrines on every mountain peak, at which the indwelling *kami* are invoked and honored with a combination of occult practices, purification rites, and elaborate ceremonies. Organized bands of pious pilgrims climb to the tops of sacred mountains to exalt the holy dwelling places of the deities. Although all mountains are believed to harbor *kamis,* Mount Fuji and Mount Ontake are the most sacred (and the most popular). Believers strive for simplicity and purity in their everyday lives and for universal brotherhood and love of humankind.

Purification Shinto. Almost all Shinto sects perform some form of purification rites, but two sects, Shinshu-kyo and Misogi-kyo, place special emphasis on ceremonial purity. Their performances of ritualistic purification are perpetuations of age-old ceremonies associated with purity of soul, mind, and body. Followers of the two sects worship ancient Shinto deities, accept the Kojiki and the Nihongi as scriptures, and uphold filial piety, moral living, dutiful citizenship, and emperor loyalty. The Shinshu-kyo purification rites include a fire-subduing ceremony, a hot-water ritual, the twanging of bowstrings, and a rice-cooking ceremony, all performed together with the recitation of prayers. The rites of Misogi-kyo consist of several rituals; the most important is the act of proper breathing, by which one can commit the direction of one's life to the divine will. Proper breathing is also considered as contributing to physical and mental well-being, because breathing is the source of life.

Redemptive Shinto. This group of three sects represents a radical departure from traditional Shinto. The Kurozumi-kyo, Konko-kyo, and Tenri-kyo sects were founded by modern individuals whose revelatory experiences are characterized by a message of redemption. The label *redemptive* is misleading, however; they also are known as "faith healing" sects or sects of "peasant origin," because faith healing plays a part in all three sects and because two of the three founders were of peasant origin and at first, drew their strongest support from peasant folk. The popularity of these sects can be attributed, at least in part, to the magnetic personalities of the founders. All three sects are theistic and attribute the source of all existence to a divine power and the achieve-

A *shugendo* priest (wandering mountain ascetic) in traditional costume blows the *horagai*, or trumpet shell.
Courtesy of Japan Information Center, Consulate General of Japan, Toronto.

ment of a happy and healthy life to "pure" faith in the divine source. The question of who or what is divine is not considered important, provided that adherents recognize their inner divine qualities and strive to actualize that divine power in everyday life. A vital missionary spirit, which may account for the successful and extensive influence of these sects, pervades each of them.

Kurozumi-kyo. This Redemptive Shinto sect was founded by Kurozumi Munetada (1780–1850), the son of a chief priest of a sun goddess shrine. Three religious crises, or revelations, marked the beginning of Kurozumi's mission in 1814. He received his sacred commission in his third experience, which took place while he was praying to the rising sun goddess. In obedience to her will, he set out to convert the world to the belief that the sun goddess was the source of all happiness and health. Although numbering other Shinto deities in his sectarian pantheon, Kurozumi believed that the sun goddess was the all-inclusive, universal parent spirit, the source of all things, and the sustaining guide of all believers. Followers were enjoined to keep the Seven Rules of the Divine Law, which consisted of faith, humility, self-possession, compassion, sincerity, gratitude, and industry.

After Kurozumi's death, his followers recognized his poems, letters, and written observations as sacred scriptures. Kurozumi himself was deified and is now worshiped along with Shinto deities and the sun goddess not only in Japan but also in Korea and Manchuria, where proselytizing activity has won converts.

One of the chief attractions of the Kurozumi-kyo sect is faith healing, which is achieved by faith and the recitation of purification ritual, by the rubbing of affected parts of the body to transfer therapeutic energy from the healer to the patient, by hypnosis, and through the agency of consecrated water drunk by the patient, sprayed over the patient from the priest's mouth, or even sprinkled on a piece of paper bearing the patient's name.

Konko-kyo. This sect was founded by the peasant Kawade (1814–1883), who, in a vision in 1859, was assigned to mediate between Tenche-kane-no-kami (Great Father of the Universe) and humanity. Tenche-kane-no-kami is a modern accretion to Shinto who is described as the source and eternal spirit of everything, the *kami* of infinite love and mercy. Believing that all human suffering and calamity result from two basic defects — ignorance of Tenche-kane-no-kami's love and violation of his laws — adherents of Konko-kyo hold that all people should have faith in the Great Father of the Universe, love each other, fulfill their respective responsibilities, and pray for peace, happiness, and prosperity in the world.

Kawade left no writings, but his followers compiled his teachings and ideas into what are now considered the sacred scriptures of the sect. Adherents pay special reverence to Kawade as the founder of their religion, but he is not considered a deity. They reject all occult activities, ascetic practices, and religious austerities. Believers are enjoined to rely on their inner creative spiritual powers, the gift of the Great Father of the Universe. Although Konko-kyo is strongest in southeastern Japan, missionary efforts have extended this Redemptive Shinto sect to northern and central China, Taiwan, Singapore, Hong Kong, and Hawaii.

Tenri-kyo. This sect was founded by Nakayama Miki (1798–1887), a peasant woman and a former Buddhist of the Pure Land sect who claimed to have been possessed during a trance in 1838 by a god calling himself Tenri-o-no-mikito (the God of Divine Reason). He commanded her and her whole family to dedicate everything to his cause for the sake of humankind. In keeping with those directions, Nakayama gave away all her property and devoted herself to the teaching of the true God, Tenri, supplemented by mental cures and faith healing.

Nakayama taught that human life is based on reason and that ultimate reality is Divine Reason, Tenri. Those who live according to reason prosper; those who violate it perish. According to Nakayama, happiness and prosperity in this life are the will of Divine Reason, which human beings oppose by substituting misfortune and suffering in pursuit of their own selfish ends. Original purity can be restored if one can get rid of the accumulated "dust" of inner vices. Through faith in Tenri, or Divine Reason, one can gain mastery over vices, sweep off the "dust," attain divine favor, and reach ultimate contentment.

The activities and the institutions of Tenri-kyo are nationwide, and its missionary efforts have extended to various countries in Asia. To date, Nakayama's direct descendants hold the office of chief priest. A strong, organized, central administrative system, public services, and faith healing, among other factors, account for the rapid growth of this Redemptive Shinto sect.

Folk (Popular) Shinto

Various Shinto beliefs and practices generally are not included in Sectarian or Shrine Shinto because they are so diversified and so disorganized. For the lack of a more descriptive label, such religious tendencies usually are referred to as Folk (or Popular) Shinto. Generally speaking, Folk Shinto emphasizes aspects of Shinto worship that are common but peripheral elements of other sects. Its most common features are superstition, occult practices, and devotion accorded to innumerable deities, whose images or symbols dot the countryside.

As would be expected, household rituals and ceremonies are of primary importance in Folk Shinto, especially in celebration or remembrance of family on such occasions as births, marriages, business ventures, deaths, and anniversaries associated with relatives and ancestors. Rituals are centered on the *kami-dana* (*kami* shelf), a miniature shrine that serves as a family altar, usually mounted in a small alcove above a closet door in the main room. Well-to-do families maintain small shrines in gardens. A devout Shinto steps in front of the *kami-dana* early in the morning, after washing or bathing, to pay homage to the deity. The devotee bows, claps hands twice (to get the attention of the deity), then bows again for a moment before going to work or beginning the day's chores.

On special occasions, worshipers purify themselves first by bathing and then by waving a small branch of the sacred *sakaki* tree (or an imitation made of hemp and paper) at each shoulder while standing in front of the *kami-dana*. It is also customary to announce special occasions (such as visits to the tutelary shrine) before the *kami-dana*.

Similar rituals are associated with the thousands of popular deities whose images and symbols are found throughout Japan. Prominent among such deities are Daikoku-ten, the god of luck and good fortune; Ryujin, the serpent deity who controls the rain and the wind and who acts as the guardian god; Dosojin, the guardian deity of the crossroads; and Kamado-no-kami, the deity who presides over the kitchen fires.

Simple rituals express the devotion of a devout Shinto worshiper. A passerby usually stops before any symbol or image of a deity, claps the hands twice, and bows in silence before going on. A tossed stone that happens to land on an image is considered a sign of good fortune.

Slightly different are the ceremonies and rituals connected with the purification of land used for construction. Ceremonies in such cases usually are performed before the earth is broken, to appease the particular *kami* of the land. Appropriate rituals also are performed to guard against accidents on bad corners, broken or shaky bridges, sagging roofs, unlucky days, and so on.

Generally speaking, Folk Shinto gives credence to people—usually women distinguished by wild appearance and behavior—who claim

The tea ceremony in Japan is practiced as a means of improving one's spiritual qualities in cultivating unity of body and mind.

Courtesy of Japan Information Center, Toronto.

to possess the power to communicate with the spirits of the dead or to invoke any of the deities. That people still consult "spirit-possessed" authorities for advice on queer feelings, strange behavior, unusual events, or physical disabilities testifies to a widespread and popular reliance on black magic, witchcraft, and numerous other occult practices.

New Religious Groups

Hundreds of religious sects have emerged since World War II and have categorized themselves as "new religions." Many of them, however, were in existence prior to World War II as involuntary affiliates of officially recognized Sectarian Shinto sects. Other sects are of such recent origin that their founders are still living—a circumstance that does not make analysis of their teachings any simpler, since the leaders guide their followers by means of oracles or revelations. Similarly, there are no reliable estimates as to the number of new sects and no satisfactory criteria for classification. Consequently, only a general characterization of new Shinto sects can be offered.

Frequently a charismatic personality who has had an unusual experience and who possesses an extraordinary ability becomes the central figure of a new movement. Next, an organizational figure is required to ensure continuity of the new sect. Innovations combined with ancient traditions, uncomplicated rituals, and promises of physical and material benefits accruing from purposeful daily activity are the core features of new sects.

The teachings of most new sects are a reconstitution of traditional values and a reformulation of the general metaphysical outlook derived largely from one or more of the following backgrounds: Shinto, Buddhist, Confucian, Taoist, and Christian. The characteristic function of such groups is to provide followers with a stable basis for coping with pressing contemporary problems. Unfortunately, no reliable evidence exists of their strength or influence, although undoubtedly, like so many other religious groups, they will leave their mark on Shinto character as a whole.

The Status of Women

There is some evidence that early Japan was politically matriarchal, and priestesses and shamanesses played an important role in early Shinto. All that changed when Japan came into contact with China and wholeheartedly adopted Confucian ethics. By the eighth century, women no longer were permitted to rule, and by the fifteenth century they had lost virtually all civil rights. Only during periods of severe crisis were some women politically influential, but only briefly.

Contact with the West during the nineteenth and twentieth centuries has done little to change the rights of women. Modern Japanese males simply have shifted their allegiance from feudal lords to corporations and businesses. Husbands still consider their wives to be functional creatures essential to the fulfillment of family life: as mothers of their children and managers of their households. In traditional Confucian style, the ideal Japanese family consists of three generations living under one roof. Marriage provides a line of heirs for the "ancestral house." Marriages still are arranged by parents, and a barren woman is promptly returned to her parents' home.

Another role symptomatic of the status of women in urban Japan is that of *geishas*. A *geisha* is principally an accomplished entertainer, a sympathetic listener, and a graceful hostess, not simply a lover or prostitute, and hers is a secondary—never a primary—role. Large firms subsidize all-male gatherings at *geisha* houses, where business often is conducted and ties among coworkers strengthened. Female employees, numerous as they are in the Japanese business world, have few opportunities beyond jobs as clerks or secretaries.

In rural areas, women who function as mediums and diviners still exert a strong influence. Their practices involve fortune-telling, praying for and healing the sick, and contacting the *kami*—the spirits of the dead. Many of these women are charismatic leaders who claim to have received a vision and to possess the power of healing. A few have been social reformers; others have founded "new religions."

There are relatively few Japanese feminist leaders. On the whole, Japanese women tend to accept male dominance. Confucian tradition by and large prevails, and society expects women to settle down to marriage and a family life. Women's rights and full equality seem to be a distant dream.

The bride and the bridegroom are seated in front of the alcove, which is decorated by a scroll painted with a pair of cranes, symbol of longevity, and a flower vase arranged with pine branches, symbol of continuing happiness. Nuptial cups will be filled with *sake*, (Japanese wine), which the couple will exchange in the presence of their parents.
Courtesy of Japan Information Center, Consulate General of Japan, Toronto.

SHINTO OBSERVANCES

Shinto observances involve religious and cultural practices that include folklore, magic, pilgrimage, ritual, worship, and nationalism. The complexity of Shinto practices emerged from the vigorous flow of Japanese religious and social history. The result has been a phenomenal growth of ritual evolving from diverse origins and reflecting a wide variety of influences. Elements of animism, fertility rites, ancestor and hero rites, and nature worship are only a few ingredients.

Rites of Passage

At the birth of a child, the usual custom is to register the baby at the Shinto shrine where the family normally worships. Children are also taken to the shrine during their third, fifth, and seventh years. Marriages usually take place at a Shinto shrine with a Shinto priest officiating. Funerals, however, are frequently conducted by a Buddhist priest, and on those occasions the mourning family visits the local Buddhist temple.

Devotional Acts

Ceremonial rites are performed daily by the priests in Shinto shrines. Individuals visit shrines at any time for personal devotion or to obtain charms or talismans. On entering the shrine, devotees bow toward the *honden* (*kami* altar), make a special offering, and clap their hands as a symbol of communication with the *kami* before advancing farther.

In addition to visiting local shrines, many Shintos maintain a *kami-dana* in their homes, business places, and workshops. Memorial tablets made of wood or paper, each inscribed with the name of an ancestor or a patron *kami,* are placed on the *kami-dana.* A miniature shrine containing a sacred mirror, strips of paper inscribed with sacred texts, and charms or talismans occupy the center of most *kami-danas.* On special family occasions, such as births, weddings, or anniversaries, the family head lights candles at the *kami-dana* and offers flowers, food, and *sake* (an alcoholic beverage made from rice), while the other family members sit on the floor with bowed heads. The more important the occasion, the more elaborate the ceremony.

Festivals

Great preparations and special family observances take place in anticipation of the New Year festival. Houses are cleansed of the evil influences of the past, and the *kami-dana* is renewed with fresh memorial tablets, strips of sacred texts, charms, flowers, and so on. Both actions invite good fortune for the future. Bills are paid as well, and special food is prepared to obviate the necessity of cooking during the first three days of the New Year. Pounded rice, prepared with special care and ritual, is the appropriate New Year's dish. Homes are decorated with special arrangements of flowers, pine branches, bamboo sticks, straw, and white paper (to indicate purification). Where possible, 108 peals of bells are rung at Shinto shrines on New Year's Eve, marking the banishment of evil in preparation for the New Year.

The Girls' Festival (also called the Dolls' Festival), a fête that emphasizes family and national life, is celebrated annually on March 3. Fifteen or more dolls are arrayed on ascending ceremonial shelves. The highest shelf is occupied by a brilliantly costumed emperor and empress, followed, in descending order, by ladies-in-waiting, ministers of the court, musicians, and footmen. At the lowest level are dolls' furniture and utensils.

The Boys' Festival, which is celebrated on May 5, provides each family with an opportunity to proclaim to the community its good fortune in begetting sons. Colored paper carp, representing a family's sons in order of age, are suspended one below the other. Inside the house, *samurai* dolls and weapons symbolize courage, loyalty, and patriotism.

A great festival of the dead, called Bon, is held sometime during the middle of the year. The souls of the departed are believed to return to their homes, where they are entertained and fed by their families. When the feast is over, farewell fires, adapted to the local environment, light the souls on their return journey. In coastal communities, for instance, tiny paper or wooden boats bearing lanterns and food are set adrift on the water.

Numerous other festivals commemorate either important dates in the long annals of Japanese imperial history or seasonal events. For instance, an especially elaborate ceremony, Nihi-name, occurs in October-November and celebrates the offering of the first fruits of harvest. Singing, dancing, and feasting are the main events of Nihi-name. Strict Shintos do not eat the new season's rice until the entire ceremony is performed and the rice *kami* is honored. During seasonal flower festivals to celebrate the blossoming of peach trees and irises, flowers, dolls, and lanterns are carried about in celebration.

Regional festivals are conducted to honor particular aspects of a local shrine. Artisans of most kinds venerate their own patron *kamis* and observe special days in their honor. Shinto *kamis* are recognized by their own special festivals, when flowers and other gifts are brought to the shrines. Almost every Shinto sect celebrates the birth and death of its founder in public services.

Shinto has adopted numerous Buddhist festivals, and other festivals, such as Christmas, have begun to infiltrate Shinto observances. That is

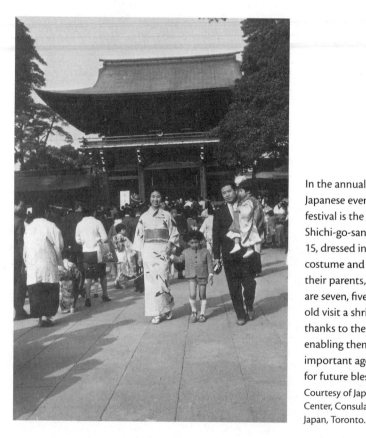

In the annual calendar of Japanese events, one unique festival is the festival of Shichi-go-san. On November 15, dressed in traditional costume and accompanied by their parents, children who are seven, five, and three years old visit a shrine to offer their thanks to the deities for enabling them to reach those important ages and to pray for future blessings.
Courtesy of Japan Information Center, Consulate General of Japan, Toronto.

especially true in large urban centers and among merchants and advertisers. Regardless of their origin, all festivals express Japanese sentiments of patriotism and national pride.

STUDY QUESTIONS

1. Define the term *Shinto* as understood by the Japanese.
2. Explain the role and the significance of *kami.*
3. What is the importance of the *hara-kiri* ritual?
4. What writings are considered Shinto scripture?
5. Recount the traditional Shinto version of creation.
6. Describe what is known as the early period of Shinto.
7. Discuss the impact of Chinese civilization on Japanese culture.
8. Examine the effect of Buddhism on the Japanese people.
9. Explore the Japanese reaction to Christianity.
10. Describe briefly the historical fate of State Shinto.
11. How does Shrine Shinto differ from Sectarian Shinto?
12. Describe the household rituals and ceremonies important to Folk Shinto.
13. What characteristics are basic to the "new religions"?
14. Discuss the role and the status of women in Japanese history.
15. What are some of the more important Japanese festivals?

Suggested Reading

Earhart, H. Byron. *Religions of Japan.* Hagerstown, Md.: Torch Publishing Group, 1984.

Ellwood, Robert, and Richard Pilgrim. *Japanese Religions.* Princeton, N.J.: Princeton University Press, 1985.

Hardcare, Helen. *Shinto and the State, 1868–1988.* Princeton, N.J.: Princeton University Press, 1989.

Kitagawa, Joseph M. *On Understanding Japanese Religion.* Princeton, N.J.: Princeton University Press, 1987.

Nelson, John K. *A Year in the Life of a Shinto Shrine.* Seattle: University of Washington Press, 1996.

Picken, Stuart D. B. *Essentials of Shinto: An Analytical Guide to Principal Teachings.* Westport, Conn.: Greenwood Press, 1994.

Plutschow, Herbert E. *Matsuri: The Festivals of Japan.* Richmond, Eng.: Japan Library, 1996.

Reader, Ian T. *Religion in Contemporary Japan.* Honolulu: University of Hawaii Press, 1991.

Yamamoto, Y. *Way of the Kami.* Stockton, Calif.: Tsubaki American
Publication, 1987.

Note

1. Cited in Harold Coward, Eva Dargyay, and Ronald Neufeldt, *Readings in Eastern Religions* (Waterloo, Ont.: Wilfrid Laurier University Press, 1988), p. 345.

8 Egyptian Religion

Of the various ancient civilizations that once dominated the arena of history, four left records extensive enough to permit our understanding of the religious beliefs and practices that died with them. Those four are the Egyptian, Mesopotamian, Greek, and Roman civilizations. A number of fundamental religious ideas and practices in Judaism, Christianity, and Islam can be traced back to one or more of those ancient civilizations.

EGYPTIAN CIVILIZATION

Long before the advent of the pharaohs, the Egyptians were already an ancient people with roots in the Old Stone Age, when scattered groups of hunters wandered along the mud strip of the Nile River. Sometime between 10,000 and 7000 BCE, a pastoral group settled along the fertile Nile valley. Between 7000 and 3000 BCE, those settlers organized themselves into independent villages with buildings constructed of wood, brick, and stone. By about 3000 BCE they had developed the art of hieroglyphic writing (picture script), an advance followed shortly afterward by the unification of many village communities into a single kingdom under one imperial ruler, called the pharaoh. The pharaonic dominion of a united kingdom of Egypt, extending at its apogee (before 1800 BCE) to include the littorals of modern Israel and Syria, lasted until 332 BCE, with a few interruptions. One such break occurred sometime around 2200 BCE, when the authority of the pharaohs was broken by the emergence of several petty states, only to be restored two hundred years later. Another interregnum of two hundred years occurred around 1800 BCE, when Egypt was ruled by the Hyksos, a group of Asiatic nomads

Egyptian Religion

BCE

c. 3100 Unification of Egypt under Menes
c. 3000 Invention of writing in Egypt
c. 2700 Construction of great pyramids in Egypt; composition of Pyramid Texts
c. 2050 Composition of the *Coffin Texts*
c. 1370 Akhenaton's "monotheistic" reform
c. 1360 Composition of the hymn to Aton
c. 1350 Composition of *The Book of the Dead*
    525 Persian conquest of Egypt
    332 Conquest of Egypt by Alexander the Great

whose origins are still a subject of controversy. Then, for over a thousand years, the royal authority of the pharaohs was supreme, until a series of incursions, first by the Assyrians, then by the Persians, and finally by Alexander the Great in 332 BCE, brought the Egyptian kingdom to an end.

EGYPTIAN RELIGIOUS THOUGHT

Pharaoh Worship

The development of Egyptian religious traditions was a long, continuous process uninterrupted and unaffected by developments in other civilizations. From about 3000 BCE, the official religion recognized every pharaoh as the incarnate son of the sun god and a god himself. It was unnecessary, then, to seek the will or the mandate of the sun god, because that mandate was expressed through the pharaoh-god. Justice was based not on a code of laws but on the pharaoh's own decisions made in accordance with custom. Those who resisted the pharaoh's supreme authority were punished as rebels.

The cult of the pharaoh was perhaps best expressed by the immense structure of the pyramids. The divine tombs were central to the cult of the pharaoh-god, who in death was assumed to have returned to the company of all pharaoh-gods as the next pharaoh-god succeeded to his earthly mandate. The sight of those monuments suggested to the Greek invaders, centuries later, harsh, forced labor imposed by a hateful tyrant. Such a view was a misunderstanding of the religious conviction and mentality of the Egyptians, who willingly accepted the obligation to work on monumental projects as service befitting the incarnate pharaoh-god.

Animal Cult

Along with the pharaoh cult, Egyptian religion embraced a remarkable variety of gods and goddesses. Each region in Egypt had its own deity, and cities and villages in each region recognized local extensions to regional pantheons. The most striking feature of Egyptian religious tradition, however, was not its polytheistic nature or its sheer quantity of gods; rather, Egyptian religion was distinguished by the remarkable qualities of its deities. Egyptian gods and goddesses were thought of either as complete animals or as semihuman and semianimal forms. Horus, the god of the delta region, was represented by a human body and a falcon's head. The goddess Hathor had a woman's head and a cow's body. Anubis featured a man's body with the head of an ibis' or a jackal. The goddess Sekhmet was distinguished by a woman's body and a lioness's head. Tueris had a crocodile's head, a hippopotamus's body, a lion's feet, and the arms of a human. Other deities appeared as complete animals in the forms of a crocodile, a cat, a frog, an eel, a hippopotamus, and so on.

Modern scholars are, to say the least, puzzled by those strange representations. Some speculate that the animal-shaped deities were vestiges of prehistoric totemism or simply symbolized animal guardians. Others argue that ancient Egyptian religious traditions blurred distinctions and incompatibilities among gods, humans, and beasts, all of whom shared common supernatural characteristics. Still others postulate that since the pharaoh was a god in human form other divinities also could appear in animal, semianimal, or semihuman form. Whatever the underlying concept, the Egyptians saw no difficulty in the worship of powers with human or animal characteristics.

Egyptian Deities

Besides the sun god and deities endowed with animal forms, Egyptian religion recognized a host of other divinities. Among them were various cosmic deities, such as the earth god Geb, the heaven goddess Nut, and the air god Shu. (Note the reversal of the usual assignment of the sexes in ancient religions—a male earth god and a female god of heaven.) Among the astral deities, the sun god Horus initially was the most prominent. He was not the only sun god, however; others were Kheprer, Atum, and Re (or Ra), who in time eclipsed Horus.

Like the rising sun, Horus was symbolized by the widespread wings of the mounting falcon. Each morning the sun god rose out of the ocean to traverse the sky in his majestic ship; each evening he descended through the ocean to the underworld, where a great serpent daily attempted to overturn him, to no avail. Horus's substitute, the moon god Thoth, presided in the sky in Horus's absence.

More unusual than the falcon imagery was the identification of the sun god with the scarab, or dung beetle. Just as the scarab diligently rolled its dung ball as a repository for its eggs, so also the sun god Kheprer (or Khapri) rolled the huge sun ball across the sky.

Around 2000 BCE, the sun god acquired another characteristic by becoming Amon-Re. Amon, originally the local god of the city of Thebes, had become a national god and was assimilated with Re to become Amon-Re, the greatest of the gods.

Besides those deities, there were others who were represented as entirely human or, sometimes, as abstract concepts. The list is long, so

Each pharaoh built a pyramid complex, which was both a symbol of his power and his final resting place. This pyramid-sphinx complex, built at Giza, is that of King Khafre (Chephren) of the Fourth Dynasty of the Old Kingdom (c. 2613–2494 BCE). The pyramid measures 471 feet high and 708 feet to a side. An existing natural rock in a nearby valley was transformed by the king's sculptors into a guardian sphinx, the largest sculpture ever carved by human hands. The sphinx is in the form of a recumbent lion with a royal human head, in which the features of Khafre are thought to have been carved.
Courtesy of Richard Arthur Couche.

a few examples will have to suffice: Maat, the goddess of truth and world order; Safekht, the goddess of writing; Hu, the god of taste; Anubis, the guardian god of the cemetery; Neit, the goddess of hunting; and Ptah, the creator god who conceived the world in his heart and ordered it to rise from primordial mud by an utterance of his tongue.

Attempts by the priests to organize the amorphous collection of deities and beliefs into some sort of system resulted in a variety of family groupings. Some deities, such as the creator god Ptah, the war goddess Sekhmet, and the medicine god Imhotep, were identified in a triad as father, mother, and son, as were the sun god Amon-Re, the Nile goddess Mut, and their son, the moon god Khonsu. Other deities were grouped into a four-generation family of nine: Atum, the hill god who emerged from the primordial sea; Atum's son, the air god Shu, and daughter, the dew goddess Tefnut; Shu and Tefnut's children, the earth god Geb and the sky goddess Nut; and Geb and Nut's two sons, Seth and Osiris, and two daughters, Nephtys and Isis.

Isis-Osiris-Horus

No grouping of deities stirred popular interest more than the family that included the Isis-Osiris-Horus group. According to the earliest Egyptian version of the story (the Pyramid Texts, assembled from fragments of funerary hymns and rituals), Osiris was a good and beneficent god-king who was killed by his evil brother, Seth. Seth made good his escape, taking Osiris's "third eye" (symbolic of kingship) with him. Meanwhile, Isis and Nephtys found their brother's body; while Isis wept and embraced the corpse, Osiris suddenly came to life long enough to impregnate her. The result of that union was the child god Horus, who, as soon as he was old enough, was asked by Isis to avenge his father's death.

Horus first appealed to the court of deities, accusing Seth of murdering his father. Because the court was slow to act, Horus then took the law into his own hands, killing Seth and recovering his father's third eye. As soon as Horus replaced the eye in his dead father's corpse, Osiris was resurrected. From then on, Osiris presided over the underworld as judge of the dead. He bequeathed his third eye to Horus, who wore it as the ruler and sun god of Egypt.

According to a later, Greek account of the same story, attributed to Plutarch in the first century CE, the good and beneficent King Osiris was tricked by Seth and a group of fellow conspirators. Seth had a handsome coffin specially made to measure for Osiris, and at a banquet he promised to give the coffin to anyone who could fit in it exactly. The attempts of various guests having failed, Osiris lay down and fit into it perfectly. Seth's fellow conspirators then closed the coffin, carried it to the water, and threw it into the Nile, which swept it out to sea. When she heard the news, Isis, overcome with grief, set out in search of her brother's corpse, which she finally found washed up on the Phoenician coast (the coastline of modern Israel and Syria). Taking the form of a kite, Isis hovered with wings extended over the body of Osiris until it stirred and Osiris was restored to life. The Greek account, like the early Egyptian version, relates how Osiris left the living in favor of descending to rule the realm of the dead.

Although no complete version of the story has survived, these accounts have provided modern scholars with insight into the views and ideals held by a large number of the adherents of Egyptian religious practices. The prevailing view is that Osiris's story represents the victory of good over evil and that the third eye of the sun god–king brings life and resurrection to the grain in the soil. As for Isis, worship of her centered at first around Memphis, then spread throughout Egypt. By about 100 BCE, Isis worship had become one of the popular mystery religions adopted by Greeks and Romans, lasting until the fifth century CE, when Christian suppression ultimately brought it to its end.

Aton

A radical break from the established traditional Egyptian religion took place during the reign of the Pharaoh Amen-hotep IV (c. 1380–1362 BCE), who moved his capital from Thebes to Tell-el-Amarna, changed his

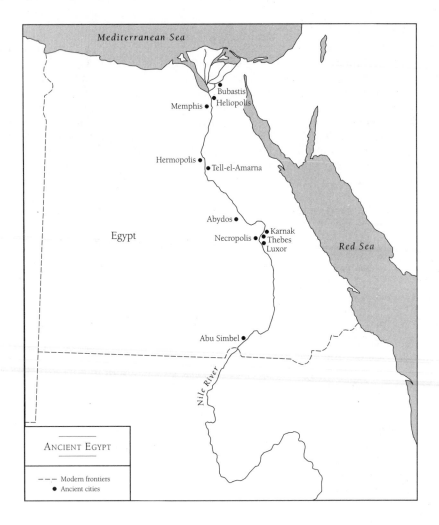

Mediterranean Sea

Bubastis
Heliopolis
Memphis ●

Hermopolis ●
● Tell-el-Amarna

Abydos ●

Egypt

● Karnak
Necropolis ● ● Thebes
Luxor

Red Sea

Abu Simbel ●

Nile River

ANCIENT EGYPT

--- Modern frontiers
● Ancient cities

name to Akh-en-Aton (or Ikhnaton) and instituted the exclusive worship of Aton, the sun disk, as the creator and sustainer of all things.
Moreover, he ordered the priests to expunge the names and images of
all deities other than Aton from all public records, monuments, and
temples. He then created new centers throughout his empire, from Syria
to Nubia, for the sole worship of Aton.

Because Akh-en-Aton was devoted to only one god and because he
identified that god as exclusive and supreme (not merely the highest
god among many), some scholars, though not all, have regarded him as
the founder of monotheism. His monotheistic beliefs are best expressed
in a hymn (composed c. 1370 BCE) that is strikingly similar to Psalm 104
in the Old Testament hymn that praises God for his work of creation.
The following parallel selections illustrate the generic similarities between the two compositions.

HYMN TO ATON[1]

Thou dost appear beautiful on the horizon of heaven O living Aton, thou who wast the first to live. When thou hast risen on the eastern horizon, Thou hast filled every land with thy beauty. Thou art fair, great, dazzling, high above every land. Thy rays encompass the lands to the very limit of all thou hast made.

When thou dost set on the western horizon, The earth is in darkness, resembling death. . . . Every lion has come forth from his den. . . . At daybreak, when thou dost rise on the horizon. . . . the two lands are in festive mood . . . the whole land performs its labour.

All beasts are satisfied with their pasture; trees and plants are verdant. The birds which fly from their nests, their wings are (spread) in adoration to thy soul; all flocks skip with (their) feet; all that fly up and alight live when thou has risen (for) them.

How manifold is that which thou has made, hidden from view! Thou sole god, there is no other like thee![3] Thou didst create the earth according to thy will, being alone: mankind, cattle, all flocks, everything on earth which walks with (its) feet, and what are on high, flying with their wings.

PSALM 104[2]

O lord my God, thou art very great! Thou art clothed with honor and majesty, who coverest thyself with light as with a garment, who hast stretched out the heavens like a tent, who hast laid the beams of thy chambers on the waters, who makest the clouds thy chariot, who ridest on the wings of the wind, who makest the winds thy messengers, fire and flame thy ministers.

Thou makest darkness, and it is night, when all the beasts of the forest creep forth. The young lions roar for their prey, seeking their food from god.
When the sun rises, they get them away and lie down in their dens. Man goes forth to his labour until the evening.

They give drink to every beast of the field; the wild asses quench their thirst. By them the birds of the air have their habitation; they sing among the branches. From thy lofty abode thou waterest the mountains; the earth is satisfied with the fruit of thy work.

O Lord, how manifold are thy works! In wisdom has thou made them all; the earth is full of creatures. Thou didst set the earth on its foundations, so that it should never be shaken.

The similarity in spirit and in wording of the Egyptian hymn to Psalm 104 has often been noted and discussed by scholars. Sigmund Freud offered in his book *Moses and Monotheism* (1939), the ingenious suggestion that Moses, who was raised in the Egyptian royal palace around that time, was influenced by Akh-en-Aton's monotheistic belief. Few scholars, however, take that proposal seriously.

Whatever links there were between Atonism and Mosaic religious traditions, the reforms instituted by Akh-en-Aton failed to survive his death. In fact, the new capital he founded was destroyed, his memory effaced, and the name of Aton obliterated from every public place. The succeeding pharaoh, Tut-ankh-Aton, changed his name to Tut-ankh-Amon (more popularly known today as King Tut) and yielded to the entreaties of his priests to return to traditional religious structures. Osiris, Isis, Horus, Amon-Re, and many other deities resumed their former status and survived until Christianity discredited them beyond hope of redemption.

Death, Heaven, and Hell

The erection of the pyramids and the process of mummification (embalming) are perhaps the best-known symbols of an Egyptian preoccupation with the afterlife. The Egyptians perfected the technique of mummification to such a degree that a corpse could be preserved from decomposing almost indefinitely.

Retribution for the deeds of this life pervaded the thinking behind mummification. After death, so the Egyptians thought, everyone was fated to appear before the tribunal of Osiris. There, in the presence of Osiris and forty-two divine jurors, the newly dead were expected to confess to and exonerate themselves of various crimes, sins, and misdemeanors. To do that, the dead were buried with a guidebook or mortuary text, a collection of hymns, prayers, mythologies, and magical formulas gathered by scholars under the title *The Book of the Dead*. The mortuary texts described the important experiences awaiting the deceased, along with a long list of "negative confessions," or protestations of guiltlessness, which the dead had to recite to certify themselves as worthy to enter the land of Osiris. Here is a short portion of that long confessional list, taken from Chapter 125 of *The Book of the Dead*:

> Hail to thee, great god, lord of Truth. . . .
> I have committed no sin against people. . . .
> I allowed no one to hunger.
> I caused no one to weep.
> I did not murder.
> I caused no man misery.
> I did not decrease the offerings of the gods.
> I did not commit adultery.
> I did not diminish the grain measure.
> I did not diminish the land measure.
> I did not deflect the index of the scales.
> I did not take milk from the mouth of the child.
> I did not report evil of a servant to his master.
> I did not catch the fish in their pools.
> I am purified four times.[4]

After the plea, the Egyptians envisioned that the heart of the deceased person was weighed on a scale against an ostrich feather, the

symbol of truth. If the heart overbalanced the scale, retribution followed. One view held that the guilty were destroyed by the "De-
vouress," a terrifying and frightful creature. Another view was that
retribution took the form of a fiery hell, where the guilty writhed in
nameless agony. If, however, the scales were balanced, the dead were
permitted to enter the world of the blessed. There they were free to
make use of the funerary articles stored in their tombs to speed their
journey and ease their transition to the netherworld: chairs, beds, chari-
ots, boats, kitchen utensils, combs, hairpins, cosmetics, gilded and silver objects of art, foodstuffs (such as jars of water, wine, grain, dates,
cakes, portions of beef and fowl), and models of women and servants.
Spells and incantations were provided to vivify the models of women
and servants so they could be put to work as soon as their masters or
mistresses arrived in the world of the blessed.

EGYPTIAN MYTHOLOGY

Egyptian mythologies are embodied largely in the mortuary texts and
cover the most disparate themes. The themes of creation and the origin
of all things, rivalry among the gods (such as Seth's enmity toward
Horus), family life among the gods, the good fortune of those who have
passed from the tomb to life everlasting, the fields of paradise, a legend

The massive mortuary temple of Queen Hatshepsut (1490–1469 BCE), carved from existing
rocks at Deir-el-Bahri.
Courtesy of Richard Arthur Couche.

about seven years of famine, and a story about a princess possessed by spirits reflect the rich variety of Egyptian mythologies, several of them common to many religions. But unlike some religions, the mythology of Egypt does not provide a uniform pattern or an explanation for various phenomena. On the contrary, several mutually exclusive — and sometimes contradictory — conceptions coexisted. For example, instead of a single account of the origin of things, there are several creation myths.

Creation is attributed to the creator god Atum (or Atum-Kheprer), who created air, moisture, earth, sky, and the deities and put his own vital force into the first creatures. But the Egyptians also viewed the god Ptah as the First Principle, taking precedence over other creator deities. Alternatively, they saw the origin of everything as the work of Kheprer, the morning-sun god conceived of as a scarab beetle.

Attribution of creation to at least three divine agents is only one example of many apparent contradictions implicit in Egyptian mythology. Another contradiction involves the notion of the sky as being supported, variously on posts, on walls, on a cow, by a goddess whose arms and feet touched the earth, or by a god. It is difficult, if not impossible, to establish which of those mythologies most appealed to the Egyptians. Possibly they represented regional or local variations on common themes or were beliefs held at different times.

EGYPTIAN OBSERVANCES

Temples, Sphinxes, and Pyramids

Egyptian intellectual activity, cultural life, and religion revolved around the temples. The temples were independent and well-organized social, economic, and religious centers that contained statues of the deities. Various classes of specialized attendants, both male and female, were organized hierarchically to perform the necessary duties. High priests, their acolytes (attendants), scribes, readers, purifiers, sacrificers, singers, prophets, and musicians all served various functions in temple activities.

Priests performed daily ceremonies in the temples. After a preliminary purification, the priest appointed for the occasion entered the sanctuary or temple and censed the entire area. Next, he broke the seals and unlocked the doors of the holy sanctuary. Standing before the statue of the deity, he offered a brief prayer, followed by the awakening, washing, perfuming, and reclothing of the statue of the deity. A meal was then offered to the deity and set alight to be burned in the deity's presence before the priest withdrew. The ceremony concluded with the priest relocking and resealing the doors of the holy sanctuary.

The pyramids are striking evidence of royal power and confirmation of Egyptians' belief in the pharaoh's continuing life after death. The massive structures were the tombs of the god-kings. To the Egyptians, it was only natural that people of divine origin should have grandiose tombs as an assurance of a full and untroubled existence in the next world. Funerary temples or shrines built in conjunction with the pyramids consisted of either simple chapel constructions or elaborate rock hollows arcaded by several terraces.

Religious Festivals

In addition to daily worship in the temple, great seasonal, agricultural, and fertility festivals were held that varied from center to center and from one local deity to another. During the festivals, the statue of the deity was brought out of its holy sanctuary and carried in procession through the town or city. At times, devotees reenacted some episode in the life of the deity, for instance, the conflict between Osiris and Seth: the murder of Osiris by Seth, the mourning of Isis, and the resurrection of Osiris by Horus. Undoubtedly, the solemn performances drew large crowds of pilgrims from all over Egypt. Centuries later, the Greek historian Herodotus described the celebration of the festival of the cat goddess Bast in the city of Bubastis.

When they congregate at Bubastis, they go by river, men and women together, many of both in every boat; some of the women have rattles and rattle with them and some of the men play the flute all the way; the rest, both sexes alike, sing and clap their hands. At every city they find in their passage, they bring their boats close to the bank, and some of the women continue with their music while others shout opprobrious language at the women of the place, some dance and some stand up and pull up their garments. And this they do at every town that stands by the shore. When they come to Bubastis, they celebrate the festival with great sacrifices, and more wine is drunk at this feast than in all the rest of the year. For the people of the place say that seven hundred thousand men and women, apart from children, assemble there.[5]

Ceremonials on behalf of deities and pharaohs were detailed and elaborate. Egyptian religion was characterized by a high degree of ritual, ceremony, and festival.

Occult Practices

Another characteristic feature of Egyptian religion among the general population was its magical element: charms, curses, and threats. Magical curses were leveled against anyone who violated royal decrees or defamed the name of a dead pharaoh. Similarly, threatening magic was invoked against anyone who violated a tomb. Here, for instance, is the inscription on the tomb of the Egyptian vizier (royal executive) Ankh-ma-Hor:

May it go well with you, my successors; may it prosper you, my predecessors! As for anything you may do against this tomb of the necropolis, the like shall be done against your property.[6]

Another inscription, found on the tomb of the Egyptian official Meni, invokes vengeance and retribution against violators of the tomb:

The crocodile be against him in the water, the snake be against him on land—against him who may do a thing to this tomb.[7]

Mummy of an adult male about 20 years old. The head and chest are covered by a gilded mask (Ptolemaic period c. 200 BCE).
Courtesy of D. van Eeken.

However, even vandals had some recourse in ancient Egypt. A person anathematized by the most terrible imprecations or even threatened by a real or potential enemy could exorcise the threat by inscribing the name of the foe on a bowl or figurine and then smashing it, thereby shattering or breaking the power of the enemy.

STUDY QUESTIONS

1. Give a brief account of the history of Egypt.
2. Describe the role and the status of the pharaoh.
3. What theories have scholars proposed to explain the animal representations of Egyptian deities?
4. Recount the variety of family groupings of the deities.
5. Compare the Egyptian and Greek versions of the Isis-Osiris-Horus story.
6. Examine the view of Aton and his monotheistic faith.
7. What was the Egyptian notion of death and the hereafter?
8. Discuss some of the views on creation held by the Egyptians.

9. What was the purpose of pyramids and sphinxes in Egyptian religion?

10. Describe some of the magical elements employed in Egyptian religion.

Suggested Reading

Allen, Thomas George (trans.). *The Book of the Dead, or Going Forth By Day*. Chicago: University of Chicago Press, 1974.

Assmann, Jan. *Egyptian Solar Religion in the New Kingdom: Re, Amun and the Crisis of Polytheism*. Trans. by Anthony Alcock. London and New York: Kegan Paul International, 1995.

Faulkner, Raymond Oliver. *The Ancient Egyptian Coffin Texts*. Warminster, Eng.: Aris & Phillips, 1973.

Griffiths, John Gwyn. *The Origins of Osiris and His Cult*. Studies in the History of Religions: Supplements to Numen; 40. Leiden, The Netherlands: E. J. Brill, 1980.

Ions, Veronica. *Egyptian Mythology*, rev. ed. New York: P. Bedrick Books, 1988, c1982.

Johnson, Sally Barber. *The Cobra Goddess of Ancient Egypt: Predynastic, Early Dynastic, and Old Kingdom Periods*. Studies in Egyptology. London and New York: Kegan Paul International, 1990.

Kemp, Barry J. *Ancient Egypt*. New York: Routledge, 1991.

Meeks, Dimitri, and Christine Favard-Meeks. *Daily Life of the Egyptian Gods*. Trans. by G. M. Goshgarian. Ithaca, N.Y.: Cornell University Press, 1996.

Morenz, Siegfried. *Egyptian Religion*. London: Methuen, 1973.

Redford, Donald. *Akhenaten: The Heretic King*. Princeton, N.J.: Princeton University Press, 1987.

Ritner, Robert Kriech. *The Mechanics of Ancient Egyptian Magical Practice*. No. 54 of *Studies in Ancient Oriental Civilization*. Chicago: Oriental Institute of the University of Chicago, 1993.

Watterson, Barbara. *The Gods of Ancient Egypt*. New York: Facts on File, 1985.

Notes

1. The translation is by Ronald J. Williams in D. Winton Thomas, ed., *Documents from Old Testament Times* (New York: Harper & Bros., 1961), pp. 145–150.

2. The biblical citation is from the Revised Standard Version (RSV), to match the archaic translation of the Hymn to Aton.

3. This statement is commonly cited as evidence of the monotheistic faith of Pharaoh Amenemhotep IV. For a critical study, see Donald B. Redford, *Akhenaton: The Heretic King* (Princeton, N.J.: Princeton University Press, 1984).

4. T. C. Allen (trans.), *The Book of the Dead, or Going Forth by Day* (Chicago: University of Chicago Press, 1974), p. 97.

5. *Herodotus*, II. 60, trans. by H. Carter (Oxford: Oxford University Press, 1962), p. 117.

6. J. B. Pritchard (ed.), *Ancient Near Eastern Texts Related to the Old Testament* (Princeton, N.J.: Princeton University Press, 1955), p. 327.

7. Ibid.

9 Mesopotamian Religion

The civilization of Mesopotamia (modern Iraq) developed at about the same time as that of Egypt, starting around the middle of the fourth millennium BCE. But the history of Mesopotamia was totally different from Egypt's. The Mesopotamian territory was exposed to continuous invasions, and no significant unity was achieved except for brief periods. During most of the twenty-four hundred years from the thirtieth to the sixth century BCE, a succession of governments, which differed politically and sometimes ethnically, developed what is called a "Mesopotamian" civilization. First, the Sumerians created a great empire; by 1800 BCE, most of the area was unified as the Babylonian Empire. Next came the Assyrian Empire in about the ninth century BCE, until the Persian conquest in the sixth century BCE.

MESOPOTAMIAN CIVILIZATION

The Sumerians, the Babylonians, and the Assyrians

Archaeological evidence suggests that during the third millennium BCE the Sumerians emerged as an established people in the area of Mesopotamia, in the southern part of modern Iraq. That was not their true starting point, however. The Sumerians (named after their city of Sumer) were a non-Semitic, non-Indo-European people (the terms *Semitic* and *Indo-European* refer to language families, not cultural groups) of unknown origin who invaded the Tigris-Euphrates valley either from the south by sea or from the east across the mountains, sometime in the fourth millennium BCE. The ensuing struggle between the indigenous population and the Sumerians lasted for almost two thousand years, until Sargon the Great (a Semitic king) united Mesopotamia around

Mesopotamian Religion

BCE

c. 3000   Invention of writing in Mesopotamia
c. 2350   Founding of Babylonian dynasty by Sargon the Great
c. 2000   Composition of *Epic of Gilgamesh*
c. 1750   Hammurabi's Law Code
c. 1300   Composition of *Epic of Creation*
   331   Conquest of Mesopotamia by Alexander the Great

2350 BCE and pressed northward and westward into what is presently Syria and Turkey.

Sargon

The story of King Sargon's success and the dynasty that he founded is intriguing. Its theme of the "exposed child" rescued by chance would recur in the stories of Moses, Perseus, Oedipus, and Romulus and Remus, among others. Briefly, the baby Sargon was abandoned by his mother, and set adrift in a reed basket on the river. The baby was rescued by the king's gardener, and through the love goddess Ishtar, Sargon eventually triumphed. As the chronicler records,

> Sargon, the mighty king, king of Agade, am I.
> My mother was a changeling (?), my father I knew not.
> My changeling mother conceived me, in secret she bore me.
> She set me in a basket of rushes, with bitumen she sealed my lid.
> She cast me into the river which rose not over me.
> The river bore me up and carried me to Akki, the drawer of water.
> Akki, the drawer of water, lifted me up. . . .
> Akki, the drawer of water, took me as his son and reared me.[1]

Hammurabi

King Sargon's dynasty survived for some two centuries, until a group called the Gutians arrived around 2150 BCE to ravage and rule the area. The Gutians were succeeded a century later by a Semitic group called the Amorites, who united all of Mesopotamia under one of their rulers shortly after 1800 BCE. That ruler was the great and powerful King Hammurabi of Babylon, whose fame derives from the impressive legal code and juridical document attributed to his administration. The Code of Hammurabi stipulated that in his kingdom, among other things, the weak were to be protected, justice was to extend even to the orphan and the widow, inheritance was to be based on legitimate succession, and judicial proceedings were to take place before judges.

Around 1530 BCE, an invasion of Kassites from the Iranian mountains brought Hammurabi's Babylonian dynasty to an abrupt end. Meanwhile, the Assyrians in northern Mesopotamia gradually rose to power. Their expansion followed paths spearheaded by military advances and reached its zenith around the seventh century BCE, under King Esarhaddon. The entire area from the Tigris-Euphrates to the Nile was united in a single but short-lived Assyrian Empire. Then the Medes, followed by the Persians, swept down from the Iranian plateau in the sixth century BCE. Three centuries later, in 331 BCE, Alexander the Great conquered the area and brought the history of the Mesopotamian empires to an end.

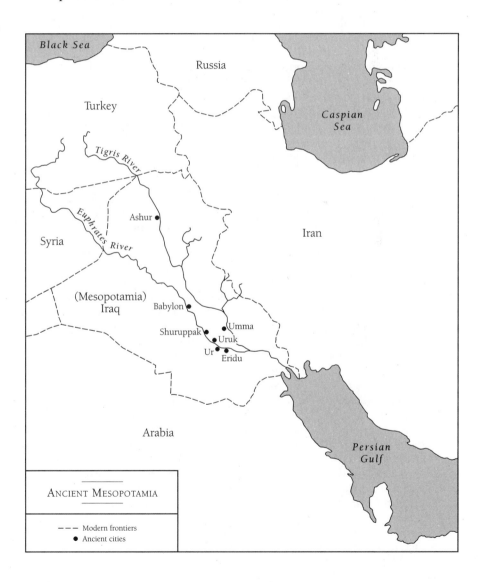

MESOPOTAMIAN RELIGIOUS THOUGHT

Mesopotamian Deities

Mesopotamian religion was a "naturalistic polytheism": the natural forces of the universe — the forces that govern rivers, vegetation, climate, astral laws, birth, death, and so on — were all regarded as laws instituted by gods and goddesses who needed to be evoked or worshiped. An overlapping function of many deities was supervision of the destiny of particular cities. In other words, a cosmic god was also the tutelary god (guardian) of a city, even though other gods were worshiped in that city. Thus, An (Anu),[2] the sky god, was considered not only the king and ruler of all the other gods but also the tutelary god of the city of Uruk. Similarly, Enlil (Bel), the air god, lord of the wind and storm, was the chief deity of the city of Nippur; Nanna (Sin), the moon god, reigned over Ur (the city of the biblical Abraham); Utu (Shamash), the sun god, ruled Larsa until it was destroyed and then became the tutelary god of Sippar; and Enki (Ea), the god of water and wisdom, reigned over Eridu.

The list of Mesopotamian deities is incredibly long — about two thousand names! More interesting than the sheer number of gods, however, are their characteristics and interrelationship. Although the deities represented natural forces and cosmic elements, they assumed or were invested with the likenesses of human beings. Thus, the deities were robed like sovereigns but in vestments more dazzling. Like human beings, the deities represented both sexes, had families, made love, hated, and fought among themselves, but on a much grander and more terrible scale. The deities were immortal models of humans.

City Gods. Although the population of a city might recognize and worship subsidiary gods, there was one supreme god or absolute lord of the city whose will was manifested through various portents. The human ruler or sovereign of the city was the earthly representative of the absolute lord. It was the ruler's task to interpret the mandates of the god and to honor the divine metropolitan mentor by erecting temples and building canals so that prosperity might follow. The social and political fortunes of the city hung in the balance and were determined by its tutelary god. Drought and famine resulted from mortals' neglect of the god's temple. Human sovereignty was determined by divine decree, and victory or defeat in war was the result of divine favor or disfavor.

Every human endeavor or activity, therefore, depended on the city god, so every social and political enterprise was performed for the benefit of the city god. The temple of the city god was centrally located and surrounded by other temples belonging to the god's spouse, children, and related deities. In that way, the greatest landowner of the city became the city god because most, if not all, of the land in the city was temple land. The inhabitants of the city, accordingly, earned their livelihoods as servants of the city god and of other deities. As a matter of fact, Mesopotamians held the view that humans had been created to relieve the deities from the labor of maintaining their estates.

Marduk and Ashur. As different groups of people ruled the area, new local divinities succeeded established deities. For instance, the ascendancy of the god Marduk and his authority over all the other deities resulted from the political ascendancy of the Babylonian dynasty. The honor accorded to the god Ashur was characteristic of succeeding Assyrian rulers. Each major political change catapulted the victor's supreme hometown deity to national prominence as the true creator and orderer of the universe.

Life after Death

The discovery of entire retinues interred beside their dead sovereigns in the royal tombs at Ur confirms that the Mesopotamians believed in life beyond the tomb. However, the prospect as conceived by Mesopotamian religion was cheerless and uninviting, "with poor possibilities and overshadowed with gloom."[3] Mesopotamian religious beliefs saw the dead as wretched, abandoned, and restless, haunting the living and subsisting on dust and dirty water.

MESOPOTAMIAN MYTHOLOGY

Among the various Mesopotamian religious literary works, those of mythology were prominent. Mesopotamian mythology featured the adventures and interrelationships of the gods, the origin of the universe, the creation of humanity, the netherworld, the cycle of vegetation, and "the flood."

The Story of the Flood

The story of the flood is of Sumerian origin and perhaps derived from grim experiences associated with the flooding of the Tigris and Euphrates rivers. The Sumerian account relates how an assembly of gods decided, for reasons that are unclear, to punish humanity by a flood. The decision was "leaked" by one of the deities to a god-fearing man called Ziusudra (the counterpart of the Babylonian Utnapishtim and the biblical Noah), who built an ark and embarked in it with his entire family and as many animals and birds as the ship could accommodate. The well-preserved Babylonian version continues:

> After I had caused all my family and relations to go up into the ship,
> I caused the game of the field, the beasts of the field (and) all the craftsmen to go (into it). I viewed the appearance of the weather; the weather was frightful to behold. I entered the ship and closed my door. . . . Six days and [six] nights the wind blew, the downpour, the tempest (and) the flood overwhelmed the land. When the seventh day arrived, the tempest, the flood, which had fought like an army, subsided in (its) onslaught. The sea grew quiet, the storm abated, the flood ceased. . . .
> I looked upon the sea, (all) was silence, and all mankind had turned to clay. I sent forth a dove and let (her) go. The dove went away and came back to me; there was no resting-place, and so she returned . . . . (Then)

I sent forth a raven and let (her) go. The raven went away . . . (and) did not return. (Then) I sent forth (everything) to the four winds and offered a sacrifice. I poured out a libation on the peak of the mountain.[4]

The relationship between the Mesopotamian flood story and the biblical account (Genesis 7–8) is obvious.

Gilgamesh

The adventures of the deities, life and death, the origin and destiny of the universe, and the remarkable feats of heroes played large roles in Mesopotamian mythology. One outstanding heroic figure was Gilgamesh (considered by some scholars to be the Sumerian antecedent of Hercules), whose fate mirrors the inevitable fate of all human beings—death.

In the story, Gilgamesh, the ruler of the city of Uruk (Erech) appeals to Utu, the sun god, to allow him to undertake the long and perilous journey to "the land," the home of the gods, to assure himself of an immortal name, because he is not on his own account eligible for immortality. Utu grants Gilgamesh's plea, whereupon the latter, accompanied by his trustworthy friend Enkidu and fifty loyal volunteer citizens, sets off on his enterprise. After crossing several perilous mountain barriers, the companions finally look down on "the land," with its vast forest and its guardian monster, Huwawa. In spite of his friends' warnings, Gilgamesh is determined to confront the unknown by seeking out and overcoming the monster, whose corpse he presents to the gods.

Another version of the story has the death of Gilgamesh as its main theme. According to that account, Enkidu, the wild but trustworthy friend of Gilgamesh, dies prematurely for offending Ishtar, the goddess of love. Forced to set out in search of immortality on his own, Gilgamesh travels to the realm of the immortals, among whom his ancestor Utnapishtim lives after having escaped the flood. Utnapishtim helps Gilgamesh to find the herb of immortality at the bottom of the sea, but fate intervenes in the shape of a serpent that swallows the herb and so robs Gilgamesh of immortality. The pathos of human disappointment in the face of imminent death is beautifully described in the following inscription:

Gilgamesh, whither runnest thou? The life which thou seekest thou wilt not find. (For) when the gods created mankind, they alloted death to mankind; (but) life they retained in their keeping.[5]

The story of Gilgamesh being robbed of immortality by an act of the serpent somewhat parallels the story of Adam and Eve in Genesis 3.

MESOPOTAMIAN OBSERVANCES

Cult Practices

The worship of deities in Mesopotamian religion took the form of a complex and highly developed system of rites and rituals, temple celebrations, sacrificial festivals, and occult practices. Whereas gods and

This Assyrian scene from about 865–860 BCE was found in the city of Nimrud (Calah in the Bible) and is representative of the polychrome carved stone reliefs that decorated imperial monuments. Most of the bas-reliefs uncovered depict royal affairs and concentrate on scenes depicting hunting and warfare. The Assyrians were known as a warrior people and spent so much time, energy, and manpower expanding and protecting their empire that they eventually had to import food.
From the private collection of the author.

goddesses protected human beings and provided them with material blessings, demons and demonesses brought terror and torment. For the most part, demons were wicked, restless spirits of the dead who lived in tombs, in darkness, and in desolate places. They were insatiable in their greed and relentless in their pursuits, but they could be exorcised and their intent frustrated by incantations and occult practices.

Confronted by such forces, Mesopotamians divided religious functions among both men and women to meet the conflicting demands of service to one class of gods and vigorous offensive action against the others. Religious officials were classified according to the function they performed: magic, sorcery, divination, wailing, singing, sacrificing, and so on. Animals, birds, fish, vegetation, cooked food, milk, wine and beer, clothing, and perfumes were either sacrificed or offered to deities.

Divination

The most widespread cultic practice was *divination* based on scrutiny of animal livers. An entire class of occult practitioners were qualified to read omens and to draw conclusions for practically every event in life through a detailed analysis of the liver of a sacrificial animal. Another divinatory practice was based on astronomy. Because the position, movement, and conjunction of the stars were believed to pronounce omens, observatories were built on temple tops to record accurately the courses of the stars and to predict eclipses, a scientific bonus at least as significant as the guidance such celestial research provided. Divination also was practiced by oracles (priests and priestesses through whom divine communication was transmitted). Kings consulted oracles before setting out for war and regulated their plans in accordance with the answers.

Religious Festivals

Festivals seem to have played a central role in Mesopotamian religion. There were two kinds of festival: the fixed feasts of the New Year and the new moon and the movable feasts dedicated either to particular deities or to special occasions, such as temple dedications, royal coronations, wars, and victories.

The New Year's festival, celebrated in the spring, was the central point of the Mesopotamian religious year. For twelve successive days, purificatory rites, prayers, and sacrifices were offered, while the king paid special homage to the national god and the other deities. The main feature of the ceremony, however, was the celebration of the death and resurrection of the god Marduk. Although scholars still dispute the mythical texts and, consequently, the rites connected with the feast, the celebration probably involved reenacting the story of Marduk's captivity in the underworld (indicating his death) and his triumph in returning to life (indicating his resurrection). The celebration was an expression of faith in the earth's cycle—the renewal of nature. Just as life followed death and order followed chaos, so the seasonal vegetation that had died in the winter would emerge anew in the spring.

Ziggurats

Mesopotamian religious activity centered around the city temples and their sacred precincts or courtyards. The temples contained altars with offering tables and images of gods, rooms for priests, storerooms, and rooms for various other purposes. The largest and most splendid of Mesopotamian temples was that of Marduk, the tutelary god of Babylon. Situated on the eastern bank of the Euphrates River and surrounded by high, turreted walls, Marduk's temple complex included a great rectangular temple tower, known as a ziggurat (the biblical Tower of Babel). A succession of stairways and ramps led to the sanctuary at its summit.

Apart from the conclusion that ziggurats played an important part in Mesopotamian religion, modern scholars are uncertain of their function. Were they, like Egyptian pyramids, tombs for deified kings? Were they the abodes of the gods? Were they simply outward expressions of a need to approach the deities? Did they symbolize the link between heaven and earth, between gods and mortals? Were they astronomical observatories for astrological prophesy? They may have fulfilled any or all of those functions.

STUDY QUESTIONS

1. Briefly recount the history of Mesopotamia.
2. State the characteristics of Mesopotamian deities.
3. Discuss the Mesopotamian stories that parallel biblical accounts.
4. Compare and contrast the story of "the flood" in Mesopotamian and biblical accounts.
5. What was the most widespread religious practice in Mesopotamia?
6. Recount some of the stories written about Gilgamesh.
7. Why did the New Year's festival play a central role in Mesopotamian religion?
8. State some of the theories proposed regarding the ziggurats.

Suggested Reading

Jacobsen, Thorkild. *The Treasures of Darkness: A History of Mesopotamian Religion*. New Haven, Conn.: Yale University Press, 1976.

Oppenheim, Leo. *Ancient Mesopotamia*. Chicago: University of Chicago Press, 1976.

Ringgren, Helmer. *Religions of the Ancient Near East*. London: SPCK, 1976.

Roux, Georges. *Ancient Iraq*, 2d ed. London: Penguin Books, 1980.

Notes

1. James B. Pritchard, ed. *Ancient Near Eastern Texts Relating to the Old Testament* (Princeton, N.J.: Princeton University Press, 1955), p. 119.
2. Names that appear in parentheses are the Semitic/Akkadian counterparts of the original Sumerian deities.
3. S. Moscati, *The Face of the Ancient Orient* (Garden City, N.Y.: Doubleday, 1962), p. 29.
4. Translated by A. Heidel, *The Gilgamesh Epic and Old Testament Parallels* (Chicago: University of Chicago Press, 1951), pp. 84–87.
5. Ibid., p. 70.

10 Greek Religion

The origins of the earliest inhabitants of mainland Greece and the adjacent islands are far from clear. What is certain is that by 2000 BCE, Crete, the largest adjacent island, had developed the first flourishing Hellene culture. The Cretan culture, also called Minoan culture (after the legendary King Minos of Crete), extended its influence northward to the cultural center of Mycenae in southern mainland Greece. Agamemnon, the legendary king of Mycenae, was regarded as the most powerful and richest ruler on the mainland.

From 1200 to 1000 BCE, groups of migrating tribes invaded Greece from the north and destroyed the existing Minoan-Mycenaean cultures. At the end of those migrations, three cultural groups dominated: the Aeolic in northern Greece, the Ionic in central Greece, and the Doric in southern Greece.

From 800 to 600 BCE, the Greeks expanded their culture by colonization. The Ionians moved northeastward to the Black Sea, the Aeolians westward to France and Spain, and the Dorians to Sicily and southern Italy. Several centuries later, the Greeks were forced to contend with the Persians. After several attempts, the Persian army crossed the Hellespont (the modern Dardanelles) in 480 BCE and marched into Greece. They captured Athens and burned the Acropolis before their fleet was routed by the Athenians and their allies in the naval battle of Salamis.

A period of great cultural and intellectual achievement followed, before power politics between Greek city-states led to political decay and warfare. In the fourth century BCE, King Philip II of Macedon conquered Greece. Philip's son, Alexander the Great, gathered an army of Greeks and Macedonians and crossed the Hellespont to attack the Persians. In ten years, he conquered western Asia as far as modern India and overran Egypt. Over time, Greek cities were established everywhere

Greek Religion

BCE

c. 3000 Beginnings of Minoan culture
c. 2100 Construction of royal palace at Knossos
c. 2000 Achaean invasion of Greece
c. 1400 Destruction of the palace at Knossos
c. 800 Composition of Hesiod's poems
776 Olympic games first held
490 Darius I defeated by the Greeks at Marathon
356 Birth of Alexander the Great (d. 323 BCE)

throughout western Asia and in Egypt, and Greek civilization and language predominated in the vast area in spite of Alexander's untimely death in 323 BCE.

The period that followed Alexander the Great is called the Hellenistic Age. As the power of Macedon declined, many Greek city-states formed independent leagues. Then, in 197 BCE, the Romans arrived and conquered Macedon and Greece, an event that precipitated a fifty-year struggle between the Romans and the Greeks. Finally, the Romans destroyed Macedon in 148 BCE and a year later made Greece a Roman province. The Romans gradually completed their conquest of most of the Hellenistic world between 146 and 127 BCE.

EARLY GREEK RELIGION

Greek Deities

The roots of Greek religion go as far back as Neolithic times, when the Indo-European sky god, variously known as Zeus, Jupiter, and Dyaus, was believed to control the weather. As waves of Greek-speaking tribes moved into mainland Greece, they absorbed Pelasgian (pre-Greek) cults, such as that of the horse-headed Demeter and the oracles of Zeus centered at Dodona. Each Greek deity possessed its familiar beast or bird, although it is uncertain whether deities ever were visualized in animal forms. Some deities, such as the hearth goddess Hestia, were only vaguely personified. Others, such as Apollo, Hermes, and Dionysus, often were represented as posts, columns, or stones.

The deities in Greek religion were regarded as the immortal controllers of natural forces. Zeus was the weather god, known also as Zeus Maemactes (Storm) or Zeus Cataebates (Striker). The Greeks visited his shrines, sited on mountaintops, in times of drought. Apollo was the god of plagues and herdsmen; he also sanctioned purification rites. Hades (or Pluto) was the god of the underworld. Poseidon was the god of the

sea and of horses. Themis personified justice; Aphrodite and Eros
aroused love and sexual passion. The list goes on and on.

All of life's major events, such as births, marriages, and deaths, required the invocation of a deity. No occupation or journey was undertaken without a deity's prior approval. In fact, the ancient Greeks invoked the gods for help and guidance on any and every occasion.
Between them and their deities was a natural, everyday, down-to-earth
interaction, free of any sense of servitude or fear.

In Crete, the cult of the Mother Goddess seems to have played an important part. The Mother Goddess combined a number of different
functions. She was associated with vegetation, depicted as a mountain
deity, worshiped as ruler of the netherworld, and thought of as mistress
of all beasts. Sometimes she was shown as a female figure holding
snakes in each outstretched hand, and sometimes she was accompanied
by a male deity. Her cult was later submerged by that of the Olympian
gods, but her importance survived in the mystery religions of occult
practitioners (discussed at greater length later in the chapter).

Homeric Deities

The Greek poet Homer, whose birthplace and birth date are unknown
(the conjecture is that he lived some time between 1000 and 800 BCE),
left an artistic and intellectual picture of the Greek deities. To serve the
purposes of his epic poetry, Homer assembled all the major deities on
Mount Olympus and portrayed them as fair in form and of superhuman size yet capable of moving with the lightness of birds. The Homeric
pantheon was a divine aristocracy ruled by Zeus, a splendid sky god
who held dominion over clouds, thunderbolts, and rain. As father of
the gods, Zeus was involved in numerous generative relationships, but
his permanent consort was Hera. Other important deities in the Homeric
pantheon were Apollo, Poseidon, Aphrodite, and Athena. Apollo was
identified as the god of light and had a wide range of interests, including the care of animals, music, and medicine. The oracle at Delphi was
identified with his voice.

On the whole, the Homeric deities were stripped of their primitive
characteristics. Earlier views of the deities in animal form, of the Mother
Goddess, and of the Minoan and the Pelasgian cults were either absent
or modified. Those deities, although immortal, were attractive, charm-
ing, and amusing; indeed, they were like humans—moody, passionate,
jealous, and prone to indulge their own whims. Homer's deities, in contrast, exercised great power over human lives. Cities rose or fell, armies
triumphed or failed, individuals lived or died according to the will of
the deities. And the gods showed little, if any, concern for justice in the
modern sense. Rather than justice, tribute—a due regard for their divine status or power along with sacrificial rituals— governed the relationship of the gods toward humans and the manner in which the gods
bestowed or withheld their favors.

The influence of the Homeric pantheon in guiding the imagination
of Greek artists was considerable. Humans could now gaze with awe
and wonder at bronze and marble embodiments of the gods in temples,

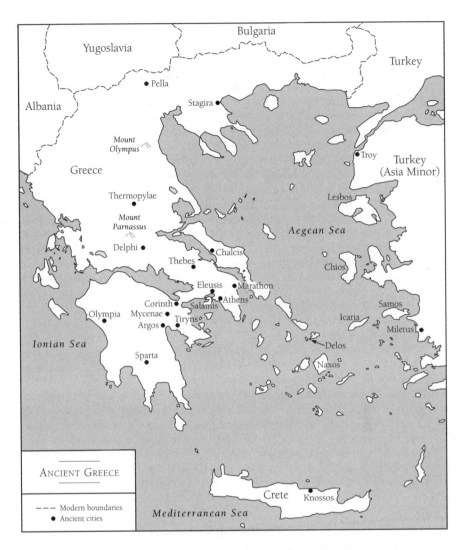

ANCIENT GREECE

- - - Modern boundaries
● Ancient cities

acropolises (city citadels), and marketplaces. But transcending even Zeus was a power that Zeus might change by force of will but to which he also submitted. That power was identified as Moira (fate) and Ker (doom)—the destiny allotted to each individual. Sometimes Zeus was the instrument of fate, but he was powerless to control it. So, although the Homeric deities were represented as superhuman beings, their powers were not boundless.

Greek Mythology

Greek religion in all its manifestations—intellectual, popular, and mysterious—was so rich in myths that even the barest outline would require more space than is available here. The origins of many Greek myths are lost. What remains is the creation of the poets, starting no earlier than 1000 BCE with Homer and his epic poem the *Iliad*. Greek mythology does not portray prehistoric humankind, but it clearly reveals what early Greeks thought and imagined. The Greeks, unlike the Egyptians and the Mesopotamians, made their gods in their own image. Greek deities were real, normal, and natural: they ate, drank, feasted, made love, and amused themselves as human beings did. Naturally, the deities were powerful and dangerous when they were angry, so they were to be feared. Yet with proper care, a person could be at ease with them, sometimes even laugh at them. In fact, the Greek gods were not only exceedingly human but also very attractive.

The terrifying, irrational world of spooky monsters was lacking in Greek mythology, and demonic creatures were few. The world of Greek mythology was, by and large, far from a place of terror. What stood out in Greek mythology were the stories and adventures of gods, goddesses, heroes, and heroines—the mighty Zeus, who was all too human; Hera, his wife, the prototype of the jealous woman; the love affairs of Cupid and Psyche, Pygmalion and Galatea; the adventures of Jason in his quest for the Golden Fleece; the superhuman achievements of Odysseus and Heracles; the tragic fates of Oedipus and the heroic Antigone—all contributed to the texture of the Greek mythological tapestry.

INTELLECTUAL VIEWS

To an extent unknown in Egypt or Mesopotamia, the Greeks intellectualized religious beliefs and concepts. Dramatists and philosophers, not content with chronicling the activities of the gods or explaining religious concepts, continually examined the bases of religious beliefs, searching for fundamental intellectual and moral values. Their rationalistic, even skeptical, attitude toward traditional religion was to exert a profound influence on the future course of Western religions.

Dramatists

Human destiny was a recurrent theme of the great dramatists of the sixth and fifth centuries BCE, especially Aeschylus, Sophocles, and Euripides. The question they addressed was whether the gods or fate controlled human destiny. Both Aeschylus and Sophocles exalted Zeus as the administrator of cosmic justice. They took the position that all other deities yielded to Zeus's will when he overruled them in the name of justice. Aeschylus portrayed Zeus in command of fate and in control of human destiny. Sophocles, however, softened that implacable image by attributing to Zeus a judgment tempered by mercy, although he acknowledged that Zeus's favor was not easily gained without purity in word and deed. In contrast, Euripides, who was influenced by humanist sentiments, expressed skepticism about the justice and integrity of the gods. He pitied human beings, whose destiny lay at the mercy of uncaring, unfeeling, and unseeing deities. The following excerpt reflects his sentiments:

Athena, patron goddess of Athens, who was also worshiped in other parts of Greece. A virgin goddess, Athena personified wisdom, and she was the patron of arts and crafts and closely connected with war. According to Greek mythology, her birth occurred when she leapt, fully armed, from the head of Zeus, which had been split open by an axe. Her most famous shrine is the Parthenon, on the Acropolis of Athens.

Courtesy of Tom G. Elliott.

> Ah pain, pain! O unrighteous curse . . .
> Thou Zeus, doest see me?
> Yea, it is I; the proud and pure, the server of god;
> The white and shining in sanctity!
> To a visible death, to an open sod, I walk my ways;
> And all the labor of saintly days lost, lost without meaning![1]

Philosophers

Greek philosophers in the fifth century BCE also attempted to come to terms with contemporary beliefs in the gods. On the whole, they maintained a reserved, if not skeptical, attitude toward traditional views. Xenophanes, born in Colophon around 540 BCE, favored the concept of a divine, creative power—one god who was the greatest among deities and human beings and who thought all, saw all, and heard all. He ridiculed the human proclivity to represent such a god in the likeness of another human, thus perpetuating what he saw as an anthropomorphic fallacy. If animals were able to think and act, argued Xenophanes, they too would represent the deities in their own likeness or form:

> Mortals think that the gods are begotten, and wear clothes like their own, and have a voice and a form. If oxen or horses or lions had hands and could draw with them and make works of art as men do, horses would draw the shapes of gods like horses, oxen like oxen; each kind would represent their bodies just like their own forms.[2]

Socrates, born in Athens about 470 BCE, left no writings. We depend almost entirely on what Plato and Xenophon, his two most famous pupils, wrote about him. Socrates taught in a very informal way, not in a school. He was gifted in the use of questions and answers — the dialogue type of instruction. He engaged interested persons, especially the youth, in conversation. His concern was to show his listeners how to think clearly and how to arrive at sound conclusions. He could lay bare, with a few bold strokes, every form of pretense, sham, and hypocrisy. Logic and ethics were therefore his basic concerns. In fact, he identified virtue with knowledge and placed religion on the basis of one's inner motives. He was brought to trial and accused of destroying faith in the deities worshiped by the Athenians, and of corrupting the youth. Socrates was, indeed, critical of the myths and legends of the Greek deities. However, before he died from the cup of hemlock he had been condemned to drink, he is supposed to have said that "no harm can come to a good man in life or death."

Plato, born in Athens in 429 BCE, continued where Socrates left off, but his interest led him into the field of metaphysics. He criticized the Homeric pantheon and advocated a revision of traditional tales of the gods to censor passages to which he objected. Plato did not deny the existence of the deities so much as he rejected the Homeric representation of them as wayward and fallible. Plato also disagreed with mystery religions for representing the deities as easily swayed from impartial justice.

For Plato, the highest of all values was the Good, the beginning of the realm of ideal forms, the "creator" above and behind all other things. Gods, humans, animals, mountains, plains, and seas all embodied the Good in various degrees. Consequently, the gods required none of the magical or superstitious rituals that contemporary human beings considered to be the gods' rightful due. Each human being, Plato argued, was a soul encased in a body, and all that the gods required was that each soul should seek to grow toward the highest good in order to move into a timeless, eternal realm where the soul would see and enjoy ideal forms in all their truth, beauty, and goodness.

Plato's conception of a timeless realm lying beyond the reach of the senses and culminating in the form of the Good impressed students and fellow philosophers alike. Aristotle, born in Stagira, Macedon, in 384 BCE and a student in Plato's school of philosophy for twenty years, postulated a pattern of thought that affected all subsequent philosophers, scientists, and theologians. In his philosophy, Aristotle dispensed with the traditional Greek deities. Instead, he posited as the highest type of being the Prime Mover, a motionless being who caused all the movements of celestial and terrestrial bodies by attracting them toward himself.

POPULAR RELIGION

Even as the philosophers seriously challenged traditional religious beliefs, Greek popular religion flourished along with the various civic cults. People worshiped all sorts of nature spirits and local deities. Magic, spells, and witchcraft were widespread. Religious civic festivals attracted large gatherings and punctuated daily life. The oracles, with their claim to reveal the future, were eagerly consulted by individuals as well as states.

The most persistent form of Greek religion was that of simple and unlettered peasants. Gods were often overthrown and forgotten, but nature spirits, demons, nymphs, and heroes persisted in the memories and day-to-day activities of ordinary people.

Demons, Nymphs, and Heroes

Demons seem to have been of two types: *centaurs* and *seilenoi*. Centaurs, which inhabited bodies that were half-human and half-horse, were believed to have originated as spirits of the precipitous mountain torrents. They represented the nature spirits of wood and wilderness, that is, the rough and violent aspect of nature. *Seilenoi* were demons distinguished by the head, torso, and arms of a man atop the hindquarters (legs, tail, and testicles) of a horse. In Greek mythology, the *seilenoi* (and their Roman counterparts, the satyrs) had sexual intercourse with nymphs, the female spirits of nature. Nymphs were always thought of as human in shape. They were beautiful, omnipresent, and benevolent, although at times capable of anger and threatening behavior. Their usual habitats were groves, caves, meadows, and mountains, but there were also sea nymphs and tree nymphs. Artemis, the great and most popular goddess of Greece, was associated with trees, rivers, and springs and haunted mountains and meadows; she was viewed as the leader of the

This statue of Diana found in the Capitoline Museum in Rome is a copy of the Greek original of the fourth century BCE. Artemis, whose worship was widespread in ancient Greece, is identified with Diana. Both were virgin goddesses closely identified with the hunt, marriage, and childbirth. Both Diana and Artemis were also associated with the moon.
Courtesy of Tom Elliott.

nymphs. She protected women in childbirth and watched over children, but she was also the goddess preferred by hunters and was considered the virgin twin sister of Apollo.

Heroes in ancient Greece were regarded as inferior to gods, even though some, such as Heracles, Asclepius, and the Dioscuri, were not far removed from divinity. Not necessarily heroic figures in the modern sense, the Greek heroes were people who in death transcended the admiration they had earned in life and continued to walk the earth in corporeal form. The cult of heroes centered on their tombs or the relics buried in the tombs. For that reason, the bones of heroes were sometimes dug up and transferred to another place during wartime. The Lacedaemonians, for instance, with some difficulty recovered the bones of Orestes at Tega and transferred them to Sparta to help the Spartans fight the Arcadians. In the battle of Marathon (490 BCE), King Theseus was said to have risen from his tomb to fight with the Athenians against the Persians. Heroes and heroines in ancient Greece were so numerous that their tombs and shrines dotted the countryside. They were believed to appear in concrete form, and any individual could call on them for help in all matters of life.

Oracles

Another important aspect of Greek religion was that of oracles — answers to specific questions vouchsafed by a deity to the human inquirer, usually through a priest or priestess. Methods of inquiry included the casting of lots; incubation, a process by which an inquirer sleeping in a holy precinct would receive a response from the deity in a dream; and oracular pronouncements in response to questions delivered orally by a human agent. Responses were supposed to emanate by supernatural inspiration through a human agent or some object. In either case, the idea was that a power took possession of a person or a thing and made the person or thing a medium of response.

Among the famous oracular shrines were those of Zeus at Dodona and Olympia, of Apollo at Delphi and Delos, and of Asclepius at Epidaurus. The most ancient oracular shrine was at Dodona, where priests (later, priestesses) revealed the responses of Zeus from the rustling of oak trees, a sacred spring, and the striking of a gong. The most popular oracular shrine was that of Apollo at Delphi, where the medium was a woman known as Pythia. After certain introductory rituals, she became possessed by the god while she sat on a sacred tripod, and her ecstatic utterances were passed on by priests to the inquirer. The inquirers were either private citizens, who consulted the oracle for personal matters, or kings, who sought the advice of the deity in matters of war or politics. At times, priests had difficulty understanding the oracle and consequently passed on the response in the form of ambiguous verse. For instance, Croesus, king of Lydia, consulted the oracle before he invaded Cappadocia. The answer he received stated that if he invaded the country he would "bring ruin to the empire." Croesus jumped to the conclusion that the empire the oracle referred to was Cappadocia. He was wrong, but he did not realize his mistake until he had lost his own empire.

The influence of the Delphic oracle waned during Roman times, and ultimately the sanctuary was closed by the Christian Roman Emperor Theodosius in 390 CE.

MYSTERY RELIGIONS

Another major component of Greek religious life addressed a human need largely untouched by the intellectual speculations of the philosophers and the formulaic prescriptions of traditional religious forms. People seeking an intensely personal, emotionally satisfying religious experience turned to the mystery religions, or *cults*. Initiates of such religious movements underwent purification rites, received instruction in mystical knowledge, viewed sacred objects, watched the enactment of a divine story, and were crowned as full-fledged members. The initiation was spread over several days and included various celebrations and processions. The experiences were referred to as "mysterious" rather than "mystical" because the rites were kept absolutely secret from all except the initiates. Individuals who wished to join any of these religious movements were initiated to the secret rites by a *hierophant*, a revealer of sacred mysteries and esoteric principles. Initiates were sworn to secrecy and put to death if they broke their vows.

So passionately devoted were the members of the mystery religions that they carried on with their rites even during public crises. According to the historian Herodotus, while Attica was being ravaged by the Persians and the Greek fleet at Salamis was in danger, thousands of devotees of the Eleusinian mysteries marched in a procession from Eleusis to Athens, chanting their mystical hymn to Dionysus.[3] The mystery religions, then, provided not only a personal religious satisfaction but a deep sense of a mystic reality—the reality of sharing the immortal nature of the gods.

Eleusinian Mysteries

The Eleusinian mysteries were by far the greatest of all Greek mystery religions. The three deities involved were the grain goddess, Demeter; her daughter, Kore; and the underworld god, Hades. The story underlying the Eleusinian mysteries went as follows. After Hades carried off Kore to the underworld to be his bride, the grieving Demeter searched for her daughter everywhere with a lighted torch, until finally she arrived at Eleusis exhausted and in utter despair. During that state, the goddess refused to make the grain grow, and so terrible was the resultant famine that the deities persuaded Zeus to ask Hades to return Kore to her mother. Hades agreed to let Kore return to earth, but only after he had cunningly persuaded her to eat a pomegranate (the fruit that symbolized marriage), thus ensuring her return to the underworld. Zeus then effected a compromise, whereby Kore had to return to the underworld for only one-third of each year. Consequently, Kore was identified in Greek mythology with Persephone, queen of Hades. Some time later—precisely when is not clear—the god Dionysus was incorporated into the Eleusinian mysteries.

The content and the nature of the mysteries were kept secret, although the public could watch the procession of candidates going down to the sea for ritual purification. Several days later, after the candidates had gone through their initiation rites, the public was allowed to witness the procession of the *mystae* (initiates) from Athens to Eleusis and back. As new members of the religion, the mystae could claim knowledge to the secret of happiness after death.

The main ceremonies of the Eleusinian mysteries eventually became common knowledge throughout the Hellenic world and, later, the Roman Empire. (Several Roman emperors became mystae.) Only the destruction of the temple at Eleusis following the invasion of Greece by Alaric the Goth in the fourth century CE put an end to the Eleusinian mysteries.

Dionysian Mysteries

Dionysus originally was a god in Phrygia, in Asia Minor. He came to Greece through Thrace and became the central figure of yet another extravagant mystery religion. The practices of the Dionysian mysteries normally were held in remote places, such as mountainsides, where devotees, predominantly women, gathered to express their religious excitement in eating, drinking, music, and dancing. The ritual culminated in tearing apart and eating the raw flesh and drinking the blood of a bull or a kid, both of which were identified with Dionysus. The blood, the raw flesh, the wail of music, the whirling dance, and the glow of torches all heightened the consciousness of the devotees to a state of divine possession. They felt themselves identified with Bacchus, one of Dionysus's aspects as god of the vine. The devotees thus were known as bacchants or maenads ("mad ones"). Some time around the sixth to fifth centuries BCE, the wildness and frenzy of Dionysian mysteries aroused criticism and hostility among followers who respected tradition. Nevertheless, the ecstatic practices continued up to Roman times.

Orphic Mysteries

The Orphic movement was said to have been founded in the fifth century BCE by Orpheus, legendary poet and musician of Greek mythology, a victim of *sparagmos* ("tearing to pieces") by the maenads in Thrace. According to Orphic tradition, Dionysus, under the name Zagreus, was the offspring of Zeus and Persephone. The Titans, an ancient race of giant gods, killed the infant Zagreus and ate his flesh. In retaliation, Zeus burned the Titans with his thunderbolts and formed the human race from the ashes. Humans, then, were conceived as a combination of good and evil—the ashes of the Titans (evil) containing the substance of Zagreus (good). However, Zagreus, as it turned out, had not been entirely swallowed by the Titans. The goddess Athena had managed to rescue the infant's heart, which was swallowed by Zeus. Zagreus then was reborn as the son of the earth goddess, Semele.

Through ascetic (not, as in the Dionysian mysteries, ecstatic) practices, such as food restrictions, self-denying practices, and purification rites, devotees of the Orphic mysteries attempted to liberate themselves from bodily entanglements and to achieve immortal life.

Strangely enough, Orphic ideas were incorporated into the philosophies of both Pythagoras (c.582–507 BCE) and Plato. In fact, the Pythagoreans insisted on the need for purity, food taboos (forbidden food), and a belief in reincarnation. Their studies in mathematics, medicine, music, astronomy, and philosophy were designed to awaken the divine elements in humans so they could regain the state of purity and end their earthly transmigration.

FESTIVALS

Festivals were large gatherings that expressed the social aspect of religion. Basically agrarian in origin, festivals were seasonal, often were held at the full moon, and always included animal sacrifices. They were not always strictly religious in nature. Some served as occasions for official functions, such as honoring citizens or receiving foreign embassies. Others, such as the Pan-Hellenic Pythian and Olympic festivals, expressed the unity of the Greek peoples and included dramas, poetry recitals, music, and athletic contests. No rigid distinctions were drawn between the artistic expression, the political life, and the religious concerns of the populace.

The precise details of many festivals are obscure. In Athens, some seventy festivals were celebrated in a year. The Athenians honored their deities by seasons of the year: Apollo, Athena, and Demeter in the summer and fall; Dionysus and Artemis in the spring. The manifold functions of Zeus made him an exception — he received honors year round.

Panathenaea

Among the more elaborate Athenian festivals was the Panathenaea, which honored Athena, the patron goddess of the city. The festival was held annually in midsummer and on a more splendid scale every fourth year. Its purpose, besides the offering of sacrifices, was providing the image of Athena, housed in the temple on the Acropolis, with a newly embroidered mantle woven by Athenian women. Every fourth year, the celebration included, in addition to the procession, a torch race, bardic recitations, mock fights, and athletic contests.

Dionysia

Another important festival celebrated in Athens in the spring was the Dionysia, to honor the god Dionysus. At the end of this six-day ritual, the image of Dionysus was escorted to the theater, where it presided over dramatic performances of works by Aeschylus, Sophocles, Euripides, and Aristophanes.

Heracles (Hercules to the Romans) was the most popular and
widely worshiped of Greek heroes. Of his celebrated twelve
endeavors, three had to do with the conquest of death, giving
Heracles the character of a savior. (It is possible that he thus
affected the development of Christology.) As the Roman god of
victory and traders, an ancient altar was built in his honor in the
Forum Boarium (Cattle Market). His emblems are the lion skin, the
club, and the poplar tree.
Courtesy of Tom G. Elliott.

Pan-Hellenic Festivals

The Pan-Hellenic festivals were the most famous: the Olympic, held at
Olympia in honor of Zeus; the Pythian, held at Delphi in honor of
Apollo; the Isthmian, held at the Isthmus of Corinth in honor of Posei-
don; and the Nemean, held at Nemea in honor of Zeus. All travelers to

the Pan-Hellenic festivals were guaranteed safe passage, even in wartime.

The Olympic festivals, which were celebrated every fourth summer in Zeus's sacred precinct in the western Peloponnesus, attracted large numbers of athletes from all parts of the Greek world. A nationwide truce was proclaimed, to allow warring Greeks to compete, and the celebrations lasted five days. After sacrifice and libation were offered at the altars of Zeus and Hestia and at the tomb of Pelops, the judges and competitors took the oath to observe the rules. Then followed processions, bardic recitations, and the honoring of the winners at state banquets. Women were banned from the celebration, although they competed at the festival of the goddess Hera. The festivals in honor of Apollo at Delphi and of Poseidon at Isthmus followed the Olympian pattern.

HELLENISTIC SYNCRETISM

Because of the conquests of Alexander the Great, the Greeks and the Macedonians came into contact with a number of impressive Oriental religious cults, such as Cybele, Attis, Isis, and Osiris. The international associations and racial mixture that resulted from Greek contact with Asiatic peoples created opportunities for cultural and religious diffusion. That did not mean that traditional Greek religion and cults disappeared; rather, an ever increasing number of people came in contact with "foreign" beliefs and practices. Thus, the assimilation of various deities led to unification. Greek and, later, Roman monarchs, like Oriental monarchs, were considered emanations of gods. Indeed, the deities of Greece, Egypt, Asia Minor, and Persia attracted all Greeks.

The Roman conquest in the second century BCE ultimately absorbed Greece into a wider political world. Greek religion, like most other aspects of Greek life, had a considerable impact on Roman religion. Greek and Roman deities mingled, and a process of syncretism took place. Greek religion survived in that form until 529 CE, when the Christian Roman Emperor Justinian dealt a death blow by closing the Athenian schools of philosophy.

STUDY QUESTIONS

1. Give a brief account of the origins and development of Greek peoples.
2. Compare the Homeric view with earlier views of deities.
3. What role did the Mother Goddess play in Crete?
4. Compare Greek mythology with that of Egypt and Mesopotamia.
5. What was the recurrent theme of the dramatists?
6. Discuss the contribution of Greek philosophers to Greek religion.

7. Examine Plato's concept of the Good.

8. Describe the role and the function of demons, nymphs, and heroes.

9. Why were oracles of great importance? Where were the sites of the most famous oracular shrines?

10. How did the mystery religions provide personal satisfaction?

11. List the main ceremonies associated with the Eleusinian mysteries.

12. How did the devotees of the Dionysian mysteries conduct themselves?

13. How did the devotees of the Orphic mysteries achieve immortality?

14. Describe the celebration performed in honor of the patron deity of Athena.

15. Discuss the Pan-Hellenic festivals.

Suggested Reading

Abrahamsen, Valeri Ann. *Women and Worship at Philippi: Diana/Artemis and Other Cults in Early Christian Era*. Portland, Maine: Astarte Shell Press, 1995.

Avagianou, Aphrodite. *Sacred Marriage in the Rituals of Greek Religion*. Bern: P. Lang, 1991.

Bremmer, Jan N. *Greek Religion*. Oxford: Oxford University Press, 1994.

Burkert, Walter. *Greek Religion*. Cambridge: Harvard University Press, 1985.

Dietrich, Bernard Clive. *The Origins of Greek Religion*. New York: De Gruyter, 1974.

Garland, Robert. *The Greek Way of Life: From Conception to Old Age*. Ithaca, N.Y.: Cornell University Press, 1990.

———. *Introducing New Gods: The Politics of Athenian Religion*. London: Duckworth, 1992.

Lyons, Deborah. *Gender and Immortality: Heroines in Ancient Greek Myth and Cult*. Princeton, N.J.: Princeton University Press, 1997.

Martin, Luther H. *Hellenistic Religions: An Introduction*. New York: Oxford University Press, 1987.

Meyer, Mervin (ed.) *The Ancient Mysteries, A Sourcebook: Sacred Texts of the Mystery Religions of the Ancient Mediterranean World*. San Francisco: Harper & Row, 1987.

Richer, Jean. *Sacred Geography of the Ancient Greeks: Astrological Symbolism in Art, Architecture and Landscape*. Albany, N.Y.: SUNY, 1994.

Notes

1. G. Murray (trans.), *The Plays of Euripides* (Newton, Wales: Gregynog Press, 1931), p. 1347.

2. Cited in F. M. Cornford, *Greek Religious Thought from Homer to the Age of Alexander* (London: Dent, 1923), p. 85.

3. *Herodotus*, VIII. 40–68, trans. by H. Carter (Oxford: Oxford University Press, 1962), pp. 506–515.

11 Roman Religion

No one knows how or when Rome was founded. One story, popularized in Virgil's *Aeneid,* held that the Trojan warrior Aeneas set up a kingdom in Italy after the fall of Troy, around 1100 BCE. Another legend described how Romulus and Remus, twin brothers, founded Rome around 753 BCE. According to that story, the twin infants were placed in a basket and set adrift on the Tiber River, which carried them to the foot of the Palatine Hill. There, a she-wolf cared for the boys until the shepherd Faustulus found them and took them to his house. (Up to that point, the legend bears a striking resemblance to stories about the Mesopotamian King Sargon and the biblical Moses.) Faustulus reared the boys with his own children. Later, the brothers decided to build a new city at the spot where their lives had been saved, but an argument about the exact site of their deliverance culminated in the death of Remus at the hand of Romulus. The building of the city of Rome followed, with Romulus its founder and leader.

Archaeological study has offered no evidence to support the legendary claims of either Aeneas or Romulus as the founder of Rome. Excavations show that the city of Rome was the site of a small farming village of Latin inhabitants as early as the eighth century BCE. The simple community later became the capital of a huge empire, whose boundaries at its height, during the reign of Emperor Trajan in the second century CE, included most of Europe, part of the Middle East, and the northern coastal area of Africa. Its millions of people, speaking many languages and worshiping different deities, were united by the military power and imperial administration of the Romans.

Roman Religion

BCE

  753 Legendary date of Rome's founding

c. 210 Worship of Cybele introduced at Rome

  149 Destruction of Carthage

   c. 4 Birth of Jesus Christ (d. CE 28)

CE

   70 Destruction of Jerusalem and burning of the temple by the Romans

  311 Edict of Milan

  354 Birth of St. Augustine (d. 430)

c. 453 St. Patrick in Ireland

  476 End of Western Roman Empire

ROMAN RELIGION

Numina

Roman religion involved belief in the potency of a supernatural quality called *numen* (pl., *numina*), from which the term *numinous* is derived. The *numina* were thought of in a personal way and were associated with deities, humans, and particular places, functions (such as procreation, healing, and fighting), and things (such as homes, kitchen utensils, trees, rivers, and boundary stones). The deities derived their power and greatness in proportion to the strength of their *numina*. Jupiter, as the chief deity, had more *numen* than did other deities. Appropriate sacrifices performed by humans enhanced the *numen* of the deities to whom they were offered. Humans, particularly groups or tribes, also possessed *numen*. *Numen* was transferable and was conferred by a deity on a person, a tribe, a farm, a tool, and other elements.

The importance of the concept of *numen* in Roman religion led to an ambiguous definition of divine characteristics. There was a lack of distinct personality, sometimes even of sex, among the various deities. No anthropomorphic images, no divine genealogies, and no mythical histories seemed to have intrigued the imaginative faculty of the Romans. Roman religion focused on the diverse functions of *numina*, not on the characteristics and personal histories of the deities.

To ensure success in any endeavor, the Romans invoked the relevant *numina*. In the cultivation of grain, for example, Saturnus represented the best source of *numen* in sowing, Ceres in growing, Consus in harvesting, and Ops in storing. Pales was the *numen* in pasture, Faunus in woods and forests, and Lares in sown fields, family estates, and crossroads. In the home, Janus was the *numen* in the door, Vesta in the hearth.

Penates were the *numina* in the cupboard or storeroom; Lar Familiaris the *numina* in the whole household.

A few important *numina* are hard to define. Genius was the *numen* in every male, representing the energy, vitality, and essence of manhood. Juno was the *numen* in every female, representing the energy, vitality, and essence of womanhood. The Manes were the *numina* of the dead, which had to be propitiated with appropriate burial rites to secure entrance of the dead to the underworld. To do less was to risk the haunting presence of Lemures, unhappy spirits denied entrance to the underworld, spreading misfortune among the living.

The Roman *numina* were propitiated and honored by a variety of magical acts, ceremonial rituals, and festivals, which were regulated by certain principles that were carried out with formal exactness. Any deviation from appropriate formulas rendered the exercise ineffective.

Roman Deities

It has been said of the Roman pantheon that the deities were as alike as peas in a pod, and there is some justification for such a conclusion. Many Roman dieties survived in name only, having lost their following or appeal or having been superseded by or incorporated into new systems of worship or belief, so that little or nothing is known about them. Some, however, retained their prominence through the centuries by virtue of art or literature and merit some comment.

Jupiter was the ancient Indo-European Dyaus Pitar (or Diovis Pater or Zeus Pater), whose exalted title was Optimus Maximus. He was the god of light, lightning, thunder, rain, and storm. He prescribed and ordered human affairs, which augurs or soothsayers could predict by signs in the heavens or the flight of birds, and he was the guardian of laws and oaths. His sanctuary, or temple, was on the Capitoline Hill, called Jupiter Capitolinus. In later years, he was associated with the imperial glories of Rome and acquired various titles: the Victor, Invictus, Imperator. His consort was Juno, whom the Greeks identified as Hera.

Mars, originally the protector of fields and herds, was best known as a war god; his sacred symbols were the lance and shield and his sacred animal was the wolf. Mars was honored in the first month (later changed to the third month) of the Roman calendar. March (from *Martius*) was named after him, and the priests of Mars *(salii)* celebrated the festival with dancing in the street. Quirinus was another war god, of whom little is known. He was served by a *flamen*, a priest assigned to a particular god, and an annual festival called Quirinalia was dedicated to him.

Janus was the god of beginnings and was invoked at the opening of almost any event or the threshold of almost any structure: the New Year (January, derived from Janus), the first day of every month, the first hour of the day, the entrance (door) of a home, or a city gate. His symbol was an opening or entrance; in Rome, it was the gateway to the Forum.

Minerva was the goddess of wisdom and patroness of the arts and trades. Later, she was associated with war and was therefore represented as wearing a helmet and carrying a shield and a spear.

Priests and Diviners

The Romans also believed that the health, safety, and welfare of the family and the state depended on the protection and goodwill of the deities. Thus, the state assumed the performance of all religious rituals and the emperor was vested with priestly power in addition to secular power.

During the republic, the administrative responsibility for state religious affairs was held by an official with the title Pontifex Maximus, who had the power to appoint high-level priests from a well-defined hierarchy divided into colleges or guilds or according to specific functions. The *sacerdos*, for instance, was a priest whose function was to officiate at sacrificial rites, especially animal sacrifices, which were central to worship in public temples. In addition, each deity had his or her own *flamen*, or priest, whose duty was to light the altar fires. Then there was the board of augurs (consisting originally of three members but later increased to sixteen), who specialized in interpreting any unusual event or phenomenon by the flight of birds and the movements of fowl. Important decisions about state matters often were delayed until a propitious augury was obtained from the board of augurs.

The Romans also solicited omens, portents, and divine messages beyond their own borders. The Etruscan *haruspex*, an expert diviner, was consulted for important matters. Messengers were sent to the renowned Greek temple of Apollo to receive his oracles. Later, both methods were imported into Rome.

Magic and Astrology

Magic, on the whole, was a discredited practice and a disreputable occupation in Rome, although fortunetelling by magical means was common enough. According to an ancient Roman code of law, two forms of sorcery were forbidden: the use of a noxious charm and the practice of making a neighbor's crops magically leap over to a sorcerer. Expert sorcerers were believed to have the power to bring themselves into contact with a deity or to induce a deity to exercise his or her *numen* in a specific way to achieve a particular objective. By performing the proper rites — that is, by applying magical arts — a powerful sorcerer could achieve the desired results. However, the the Romans did not rely on magic to the same degree that many of their neighbors did.

Almost a corollary of magic was astrology. Several philosophical schools insisted that the stars were divine and that celestial motions, especially solar or lunar, had a religious significance far beyond their surface appearance as natural phenomena. The positions of the heavenly bodies at the time of someone's birth were believed to determine the destiny of that individual. Even though predictions did not always satisfy expectations raised by complicated astrological rules and formulas, forecasts gained considerable credence among the public — so much so that state officials often opposed astrologers.

Private Associations

More numerous than public congregations of worshipers were private associations that had religious purposes. Members of such associations described themselves as *cultores,* or cult devotees. A decree of the Roman Senate stipulated the maximum number of meetings such associations could hold annually and the limitations placed on their activities. The private associations, however, did not seem to be really more than burial cult clubs. Members paid a subscription and in return received a respectable funeral at the time of their death, which included the rite of a funeral feast. Although very little is known about the private cults, it seems they provided their members with an assurance or hope of a better life in another world.

Emperor Worship

One of the main features and last manifestations of Roman religion was the deification of the emperors, which took hold in the first century CE, at the end of the republican period and the beginning of the empire. At that time, many native Roman gods were losing popularity and their temples were being deserted. Patriotic statesmen and influential poets started to endow emperors with divine qualities, elevating them beside the old Roman gods as objects of worship. Thus, upon their deaths, if not during their lives, the emperors were raised to the status of Roman deities.

Some scholars consider the deification of the emperors to have been rooted in the ancient Roman view of the quality or attribute that Romans identified as *genius* (a family or ancestral spirit, derived from the *numen* Genius) that was bequeathed or transmuted from the dead as a divine force to the clan. (A clan is a social unit smaller than a tribe but larger than a family.) Other scholars speculate that the practice was borrowed from Egyptian pharaoh worship. Whatever its ultimate origins, emperor worship was initiated with Julius Caesar, when the Senate declared him a god in 44 BCE, before his death. Emperor Augustus, the adopted son and successor of Julius Caesar, further honored his father with a temple erected and dedicated in his name (Divus Julius). Henceforth, it became customary to add the divine epithet *divus* to the emperor's name after his death.

Emperor Augustus himself permitted the erection of shrines in which his *genius* was worshiped. In fact, paying reverence to the emperor's *genius* (and sometimes to the emperor himself) became a sign of loyalty to the Roman Imperium. In due time, the aura of divinity was accorded to every emperor as a matter of course during his lifetime. Emperors Nero, Caligula, Domitian, and Trajan were among those who demanded the status of gods during their lifetime. Emperor Nero is said to have enjoyed being equated with Apollo.

As an expression of patriotism, emperor worship perhaps attained a degree of success, but it failed as a unifying element to give various religious faiths one inclusive meaning or purpose as a focus for Roman citizens and society.

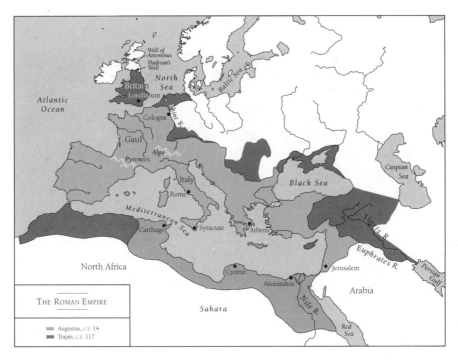

Source: Lanny B. Fields, Russell J. Barber, and Cheryl A. Riggs, *The Global Past* (Boston: Bedford Books, 1998), p. 192.

FOREIGN ACCRETIONS

From about the sixth century BCE onward, the Romans came in contact with the Greeks and then with the peoples of the Middle East. The result was a progressive identification of the deities within and between the various religions and the reinforcement of the anthropomorphic strain in Roman piety. Thus, the Roman god Jupiter was equated with the Greek god Zeus, Juno with Hera, Mars with Ares, Minerva with Athena, Neptune with Poseidon, Venus with Aphrodite, and so on. More important, however, and of far-reaching ramification, was the importation of a collection of Greek oracles—the famous Sibylline Books. The books were stored in the basement of the Capitoline temple, and two priests were appointed to take charge of consulting the oracles. Later, the number of priests was increased to ten and, later still, to fifteen. The contact with the Greek oracles helped the Romans add an entirely new dimension to their religion—personalized deities.

Soon, temples were erected to Apollo, the god of healing; Mercury, the god of commerce; Fortuna, the goddess of luck and good fortune; and many other deities who were represented as wooden figures, elegantly dressed and reclining on couches beside a table laid for a sacramental meal. Along with the adoption of personalized deities, the

Temple of the goddess Hera at Paestum, Italy, dated c. 450 BCE. Hera (Juno to the Romans),
queen of the gods and the sister and wife of Zeus, was associated with marriage and the sexual
life of women. Her temples at Olympia, Argos, and Samos are renowned.
Courtesy of Tom G. Elliott.

Romans also showed a keen interest in Greek myths and epics. Some
Greek mythologies were recast in a Roman context, while other stories
were adopted with little change.

The influence of the Greeks on the Romans was felt not only in religious matters but also in philosophical systems. Starting in the first century BCE, the teachings and ideals of Epicurus (342–270 BCE), Zeno
(335–263 BCE), and Plato (427–347 BCE), among others, attracted the
attention of many educated Romans. The masses, however, were far
less interested in Greek philosophical systems than they were in various Greek and Middle Eastern mystery cults, which provided them
with a more personal, less formal religious experience.

Cybele and Attis

The first Middle Eastern mystery cult adopted by the Romans as a result of an oracular command was the worship of Cybele, the goddess of
the Phrygians. In 204 BCE, a black meteorite stone representing the foreign goddess was solemnly installed on the summit of the Palatine amid
public cheering and incense fumes. Next, a temple was erected on the
spot and an annual celebration was held from April 4 to 10 in commemoration of the arrival of the goddess, whom the Romans named the
Great Mother Goddess of Idaea (or Ida). In a short time, however, the

cult of Cybele encountered resistance from both the civil administration and the public, because of the orgiastic acts of its priests during the annual festival.

The annual festival of Cybele-Attis was held on the spring equinox and lasted four days, from March 22 to 25. On the first day, the trunk of a pine tree wreathed with violets and swathed with woolen cloth was carried ceremonially into the temple. Then, an effigy of the god Attis, Cybele's lover who was reputed to have died by emasculating himself under a pine tree, was fastened to the decorated tree trunk. On the second day, a procession of mourners followed the statue of the goddess Cybele through the streets. They screamed, whirled, leaped, and in their frenzy slashed themselves with knives and swords. On the third day, the bloody passion-drama reached its climax. The novitiates sacrificed their virility by emasculation, so they could share Attis's resurrection. The severed organs were offered on the altar of the goddess Cybele. The effigy was then removed and laid in a tomb, while the castrated initiates watched and fasted until the next morning. Early at dawn on the fourth day, the tomb was opened and the crowds of worshipers shouted in joy, because the god Attis was resurrected and the tomb was empty. The festival ended with a huge and joyous procession carrying the black meteorite stone (representing Cybele) to the river, where it was ceremonially bathed, after which it was returned to its sacred place in the temple.

In addition to that festival, there were some rituals performed only by the emasculated initiates. Those ceremonies consisted of an initiatory rite, known as the *taurobolium,* and a sacramental meal. The *taurobolium* was a baptismal font in the form of a pit into which the newly inducted members descended, to stand under a grating that supported a sacred bull. The sacrificial bull was ceremonially slain on the grating so that its blood ran over the inductees below, who, by the ritual, were considered to be purified. The ritual of purification was followed by a sacramental meal, at which the inductees shared a sense of oneness or of unity as they ate from a common drum and drank from a common cymbal.

The similarity between some aspects of the rites associated with Cybele-Attis and the Christian celebration of the resurrection of Christ is striking. Two coincidences stand out: first, the site of Cybele's temple is where the basilica of St. Peter's stands today; and second, the annual spring celebration of the death, burial, resurrection, and discovery of an empty tomb are features both of the ancient rites of Cybele-Attis and of the annual spring celebration of Easter, or Pascha, which commemorates the death, burial, resurrection, and discovery of the empty tomb of Jesus Christ.

Isis and Serapis

The worship of the Egyptian goddess Isis was introduced to Rome in about the second century BCE, but long before that the popularity of her cult had spread far and wide. Her statues and temples adorned Syria around the seventh century BCE, and three centuries later a great temple was built for Isis at the foot of the Acropolis in Greece. Soon every Greek city and village had a temple and a statue of Isis. The statue of Isis, which represented the Mother Goddess with her suckling infant son, Horus, became an object of veneration in the Greco-Roman world. Some scholars are of the opinion that Christian images and statues of the Madonna and child (Mary and the infant Jesus) resemble those of Isis and her son.

The goddess Isis was regarded as the symbol of maternal love, protection, creative life, and chastity, and she was regarded as the queen of heaven. Because she encompassed such virtues, her cult attracted a large number of followers. Two festivals, one in spring and the other in autumn, were celebrated in her honor. The spring festival coincided with the Egyptian harvest, while the autumn celebration consisted of a four-day dramatic festival. On the first day of the autumn festival, actors impersonated several Egyptian deities, including Isis and Horus, who wept, wailed, and searched for the body of Osiris. On the next two days, portions of the body of Osiris were found, reconstituted, and resurrected by Isis. On the fourth day, a great rejoicing took place, because Osiris had been resurrected and become immortal. Devotees of Isis could celebrate her assurance of life after death and immortality by drinking the milk of Isis from a chalice in the shape of a woman's breast. Those who put their trust in Isis did so in the conviction that she would intercede on their behalf with Osiris when they appeared before his throne of judgment and that Osiris would in no way deny immortality to those for whom Isis interceded.

The Egyptian god Serapis also was closely associated with the mythology surrounding Osiris. The name was a Hellenized combination of Osiris and Apis, the Egyptian bull god. His cult originated in Alexandria, Egypt, and from the beginning was identified with Osiris, the god who ruled the dead and shared immortality with them. Its adoption by the Romans began around the second century BCE, although a century later the Roman Senate took strict measures to stop its diffusion. Nevertheless, the worship of Serapis, like the cult of Isis, invaded Italy and every imperial province. Not until five centuries after they had been adopted by the Romans were the cults of Isis and Serapis finally suppressed. In 390 CE, the Patriarch Theophilus, with the aid of the Roman Emperor Theodosius, consigned the temple of Serapis in Alexandria to the flames. Between the reigns of the emperors Theodosius and Justinian, an interval of about two hundred years, the worship of Isis, Serapis, Cybele, Attis, and all other Greek, Roman, and foreign deities was extirpated in favor of Christianity.

Mithra

Of all the foreign religions adopted by the Romans, the worship of the Persian (Iranian) god Mithra became the most popular and the most widespread. Introduced into the Roman Empire in the first century BCE, Mithraism spread so rapidly that in a very short time hundreds of Mithraeums (temples) had been established from India to Scotland through the agency of zealous Mithraic proselytes, who communicated their convictions with missionary fervor along the ancient trade routes of Africa, Italy, Germany, Spain, France, and Britain. Roman emperors, senators, soldiers, and civil servants were among the most ardent supporters of Mithra. That was not surprising, because Mithra was the invincible god of war, the protector of stable government, and the upholder of social justice and brotherhood.

Mithra was an ancient Indo-Aryan god that appeared in the religion and mythologies of the Persians (ancient Iranians) and the Indians. As the lord of heavenly light, he was identified with the sun, but he was also the god of cattle, agriculture, war, and truth. In addition, Mithra was one of the judges who welcomed the souls of humans after death and, as the god of immortality, conferred everlasting life on his faithful followers. No documents or scriptures are extant on Mithra, but scholars have been able to analyze the cult based on fragmentary references, inscriptions, bas-reliefs, and sculptures. On the basis of all that material, scholars have reconstructed the following story about Mithra.

According to the story, the god Mithra was born miraculously in a cave on December 25. The event was witnessed only by some shepherds

A Mithraeum at Carrawburgh on Hadrian's Wall, the Roman line of defense across northern England. Built in the early third century CE, it was destroyed in the fourth century. Three altars, side benches, and the statue of the torchbearer Cantes remain. Courtesy of Roger Beck.

who came to worship the newborn god with their gifts. From infancy, Mithra's mission was to become master of the earth. To that end, he made the sun subject to his will and consequently was identified with it. Next, he considered it his duty to sacrifice a bull, the pristine creation of the ancient Iranian god Ahura Mazda (see Chapter 12, "Zoroastrianism"). That sacrifice was imperative, because the Persians believed that the soul of the bull was the generative source of all celestial elements and its body the source of human life and all life on earth: all useful herbs from its carcass; wheat from its spinal marrow; all useful animals from its semen; and grapes, which produced the sacramental wine consumed during Mithraic rituals, from its blood. Mithra, therefore, was identified with the slain bull as the creator of all beneficent creatures and herbage. Above all, Mithra was the savior god who protected his devotees in this world and granted them salvation in the next.

Mithraic congregations consisted only of male communicants, who gathered in small numbers of perhaps a hundred or so in underground or subterranean meeting places, because Mithra was born in a cave. Members passed through seven orders or degrees, including an initiation ritual, in which the outline of a cross was branded on their foreheads. Newly inducted members, like their counterparts in Cybelian *tauroboliums,* stood under a grating on which a sacred bull was ceremonially slain, drenching them in the bull's blood. They also took an oath never to reveal the secrets of the order or the mysteries of Mithra. Induction into higher orders involved purification; baptism by fire, in a ceremony that required postulants to submit to a sign marked on their foreheads with a hot iron; and the sacraments of bread and wine, representing mystical union with the god Mithra.

Sunday was holy to the followers of Mithra, because it glorified the sun god, Mithra. December 25 was hallowed because it was the birthday of Mithra, and devotees kept a vigil on the preceding night.

The striking parallels between Mithraism and Christianity hardly need to be pointed out. Both taught that their founders were mediator savior gods, through whom the salvation of mankind was possible and through whom the world would be judged. Both taught the doctrines of heaven and hell, the last judgment, and the immortality of the soul; that the forces of good and evil were in a state of perpetual conflict; and that self-control and abstinence were requisites to acceptance. Both offered the sacraments of baptism and communion and observed Sundays and December 25 as holy days.

For five centuries, followers of Mithraism enjoyed complete freedom of worship throughout the Roman Empire. However, the accession of Emperor Constantine in 311 CE and his encouragement and support of Christianity drastically changed that situation. The hatred that Christians exhibited toward Mithraism and the terrible persecution they perpetrated against its adherents ultimately destroyed it. The most extreme measures against Mithraism came during the reign of Emperor Theodosius in the fourth century, when the once widespread mystery cult of Mithra was completely extirpated by the followers of Christianity.

FESTIVALS

The Roman religious festivals, especially those celebrations connected with the deities, were of two kinds: fixed feasts and movable feasts. The first type, like similar festivals in modern religions, occurred on the same, fixed date or dates each year. The second type of festival was celebrated on dates that were determined from year to year. The nature of some Roman religious festivals is known; the records of others are limited to a list of names and dates that indicate only the time of year at which festivals were held.

Religious public festivals, as prescribed and set down on the state calendar, occupied 104 days of the year. Priests of the various deities or cults performed a long order of ceremonies and sacrifices. Their performances were meticulously enacted, whether or not anyone else attended. A description of some of the best known festivals indicates the importance and seriousness of the religious ceremonies.

The festival of Equirria was conducted by the *salii*—the priests of Mars—twice a year, on the first day of March and on the last day of October. The centerpieces of both festivals were races of warhorses (in October, the winning horse was solemnly sacrificed to Mars, as a way of contributing to the deity's *numen*). On March 19 and October 19, the same priests performed a lustration, or purification, ceremony of the weapons of the Roman legions. The ceremony consisted of a dance, in which the legionnaires brandished their spears and clashed their shields in an act of war magic. On March 23 and May 23, the *salii* again performed lustration of the war trumpets, the magical effects of which were associated not with war but with farmers and herders.

The festival of Fordicidia was observed on April 15 with the sacrificing of pregnant cows to the goddess Tellus in the hope that the fields would yield good crops. Each calf fetus was carefully removed and burned, and its ashes were buried by vestal virgins (virgins consecrated to Vesta, goddess of the hearth), to ensure the fertility of sheep. The vestal virgins, who were chosen from patrician families, were priestesses who had taken a vow of chastity, violation of which was punishable by death. Only six vestal virgins served at a time, each for thirty years; their chief function was to tend the holy fire of Vesta (the hearth fire) in the national shrine in Rome. An annual festival, called Vestalia, was held for nine days, June 7 to 15. During that period, women came barefoot to Vesta's shrine with their offerings, which were burned in Vesta's fire in preparation for the approaching harvest.

At the festival of Parilia (April 21), sheep were made to jump through a ring of burning straw or laurel, as a magical act of purifying the animals. The festival of Cerealia was held on April 19 by the priests of Ceres to promote the growth of grain sown in the fields. At the festival of Robigalia, held on April 25 in a grove, a red dog was sacrificed to prevent red rust from endangering the grain crops.

At least six festivals observed in August were devoted to the various phases of the harvest. There were also six festivals in December, including the festival of Saturnalia, when friends and relatives exchanged gifts. Perhaps the most famous of the festivals was that of Lupercalia, which started with the sacrifice of several goats and a dog and concluded with the priests running in two bands around the walls of the Palatine settlement, striking women who suffered from sterility with thongs cut from the skins of the sacrificed animals.

STUDY QUESTIONS

1. Relate the legendary account of the founding of Rome.
2. Discuss the significance of the concept of *numen*.
3. What were the roles of the deities Jupiter and Mars?
4. Describe the functions of the *sacerdos* and the *flamen*.
5. What were the connection between magicians, astrologers, and state officials?
6. What do we know about the private associations?
7. Analyze the significance of the practice of emperor worship.
8. What transpired when the Romans came in contact with the Greeks?
9. Describe the mystery cult of Cybele and Attis. Make specific reference to its similarity with Christianity.
10. Discuss the worship of the Egyptian deities Isis and Serapis by the Romans.
11. What were the striking parallels between Mithraism and Christianity?
12. Explain the role of the vestal priestesses.
13. Who were the *salii* and what did they perform?

Suggested Reading

Cumont, Franz V. M. *The Oriental Religions in Roman Paganism.* New York: Dover, 1956.

Feeney, Denis. *Literature and Religion at Rome: Cultures, Contexts and Beliefs.* New York: Cambridge University Press, 1998.

Ferguson, John. *The Religions of the Roman Empire.* London: Thames & Hudson, 1970.

Hornum, Michael B. *Nemesis, The Roman State and the Games.* Vol. 117, *Religions in the Graeco-Roman World.* Leiden, The Netherlands: E. J. Brill, 1993.

Orlin, Eric M. *Temples, Religion, and Politics in the Roman Republic.* Leiden, The Netherlands: E. J. Brill, 1997.

Spaeth, Barbette Stanley. *The Roman Goddess Ceres.* Austin: University of Texas Press, 1996.

Takacs, Sarolta A. *Isis and Sarapis in the Roman World*. Vol. 124, *Religions in the Graeco-Roman World*. Leiden, The Netherlands: E. J. Brill, 1995.

Ulansey, David. *The Origins of the Mithraic Mysteries: Cosmology and Salvation in the Ancient World*. New York/Oxford: Oxford University Press, 1989.

Vermaseren, Maarten Jozef. *Cybele and Attis: The Myth and the Cult*. London: Thames & Hudson, 1977.

Watson, Alan. *The State, Law, and Religion: Pagan Rome*. Athens, Ga.: University of Georgia Press, 1992.

Witt, Reginald Eldred. *Isis in the Graeco-Roman World*. London: Thames & Hudson, 1971.

12 Zoroastrianism

Zoroastrianism emerged in ancient Persia (modern Iran) from the Indo-Iranian, or Aryan, faith. Today, Zoroastrianism is the religion of a tiny ethno-religious community that still resides in its ancient homeland in modern Iran. Some Zoroastrians migrated from Iran during the ninth and tenth centuries CE and settled on the west coast of India. Their number at present is still small, and they are popularly known as *Parsees* or *Parsis,* a name that refers to the province of Fars in ancient Persia. Since the rise of European imperialism, Zoroastrians from both Iran and India have migrated and established small communities in almost every major city in the West.

ZOROASTER

Traditional Account

Of all the great religious founders, Zoroaster is certainly one of the least known. Modern scholars have tried to reconcile evidence from a variety of sources, such as the traditional Zoroastrian writings, ancient Greek sources, and Islamic sources dating from the ninth century CE, but their efforts add up to no more than speculation. The dates proposed for his birth range from 1400 BCE to 500 BCE, and prevailing ideas about his birthplace range from eastern to western Iran.

The accounts of Zoroaster's infancy and later life abound with miracles. Of his mother it is said that at the age of fifteen she conceived and gave virgin birth to Zoroaster. He is said to have been born laughing instead of weeping and, as an infant, to have escaped numerous attempts on his life through the intervention of animals. First, a bull stood over him to protect him from the hooves of cattle; then, a stallion saved him

Zoroastrianism

BCE

c. 5000   Rise of civilizations in the ancient Near East
c. 628   Traditional birth date of Zoroaster (d. 551 BCE)
   550   Persian empire established by Cyrus II
   538   Jews allowed to return to Jerusalem by Cyrus II
   490   Darius I defeated by the Greeks at Marathon
   330   Darius III defeated by Alexander the Great

CE

   224   Sassanid Empire (ended 651) established by Ardashir
   651   Fall of Sassanian Empire to Muslim Arabs
  800s   Flight of Zoroastrians to India
c. 1010   Completion of the *Shah-nama* by Firdausi (Ferdowsi)
 1500s   Beginning European awareness of Zoroastrians
 1600s   Composition of the *Quissa-i Sanjan* by Bahman, son of Kaikobad
 1700s   Beginning of Zoroastrian immigration to the West

in the same way from being trampled by horses; finally, a she-wolf accepted him among her cubs instead of devouring him.

Whatever his father's own career may have been, Zoroaster was trained to be a priest. It is said that he left home at the age of twenty against the wishes of his parents. He married three times and had three sons and three daughters (three daughters and a son from the first marriage and two sons from the second). Ten years after leaving home, Zoroaster's quest for truth culminated in several visions or revelations.

This first vision occurred, it seems, while Zoroaster was attending the celebration of the spring festival and, according to ancient custom, was fetching water at dawn from a nearby river for a special ritual. As he was returning to the bank from midstream, he saw the shining figure of the archangel Vohu Mana (Good Intention), who led Zoroaster into the presence of Ahura Mazda (Wise Lord) and the five Immortals, where he was taught the cardinal principles of the "true religion." That vision was repeated a number of times, and on each occasion Zoroaster saw, heard, or felt conscious of Ahura Mazda. Tradition states that Zoroaster's religious experience led him to believe that he was commissioned by Ahura Mazda to preach the true religion.

His mission, therefore, started at the age of thirty. During the next ten years, he was successful in converting only one person, his cousin Maidhyoimah. Those long, discouraging years brought Zoroaster into sharp conflict with the priests of his day. His eventual triumph began with his conversion of King Vishtaspah and the royal court in Bactria (in northwestern Iran). As the story goes, three days of debate at a great assembly convened at the royal palace confirmed the hostility of priests against Zoroaster. The functionaries were instrumental in getting Zoroaster thrown into prison, where he remained until he won the willing ear of King Vishtaspah by curing the king's favorite horse of paralysis. The event, which, according to Zoroastrian tradition, took place when the prophet was forty-two years old, marked a turning point in Zoroaster's career. So impressed were King Vishtaspah, his queen, and the entire royal court that they all accepted Zoroaster's teachings wholeheartedly. Such recognition helped to spread his doctrines as far as China.

Practically nothing is known of the way in which Zoroaster's teachings spread. Some evidence suggests that Zoroaster organized, perhaps in an informal way, a fellowship or brotherhood of his followers, called the Maga brotherhood. Most authorities consider the Maga group to be the Magi (from which the word *magic* is derived), a powerful, hereditary priestly class probably of Median origin. Their role, which entitled them to religious and political privileges, was important. They performed the coronation of the king, accompanied the army to celebrate all religious duties, interpreted dreams, and educated the young men. Matthew, one of the Christian gospel writers, states that the Magi—the "wise men from the east"—traveled to Jerusalem to worship the newborn Jesus by following the course of a star (Matthew 2:1–12).

Zoroaster's Message

Zoroaster tried to reform the traditional pantheistic religion into which he was born by promoting the supremacy of one God, Ahura Mazda. With Ahura Mazda as the only God, traditions hitherto associated in the Indo-Iranian cosmology with many gods and devils became subordinate to the one God. And perhaps without losing all their primitive meaning, those traditions were incorporated by Zoroaster into the powers and characteristics he attributed to Ahura Mazda. Furthermore, Zoroaster welded the elements of tension that lay dispersed in the ancient myths of gods, demons, and monsters into a single universal conflict, good versus evil, in which God and humans took part together.

Witnessing the religious corruption of his day, Zoroaster was deeply offended by two types of ritual practiced by the priests: animal sacrifice and the rite of consuming the juice of the sacred *haoma* plant. Those rituals must have been an unseemly and orgiastic affair; the slaying of a bull or an ox was accompanied by shouts of joy by priests intoxicated through excessive use of the juice of the *haoma* plant. Zoroaster denounced the "filthy drunkenness" of the priests and their attempts to deceive the people. He condemned them as followers of the *daevas* (malevolent gods), obstructors of the "Good Mind," and frustrators of the divine purpose of Ahura Mazda. Knowing that his challenge of the priests would provoke hostility and invite persecution, he still spoke courageously against them, calling them willfully blind and deaf and accusing them of hindering "cultivation, peace and perfection of creation through their own deeds and doctrines" (Yasna 51.14). Zoroaster's

Worshipers offer homage and prayers at home in front of
a small altar. The altar includes the image of the prophet
Zoroaster and the fire urn, symbol of Ahura Mazda's power.
Courtesy of *Illustrated Weekly* of India.

vigorous, radical preaching earned him the enmity of many, because
his reform meant, for the priests, the loss of their lifework and their
income.

Against a pantheon of deities, some benevolent, others malevolent,
Zoroaster maintained the supremacy of Ahura Mazda. For Zoroaster,
Ahura Mazda, the lord of life and wisdom, was "the first and also the
last" (Yasna 31.8). Believing his God to be holy, eternal, just, omniscient,
the primeval being, the creator of all, and the origin of all goodness,
Zoroaster chose Ahura Mazda as his sole master.

Furthermore, Zoroaster saw humanity as divided into two opposing parties: the *asha-vants* (followers of truth), who were just and God-
fearing, and the *dreg-vants* (followers of evil), among whom were
classed all evil rulers, evil doers, evil speakers, those of evil conscience,
and evil thinkers. What Zoroaster saw on earth as basic dualism he
projected to the whole cosmos. He came to the conclusion that the fundamental tension between good and evil existed in the material as well
as in the spiritual sphere. Against a transcendental good mind stood
an evil mind, against a good spirit stood an evil spirit, and so on. On
every level a choice had to be made. That insistence on freedom of
choice was a marked characteristic of Zoroaster's teachings, which was

distinguished not by the ethical dualism of good versus evil but by the importance of the individual as an arbiter between them. Each individual, he taught, was ultimately faced with making a choice between good and evil.

Side by side with the fundamental principle of freedom of choice, Zoroaster taught that goodness was its own reward and that happiness and misery were the consequences of a person's good and evil deeds. He anticipated a final consummation of creation, at which time Ahura Mazda would come with his "three powers," sinners would surrender deceit (evil, lies) into the hands of truth, and eternal joy would reign everywhere. Moreover, the souls of humans would be judged at the "bridge of the requiter," where the just would receive their eternal reward, the wicked their final doom. Hell was the abode of all evil rulers, evil doers, evil speakers, those of evil conscience, and evil thinkers. Heaven was the abode of the righteous, who would be blessed by Ahura Mazda with perfection and immortality.

THE SPREAD OF ZOROASTRIANISM

The paucity and varied nature of sources make it difficult, if not impossible, to describe the historical development of Zoroastrianism. Indeed, the evidence is so scanty and so obscure that it is impossible to determine what the status of Zoroastrianism was. All that is known is that Alexander's conquest of Persia (c. 330 BCE) was a disaster for Zoroastrianism. Alexander is remembered in Zoroastrian tradition as "the accursed Iskander" (Iskander = Alexander) because Alexander burned the royal capital at Persepolis and destroyed the definitive copy of the Zoroastrian scripture, which had been meticulously transcribed in gold on thousands of oxhides.

The lack of evidence makes the subsequent history of Zoroastrianism as difficult to reconstruct as its early history. In 651, the entire Persian Empire fell to the Muslim Arabs without much resistance. Zoroastrian tradition speaks of "the ruin and devastation that come from the Arabs," but how and why such disasters occurred are not known. At any rate, a minority group of Zoroastrians, called by Muslims *gabar* or *gavour* ("infidels"), survives to this day in modern Iran.

Another small group of Zoroastrians left Iran in the eighth and ninth centuries to seek asylum in India. As descendants and survivors of the ancient Persians, they were (and still are) called Parsees (or Parsis). Most settled in Bombay and neighboring areas, and like their Iranian counterparts, they have managed to survive to this day. Unfortunately, nothing is known of the long history of Zoroastrianism in either India or Iran after the conquest by Islam. Only after the arrival of Europeans in India in the sixteenth century did Western scholars become aware of the surviving adherents of Zoroastrianism in India. For centuries, that small group of Zoroastrians had resisted assimilation. Clinging tenaciously to their religion and observing many of its ancient rites and ceremonies, they succeeded in the struggle to preserve their religion from near extinction.

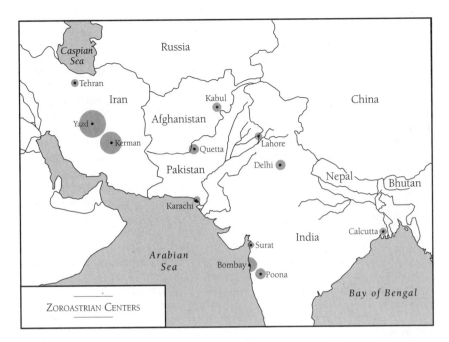

Source: David S. Noss and John B. Noss, *A History of the World's Religions*, 9th ed. (New York: Macmillan, 1994). Reprinted by permission of Prentice-Hall/Pearson Higher Education.

Today, Zoroastrianism in India and elsewhere (except Iran) has been irresistibly drawn into the unsettling orbit of Western technology and influence. Like most other faiths, Zoroastrianism is subject to the transforming power of western ideas, particularly those of agnosticism and skepticism. Ancient customs are being questioned and traditional patterns threatened. As a result, conservative and reformist forces are in conflict, with neither side winning a clear victory.

ZOROASTRIAN SACRED TEXTS

The Avesta

The collection of sacred writings of the Zoroastrian religion is known as the Avesta, which comprise four principal groups of writings.

- The Yasna is a collection of prayers and liturgical formulas that contains the Gathas, a group of hymns believed to have been written by the prophet Zoroaster.

- The Visparat was composed in honor of and as an invocation to the celestial lords.

- The Videvdat (Vendidad) is a body of writings primarily concerned with ritual purification.

- The Khorde Avesta ("Smaller Avesta") is a book of daily prayers that includes the Yashts, a collection of hymns addressed to individual deities and epic narrations concerning kings and heroes.

The entire Avesta is believed to have been written over a period of a thousand years. The earliest portion probably was composed before the sixth century BCE and the most recent excerpts around the fourth century CE. According to tradition, the Avesta once comprised a vast literature, only a small part of which survives.

The Gathas fill seventeen out of the seventy-two chapters of the Yasna. Scholars believe those seventeen chapters are older than the writings in the rest of the Avesta, and they have found a close link between the language and history of the Gathas and the language and history of the Rig Vedas (the collection of sacred texts of ancient India and the oldest known documents in Sanskrit). That discovery seems to support the belief of many scholars that both writings have a common cultural and linguistic origin. Although the generally accepted view is that the Gathas represent the words of Zoroaster, the opinions of experts differ widely. Some think that Zoroaster composed and wrote the Gathas; others think that the Gathas were composed in the main by him but that his disciples added occasional verses. Still others suggest that the Gathas, although originally composed by Zoroaster, were preserved only in memory for centuries before they were written down. Whatever theory is held about their composition, the general view is that the Gathas are the only authentic documents concerning the life and teachings of Zoroaster.

Other Writings

In addition to the Avesta, there is an extensive literature, probably dating from the ninth century CE, that deals with religious subjects. Of the at least fifty-five known works, the most important are the Bundahishn, which deal with cosmogony, mythology, and history; the Dinkard (Denkart), which deal with religious doctrines, customs, traditions, history, and literature; the Datastan-i Denik, which are the religious opinions of the high priest Manushkihar written in response to ninety-two questions; the Zad-sparam, written by the younger brother of Manushkihar; the Shayast Na-shayast, a miscellaneous compilation of laws and customs concerning sin and impurity; and the Arday-Viraf Namak, or Book of Arday-Viraf, which describes his visit to heaven and hell while in a trance.

ZOROASTRIAN TEACHINGS

God

The supreme god of the Zoroastrian faith is known as Ahura Mazda (or Ohrmazd, meaning "Wise Lord"). He is self-created, omniscient, omnipresent, holy, invisible, and beyond human conceptualization. He is neither begotten, nor is there anyone who is his equal. He is, as his name implies, the Wise Lord, the Most Knowing One, and the Most Far-Seeing One (Yasht 1.7, 8, 15).

Ahura Mazda's infinite wisdom, or omniscience, is absolute, so he knows everything before it happens. Consequently, he is all-pervading, and there is no conceivable place where he is not. He is also changeless, first and foremost the most perfect being, the greatest, the most powerful, the one who was, is, and will be forever.

Ahura Mazda is the creator of the universe, the author of the celestial and terrestrial worlds. He brought forth rivers, trees, forests, wind, clouds, sun, moon, stars, and the seasons. He guards heaven and earth from falling, and everything follows the sequence he has ordained from the beginning. He created the human body and endowed it with life, mind, and conscience. He is the dispenser of every material good and spiritual blessing, because it is in his nature to be beneficent to all his creation.

As father and creator of all good things, Ahura Mazda created the two realms: the spiritual *(menog)*, which cannot be seen, and the material *(getig)*, which can be seen and is liable to destruction. Of Ahura Mazda's mundane creations *(getig)*, the first was the sky, the second water, the third earth, the fourth vegetation, the fifth animals, the sixth mankind, and the seventh fire. Ahura Mazda's spiritual powers *(menog)* consist of a group of six celestial beings (sometimes thought of as archangels) called Amesha Spenta (or Amahraspand, meaning "Holy Immortal" or "Bountiful Immortal"), who stand second in rank to Ahura Mazda and who, with Ahura Mazda at their head, form a heptad (mystical potency is attributed to the number seven).

Ahura Mazda is synonymous with light, and the sun is spoken of as his most beautiful form — in fact, it is called his eye. "Radiant" and "glorious" are the two epithets most frequently used in the Avesta as an opening invocation to the divinity. The first Yasht, which is dedicated to Ahura Mazda, enumerates seventy-four attributes, all descriptive of his wisdom, power, justice, righteousness, and mercy.

Satan

In contrast to the divine forces created by Ahura Mazda to represent the principles of goodness are the forces created by Ahriman ("the Adversary," or Satan) to represent the principles of evil. Evil, in the Zoroastrian faith, is considered to have as independent and as complete an existence as good. Both exist entirely separate from each other and are primeval. Good does not originate from evil, nor evil from good. The fundamental purpose of all human beings is to maintain the well-being of the created order of Ahura Mazda. He is absolutely good and, therefore, cannot be considered the creator of any kind of evil, natural or moral. All the evil in the world is the creative work of Ahriman.

Ahriman, then, is considered to be the inveterate foe of the supreme God, Ahura Mazda, and the origin of all suffering, affliction, bodily deformities, evil, and death. His place was originally in the pit of endless darkness, but in the beginning of Ahura Mazda's creation of the universe, he rushed upon the entire world to bring harm and destruction. For every one of Ahura Mazda's benevolent spiritual powers, Ahriman conjured up an opposing malevolent power of equivalent rank to counterbalance every good creation of Ahura Mazda with an evil one of his own. Thus, the phenomenal world consists of pairs of conflicting opposites: light/dark, truth/falsehood, health/sickness, rain/drought, pure/impure, good creatures/noxious creatures, life/death, heaven/hell.

Because Ahriman is not omniscient, he cannot foresee his own final defeat. And because he is an after-thinker, he knows nothing of events to come. He is stupid, ill-informed, totally ignorant, and blind. Ahriman was not even aware of the existence of Ahura Mazda until he arose from his eternal place in the abyss.

Ahriman prompts all human beings to perform evil deeds and instigates discord, violence, and licentiousness. He deceives human beings and obstructs them from hearing and accepting the message of Ahura Mazda. He is a father of lies, a murderer from the beginning and the source of death. He is an oppressor of mankind's happiness as well as the inveterate enemy of Ahura Mazda. He rules over a large host of evil spirits, all of whom will be defeated eventually in a decisive battle.

One of many of Ahriman's malicious acts was to infest the earth with noxious creatures, such as snakes, scorpions, lizards, and frogs. Hence, Zoroastrians consider killing a noxious creature a meritorious deed. Ahriman also introduced evil into vegetation by producing weeds, thorns, poison ivy, and many other harmful elements of nature. But little does he realize that his evil existence will cease at the hands of Ahura Mazda when the end of his allotted time arrives.

Cosmic Dualism

The Zoroastrian concept of dualism is the dualism of two opposing personified forces in the universe: a good god and an evil adversary. That type of thinking can be described as cosmic *dualism,* that is, the entire cosmos — heaven, earth, and the underworld, along with their inhabitants — is involved in the opposition between the powers of good and evil.

Ahura Mazda personifies the principle and the source of all good; Ahriman embodies the principle and the source of all evil. The struggle of Ahura Mazda and Ahriman in Zoroastrian teachings extends over the entire seen and unseen world. The world is a great battlefield in which the beneficent powers of Ahura Mazda ceaselessly contend with the baleful forces of Ahriman. Light struggles with darkness, the vivifying waters with drought and barrenness, warmth with icy conditions, useful animals with beasts of prey, industrious peasants and herdsmen with marauding nomads, civilized people with barbarians; the destructive forces in both nature and society are not guided by chance or blind laws but by the warring of benevolent and malevolent powers.

To Zoroastrians, therefore, the universe is an eternal battleground where a pair of coexistent, divine, and warring principles combat. In every sphere and in every situation that demands a decision between two opposites, human beings have to make a choice between two principles. The consequences alone imply that the principle of good is more powerful than the principle of evil and, therefore, that Ahura Mazda eventually triumphs.

Zoroastrian fire temple with the winged symbol of Ahura Mazda in Bombay, India.
Courtesy of Yazdi Antia.

Human Choice

According to Zoroastrian teaching, the implication of cosmic dualism is that human beings are not merely passive spectators of the war between Ahura Mazda's and Ahriman's hosts of allies, on which human beings' fortunes and their very existence depend. Every individual is by choice engaged in the cosmic warfare contending for the defeat of Ahriman and the ultimate triumph of Ahura Mazda. The whole conflict is a war of moral choices: right or wrong, truth or falsehood, justice or injustice. In one sense, then, human life is regarded as a war, a personal defense against evil spirits. Those persons who pray to Ahura Mazda daily and live a pious life; who are humble, patient, truth speakers and pure of heart; who possess virtues and good characteristics; and who avoid wrath, greediness, jealousy, enmity, lying, stealing, laziness, and asceticism—they establish the proper relationship with the spiritual powers and maintain the purity and well-being of the created order of Ahura Mazda. Asceticism, renunciation, celibacy, and fasting have no place in Zoroastrian teaching.

That means the whole human drama—indeed, the ultimate purpose of existence—is reduced to just one element: choice. Every person is genuinely free to pursue either of two paths: good or evil. The freedom to choose between good and evil and the inevitable consequences of such a choice evolve from a moral triad and its evil opposite: purity of thoughts, words, and deeds versus impurity of thoughts, words, and deeds.

Eternal Destiny

The sum and substance of the moral triad also determines the fate of every individual after death. At death, according to Zoroastrianism, the soul of an individual stays with the body for three days. On the fourth day, the soul journeys to the place of judgment by crossing the Chinvat Bridge (possibly over an underground river and guarded by supernatural dogs), which spans the abyss of hell and leads to paradise on the other side. If the record of the soul's life on earth is represented in the balance by a weighty accumulation of good thoughts, words, and deeds, then the soul meets its own conscience in the shape of a "fair maiden" and crosses without difficulty to paradise. But if the reverse is the case, passage over the Chinvat Bridge becomes an entirely different experience for the soul. The bridge turns on its side, presenting a knife-edge footing like the edge of a sword; the soul perceives its own conscience in the shape of an "ugly hag" and plunges into the abyss of hell.

Paradise is a place of beauty, light, pleasant scents, and bliss to be enjoyed by those who adhere in life to the Zoroastrian moral and ceremonial teachings; hell is a place of horror, misery, darkness, evil smells, and suffering for those who violate in life the same Zoroastrian teachings. If the good and evil deeds done in life balance, the soul remains in an intermediate place called *hamestagan* (or *hamestagna* or *hamestakan;* the purgatory of Christianity) until the day of resurrection and final judgment. There the soul suffers no torment except the seasonal temperatures of heat and cold. That "limbo" state is conceived to be located in the region between heaven and earth and is of considerable discomfort but imposes no intense torture.

Neither the bliss of souls in heaven nor the torment of those in hell is regarded as a final state. When the appointed time arrives, three saviors—namely, Hushedar, Aushedar-Mah, and Saoshyant—will appear at intervals of a millennium to herald the Messianic Age. The three saviors will bring to completion and perfection the work of reclaiming humanity from evil, and they will regenerate the universe. Each savior will be a direct descendant of Zoroaster and born through a virgin birth. Each will be attended with portents and miraculous signs.

The appearance of Hushedar will be preceded by successively degenerating regimes. All people will become deceivers, and affection will depart from the world; brothers, even father and son, will hate each other. All sacred rites and ceremonies will be treated with contempt. Wrath and avarice will precede total apostasy. Then, in those horrible days, the sun and the moon will show signs; there will be frightful earthquakes and terrible storms. Wars and battles will greatly increase, and many soldiers will be slain (cf. Matthew 25 and Revelation 21–22).

However, from the moment of the first savior's appearance to the end of the period of the last savior, righteousness will prevail more and more in the world. Before the arrival of the day of the resurrection of the dead and of the renovation of the universe, the ideal teachings of Zoroaster — "the good religion" of Ahura Mazda — will be spread to the ends of the world. All evil and wickedness will perish, because the entire human race will embrace righteousness by practicing "the good religion." All those who happen to be living at that time will join the ranks of those resurrected from the dead.

When the appointed time arrives, all the dead, righteous and wicked alike, will arise on the spot where they died. Thus, earth and sea will surrender their dead, and all will be gathered before the judgment seat. The souls of both the righteous and the wicked will be reunited with their bodies — the bones being demanded back from the earth, the blood from water, the hair from plants, and the life from fire — so they are reconstituted once again in their original materials. Then, the reconstituted individuals will assemble in one place and know of each other's deeds performed on earth. Next, the righteous and the wicked will be separated from each other and sent in their reconstituted forms to heaven or hell for three days. The wicked will be cast into the depths of hell, where frightful punishments, torture, filth, and darkness will be their share. The righteous, on the other hand, will enter heaven and enjoy every imaginable bliss in the realm of endless light. All those in whom good or evil does not outweigh the other will remain in the intermediary place called *hamestagan*.

Three days later, both the righteous and the wicked will be purified by walking through molten metal. All will speak in one tongue and proclaim their praise to Ahura Mazda and his entities. Then an ambrosia of immortality will be given to all. As a result, adults will be restored as men and women of forty, children as youths of fifteen. Life will be restored back to its pristine state, with each man having his wife and his offspring without procreation.

In the meantime, Ahriman will be able to mobilize a vast army for the great and final Armageddon battle. There will be so much slaughter that the rivers of blood will reach the girths of the horses. Nevertheless, the result will be the ultimate triumph of Ahura Mazda. Then will come the great conflagration, in which the world will burn in a fantastic holocaust. Ahriman and his followers, including the inhabitants of the pit of hell, will be burned and annihilated. Everything will be destroyed, and a new universe will come into being. Finally, there will follow an eternity of bliss, and the will of Ahura Mazda shall prevail supreme.

The striking resemblances (and differences) between some characteristic Zoroastrian teachings and practices and those of Judaism, Christianity, and Islam are obvious. Evidence of the similarities between Zoroastrianism and Judaism, Christianity, and Islam are diverse and range from theological to ethical to eschatological matters. Of particular interest are the following shared concepts and beliefs:

- God and Satan (or the devil)
- Angels and demons
- Heaven and hell (and purgatory in Christianity)
- Resurrection of the body and life everlasting

- Individual judgment at death and cosmic last judgment
- Arrival of a Messiah
- Cosmic events during the end of the world
- The Armageddon battle followed by a millennium period

ZOROASTRIAN OBSERVANCES

Zoroastrians observe a number of rituals and ceremonies associated with the different stages of life, seasonal feasts, religious anniversaries, and historical events. No Zoroastrian ritual or religious ceremony is complete without the presence of the fire.

Sacred Fire

Atash, or fire, is an important, central symbol in Zoroastrianism. For that reason, Zoroastrians maintain a perpetual sacred fire both in their homes and in the fire temples. Devout Zoroastrians attend the fire temple daily, but many believers are satisfied with four visits a month. In the *Atash Niyayesh* (fire prayer or litany), fire is invoked as "worthy of sacrifice, worthy of prayer, in the dwellings of human beings." From the time of the Indo-Iranians to the present, the house fire has remained a cult object. Each Zoroastrian family maintains a house fire in a pot or an urn. Prayers are made regularly in the presence of the house fire, because fire, like the sun, represents divine purity, light, power, and warmth. No sin is as grave as that of extinguishing one's fire.

Rites of Passage

Zoroastrian rituals associated with the important points in life (normally identified with rites of passage) consist of prebirth, birth, initiation, marriage, and death.

On the occasion of the completion of the fifth and seventh months of pregnancy, most Zoroastrian households light a lamp of clarified butter (*ghee*). On the birth of a child, a lamp is lighted again and kept burning for at least three days in the room where the mother of the child is confined. Some households keep the lamp burning for ten days while others maintain it for forty.

The first birthday of a child also marks an important occasion. On that day, the child is taken to the fire temple, where during a religious ceremony blessings are invoked and spent ashes from the sacred fire are placed on the child's forehead. A special ceremony, known as *naojote,* takes place for each child between the ages of seven and ten. *Naojote* is an initiation ceremony that makes a child responsible for honoring Zoroastrian religious observances. The ceremony, which usually, though not necessarily, takes place in the home, consists essentially in investing the child with a sacred shirt (*sudreh* or *sadre*) and a sacred thread (*kusti*), which he or she is to wear throughout life. Prior to investiture, the child is given a ritual bath in sacred or holy water by the officiating priests and then taken to a room where parents, relatives,

The *naojote* ceremony, in which a youth is made responsible for honoring the Zoroastrian faith. The rite of investiture with the sudreh and the kusti is performed by the Zoroastrian priest.
Courtesy of Yazdi Antia.

friends, and various priests are assembled. There, the child sits facing eastward (the direction of the rising sun) on a low stool in front of one of the officiating priests. The ceremony includes recitation of various prayers, declaration of the Zoroastrian faith, the drinking of a few drops of consecrated cow's or ox's urine (now often replaced by a soft drink), and the child's investiture with the sacred shirt and thread. The entire ceremony ends with a festive banquet in honor of the Zoroastrian initiate.

The institution of marriage offers yet another occasion for celebrating an important religious ceremony. On the day of the wedding, the bride and the bridegroom take ritual baths. The ceremony itself generally is performed in the evening, shortly after sunset. Just as light and darkness are united at twilight, so do the bride and the groom unite to share prosperity and adversity, happiness and grief. The officiating priests perform the ceremony of union, which includes symbolic rituals, the exchange of vows, prayers, admonitions, and benedictions. All the assembled guests are then entertained at a marriage feast.

Religious observances associated with death and disposal of the corpse are among the most difficult for Zoroastrians to implement outside their homeland. Zoroastrians who do not live in India or Iran are forced to conform to local conditions and usually choose the crematorium rather than the cemetery. Wherever possible, they observe the following sequence of solemn ritual. First, the corpse is placed on slabs of stone in the house. Next, a "four-eyed" dog (i.e., one with a spot over each eye) is brought to the corpse; such dogs are thought to act as living intermediaries between the seen and the unseen. The ritual is repeated five times a day for three days. Then the corpse is removed to the *dakhma,* or Tower of Silence, a massive, towerlike building generally raised on a hill or elevated ground, where the corpse is exposed to the sun and to flesh-eating birds. In India, the dry bones are then swept into a deep central well with deposits of lime and phosphorus. The reason for that dramatic practice is the Zoroastrian reverence for the elements: air, earth, fire, and water. Cremation pollutes air and fire, while burial contaminates the earth and water. Exposure to flesh-eating birds provides a convenient solution to the dilemma.

Purity-Impurity

The Zoroastrian concept of a universal conflict between the forces of good and evil is best exemplified in the ritual linked with the paired concept of purity and impurity, symbolizing good and evil, respectively. Ritual practices and symbolic gestures sustain the Zoroastrian doctrine of cosmic dualism, and there is no better evidence for that than the purificatory observances. They provide the best means whereby each Zoroastrian becomes the central protagonist in the cosmic battle between the forces of good and evil in the material world. Any violation of purity rites is considered an act of impurity, which furthers the cause of evil. That means that Zoroastrian acts of purification serve as a means to ensure on both a personal and a communal level the triumph of good over evil. In no way do the acts provide an expiation from sin—a notion central to Judaism, Christianity, and Islam. Zoroastrian purification ceremonies assist in vanquishing evil.

Zoroastrian purificatory rituals usually are grouped into three categories. The most important category is the *Bareshnum* (or *Barashnum i no shab*), which every devotee should undertake at least once in his or her lifetime. The next category comprises three rituals observed on special occasions: *Padyab, Nahn,* and *Riman.* The final category includes various acts to ensure a continuous state of personal and communal virtue and purity.

Certain bodily substances, such as hair, nails, skin, breath, saliva, blood, urine, feces, semen, and menstrual fluid, are considered to be impure once they leave or are separated from the body. Any contact with such severed substances (known as *hikhra* or *hixra,* meaning "excrement") renders a Zoroastrian ritually impure, thereby necessitating certain purificatory acts to return to a state of purity. Elaborate codes

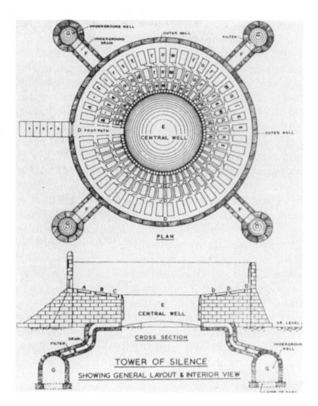

The Tower of Silence, a circular platform consisting of three rows of stone slabs. Row A is for men, row B is for women, and row C is for children. The path marked D is for corpsebearers. The corpses are placed in the tower, where the flesh and organs are consumed by vultures. The bones then dry and slip into the central well (E), where they mix with lime and phosphorus and disintegrate. The holes in the inner side of the well lead rainwater into four underground drains (F), which in turn lead into four underground wells (G), whose bottoms are covered with a thick layer of sand. A mixture of charcoal and sandstone, renewed from time to time, is placed at the end of each drain to purify the rainwater that flows over the bones.
Courtesy of *Illustrated Weekly* of India.

also exist to prevent food, utensils, clothing, and homes from contamination with severed substances.

Thus, there are specific rituals to be performed for cutting hair and paring nails. Indeed, a proper fulfillment of the ritual requires a proper disposal rite. Although variant forms of practices among Iranian and Indian Zoroastrians have continued into modern times, at present only priests and a few orthodox Zoroastrians still follow the elaborate ritualized order for trimming hair and paring nails. Most have discarded the prescribed rituals and now visit a professional barber or hairdresser, and pare their nails without any precautionary or purificatory acts.

Precautions still are taken to prevent the state and spread of impurity to the seven creations of Ahura Mazda (vegetation, animals, earth, water, metal, fire, and human beings) by breath and saliva. Naturally, measures against such impurity are hard to practice in everyday activities, but the release of breath and saliva must be controlled as much as possible to avoid contact with any sacred elements or substances. Safeguards are strictly enforced during religious rituals. Every priest engaged in a religious rite wears a white veil covering mouth and nose so as not to transmit any impurities released by his breath or spittle to the sacred elements.

All Zoroastrian purificatory acts, including the consecration and use of sacred elements and utensils, are ultimately directed to combat cosmic evil. That symbolic value has played a significant role in the survival of the Zoroastrian faith throughout the centuries. But it is also equally important to realize that purity practices, even in their simplified versions, have served—and still do serve—as a means of expressing symbolically the essential Zoroastrian doctrine of eschatology. Every Zoroastrian devotee yearns for the final salvation of the universe and the immortality of human beings. By performing purificatory rituals, every devotee is reminded that evil, pain, suffering, and death can be counteracted and transcended until the final day of victory when perfection and immortality shall reign forever.

Festivals

Zoroastrians observe numerous seasonal festivals, or *gahambars*. Tradition states that Zoroaster chose six *gahambars* as celebrations for his people. Today, Zoroastrians celebrate the Sada (Hundred Days feast), an ancient fire festival held nowadays close to a stream. Other Zoroastrian ceremonies mark the memory of the departed (similar to the Christian festival of All Souls' Day), the deities who preside over the Gathas and over each day and each month of the Zoroastrian year, the feast of waters, and the birthday and death of Zoroaster.

The dates of the religious festivals have caused a split among Zoroastrians. The Zoroastrian division is based on the religious calendar, not on different religious convictions. The dispute is centuries old and around 1730 caused a permanent schism. Currently, three groups celebrate Zoroastrian seasonal festivals at different periods of the year, based on differences in the calendars they recognize and in the ways they calculate time.

- The *Shenshahi* (Imperial) observe the New Year in autumn (August or September, by the Gregorian calendar).
- The *Qadimi* (Ancient) observe the New Year in summer (July or August).
- The *Fasli* (Seasonal) observe the New Year at the spring equinox (about March 21).

Zoroastrian priests performing the Yasna (dedication) ceremony within a demarcated area. Each priest wears a mouth veil to avoid contaminating the consecrated implements or the sacred fire with their breath.
Courtesy of the author.

The date of the observance of the New Year (Naw Ruz or Noruz) sets the dates for observing other festivals throughout the year. In spite of the differences in calendar and time reckoning, all three groups attach great religious importance to the Zoroastrian seasonal festivals.

STUDY QUESTIONS

1. Recount the traditional story of Zoroaster.
2. Discuss the teachings ascribed to Zoroaster.
3. Describe the fate of Zoroastrians from the early period to modern times.
4. Describe the collection of writings that attained the status of scripture.
5. What are the most important attributes of Ahura Mazda?
6. Describe the creative works of Ahriman.
7. Analyze the concept of cosmic dualism.

8. How is human choice understood in Zoroastrianism?

9. What is the fate of every individual after death?

10. Discuss the notion of the appearance of saviors at certain intervals.

11. Describe the significance of the sacred fire.

12. What ceremonies are associated with the rites of passage?

13. Discuss the value placed on the observances connected with purificatory acts.

Suggested Reading

Boyce, Mary (ed.). *Textual Sources for the Study of Zoroastrianism.* Chicago: University of Chicago Press, 1984.

―――. *Zoroastrians: Their Religious Beliefs and Practices,* 3rd ed. London: Routledge & Kegan Paul, 1988.

―――. *A History of Zoroastrianism.* 3 vols. Leiden, The Netherlands: E. J. Brill, 1975–1991.

―――. *Zoroastrianism: Its Antiquity and Constant Vigour.* Costa Mesa, Calif.: Mazda Publishers, 1992.

Choksy, Jamsheed Kairshasp. *Purity and Pollution in Zoroastrianism: Triumph over Evil.* Austin: University of Texas Press, 1989.

Gnoli, Gherardo. *Zoroaster's Time and Homeland: A Study on the Origins of Mazdeism and Related Problems.* Naples: Istituto Universitario Orientale, 1980.

Hinnells, John R. *Zoroastrianism and the Parsis.* London: Ward Lock Educational, 1981.

―――. *Zoroastrians in Britain.* Oxford: Clarendon Press, 1996.

Luhrmann, Tanya M. *The Good Parsi: The Fate of a Colonial Elite in a Postcolonial Society.* Cambridge: Harvard University Press, 1996.

Mehr, Farhang. *The Zoroastrian Tradition: An Introduction to the Ancient Wisdom of Zarathustra.* Rockport, Mass.: Element, 1991.

Mistree, Khojeste P. *Zoroastrianism: An Ethnic Perspective.* Bombay: Zoroastrian Studies, 1982.

Nigosian, Solomon A. *The Zoroastrian Faith. Tradition and Modern Research.* Montreal: McGill-Queen's University Press, 1993.

Pangborn, Cyrus R. *Zoroastrianism: A Beleaguered Faith.* New York: Advent Books, 1983.

Williams, Ron G. *Ritual Art and Knowledge: Aesthetic Theory and Zoroastrian Ritual.* Columbia, S.C.: University of South Carolina Press, 1993.

Zaehner, Robert Charles. *The Dawn and Twilight of Zoroastrianism.* London: Weidenfeld & Nicolson, 1961.

13 Judaism

Judaism, one of the oldest surviving religions, originated in the Middle East sometime during the middle of the second millennium BCE. It is practiced today by millions of Jews living both in Israel and all over the world. To understand the religion of Judaism, we need to keep in mind the following important points.

First, the geographical environment and the political situation shaped the thought patterns and culture of the Jewish people. In other words, historical events were — and still are — crucial to the formation of the religion of Judaism.

Second, Jews and Judaism have survived assimilation and proscription since the beginning of recorded history. It is one factor that makes the Jewish people unique.

Third, Jews consider themselves direct descendants of Abraham, with whom God established a *Covenant*. The significance of that concept is clear: Jews consider Judaism to be an extension of biblical religion and think of themselves as successors or inheritors of the "Chosen People" recorded in the Tanakh (Jewish scriptures; known as the Old Testament by Christians). One cannot penetrate into the mind and spirit of Judaism without a proper understanding of the concept of Covenant. From biblical days to the modern period, historical events have always been understood in terms of that unique Covenant between God and the Jewish people.

Judaism, like Shinto and Hinduism, has no identifiable founder analogous to most other religions (e.g., Buddhism, Christianity, Islam). The Jewish people consider Abraham their ancestral "father" who obeyed the divine command and Moses the one who received and transmitted the divine Torah ("Instruction" or "Guidance"). The real question is not who is the founder of Judaism. Rather, it is who are the Jewish people. When, where, and how did they originate in history?

Judaism

BCE

c. 5000 Rise of civilizations in ancient Near East

c. 1700 Abraham's migration from Mesopotamia to Egypt

c. 1275 Exodus of Jews from Egypt

c. 1000 Reign of David

   922 Northern kingdom separated upon King Solomon's death

c. 750 Rise of the prophets

   721 Northern kingdom conquered by the Assyrians

   621 King Josiah's reform based on *Deuteronomy*

   585 Jerusalem destroyed; beginning of exilic period

   538 Jewish exiles allowed by Persian king to return to Jerusalem

c. 400 Final compilation of the *Torah*

   331 Alexander the Great enters Palestine

c. 200 Final compilation of *The Prophets*

   164 Maccabean uprising and rededication of the Temple

CE

    70 Destruction of Jerusalem and burning of temple by the Romans

c. 100 Final compilation of *The Writings*

  500s Completion of the Babylonian *Talmud*

  1075 Birth of Judah Halevi (d. 1141)

  1135 Birth of Maimonides (d. 1207)

  1187 Recapture of Jerusalem by Salah ed-din (Saladin) for Islam

  1698 Birth of Baal-Shem-Tov (d. 1760)

  1729 Birth of Moses Mendelssohn (d. 1786)

  1791 Granting of citizen rights to French Jews

  1860 Birth of Theodore Herzl (d. 1904)

  1941 Beginning of Jewish Holocaust (ended 1945)

  1948 Founding of the state of Israel

No single definition is broad enough to encompass all Jews. Strictly speaking, they are not a race. Most Jews are Caucasians, but there are Falasha (black) Jews, Chinese Jews, Japanese Jews, and Indo-Mexican Jews. Jews do not represent a nation in the full and proper sense of the word. Jews in Israel proudly refer to themselves as a nation, but there are no national ties that unite all Jews throughout the world. Israel is a Jewish nation just as Great Britain can be said to be a Christian nation and Iran an Islamic nation. True, most Jews share a sense of kinship — the legacy of a common history, a vast literature, and a sense of common destiny — but there are many Jews (and Irish and Italians) who feel more at home in Brazil, Canada, or the United States than they do in Israel (or Ireland or Italy). Jews represent no particular nation any more than Christians do.

Are Jews a religious group of people? Certainly a vast number of Jews adhere rigidly to their age-old faith and tradition, but there is also a large segment of Jews who have totally eliminated religion from the way they live.

Perhaps the most appropriate definition of the Jewish people is still the biblical one: *beth yisrael*, the House of Israel. The name implies family, a sense of kinship expressed in custom and practice, a sense of filial obligation and duty even amid quarrels and conflicts, and a sense of experiences shared, all of which have linked the Jewish people in a common tradition. The "father" of the common tradition of the House of Israel is none other than Abraham.

BIBLICAL TRADITION

Abraham

The early records of the religious history of Judaism date from the classical period of the ancient Israelites, a Semitic group that roamed the northern Arabian desert. Just as other nomadic groups lived in tribes structured with a chieftain in authority over the group's members, so around the second millennium BCE the patriarch Abraham and his people lived and traveled on the fringes of the desert, seeking pasture for their animals. They normally camped beside springs and oases, but because vegetation was sparse they had to be on the move continuously. Crossing and recrossing desert wastes of pebbles and shifting sand, they traveled in search of fruit, vegetation, and water.

Biblical tradition quite specifically identifies the beginnings of Jewish history with a series of *avot* (fathers or patriarchal figures): Abraham, Isaac, Jacob, and Jacob's twelve sons. Scholars have been tempted to establish a connection between the advent of Abraham and the incursion into Canaan (modern Israel) around 1900–1800 BCE of the Amorites, a Semitic group from western Asia. But the accuracy of events attributed to the *avot*, especially the question of their relationship to each other, has often been challenged. Some scholars consider Isaac, Jacob, and the rest as the direct descendants of a single clan head, Abraham. Others view the *avot* as tribal chiefs, not necessarily related, whose popular legends gradually developed into a single narrative.

Whatever the historical truth of the matter, biblical tradition holds that Abraham's God promised him and his descendants a permanent territory in an area inhabited by the Canaanites. So Abraham, along with the members of his tribe and their flocks and herds, emigrated to Canaan, the biblical name for modern Israel, the region between the Jordan River and the Mediterranean Sea. After Abraham's death, his son Isaac and then his grandson Jacob took his place. Then a terrible famine forced Jacob and his family into a second emigration, this time to Egypt.

Tradition records that everything went well in Egypt for several centuries, until the Egyptian throne was occupied by a pharaoh whose passion for building large cities and monumental temples led him to resort to forced labor and slavery. Among the people so enslaved were Jacob's descendants. They were delivered from bondage some time in the thirteenth century BCE by a leader called Moses, who claimed to have had a revelation from the God of the *avot*. The result was the Exodus, the departure of the Jews from Egypt, and their subsequent experience at Mount Sinai in the desert.

Moses

The story of Moses is the cornerstone of Jewish religion. Scholars — particularly Christian scholars — disagree dramatically in their views of the historicity of the traditional narrative of Moses and of subsequent events. Some maintain that much of the account is a later pious fabrication. Others argue that all the events occurred precisely as described. Still others insist that although much of the account was embellished in many ways by later editors, the memory of past experience is, in its major points, recorded correctly. Even the most skeptical critics, however, admit that *something* happened to give the Jewish people a new sense of destiny.

Tradition states that after centuries of living in Egypt, the Jewish population had grown to such a degree that the Egyptian government feared the Jews would become too numerous to control. Consequently, the pharaoh ordered that all male babies born to Jewish families be killed. Moses, who was born during that period (perhaps the thirteenth century BCE), was hidden at home for three months, until the consequences of discovery prompted his mother to set her baby adrift in a waterproof basket in the rushes along the Nile River. There he was discovered by the pharaoh's daughter, who reared him in her palace as her adopted son.

As a young man, Moses witnessed a scene that became a turning point in his life: an Egyptian beating a Jew. Moved by a sudden outburst of anger, he killed the Egyptian on the spot; soon after, Moses fled eastward and found refuge with a Midianite priest named Jethro. Eventually, he married one of Jethro's daughters, Zipporah.

A second turning point occurred while Moses was herding Jethro's flock of sheep near Mount Horeb. There he experienced the presence of a divine being in a burning bush — an incident that not only changed his life but that altered the destiny of his people in Egypt. The divinity charged Moses with bringing the Jews out of the land of their enslavement and taking them to the "promised land" — the land of the Canaanites, where their ancestors had lived. Moses was assured by the divine presence, or God, that he would receive all the power necessary to persuade the pharaoh to let the Jewish people go.

The Exodus

When Moses returned to Egypt, however, he found the pharaoh impervious to his pleas. Moses, directed by God, first threatened and then struck Egypt with nine terrible plagues in succession. Finally, the tenth plague, which struck and killed all the first-born sons of the Egyptians, including the pharaoh's, forced the pharaoh to let the Jews go. Only the Jewish children were "passed over" (remained unharmed), and to this day the incident is commemorated as the "night of the Passover" or the Passover feast.

Moses then led the Jews miraculously through the waters of the Red (or Reed) Sea and across the desert to the foot of Mount Horeb (sometimes referred to as Mount Sinai). The exact location of the mountain is still debated, but the events that followed are not.

The Covenant

With Moses acting as the intermediary, a confrontation between God and the Jews resulted in a solemn pact, commonly known as the Covenant. Tradition relates how Moses left the people at the foot of the mountain while he went up to communicate with God. Several days later, he returned with two stone tablets delivered to him by God and inscribed with the commandments of God, the familiar code known as the Ten Commandments.

THE TEN COMMANDMENTS

1. I am the Lord your God, who brought you out of the land of Egypt, out of the house of bondage. You shall have no other gods besides me.

2. You shall not make yourself a graven image, or any likeness of anything that is in heaven above, or that is in the earth beneath, or that is in the water under the earth; you shall not bow to them or serve them; for I the Lord your God am a jealous God, visiting the iniquity of the fathers upon the children to the third and fourth generation of those who hate me, but showing steadfast love to thousands of those who love me and keep my commandments.

3. You shall not take the name of the Lord your God in vain, for the Lord will not hold him guiltless who takes his name in vain.

4. Remember the Sabbath day, to keep it holy. Six days you shall labor, and do all your work; but the seventh day is a Sabbath to the Lord your God; in it you shall not do any work, you, or your son, or your daughter, your manservant, or your maidservant, or your cattle, or the sojourner who is within your gates; for in six days the Lord made heaven and earth, the sea, and all that is in them, and rested the seventh day, therefore the Lord blessed the Sabbath day and hallowed it.

5. Honor your father and your mother, that your days may be long in the land which the Lord your God gives you.

6. You shall not kill.

7. You shall not commit adultery.

8. You shall not steal.

9. You shall not bear false witness against your neighbor.

10. You shall not covet your neighbor's house; you shall not covet
your neighbor's wife, or his manservant, or his maidservant, or
his ox, or his ass, or anything that is your neighbor's. (Exodus
20:1–17; cf. Deuteronomy 5:6–21)

Tradition maintains that the Jews constructed a portable shrine,
known as the Tabernacle of God, within which stood a box or chest containing the two stone tablets marked with the terms of the Covenant.
As the Jews continued their journey, Moses was able to commune with
God in the interior of that portable shrine.

The Promised Land

When Moses finally led the Jews to the borders of Canaan, with the
intention of invading it, they lost courage and rebelled against both
Moses and God, bringing upon themselves years of wandering in the
wilderness. Only under Joshua, Moses' successor, did the Jews cross the
River Jordan into the promised land of Canaan.

The incursion into Canaan—the transition from a nomadic life to a
settled, agrarian one—coincided with the adoption of Canaanite gods
and practices. The traditional narrative of this period is characterized
by the theme of the Jewish people in pursuit of "foreign gods" and the
unhappy consequences of such misplaced devotion. Any ill that befell
the Jews was interpreted as God's punishment for attachment to
foreign gods. That the people did indeed worship other gods is unques-
tionable. Archeological discoveries and numerous biblical passages
attest to the willingness of the Jewish people to embrace the gods and
religious practices of the Canaanites and neighboring peoples.

The Jewish Kingdom

Eventually the Jewish people conquered the territories on the east bank
of the Jordan River. Around the eleventh century BCE, under King
David, they captured Jerusalem and extended their dominion over
various parts of Palestine. King Solomon, David's son and successor,
built a magnificent temple in Jerusalem and consolidated all religious
practices, such as prayers, sacrifices, and festivals, in that center.

The Jewish kingdom did not last long, however. A little over a century after its establishment, it split in two. The northern part, which was
called Israel and was the larger of the two, was destroyed by the Assyrians
in the eighth century BCE. The southern part, called Judah, survived until
the sixth century BCE, when it was destroyed by the neo-Babylonians
(better known as the Chaldeans). The era of the kings prior to the destruction of the Jewish kingdom did not purge Jewish religion of polytheism. On the contrary, the establishment of the monarchy gave rise to a
nobility that was highly influenced by Canaanite elements. The result
was an inevitable mixture of religious practices.

The rulers of the split kingdoms that succeeded Solomon's reign
invited an even wider acceptance of extraneous forms of worship and
occult practices. In the north, King Jeroboam introduced the worship of
two golden calves and established various occult rites and practices
that were quickly adopted by the people and by succeeding rulers,

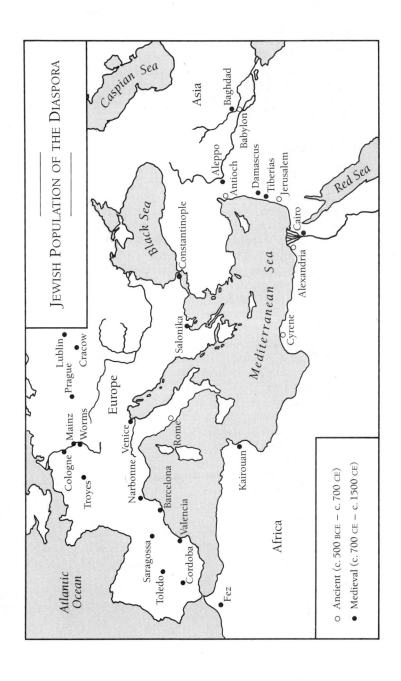

JEWISH POPULATION OF THE DIASPORA

○ Ancient (c. 500 BCE – c. 700 CE)

● Medieval (c. 700 CE – c. 1500 CE)

including Jehu and Omri. The policies of those monarchs and the willingness of the people to incorporate the religious practices of their neighbors are well documented in the biblical records (e.g., 2 Kings 17:7–18; 21:1–7).

The failure of the reforms attempted by both King Hezekiah and King Josiah indicates how deeply rooted was belief in the efficacy of magical practices and divinatory arts. Many feared, worshiped, and, with the help of occult practitioners, offered sacrifices with libations to numerous deities and demons to avert or mitigate plagues, diseases, and all other mishaps.

Role of the Prophets

The chief and most articulate critics of rival cults and factions were the prophets, whose role within Jewish society grew in importance. Their deep concern with the social systems, religious institutions, and ritual practices of their time led them to assume responsibility for the character and development of the Jewish religion. The prophets were a diverse group. Some were strong individualists; others were members of organized groups. Some restricted their activities to the role of experts delivering oracles; others accepted the challenge and the risk of delivering moral judgments. Some were associated with the royal courts; others openly revolted against the ruling king. Some were ecstatic; others opposed ecstasy. Some were highly regarded and respected; others were objects of suspicion or contempt.

One band of ecstatic prophets seems to have moved about the country and played various musical instruments. Another prophetic band lived together in semimonastic fashion, taking meals in common and living together. The size of the communal prophetic orders varied from one hundred to as many as four hundred. Each prophetic band was organized under a leader and was financially dependent, by and large, on the gifts of adherents or supporters.

Jewish kings retained in their courts many prophets who were qualified to interpret omens and to deliver important oracles. Among the court prophets were some staunchly independent thinkers who reacted strongly against corrupt regimes and unjust social behavior and who rebuked hypocritical attitudes and religious formalism. To those prophets, ethical principles and moral obligations related to human character and conduct were more important than methods and forms of ceremonial religiosity. They portrayed their God as a merciful, righteous, just, and holy deity who despised religious ceremonies, fasts, or prayers performed by suppliants who tolerated, condoned, or practiced social injustice, oppression, and cruelty. Stressing the inward quality of religion, those prophets defined true piety as the personal relationship of an individual to God.

Exile

Despite the denunciatory voices of the prophets, polytheism and occultism persisted as legitimate and accepted norms of Jewish society until the period of exile (sixth century BCE). All in all, there were three exiles, or deportations, of Jews to Babylonia. The first, in 598 BCE, included King Jehoiachin, his mother, his palace retinue, along with palace and Temple treasures, and innumerable captives. (A vivid description of the Jewish-Babylonian struggle is given in 2 Kings 24:12–16.) The second, in 587 BCE, followed an uprising against the ruling Babylonians, led by the vassal king of Judah, Zedekiah, and his nobles. That uprising was the most catastrophic event in Jewish history: the Temple, the royal palace, and hundreds of homes were burned, the walls of the city destroyed, and thousands of people deported. (Again, a description is given in 2 Kings 25:8–21). The third exile was in 582 BCE, when Gedaliah, the governor of Judah appointed by the Babylonians, was assassinated by Ishmael, leader of a band of nationalists in league with the Ammonite king. The Babylonian reprisal was swift: more deportations to Babylonia. During each of the three conflicts, many Jews fled to Egypt, lest they too become targets of Babylonian vengeance.

Gone was the mass following of various gods, goddesses, and occult activities. Gone too was Solomon's Temple, after existing for some 350 years. Those who remained in Palestine were common people who, by and large, were accustomed to the practices that had persisted through the centuries and who were now isolated from their roots by an immigrant population of colonists. Obviously, such people could not revive the worship of one God. Instead, it was left to the exiles who returned to Jerusalem in the fifth century BCE to fulfill that task. They did so with a deliberateness and exclusiveness that had been uncharacteristic of them in the past.

THE RISE AND DEVELOPMENT OF JUDAISM

Emergence of Synagogues

The years following the downfall of the kingdom of Judah in the sixth century BCE saw the beginning of the *diaspora*, the scattering of the Jewish people all over the world. Many critics consider that period as marking the end of biblical religion and beginning the rise of Judaism. Far from their place of worship, the Temple in Jerusalem, the Jewish people were forced to adopt a new institution of worship—the synagogue, a term of Greek derivation meaning a meeting place or an assembly. With the synagogue appeared the figure of the rabbi, the Jewish religious leader, teacher, or master. Unfortunately, we do not know how or when that innovation came into being. It is possible that synagogues gradually developed some time between the fifth century BCE and the first century CE.

Rebuilding of the Temple

When the Persian King Cyrus conquered Babylon in 538 BCE, he allowed those Jews that wished to do so to return to their homeland. The estimated 40,000 Jews who made their way back home, however, were soon disillusioned and disheartened by the conditions they found in Jerusalem. One of the main projects of the returning exiles was to rebuild the Temple. At first, the community proved unequal to the task; then, at the urging of the prophets Haggai and Zechariah, the project was carried through to completion in 516 BCE. Thus, seventy years after the destruction of the first temple, a second one arose on its ruins.

Recognition of the Torah

Meanwhile, the Jews who had remained in Babylon achieved positions of wealth and influence and developed a vigorous religious life. They founded their own institutions, built up a new polity, and centered their religious life on the Torah (Law), the first five books of the Bible, believed to have been written by Moses. From the ranks of the Babylonian Jews came Ezra the scribe and some 1700 others who arrived in Jerusalem in 458 BCE to disseminate knowledge of the Torah. Twelve years later, Ezra was joined by Nehemiah; together their forces brought about religious reforms. Two issues addressed by Ezra and Nehemiah had a far-reaching effect on the religion and history of the Jewish people: the status of the Torah and the issue of foreign marriages.

Ezra and Nehemiah

The ultimate aim of Ezra and Nehemiah was to establish the Torah as the supreme, authoritative source of instruction in all facets of life. They achieved that not merely by reading from the Torah but by applying it to their own times and by interpreting and explaining its contents to fit the circumstances and conditions of life. Ezra, for example, dramatized his disapproval of foreign marriages by begging for forgiveness from God on behalf of those who had married foreign partners, while Nehemiah resorted to the use of intimidation to encourage adherence to marriage norms that he felt were crucial to the survival of Judaism.

Ezra and Nehemiah established a new theocratic state in which power was vested in the priests. They made the people take a solemn oath to observe the Torah and to strictly fulfill the requirements of tithing, sacrifices, and festivals. Later, a demand for specialists to copy and interpret the Torah was soon filled by a class of scribes known as *sopherim*. Those who developed a special talent came to be known as rabbis, or masters. Others diligently applied themselves to the literary labor of writing down the Hebrew canon and scripture.

Impact of the Persians

The postexilic period, particularly the period of Jewish-Persian contact (sixth to fourth centuries BCE), was in many ways decisive for the subsequent development of Judaism. The exile forced the Jews to come to terms with certain ideas and practices. Special emphasis was placed on God's uniqueness. He alone was God, the living Lord, king of the universe, and the sovereign of all authority. Terms such as the Almighty, the Exalted One, the Great Holy One, the Lord of Glory, the Lord of Hosts, and the King of Kings were used to stress God's transcendence, that he was beyond the range of human grasp, reason, description, or experience. A tendency also developed to avoid the use of the divine

The Torah scroll, kept inside the Ark of the Covenant in the synagogue. The other two scrolls represent the Neviim and the Kethuviim. The Jewish worshiper is wearing both *tallit* and *tefillin*.
Courtesy of Ray Kurkjian.

name YHWH. Instead, it was replaced by *Adonay* (Lord). And God's presence and relationship with human beings came to be referred to by the word *shekinah* (literally, "dwelling").

The substitutes for the divine name and God's activity created another concept: the Spirit or the Holy Spirit (cf. Isaiah 63:10–11). The Spirit was conceived of as an ethical principle that permeates the world and holds it together—a divine force that teaches human beings God's will. Centuries later, it was represented in rabbinic literature as a mediator of divine revelation in the scriptures. In addition, the ancient concept of God's heavenly court was transformed in the postexilic period into a highly developed doctrine of angels. Angels were holy, eternal, and immortal beings made by God on the first day of creation to serve, praise, and glorify him and, most important, to carry out his will. Angels also received the prayers offered by the pious, intervened in perilous situations, and carried out God's punishment against the wicked. Their number and division into various ranks are not known.

Judaism's angelology may have developed under Babylonian and Persian influence. Scholars have pointed out the similarities between the Jewish angelology and the astral deities of Babylonia as well as the Zoroastrian Amesha Spentas. The matter has not been conclusively resolved, but it is hardly conceivable that Judaism's angelology came into being without Persian influence. That is even more true regarding Judaism's ideas of Satan, demons, resurrection, and the Messianic Age.

One must reckon with the powerful influence of Persian ideas, no matter how difficult it is to give any particulars about the nature of that influence.

Preexilic Jews believed that everything, both good and evil, derived from God. In postexilic times, that conception changed. God was perceived of as exclusively good and Satan as the author and representative of evil. The appearance of Satan as God's antagonist (called "the adversary" in the book of Job) was introduced in the postexilic period. Later developments represented Satan, along with his angels and powers, as one who constituted the realm of evil, who sought to lead individuals to wickedness and destruction, and who caused evil, sin, and death. He stood in complete antithesis to God, who would bind and destroy him at the end of the world.

But Judaism never maintained the thoroughgoing dualism of Zoroastrianism. Nor did it reach to the Zoroastrian conclusion that Satan and God were two coequal but not coeternal powers. Instead, Judaism explained the appearance of evil as a fall within God's creation, because God, being good, could not have created evil. Certain Jewish documents, mainly from the Greco-Roman period, present the explanation that the angel Satan exalted himself above the stars, refused to worship Adam as the likeness of God, and was consequently cast down from heaven. That story has some connection with the myth of the fallen day star mentioned in Isaiah 14:12ff. The Latin term for the day star, *Lucifer,* consequently came to mean Satan.

The admixture of Persian ideas also can be seen in the Jewish conception of demons, or evil spirits. The story of the angels or "sons of god" in Genesis 6:1ff., usually serves as a background explanation. The so-called angels were once created by God, but they fell from God's grace and were imprisoned. Their descendants, the demons or evil spirits, now inhabited the earth, and their primary function was to tempt individuals to commit sin. Later, there developed the conception of a structured realm of evil spirits, serving as Satan's ministers and hostile to God's sovereignty.

The Zoroastrian view of resurrection and life after death caused a sharp division among postexilic Jews. One group persisted in maintaining the old conviction that the dead led a shadowy existence in the underworld (*sheol* in Hebrew, *hades* in Greek); the other group became attracted to the belief that "those who sleep in the dust of the earth shall awake, some to everlasting life, and some to shame and everlasting contempt" (Daniel 12:2). Unfortunately, nothing is known about the mechanism of resurrection to make any possible conclusions. The same applies for the transition from preexilic prophetic ideas to postexilic eschatological ideas (ideas pertaining to the last things or final age), which depict the end of history and a new world in which God alone is sovereign. All that can be deduced is the tendency among Jews to regard the present age as evil, the order of nature disturbed, the heavenly bodies thrown into disorder, and terror reigning over the earth. Toward the end of time, it was further thought, portents were to appear, God was to intervene in history, a great judgment was to follow, the righteous were to enter the new world (the kingdom of God), and the wicked were to be judged.

Details regarding the sequence of events leading to the end of time are lacking. What is known is that some time near the end of this present age but prior to the ushering in of the new age, a Messiah ("Anointed One") was to appear. That human, God-appointed ruler would be endowed with extraordinary qualities of righteousness, wisdom, and power. His mission would be to establish his kingdom in Zion (Israel) and destroy the hostile world power. Those eschatological views, long central to the Zoroastrian religion, found their way into postexilic Judaism.

Impact of the Greeks

In 332 BCE, the theocratic state centered in Palestine came under the powerful influence of Greek civilization through Alexander the Great and his successors. The Greek way of life — education, sports, theaters, libraries — quickly was adopted by educated as well as uneducated Jews. King Antiochus IV (175–164 BCE), however, was determined to hasten the process of Hellenization among Jews who stubbornly resisted change. He prohibited the Jews, on pain of death, to practice circumcision, to own any copies of the Torah, or to keep the Sabbath (holy day of rest and worship). In addition, he attempted to force them to worship Zeus by erecting an altar to that deity in the Temple at Jerusalem and by sacrificing pigs. The horror and indignation inspired by such sacrilege among Jewish believers led to open rebellion against the king and a call to all Jews to return to the "way of their fathers."

The Maccabean Revolt

The Maccabean Revolt was led by an aged priest called Mattathias, who killed a commissioner who had ordered him to sacrifice to Zeus. Together with his five sons and a large following of supporters, Mattathias took to the desert. In 165 BCE, one of his sons, Judas Maccabeus, recaptured most of Jerusalem and restored Jewish worship in the Temple. The period of Maccabean independence (celebrated today as Hanukkah) lasted until 63 BCE, when animosity between divergent Jewish parties led to violence, bloody massacres, and, eventually, civil war. The Roman general Pompey, then stationed in Syria, was called upon to arbitrate; instead, he promptly occupied Palestine and declared it to be a Roman province.

Impact of the Romans

During the period of Roman occupation, the pervasive influence of Hellenistic culture on Judaism became quite obvious. The biblical books of Ruth, Esther, Jonah, Job, and Ecclesiastes, among others, appeared. In addition, the Septuagint (the translation of the Hebrew scripture into Greek for Greek-speaking Jews) was completed by the second century BCE.

A cantor lighting the candelabrum for
the annual celebration of Hanukkah,
the Festival of Lights.
Courtesy of Ray Kurkjian.

The era also was distinguished by the advent of various new Jewish
groups and parties. A wealthy, aristocratic, and somewhat liberal group
known as the Sadducees displayed a keen interest in disseminating
Greek culture. Another group, the Pharisees, represented pious members of society whose main passion was the Jewish religion. They paid
great attention to oral tradition, harnessed their aspirations to Messianic
expectations, preached concepts related to resurrection, and struggled
for liberation from worldly preoccupations.

Three other influential groups were founded during the Roman
occupation of Palestine. The Herodians supported the Roman government, the house of Herod, while the Zealots opposed the Roman government because, in their view, submission to the Romans meant forsaking God. Their recourse was to the sword, which the Zealots
believed could hasten the Messiah's coming. The third group, the
Essenes, lived in a monastic commune, practiced nonviolence, and
awaited the end of the world, at which time they, as the "sons of light,"
would triumph over the "sons of darkness." The famous Dead Sea
Scrolls, found near Qumran, have been attributed to the Essenes.

Masada

In 66 CE, toward the end of Emperor Nero's reign, the discontent of the
Jews against the Romans broke into open rebellion, which the Romans
suppressed with savagery and slaughter. In 70 CE, Jerusalem was razed
and the Temple set on fire. Three years later, a band of Zealots at
Masada fought against the Romans until starvation led them to commit

suicide rather than submit. A final attempt to liberate Palestine from Roman rule was made by Bar Kokhba, supported by Akiba, the greatest rabbi of the time. After three years of struggle (132–135), the Romans crushed the rebellion, and the Jewish population of Palestine was largely scattered throughout the Mediterranean basin.

JEWS UNDER CHRISTIAN AND MUSLIM RULE

Spanish Jews

The center of Jewish life and thought remained in the eastern Mediterranean until the Muslim conquest of Spain in the eighth century CE. Under the relatively tolerant Muslim administration, Spanish Jews flourished and became the leaders of worldwide Judaism. Entering the fields of government, science, medicine, philosophy, and literature, they made outstanding contributions in every field.

The restoration of Christian rule in Spain in the fourteenth century disrupted Jewish life. For almost a century, Spanish Jews lived under the threat of persecution. Ultimately they were expelled from Spain, and thousands fled to Portugal, Italy, Turkey, Morocco, and other parts of Europe where Jews had taken refuge ever since the time of the Roman Empire. (By the end of the tenth century, for instance, there were already large Jewish colonies in Italy, Germany, France, and England.)

European Nations

By the end of the fifteenth century, almost every European nation had maltreated and expelled their Jewish populations. Jews fled once more, this time to eastern Europe and to the Muslim states of the Ottoman Empire. Jewish refugees from Spain and Portugal who settled in the Ottoman world came to be known as Sephardim. They developed their own language, mainly Spanish mixed with Hebrew. Jewish refugees in eastern Europe came to be known as Ashkenazim. They, too, developed a language, known as Yiddish, a combination of German and Hebrew.

Jewish Ghettos

The treatment of Jews in sixteenth- and seventeenth-century Europe was no more tolerant or enlightened than it had been in preceding centuries. The establishment of the Inquisition by the Roman Catholic church affected not only dissident Christians but the Jews as well. A papal decree, issued in 1555, authorized the containment of Jews within special quarters, known as ghettos, and the restrictions imposed by a daily curfew forced the Jews to live in miserable conditions. Such irrational intolerance also was characteristic of the treatment of Jews during the uprising of Ukrainian (Cossack) peasants against the Polish nobility in 1648. The Jews became part of the general slaughter in an event known as a Jewish pogrom.

Jewish Emancipation

The late eighteenth and early nineteenth centuries saw the emancipation of the Jews in Europe, particularly after the French Revolution, in 1789. Soon, Jews were allowed to mix freely in social circles that had been closed to them in the past, to pursue various trades and professions that had denied them entry, to attend centers of higher learning, and to follow the religious life bequeathed to them by their ancestors.

The upsurge of nationalism in nineteenth-century Europe also affected the Jewish people. Theodore Herzl and other Jewish leaders came to the conclusion that despite the liberty accorded to Jews by European countries, the Jewish people never would be treated as equals except in their own homeland. In the late twentieth century, that aspiration for status as a nation coalesced with the development of Zionism, a movement dedicated to the formation of a national homeland in the former ancient territory of the Jewish people, Palestine. In the meantime, a catastrophic event reduced the total population of the Jews by as much as one-third.

The Holocaust

That terrible incident was the Holocaust of 1941–1945, in which the German Nazis under Adolf Hitler applied the most effective method of exterminating the Jews that they could devise: asphyxiation by gas.

The Holocaust (and World War II) confirmed Zionists' determination to establish a homeland in Palestine. Consequently, in 1948, the independent state of Israel came into being, thus ending the long centuries of exile and accelerating the "ingathering" of the exiles.

The State of Israel

The chain of events that led to the startling reality of an established Jewish state is so recent and so well documented that it does not need to be recounted here. However one wishes to interpret the sequence of events that led to that consummation, one cannot deny that Judaism provides a graphic illustration of the long arm of history reaching into the present to influence the future. The modern state of Israel and the effect it has had and continues to have on its neighbors are manifestations of the Jewish faith and 3500 years of Jewish history.

A number of specific historical events have a particular significance to those Jews who see Israel as their birthright and their homeland. One event is, of course, the Exodus from Egypt. Other events are associated with the Temple in Jerusalem: the dedication of the first Temple during the reign of King Solomon in the tenth century BCE; the total destruction of the Temple by the neo-Babylonians in August 587 BCE and its rededication under Persian sovereignty in March 516 BCE; and Judas Maccabeus's reclamation of the Temple from the Seleucids (descendants of Seleucus, a general and successor of Alexander the Great) in 135 BCE and its rededication. Those events in Temple history are eclipsed by the final catastrophe in 70 CE, when the Romans leveled the Temple once and for all. Even to this day, Jews gather at the ruined western wall

The main gate at the Auschwitz death camp, with an inscription in German "ARBEIT MACHT FREI," meaning "work makes (one) free." Led by Adolf Hitler, German Nazis established numerous death camps, at Auschwitz (Oswiecim, Poland) and elsewhere, where they systematically and gruesomely murdered millions of Jews.
Courtesy of Wolf Arnold.

in Jerusalem to pray for the reconstruction and rededication of their ancient center of worship, whose site is now occupied by an Islamic mosque.

The indescribable horrors suffered by the Jewish people during the twenty centuries of exile that followed the Roman sack of the Temple are well documented. The long, bloody centuries of hardship underline the significance of the proclamation of May 14, 1948, confirming the establishment of the modern state of Israel. It represents, perhaps, the most decisive event in the entire history of Judaism. The long Jewish struggle for national and religious independence was finally crowned with success on that date, which marked the end of two thousand years of exilic survival.

Hundreds of thousands of Jewish people, scattered throughout central and eastern Europe and western Asia, converged on Israel, which they saw as their homeland restored. The four wars of 1948, 1956, 1967, and 1973 did more than demonstrate their capacity to survive in a hostile environment. The wars resulted in territorial gains, the recovery of the Temple wall, and the confirmation of a "Messianic vision" eloquently expressed by David Ben Gurion, the first prime minister of Israel:

The suffering of the Jewish people in the Diaspora, whether economic, political, or cultural, has been a powerful factor in bringing about the immigrations to the Land of Israel. But it was only the Messianic vision which made that factor fruitful and guided it towards the creation of the State. Suffering alone is degrading, oppression destructive; and if we had not inherited from the prophets the Messianic vision of redemption, the suffering of the Jewish people in the Diaspora would have led to their extinction. The ingathering of the exiles, that is, the return of the Jewish people to its land, is the beginning of the realization of the Messianic vision.[1]

Thus, for the Jewish people, historical events are far more than a mere sequence of names and incidents. To them, historical events are acts of a God who is deliberately and purposefully guiding his people onward. Jewish people see all historical events as crucial to the formation of their religion.

JEWISH GROUPS IN THE MIDDLE AGES

The period between the seventh and fourteenth centuries saw the rise of several new Jewish groups and parties, notably the Karaites, the Kabbalists, and the Hasidics.

The Karaites

The Karaites flourished in the Middle East, especially in Babylonia (modern Iraq) from the ninth to the twelfth centuries. The name *Karaite* literally means "readers of scriptures." They were so called because of their exclusive adherence to the Bible as the only source of religious authority in Judaism. They repudiated the Talmud as a spurious invention of the rabbis.

The Kabbalists

Although the Kabbalistic movement may have originated in Palestine, its systematic development took place in Babylonia. The term *kabel* means "to receive" and the name Kabbalist at first described any Jewish mystic who was a teacher of secret or inward revelation. Hence, Kabbalist became the name associated with those Jews who were particularly concerned with the philosophical mystic lore of Judaism based on an occult interpretation of the Bible handed down as secret doctrine to the initiated. During the ninth and tenth centuries, the Kabbalistic movement spread to Europe, especially to Italy, Spain, and Germany.

The two most important books of the movement composed and edited in Babylonia were the Sefer Yitzirah (The Book of Formation) and the Shiur Komah (The Measure of the Height). The former chiefly concerned the creative powers of letters and numbers, while the latter described in human terms the dimensions of the Deity. However, the book that came to be regarded as the most sacred of all Kabbalistic writings and the very epitome of Jewish mysticism is the Zohar. The word *zohar* means "splendor" or "brightness" and is derived from Daniel 12:3. The book records the revelations said to have been received in the second century CE by Rabbi Simeon ben Yochai during the thirteen years he was hiding in a cave and transmitted by him to his disciples. Compiled and made public in 1300 by Moses de Leon of Granada, Spain, the Zohar come to be regarded as the Bible of medieval mysticism. The Zohar is a compendium of Jewish mystic lore on the nature of God, the mysteries of the Divine name, God's attributes and dimensions, the evolution of the universe, a person's place in the universe and the nature of the human soul, the characteristics of heaven and hell, the order of the angels and demons, magic, astrology, as well as expositions on many ethical themes and ceremonies.

The Hasidics

The Hasidics (the term *hasid* means "pious") are a mystical group still represented in modern Judaism; their origins go back to the Kabbalist Israel Baal-Shem-Tov (1700–1760), who was born in the Ukraine but later settled in Poland. Famed as a miracle worker and healer, he was regarded as a true saint and mystic. By the efforts of a number of his disciples, the movement attracted a large following, especially among the Jews of the Polish Ukraine. In contrast to Kabbalistic mysticism, which was difficult to understand and appealed particularly to intellectuals, Hasidic mysticism became a vital, singing faith of the masses. Its appeal lay less in visions of speedy Messianic deliverance than in relieving the gloom and depression of an impoverished people. Without suppressing the natural impulses within humans, Hasidic mysticism promoted contentment coupled with meekness and modesty.

The Hasidic movement, with its emphasis on mysticism and ecstasy, transformed the face of east European Jewry in the eighteenth and nineteenth centuries. Despite bitter persecution by members of the "orthodox" rabbinic school, who viewed Hasidism as a threat to Jewry, the movement spread rapidly, until it included almost half of traditional rabbinism in its ranks.

MODERN JEWISH GROUPS

Imbued with nineteenth-century European idealism, another group of Jews was determined to reform Jewish belief and practice by placing more emphasis on ethics. The so-called Reform movement spread rapidly throughout Europe and, later, the United States. Today, four modern variations of Judaism predominate in North America: Orthodox, Reform, Conservative, and Reconstructionist.

Orthodox Judaism

The Orthodox, the largest group in contemporary Judaism, are committed to remain as true as possible to biblical and Talmudic regulations. Strict observance of the Sabbath is stressed, as is firm compliance with regulations governing food. (Orthodox Jews eat only kosher food, food that is ritually sanctioned.) In general, men and women sit in separate areas of the synagogue, and both sexes cover their heads once they step inside.

Reform Judaism

Reform Judaism reflects the spirit of the modern age by omitting many traditional practices. Talmudic restrictions on the Sabbath and on diet have been modified to make them less rigorous. Synagogue services, which are conducted in the vernacular as well as in Hebrew, are usually held on Friday nights. Men and women sit together and are not obliged to cover their heads.

Conservative Judaism

The followers of Conservative Judaism depart from a number of ancient practices but attempt to abide by biblical and Talmudic regulations regarding diet and Sabbath observance. Unlike Reform Judaism, Conservative Judaism has retained Saturday morning services and the requirement that men cover their heads. As in Reform Judaism, however, synagogue services are conducted in both the vernacular and Hebrew. Conservative Judaism also can be distinguished from Orthodox Judaism by a general concern with the scientific study of biblical and Talmudic material.

Reconstructionist Judaism

Reconstructionist Judaism is a recent American movement founded by Mordecai M. Kaplan. In this new context, Judaism is understood not only as a religion but as an ongoing tradition with a unique culture that comprises aspects such as its history, law, art, and music. Proponents of this point of view are chiefly concerned with persuading the Jewish community that Judaism is more than a religion. They hold that culture and tradition in their entirety have to be experienced rather than studied in isolation.

Other Jewish Groups

Numerous smaller Jewish sects also have spread throughout the world. The Falashas of Ethiopia practice a form of Judaism that seems to be rooted partly in ancient observances and partly in traditions that lie beyond the mainstream of Judaism. That is also true of Jewish sects in Yemen, India, China, and other parts of the world.

THE BIBLE

For many centuries, the stories, ballads, laws, and religious activities of the Jews were transmitted orally from generation to generation. A few oral traditions may have been put into writing as early as 1000 BCE. During the period of the monarchy, Jews required codification of their oral

The western wall (Wailing Wall) of the Temple in Jerusalem. Orthodox Judaism requires
separation of the sexes during prayer. Recently, delegations of Reform Judaism have
attempted mixed prayer services at the Wall, which were met with impassioned
demonstrations from Orthodox adherents. The Wall, one of Judaism's holiest sites,
is a remnant of the second Temple, which was destroyed in 70 BCE.
Courtesy of Israel Government Tourist Office, Ministry of Tourism, Toronto.

traditions in response to the needs of an increasingly complex society.
That process continued for several centuries, until the collection of sacred writings attained the status of Bible.

The term *Bible* is derived from a Greek word that means "books";
both Jews and Christians use the term *Bible* to mean their sacred books.
Originally, the writings were written on skin or parchment and made
up into individual rolls or scrolls.

Of course, there are many ancient copies of the Jewish Bible (called
the Old Testament by Christians), often referred to as "manuscripts."
Until the discovery of the Dead Sea Scrolls in 1947, it was thought that
the oldest manuscript dated from the ninth century CE. However, manuscripts discovered in caves beside the Dead Sea have been dated as far
back as the second century BCE.

Because the common language in the early days of the Jews was Hebrew, the Jewish Bible was written in that language except for small
portions of the books of Daniel and Ezra-Nehemiah, which were written in Aramaic (a Semitic dialect closely related to Hebrew). The Jewish
Bible, in its present form, contains twenty-four books and is divided
into three main sections.

- The Torah (Law or Instruction) consists of the books of Genesis, Exodus, Leviticus, Numbers, and Deuteronomy.

- The Nebi'im (Prophets) consists of the books of Joshua, Judges, Samuel, Kings (referred to as Former Prophets), Isaiah, Jeremiah, Ezekiel, and the twelve "minor" prophets (referred to as Latter Prophets).

- The Kethubim (Writings) consists of the books of Psalms, Proverbs, Job, Song of Solomon, Ruth, Lamentations, Ecclesiastes, Esther, Ezra-Nehemiah, Chronicles, and Daniel.

Today, the Jewish people refer to their scriptures as *Tanak,* an acronym made up of the initial consonants of the three major divisions. A brief description of each section will help us understand the importance of the religion of Judaism.

The Torah

The most significant section of the Jewish Bible is the Torah, the authorship of which is traditionally ascribed to Moses. Scholars have traced some of the basic ideas in the Torah to Moses, but the collection of writings, as it appears today, came into existence over a period of six to seven hundred years. The Torah recounts the history of the Israelites from the days of their departure from Egypt, under the leadership of Moses, to the eve of their triumphant entry into the land of the Canaanites. Prefaced to this account are two other histories: the origin of the universe and of humankind and the stories and sagas of the patriarchs. Scattered among the accounts are various legal, social, and religious instructions or codes.

An enormous amount of study has been devoted to the identification of the authors, the dates, and the sequence of revisions of the Torah. The consensus is that there were at least four sets of editorial revisions, the last of which was undertaken by the priests during the exile in Babylon in the sixth century BCE. By 400 BCE, the five books of the Torah as it appears today attained the status of scripture.

The Nebi'im (Prophets)

Many works and oracles believed to have been written by prophets gradually won an influential place in Jewish tradition. Although never attaining the same level of authority as the Torah, the collections in the Nebi'im nevertheless came to be regarded as important works, and by 200 BCE they had attained the status of scripture.

The books of Joshua, Judges, Samuel, and Kings constitute the category of the so-called Former Prophets, following immediately after the Torah. The four works deal mainly with the historical events that occurred from the death of Moses to the downfall of the Jewish kingdom, a period of about seven centuries. It generally is assumed that the books of the Former Prophets had a complex compositional history, but no consensus exists among scholars about the course of that history. Possibly, the books were not completely composed until shortly before, or even during, the neo-Babylonian exile in the sixth century BCE. Virtually nothing is known also about their authorship. Undoubtedly, the books from Joshua to Kings represent in their present form the final stage of a lengthy editorial process.

The collections of the Latter Prophets deal mainly with social systems, political activities, moral norms, and religious practices. Written and compiled some time between the eighth and fourth centuries BCE, they address the principles related to human conduct by condemning hypocritical attitudes and religious formalism.

The Kethubim (Writings)

The works included in the Kethubim contain poetic, proverbial, liturgical, and philosophical material written by unknown sages over several centuries and finally recognized as scripture by 100 BCE. The striking feature of the Kethubim is a shift in outlook. The writers are chiefly interested not in Judaism or in national concerns but in humanity. They address their listeners with common, human problems arising from family relations, personal affairs, social and business matters, public interests, manners, and morals.

THE TALMUD AND THE MIDRASH

By the time the Bible had been completed and assembled, great changes had taken place in Judaism, changes that gave rise to oral interpretations and traditions concerning many of the written laws. Although Judaism affirmed the binding character of the Torah, it also sanctioned and endorsed the traditions that came to be known as the Talmud and the Midrash.

The Talmud is a collection of commentaries, traditions, and precedents that supplements the Bible as a source of authority. The Midrash is a collection of literary works containing scriptural expositions and interpretations of both legal and nonlegal matters. Next to the Bible, the Talmud and the Midrash are the most sacred Jewish books. School children use them as textbooks; rabbis, particularly Conservative and Orthodox ones, study them as sources of precepts and teachings; and pious Jews read them as guidebooks for day-to-day living. Biographical sketches, humorous anecdotes, parables, epigrams, treatises, and scholarly commentaries in the Talmud and the Midrash provide not only an intimate glimpse into ancient Jewish life but also moral insights and spiritual values that have universal application.

The Talmud and the Midrash are often thought of as the "oral" Torah, in contrast to the "written" or "revealed" Torah. Jewish tradition maintains that from the very moment that Moses accepted the written Torah on Mount Sinai there existed an oral Torah that was handed down from generation to generation. It is more probable that oral traditions developed over hundreds of years, until the volume of accumulated tradition taxed the capacity of each succeeding generation to sustain it. As a result, the traditions were written down and codified in legal form.

Students studying the Talmud in one of the yeshivas (schools) in the reconstructed Jewish area of the Old City in Jerusalem.

Courtesy of Israel Government Tourist Office, Ministry of Tourism, Toronto.

The product of two distinct Jewish centers of learning, the Talmud exists in two versions: the Palestinian version and the Babylonian version. The differences between the two versions in subject matter, method, presentation, and language may reflect the differing life-styles of the Jews who lived in Palestine and those who lived in Babylonia. Biblical commandments had to be applied differently in different circumstances. Today, decisions in matters of religious law are rendered on the basis of the Babylonian Talmud.

JEWISH TEACHINGS

God

Affirmation of the existence of one supreme deity is the first fundamental tenet of Judaism. God is one, omnipotent, omniscient, and without limitations or form. He is not only the creator and master of the universe but also an active participant in human affairs. He is holy and the embodiment of moral perfection. He is the God of mercy, love, and justice. In Judaism, God is the only creative cause of existence. Everything has come into existence by his will.

The importance of God in Judaism is rooted in the basic concepts and fundamental views found in the Torah. Three interconnected central themes dominate the Torah: (1) God, (2) the universe, and (3) human beings.

"In the beginning God created the heavens and the earth," are the opening words of the Torah. There is no question in the Torah as to whether or not God exists—he is, and he is only One. Again, the Torah represents God as a personal God, not in the sense that he has a physical body, but in that he enters, instructs, and directs the life of every human being. He is, moreover, regarded as "merciful and gracious, slow to anger, and abounding in steadfast love and truthfulness" (Exodus 34:6–7). He is "God of gods and Lord of lords, the great, the mighty, and the terrible God" (Deuteronomy 10:17), who executes justice for the orphan and the widow. Nevertheless, he is a "jealous God, visiting the iniquity of the fathers upon the children to the third and fourth generation of those who hate him" (Exodus 20:5).

The Torah represents the nature and attributes of God in the following manner: those who love God and keep his commandments, or instructions, benefit from his love, mercy, and grace; those who disobey his commandments reap only his anger and justice. Nowhere in the Torah is the paradox or the apparent problem between God's mercy and justice tackled, let alone resolved. Centuries later, rabbinic commentary explained it this way: if the world had been created on the basis of God's mercy alone, the sins of the world would have been many; if, on the other hand, the world had been created strictly on the basis of God's justice, the world would not have been able to exist. To maintain a proper balance, God created the world with both his attributes—justice and mercy.

The opening statement in the Torah suggests that God is the only creative cause of the universe. Nowhere does the Torah suggest that the universe is self-created. God is regarded as the creator of the heavens and earth: everything that is has come into being by his command. In fact, the Torah states (Genesis 1) that God's commanding word separated darkness from light, night from day, the heaven from the earth, and the seas from the dry land. At his word, the sun, the moon, all heavenly bodies, all water creatures, all vegetation, and all creatures and animals came into being. God's last act of creation was man and woman.

The Torah repeatedly insists that God is not a spirit in nature nor part of nature, but above and distinctively apart from nature. Neither the stars nor the moon nor any other heavenly or earthly phenomenon is to be worshiped or thought to have godlike (i.e., divine) characteristics. God alone brought everything into existence and thus is the preserver and the ruler of the universe. And, according to the Torah (Genesis 1), the created universe is "good."

Another viewpoint central to the Torah is that man and woman are created in the "image" of God (Genesis 1:26, 5:21). To be created in the image of God means, in the modern Jewish view, to be divinely ordained to demonstrate God's justice and mercy. Nowhere does the Torah instruct an individual to abandon the world (as do Christian, Hindu, and Buddhist ascetics or monastics) to please God. On the contrary, life is to be responded to with piety and reverence. In other words, a person ought to love the world and hallow life in such daily activities as eating, drinking, working, and pleasure, by raising them to their highest level so that every act is sacred and reflects the divine image. The Torah instructs how an individual's behavior must be governed from the cradle to the grave by moral codes. Naturally, a person is free to choose and is morally responsible for the choices made.

The Torah makes no attempt to offer philosophical explanations for those views. Only the following assertions are made: God exists, he is the sole creator, he is absolutely without a rival (or an incarnation), he needs no representation of any sort, the universe he created is good, and the purpose of human life is to serve God and fellow individuals. The importance of the Torah is illustrated in the following well-known Jewish story.

> A heathen once came to the Jewish scholar Shammai and said that he would become a proselyte (convert to Judaism) on condition that he be taught the entire Torah while standing on one foot. Shammai chased him away. So the man appealed next to Hillel, another Jewish scholar. "Whatever is hateful to you," said Hillel to the man, "do not do to your neighbor; that is the entire Torah. The rest is commentary—go and learn it."

The Chosen People

The second basic tenet of Judaism is that a Jewish person is free to accept or reject the *mitzvot* (commandments) of God, which, according to tradition, were offered to and accepted by his people during the revelation at Mount Sinai. Judaism views human beings as autonomous agents neither wholly evil nor wholly good in nature, who can suppress their potential for evil by following God's commandments.

The essence of that obligation is perhaps best expressed in the Jewish legend telling of how God, having completed the requirements he demanded of humankind, offered them in the form of a scroll (the Torah) to various nations. All except the Jewish people refused, on the grounds that the Torah placed too many restrictions on their lives. Only the Jewish people were willing to accept God's mandate without reservation. Modern Judaism, therefore, represents Jews as a choosing, not a chosen, people. God's acceptance of Israel can be explained in terms not of divine preference but of human choice. There is no question of favoritism; on the contrary, Jews consider themselves committed to maintain a special sense of responsibility toward God and his commandments.

The story of God's continual activity in history, particularly in the history of the Jewish people, is the underlying concept of all Jewish teachings. Judaism cannot be defined in terms of Christian theological categories or Christian catechism. Yet there is a logic immanent in Judaism that sooner or later becomes evident to the careful investigator. What is striking in Judaism is that faith is grounded on divine-human actions for a specific divine purpose: the establishment of peace and well-being in this world among humanity. But that divine-human action is understood in a twofold way. On the one hand, Judaism makes the claim that God "chose" the Jewish people from among the nations for the task of applying the strictest obedience to the Torah as an instrument for enhancing the well-being of all humanity. On the other hand, Judaism asserts that God's universal love and care will lead humanity to the day when all shall know that God is the only one. Consequently, Jews believe that their absolute loyalty and obedience to God's ordinances will result in the redemption of the entire human race.

Attempts to defend or reject the religious concept of singularity have been made through the ages, and today it is increasingly subject to attack. Several modern Jewish thinkers and some forms of Zionism have sought to abandon that problematic view. Other leading Jewish thinkers, however, continue to affirm the notion, reassuring the Jewish people of their divine election. To such individuals, the sanctity of Jewish life and faith, the modern land of Israel, and the very existence of the Jews — in a word, Judaism itself — is inconceivable without the concept of chosenness. The special covenantal relationship between God and his people does not in any way negate the universal rule of God. On the contrary, it is precisely that particular relation (God-Jews) that underscores the universalistic position (God-humanity). Humanity is neither expected nor obligated, as Jews are, to live within the jurisdiction of the Torah. The responsibility of non-Jews is only that they accept seven basic obligations: (1) not to profane God's name, (2) not to worship idols, (3) not to commit murder, (4) not to steal, (5) not to commit adultery, (6) not to be unjust, and (7) not to cut limbs from living animals (Genesis Rabbah 34:8). From the perspective of Jewish faith, the two sovereign aspects of God (the particular and the universal) are not two sets of contradictory assertions; rather, both are true as a description of Judaism, since neither is true without the other. God's purpose, it is argued, lies beyond the limits of mere human logic and reason.

The Arrival of a Messiah

Jews also believe that Judaism has a particular role to play in the task of world redemption. Since ancient times, Jewish tradition has asserted that a Messiah, endowed with strong leadership and great wisdom, will come to redeem humankind and establish God's kingdom on earth by ushering in an era of perfect peace. The Messiah is expected to be a human rather than a divine being, a descendant of the house of David.

Many Jews today still pray for the arrival of such a Messianic Age when they gather to worship in the synagogue. Others have reinterpreted this traditional belief. Instead of pinning their faith on an individual who will usher in the Messianic Age, they consider that some day humanity collectively will reach a level of transcendent enlightenment, justice, and kindness that will create the climate for God's kingdom on earth. Regardless of the interpretation placed on the Messianic tradition, Judaism is more concerned with this world than the next in striving toward the ideal.

JEWISH OBSERVANCES

Judaism has always defined itself in terms of rites and religious acts. Such observances either mark stages in individual life cycles or are related to the cycle of the religious calendar.

Rites of Passage

The most important and distinctive of all Jewish rites is the circumcision of all male children eight days after birth as an external symbol of the Covenant and of commitment to Judaism. Another religious obligation is the *Bar Mitzvah* for boys reaching the age of thirteen. Recently, a *Bat Mitzvah* has been introduced by some groups, although not all, as a parallel ceremony for girls. In the rite, the young are recognized as responsible adults, members of the Jewish community and faith.

The marriage ceremony is largely a matter of local practice, but certain religious observances are common to most Jewish communities. The marriage vow is taken under a canopy that symbolizes the couple's home. At the end of the ceremony, the bride and the groom share a cup of wine, which symbolizes their common destiny. They also sign the marriage document as a legal contract. Jewish tradition makes provision for divorce in case a marriage breaks down. Divorced persons are encouraged to remarry and may wed another partner in the synagogue.

Death is attended by an extremely detailed ceremonial pattern governed primarily by an overriding concern to comfort the bereaved. Burial takes place within twenty-four hours of death, except when a Sabbath or a holy day intervenes. (Some groups have relaxed that rule somewhat, although no group allows the body to lie in state for any length of time.) The burial is followed by a seven-day period of mourning, usually called *shiva* (meaning seven), limited to the immediate next of kin. The bereaved remain at home, except for Sabbath worship, and services are held there each evening. A general period of mourning continues for the next eleven months, after which a memorial stone is placed at the graveside.

The Sabbath

The most important of all Jewish observances is the Sabbath (the Hebrew word *Shabbat* means rest), which starts every Friday evening at dusk and continues until dusk on Saturday. To proclaim the Sabbath, the woman of the house lights the candles while the man of the house recites a special benediction over the wine and bread. The ritual is followed by a festive meal.

Orthodox Jews usher in the Sabbath by attending synagogue services on Friday, before dinner. Some Conservative and Reform Jews attend a late evening service. For all three groups, however, Saturday is a day of

Jewish children celebrating both Bat Mitzvah and Bar Mitzvah in moving ceremonies at the Wailing Wall in Jerusalem.

Courtesy of Israel Government Tourist Office, Ministry of Tourism, Toronto.

synagogue worship. On that day, Orthodox Jews refrain from any type of work, a term that includes such activities as lighting or extinguishing a light or riding in an automobile. A symbolic ceremony in the home concludes the Sabbath. A lighted candle is extinguished in wine, and a spice box is passed around from hand to hand for the family to taste or smell, as it were, the sweetness of the Sabbath as it closes.

Devotional Acts

Adherents of Judaism seek continually to know God's will and to implement it in everyday life. One of the responsibilities of a devout Jew is to recite twice a day the basic prayer called *Shema* ("Hear!"), recorded in Deuteronomy 6:4–9:

> Hear, O Israel: the Lord our God is one Lord; and you shall love the Lord your God with all your heart and with all your soul and with all your might. And these words which I command you this day shall be upon your heart; and you shall teach them diligently to your children, and shall talk of them when you sit in your house, and when you walk by the way, and when you lie down and when you rise; and you shall bind them as a sign upon your hand, and they shall be as frontlets between your eyes. And you shall write them on the doorposts of your house and on your gates.

The injunction that the words affirming the oneness of God and the response to love God be engraved on the heart, between the eyes, and on the doors of every home is taken quite literally by Jews. *Tefillin*, little boxes containing the *Shema*, are strapped on the left arm (which is close to the heart) and the forehead (which is close to the mind and eyes). Similarly, *mezuzah*, small receptacles containing the *Shema*, are permanently fastened to the doorposts of Jewish homes, offices, and schools.

Two other external symbols associated with prayer are the *tallith* and the skull cap. The *tallith* is a prayer shawl (or stole or robe) decorated with tassels or fringes on all four corners that is worn by most pious Jews during daytime prayers or services (but not at night). Most male Jews wear a skull cap at all times, not only during prayer. Pious Jewish women wear a wig as a mark of piety and reverence.

Women's Responsibilities

Perhaps the most important and distinctive change in this century is the matter of a woman's religious responsibilities. Historically, men dominated public life as leaders, teachers, and priests; women tended the home and the children. Throughout the centuries, Jewish women accepted that role as a dignified responsibility with many rights and in no sense inferior, or unequal, to the role played by men. However, males began to assert their dominance as time went on, particularly because men were not burdened by pregnancies or the nursing of babies. Soon strictures became generalized. Women were not allowed to perform certain religious duties, such as reading and studying the Torah or wearing the *tallith* and *tefillin*. Males excluded women from being counted among the *minyan* (a quorum of ten, for purposes of public worship or for constituting a congregation) and segregated them (often by a curtain) during synagogue services. In addition, women came to be regarded (though not by all) as temptresses who threatened the purity of men. Worse still, the traditional Jewish prayerbook contained the following benediction for men: "Blessed are You, God . . . who has not made me a woman."

Male superiority and dominance were never so absolute in the Torah, in which women took leadership positions when the need arose. For instance, Miriam, the sister of Moses, was an organizer and leader (Exodus 15:20); Deborah served both as a judge and a general (Judges 4–5); Huldah was a prophetess (2 Kings 22:14–20); Esther was a skilled diplomat (Book of Esther); and the Torah granted women many legal rights, including a share in real estate (Numbers 27:1–11). However, Talmudic injunctions barred women from becoming judges, leaders, rabbis, or cantors; instead, they were assigned undisputed power in ruling the home and raising children. The statement in the Torah that "he shall write her a bill of divorce" (Deuteronomy 24:1) was interpreted to mean that a woman could not divorce her husband against his will, whereas a man had the power to divorce his wife at any time. Moreover, a woman was in no legal position to remarry if her husband had disappeared or if his death was not properly certified by witnesses, whereas a man could remarry under similar circumstances.

Today, however, Jewish women (except in conservative groups) are quite active in business, the professions, politics, and the military. In matters of religious responsibilities, Jewish women are gaining ground in their demand for equal rights to study the Torah and the Talmud, to wear the *tallith* and *tefillin*, to be cantors, to be ordained as rabbis (a measure that Orthodox Jewry has strongly attacked), and to be counted among the *minyan*. Those bold decisions are based on the interpretation

Jewish adult males use special objects in worship: a prayer shawl *(tallith)* woven of wool or silk, with fringes attached to the four corners as ordained in Numbers 15:37–39; two small boxes of black leather *(tefillin)*, containing parchment slips on which are inscribed four texts (Exodus 13:1–10, 13:11–16; Deuteronomy 6:4–9, 11:13–21), which are bound to the forehead and the left arm by straps; and a skullcap.

Courtesy of Ray Kurkjian.

of Jewish *halakah* (the guiding law of Jewish life) in a new spirit of gender equality.

Relinquishing or allotting to women a share in roles traditionally performed by or reserved for men is still not an easy matter for most males and many females with conservative views. But it is generally conceded that the inferior role of women in traditional Judaism is not tenable in modern society.

High Holy Days

A unifying factor that brings together both genders as well as Jews of all degrees of belief and practice is the holy days on which the great historical events are remembered. Many portions of the Jewish annual festivals are carried out in the home, but most depend on the community meeting in the synagogue.

Rosh Hashanah (New Year). Rosh Hashanah, one of the two most sacred holy days in the Jewish calendar, is celebrated in the autumn (September or October), and ushers in a ten-day period of penitence. Orthodox and Conservative Jews, following ancient tradition, celebrate the occasion for two days; the Reform group, for one day only. The most important symbol of the festival is the *shofar* (ram's horn), which is blown in the synagogue during the service on New Year's Day and on each of the following ten days.

Yom Kippur (Day of Atonement). Yom Kippur is the second sacred Jewish holy day and is celebrated at the end of the ten-day period of penitence following Rosh Hashanah. A day-long ritual of solemn prayers and fasting in the synagogue, including the confession of a catalog of shortcomings, transgressions, and sins, marks this important event. Just before sunset, the entire congregation in the synagogue chants the *Kol Nidré,* a prayer of forgiveness for unfulfilled vows made to God. Candles are lit, and members of the family ask forgiveness of each other. Fasting ends at sunset the next day, and the entire family gathers for a festive meal at home.

Religious Festivals

Sukkot (Feast of Tabernacles). This celebration follows five days after Yom Kippur and continues for eight days (seven for Reform Jews). It is a joyous festival that marks the harvest festival of thanksgiving. A *sukkot* (a booth or tabernacle) is improvised by many families as a reminder of the temporary shelters that housed the ancient Jewish people during their wanderings in the desert. A table, chairs, and fruits furnish the improvised *sukkot,* and during the week of the festival the family meal is served there. Nowadays, many choose to celebrate Sukkot as a community or synagogue gathering. Special services are held in the synagogue on the first two and last two days of the festival, except among Reform Jews, who observe only the first and last days of the ritual.

Simhat Torah (Glorification of the Torah). This festival, celebrated at the end of Sukkot, is dedicated to the glorification of the Torah. It marks the end of one annual cycle of readings from the Torah in the synagogue and the beginning of another cycle. On this occasion, worshipers read from the last chapters of the book of Deuteronomy and the first chapter of the book of Genesis in the Torah to symbolize the eternal continuity of the Torah.

Hanukkah (Festival of Lights). Observed in the month of December, Hanukkah commemorates the Jewish battle for religious liberty led by Judas Maccabeus against the Syrian-Greek overlords in 165 BCE. The event is marked at home by the lighting of a candle on a nine-branched *menorah* (candelabrum) every evening for eight successive evenings. Rabbinic tradition holds that when Judas and his supporters entered the Temple, they found the menorah (candelabrum) damaged beyond repair. They immediately improvised a makeshift menorah out of their spears, unconsciously transforming their weapons into religious artifacts — symbols of peace. They found enough sacred oil to keep their menorah lit for one day. Miraculously, the oil lasted for eight days, the precise number of days it would take to secure and sanctify a new supply of sacred oil. Consequently, it was ordained that this miraculous event be celebrated annually in every Jewish home by the kindling of lights for eight days. Hence the term, Festival of Lights.

A nine-branched menorah is the form hallowed by tradition. Some types of menorah burn oil, but candles are also permissible. The center light is used for kindling each of the other eight tapers, one taper on each successive evening. Matching the spirit of Christmas, Jewish homes are decorated with a variety of Hanukkah symbols, Jewish schools commemorate the victory for freedom of worship with pageants and plays, and young and old exchange gifts.

Purim (Festival of Lots). Celebrated in February or March, Purim commemorates the rescue of Persian Jews from destruction at the hands of Haman the oppressor through the boldness of Esther (who, though a Jew, was the Persian queen) and her uncle Mordecai. Because the Persians cast lots to determine the appropriate day for the Jewish massacre, the festival is known as Purim (Lots). On this day, the scroll of Esther is read and gifts are exchanged.

Pesach (Passover). The most important family festival in Judaism, this feast, sometimes referred to as the Feast of Freedom, is celebrated in March or April and lasts for eight days (seven among Reform Jews). It commemorates the deliverance of the Jews from Egypt. At special synagogue services held to mark the occasion, the Torah is read, the story of the Exodus recounted, and psalms of praise chanted.

Shavuot (Weeks). Shavuot is celebrated fifty days after the festival of Pesach. Celebrated for two days (one day by Reform Jews) in May or June, this festival originally marked the wheat harvest. It now commemorates the anniversary of the giving of the Torah by God to Moses on Mount Sinai. Homes and synagogues are decorated with fresh fruits, plants, and flowers. Readings from the Torah include the books of Exodus and Ruth (a Moabite girl who adopted the Jewish faith).

Other Celebrations. Jews observe other religious celebrations, depending on local customs and the country in which they live. The various groups within Judaism follow different styles of observances. Members of certain groups do not feel necessarily bound by traditional restrictions imposed on activities defined as work. Moreover, various popular forms of celebration have emerged in modern Israel, sometimes replacing traditional ones. All variations reflect different expressions of Jewish faith.

STUDY QUESTIONS

1. What is the proper perspective for understanding Judaism?
2. What are the role and the function of Abraham in Jewish thinking?
3. Recount the traditional biography of Moses.
4. Describe the role and the activities of the prophets during and after the monarchy.
5. Trace the events associated with the rise of Judaism after the exile.

6. Discuss the Persian ideas identified in Jewish religious conceptions.

7. Distinguish the cause(s) and effect(s) that led Mattathias to revolt.

8. How did Judaism fare during the Roman occupation of Palestine?

9. Describe the treatment of Jews by Christian and Muslim powers.

10. Discuss the chain of events that led to an established Jewish state.

11. Describe the various Jewish groups from early to modern times.

12. What collections are included in the three major divisions of the Jewish scriptures?

13. Discuss the significance of the Talmud and the Midrash in Jewish life.

14. Present the fundamental views and concepts of Judaism.

15. What are the distinctive rites of passage?

16. What are the purpose and the function of the Sabbath?

17. Describe the religious role of women from early to modern times.

18. State the most significant holy days.

Suggested Reading

Baskin, Judith R. (ed.). *Jewish Women in Historical Perspective.* Detroit: Wayne State University Press, 1991.

Brown, Moshe. *The Jewish Holy Days: Their Spiritual Significance.* Northvale, N.J.: Jason Aronson, 1996.

Bulka, Reuven P. *Dimensions of Orthodox Judaism.* New York: KTAV Publishing, 1983.

Cohn-Sherbok, Lavinia. *A Short Introduction to Judaism.* Oxford: Oneword Publications, 1997.

Epstein, Perle S. *Kabbalah: The Way of the Jewish Mystic.* Boston and London: Shambhala, 1988.

Fackenheim, Emil L. *Jewish Philosophers and Jewish Philosophy.* Bloomington: Indiana University Press, 1996.

Greenberg, Irving. *The Jewish Way: Living the Holidays.* New York: Summit Books, 1988.

Greenstein, Howard R. *Judaism, an Eternal Covenant.* Philadelphia: Fortress Press, 1983.

Hammer, Reuven. *Entering Jewish Prayer: A Guide to Personal Devotion and the Worship Service.* New York: Schocken Books, 1994.

Johnson, Paul. *A History of the Jews.* New York: Harper & Row, 1987.

Lacks, Roslyn. *Women and Judaism: Myth, History and Struggle.* New York: Doubleday, 1980.

Levitt, Laura. *Jews and Feminism: The Ambivalent Search for Home.* New York: Routledge, 1997.

Neusner, Jacob. *The Way of Torah: An Introduction to Judaism.* 6th ed. Belmont, Calif.: Wadsworth Publishing Co., 1997.

Nigosian, Solomon A. *Judaism: The Way of Holiness.* Wellingborough, Eng.: Thorsons, 1986.

Reznick, Leibel. *The Mystery of Bar Kokhba: An Historical and Theological Investigation of the Last King of the Jews.* Northvale, N.J.: Jason Aronson, 1996.

Seltzer, Robert M. *Jewish People, Jewish Thought: The Jewish Experience in History.* New York: Macmillan, 1980.

Trepp, Leo. *Complete Book of Jewish Observance.* New York: Summit Books, 1980.

Wolowelsky, Joel B. *Women, Jewish Law and Modernity: New Opportunities in a Post-Feminist Age.* Hoboken, N.J.: KTAV Publishing, 1997.

Note

1. Cited in I. Epstein, *Judaism: A Historical Presentation* (Harmondsworth, Eng.: Penguin Books, 1959), p. 321.

14 Christianity

Christianity, like Buddhism and Islam, is a worldwide religion. It covers all of Europe, Britain, Canada, and the Americas. It also has many followers in Africa, Asia, and Australasia. Numerically, it is by far the largest religion in the world, with an estimated following of more than 1,780,000,000.

THE ROMAN EMPIRE

Christianity takes its name from the title attributed to Jesus, "Christ" (from the Greek *Christos*, which means "Anointed"; the Hebrew word for "Anointed" is *Mashiah,* hence the English word, Messiah). It emerged in Palestine (modern Israel) in the shadow of the Roman Empire, which was at its zenith. The Romans had conquered Palestine in 63 BCE, and by the time of the birth of Jesus, their empire had imposed a political unity on the lands bordering the Mediterranean that greatly facilitated the spread of various religions (see Chapter 11).

Religiously, the Roman Empire was pluralistic. Greek and Roman religions were tolerated from the earliest times, and in the first century BCE emperor worship was encouraged, chiefly as a means of promoting loyalty to the empire. Mystery cults, largely of Middle Eastern origin, were popular and widespread. Because the temper of the age was syncretistic, the mystery religions borrowed extensively from one another, and over time they came to share a number of common attributes. Of most importance, every cult centered around a "savior god" who had died and been resurrected. Adherents attained immortality by sharing symbolically in the death and resurrection of the savior god, whether he was called Mithras or Osiris, Adonis or Attis, Orpheus or Dionysus.

Ultimately, the religion of the savior god Jesus triumphed over all the others, but that must have seemed an unlikely outcome of events in

Christianity

CE

c. 30 Death of Jesus
c. 65 Death of Paul
c. 301 Baptism of Armenian King Tiridates III
313 Christianity legalized by Edict of Milan
325 First Council of Nicaea
354 Birth of St. Augustine (d. 430)
381 Establishment of five Christian Patriarchates
382 Complete listing of the books of the Old and New Testaments
        provided at a council held in Rome
451 Council of Chalcedon
c. 453 St. Patrick in Ireland
529 Athenian academy closed; Benedictine monastery opened
862 Cyril and Methodius in Moravia
1054 Split between Constantinople and Rome
1095 Beginning of the Christian crusades (continued until 1300)
1099 Capture of Jerusalem by Christian crusaders
1187 Recapture of Jerusalem by Salah el-din (Saladin) for Islam
1225 Birth of Thomas Aquinas (d. 1274)
1233 Inquisition begun by the Dominican order of priests (continued
        until 1834)
1517 Martin Luther's protest and the beginning of Protestantism
1534 Founding of the Society of Jesus (Jesuits) by Ignatius of Loyola;
        Henry VIII made head of the Church of England
1703 Birth of John Wesley (d. 1791)
1724 Birth of Immanuel Kant (d. 1804)
1818 Birth of Karl Marx (d. 1883)
1856 Birth of Sigmund Freud (d. 1939)
1869 Vatican Council I convened (concluded 1870)
1948 First assembly of World Council of Churches (WCC)
1962 Vatican Council II convened (concluded 1965)
1987 Desmond Tutu named the first black head of Anglican Church in South
        Africa and Archbishop of Cape Town
1991 Disestablishment of the Communist regime in Soviet Russia
1994 First South African election in which all people can vote; Nelson Mandela
        elected President

the early days of Roman tolerance. Not only were many religions tolerated, but so were many sectarian and nonconforming groups within religions. In Judaism, for instance, the Pharisees, who acted as the representatives of Jewish beliefs and practices, were concerned mainly with preserving the Jewish faith from compromises with Hellenism. The Sadducees, heavily represented in the wealthy elements of the population, controlled the central Temple in Jerusalem. The Zealots were fanatic patriots who refused any compromise with Rome and opposed all attempts to make Palestine subservient to Roman powers. Their revolt in 66–70 CE, which the Romans ruthlessly crushed, resulted in the burning of the Temple in Jerusalem and the dispersion of the Jews. The Essenes, a small communal group that lived in the vicinity of Qumran by the Dead Sea, opposed violence, lived by strict monastic rules, and patiently awaited the coming of the Messiah ("Anointed One of God"), who would deliver the Jews from foreign oppression.

The Jews had held hope of the coming of a Messiah (as an ideal king and savior) during their captivity in Egypt, long before they returned to Israel. Saul and David, the first two kings of Israel, were initiated into their royal office by anointing. Later generations that faced misfortune and destruction looked back to David as the ideal king and longed for a scion (son) of David who would deliver them from their oppressors and restore their ancient glory. During the exilic period, that longing took the form of a Messianic hope—that God would send his Anointed One (Messiah) to deliver his people from their enemies. Under the Greco-Roman rule, particularly in the first and second centuries CE, Messianic hope became so strong among the Jews that many self-proclaimed Messiahs appeared. Jesus, among others, was recognized by his immediate followers as a Messiah.

JESUS CHRIST

Sources of Information

Jesus left no writing of his own, so scholars have had to rely on three other sources of information about his life and teachings. The most important source comprises the four Gospels of Matthew, Mark, Luke, and John. Next are the writings of Paul, although he had no close relationship with Jesus. Finally, there are a few references to Jesus by classical writers of the first and second centuries CE; what they say about Jesus, however, does little more than establish his historical existence.

The four Gospels and the writings of Paul are not merely accumulations of historical facts. Rather, they are documents of faith and as such are primarily concerned with the theological implications of the life and death of Jesus. Historians generally assume that after the death of Jesus some of his disciples recorded his sayings before they were forgotten. That group of documents is called Q (from the German word *Quelle*, meaning "source"). It is further assumed that the Q documents, although on the whole authentic, were colored by presuppositions and included sayings mistakenly ascribed to Jesus. Furthermore, the Gospel writers—particularly Matthew and Luke—are assumed to have used a great deal of material from the Q documents. Whether or not that hypothesis is correct, two conclusions remain undisputed: that Jesus himself wrote nothing and that the content of the Gospels suggests or implies two sources. One is a record of sayings ascribed to Jesus, and the other is contemporary opinion reflecting the understanding of early Christians.

Biblical Tradition

The date and the place of Jesus' birth cannot be determined with certainty. According to the Gospel of Matthew, Jesus was born in Bethlehem in the days of King Herod, who died in 4 BCE. The Gospel of Luke, however, suggests two other dates: first, that Jesus was born in Bethlehem when Quirinius was governor of Syria, which was 6–9 CE; second, that Jesus was baptized at age thirty in the fifteenth year of the reign of Emperor Tiberius (26 or 27 CE), suggesting a date for the birth of Jesus of 4–3 BCE.

It was not until the sixth century CE that a Christian monk divided history into BC ("before Christ") and AD (*Anno Domini*, "year of our Lord"), to relate the birth of Jesus to the ancient Roman calendar. Whether that monk's calculation was correct or not, the beginning of the Christian era is assumed to date from the birth of Jesus. This reckoning has been accepted by the church and hallowed by long use.

As to the place of Jesus' birth, the Gospel writers vacillate between Bethlehem in Judea (Matthew 2:1) and Nazareth in Galilee (Luke 1:26–27, 57; John 1:45), locations some 200 miles apart. The early Christians (and hence the Gospel writers) may have been influenced by the desire to make Jesus a descendant of King David from Bethlehem and thus link him with Old Testament prophecies concerning the Messiah. But because all the Gospel writers agree that the family of Jesus lived in Nazareth, scholars have been inclined to attach greater credibility to the theory that the latter was Jesus' birthplace.

Jesus' Early Years

Little is known about the childhood and youth of Jesus. Mark and John make no mention at all of Jesus' virgin birth, childhood, or youth. On the other hand, Matthew and Luke declare that Jesus was born from the virgin Mary and that supernatural events occurred at the time of his birth (Matthew 1:18–25; Luke 1:26–45). Luke goes on to describe Jesus' circumcision rite when he was eight days old and his learned conversation with the Jewish rabbis in the Temple at Jerusalem when he was twelve (Luke 2:42–50). Mark and Matthew imply that Jesus' trade, like that of Mary's husband, Joseph, was carpentry, and that he had four brothers and a number of sisters (Mark 3:31, 6:3; Matthew 12:46, 13:55–56). Almost nothing else is known of his early years.

The Baptism and Temptation of Jesus

The Gospels relate that when Jesus was about thirty years old, a stern Jewish ascetic called John the Baptist appeared in Galilee and announced the coming judgment of God in the person of a Messiah, who would deliver the Jews from Roman rule. Standing by the River Jordan, he proclaimed, "Repent, for the kingdom of heaven is coming!" Jesus was among those whom John the Baptist baptized in the river.

That incident may have marked the turning point in Jesus' life. He at once withdrew to the wilderness beyond the Jordan before finally deciding on his future career. What actually happened during his forty days in the wilderness is a mystery. Mark states that Jesus lived there with the wild beasts and that angels ministered to him (Mark 1:13). Matthew and Luke say that Satan appeared in person and challenged Jesus with three temptations (Matthew 4:3–11; Luke 3:1–13).

As soon as Jesus came out of the wilderness he returned to Galilee to find that John the Baptist had been arrested and imprisoned. Jesus felt that the time had arrived for him to assume his role. He now repeated John's message: "Repent, for the kingdom of heaven is coming!"

Jesus' Mission and the Crucifixion

Jesus gradually attracted a group of twelve disciples, who constantly traveled with him from place to place proclaiming the "good news." Some of his disciples were fishermen, others were artisans, and one was a tax collector—a profession widely despised because it was identified with graft and subservience to Rome. At first, Jesus spoke in Jewish synagogues, but when the crowds grew too large, he resorted to open places.

The events recorded in the Gospels establish Jesus' authoritative personality, his keen interest in and compassion for people, and his reputation for healing. His forceful speeches and imaginative use of parables attracted large crowds. Relating easily with people of all types, including prostitutes and social outcasts, he apparently disdained social barriers and prejudices.

He also made enemies, chiefly by challenging time-honored assumptions. He ignored a number of Jewish traditions, such as Sabbath restrictions and ritual cleanliness, and scorned those who in his view had substituted social and ceremonial practices for inward morality. Sternly rebuking those who professed to be religious but were insincere and hypocritical, he offended Jewish scribes and leaders by openly attacking them for their views and behavior regarding authority, the Torah, divorce, taxes, and resurrection. His reputation varied according to the viewpoints of three disparate groups: to the scribes, he was an imposter and a deceiver; to much of the public, he was a prophet; to his disciples, he was the Son of God (Matthew 14:33).

The mission of Jesus lasted only a year or two before he, like John the Baptist, was arrested. The reasons for his trial and execution, as implied in the Gospels, are puzzling and contradictory. The only fact that is clearly and unambiguously recorded is that Jesus met his death on the cross, just like any other convicted rebel or criminal under the Roman administration.

Resurrection and Ascension

The events that followed the death of Jesus were of greater importance to early Christians than were the events that preceded it. The Bible records three phenomenal incidents. First, Jesus was resurrected three days after his crucifixion, and he subsequently appeared to many of his followers on numerous occasions. Second, forty days after his resurrec-

A procession of worshipers, led by priests, carry the cross along the Via Dolorosa (Latin for "sad road") to the Church of the Holy Sepulchre in Jerusalem during Easter week.
Courtesy of Israel Government Tourist Office, Ministry of Tourism, Toronto.

tion he was lifted up to heaven in the presence of a group of people who heard a voice saying, "Men of Galilee, why do you stand looking into heaven? This Jesus, who was taken up from you into heaven, will come in the same way as you saw him go into heaven" (Acts 1:10–11). Third, ten days after the ascent of Jesus—on the day of the Jewish festival of Shavuot—a group of Jesus' followers spoke in "strange" languages and claimed to have been filled with the Holy Spirit.

All those events laid the groundwork for various new insights among the followers of Jesus, in particular, the attribution of godhood to him and the proclaiming of him as the "Son of God." That Christian insight steadily spread to various parts of the Roman and Persian empires.

TEACHINGS ATTRIBUTED TO JESUS

In his Gospel, John states that if everything Jesus did and taught were to be recorded, "the world itself could not contain the books that would be written" (John 21:25), suggesting that Jesus said much more than was recorded in the Gospels. Consequently, identifying precisely what Jesus taught is as difficult as establishing his identity. As has been pointed out, Jesus left no written records. Sources of information that have survived are restricted primarily to the four Gospels, which do not read like verbatim reports of Jesus' words. Rather, the contents of the Gospels suggest that each writer used the material according to his own purposes and prejudices. That is not to imply that the Gospel writers distorted the message of Jesus, merely that what they wrote is likely to have been affected by their own perspectives as members of a community of early Christian believers.

Nonetheless, biblical scholars have carefully examined the Gospels as primary material in an attempt to discover the basic message of Jesus. Based on current knowledge and methodology, a number of biblical scholars recognize that the Gospels contain both reliable historical memories of the words and deeds of Jesus as well as information that is unhistorical but that has been attributed to Jesus by later Christians; scholars do, however, differ widely over how to classify specific Gospel passages. Hundreds of books have been written, each asserting that the most fundamental teaching of Jesus encompasses one or more of the following concepts: the Fatherhood of God, the Kingdom of God, God's love of humankind, and God's universal plan of salvation. The crucial question underlying those concepts is whether Jesus considered himself to be God incarnate or his followers endowed him that status after his death. The question remains unresolved because the Gospels present clear evidence justifying both views. Although it is impossible to examine in a few pages all those views, an attempt is made here to consider the basic concepts and teachings of Jesus, as recorded in the Gospels by some of his followers.

God

From the time of his baptism by John the Baptist to the end of his short life, the reality of God occupied the central place in the thoughts of Jesus. His own intimate relationship with God deeply impressed his disciples, as he strongly emphasized the Fatherhood of God. He regarded every human being as more than just a creature or servant of God—each individual was a child of God.

When his final hours of life on this earth were approaching, Jesus celebrated the Jewish annual Passover feast with his disciples for the last time and spoke to them after what has become known as the Last Supper. The Gospel of John gives us a vivid account of what Jesus spoke about. It is there (John 14–17) that Jesus reveals not only his deep relationship and intimacy with the Father, but how that relationship signifies to him complete union or oneness with the Father:

> If you had known me, you would have known my Father. . . . He who has seen me has seen the Father. . . . I am in the Father and the Father in me. (John 14:7, 9, 11)

Nevertheless, "the Father is greater than I," said Jesus, and "I do as the Father has commanded me" (John 14:28–31). Then suddenly he stopped and prayed:

> Father, the hour has come; glorify your Son that the Son may glorify you. . . . Holy Father, keep them [disciples] in your name which you have given me, that they may be one, even as we are one. . . . Now I am coming to you . . . O righteous Father, the world has not known you, but I have known you. (John 17:1)

Touched by Jesus' insight and prayer, the disciples followed him to the garden of Gethsemane. Deeply distressed and full of sorrow, Jesus fell to the ground and earnestly prayed once again:

> Father, all things are possible to you; remove this cup from me; yet not what I will, but what you will. (Mark 14:32–36)

When finally Jesus was crucified between two criminals, his words once again revealed his close relationship with God:

> Father, forgive them; for they know not what they do. (Luke 23:34)

And his last words on the cross were:

> Father, into thy hands I commit my spirit! (Luke 23:46)

That personal closeness with the Father was the characteristic feature of Jesus' teaching. In fact, he taught that God was everyone's Father and that every person could communicate directly and intimately with him, regardless of place or time. "Beware of practicing your piety before men in order to be seen by them," said Jesus, "For then you will have no reward from your Father who is in heaven" (Matthew 6:1).

Jesus not only made all who heard him distinctly aware of their relationship with God but directed their attention to the coming Kingdom of God, which he referred to as the "Kingdom of Heaven." (See Matthew, chapters 13 and 18–21, for parables of the Kingdom.) "The Kingdom of heaven may be compared to. . ." was the way Jesus began much of his teaching about God's Kingdom. His analogies regarding the Kingdom of Heaven covered a wide range of everyday activities that everyone could understand.

Whatever else Jesus may have implied by teaching about the Kingdom of Heaven, this much is certain: he urged everyone to seek primarily the Kingdom of God and His righteousness. He assured his hearers that God as a Father cared for every individual; no person was unworthy of receiving the Father's grace. Moreover, no person was to be excluded from the Kingdom of Heaven, for it was accessible to all who asked (Matthew 7:7–8).

A person's relationship with God is reasonably clear from the teachings of Jesus. What is less clear is how Jesus saw himself in relationship to God. Did he think of himself as a child or son of God in the same sense as he taught that everyone was a child or son of God? Or did he consider himself to be the "Son of God" in a special sense? Did he regard himself as the Messiah (the Lord's anointed), or was it his disciples who later thought of him as the Messiah?

Obviously, those questions have represented, and still represent, the knottiest issues of interpretation in the history of Christianity. And perhaps such crucial problems never can be finally answered. Nevertheless, one thing is beyond doubt: Jesus knew that he was "sent" to proclaim the Kingdom of Heaven and the Fatherhood of God (Luke 4:16–21, 43). Hence, he proclaimed that the Father's love for a person is so great and boundless that it is not governed by a person's goodness or wickedness. God manifests his love and mercy to all human beings — both good and bad — without regard to need or merit.

Humankind

Jesus taught that the two concepts, the Fatherhood of God and the union of humankind, are inseparable. An individual who experiences an intimate fellowship with God the Father must of necessity love humankind. Because the nature and the character of the Father are to love and be compassionate to all, it follows that the son should reflect the nature of the Father (Luke 18:23–25). In fact, anyone who does not love humankind can know nothing about God, let alone be associated with him. To love the individual who is unjust, cruel, deceitful, ugly, and unlovable; to love the murderer, the social outcast, and one's enemy as much as the good and the lovable is to love God. To feed the hungry, to clothe the naked, to welcome the stranger, to cheer the sick, to visit the imprisoned — in short, to love and serve humanity is to love and serve the Father (Matthew 25:24–46).

That teaching of Jesus so impressed the minds of many that an expert in Judaic Law (the Torah) once asked Jesus to explain what he meant by "loving one's neighbor as oneself" (Luke 10:29–37). Jesus replied by telling the story of a man who was robbed, beaten, stripped, and left to die on the road. A priest and a teacher who happened to pass that way saw the man but ignored him and traveled on. A Samaritan (one of the Jewish group regarded as enemies by traditional Jews at that time) who was the next traveler to pass pitied the man, stopped, helped him, and took care of all his needs.

"Which of these three," said Jesus, "do you think, proved neighbor to the man who fell among the robbers?"

"The one who showed mercy to him."

"Then go and do likewise," said Jesus.

Sin

For Jesus, the principles of love and mercy far outweighed any others. There was no question in his mind that the highest goal in life, the most valuable element in living, was to demonstrate God's nature: love, mercy, and compassion to one and all. One question, however, still eludes us. What was Jesus' own view about human nature? Did he agree that one was "born in sin" and inherently evil? Is evil part of one's makeup, like one's lungs or the hair on one's head?

Two of the Gospel writers, Luke and John, have nothing to say about the problem of original sin. The other two Gospel writers, Matthew (15:1–20) and Mark (7:1–23), however, record a discussion among Jesus and certain Jewish religious authorities who questioned him regarding the Tradition of the Elders.

"Why do your disciples transgress the Tradition of the Elders, and eat with hands defiled [ritually unwashed]?" they asked.

"And why do you transgress the commandment of God for the sake of your Tradition?" Jesus asked.

Then Jesus turned to all who were present there and said, "Hear me, all of you, and understand: not what goes into the mouth defiles a man, but what comes out of the mouth, this defiles a man." When his disciples showed by their questions that they did not understand what he was talking about, Jesus went on to say, "Do you not see that whatever goes into a man from outside cannot defile him, since it enters not in his heart but his stomach, and so passes on? What comes out of a man is what defiles a man. For from within, out of the heart of man, come evil thoughts, fornication, theft, murder, adultery, coveting, wickedness, deceit, licentiousness, envy, slander, pride, foolishness. All these evil things come from within, and they defile a man." (Matthew 15:1–20)

Thus, Jesus declared that sin lies deep in the heart of a human being. It is what lies in the heart—the hidden attitudes and motives—rather than outward actions that should be judged. But his statement offers no explanation of the nature of sin. Nor does he mention anything about original sin. It may be that his idea of the nature of sin was similar to one of the then current Judaic concepts, but certainly he shows no interest in defining sin or its origin in the abstract sense. Nevertheless, the presence and the problem of sin have been—and remain—a cause of dispute, schism, counterclaims of heresy, and even war among Christians. And no other person had more impact on the question of sin than Paul.

PAUL

Paul frequently has been called the real founder of Christianity, because his views came to shape and dominate subsequent Christian thinking. Paul's unique philosophy is particularly apparent in his writings collected in the New Testament, in which he applies terms such as *sin, redemption, justification*, and *reconciliation* to create the vocabulary of Christian theology. According to Paul, the human race sinned through Adam's disobedience and consequently lost its freedom and was condemned to death. The death of Jesus Christ was the payment or atonement that redeemed humanity, that is, won for it freedom and eternal life. Here is how Paul described it:

> As one man's trespass led to the condemnation for all men, so one man's act of righteousness leads to acquittal and life for all men. For as by one man's disobedience many were made sinners, so by one man's obedience many will be made righteous. (Romans 5:18–19)

> In fact, Christ has been raised from the dead, the first fruits of those who have fallen asleep. For as by a man came death, by a man has come also the resurrection of the dead. For as in Adam all die, so also in Christ shall all be made alive. (I Corinthians 15:20–22)

Paul was a non-Palestinian Jew. Born at about the same time as Jesus in the famous town of Tarsus in Cilicia (Turkey), he was a fanatically devoted Pharisee. He presumably purchased Roman citizenship and therefore enjoyed the legal status of a free-born Roman. He strongly opposed religious ideas that accommodated Hellenism or were compromised by Hellenistic influences, and he knew something about the adherents of the mystery cults, who claimed to have attained immortality by identification with a dying and rising savior god. To Paul, the Jew, those cults—and that included the cult of Jesus Christ—were anathema. He was one of the spectators at the stoning of the Christian Stephen and joined in the persecution of the early Christian group.

On a journey to Damascus to arrest Christian believers, however, Paul experienced a traumatic event that convinced him that the dead and resurrected Jesus of the Christians had appeared to him as he had appeared to others. In an instant of revelation, his fierce opposition to the Christian movement gave way to unquestioning support of it. Over the next three years, he developed a number of basic Christian theological concepts, the effects of which have dominated Christian thinking ever since.

At the heart of Paul's teaching was the concept of the Lordship of Christ. To redeem individuals from sin and death, Christ, a divine being possessing the nature of God, assumed a human form and humbled himself to die on the cross. His subsequent resurrection and ascension into heaven were proof of his triumph over death and sin—a triumph that could be shared by all who bound themselves to him by faith. Consequently, Paul declared, it was unnecessary to abide by the Jewish Torah (Law) to attain righteousness in the sight of God. Belief in and acceptance of Jesus Christ was the true path to righteousness. Those who believed in Christ, regardless of whether or not they followed the precepts of the Torah, were declared righteous in the sight of God. The following quotations illustrate Paul's teaching:

> Now we know that whatever the Law [Torah] says it speaks to those who are under the Law. No human being will be justified in His sight by works of the Law, since through the Law comes knowledge of sin. But now the righteousness of God has been manifested apart from the Law . . . the righteousness of God through faith in Jesus Christ for all who believe. (Romans 3:19–22)

> But now we are discharged from the Law, dead to that which held us captive, so that we serve not under the old written code but in the new life of the Spirit. (Romans 7:6)

> For the wages of sin is death, but the free gift of God is eternal life in Christ Jesus our Lord. (Romans 6:23)

> We rejoice in God through our Lord Jesus Christ, through whom we have now received our reconciliation. (Romans 5:11)

Paul then set out on his famous missionary journeys, during which he established Christian churches in many of the principal cities of the Roman Empire. His teachings—especially his criticism of the Torah—brought him into conflict with Jewish religious leaders, who were instrumental in his arrest in Jerusalem and indirectly responsible for the distrust in which Paul was held by the Roman authorities. Ultimately, he was taken into custody in Rome, where, according to tradition, the Romans executed him for the crime of disturbing the peace.

EARLY CHRISTIANITY

Persecution and Triumph

The first few centuries were critical times for Christianity. To begin with, a series of persecutions threatened its survival. Accused of holding secret orgies and charged with infanticide, incest, and cannibalism, Christians were tortured. Emperor Nero (57–68 CE) used Christian victims for the bloody Roman arenas. Other emperors, such as Decius (249–251) and Diocletian (284–305), employed ruthless measures in an attempt to stamp out Christianity. Christians not only survived those early trials but by the middle of the fifth century, emerged as the sole state religion of Rome.

The two emperors most instrumental in that development were Constantine (with his coemperor Licinius) and Theodosius II. (Under Diocletian, the empire was divided, for administrative purposes, into eastern and western parts, which eventually were ruled by coemperors.) The so-called Edict of Milan, issued in 313 by the coemperors Constantine and Licinius, stated that "concerning the Christians . . . all who choose that religion are to be permitted to continue therein, without any difficulty or hindrance, and are not to be in any way troubled or molested."[1] But the Edict of Theodosius, issued around 395, went further in prohibiting, on pain of death, the existence of any religion except Christianity:

> We interdict all persons of criminal pagan mind from the accursed immolation of victims, from damnable sacrifices, and from all other such practices that are prohibited by the authority of the more ancient sanctions. We command that all their fanes, temples, and shrines, if even now any remain entire, shall be destroyed by the command of the magistrates, and shall be purified by the erection of the sign of the venerable Christian religion. All men shall know that if it should appear, by suitable proof before a competent judge, that any person has mocked this law, he shall be punished with death.[2]

The Threat of Gnosticism

Another challenge that the early Christians had to face after the first generation of apostles had passed away was the movement commonly known as gnosticism. The Greek term *gnosis* means "knowledge"; for those initiated into the movement, *gnosis* meant secret or mystical knowledge about the constitution of the universe, human nature, and destiny.

The origins of gnosticism are obscure. Until the discovery of the Nag Hammadi documents (discovered in Egypt in mid-twentieth century), most of our knowledge came from works of its Christian opponents.[3] It seems that the gnostic movement was current in the Greco-Roman world during the second and following centuries, that it consisted of many sects in various places and under various leaders, and that the teachings among the differing groups ranged from beliefs that incorporated astrology and a complex mythology to beliefs that were elaborated in contemplative and philosophical terms.[4]

Despite the many differences in teaching and practice, the gnostics basically accounted for human nature as being compounded of a mortal material body and an immortal ethereal soul. The human condition was explained in terms of a cosmogony. There are two divine beings: a Supreme Being and a Demiurge, who emanated from and is inferior to the Supreme Being. The Supreme Being is often equated with mind (Greek, *nous*), life (Greek, *zoe*), and light (Greek, *phos*). The world was created by the Demiurge. Between the Supreme Being and the world are a series of entities (Greek, *aeons*), among which are the demonic powers who inhabit the planets and rule the world. Human beings resulted from the union of nature (Greek, *phusis*) and an archetypal man (Greek, *anthropos*), who had descended from the Supreme Being. Consequently, humans have a dual nature, material and spiritual. By acquiring true knowledge or *gnosis,* humans can be saved from their wretched state and free their spirits to return to communion with the Supreme Being.

Among the early Christian community were many gnostic Christians (e.g., Basilides, Cerinthus, Clement of Alexandria, Valentinus, Marcion), whose views cut at the roots of Christian beliefs. Basically, they held that the earthly life of Jesus was an apparition in human form, not an incarnation of the Supreme Being. In other words, the gnostic Christians claimed that Jesus did not take on material existence but appeared as a Redeemer from the realm of the spirit. He came to show humans the way to *gnosis* and to union with the Supreme Being. Humans could be saved from evil matter by acquiring true *gnosis* of their real nature and by following a prescribed discipline of abstinence, celibacy, and asceticism.

Some gnostic groups turned in the opposite direction. Rather than asceticism and withdrawal from the material world, they instituted orgiastic cults through which adherents expressed their spiritual nature by rising above good and evil.

Threat of Manicheism

The final triumph of Christianity over both gnosticism and state persecution was accompanied by an ironic role reversal: the persecuted, in league with the state, became the persecutors. No religious group was persecuted as ruthlessly or ferociously as were the followers of Manicheism, a religion founded by Mani (216–276) in the Persian Empire. If the exact reasons for such universal opprobrium remain difficult to isolate, it is clear that Mani's teachings and practices were perceived as a major threat to Christianity.

In his teachings, Mani made a deliberate effort to combine various Zoroastrian, Mesopotamian, Buddhist, and Christian elements, adapting or discarding whatever he felt was appropriate from other creeds. He was quite prepared to concede to his predecessors, such as Buddha, Zoroaster, and Jesus, the credit they deserved. But he considered himself the promised "Paraclete" of Jesus — the seal (end of the line of succession) of all previous prophets. He claimed to have ascended to heaven and there to have received the divine revelation in the form of a book. As recipient of the divine revelation, he regarded himself as the sole possessor of absolute truth.

At the center of Mani's system stood the doctrine of two eternal elements: God and Matter (alternatively, Good and Evil, Light and Darkness, or Truth and Falsehood). Mani taught that those aspects should not be recognized as two gods but rather as two primary elements, one called God and the other Matter, of which God is superior.

Mani's concept of the future life subsumed humanity under three classes: the Elect, the Hearers, and the Wicked. Immediately after death, according to Mani, the Elect ascend to the moon and are then conveyed to paradise; the Hearers pass through a long process of wandering and purification before they may join the Elect; and the Wicked roam around the universe in hopeless misery until they are consigned forever to the realm of darkness.

At the time of Mani's death, his religion had evolved into a highly organized system that had spread beyond the borders of the Roman Empire into Arabia, Iran, India, and China. Nothing is known for certain about the introduction and spread of Manicheism in the Roman Empire except for the evidence that it reached beyond Iran to Egypt, northern Africa, and Spain and from Syria to Turkey, Greece, Italy, and France. Its prevalence is attested to by the determined opposition of the Christian emperors who showed as much intolerance toward Manicheism as did Iranian rulers. Emperor Diocletian, for instance, drew up an edict against the Manicheans in 297. His prescriptions were draconian: all Manichean written materials and their authors, together with all ringleaders, were to be burned; all adherents were to be put to death and their properties confiscated; and anyone who held a position of high rank or status in society and was found to follow the Manichean religion was to be condemned to a fate far worse than death — compulsory labor in the mines. Opposition to Manicheans was no less vigorous from Christian leaders. Christian writers from Syria, Iraq, and Armenia allude to the Manichean religion as a "dangerous, wicked" faith. Greek and Latin authors considered the Manichean religion to be an "insane heresy," that is, opposed to established dogma. By far the most celebrated of Western authorities on Manicheism was the Catholic saint Augustine, who for nine years (373–382) before his conversion to Christianity had been a professed Manichean. After his conversion, Augustine wrote several works arguing against Manicheans. Pope Leo I (440–461) played an especially prominent part in the persecution of the Manicheans. Little is known about the history of Manicheism in Europe after the sixth century, because by that time the term *Manichean* had come to be used loosely to designate any heretical group.

Internal Disputes and Divisions

The early period of Christianity was also characterized by the first signs of differentiation and schism within the Christian movement. To protect the message of Christianity, many men withdrew from worldly contact and lived as hermits in deserts and other lonely places around the Mediterranean; that movement led to the establishment of monasticism (organized asceticism practiced by orders of monks and nuns). At the same time, internal disputes began to threaten the survival of Christianity as the persecutions by the Roman emperors had never done. As the disputes gave rise to numerous heretical movements, the Christian church was compelled to formulate an official creed (statement of belief) and to canonize certain writings as sacred scriptures. Also, the political and linguistic division of the Roman Empire into eastern and western parts in the fourth century created a basic rivalry for the leadership of Christianity. Rome was the center of the west, where Latin was the dominant language; Constantinople (modern Istanbul in Turkey) was the center of the east, where Greek predominated. Inevitably, the Christian establishments in the two centers competed for leadership. The issue was temporarily resolved at an ecumenical council convened in Constantinople in 381 that established five important ecclesiastical provinces, better known as Patriarchates: Rome, Constantinople, Alexandria, Antioch, and Jerusalem.

Various decisions, formulated at subsequent councils, hastened the fragmentation of Christianity. The first major rift came in the fifth and sixth centuries, when, discontented with certain issues and unwilling to be dominated by Constantinople, the Christian groups of Persia (also known as the Nestorian Church), Armenia, Syria (the so-called Jacobite Church), Ethiopia, Egypt (the Coptic Church), and India broke away from the rest of Christendom. To date, all have maintained autonomous existences. An even larger schism, between east and west, is conventionally dated to the year 1054 but will be dealt with here because its roots lay in the east-west division of the Roman Empire. From 1054, the churches in what had been the western part of the Roman Empire came to be known as the Roman Catholic churches, a strong, centralized organization headed by the pope (originally, merely the bishop of Rome). The churches in the eastern part of the Roman Empire, known as the Byzantine Empire, came to be called the Eastern Orthodox churches, each division of which was administratively independent and headed by its own patriarch. The four eastern patriarchs of Constantinople, Alexandria, Antioch, and Jerusalem loosely acknowledged the Roman pope as a "primary among equals," but the extent and the exact nature of the pope's authority never was clearly defined and agreed on. The result was the gradual and painful separation of the eastern and western parts of the Christian church.

Today, the Eastern Orthodox churches comprise the four ancient Patriarchates of Constantinople, Alexandria, Antioch, and Jerusalem; four more recent Patriarchates of Moscow, Serbia, Romania, and Bulgaria; the independent churches of Greece, Cyprus, Georgia, Albania, Finland, and Poland; and a number of national bodies. This federation of churches has no central authority; each church is self-governing.

Further movements within Eastern Orthodox churches in the sixteenth century led to the separation of the Uniates, or Eastern Catholic churches. These Eastern Orthodox churches reestablished communion with the Roman Catholic church while retaining their ancient rites of worship and liturgy.

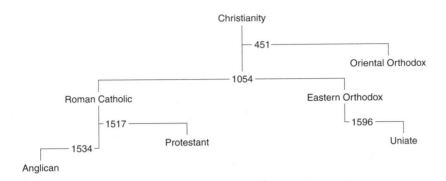

Anglican	Protestant	Eastern Orthodox	Oriental Orthodox
Church of England	Adventist	*Ancient Patriarchates*	Syrian
Church of Wales	Baptist		Coptic
Church of Ireland	Brethren	Constantinople	Armenian
Church of Scotland	Christian Scientist	Alexandria	Syro-Indian
Church of Canada	Church of God	Antioch	Ethopian
Episcopal Church U.S.A.	Swedenborgian	Jerusalem	
Archbishopric of Jerusalem	Congregationalist		*Uniate*
Church of Australia/Tasmania	Disciples of Christ	*Autocephalous*	Poland
Church of New Zealand	Evangelical	Russia	Ukraine
Church of South Africa	Friends	Romania	Antioch
Church of East Africa	Jehovah's Witnesses	Serbia	and others
Church of West Africa	Mormon	Greece	
Church of Central Africa	Lutheran	Bulgaria	
Church of West Indies	Mennonite	Georgia	
Nippon Sei Ko Kwai	Methodist	Cyprus	
Chung Hua Sheng Kung Hui	Moravian	Czechoslovakia	
Church of Uganda-Ruanda-Urandi	Nazarene	Poland	
Church of India, Pakistan,	Old Catholic	Albania	
Burma, Ceylon	Pentecostal	Sinai	
	Presbyterian		
	Reformed	*Autonomous*	
	Salvation Army	Finland	
	Spiritualist	China	
	Unitarian	Japan	
	Universalist		
	United Church		
	and others		

The Expansion of Christianity

In addition to unresolved disputes and internal disharmony, Christianity suffered severe setbacks after the rise of Islam in the seventh century. Within a century, the Arabs, inspired and united by Islam, conquered Syria, Palestine, Egypt, Sicily, Sardinia, Corsica, and Crete, as well as the entire Persian Empire. Despite this challenge to its monopoly on faith around the Mediterranean, Christianity slowly spread to the far corners of Europe, Africa, and Asia.

Between the fifth and eighth centuries, Christianity penetrated France, Britain, Ireland, and Scotland. Mainly through the efforts of Charlemagne, the Frankish ruler, the conversion of Germany was

St. Basil's Cathedral in Red Square, Moscow, built in the sixteenth century, now a tourist attraction. The early center of Russian Orthodoxy was Kiev, in the Ukraine. In 1590, the Council of the Orthodox Patriarchs in Constantinople (modern Istanbul, Turkey) formally recognized the Patriarchate of Moscow as the "Third Rome," after Rome and Constantinople.
Courtesy of the author.

accomplished late in the eighth century. In the tenth and eleventh centuries, Christianity spread to Norway, Sweden, and Denmark. About the middle of the tenth century, the Germans extended their political power and their Christian faith over Poland and the Baltic lands; by the thirteenth century, Estonia and Latvia were converted, mainly through German conquest. Similarly, Christianity prevailed in Finland, through Swedish conquest, around the thirteenth century.

In contrast to most of western Europe, where Christianity looked to Rome, the Christianity of eastern and central Europe looked to Constantinople. The Byzantine form of Christianity spread to the north and

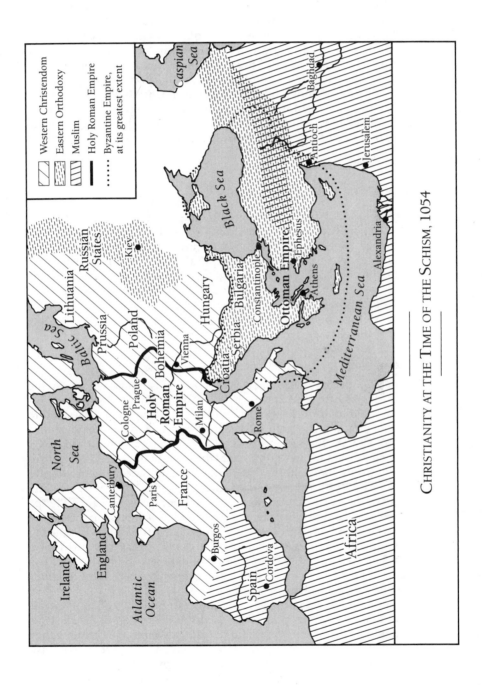

CHRISTIANITY AT THE TIME OF THE SCHISM, 1054

Legend:
- Western Christendom
- Eastern Orthodoxy
- Muslim
- Holy Roman Empire
- Byzantine Empire, at its greatest extent

Labels on map: Caspian Sea, Baghdad, Antioch, Jerusalem, Black Sea, Russian States, Kiev, Lithuania, Ephesus, Ottoman Empire, Alexandria, Constantinople, Athens, Mediterranean Sea, Hungary, Bulgaria, Serbia, Baltic Sea, Prussia, Poland, Vienna, Croatia, North Sea, Cologne, Prague, Bohemia, Holy Roman Empire, Milan, Rome, Canterbury, Paris, France, Ireland, England, Atlantic Ocean, Burgos, Spain, Cordova, Africa the west of Constantinople. In the ninth century, two Greek brothers from Thessalonica, Cyril and Methodius, were sent by Photius, the patriarch of Constantinople, as missionaries to the Slavic peoples, the Bulgars and the Serbs. Partly due to the efforts of those two men, Christianity gained a foothold also in Moravia (approximately the present-day location of Czechoslovakia). Around the tenth century, Byzantine Christianity penetrated into Kiev and later to various parts of Russia. Nestorians and some contingents of other Eastern Christianity also spread the faith to central and eastern Asia, but the numerical gains in those areas represented distinct minorities in continents dominated by Hinduism, Buddhism, Islam, and other religions.

CHRISTIANITY IN THE MIDDLE AGES

Several important and interesting, though perhaps paradoxical, developments coincided with the spread of Christianity. Particularly significant in the history of western Europe was a contest for supremacy between the papacy and various temporal states, in which each side asserted its authority and consequently denounced the other. Repeated attempts to resolve the tension came to nothing until changing times and circumstances reduced armed conflict to the level of an academic debate. Modern politics and society in the Western world have largely relegated the concept of ecclesiastical power to limbo.

The Crusades

Another significant development was a series of attempts to reform the standards of faith in Western Christianity. To that end, a number of popes sought to improve the credibility of the clergy and struggled to eradicate simony (the selling of indulgences), clerical marriage, and concubinage. At the same time, various monarchs who were either deeply concerned for the survival of Christianity or desirous of territorial gain (more likely, both) dreamed of a reinvigorated Christianity reconquering the lands that had fallen to Islam. Apparently with no thought of inconsistency and as a phase of the reform movement, Pope Urban II appealed to Christians in 1095 to fight a "holy war" to regain the places held sacred by the Christians. The result was a crusading movement, more popularly called the Crusades, that continued until nearly 1300 and gave rise to many acts of violence and barbarism. The net effect of the Crusades was to embitter relations between Christians and Muslims permanently.

Although most religions engage in varying degrees of conflict and persecution, only two religions have attempted to exterminate all rivals and dominate the globe: Christianity and Islam. From the first time they collided, both Christianity and Islam displayed exclusive, uncompromising, intolerant, and aggressive attitudes. Both proclaiming a monopoly on absolute truth, each regarded all other religious values and spiritual qualities to be false and invalid. Both felt a pressing need to convert the whole world to the truth each upheld. To that end, both used military force unhesitatingly. The record on both sides is stained with acts of violence, barbarism, and atrociousness.

The Inquisition

Another aspect of reform was the attempt of the Christian leadership to stamp out all forms of heresy. In 1179, the Third Lateran Council invoked the aid of secular powers to prosecute deviants from the Christian faith. Consequently, the papacy established a tribunal to identify individuals or groups whose views did not correspond to the teachings of the Roman Catholic church. In 1233, under the special direction of the Dominican order of priests, the Inquisition was established as a general court with almost unlimited powers. Imprisonment, exile, physical torture, public burning, and a host of other horrors were inflicted on all those whose religious views differed from papal orthodoxy.

The measures seem barbarous now, but by thirteenth-century standards they were not. They were simply the concomitants of power. Centuries later, Protestantism, which criticized the intolerance and interference of the Roman Catholic church, adopted the same brutal methods in imposing its own views on those who refused to conform. Apart from Protestantism , the Inquisition managed to suppress all groups or movements branded by the Roman Catholic church as heretical; it also was used as a weapon against the Jews and the Muslims before finally being abolished in 1834.

Persecution of Jews

The era 500–1800 was the darkest and most unfortunate period in the history of Christianity, not least because of continual and relentless persecution of the followers of Judaism. The story of Christian attempts to forcibly convert Jews, by methods paralleling in ferocity those leveled against the Manicheans, makes sad reading. The centuries of cruelty suffered by the Jews at the hands of Christians demonstrates the wickedness (and futility) of attempting to spread Christianity (or any other religion) by the use of sheer force. The fact that many Christian leaders once looked on the persecution of Jews as a religious duty is revealed in the words of a ninth-century Christian preacher at Beziers, France:

> You have around you those who crucified the Messiah, who deny Mary the Mother of God. Now is the time when you should feel most deeply the iniquity of which Christ was the victim. This is the day on which our Prince has graciously given us permission to avenge this crime. Like your pious ancestors, hurl stones at the Jews, and show your sense of His wrongs by the vigour with which you resent them.[5]

Attempts to convert Jews by force or persecution were carried out in all areas of Europe, but with particular cruelty in Spain, where they were linked in the public mind with the bitter, centuries-long struggle to reconquer the country from the Arabs. In 1296, the passions of the Spanish Christian populace of Toledo were so aroused against the Jews that synagogues were pillaged or utterly destroyed and thousands of

Jews were butchered. In 1391, similar massacres were perpetrated in Cordova, Valencia, and Burgos, and in 1460 in Andalusia and Castile. Needless to say, many Jews converted to Christianity to save their lives or the lives of their families.

Conquest of the Americas

During their conquest of Central and South America in the sixteenth century, the Spanish also attempted the last forced mass conversion to Christianity. Cortés and his Spanish troops entered Tenochtitlán (near modern Mexico City), the capital of the Aztec Empire, in 1519. Two years later, aided by thousands of American Indians, they completely leveled the ceremonial center, thus accelerating the forced conversion of the native people. But the Spanish conquest and widespread conversion to Christianity did not prevent the Aztec descendants from retaining some of their magical rites and religious beliefs, which have survived to the present day. In fact, many descendants of the Aztecs still live in small villages around Mexico City, speak their ancestral language, and, in many cases, combine their Christian religion with the ancient religion to form a peculiar style of Mexican Catholicism.

The Reformation

The tides of reform that surged and ebbed through Western Christianity in the Middle Ages failed to eradicate abuses in church practices, such as simony, or to reverse what many saw as the increasing worldliness, venality, and power hunger of the church clergy and hierarchy, up to and including many popes. At the same time, the medieval ideal of a unified Christendom was fast losing whatever hold it had exerted on the popular imagination, as emerging nation-states came to realize that Rome's agenda was not their own. Those trends, along with others, led to the religious movement commonly known as the Reformation.

Throughout the Middle Ages, religious movements branded as heresies by Rome had flared up in various parts of Europe. None were as threatening to Rome, however, as the Hussite movement, so called after Jan Hus (1369?–1415), a Czech priest who attacked clerical privileges and abuses, denied papal infallibility, and espoused state supervision of the church. Jan Hus presented a serious problem to the church authorities, because his calls for reform struck a responsive chord in the laity while infuriating the clergy, and his denial of Rome's authority became a rallying point for Czech nationalists (including King Wenceslaus IV). Hus was burned at the stake in 1415, but the religious and historical forces behind his views proved too powerful for the church to eradicate.

Martin Luther

On October 31, 1517, the German monk Martin Luther, following a common practice in university circles, affixed to the chapel door at the University of Wittenberg ninety-five theses challenging various church practices and doctrines. That date generally is regarded as marking the beginning of Protestantism, a religious movement whose numerous in-dependent churches were united chiefly by a rejection of the religious authority of the papacy and an emphasis on the individual's responsi-bility for his or her own salvation through faith. Both doctrines ap-pealed not only to the many Christians disgusted with the corruption rampant among the clergy but also to princes and kings eager to be rid of Rome's authority over their subjects. Royal patronage ensured the survival of the nascent Protestant churches. It also ensured that what had begun as a reform movement within the church would become in-extricably intertwined with political disputes. Religious warfare, at-tended by persecution and civil strife, plagued Europe for the next 150 years. By the end of that period, Catholicism (as the church of Rome was now known) had succeeded in checking the advance of the Protes-tant churches, while the latter had succeeded in establishing their inde-pendence from Rome.

The Spread of Protestantism

A concerted effort to halt the spread of Protestantism was launched by the Council of Trent in 1545. The chief accomplishments of the Counter-Reformation, as it became known, were the abolition of simony, the re-form and reinvigoration of the clergy, and the encouragement of educa-tion and proselytization as the most effective means of fighting Protestantism and advancing Catholicism. Spearheading that last effort was the Society of Jesus (Jesuits), founded by Ignatius of Loyola in 1534. A militant, highly disciplined, and well-educated religious order, the Je-suits not only helped check the advance of Protestantism but also estab-lished Roman Catholic missions in India, China, Japan, and the Ameri-cas. Protestant reformers, in contrast, were late in introducing their form of Christianity to non-European peoples. Not until the nineteenth and twentieth centuries were they able to compete with Roman Catholic missionaries on anything like equal footing outside Europe. That they finally were able to do so was largely due to the spread of imperialism and colonialism. In the meantime, various forces were changing, with increasing rapidity, the shape of Western civilization.

The Enlightenment

While various groups were developing Protestant principles in differ-ent directions and forming a multitude of churches, a succession of philosophers such as René Descartes, David Hume, Immanuel Kant, and G. W. Leibniz were turning away from theology to mount a ratio-nalistic investigation of human nature. Similarly, scientists such as Galileo and Isaac Newton pursued their experiments on and investiga-tions into natural phenomena independent of theological dogma. In art, history, and literature, theological issues and themes also were gradu-ally superseded by an interest in human activity and behavior. Those trends coalesced into the most influential intellectual movement in Western civilization prior to the twentieth century: the Enlightenment.

The Enlightenment began in the mid-seventeenth century in England and the Netherlands, but it was nowhere more eloquently

Indian converts worshiping in the Catholic church of Our Lady
of the Mount, Bombay, India. The introduction of Roman
Catholicism to India dates from the beginnings of Portuguese
activity in Asia in the fifteenth century CE. Today, only a tiny
percentage of Indians have converted to Christianity.
Courtesy of Government of India Tourist Office, Toronto.

articulated than in Germany and France. Leibniz, G. E. Lessing, and
Kant in Germany, and Voltaire (the pen name of François Marie Arouet),
Claude Adrien Helvétius, and Auguste Comte in France were its foremost philosophical offspring. Immanuel Kant (1724–1804), one of the
most influential of all Enlightenment thinkers, rejected biblical, concil-
iar, and any other nonrational accounts of human nature and the universe. Kant, followed by G. W. F. Hegel, believed that human beings
possessed a reasoning faculty that was capable of unraveling truth from
tradition and reality from myth. Consequently, Kant and Hegel dismissed the domain of the transcendent as irrelevant and defined religion as a manifestation of human self-expression.

    Widespread disenchantment with religion after over a century of re-
ligious wars and distaste for church dogmatism were two of the most
important factors that shaped the Enlightenment's optimistic perception of human, mortal, temporal potential. In the field of sciences, the
evidence of empirical discoveries led to conclusions that seemed to oppose theological judgments and affirmations of faith. The rubric of religion represented such a ponderous mass of absolute authority, superstition, and anti-intellectualism that many thinkers found themselves

forced to choose between Christian principles and love of humanity. The social thinker Auguste Comte (1798–1857), for instance, advanced the idea that humans pass through three evolutionary stages in their quest for an understanding of natural phenomena: (1) a search for a theological or supernatural explanation; (2) a search for a metaphysical or abstract explanation; and (3) a search for a social explanation. In Comte's view, humanity by the nineteenth century had reached the third stage, having graduated, as it were, from theology and philosophy.

Comte's sociological views led other thinkers, such as Hegel and Karl Marx, to amplify his emphasis on human autonomy and consciousness in different ways. The response of Christian churches was predictable. They branded anyone who had the temerity to reject ecclesiastical authority and to discard Christian doctrines and ethics as a godless sinner doomed to eternal damnation without hope of redemption. Such prospects, however, did not in any way arrest the intellectual and political aspirations of enthusiastic exponents of the spirit of the Enlightenment and their followers. On the contrary, secular rulers increasingly relegated religion to the private sector and demonstrated their reluctance to sanction state approval of one religious group at the expense of others. Similarly, with the authority of theology diminished, scientific data increasingly challenged the credibility of biblical accounts. Scientists grew increasingly confident that they soon would unlock all the mysteries and secrets of nature, including human nature.

Understandably, church leaders reacted strongly (as some still do) to the primacy of empirical reasoning and human rationality, arguing that denial of the transcending power of Christian revelation would only lead to an extension of human evil, an increase in the dehumanization of society, and total perdition. The evidence has not been conclusive or particularly reassuring on either account. In view of the horrors and bloodbaths of the French Revolution in 1789 and of the increasing degree and scale of horror culminating in the threat of a nuclear apocalypse, the application of Enlightenment beliefs has not proved an unqualified boon to humanity. Although the Age of Enlightenment was distinguished as much by its benefits as by its excesses—particularly in terms of human freedom, growth, and development and in the recognition of women in their own right—the legacy it bequeathed to the twentieth century has not diminished the debate among Christians over the issue of faith versus reason. Events have a habit of overtaking debates. In the interval, various forces paved the way for drastic changes.

CHRISTIANITY IN MODERN TIMES

Religious Movements

To meet the challenges of the changes provoked especially by the Industrial Revolution and the growth of cities, a variety of religious movements emerged in the nineteenth century. In 1844, the Young Men's Christian Association (YMCA) was founded by George Williams, an Englishman whose aim was to improve the physical, social, intellectual, and religious level of the young men in lower- and middle-income groups. The International Red Cross was organized in 1863, mainly through the efforts of the Swiss Henri Dunant, to take care of the sick and wounded in war. In 1878, the Salvation Army was begun by another Englishman, William Booth, in an effort to uplift, both physically and spiritually, the poor and downtrodden. In 1889, the Christian Social Union (CSU) was founded in England, mainly to resolve management-labor disputes by applying Christian principles.

Ecumenism

The outstanding movement among Christians in the twentieth century has been ecumenism, the trend toward worldwide unity or cooperation among churches. Paradoxically, Protestant reform that resulted in fragmentation in earlier centuries is now being countered by reform aimed at reunion, two types of which in particular are distinguishable.

The first consists of mergers of two or more religious groups to form one new institution. The United Church of Canada, for example, was formed in 1925 from groups of Methodists, Congregationalists, and Presbyterians. The Reformed Church of France was created in 1938 by the union of the Evangelical Methodist Church of France, the Reformed Evangelical Church of France, the Reformed Church of France, and a union of Evangelical Free Churches. The Church of Christ in Japan grew in 1941 from a union of fifteen religious bodies. In 1947, the Church of South India resulted from the union of four denominations. Twenty-seven independent regional churches joined in 1948 to form the Evangelical Church in Germany. Finally, the United Church of Christ in the United States was formed in 1961 by the amalgamation of the Congregational Christian churches with the Evangelical Church and the Reformed Church, both of which were the products of prior mergers.

Ecumenism also has taken the form of the convocation of international and independent Christian denominations for cooperation and federated action. The most visible manifestation of such a reunion was the organization of the World Council of Churches (WCC), which first met in 1948 in Amsterdam. Initially, only several Protestant denominations and a few representatives of Eastern Orthodoxy supported the organization. Since then, the WCC has convened several more times. Many Protestant denominations and various Eastern Orthodox contingents, including the Russian Orthodox church, have joined the organization and regularly send delegates to the conferences. Since 1961, the Roman Catholic church has sent official observers.

Although it is too soon to predict the long-term effects of the ecumenical movement, one benefit seems evident: it has forced Christians with similar allegiances but differing convictions to examine the paradox of a single church divided against itself—a parody of Christian ideals.

Religious Pluralism

The age of cultural isolation and religious imperialism finally has given way to one of cultural diversity and religious pluralism. The decisive nature and the sociological ramifications of this phenomenon are,

A Greek Orthodox secular priest on his way to church. In both the Greek
Orthodox and the Roman Catholic churches, priests play an important role.
In contrast to the Roman Catholic Church, the Greek Orthodox Church
distinguishes between "religious" and "secular" priests. The former are celibate
(unmarried), while the latter are permitted to marry.
Courtesy of Wolf Arnold.

undeniably, quite momentous. At no other time in history — except, perhaps, during the Roman period — has Christianity been more attracted
to the fusion of East-West religious ideas and practices. Experimentation with alternative religions is a burgeoning phenomenon in modern
society. The responses of various Christian thinkers, Roman Catholic
and Protestant, to religious pluralism have led to the development of
five important perspectives: exclusive, teleological, relative, single world
religion, and dialogic.[6]

Exclusive Perspective. To exclusivists, only one religion is true or valid; all other religious traditions are dismissed as false. From this perspective, the imperative role of the true religion is to replace all other religions by confronting their adherents with an uncompromising alternative.

Teleological Perspective. Those who take the teleological perspective view one particular religion as the pinnacle and completion of all other religions; in other words, one religion is seen to be the fulfillment of what is best and true in the others. The difference between this view and the exclusivists' position is only one of degree. The exclusive view idealizes a particular religious tradition and consequently considers all other religions to be false and invalid, while the teleological view affirms the superiority of one religious tradition and the inferiority of all the rest.

Relative Perspective. A somewhat similar position is held by those who see all other faiths as a *praeparatio evangelica*, "preparation for the Gospel." The relative argument is that in Christianity reposes the divine initiative; in all other religions, the human initiative reigns. In Christianity, God through Christ moves authentically to people, whereas in other religions people move toward God. Christianity is indubitable and inclusive, whereas other religions are dubious and partial.

Those who take a relative perspective argue that all religions have identical goals and, therefore, represent different ways of reaching ultimate truth. No religion possesses absolute truth — only relative truth. As a result, all religious traditions are considered to be simply different paths to the same goal.

Single-World Religion. Advocates of a single-world religion maintain that the same forces that inevitably will transform the present world into a world community also will give rise to one world religion. At least three ways of achieving that one religion have been postulated. The most simplistic is that one of the living religious traditions eventually will become the world religion by displacing all the rest. The second way is that the best insights from all the religious traditions will be selected and adapted to produce one new religion. And the third way, which lies somewhere between the first two, theorizes that the more each religion is forced (by the impact of religious pluralism and the emergence of a world culture) to go through the process of reconception — that is, the rediscovery of what is essential in its own particular religion — the nearer all will come to constituting one world religion.

Dialogic Perspective. From a purely practical point of view, *dialogic* simply means communication: open and frank discussion among persons who seek mutual understanding or harmony. Supporters of this view seek to put aside all preconceptions about other religions and to be prepared to listen and understand other religionists, even those whose utterances or behavior seems unintelligible. The act of dialogue is really a means whereby members of different religions learn how to communicate honestly and openly. It usually is argued that it is good for adherents of different religions to meet, seriously and sympathetically, to find out on what they agree and on what they differ. Some people insist, that the only appropriate mode of interreligious relationship is the act of dialogue, through which future relationships among adherents of various religious persuasions will develop differently from those anticipated now.

The dialogic perspective has become exceedingly popular, not least because it seems to offer the most promising and valid tool whereby people of different religious traditions can find a common ground to serve humanity in cooperation with one another.

The Emancipation of Women

Another outstanding movement among Christians is the emancipation of women. Until recently, Christian churches of all types generally supported the cultural conventions that conferred on women, in legal terms, a status of subservience and incompetence. The courage and determination of pioneering leaders of women's rights to fight against longstanding customs of the church and society have brought about important breakthroughs in different ways and in varying degrees. Emma Hart Willard (1787–1870), regarded as the first American woman to support publicly higher education for women, founded a girl's seminary in Watertown, New York, which was later moved to Troy, New York. In 1824, Catharine Beecher led the establishment of a seminary for women in Hartford, Connecticut. Soon thereafter, women started to pray aloud in mixed church assemblies; after a long period of resistance, they formed their own voluntary missionary societies.

Several prominent Christian advocates of women's rights identified themselves with the struggle for the abolition of slavery, notably, Sarah and Angelina Grimke, Lydia Child, Elizabeth Stanton, and Harriet Beecher Stowe. Stowe's novel *Uncle Tom's Cabin* published in 1851, made a vivid and unforgettable impression and touched many consciences.

Most Christian churches have not moved much beyond that point, however. Many do not reflect the cultural conventions of the present but preserve those of the past. In general, women have been kept out of power in church life, home and foreign missions, leadership, administrative positions, and policy making. William Augustus Muhlenberg (1796–1877), an Episcopalian clergyman, aroused strong opposition among his fellow religionists when he established an order of deaconesses in 1857 in New York. Not until the beginning of this century did other Christian churches follow suit.

If the emergence of feminist and women's liberation movements in church and society in modern times has posed a challenge to the old, familiar Christian patterns, it also has brought about fresh sources of energy and insight. Women have been elected to executive positions in churches of many denominations, and several churches have pioneered in ordaining women to the ministry and, occasionally, electing them to the highest church rank (e.g., several Protestant churches have elected women as moderators of their general assemblies).

The Roman Catholic church has made some progress in women's rights, particularly after Vatican II (the Ecumenical Council of 1962–1965). No such transformation had taken place since the Council of Trent, in 1546. Since Vatican II, many familiar features of church life, such as ecclesiastical administration, devotional practices, the form and the language of worship, ecumenical relationships, attitudes to non-Christians, and the role of nuns and women, have changed. Female laity have been given active roles in church life and in educational institutions, and they now are appointed to advisory school boards, parish councils, and diocesan senates. As a result, many Catholic women, including several nuns, have become prominent in social service and civil rights activities. Since the 1970s, the National Coalition of American Nuns has sought from the Roman curia (the papal court of the Roman Catholic Church) full equality with priests, challenging the church's justification of an all-male priesthood. That they have failed says much about the inherent conservatism of the church hierarchy.

The extent of the injustices and inequalities suffered by all women throughout the world can never be fully estimated. To this day, women in the arts, the sciences, business, politics, education, and religious institutions have remained "the second sex," in the words of the French philosopher Simone de Beauvoir. Feminists and women's liberation advocates are seeking to remedy the situation on several fronts. Some women, such as Sally Cunneen and Rosemary Reuther, are striving to change the masculine image projected in the Godhead, in Christian theology, and in religious symbols. Others, such as Angela Davis and Michelle Wallace, are attempting to change the lamentable status and condition of black women. Issues related to the role of women in Christian churches undoubtedly are complex, but the combined efforts and courageous accomplishments of female leaders are bound, in the long run, to remedy the inequalities that still remain.

THE BIBLE

Of all the major living religions, Christianity is the only one that reveres and includes in its sacred writings the whole scripture of the Jewish Bible, called the Old Testament by Christians, suggesting the "old Covenant" God made with Moses at Mount Sinai. Added to the Old Testament in Christian scripture is a collection of writings known as the New Testament, the "new Covenant" Jesus made with his disciples at the Last Supper. Together, the Old Testament and the New Testament books constitute the sacred writings of Christianity and are commonly referred to as the Bible.

The Old Testament

The early Christian community inherited the scripture of the Greek-speaking Jewish community, known as the Septuagint (abbreviated as LXX). The collection of books in that scripture included some writings that originated between 200 BCE and 100 CE but were never part of the Jewish Bible or Hebrew collection. We do not know exactly what authority the Greek-speaking Jews attributed to those writings. We do know, however, that the Greek-speaking Jews completely abandoned the Septuagint text early in the second century CE. That action did not affect the position of the early Christians. They not only adopted the Septuagint version but also possessed their own unique Christian writings based on the apostles and early witnesses. Consequently, separate designations developed for the two-part Christian canon: the Old Testament and the New Testament. The former designation was first made by Melito of Sardis (c. 180 CE), the latter by Tertullian (c. 200 CE).

Although the early Church accepted all the books listed in the Septuagint as canonical (divinely inspired), the decision over the additional books did not arrive so easily. Melito of Sardis, Athanasius, Cyril of Jerusalem, and Jerome, among others, disputed the canonicity of books that were excluded from the Hebrew text of the Jewish Bible. Jerome (346–420 CE) was the first to suggest that the books found in the Septuagint and Latin scriptures, but not in the Hebrew, be considered as *Apocrypha* (i.e., of mysterious origin).[7] Nevertheless, Jerome included those extra books in his Latin Vulgate by official orders of the bishops *(Prologus in Tobiam)*.

The Council in Laodicea in Phrygia (362 CE?) listed only the collections of the Hebrew text in the canon. Later, the local councils of Hippo (393 CE) and Carthage (397 and 419 CE) listed the additional books in the canon. The debate over those books emerged in subsequent councils, the Council in Trullo (692 CE) and the Council of Florence (1441). Finally, the Council of Trent (1546) settled the matter decisively for Roman Catholics. The authoritative pronouncement of the Roman Catholic Church reaffirmed its official consensus regarding the Old Testament canon. All the books listed in the Hebrew text were recognized as canonical; in addition, it accepted seven other Jewish writings: Tobit, Judith, Book of Wisdom, Ecclesiasticus, Baruch, and 1–2 Maccabees. Those seven writings plus additional parts of Esther and Daniel are considered by Roman Catholics as Deuterocanon (i.e., of secondary canon), a term coined in the sixteenth century to designate scriptural books whose canonicity was disputed but later accepted. During that same period (i.e., sixteenth century CE) the Protestant reformers, including Martin Luther, accepted only those books included in the Hebrew text as canon. Luther's translation of the Old Testament into German (in 1534) comprised the Hebrew text plus the additional works, which he entitled *Apocrypha* (meaning useful and good for reading but not of canonical nature), and set them apart from the rest of the Old Testament. Today, Protestants consider the extra works as the Apocrypha and assign them inferior status, often ignoring them as having no part in the canon.

As to the Eastern Orthodox canon, its books have not corresponded entirely with those of the Roman Catholic canon. Throughout the centuries, sometimes the longer and sometimes the shorter canon prevailed. The important Council of Jerusalem (1672) established the longer canonical list, varying only slightly from that of the Roman Catholic canon.

The New Testament

Naturally, many writings and collections of stories circulated widely during the first four hundred years of Christian history. Eventually, twenty-seven writings were assembled to form the New Testament and accepted as canonical. First in order are the four Gospels (Matthew, Mark, Luke, and John), which record the life and teachings of Jesus. They are followed by the book known as the Acts of Apostles, which chronicles the history of the early Christian missionaries. Succeeding the Acts are a number of Epistles—letters written by various disciples (most notably Paul) either to individuals or to Christian communities. The last book, Revelation, is a visionary account of the final triumph of God.

In its earliest form, Christian literature consisted of letters, or epistles. The epistles of Paul are probably the earliest writings in the New Testament. Some time during the first century, a number of Paul's letters circulated among Christians. The four Gospels of the New Testament also appeared in the same century. However, there seemed to be no attempt on the part of the early Christian community to regard those writings as scripture. During the second century, a flood of gospels and other literature forced Christians to make selections in their estimation of an authoritative Christian literature. The earliest exact reference to the current collection of books in the New Testament appeared in 367 in a letter of Athanasius, bishop of Alexandria. A complete listing of the books of the Old and New Testaments was provided at a council held in Rome in 382. Thus, the Christian bible took its final shape by the late fourth century.

The Christian Canon

The word *canon* is a Greek transliteration of the Semitic word *qaneh* meaning "reed." Because the reed was used in early times as a measuring rod or device, the word *canon* came to mean a rule, guide, or standard. As far as we know, the term was first used in the sense of divine rule or guide for the books of the New Testament by the Christian Athanasius in the fourth century CE (*De decretis Nicaenae synodi*, 18.3). Thus, the idea of a canon (i.e., a list of recognized, authoritative books) derived from the Christian period.

CHRISTIAN TEACHINGS

Creeds

Several principles that throughout the ages have been accepted as fundamental tenets of Christianity are explicitly summarized in the professions of faith known as creeds (from the Latin *credo*, "I believe"). Of the various creeds promulgated through the centuries, two have emerged as predominant in contemporary Christian churches, the Apostles' Creed and the Nicene Creed.[8]

I believe in God the Father Almighty, Maker of heaven and earth, and in Jesus Christ, His only Son, our Lord, Who was conceived by the Holy Ghost, born of the Virgin Mary, suffered under Pontius Pilate, was crucified, died, and was buried; He descended into hell; the third day He rose again from the dead. He ascended into heaven. And sitteth on the right hand of God the Father Almighty; from thence He shall come to judge the quick and the dead. I believe in the Holy Ghost, the holy Catholic Church; the Communion of saints; the forgiveness of sins; the resurrection of the body; and the life everlasting.

THE NICENE CREED

I believe in one God, the Father almighty, maker of heaven and earth, and of all things visible and invisible. And in one Lord Jesus Christ, the only-begotten Son of God. Born of the Father before all ages. God of God, light of Light, true God of the True God. Begotten not made; being of one substance with the Father; by whom all things were made. Who for us men, and for our salvation, came down from heaven. And was incarnate by the Holy Ghost of the Virgin Mary and was made man. He was crucified also for us, suffered under Pontius Pilate, and was buried. And the third day He rose again according to the Scriptures. And ascended into heaven. He sitteth at the right hand of the Father. And He shall come again with glory to judge both the living and the dead; of whose kingdom there shall be no end. And I believe in the Holy Ghost, the Lord and giver of life; Who proceedeth from the Father (and the Son); Who together with the Father and the Son is adored and glorified; Who spake by the Prophets. And in one, holy, catholic and apostolic Church. I confess one baptism for the remission of sins. And I look for the resurrection of the dead. And the life of the world to come.

The Trinity

At least three fundamental beliefs can be distinguished in the two creeds. First, Christians affirm the existence of one God in the form of the Trinity: the Father, Son, and Holy Spirit (Holy Ghost). The concept of Unity in Trinity or Trinity in Unity is considered to lie beyond the limits of human comprehension and therefore to be a divine mystery. The idea is not entirely foreign to human experience, however; water, for instance, retains its chemical identity regardless of whether it takes the form of ice, liquid, or steam. To a Christian, the idea of the Trinity is not analogous to three roles played by a single person (e.g., a man who simultaneously assumes the roles of son, husband, and father); rather, it signifies three distinct beings that are yet fully one God.

Incarnation

The second basic Christian doctrine is that of Incarnation: the belief that, in Jesus, God assumed a human body. To Christians, Jesus was not merely a prophet or a teacher but "the only-begotten Son of God," who was at the same time genuinely human and genuinely divine. Thus,

Saint Peter's Basilica in Vatican City, the mother church of Catholicism. Tradition holds that the apostle Peter died here on a cross about 64 CE. The present structure dates from 1506. Courtesy of C. LaVigna.

Jesus is identified with God as well as with humanity—he is God-man, truly God and truly human simultaneously. Further, Christianity claims that even though Jesus was put to death, he was resurrected three days later, ascended into heaven, and is presently with God the Father, awaiting the time of his return to judge every person, dead or alive, and to establish his eternal kingdom.

Reconciliation

Finally, Christianity firmly holds to the doctrine of reconciliation, or atonement. In the view of Christians, Adam, the father of humankind, estranged humanity from God by his disobedience, as a consequence of which all humans are sinners. But if Adam represents humankind, so does Jesus, whose death is viewed as a self-sacrifice that atoned for the original sin of Adam. Jesus' resurrection is interpreted as proof of universal atonement and a triumph over death. All those who believe in Jesus thus are no longer alienated from God but are his children.

Variations within Christianity

Naturally, around those basic themes are many variations within the body of Christianity, especially among the Eastern Orthodox, Roman Catholic, and Protestant branches. The distinctions among the three main branches are complex. Suffice it to say that Protestants not only reject the doctrinal authority of the Roman Catholic and Eastern Orthodox churches, they also maintain that the Bible is the only source of authority and that the Holy Spirit, rather than the Roman Catholic or Eastern Orthodox church, illuminates the minds of individuals who read and study the Bible. Moreover, many Protestants repudiate the following fundamental elements upheld by both Eastern Orthodox adherents and Roman Catholics: apostolic succession (the line of succession from Jesus, through the apostles, to the popes and patriarchs), hierarchical structure, an episcopate (office of bishop), a system of priesthood, prayers offered to saints, intercession for the departed, and various other, minor issues. By the same token, Eastern Orthodox groups reject the supremacy of the pope and papal infallibility (the doctrine that formal papal decrees on matters of faith must be accepted as true). Instead, Eastern Orthodox churches assert the supremacy of the College of Bishops among their own ranks, stressing the infallibility of the church as a whole.

CHRISTIAN OBSERVANCES

Sacraments

All three branches of Christianity—Eastern Orthodox, Roman Catholic, and Protestant—have developed a variety of teachings and practices based on the same fundamental Christian principles. The differences between the groups are even more pronounced in the observances of Christian sacraments and festivals.

Christians express themselves in several religious acts that are considered sacraments. A *sacrament* is an outward sign or the performance of a rite through which divine grace is sought and conferred. Both Roman Catholics and Eastern Orthodox adherents regard seven rites as sacraments: Baptism, Confirmation/Chrismation, Penance/Confession, Eucharist/Holy Communion, Matrimony, Holy Orders (ordination), and Holy Unction/Euchelaion (last rites). Many Protestant groups consider only two sacraments: Baptism and Holy Communion. Brief descriptions of the seven sacraments will serve to indicate their correspondence to the different stages of life.

- Baptism is recognized as the first stage of initiation into the Christian faith. Most Christian churches baptize the candidate in infancy, although a few Protestant subgroups wait until adolescence or adulthood.

- Confirmation or Chrismation is the next stage, performed by the Eastern Orthodox Church (Chrismation) immediately after the infant's baptism and by the Roman Catholic Church (Confirmation) on children between the ages of seven and fourteen.

- Penance/Confession of sins is the third sacrament, followed by the granting of absolution, or formal forgiveness.

- Eucharist or Holy Communion is the fourth sacrament, in which the believer partakes of bread and wine, representing, respectively, the body and blood of Jesus.

- Matrimony, the fifth sacrament, differs in form from one church to another, according to local customs; in all cases, however, its purpose is to confer divine sanctification upon the union of a man and a woman.

- Holy Orders, the sixth sacrament, is the rite in which clergy are ordained.

- Holy Unction or Euchelaion, the seventh sacrament, is administered to Roman Catholics (Holy Unction) whose death seems imminent. Among Eastern Orthodox adherents, Euchelaion (the offering of prayer and anointing with oil) is administered as often as may be necessary to comfort and heal the sick.

Protestants differ among themselves on questions of theology and church policy, but most insist that Christ instituted only two sacraments, Baptism and Communion.

Veneration of Saints

Eastern Orthodox, Roman Catholic, and Anglican churches observe the feasts of saints concurrently with the liturgical festivals. The feasts celebrated include those of Mary, the mother of Jesus (the Blessed Virgin Mary); Joseph, the husband of Mary; the archangels; and the apostles. In addition, there are the feasts of numerous patron saints, who intercede with God on behalf of those who pray to them for help. The lists of saints and martyrs recognized by Eastern Orthodox, Roman Catholic, and Anglican churches differ widely. However, the importance of the saints and martyrs in popular devotion is incalculable.

Many Protestant churches renounce on theological grounds any sort of veneration of saints. Instead, they observe Reformation Sunday (the Sunday nearest to October 31), which represents the day when Martin Luther nailed his ninety-five statements to the door of the church.

Festivals

Christian festivals gravitate around two great events: Christmas and Easter. Christmas is a fixed festival commemorating the birth of Jesus Christ and is celebrated by most Christians annually on December 25. Preceding Christmas is Advent, a solemn period of expectation and preparation. Advent marks the beginning of the ecclesiastical year and starts four Sundays before Christmas. Following Christmas is the celebration of the Epiphany (manifestation of Jesus Christ), observed on January 6. Two incidents are commemorated to recall that manifestation: the baptism of Jesus and the visit of the Wise Men (Magi) to Bethlehem.

Not all Christians mark all those days. Eastern Orthodox churches, for example, do not celebrate Christmas on December 25; rather, they celebrate the Epiphany, on January 6. Also, Roman Catholics, Angli-

An officiating Armenian priest consecrating the hosts in preparation for
the Holy Eucharist (Holy Communion). Tradition ascribes the introduction
of Christianity to Armenia to the missionary activity of two Apostles,
Thaddeus and Bartholomew. Armenians claim that the baptism of King
Tiridates III in 301 CE constitutes the first establishment of Christianity as a
state religion in the world.
Courtesy of the Armenian Church Diocese of North America.

cans, and Protestant groups differ as to the length of Advent (from
twenty-two to twenty-eight days). Roman Catholics, Eastern Orthodox
adherents, and Anglicans, but not Protestants, observe the Epiphany on
January 6. Roman Catholics, however, disassociate the incident of the
baptism of Jesus from the visit of the Wise Men.

Mausoleum in a cemetery in Nowy Sacz, Poland. Sometimes, as here, the figure of Saint Joseph (the earthly father of Jesus) holding the baby Christ, rather than the Madonna figure, is used for perpetual protection.
Courtesy of Wolf Arnold.

Differences exist also in the observances associated with the Easter cycle of events. The date of Easter is movable and is calculated on the basis of both the Gregorian calendar and the Julian calendar. Roman Catholics, Anglicans, and Protestants follow the Gregorian calendar. Thus, Easter is observed on the first Sunday after the first full moon following the vernal equinox (around March 21), usually rotating between March and April. Eastern Orthodox churches follow the Julian calendar and consequently celebrate Easter on a different date, usually several weeks after the Gregorian date.

Again, variations exist in the observances that precede Easter. Roman Catholic, Eastern Orthodox, and Anglican churches observe the solemn period of fasting and prayer known as Lent, including Holy Week, although the methods and durations of observance differ among them. In recent years, some Protestant groups have introduced the observance of Lent in their churches. As to the two feasts that follow Easter, Ascension Day and Pentecost Sunday, all Christian churches except the Unitarians and a few Protestant groups observe them, although their role and significance vary from church to church.

STUDY QUESTIONS

1. Give the biblical account of the infancy and boyhood of Jesus.
2. List the events that occurred before and after Jesus' crucifixion.
3. What was Jesus' understanding of God, according to the Gospels?
4. Analyze the concepts of sin, redemption, and justification according to Paul.
5. What factors were involved in the early struggle and triumph of Christianity?
6. How did Manicheism threaten Christianity?
7. Identify the internal disputes that threatened the survival of Christianity.
8. Compare the spread of Byzantine and Roman forms of Christianity.
9. Explain the causes and effects of the Crusades and the Inquisition.
10. Name the most influential figures associated with the Reformation.
11. Describe the origin and the development of the intellectual movement known as the Enlightenment.
12. Distinguish the views and counterviews of the Enlightenment thinkers.
13. Discuss the rise and growth of religious movements since the nineteenth century.
14. Compare the responses by Roman Catholics and Protestants to pluralism.
15. Discuss the rise of feminist and women's liberation movements.
16. Give a brief account of the books that constitute the Christian Bible.
17. Discuss the Christian teaching on Incarnation and Reconciliation.
18. Compare the seven sacraments recognized by Eastern Orthodox and Roman Catholics.
19. Distinguish the institutional and ritualistic differences among the three major branches of Christianity.
20. Describe the more important Christian celebrations and festivals.

Suggested Reading

Borg, Marcus. *Jesus, A New Vision: Spirit, Culture, and the Life of Discipleship.* San Francisco: HarperCollins, 1987.

Brasher, Brenda E. *Godly Women: Fundamentalism and Female Power.* New Brunswick, N.J.: Rutgers University Press, 1998.

Cahill, Lisa Sowie. *Sex, Gender, and Christian Ethics.* Cambridge, Mass.: Cambridge University Press, 1996.

Carmody, Denise L., and John T. Carmody. *Roman Catholicism: An Introduction.* New York: Macmillan, 1990.

Carpenter, Humphrey. *Jesus.* Oxford: Oxford University Press, 1980.

Carroll, Michael P. *The Cult of the Virgin Mary: Psychological Origins.* Princeton, N.J.: Princeton University Press, 1986.

Chaves, Mark. *Ordaining Women: Culture and Conflict in Religious Organizations.* Cambridge: Harvard University Press, 1997.

Crossan, John D. *Jesus: A Revolutionary Biography.* San Francisco: HarperCollins, 1994.

Crotty, Robert B. *The Jesus Question: The Historical Search.* North Blackburn, Victoria, Australia: HarperCollins Religious, 1996.

Dillenberger, John. *Protestant Christianity: Interpreted through Its Development.* 2nd ed. New York: Macmillan, 1988.

Donaldson, Terry. *Paul and the Gentiles: Remapping the Apostle's Convictional World.* Minneapolis: Fortress Press, 1997.

Griffith, Ruth Marie. *God's Daughters: Evangelical Women and the Power of Submission.* Berkeley, Calif.: University of California Press, 1997.

Herrin, Judith. *The Formation of Christendom.* Princeton, N.J.: Princeton University Press, 1987.

Martin, Brice L. *Christ and the Law in Paul.* Leiden: E. J. Brill, 1989.

Marty, Martin E. *Protestantism.* New York: Doubleday, 1974.

Neill, Stephen A. *A History of Christian Missions.* Harmondsworth, Eng.: Penguin Books, 1975.

Pelikan, Jaroslav J. *Jesus through the Centuries: His Place in the History of Culture.* New Haven: Yale University Press, 1985.

Sanders, E. P. *Paul and Palestinian Judaism.* Philadelphia: Fortress Press, 1977.

Stendahl, Krister. *Paul among Jews and Gentiles, and Other Essays.* Philadelphia: Fortress Press, 1976.

Tavard, George Henry. *Women in Christian Tradition.* Notre Dame, Ind.: University of Notre Dame Press, 1985.

Theissen, Gerd. *The Historical Jesus: A Comprehensive Guide.* Minneapolis: Fortress Press, 1998.

Ware, Timothy. *The Orthodox Church.* Harmondsworth, Eng.: Penguin Books, 1984.

West, Angela. *Deadly Innocence: Feminist Theology and the Mythology of Sin.* London: Mowbray, 1995.

Witherington, Ben. *The Jesus Quest: The Third Search for the Jew of Nazareth.* Downers Grove, Ill.: InterVarsity Press, 1995.

Woodrow, Alain. *The Jesuits: A Story of Power.* London: Geoffrey Chapman, 1995.

Zernov, Nicolas. *Eastern Christendom: A Study of the Origin and Development of the Eastern Orthodox Church.* London: Weidenfeld & Nicolson, 1961.

Notes

1. Cited in H. Bettenson, ed., *Documents of the Christian Church,* 2nd ed. (London: Oxford University Press, 1963), p. 16.

2. Theodosian Code XVI.10.25 (435), in *The Theodosian Code and Novels and Sirmondian Constitutions* (Princeton, N.J.: Princeton University Press, 1952), p. 476.

3. Among the many documents discovered at Nag Hammadi is the *Gospel of Thomas,* a text that the church did not recognize as scripture. Some modern scholars, however, think that that gospel was written during the lifetime of Jesus because it presents his sayings as though he were still alive.

4. A tiny gnostic community called Mandeans (from the Aramaic and Syriac *manda,* meaning "knowledge") still exists today in southern Iraq. In recent years, the community has been called Christians of Saint John.

5. Cited in C. H. Robinson, *The Conversion of Europe* (London: Longmans, Green, 1917), p. 547.

6. See S. A. Nigosian, "The Challenge of Religious Pluralism," *The Ecumenist,* 16/4 (May–June 1978), pp. 58–62.

7. The term *apocrypha* is a Greek plural neuter adjective meaning "hidden books"; it refers to esoteric books containing mysterious or secret teachings. Later, the term deteriorated to mean heretical or spurious teachings contained in esoteric books.

8. From G. Brantl, ed., *Catholicism* (New York: Washington Square Press, 1967), pp. 175–176.

15 Islam

Islam is the second largest religion in the world after Christianity, with an estimated 950,000,000 adherents. It was established in Arabia in the seventh century as a result of the message of the Prophet Muhammad. Today, it is one of the world's most widely diffused religions. More than half of the total Muslim population is found in the East: China, southeastern Asia, and the Indian peninsula, including Burma and Sri Lanka. The remaining Muslims are dispersed across eastern Europe (including Turkey), the Balkan nations, Russia, the Middle East (including the Arab world), and Africa. Small groups also are found in various Western countries, including Germany, France, Britain, Canada, and the Americas.

UNDERSTANDING ISLAM

The word *Islam* has two meanings: "submission" and "peace"—submission to the will and guidance of God and living in peace with one's self and one's surroundings. The essence of Islam, therefore, lies in submission to God, which results in peace of mind and soul. The correct name for the religion is Islam, and the proper term for identifying its adherents is Muslims.

The Islamic community is at once a political and religious community. From its very beginnings, Islam has viewed religion and politics (church and state) as necessarily and rightfully inseparable. To Muslims, the notion of religion as separable from the totality of the human context is unimaginable, even detestable. All of life is sacred and must conform to the larger whole—the identity of the Islamic faith. All who belong to the great Islamic faith share a sense of identity, a sense of global community. To believe otherwise would be to deny the validity

Islam

CE

c. 570	Birth of Muhammad (d. 632)
610	Muhammad's first revelation
620	Death of Khadijah, Muhammad's wife
622	Migration of Muhammad (*hijrah* or *hegira*) from Mecca to Medina
630	Mecca controlled by Muhammad
632	Muhammad succeeded by Abu Bakr
634	Abu Bakr succeeded by Umar
644	Umar succeeded by Uthman
c. 650	Canonization of the *Qur'an*
661	Assassination of 'Ali by a Kharijite rebel; establishment of Umayyad dynasty (661–750)
680	Husayn, son of 'Ali, assassinated at Karbala
750	Establishment of the 'Abbasid dynasty (750–1258)
870s	"Disappearance" of twelfth *imam*
912	Execution of the Persian mystic Al-Hallaj
1058	Birth of Al-ghazali (d. 1111)
c. 1200	Beginning of Muslim domination of India
1526	Founding of Mogul Empire by Babar (1526–1707)
1653	Completion of Taj Mahal in India
c. 1760	Establishment of Wahabi reform movement
1924	Abolishment of the Islamic Caliphate by the Turkish government
1947	Establishment of Pakistan as separate Muslim state
1979	Shah of Iran overthrown; revolutionary Islamic regime in Iran headed by Khomeini

of one of the core concepts of Islam, that of the *umma,* or community of the faithful governed by the dictates of *shari'a* (divine law). Indeed, the very concept of a religion in the sense of a religious organization separate from other political and social structures is completely foreign to Islam.

And finally, Muslims consider their Prophet Muhammad as the highest exemplar of humanity and his message a purification and fulfillment of Judaism and Christianity.

MUHAMMAD, MESSENGER OF GOD

The origin of Islam lies either at the beginning of time, at creation, or in the sixth century CE in Arabia, depending on the point of view one wishes to take. From the orthodox Muslim perspective, the story of

Islam starts not with Muhammad (c. 570–632) but shares a common tradition with Judaism and a common biblical origin when God (Allah, in Arabic) created the world and the first man, Adam. The descendants of Adam are traced to Noah, who had a son named Shem. That is where the word *Semite* — descendants of Shem — comes from; like the Jews, Arabs regard themselves as a Semitic people. Shem's descendants are then traced to Abraham and to his wives Sarah and Hagar. At that point, two familiar stories about Abraham provide the cornerstones of the Islamic religion. The first, Abraham's attempted sacrifice of his son Isaac, demonstrates Abraham's submission to the will of God in the supreme test; hence, the word *Islam*. The second story, concerning Ishmael's banishment, gave rise to the belief that Ishmael (the son of Abraham and Hagar) went to Mecca and that eventually from his descendants the prophet Muhammad emerged in the sixth century CE.

Traditional Account

Little is known of the early life of Muhammad. Tradition states that he was born in the city of Mecca around 570, to parents who belonged to the Qurayish clan. His father, Abdullah ibn Muttalib, died before his birth, and his mother, Aminah bint Wahb, died when he was six, leaving him an orphan. Muhammad then went to live with his grandfather, who was the custodian of the holy temple known as *Ka'ba*. That arrangement lasted only two years, until the death of the grandfather. Muhammad was then left in the care of a paternal uncle, Abu Talib.

As a child, Muhammad traveled by caravan with his uncle to Syria, where a Christian monk one day drew the uncle's attention to the fact that the child bore the marks of prophethood. Like other boys of his day, Muhammad also spent time as a shepherd, leading his flock to the caves and rocks near his home. As a young man, Muhammad joined the merchant caravans, and at the age of twenty–five entered the service of a wealthy widow named Khadijah. Soon, his relationship with her deepened into love, and, although she was fifteen years older, he married her.

Divine Revelation

According to tradition, Muhammad experienced at the age of forty his first divine communication with the angel Gabriel. Like Abraham, Moses, Samuel, and Jesus, Muhammad heard a divine voice. The voice said, "Recite!" and Muhammad, overwhelmed by the voice and the appearance of the archangel Gabriel, fell prostrate to the ground. The voice repeated, "Recite!" "What shall I recite?" asked Muhammad in terror. And the answer came:

> Recite — in the name of thy Lord who created! Created man from clots of blood! Recite — for thy Lord is most beneficent, who has taught the use of the pen; has taught man that which he knew not! (Qur'an 96.14)

Terrified by the overwhelming divine presence, Muhammad rushed home and told Khadijah that he had become either "possessed" (insane) or a prophet. On hearing the full story, his wife encouraged him: "Rejoice and be of good cheer, you will be the Prophet of this people!" Such experiences recurred throughout Muhammad's life, giving him spiritual inspiration and guidance.

Some modern scholars explain Muhammad's divine experiences as epileptic seizures, because they involved intense physical trembling, sweating, and auditory hallucinations. Other critics, however, maintain that Muhammad's behavior differed very little from that of other prophets. Muhammad himself was sincerely convinced that he was *rasul'ullah,* the messenger or prophet of God (Qur'an 33.40).

Muhammad, it is further stated, was ridiculed and accused of being a sorcerer. The greatest opposition came from the leaders of the Qurayish tribe, who saw his teachings as a threat to Meccan social and economic life. Muhammad's preaching on social justice was directed essentially against the privileged, and they resented it. Consequently, the leaders of the Qurayish decided that each group within the tribe must take the necessary steps to suppress this "heretical" faith.

Muhammad was fairly safe as long as he lived under the protection of his uncle, who, although he did not accept Muhammad's religion, used all his prestige and power in the community to save his nephew's life. But in 620, both Muhammad's wife, Khadijah, and his uncle, Abu Talib, died. Their deaths stripped Muhammad of his comparative immunity from local animosity and presaged his forced departure from Mecca.

The *Hijrah (Hegira)*

The opportunity to leave Mecca arrived when a delegation from Yathrib (later renamed Medina in honor of Muhammad) invited Muhammad to mediate their tribal feuds in return for protection of himself and his followers. After completing preliminary negotiations, Muhammad and his followers arrived secretly at Medina on September 24, 622. That migration is known in Arabic as *hijrah* (Latin, *hegira,* for "flight"), and the year during which it occurred marks the beginning of the Muslim calendar.

Muhammad soon settled the tribal feuds he had been invited to mediate and won over to his faith the inhabitants of Medina. He devoted his attention not only to social and political issues but also to moral and educational concerns, initiating ordinances governing marriage, divorce, fasting, almsgiving, and the treatment of slaves, prisoners of war, and enemies. He also married a number of women, possibly to cement political alliances. Under his direction, civil and religious authority were fused, and within ten years he had succeeded in organizing his society into a Muslim state.

Muhammad's Relationship with Jews, Christians, and Unbelievers

During this period, Muhammad's religious interests were governed by his relationship with neighboring Jewish and Christian communities. He had hoped that they would convert to his faith, especially since he borrowed freely from both religious traditions. Instead, he embroiled himself in so many disputes with Jews and Christians that he was led to conclude that they had fallen away from the true faith and falsified the scriptures.

Later, he persuaded his followers to attack several wealthy Jewish and Christian communities in the neighborhood of Medina. Some Jews and Christians abandoned their possessions and fled for their lives. Others submitted to conditional treaties: freedom of worship in return for a substantial tribute. Still others surrendered their religion and submitted to Muhammad's political and religious authority.

The moral effect of victory over local Jewish and Christian communities led Muhammad to declare war against unbelievers — even his own countrymen — and to divide their spoils among his followers. He recruited volunteers who were prepared to raid the caravans of rival and unassimilated traders.

Subsequent and repeated attacks on unbelieving merchants yielded successes that were interpreted as divine victories. Muhammad was convinced that if his religious mission was to succeed, it was necessary to create an ordered community and eventually a state. In the absence of any stable national institution, the powerful administration and firm social structure of Muhammad's community made him a super chieftain. Gradually, various tribes sent delegations to offer their allegiance and submission to Muhammad and his new monotheistic faith. In testimony to their sincerity, they often sealed their allegiance by giving their women in marriage to Muhammad.

The Surrender of Mecca

Finally, the time came to strike at the hostile Meccans by intercepting and raiding their caravans. The first raid was spectacularly successful, both militarily and economically. A second attempt, however, ended in failure, with Muhammad being slightly wounded. In retaliation, the Meccans prepared for a grand assault. With some ten thousand men, they advanced on Medina, but Muhammad had ordered several trenches dug around the town, and the battle (known as the Battle of the Trench) ended with the retreat of the Meccans. After a skillful exercise of diplomacy and military pressure, Muhammad and ten thousand of his followers marched into Mecca in January 630. His former fellow townsmen, who had once conspired against him, put up no resistance.

One of Muhammad's first acts was to go to the holy temple, the *Ka'ba,* and reverently circumambulate, or walk around it, seven times. Next, he ordered the destruction of all the idols within the temple, including the paintings of Abraham and the angels. Then he walked over to the nearby Zamzam well, which tradition associates with the biblical story of Hagar and her son Ishmael, and sanctioned its use. Finally, he restored the boundary pillars that defined the sacred territory of Mecca. Henceforth, all followers of his faith, called Muslims (Arabic for "those who have submitted"), would be free to travel securely on a pilgrimage to Mecca.

The Triumph of Muhammad

For the next two years, Muhammad's power came to be acknowledged by all in Arabia. He unified the Arab tribes under a theocracy, governed by the will of God. Former tribal loyalties were now transferred to the *umma*, a religious commitment that was to unite them more closely than tribal ties of blood ever had.

Tradition states that in his last discourse, Muhammad proclaimed the fundamental shift in age-old loyalties in the following words: "O believers, listen to my words and take them to heart. Know that every Muslim is a brother unto every other Muslim; for you are now one brotherhood" (Qur'an 49.10). Muhammad died suddenly in 632, following a few days' illness.

ISLAMIC EMPIRES

The Four Caliphs

Muhammad's death left the Muslim community with a leadership crisis. What happened subsequently has been vigorously disputed by his followers. According to the Sunni group (the traditionalists, who make up the majority of Muslims), Muhammad left no successor. According to the Shi'ites (the partisans), Muhammad designated his cousin 'Ali (who was also his son-in-law) as his successor. The Prophet's preference may have been general knowledge, but two of his fathers-in-law met with the leaders of Medina to select a single leader. The choice fell on the aging Abu Bakr. 'Ali and his kinsmen agreed for the sake of unity, but they were deeply offended. Abu Bakr was now the *caliph* (from Arabic *khalifah*, meaning "successor"), who was to assume only the administrative responsibilities, not the office of prophethood.

That decision immediately provoked divisions among various Arab groups. Some decided to cut their ties with Medina and the newly elected caliph. Others began to follow leaders who claimed to have prophetic powers like Muhammad's. Abu Bakr dealt swiftly and firmly with the disaffected, then announced a program of expansion, mainly into Syria, which at that time was under Byzantine control. His age and his health, however, did not allow him to undertake major military expeditions. Abu Bakr's plans for conquest were to be carried out by 'Umar, who was appointed caliph by Abu Bakr before the latter's death in 634.

The amazingly rapid expansion of Islam began under the skillful leadership of 'Umar, who ruled from 634 to 644. His military campaigns were waged on two fronts: against the Byzantine Empire to the north and west and the Persian Empire to the east. From the former, he conquered Syria in 636, Palestine in 638, and Egypt in 642. For Christianity, that meant that three of the four Patriarchates (Jerusalem, Antioch, and Alexandria) came under the jurisdiction of Muslim overlords. To the east, 'Umar's forces overran Iraq and the Iranian plateau in 642. In all the conquered lands, the indigenous inhabitants were required to live in peace, accept 'Umar's protection, and pay taxes, but they were

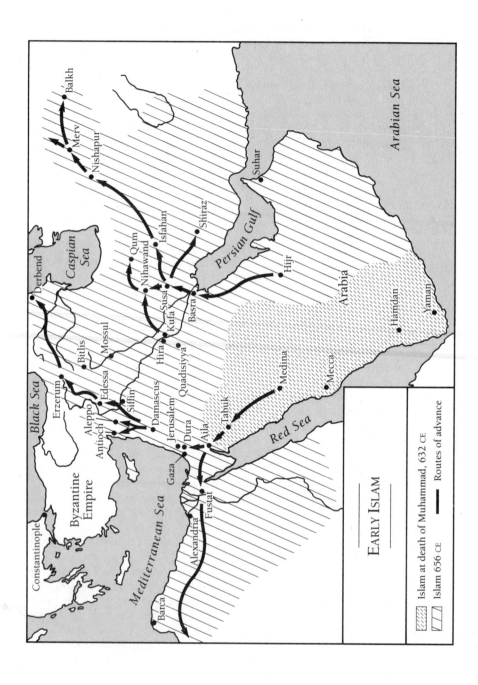

EARLY ISLAM

Islam at death of Muhammad, 632 CE

Islam 656 CE

Routes of advance

Aerial view of the Dome of the Rock (Mosque of Omar), built in 690 over the traditional site of Solomon's Temple, in Jerusalem. One of the most beautiful examples of Islamic architecture in the world, the mosque is covered with blue, green, and white tile mosaics and topped by a dome of gold leaf.

Courtesy of Israel Government Tourist Office, Ministry of Tourism, Toronto.

allowed to keep their own religions and customs. Muslim Arabs were accommodated in newly constructed towns that were supported by taxes paid by the conquered. Thus, by conquest and settlement, 'Umar laid the foundation of an empire that would incorporate both Arab culture and Islamic features.

'Umar's plans were interrupted when he was stabbed to death by an Iranian slave. The leading companions of the Prophet then met to elect a new caliph. Despite 'Ali's pleas and claims, they selected 'Uthman, another son-in-law of Muhammad and a prominent member of the Umayyad family in Mecca, as caliph. 'Uthman, who ruled 644–656, immediately strengthened the control of the Muslim Empire by placing members of his clan in key positions. That policy antagonized many devout Arab Muslims, including 'Ali, who on several occasions opposed 'Uthman's policies.

After 'Uthman was assassinated in 656 by one of his opponents, the deeply shocked people of Medina hailed 'Ali as caliph. But Meccans and a number of other leading Muslims rejected 'Ali, accusing him of collusion in the assassination plot. The fragile unity of the Muslim community finally fractured on the issue of succession, never to be reestablished. 'Ali and his partisans were challenged by Mu'awiyah I, the Muslim governor of Syria, who had the support of the Meccans and other leading tribesmen. In the ensuing flux of changing loyalties a third group emerged, called the Khariji ("seceders"), who opposed both 'Ali and Mu'awiyah. One of the Khariji assassinated 'Ali in 661, and Mu'awiyah was installed as caliph.

The Umayyad Dynasty

Mu'awiyah (ruled 661–680) was a superb statesman who moved the caliphate to Damascus, where he established the Umayyad dynasty (661–750). Under Mu'awiyah's leadership, Islamic expansion was resumed, internal feuds and revolts were stamped out, administration was centralized, and an attempt was made to systematize the legal and ethical teachings of Muhammad that affected Islamic society at large. Thus, a distinctive Islamic civilization emerged under the Umayyad caliphate.

The momentum of Islamic conquest and settlement carried the Umayyads eastward to India as far as the borders of China and westward to the Atlantic Ocean, through Libya, Tunisia, Algeria, Morocco, and across the Strait of Gibraltar into Spain, Portugal, and France. Only in 733, a century after the Prophet's death, was the Muslim advance westward halted by the Franks, at the decisive battle of Tours.

The 'Abbasid Dynasty

The Umayyad dynasty was overthrown seventeen years after the battle of Tours by the 'Abbasid dynasty (750–1258). Because the new dynasty represented the interests of the Islamicized Iraqi aristocracy, the caliphate was moved from Syria to Baghdad. Six years later, a rival caliphate was established by the Umayyads in Cordova, Spain. Under that caliphate (756–1236) and its successor, the Moorish caliphate at Granada, the Muslims of Spain built a rich and influential culture that lasted until 1492.

Although the 'Abbasid dynasty enjoyed one of the longest reigns of any in Islam, its influence gradually waned after the ninth century, as rival caliphs and independent rulers established themselves in Tunisia, Egypt, Syria, and Iran. The eighth and ninth centuries, especially the reign of Harun al-Rashid (786–809), marked the pinnacle of Islamic wealth and culture. Medicine, science, mathematics, fine arts, and philosophy flourished throughout the Muslim Empire.

Throughout the Islamic world, conquered pagan peoples had to choose between conversion to Islam and death by the sword. Jews and Christians had an alternative to conversion: they could adhere to their religions in return for payment of heavy taxes.

The conquest of Iran, Iraq, and the eastern littoral of the Mediterranean by Muslim Arabs in the seventh century brought comparative respite to the Manicheans in their homeland (see Chapter 14). When the 'Abbasid caliphs succeeded the Umayyads, however, they renewed the persecution that had been the common lot of Manicheans under Persian kings. The 'Abbasid Caliph al-Mahdi (who ruled 775–785) was determined to extirpate all heretics, including Manicheans, and for that purpose he instituted a court of inquisition. The chief inquisitor had full plenary powers, and the surviving records on the ruthless measures taken make blood-chilling reading. The religious policy of al-Mahdi generally was followed by his successors, especially the Caliph al-Muqtadir (who ruled 908–932). In spite of the worst that the 'Abbasids could do, the Manichean religion survived in the Muslim Empire, possibly until the Mongol invasion of the thirteenth century.

By the end of the ninth century, Turkish officers had made themselves masters of the 'Abbasid caliphs, dethroning them at will, appropriating the imperial revenues, and plundering the royal palaces. Local governors asserted authority over the provinces they ruled, and social and religious revolts became endemic in the empire.

Seljuk Turkish marauders swept over Syria and Palestine, capturing Jerusalem in 1070. Tales of horror and desecration perpetrated by Turks were spread by Western pilgrims to the courts of the Frankish kingdoms. The result was the launching of the Crusades. At first, common hatred of the Turks united western and eastern Christians in the capture of Jerusalem in 1099; the final outcome, however, was not only unsuccessful but disastrous for the Christians. In 1187, the Muslims recaptured Jerusalem and over the next hundred years reconquered the entire area.

Meanwhile, great movements of tribal peoples after the eleventh century were resulting in political and social dislocations throughout the Muslim Empire. First, the Ghaznavids, who originated in Afghanistan, and then the Seljuk Turks, from central Asia, raided and invaded the territories of Iran and Iraq. The Mongols, another Asiatic group, sacked Baghdad in 1258 and overthrew the 'Abbasid dynasty. Four decades later, the Mongols embraced Islam.

The Mongol Empire

Originally, Mongols consisted of loosely organized nomadic tribes in Mongolia, Manchuria, and Siberia. Sometime around 1200, a chieftain later known as Genghis Khan (his real name was Temjun) unified and organized the scattered Mongol tribes into a superior fighting force. As the undisputed master of Mongolia, Temjun and his successors set out on a spectacular career of world conquest.

The Mongols are popularly viewed as the most savage conquerors in history. They spread terror and destruction everywhere, and whenever they met resistance, they systematically slaughtered the local population. Their vast empire, however, contributed to increased contacts between peoples. At its greatest extent, during the reign of Kublai Khan (1279–1294), one of the grandsons of Genghis Khan, the Mongol Empire (c. 1200–1368) extended from the Pacific Ocean westward to the Danube River, the largest area ever controlled by one state in world history.

In 1256, Hulagu Khan, brother of Kublai Khan, marched with his Mongol army into Iran, destroying several cities. Two years later, he entered Iraq and devastated Baghdad, putting the Caliph al-Musta'sim to death and sparing only some Shi'ites and Christians. Less than forty years later, his descendants, under the leadership of Ghazan Khan (who ruled 1295–1304), embraced Islam and became patrons of Muslim culture and civilization. Yet it was not the Mongols of Iraq who restored Islam's military glory. That task was left to the Ottoman Turks, who became the last Islamic dynasty to hold on to the caliphate.

The Ottoman Empire

The empire of the Ottoman Turks (c. 1300–1922) was founded in present-day Turkey by Osman (in Arabic, 'Uthman) in 1300 and spanned a period of more than six centuries. Constantly varying in extent, it included in different epochs Turkey, Syria, Palestine, Jordan, Egypt, Iraq, parts of Arabia and North Africa, Cyprus, Crete, Greece, the Balkan states, and parts of Hungary, Austria, and southern Russia.

In their initial stages of expansion, the Ottomans were leaders of the Turkish *gazis,* warriors for the faith of Islam. Osman and his immediate successors concentrated their attacks on Byzantine territories (modern Turkey), southern and central Europe, and southwestern Asia. The Ottomans' reputation as champions of militant Islam was cemented by Sultan Mehmet II's 1453 capture of Constantinople (modern Istanbul), the last remnant of the once mighty Christian Byzantine Empire.

Sultan Mehmet accorded the patriarch of the Greek Orthodox church certain prerogatives, safeguarding his security, recognizing his jurisdiction over his prelates, and granting him some administrative authority. Nevertheless, all Christians remained outside the *umma.* In the world of Islam, Christians living in an Islamic sphere of influence belonged to the *dhimmi,* people held under or protected by the dictates of the conscience of Islam. They could retain their own religious and social customs, but they were subject to certain restrictions or bans (e.g., they were forbidden to convert Muslims to Christianity, to marry Muslim women, or to hold high governmental office) and were required to pay a special tribute. In sum, the *dhimmi* represented an alien and unassimilable element in the body politic of the *umma.*

Although conquered Christians were treated as a separate group in the Ottoman Empire, under the leadership of their own patriarchs and bishops, Muslim breakaway groups or revolutionary movements met with severe and summary punishment. The Ottoman Sultan Selim I (who ruled 1512–1520), for instance, massacred most of the Shi'ite Muslims in Turkey and forced the survivors underground.

Selim's successor, Suleiman the Magnificent (1520–1566), spearheaded a renewed Islamic advance into Europe, invading Serbia, Hungary, and Austria. He incited the newly converted Protestant princes of Germany against the pope and the Holy Roman emperor, and he made Ottoman Hungary a stronghold for Protestant groups, particularly Calvinists. For almost two centuries, support of Protestantism remained a basic Ottoman policy.

The Mughal Empire

Meanwhile, Islam in India was deeply affected by the Mughals. The term *Mughal* is the Persian version of the Indian word *Mogul,* meaning Mongol. In 1526, Babar, a descendant of the great Mongol conquerors Timur (or Tamerlane) and Genghis Khan, established the Islamic

The Daratagaha Mosque in Colombo, Sri Lanka. Mosques can be erected on large grounds or squeezed, as here, between commercial buildings. In the background is the Town Hall.

Courtesy of British Airways (BOAC).

Mughal Empire in India (1526–1857). Babar's grandson, Akbar the Great (1542–1605) conquered northern India and Afghanistan and extended his rule as far north as Hyderabad, West Pakistan. In time, great numbers of Hindus, especially from the lower classes, converted to Islam.

Mughal civilization in India fused indigenous Indian traditions with Mongolian, Iranian, and Arab elements. Under the early Mughal emperors, India flourished, but trouble developed during the reign of Emperor Aurangzeb (1658–1707), a harsh and narrow-minded ruler who tried to force Hindus and other Indians to convert to Islam. He also imposed a special tax on Hindus and destroyed many of their temples. Large numbers of Hindus were alienated by Aurangzeb's policies, and many rebelled. His long and disastrous wars sapped the economy and morale of both the army and the ruling class. Finally, he was defeated by guerrilla tactics employed by Hindus from southern India. His disastrous defeat left his descendants a troubled inheritance.

Under the early Mughal emperors, India flourished as a result of the fusion of indigenous traditions with Mongolian elements. But in the seventeenth and eighteenth centuries, trouble developed. The emperors

Jahangir and Aurangzeb, in particular, tried to force Hindus, Sikhs, and other Indians to convert to Islam, a situation that led to ever-escalating violence.

The atrocities perpetrated in the name of Islam during the centuries between 600 and 1800 were as terrible as those committed elsewhere during the same period in the name of religious hegemony. Many pious Muslims accepted (and still accept) the principle that military success is closely linked to divine favor, a belief that inevitably led to bloody and violent confrontation. But by 1800 the once proud realms of the Muslim Ottoman and Mughal empires were being humiliated by the European powers, whose military units outclassed the Muslim troops and decisively defeated them. To Muslims, the shattering reversal of the normal historical course of events remains inexplicable.

ISLAM IN MODERN TIMES

Abolishment of the Caliphate

The situation of Muslim communities in the eighteenth and nineteenth centuries was deplorable. On the one hand, European powers were gradually expanding and partitioning among themselves territory in Africa, western Asia, and India that for centuries had known only Muslim dominion. On the other hand, many Muslims dismissed the Ottoman religious establishment as an un-Islamic development and questioned whether the authority of the Ottoman sultan was truly derived from God or from the consensus of the Muslim community.

While various Muslim political organizations rose and fell according to the vicissitudes of time, the institution of the caliphate—rather, the head of state, who in theory represented the Prophet's successor—survived. The caliphate justified the claim of succeeding heads of state to the allegiance of all their subjects, both those who accepted the Islamic religion and those who paid tribute. All through Islamic history, rival dynasties ruled vast territories in the name of the caliphate, thus claiming to be the successors of Muhammad and the defenders of Islam—until March 3, 1924, when one of the most decisive moments in the history of Islam arrived.

On that date the Turkish National Assembly abolished the institution of the caliphate, thus ending almost 1300 years of unbroken historical tradition. In the course of its turbulent history, the caliphate underwent numerous modifications, was battled over by rival caliphs, and, at times, was the focus of powerful popular resentment. Nevertheless, for 1300 years it was recognized both as a moral link among Muslims and a symbol of Islamic solidarity. In 1924, however, Mustafa Kemal Attaturk, the first president of the Republic of Turkey and the champion of modern Turkish nationalists, dealt the mortal blow to the institution in this statement: "The idea of a single caliph, exercising supreme religious authority over all the peoples of Islam, is an idea taken from fiction, not from reality." Soon after, the Turkish National Assembly decreed the abolition of the caliphate and the last Ottoman holder of the title, Caliph 'Abdul Majid, was sent into exile.

The abolition of the caliphate offended Sunni Muslims everywhere, and various attempts were made to restore that fundamental institution. Three congresses were held—in Cairo in March 1926, in Mecca in July 1926, and in Jerusalem in 1931—but the fate of the caliphate remained unchanged. Similarly, the attempt of King Faruk of Egypt in 1939 to revive the caliphate met with vigorous opposition, especially from the Turkish government.

To date, nothing has replaced this institution in the Muslim world. Whether Muslim opinion is finally resigned to its loss is difficult to say. Clearly, though, the excision of the ancient title represents a self-inflicted wound that has left an indelible mark on the Muslim consciousness.

The Impact of Modernity

Another major issue that threatens the legal and creedal unity of Islam is the conflict of values between traditionalism and modernity. The vast majority of Muslims oppose modernity and accuse its champions of unfaithfulness to Islam in favor of Western ideologies. However, the ruling elites in almost all Islamic countries are educated and trained according to modern Western concepts. In the eyes of the reactionaries—rather, of antimodernists and anti-Westerners—such rulers are both unrepresentative of the Muslim masses and, more seriously, absolutely unfaithful to Islamic ideals. The goal of reactionaries is to bring their social order and political aspirations in line with the *shari'ah* (divine law), which provides guidelines for every sphere of life.

The conflict between the two sectors of Muslim society constitutes a grave problem for all Islamic societies. The struggle for freedom from Westernization and modernity has generated revolutions (such as in Iran) and ideas of nationalism that promote a holy war against all foreign domination. In virtually every area of the globe, with the exception of China, Muslims have obtained independence from foreign domination. Yet rapid population growth, industrialization, and political rivalries have created severe problems. Ironically, Islam has not lost adherents; on the contrary, it is making significant numbers of converts in recently industrialized societies, particularly in Africa.

The old longing for strong, one-man leadership that will bring religious unity and social justice still haunts popular Islamic imagination. In fact, the aspiration of such Muslims is to unify the world—by waging a holy war against unbelievers, if necessary—under the one government of God and in a culture that is Muslim in character and expression.

The Status of Women

Another major conflicting issue between Islamic tradition and Western liberalism is the status of women. According to Islamic theology and law, men and women are equal before God, but that ideal is seldom realized in practice. In ancient times, it is more than probable that, with isolated exceptions, the status of women in society did not vary appreciably from culture to culture. In the past, discrimination against women paled into insignificance beside the savage and focused brutality directed against minorities and dissenters everywhere.

Two Muslim women descending the steps of the Dome of the Rock (Mosque of Omar) in Jerusalem after worshiping.
Courtesy of Israel Government Tourist Office, Ministry of Tourism, Toronto.

It is only by modern, largely Western standards that women in Islamic communities seem to suffer discrimination today. Islamic tradition and Western liberalism offer radically opposite solutions to an issue that persists in creating tension and disruption, even in Western societies. Obviously, whatever changes are to be made must be introduced carefully in the framework of the Islamic tradition, not as models cut from Western patterns. Disenchantment about the status of women in Islamic communities is likely to be resolved in terms of how Muslim women can take their rightful place in Islamic society and carry out their obligations so they contribute fully to the development of their communities.

Muslim women, like men, are obliged to fulfill the Five Pillars of Islam: profession of faith, prayer, almsgiving, fasting, and pilgrimage. Unlike men, they enjoy certain exemptions from those duties when they are menstruating, pregnant, or ill.

To undertake a pilgrimage to Mecca at least once in a lifetime is incumbent on every adult Muslim who is physically, mentally, and financially capable of doing so. Women who wish to perform the pilgrimage must be accompanied by a husband or a male relative. To enter the state of sanctity, men are required to don a special garment consisting of two large pieces of white seamless cloth. Women, however, are permitted to wear any clothing that covers the entire body except the face and the hands, although some women prefer to veil their faces too. If menstruation occurs during the period of sanctity, women are excused from performing some rites.

The Qur'an (Muslim scripture) also embodies some important legal proscriptions. Polygamy is strictly regulated to a maximum of four wives, provided that husbands can do justice to all; if they cannot, they may marry only one woman. However, polyandry, the practice of a woman marrying several men, is not allowed under any circumstances. In general, Muslims tend to live monogamous lives.

Marriage has no sacramental status in Islam; it is simply a contractual relationship or agreement. The rights of the bride require due status, contract, and provision before any sexual relations are legitimately sanctioned. Sexual relations outside marriage are prohibited, and fornicators and adulterers are punished. Divorce is possible, but only after certain requirements are met. Inheritance laws require that females receive half as much as male inheritors.

Modesty among females is emphasized by regulations governing their appearance and conduct in society. A woman may in no way compromise the integrity of her reputation or stir the passions of males by immodest dress or conduct. Thus, the respective roles women and men assume as members of Islamic society are clearly delineated.

ISLAMIC GROUPS

Despite the ideal of a unified, consolidated community taught by Muhammad, sectarian differences arose among Muslim believers immediately after his death. Those differences arose principally out of disputes over leadership and dynastic succession.

The Khariji

In the seventh century, a group of active dissenters, the Khariji (from the Arabic word *khuruj,* meaning "rebel"), accused the elected caliphs, especially 'Uthman, of nepotism and misrule. Their discontentment led to the assassination of 'Uthman. Later, they also denounced 'Ali for submitting his claim to the caliphate.

The Khariji stressed three fundamental principles: (1) any person who committed a grave sin and did not sincerely repent ceased to be a Muslim; (2) Islamic idealism meant aggressive militancy, or *jihad* ("holy war"), which in the view of the Khariji was equal in importance to the Five Pillars of Islam; and (3) the leadership should be open not just to those who belonged to the Qurayish tribe (the Sunni position) or to the Prophet's family (the Shi'ite position) but to any individual, whatever his race or color, who had a righteous character.

The Khariji did not last long in history, but they left a permanent mark on the development of Islam. Today, a group known as the Ibadi, found in parts of Africa, is considered to have inherited the Khariji legacy, although the group applies less aggressive methods.

The Sunni and the Shi'ite

Although there are numerous groups within Islam, the major division is between the Sunni and the Shi'ite groups. The term *Sunni* derives from *sunna,* meaning "tradition," "community," or "consensus." The term *Shi'ite* (or *Shi'ah*) means "partisan." The Sunni are in the majority; the Shi'ite comprise not more than fifteen percent of the total Muslim population. The Shi'ite and their various subsects are found mainly in Iran and to some extent in India. In the ninth century, a Shi'ite subsect, known as the Ismaili, appeared in India. That group, which is headed by the Agha Khan, maintains that there is always an *imam,* or religious leader, directly representing God on earth. Another subsect originating in India in the latter half of the nineteenth century, the Ahmadiya, has been particularly active in propagating the Islamic faith, especially among Westerners.

The Sunni and the Shi'ite differ on two fundamental points: line of succession and religious authority. The Sunni follow a line of succession originated among the friends of Muhammad, beginning with Abu Bakr. The Shi'ite hold that succession in the leadership of Islam follows through the family of Muhammad; consequently, they consider that 'Ali, the son-in-law of Muhammad, was the Prophet's rightful successor. In the matter of religious authority, the Sunni maintain that the Qur'an, as interpreted by *sunna* (tradition) and the *ijma'* (agreements among scholars), is the only authoritative basis of Islam. The Shi'ite insist that Islamic religious authority is vested in an *imam,* who is infallible in all pronouncements regarding matters of doctrine and practice. All members of the Shi'ite group must recognize and submit to the authority of the *imam.* Most Shi'ite assert that there have been twelve *imams* since the death of Muhammad and that one more, who will herald the end of this world, is still to come.

The Sufi

The mystical movement in Islam goes by the name of Sufism. The origin of the term *Sufi* is complex, but the word generally is connected with the wearing of an undyed garment made of wool (Arabic *suf*). Initially, Muslims wore such garments as a mark of personal penitence. Later, wool garments became the regular uniform of Sufis.

The Sufi movement emerged from early ascetic reactions by certain Muslims against the legalistic and ritualistic expression of Islam. Groups of ascetics began to meet for the purpose of reciting the Qur'an aloud, and those recitations gradually assumed a liturgical character that evolved in the direction of mystical love. When the Sufis sought to express their views in bolder terms, however, they were charged with heresy by the orthodox Muslims. As usual, all repressive tactics proved futile, and the Sufi movement grew in strength and popularity.

Three important views are shared by most Sufi groups: (1) truth or reality may be found not by rational knowledge but by direct and personal experience, culminating in absorption or union with the godhood;

(2) Sufi *shaikhs* (masters, in the sense of Zen masters) are to be venerated in their lifetime and, after death, elevated to the rank of saints; and (3) *celibacy* (abstinence from sexual intercourse) is preferable to marriage, provided the Sufi's heart is unstained and his or her mind free from sin and lust.

The name most often associated with the Sufi movement is that of al-Ghazali (d. 1111), who combined personal experiences with philosophical ideas and mystical systems in such a way as to win an honorable place among orthodox Muslims. What al-Ghazali did not foresee was that his attempted synthesis of the philosophical and the mystical would open the door to all sorts of popular religious practices and "heterodox" intellectual ideas that would gravely debase his ideals.

The pursuit of the mystical or ecstatic state of Sufism led to the introduction of alien practices and ideas. Within the ranks of the Sufis were wide gradations, which ultimately led to the development of several Sufi orders spread throughout the Muslim world. Today, some Sufi orders are local and regional, others are global. The orders are centered around their founders, whose shrines serve as pilgrimage sites. The Sufi monastery, called *tékké* or *zawiyah,* has become the center of public religiosity, often overshadowing the mosque. Techniques of inducing autohypnotic states through certain practices, such as chanting formulas or frenzied dancing, have become the expression of religiosity. *Shaikhs* initiate novices into the practice of *dhikr* or *zikr* (meaning "remembrance of God"), provided the disciples demonstrate an unquestioning faith in their masters.

The spread of Islam outside the Muslim world largely was due to Sufi orders, because the Sufi could easily make compromises with local customs and beliefs. By the same token, many primitive elements were absorbed into Sufi practices, and superstitious cults, occultism, various kinds of miracles, saint worship, and several unorthodox practices crept into the Sufi orders. Since the nineteenth century, the Sufi orders have been in decline, largely because of reform movements aimed at purifying their accretions and superstitions, the advent of modern education, and rapid industrialization.

THE QUR'AN

Muhammad, like Jesus Christ, wrote nothing. But the utterances of the revelations he received were recorded by his supporters and organized by editors working under Caliph 'Uthman into the scriptural *Qur'an* (Koran). The Arabic word *qur'an* means "recitation," and professional Muslim reciters evoke the beauty of the Arabic language when they read with specific intonations. Besides being revered for its religious significance, the Qur'an is a perfect model of Arabic literature and therefore is used as a text to study the Arabic language. Muslims regard the Qur'an as revelations of God transmitted to Muhammad through the angel Gabriel, and they believe that all its 114 chapters, or *sura,* mirror an original text preserved in heaven.

The arrangement of the chapters seems to be determined by length, with the longest chapters placed at the beginning and the shortest ones toward the end. The only exception to such ordering is the first chapter, titled "The Opening":

> In the name of God, the merciful, the compassionate.
> Praise be to God, Lord of the worlds,
> The merciful, the compassionate,
> Master of the day of judgment.
> You alone we serve; to You alone we cry for help.
> Guide us in the straight path,
> The path of those You have blessed;
> Not of those who have incurred Your anger,
> Nor of those who go astray. (Qur'an 1)

The contents of the Qur'an are varied. Some sections deal with ceremonial and civil law, others offer theological views and moral exhortations. Various chapters refer to biblical characters such as Adam, Moses, Abraham, Mary, Joseph, and Jesus. For instance, Adam is described as the first prophet, while Satan's fall from his position in heaven among

Young Turkish student performing a pious act by illuminating a page from the Qur'an. The Qur'an, the sacred book of Islam (roughly the size of the New Testament), is held to be the eternal, uncreated word of God, inscribed on the Preserved Tablet in heaven. Courtesy of Turkish Tourism and Information Office, Istanbul, Turkey.

the angels is explained by his refusal to worship Adam on God's command. Moses is acknowledged as having "talked with God" and having given the Torah to the Jews. Jesus is regarded not only as a prophet but also as the son of Mary, a servant of God, and a "messiah," committed to "redeeming" the Jews from the bondage of the Torah, with its accretion of irrelevant rites and practices. Not only are the miracles of Jesus mentioned, but the Annunciation to Mary of the birth of Jesus, which resembles the account in Luke's Gospel, is recounted twice in the Qur'an. Moreover, there is a reference to the Last Supper and the Ascension. However, the Christian doctrine of the divinity of Jesus, in particular the dogmas of sonship, intercessor, crucifixion, and resurrection are categorically denied in the Qur'an (see Qur'an 17.110, 5.76–79, 4.155–156).

The Qur'an is, first and foremost, a scripture to be confessed by rehearsing its contents. Muslim piety and even scholarship demand memorization and recitation, of the Qur'an in Arabic. Indeed, the chanting of the Qur'an is the primary music of Islam and is reflected in the speech of all faithful Muslims. The divine command to Muhammad was to "recite." Since then, Muslims have obeyed that divine command by reciting the contents of the Qur'an. The following is a popular proverbial saying:

> If any man recites the Qur'an and memorizes it, God will cause him to enter paradise and will grant him the right to intercede successfully for ten people of his household, all of whom deserve hell fire.

Besides providing a rich, varied, and abiding source for strict memorization and recitation, the Qur'an is warning, guidance, criterion, and mercy. Its subject is human beings; its theme is the exposition of reality; its aim is an invitation to humankind to accept God's guidance in the "right" path (Qur'an 1.5). Unlike the multiple authorship of most other

A Qur'anic inscription (in Arabic) that reads: "In the name of God, the merciful, the compassionate." This statement, which is found in the opening line of every chapter in the Qur'an, is inscribed in many mosques.
Courtesy of MSA Services in Canada.

scriptures, the Qur'an is the product of one man's revelations. Though references to topics such as theology, jurisprudence, science, and history are scattered throughout the Qur'an and appear to be somewhat incoherent, the sense of divine claim and authority, the dignity of human existence, the folly of human perversity, the impending day of judgment and destiny, the eternal conditions of bliss and doom, and the reality of God's mercy are all dominant themes in the Qur'an.

While the followers of Islam respect the scriptures of Judaism and Christianity, they regard the Qur'an as the pure and final essence of divine revelation, superseding the other scriptures. Its inspiration and authority are thought to extend to every letter and title (of which there are 323,621) so that every faithful Muslim must memorize and recite the Qur'an in Arabic. Although the Qur'an has been translated into some forty languages, it is believed to lose much of its inspiration in translation; no translation has ever fully conveyed the eloquence or flavor of the original Arabic. Its religious and social influence over millions of believers can hardly be overestimated.

ISLAMIC LAW AND JURISPRUDENCE

The Hadith

Next to the Qur'an, the most important piece of Islamic literature is the *Hadith* (Tradition) which is the basis of Islamic law, theology, and custom. The Hadith is based on the actions and sayings of the Prophet Muhammad, who is regarded as the most competent and the most appropriate authority for interpreting the Qur'an. Because Muhammad never recorded his sayings, it was left to a succession of reliable narrators to record them in what gradually evolved into the Hadith. By the ninth century, the Hadith was established as the norm by which the beliefs and practices of the Muslim community were governed.

As one might suppose, there are a vast number of versions and editions of the Hadith, but no single collection has won the full acceptance of all Muslims. Certain compilers are trusted more than others, but what is accepted by one school or group is rejected by another. One of the main reasons for the disagreement is that each version of the Hadith is a unique collection of events and sayings transmitted with the authority of a particular chain of narrators. To be acceptable, the Hadith must include the name of each human link in the chain between the Prophet and the person who recorded the Prophet's life and words. Here, for example, is the opening statement of a typical Hadith:

> Al-Bukhari writes: "Abdallah ibn-al-Aswad told me: Al-Fadl ibn-al-Ata told us: Isma'il ibn-Umayya told us on the authority of Yahya ibn-Abdallah ibn-Sayfi that he heard Abu Ma'bad, the freedman of Ibn-Abbas, say 'I heard Ibn-Abbas say: When the Prophet,' the blessings of Allah be upon him, and peace, 'sent Mu'adh to the Yemen, he said to him. . . .'"

The obvious question that bothers scholars is this: What faith can be placed on the authority or reliability of each transmitter? To be sure, many Muslim scholars admit that many Hadiths are spurious, but no way has yet been devised to check or confirm the authenticity of the names mentioned in the chain or of the tradition transmitted by a particular version of the Hadith. Nevertheless, a great deal of precious information, which otherwise would have gone unrecorded, is preserved in the Hadith, for example, the moral precepts of the Prophet. True, the general principles by which all moral issues must be regulated are in the Qur'an, but not all the issues are clearly elaborated there. In addition, almost all of the early history of Islam and the religious opinions of the first generations of pious Muslims can be deduced from various versions of the Hadith. Therefore, even though the authenticity of certain versions of the Hadith may be questioned, their historical and moral value should not be underestimated.

The *Shari'a*

Both the Qur'an and the Hadith require interpretation and analysis to be applied to specific situations, be they political, social, or religious. From very early times, the Islamic community developed directives for action that were compiled and documented in legal manuals over the centuries. That legal compilation came to be known as *shari'a* (literally, "way" or "path") and is regarded as the embodiment or codification of divine law. In Islamic thought, only one who accepts the injunctions of the *shari'a* as binding is, properly speaking, a Muslim, although it may not be possible to realize its teachings or follow its commands fully.

In Islam, *shari'a* is not simply a set of teachings but a guide to human action that encompasses every facet of human life. In fact, religion to a Muslim is fundamentally *shari'a*, the universal moral principles that must be applied to all daily actions and details: eating, sleeping, marriage, procreation, divorce, trade, and prayer. In one sense, then, *shari'a* is for Islam the means of integrating human society, the way by which one gives religious significance to one's daily life.

All Muslims consider themselves to be part of the *umma*, or community of the faithful. There is no priesthood and there are no holy orders in Islam, but men trained in the *shari'a*, known as *'ulama*, guide the affairs of the community. Every Muslim is under the authority, directly or indirectly, of various religious leaders.

Some time in the eighth or ninth century, four important schools of *shari'a*, representing different interpretations of the Qur'an and the Hadith, developed: the Malaki, the Hanafi, the Shafi'i, and the Hanbali. The last two are quite conservative in their interpretation of the Qur'an and the Hadith; the Malaki depend on consensus of the community, and the Hanafi extend orthodox teaching by analogy. Of the four, the one with the fewest followers today is the Hanbali, spread between Syria and Egypt. The Malaki school is dominant in northern Africa, the Hanafi school in Turkey. The strength of the Shafi'i school has always been in Syria and Egypt.

The *shari'a* provides for Muslims the knowledge of right and wrong in matters of politics, economics, society, and religion. In the Islamic view, the *shari'a* contains definitive teachings that should form the basis

Muslims praying on a street in Cairo, Egypt. Muslims pray
wherever they happen to be: at home, in the market, at a railway
station, on board a ship, or by the roadside. Every Muslim unrolls
his prayer mat and stands barefoot facing toward Mecca. Various
formal positions are assumed during prayer: standing, bowing,
kneeling, and prostrating by touching the ground with the
forehead.

Courtesy of Robert Monroe.

of Islamic political theory. In the domain of economics, the *shari'a* contains both general principles and specific instructions on matters such as poverty, taxes, and inheritance. The social teachings of the *shari'a* constitute a vast body of prescriptions dealing with issues such as education, status, the family unit, and the functions and roles of the sexes. And in matters of religion, the *shari'a* prescribes the details of the religious duties related to the Five Pillars.

To live according to the *shari'a* is, for Muslims, to live according to divine law, according to the norm that God has provided and willed for humans. That norm is considered to be the blueprint for a perfect human and social life.

ARTICLES OF FAITH

Muhammad's teachings, as recorded in the Qur'an, constitute the well-spring of Islamic faith and practice. The following selections from the Qur'an summarize the five Islamic articles of faith:

> True piety is this: to believe in God, and the Last Day, the Angels, the Book, and the Prophets. (Qur'an 2.176)

> O believers, believe in God, and in His Messenger, and in the Book which he has sent down to his Messenger, and the Book which he sent down previously. For whosoever disbelieves in God, and his Angels, and His Books, and His Messengers, and the Last Day, has indeed strayed far in error. (Qur'an 4.135–136)

Five important teachings are immediately apparent in those scriptural declarations: God, the Last Day, Angels, Books (Scriptures), and Prophets ("Messengers").

God

Of the five tenets central to Islam, the foremost is the oneness of God. "There is no other god but God" is an assertion that Muhammad stressed, and he rejected the Christian concept of the Trinity as being polytheistic (Qur'an 4.168–169, 5.78, 112.1). He was unequivocal on that point. For Muhammad and all Muslims, there is but one God, who exists from eternity to all eternity. He is all-seeing, all-hearing, all-speaking, all-knowing, all-willing, all-powerful, and — above all — an absolute unity. Islamic theology provides one of the most comprehensive lists of devotional expressions about God, consisting of ninety-nine "most beautiful names" of God. Everything comes into being through God's divine will and creative word. He is the creator, provider, and protector of humanity and the universe.

The Islamic teaching about God is expressed in the form of adjectives, such as all-seeking, all-powerful, all-knowing, all-hearing, from which are derived the ninety-nine "beautiful names" of God. Occasionally, however, longer passages in the Qur'an attempt to describe the glory and power of God.

> God, there is no god but He, the living, the everlasting! Slumber seizes Him not, neither sleep; to Him belongs all that are in the heavens and the earth. Who is there that shall intercede with Him except by His permission? He knows what lies before them and what is after them; and they comprehend not anything of His knowledge except such as He wills. His throne comprises the heavens and the earth; the preserving of them oppresses Him not; He is the all-high, the all-glorious. (Qur'an 2.255–256)

The Qur'an makes a fundamental distinction between God and all else, including human beings, who are finite creatures. God alone is infinite as well as absolute. To point to an individual such as Jesus with delineations of birthplace and birthdate and then to say simply that he is God or the second person in the Godhead is, according to the Qur'an, impossible and unpardonable. The Qur'anic judgment against those who uphold the Christian doctrine of the Trinity is similar to its judgment against infidels.

> Those who say: "the Messiah, son of Mary, is God," are infidels. . . . Those who say: "God is the third of three," are infidels, for there is no God but One. . . . Those who associate anything with God, God will prohibit them from entering paradise, and their refuge shall be hell. (Qur'an 5.76–77)

The Last Day

The second doctrine that occupies an important place in the minds of Muslims is that of the day of judgment. Heaven, hell, and the final day of judgment are described elaborately and powerfully. Every individual will be called to account. There will be a resurrection of the body, a final judgment, and a final destiny in heaven or hell, depending on one's record on earth.

The vivid descriptions of heaven and hell and the elaborate portrayal of the final judgment are very similar to the Book of Revelation in the New Testament and yet more powerful. The events of the last day are described as cataclysmic, that is, as appearing suddenly with great cosmic changes and at a time known only to God. On that day, when the trumpet sounds, the sun shall be darkened, the stars shall fall, the heavens shall be split asunder, the mountains shall turn to dust, and the earth shall be crushed.

> When the sun shall be darkened,
> When the stars shall be thrown down,
> When the mountains shall be set moving,
> When the pregnant camels shall be neglected,
> When the savage beasts shall be mustered,
> When the seas shall be set boiling. . . .
> When the heavens shall be stripped off,
> When hell shall be set blazing,
> When paradise shall be brought nigh,
> Then shall a soul know what it has produced!
>   (Qur'an 81.1–14)

> When the trumpet is blown with a single blast, and the earth and the mountains are lifted up and crushed with a single blow, then, on that day, the terror shall come to pass. . . . And the angels shall stand upon its borders. . . . On that day you shall be exposed, not one secret of yours concealed. (Qur'an 69.14–30)

On that last day, according to the Qur'an, the graves will open and humanity will be called to account. The guardian angel of each individual will bear witness to that person's record on earth. Each person's deeds will be weighed in the divine balance, and a "book" containing one's record of life will be placed in one's hand. If the book is placed in the right hand, the individual will be among the blessed; if the book is placed in the left hand, the individual will be among the damned.

Then as for him who is given his book in his right hand . . . he shall be in a pleasing life, in a lofty garden. . . . But as for him who is given his book in his left hand, he shall say, "Would that I had not been given my book and not known my reckoning! Would it had been the end!" Take him and fetter him, and then roast him in Hell! (Qur'an 69.13–37)

The terror of the Qur'anic portrayal of hell defies description. All worshipers of gods other than God, all the proud and the evildoers are to be cast into the fires of hell. They will abide there forever, with no release from its torments. On the other hand, all the blessed and God-fearing individuals, all the humble and charitable, all those who suffered for God's sake, and all those, especially, who fought in the name of and for God are to be provided with fine garments, music, feasting, beautiful maidens, and inexpressible bliss in the garden of paradise.

Angels

A third fundamental tenet of Islam is belief in intermediary beings called angels, two of whom play especially prominent roles: Gabriel, who appeared before Muhammad to reveal to him that he had been called by God, and *Iblis* or *Shaitan* (Satan), who along with the *jinn* (rebellious angels) are destined to be judged and condemned to hell. Other angels record men's actions, receive their souls at death, and bear witness for or against them on the Day of Judgment.

Books (Scriptures)

The fourth principal teaching of Islam is the sacredness of the Qur'an. Although Muslims respect parts of the scriptures of Judaism (the Torah, Psalms) and Christianity (the Gospels), they regard the Qur'an as God's final revelation, superseding all previous revelations. Its message is addressed to all humanity, including Jews and Christians, who are considered to belong to a community defined as the "people of the book."

Prophets

The fifth important teaching Muslims profess is belief in the prophets. Islam maintains that God has communicated his divine message and guidance to humanity throughout the ages through the medium of selected members of the human race — the prophets, or messengers of God. Muslims honor a total of twenty-eight prophets of God, including Muhammad. Eighteen of those prophets are well-known biblical figures, beginning with Adam and continuing with, among others, Abraham, Noah, Isaac, Ishmael, Moses, Zechariah, John, and Jesus. According to Islamic doctrine, those men were selected to convey the divine messages to keep humanity on the right track. At a particular point in history, the seventh century, Muhammad was selected as the last messenger and commanded to convey God's complete design to the entire human race. Thus, Muhammad is thought of as the seal of the prophets, through whom God revealed his eternal message in its definitive form.

THE PILLARS OF ISLAM

Just as every faithful Muslim must accept five fundamental tenets, so must every devout follower perform five important religious duties: proclamation of faith, prayer, almsgiving, fasting, and pilgrimage. These requirements are usually known as the Pillars of Islam.

Shahada

The first duty of a Muslim is to recite the *shahada,* or proclamation of faith: "There is no other god but God, and Muhammad is the Prophet of God." Countless devout Muslims repeat the *shahada,* the shortest and most incisive creed of any religion, many times a day.

Prayer

The second duty of a Muslim is to pray five times a day: at daybreak, at noon, in midafternoon, after sunset, and in the late evening. Generally, Muslims go to a mosque, a building, or a place for prayer. If that is not possible, it does not matter where they pray, as long as the obligation is met. Forehead, hands, and feet must be washed as a prelude to prayer, and the courtyards of mosques are equipped with washing facilities for that purpose. If no water is available, the hands and face may be wiped with fine, clean sand. Muslims pray on a mat or a carpet, and all recite their prayers in Arabic, no matter what the linguistic and cultural background of the worshiper may be. Friday noon is set aside as a time of public prayer, and Muslims observe that religious duty collectively in their different communities.

All faithful Muslims assemble every Friday noon for solemn community prayer. It is not necessarily a day of rest but rather a day on which all business activities are suspended temporarily for an interval of communal prayer in the mosque. Behavior appropriate to the occasion includes the rite of ablution, or purification; the removal of shoes or sandals; and the performance of the prayer ritual. Facing toward Mecca, the faithful place themselves in rows behind an *imam* to perform the prayer ritual. Following the public prayer is an address, or sermon, given by the *imam,* which consists of praises of God, blessings on the Prophet, prayer from the Muslim community, a recitation from the Qur'an, and extemporaneous admonitions to piety. Also, God's blessing is invoked on the leaders of the Muslim states.

Almsgiving

The third duty is to give alms to the poor as an outward sign of true piety. Devout Muslims consider the sharing of the abundance bestowed by God a privilege.

Fasting

The fourth duty is to fast during the month of *Ramadan* (the ninth month in the Islamic calendar). What distinguishes this observance from other fasts is that during the day Muslims must abstain from drink, food, and sexual relations; the proscriptions are lifted between

Washing facility in the courtyard of a mosque in Cairo, Egypt. Washing the head, hands, and feet is part of the preparation for prayer, and the courtyards of mosques are equipped with washing facilities.
Courtesy of Robert Monroe.

sunset and sunrise. Only invalids, travelers, soldiers at war, and pregnant or menstruating women are excused from fasting, though they must make up for any days missed at some other time.

A festival celebrated with great joy and feasting takes place at the end of Ramadan, as soon as the new moon appears. The first three days are celebrated as the *'id-al-fitir* ("Festival of Fast Breaking") or *Ramazan Bairam* (Turkish for "Festival of *Ramadan*") or as *'id-al-saghir* ("Little Festival") or *Kuchuk Bairam* (Turkish for "Little Festival"). Soon after sunrise, everyone dresses in new or clean clothes, and the men assemble in the mosques for prayers. Families and friends visit and exchange presents, especially cakes and candies. Many Muslims also visit family graves to recite prayers and offer food to the less fortunate.

Pilgrimage

The fifth duty is to make a pilgrimage to the holy city of Mecca at least once in a lifetime. Long before the days of Muhammad, Mecca had been a sacred center to which Arabian people came yearly, on a pilgrimage to the sacred cube-shaped shrine known as the *Ka'ba* (cube). In the shrine is a black stone about the size of a pomegranate and oval in shape. Tradition held that the angel Gabriel brought the stone down to Abraham. Legend also said that the holy stone once had been so brilliantly white that pilgrims could be guided to the city by its radiance. Because of humanity's wickedness, the stone later turned black.

Only a few steps away from the *Ka'ba* is the sacred well of *Zamzam*, believed to contain miraculous healing powers. Later tradition connected it with Hagar, who, when she left Abraham's tent, wandered with her son, Ishmael, through the barren desert in search of water. In desperation, she left Ishmael, who was too exhausted to travel farther, lying on the hot earth, while she ran back and forth in search of water. In the meantime, Ishmael, tossing restlessly, kicked his heels and accidentally uncovered the opening to the well. Hagar and her son decided to remain there, and in the years to come the children and grandchildren of Ishmael multiplied to become the Arab race.

The black stone in the *Ka'ba* and the well of Zamzam are not the only factors that made Mecca a holy city. Eight years after Muhammad fled from Mecca to Medina, a delegation from Mecca negotiated a peaceful settlement with Muhammad. In 630, Muhammad and some 10,000 followers peacefully entered Mecca, the city of his birth. Walking first seven times around the outside of the *Ka'ba*, Muhammad entered the shrine and destroyed all of its 360 idols and images. Then he dedicated the *Ka'ba* to God and proclaimed Mecca to be the holiest city of Islam.

Each year following that incident, Muhammad came to Mecca from Medina to lead a large group of people in a pilgrimage to the holy *Ka'ba*. His first pilgrimage was in 632, when it is said that 100,000 faithful followers walked and performed many solemn rites. The pilgrimage to the holy city then became a popular means of securing God's favor.

No religious ritual has done more to unite the Muslims than the rite of pilgrimage. Every devout Muslim must make a pilgrimage to the sacred city of Mecca at least once in his or her lifetime. Only poverty, illness, or bondage can excuse a believer from this duty. The importance of the annual gathering of Muslims from many countries would be difficult to overestimate. Muslims from all walks of life and of varying colors, races, and nationalities (e.g., Arabs, Turks, Persians, Indians, Chinese) realize their equality before God as they meet on common ground. Because not all Muslims can make the costly journey to Mecca, they may make the trip by proxy through another pilgrim. In such cases, the custom is for the would-be pilgrim to contribute as much as possible so a substitute can go in his or her place. Such substitutes bring merit on all those who make their pilgrimage possible.

Before entering the holy precincts, all pilgrims wear a white seamless garment and abstain from shaving or cutting their hair. However, simply visiting Mecca is not enough. Three main rituals, along with various other duties, are prescribed.

1.   Before entering the most sacred precincts of the large open-air center where the *Ka'ba* is located, pilgrims stop to perform their ablutions, put on a white seamless garment, remove their sandals or shoes, and approach the *Ka'ba* barefoot. Then, like their prophet Muhammad, they walk around it seven times, three times quickly and four times slowly. On each circuit, they pause to kiss or—if the crowd is too great—touch with the hand or a stick the southeast corner of the *Ka'ba*, where the black stone is located.

2. The next observance commemorates Hagar's frantic search for water for her son, Ishmael. Pilgrims walk quickly seven times across the valley between the two mounds of Safa and Marwa, some five hundred yards apart.

3. The climactic ritual is a march to the Mount of Mercy, on the plain of Arafat, some fifteen miles east of Mecca. The ceremony is a day's journey on foot, but many stop to rest at the sanctuary of Mina, the halfway point. All pilgrims must, however, arrive at Mount Mercy the following morning. Once there, pilgrims "stand before God" from noon to sunset, absorbed in pious meditation. The night is then spent in the open. The following morning, pilgrims return to Mina, where animal sacrifices and three days of feasting follow. A final trip around the *Ka'ba* in Mecca and the discarding of the seamless garment complete the pilgrimage. The pilgrim is now permitted to assume the special title of *Hajj*, one who has made the pilgrimage to the holy city.

The feast celebrating the successful conclusion of the pilgrimage is known as *'id-al-azha* ("Festival of Sacrifices"), *'id-al-kabir* ("Great Festival"), or *Qurban Bairam* (Turkish for "Festival of Sacrifice") and lasts for four days. Pilgrims celebrate it in the month of pilgrimage, in the valley of Mina (where Mecca is located), while nonpilgrims celebrate it at home. Every Muslim is expected to sacrifice an animal (although that is not a legal duty except in fulfillment of a vow), just as Abraham sacrificed a sheep instead of his son. After the feasting is over, most families visit the tombs of their relatives, where palm branches are laid on the graves and food is distributed to the poor at the cemetery. Professional reciters are hired to pray at the graveside, after which the men leave the cemetery. The women maintain a vigil throughout the day; in many Muslim countries, it is customary for them to spend the night in a tent at the cemetery.

HOLY WAR (*JIHAD*)

In addition to the obligations of the five Pillars of Islam, the Qur'an enjoins Muslim believers to "strive in the way of God." What that means is spelled out in the following passages:

> O believers, fear God. Fight in the path of God against those who fight against you; but do not commit aggression. . . . Slay them wheresoever you find them, and expel them from where they have expelled you. . . . Fight against them until sedition is no more and allegiance is rendered to God alone. (Qur'an 2.186)

> Fight against those who believe not in God, nor in the last day; who prohibit not what God and his Prophet have prohibited; and who refuse allegiance to the true faith. (Qur'an 9.29)

The quality of combativeness — rather, of being actively engaged in combat against "pagans" or opponents — is called *jihad*, meaning "holy

war." *Jihad* entails an active struggle using armed force whenever necessary. The object of *jihad* is not so much the conversion of individuals
to Islam as the gaining of political control over societies, in order to govern them in accordance with the principles of Islam.

Classical Islamic teaching held that the world was divisible into three
spheres: *dar al-Islam,* or the zone of Islam; *dar as-sulh,* or the zone of
peace (areas defined in terms of peace pacts that the Muslims had concluded with neighbors); and *dar al-harb,* or the zone of war. In modern
times, the Muslim position on the zone of war has been modified in the
sense that no nation or territory is regarded as hostile unless it is actively so. Thus, *jihad* no longer is thought of as an offensive engagement
for expansion but as a defensive reaction against liberalism, modernism,
and Westernization.

ISLAMIC OBSERVANCES

Rites of Passage

Of the several solemn observances that are as binding on Muslims as
religious duties, four of the most important are birth, circumcision, marriage, and death.

Seven days after birth, the parents name the child, cut its hair, and
offer a sacrifice. The meat of the sacrificial animal is given to the poor,
and monetary gifts corresponding to the weight of the infant's hair are
distributed in alms. Circumcision of a male child usually is performed
at the age of four or later. Both occasions usually are marked by family
gatherings and festivities.

The general rule for marriage is that a Muslim male may marry a
non-Muslim (a Christian or a Jew, but not a polytheist), whereas a Muslim female may marry only a Muslim. Essential to the marriage ceremony are the presence of witnesses and a contract specifying the bride-
price. The bride-price of goods is given by the groom (or his father) to
the father of the bride. As a rule, only part of the bride-price is paid on
marriage; the remainder is paid if and when the marriage is dissolved.

When a Muslim dies, the body is washed with water, usually by
someone of the same sex, and burial follows promptly after the recitation of short prayers. All Muslims are laid to rest on their right side facing Mecca. Males and females are never buried in the same grave unless joint interment is unavoidable, in which case a partition is raised to
separate the corpses.

Memorials and Celebrations

Muslims observe several other ceremonies and celebrations. The first
month of the Islamic year, known as Muharram, begins with a ten-day
mourning observance among the Shi'ites. The occasion marks the
martyrdom of 'Ali, son-in-law of the Prophet Muhammad, and his sons
Hassan and Hussain. The incident that sets the mood for this commem-
orative day is the tragedy of Karbala rather than the assassination of
'Ali. On the tenth of Muharram (October 10, 680), Hussain, who came to

be considered the third *imam,* was killed in a revolt in Karbala, Iraq. His grave on the battlefield became, almost immediately, a shrine for pilgrims. To this day, many Shi'ites go to Karbala to die, or they ask that their bodies be transported to that "holy city" for burial; tradition asserts that those who are buried by the shrine will certainly enter paradise.

Shi'ite Muslims often commemorate the martyrdom of 'Ali and his sons by reenacting the suffering and burial of Hussain. The observance culminates with a reenactment of the "passion," or "vicarious suffering," and death of Hussain. A big procession, designed as a funeral parade, dramatizes the burial of Hussain.

The Sunni Muslims also observe Muharram, but only for one day and with a different emphasis. They believe the creation of Adam and Eve, heaven and hell, and life and death took place on this day.

There are various other Islamic memorials, but the dates and even the events they commemorate vary, depending on the history and racial background of the people. For instance, Indian Muslims observe the anniversary of the death of Hassan, the brother of Hussain. Other Muslims observe the birthday of Hussain. The Shi'ite Muslims commemorate the birthday and the death of 'Ali, and Indian Muslims commemorate the death of 'Ali on the twenty-first day of Ramadan. Another purely Shi'ite festival is the *'id-al-ghadir* ("Festival of the Lake of Humm"). The Lake of Humm is thought to be where the Prophet Muhammad nominated 'Ali as his successor. One very important observance is the *lailat al-bara'a* ("Night of Privilege"). For some Muslims (mainly from India and Indonesia), that day is set aside for the commemoration of the dead. Other Muslims (mainly from Egypt) believe that a little after sunset on that night the "Heavenly Tree" is shaken and the leaves that fall from the tree identify the human beings who will die the following year.

A number of memorial days are connected with the Prophet Muhammad and are celebrated by almost all Muslim people. Those observances include the birthday and the death of the Prophet; the Night of Fulfilled Desires, commemorating the night on which the Prophet Muhammad was conceived; and the Night of the Ascension of the Prophet.

STUDY QUESTIONS

1. What is the proper perspective for understanding Islam?
2. Describe the life of Muhammad before and after he received divine revelation.
3. Describe the incident marking the beginning of the Muslim calendar.
4. What are the reasons for the triumph of Muhammad's religion?
5. Present the rise and conflict of the first four Caliphs.
6. What factors helped the spread of Islam?

7. Describe the role of the Mughal emperors in India.

8. Give the reasons for the abolishment of the Caliphate.

9. Cite the regulations governing the appearance and conduct of women.

10. Compare the distinguishing features among the major Islamic groups.

11. Discuss the position of the Qur'an in relation to the Christian Bible.

12. Analyze the significance of the *Hadith.*

13. Describe the norm provided by the *shari'a* for Muslim conduct and behavior.

14. What are the Islamic Articles of Faith?

15. State briefly what are considered to be the Pillars of Islam.

16. List the main rituals prescribed for pilgrims in Mecca.

17. Discuss the various views offered regarding *jihad.*

18. Name and describe some of the more important observances and celebrations in Islam.

Suggested Reading

Armstrong, Karen. *Holy War.* London: Macmillan, 1988.

———. *Muhammad: A Biography of the Prophet.* New York: Harper-Collins, 1992.

Cook, Michael A. *Muhammad.* Oxford: Oxford University Press, 1983.

De Seife, Rodolphe J. A. *The Shari'a: An Introduction to the Law of Islam.* San Francisco: Austin & Winfield, 1994.

Esposito, John L. *Islam: The Straight Path,* 3rd ed. New York: Oxford University Press, 1998.

Fernea, Elizabeth Warnock. *In Search of Islamic Feminism: One Woman's Global Journey.* New York: Doubleday, 1998.

Hekmat, Anwar. *Women and the Koran: The Status of Women in Islam.* Amherst, N.Y.: Prometheus Books, 1997.

Jawad, Haifaa A. *The Rights of Women in Islam: An Authentic Approach.* New York: St Martin's Press, 1998.

Johnson, James Turner. *The Holy War Idea in Western and Islamic Traditions.* University Park, Penn.: Pennsylvania State University Press, 1997.

Lings, Martin. *Muhammad: His Life Based on the Earliest Sources.* London: George Allen & Unwin, 1983.

Majumadara, Suhasa. *Jihad: The Islamic Doctrine of Permanent War.* New Delhi: Voice of India, 1994.

Matthews, Mary. *Magid Fasts for Ramadan.* New York: Clarion Books, 1996.

McCloud, Aminah Beverly. *African American Islam.* New York: Routledge, 1995.

Mernissi, Fatima. *The Veil and the Male Elite: A Feminist Interpretation of Women's Rights in Islam.* Reading, Mass.: Addison-Wesley, 1991.

Nasr, Seyyed Hossein. *Ideals and Realities of Islam,* 2nd ed. London: Unwin Hyman, 1985.

Nigosian, Solomon A. *Islam: The Way of Submission.* Northants, Eng.: Thorsons, 1987.

Peters, Francis E. *Muhammad and the Origins of Islam.* Albany, N.Y.: SUNY Press, 1994.

———. *The Hajj: The Muslim Pilgrimage to Mecca and the Holy Places.* Princeton, N.J.: Princeton University Press, 1996.

Pinault, David. *The Shi'ites: Ritual and Popular Piety in a Muslim Community.* New York: St Martin's Press, 1992.

Rahman, Fazlur. *Major Themes of the Qur'an,* 2nd ed. Minneapolis: Bibliotheca Islamica, 1994.

Rodinson, Maxime. *Muhammad,* 2nd ed. London: Penguin Books, 1996.

Schimmel, Annemarie. *Mystical Dimensions of Islam.* Chapel Hill, N.C.: University of North Carolina Press, 1975.

———. *And Muhammad Is His Messenger: The Veneration of the Prophet in Islamic Piety.* Chapel Hill, N. C.: University of North Carolina Press, 1985.

———. *My Soul Is a Woman: The Feminine in Islam.* New York: Continuum, 1997.

Smith, Jane I. (ed.). *Women in Contemporary Muslim Societies.* Lewisburg, Penn.: Bucknell University Press, 1980.

16 Sikhism

Sikhism, the religion of the Sikh community, originated in the Punjab region of India around the sixteenth century. Some scholars view Sikhism primarily as a reform movement of Hinduism; others see it as an outstanding example of religious syncretism—a blend of Hinduism and Islam. The Sikhs, however, reject such interpretations of their religion as misrepresentations. To its followers, Sikhism is not simply the reworking of two older religions but a new, divine revelation and, consequently, a genuinely independent religion.

The self-denial, ascetical and pacifist attitude of Jainism is alien to the social involvement and political affirmation of Sikhism. In the seventeenth century, the Sikhs became involved in politics, with the result that they earned the displeasure of the ruling Mughal dynasty. During the reign of Emperor Aurangzeb (1658–1707), many Sikhs, including one of their *gurus*, were executed. The Sikhs reacted with armed resistance, which fostered the military characteristics they retain to this day.

The fact that Sikhs are an adventurous and enterprising people perhaps accounts for the numerous Sikh communities found outside India. Wherever they have gone, they have installed their Holy Book, the Guru Granth Sahib, in their homes and in their temples *(gurdwara)*. The Sikhs are distinguishable mainly by their beards, long hair, turbans, and steel bracelets, but some, especially those who live in large Western cities, have shaved off their beards, cut their hair, and discarded the turban. Whether or not they retain external symbols of their faith, Sikhs show their devotion to God in daily prayer and religious observances. Equality and democracy are the two outstanding characteristics of Sikhism, and its code emphasizes truth, good behavior, and moral courage.

Sikhism

CE
- **1469** Birth of Guru Nanak (d. 1539)
- **1479** Birth of Guru Amar Das (d. 1574)
- **1504** Birth of Guru Angad (d. 1552)
- **1528** Founding of Mogul Empire by Babar (1526–1707)
- **1563** Birth of Guru Arjun Dev (d. 1606)
- **1581** Compilation of *Adi Granth*
- **1666** Birth of Guru Gobind Singh (d. 1708)
- **1708** Installation of the Adi Granth as Guru
- **1716** Hundreds of Sikhs executed in Delhi by the Mughals
- **1757** Beginning of British domination in India (ended 1947)
- **1783** Birth of Baba Dayal (d. 1854), founder of Nirankari group
- **1816** Birth of Satguru Ram Singh (d. 1884), founder of Namdhari group
- **1849** Sikh kingdom of Punjab annexed to Great Britain by British forces
- **1860s** Namdhari Sikhs revolt against British rule in India by boycotting British goods, government schools, law courts, and postal services
- **1872** Satguru Ram Singh exiled by India's British government to Burma
- **1892** Founding of the Khalsa College in Amritsar, an educational establishment to promote education and publish books and periodicals on Sikhism
- **1947** Partition of Punjab; hopes of independent Sikh state dashed
- **1950s** Beginning of Sikh immigration to the West
- **1969** Harbhajan Singh Puri (also known as Yogi Bhajan), founded in the United States the movement popularly known as "3HO" (Healthy, Happy, Holy Organization)
- **1984** Golden Temple of Sikhs invaded by Indian army; assassination of Indira Gandhi by Sikh extremists

While Sikhs are concentrated mainly in the province of the Punjab (currently divided between Pakistan and India), a considerable number have emigrated, especially since India's independence and partition in 1947, to Great Britain, Europe, and the Americas.

GURU NANAK

The founding of Sikhism is attributed to Guru Nanak (1469–1539), who was born of Hindu parents in the village of Talwandi, some forty miles from Lahore, India. The earliest source materials on Nanak were written fifty to eighty years after his death. Most scholars, however, have rejected those sources, relying instead on the accounts of historians of the eighteenth and nineteenth centuries and on the records of Mughal court historians.

Nanak's father was the village clerk; his mother was a pious woman devoted to the family. Nanak was a reflective boy, and at an early age he studied both the Islamic Qur'an and the Hindu Shastras (scriptures). He was also greatly influenced by Kabir (1440–1518), a Muslim poet who taught the oneness of God, the union of humankind with God, the consubstantiality between Hinduism and Islam, and the irrelevance of formal creeds and dogmas.

Tradition asserts that Nanak's marriage, which took place while he was still in his teens, was unhappy. Even though two sons resulted from the marriage, Nanak left his home and, in traditional fashion, wandered around India in search of truth and wisdom. He is also believed to have made a pilgrimage to Mecca, even though he was a Hindu.

The revelation that transformed Nanak from an obscure wanderer to a *guru* came to him as he was meditating in a forest in Sultanpur, India, when he was about thirty years old. The message of the vision was that God had singled him out to proclaim the True Name. In the words of Nanak:

> The Mighty One instructed me:
>
> "Night and day, sing my praise!"
> The Lord did summon this minstrel
> To his High Court;
> On me he bestowed the robe of honor
> Of those who exalt him.
> On me he bestowed the nectar in a cup,
> The nectar of his True and holy Name.[1]

Shortly after that vision, Nanak announced his message: "There is no Muslim and there is no Hindu."

Nanak and his constant companion, the Muslim minstrel Mardana, traveled widely in India over the next few decades, preaching the essential unity of Hinduism and Islam. To illustrate his absolute conviction in this unity, he dressed in a mixture of Hindu and Muslim styles. His greatest success was in the Punjab area, where groups of Hindus and Muslims began to follow him.

The story of his death perhaps best illustrates his success in attracting followers from both groups. The story goes that in Nanak's final hours his disciples began arguing about what to do with the body — whether to burn it according to Hindu custom or to bury it as Muslims do. Nanak, who had overheard them, settled the dispute by telling both groups to lay flowers at his side, adding that the group whose flowers remained fresh the following morning could have his body. Then Nanak covered himself with a sheet and died. When the sheet was lifted the next morning, the disciples found, to their amazement, that there was no way of distinguishing one group of flowers from the other group. They were all fresh.

THE DEVELOPMENT OF SIKHISM

The Succession of Gurus

Nanak was succeeded by nine other *gurus* during the next 150 years.

Name	Birth–Death	Leadership
Guru Angad	1504–1552	1539–1552
Guru Amar Das	1479–1574	1552–1574
Guru Ram Das Sodhi	1534–1581	1574–1581
Guru Arjun Dev	1563–1606	1581–1606
Guru Har Gobind	1595–1644	1606–1644
Guru Har Rai	1630–1661	1644–1661
Guru Har Kishan	1656–1664	1661–1664
Guru Tegh Bahadur	1621–1675	1664–1675
Guru Gobind Singh	1666–1708	1675–1708

Those nine *gurus* shaped the religion of Sikhism by consolidating, institutionalizing, and contributing significantly to its social, political, and religious life. A few of the leaders merit special mention. Guru Angad, whom Nanak appointed as his successor, distinguished himself particularly by devising a Punjabi script, the script in which Sikh scriptures are written. Significant changes also occurred under the administration of the fifth *guru*, Arjun Dev, who completed his father's project of building the Golden Temple at Amritsar, which today is the holy city of the Sikhs, and pioneered the practice of making pilgrimages there. His greatest contribution, however, was the compilation of the Granth Sahib (Holy Book), the Sikh scripture.

When Guru Arjun was killed by the Mughal emperor Jahangir in 1606, he was succeeded by his son, Har Gobind, who was responsible for the development among Sikhs of a more militant and aggressive attitude toward their enemies. Under Guru Gobind, Sikhs were forced for the first time to resort to the sword and to assume a national character, factors that contributed considerably to their persecution at the hands of Mughal rulers.

One of the worst persecutions came during the leadership of Tegh Bahadur, the ninth *guru*. The Mughal emperor Aurangzeb, who was then on the throne, was a religious fanatic who was determined to convert all his subjects to Islam, by force if necessary. Guru Tegh Bahadur was beheaded because he advocated freedom of religious worship.

The "sword of leadership" was conferred on Gobind Singh, the tenth and last *guru*, who, after Nanak himself, is considered by Sikhs to have been their most outstanding leader. In his thirty-three years of leadership, Guru Gobind Singh concentrated on strengthening the political, social, and religious aspects of the Sikh religion. Men and women were trained in the use of arms, and Guru Gobind Singh led them in the struggle against the Mughal emperor. He organized a defense group

Gurdwara Hari-Mandir Sahib in Amritsar, the state of Punjab in India. The most famous *gurdwara* among Sikhs, it is often called the Golden Temple because its dome is covered with gold leaf. The temple, built above the huge watertank, was completed in the sixteenth century CE by Guru Arjun Dev, the fifth *guru*.
Courtesy of Government of India Tourist Office, Toronto.

modeled along military lines to ward off punitive attacks on the Sikh community. The group, known as the *Khalsa* ("Brotherhood of the Pure"), survives today as a vital force in the life of the Sikh community, as do several religious observances initiated by Guru Gobind Singh.

Militant Sikhism

Before his death, Guru Gobind Singh declared the succession of *gurus* at an end. Henceforth, Holy Book of the Sikhs, the Adi Granth (more commonly known as the Granth Sahib), represented the final, definitive statement of Sikhism for all Sikhs and the authority by which they were to be governed. Military leadership of the Sikhs, however, devolved on Banda Singh Bahadur (1670–1716).

At first, Banda Singh was successful in defying the Mughals, but his military career ended in disaster when he and seven hundred of his followers were captured and executed in Delhi in 1716 and the Sikh community was forced to disperse into the neighboring hills. Shortly after that incident, the Mughal Empire was completely disrupted by a series of Iranian and Afghan invasions. The Sikhs acted swiftly. Ranjit Singh (1780–1839) exploited the occasion to bring under his suzerainty a territory extending from the Jamuna River to the Indus River. After his death, Ranjit Singh's Sikh kingdom disintegrated rapidly, a consequence of the disruptive influence of internal squabbles over his succession and the advance of British forces. In a series of bitterly contested battles between 1845 and 1849, the Sikhs were defeated and the Sikh kingdom was annexed to Great Britain.

Modern Sikhism

Disillusioned by the British act of annexation, the Sikhs joined Gandhi's freedom movement, only to find their communities split in half by the division of the subcontinent into India and Pakistan in 1947. Bloody, brutal riots between Sikhs and Muslims preceding partition forced millions of Sikhs to leave Pakistan. Today, the majority of Sikhs are settled in the Indian Punjab region and maintain their separate identity, as encouraged by state legislatures and the Indian Parliament.

Two of the most pressing issues facing the Sikhs today are the establishment of a Sikh state and the status of Sikh-Hindu relations in India. Sikh religion and politics have always been intimately connected. In fact, the belief in a Sikh state is an article of faith that is chanted at the conclusion of every service: "The *Khalsa* shall rule." In 1970, a Sikh-dominated state was established in the area of Punjab, with Chandigarh as its capital.

The matter of Sikh-Hindu relations is a sensitive one. The tendency of the modern generation of Sikhs is to abandon their distinguishing characteristics and to affiliate socially with Hindus. Efforts to combat that tendency have not yielded great results.

Nonetheless, the main body of Sikhs has gradually broken away from Hindu social structure and asserted Sikh separatism. For instance, Sikh insistence on commensality — eating together at the kitchen of the *gurdwara* — destroyed among Sikhs the traditional, rigid Hindu class or caste system. However, Sikh social structure imposed an alternative, three-level system, based on ethnic differences: *jats*, made up of agricultural people; non-*jats*, comprising priests, warriors, and professionals; and *mazahabis,* converts from Hindu outcastes. The three-tiered structure is currently in a state of flux, especially among the educated, urban classes. Thus, the political, social, and religious roles of Sikhism, like those of most other religions, need reassessment in the light of modern influences and changes.

SIKH SACRED TEXT

The Holy Book of the Sikhs, Guru Granth Sahib (or Adi Granth), is in general a devotional book similar to the book of Psalms and is divided into three main sections. The first section, called the Japji, is considered by Sikhs to be the epitome of their teaching because it was written by Guru Nanak. After the Japji come the Ragas (tunes), consisting of four books. The twenty-six minor books that follow form the third section and are elaborations on the Ragas.

The Guru Granth Sahib is the focal point of *gurdwaras* (temples) and homes. It is always ceremoniously installed and treated with the utmost reverence. For instance, when the Guru Granth Sahib is installed in a

gurdwara, all stand and bow their heads. The Guru Granth Sahib is placed on cushions on a dais covered in rich hangings below a canopy. The officiating reader, who sits on a lower cushion, occasionally waves a long-haired, ceremonial whisk over it in imitation of an ancient custom once reserved for monarchs. All who enter the area hallowed by the Guru Granth Sahib must remove their shoes and cover their heads. Worshipers circle the temple clockwise and come to bow before the Guru Granth Sahib with folded hands. Prayers are addressed to the Guru Granth Sahib, an appropriate sermon accompanies the service, and the congregation joins in chanting various hymns and in eating a communal meal, commonly known as a "free kitchen."

Sikhs are expected to set aside a room in their homes to house a copy of the Guru Granth Sahib. Ceremonial rituals and daily readings chosen at random form part of obligatory observances in every household. Many Sikhs recite verses from the Guru Granth Sahib during their day-to-day activities.

SIKH TEACHINGS

The True One

Sikhism, in keeping with the teachings of Nanak, asserts that there is only one God, called Sat Nam ("True Name" or "True One"). Sat Nam is an unborn, uncreated, and immortal deity, through whom all things

Devotees at a Sikh service (photo at left and above). Worshipers first approach the Guru Granth Sahib to pay their respects before taking a seat on the floor. The officiating reader waves a fine yak-hair whisk above the Guru Granth Sahib to purify the atmosphere.
Courtesy of Wolf Arnold.

are created. Although Sat Nam is a personal God, he is formless, omniscient, omnipotent, omnipresent, and infinite — characteristics that are stated quite clearly in the Guru Granth Sahib:

> When God was himself self-created, there was none else. He took counsel and advice with Himself. What he did came to pass. Then there was no heaven or hell or the three regional worlds. There was only the Formless One Himself. (Guru Granth Sahib, 1)

Although everything is created by Sat Nam, he nevertheless is the "in-dweller of nature," filling all things and contained in everything. Thus, the immanent and transcendent qualities of Sat Nam are combined: the universe and everything in it are rooted in Sat Nam, at once containing him and being contained by him. Because he is indivisibly One and pervades everything, he is both in all else and above all else.

Moreover, Sat Nam is the God not only of a chosen group of people but of all humanity. He can be reached not through the mere accumulation of knowledge or on a merely theoretical plane but only through love and faith. Humanity's duty is to repeat the True Name, Sat Nam, while living a life of dedicated and active service. Devotion to Sat Nam manifests itself in right conduct and correct attitudes. Honesty, compassion, patience, and contentment distinguish the righteous, who are committed to denounce such vices as greed, slander, murder, robbery, and falsehood.

Rebirth

Sikhs believe that an individual is successively reborn in human form as he or she strives to attain the ultimate goal of existence; thus, every individual inherits a legacy represented by his or her performance in past existences. That goal is described as the union of the individual's spirit or soul, which is an immortal, divine spark, with its source, Sat Nam. An individual's family and racial inheritance as well as acquired characteristics also influence his or her conduct. Those who behave selfishly or cruelly, disregarding the rights and needs of others, suffer the consequences not in any future hell but in the next existence. Consequently, Sikhism, unlike many other religions, is not predicated on a Day of Judgment and its aftermath, that is, on an alternative between reward or punishment. Instead, the individual spirit, or soul, develops through countless births until it is absorbed by the infinite One.

In the last analysis, Sikhism is based on character training, on a discipline of spiritual purification designed to control five specific vices: anger, greed, false pride, lust, and an attachment to material or worldly things. The philosophy implicit in Sikhism is best expressed in this poetic passage:

> Ritual purification, though done a million times, may not
> purify the mind;
> Nor may absorption in trance silence it, however long and
> continuous.
> The possession of the world will not quench the rage of greed
> and hunger;
> A hundred thousand feats of intellect will not bring liberation.
> How then is Truth to be attained? How is the veil of illusion
> to be destroyed?
> Nanak says, through obedience to the Divine Order, which is
> written in your heart.[2]

SIKH GROUPS

All Sikhs, no matter to which sect they belong, accept the following three precepts: the oneness of God, the leadership of the ten *gurus,* and the divine revelation of the Guru Granth Sahib. Each of a number of divisions within the main body of Sikhism places a particular emphasis on one or more aspects of the religion.

A group known as the Nirankari seeks to restore the worship of the formless and invisible God to its pristine purity. Another group, the Namdhari, has developed an alternative theory of *guru*ship to that of the ten *gurus* and the Guru Granth Sahib. Yet another group, commonly known as Singh Sabha, fosters education to help Sikhs play a more significant role in the modern world. Still another group, the Sahajd-haris, rejects the militant aspects of Sikhism, and its adherents are always clean-shaven. The Udasis, basically an order of holy men, follow many of the principles that govern Indian ascetics. With a begging bowl as their sole possession, they vow celibacy and go about either naked, like Jain monks, or dressed in yellow garments, like Buddhist monks. Unlike most other Sikhs, they frequently cut their hair and shave their heads. Then there are the Singhs, the group with which the West has become the most familiar and therefore one that merits closer scrutiny.

The Singhs take their lead from the tenth and last *guru*, Gobind Singh, who assumed leadership of the Sikhs when he was nine years old, at the beginning of a period of particularly harsh persecution heralded by the execution of his father, Tegh Bahadur, the ninth *guru*. The Singhs represent the soldier-saints of the Brotherhood of the Pure, the *Khalsa*, founded by Guru Gobind Singh to ensure the survival of his followers in the face of persecution. To this day, the Singhs live by the code formulated by Gobind Singh. All members are baptized in a special ceremony and assume a common surname—Singh (Lion) for males and Kaur (Princess) for females—to symbolize their equality in the brotherhood and their repudiation of caste. All of them carry five distinguishing marks, the names of which begin with the letter *k: keshas*, uncut hair; *kangha*, a comb; *kara*, a steel bangle or bracelet worn on the right wrist; *kuchka*, a pair of shorts; and *kirpan*, a short sword or dagger. Singhs are also committed to avoid tobacco and intoxicants, the meat of animals that have not been killed by one stroke of the sword but that have been bled slowly to death, and adultery.

SIKH OBSERVANCES

Rites of Passage

Four principal ceremonies mark the life of a Sikh: naming, initiation, marriage, and death. Soon after birth, a child is taken to the *gurdwara* for a ceremony that culminates in the naming of the child. During the service and in the presence of the congregation, the Guru Granth Sahib is opened at random for a reading. The first letter of the first verse on the left page becomes the initial of the child's name.

In the initiation ceremony, the adherent acquires full membership in the Sikh community. The ritual consists of a baptismal ceremony initiated by Guru Gobind Singh, who stipulated that it must be performed by five baptized Sikhs. It is their duty to prepare the ceremonial agent of baptism, the Amrita (nectar of immortality), water and sweetmeats mixed with a double-edged sword in a steel bowl. While they stir the liquid, the five baptized Sikhs recite five prayers over the ceremonial bowl. Candidates, who are between the ages of eight and fifteen, first bathe and present themselves carrying the five marks of the *Khalsa*. Next, they kneel and, cupping their hands, receive five handfuls of the Amrita, which they drink. Their eyes and hair are also sprinkled five times with Amrita. Now they are ready to assume the responsibilities dictated by the religion and to accept the obligations implied by the five marks of the *Khalsa.*

Marriage, the third event in a Sikh's life that is celebrated with special ceremony, symbolizes the transcending and eternal union. It is celebrated in Sikh hymns that describe the human spirit as the bride of the eternal husband, God. During the marriage ceremony, the couple circle the Guru Granth Sahib four times to the accompaniment of four verses of the marriage hymn composed by Guru Ram Das.

The fourth and last ceremony that marks a stage of a Sikh's life occurs at death. The body is cremated, and a brief service is conducted for the relatives with the reading of appropriate hymns. Later, a religious ceremony generally is conducted either at home or at the *gurdwara,* during which a relay of readers maintains a continuous reading of the Guru Granth Sahib.

Devotional Acts

In addition to the four rite-of-passage observances, Sikhs follow a number of daily rituals. They begin the day with a ritual bath, followed by meditation on the name of God and the recitation of certain hymns and prayers. Every devout Sikh silently repeats as a morning devotional rite this composition (said to have been uttered by Guru Nanak):

> There is but one God whose name is True, the Creator, devoid of fear and enmity, immortal, unborn, self-existent, great and bountiful. The True One was in the beginning, the True One was in the primal age. The True One is, was, O Nanak, and the True One also shall be.[3]

Other rituals of hymns and prayers follow in the evening and before bedtime.

Sikhs also commemorate the anniversaries of the birth and the death of each of the ten *gurus.* Because Sikhs base their calculations on a combination of two factors, the Indian calendar and the lunar cycle, the dates of those celebrations vary from year to year.

Festivals

Three other festivals are important. Two of them commemorate the martyrdom of the four sons of Guru Gobind Singh: Ajit Singh and Jujhar Singh, who were slain in battle, and Zorawar Singh and Fateh Singh, who were executed by order of the Mughal emperor for refusing to accept Islam. The third festival commemorates the anniversary of the Baisakhi, the birthday of the *Khalsa.*

Local *gurdwara* committees may authorize other celebrations from time to time, but of all the Sikh festivals, only five rate as major observances: Guru Nanak's birthday, Guru Gobind Singh's birthday, Guru Arjun Dev's martyrdom, Guru Tegh Bahadur's martyrdom, and the anniversary of the Baisakhi. Those special occasions are preceded by a forty-eight-hour continuous reading of the Guru Granth Sahib from beginning to end and are concluded by the customary distribution of *karah parshad* (sweet food) to everyone present.

STUDY QUESTIONS

1. Give the traditional account of Guru Nanak.

2. Why do Sikhs consider the tenth Guru their most outstanding leader, after Nanak himself?

3. Trace the events that occurred between the Sikhs and the Mughal leaders.

4. What are the most pressing issues facing the Sikhs today?

5. Give a brief account of the role and the significance of the Guru Granth Sahib.

6. Analyze the Sikh concept of Sat Nam.

7. Compare the Sikh and Hindu concepts of rebirth.

8. What distinguishing features do all Singhs adopt?

9. List the ceremonies that mark the rites of passage in the life of a Sikh.

10. Describe the daily rituals observed by Sikh devotees.

Suggested Reading

Bennett, Olivia. *Listening to Sikhs.* London: Unwin Hyman, 1990.

Cole, William Owen, and S. Piara Singh. *The Sikhs: Their Religious Beliefs and Practices.* London: Routledge & Kegan Paul, 1978.

Draycott, Pamela. *Sikhism: A New Approach.* London: Hodder & Stoughton, 1996.

McLeod, W. Hew. *Sikhism.* London: Penguin Books, 1997.

———. *Guru Nanak and the Sikh Religion.* Oxford: Clarendon Press, 1968 (reprint 1988).

———. *The Evolution of the Sikh Community.* Delhi: Oxford University Press, 1975.

———. *Who Is a Sikh? The Problem of Sikh Identity.* Oxford: Clarendon Press, 1989.

Singh, N.-G. K. *The Feminine Principle in the Sikh Vision of the Transcendent.* Cambridge: Cambridge University Press, 1993.

Uberoi, J. P. Singh. *Religion, Civil Society, and the State: A Study of Sikhism.* Delhi/New York: Oxford University Press, 1996.

Notes

1. *The Sacred Writing of the Sikhs,* translated by Trilochan Singh, et al. (London: George Allen & Unwin, 1960), p. 82.

2. Translation by Gurbachan Singh Talib, *Japuji* (Delhi: Munshiram Manoharlal, 1977), p. 39.

3. Translation by M. A. MacAuliffe, *The Sikh Religion: Its Gurus, Sacred Writings and Anthems,* 6 vols. (Oxford: Clarendon Press, 1909), vol. 1, p. 35.

17 African Traditions

Africa was the home of human beings long before the dawn of history. Scientists believe that humanlike creatures roamed the plateaus of eastern Africa at least three million years ago. Today, archeologists are increasingly convinced that it was in Africa that humans became differentiated from other primates. Yet little is known of the beginnings of African religion, particularly in the area south of the Sahara Desert.

Archeological evidence based on several sites dating from 30,000 BCE indicates premeditation in the treatment and burial of human corpses. There are also rock paintings, depicting masked figures and serpentlike creatures, associated with some sort of religious activity. The discoveries of a variety of artifacts, particularly objects related to divination, also indicate the presence of religious activity. Naturally, many objects —including religious ones like shrines, stools, masks, and dress—from which a certain amount of historical study can be derived do not survive long in Africa's tropical climate. Consequently, archeological finds are limited in terms of what they reveal about the beginnings of African religion. Nonetheless, they provide valuable evidence of a link between past and present.

HISTORICAL OVERVIEW OF AFRICA

The Precolonial Period

The dearth of written records prevents scholars from reconstructing clearly the history of sub-Saharan Africa before the colonial period, that is, the period before the European explorations, which started in the 1400s. Nevertheless, the available information does provide some

African Traditions

BCE

c. 30,000 Evidence of rock paintings and burial of human corpses.

CE

c. 700s Rise of the kingdom of Ghana
c. 1000s Rise of the kingdom of Mali
c. 1400s Beginning of European explorations
c. 1500s Rise of the kingdom of Songhay
1502 African slaves arrive in Haiti
c. 1800s European nations consider slave trafficking an illegal enterprise
1806 British seize Cape of Good Hope
1841 David Livingstone comes to Africa
1869 Henry Stanley sent from New York to search for Livingstone
1884 European powers decide territorial rights in equatorial Africa
1900s Africa under colonial rule until 1945
1923 British take over southern Rhodesia (Zimbabwe)
1925 Hamallah founds a syncretistic religious movement
1930s Yakouba Sylla receives revelation from Fatima, daughter of prophet Muhammad.
1960 Nigeria gains independence
1963 Establishment of Republic of Nigeria
1963 Nelson Mandela imprisoned
1969 The Congo gains independence
1971 Establishment of Republic of Zaire
1990 Nelson Mandela freed from prison
1994 Nelson Mandela elected President of South Africa

significant episodes in the long development of African culture and civilization.

Long before the discovery of Africa by Europeans, Africans had developed their languages, cultures, political structures, social institutions, and religious systems. African religious systems consisted of Christianity (concentrated mainly in Egypt and Ethiopia), Islam (predominantly in northern Africa), Judaism (scattered communities throughout the continent), and a variety of indigenous religions. The contact of African culture with other cultures, particularly Islam, resulted in the creation of several great kingdoms. The best known were those of Ghana, in the interior of western Africa along the Niger River from the eighth to the eleventh centuries, and its successor Mali, which controlled trade across the desert until about 1500, when it was overthrown by the Songhay. Smaller kingdoms also flourished in other parts of Africa. In Nigeria and to the west were the kingdoms of Benin, Oyo, and Akan; to the east were the Baganda; and the territory of Sudan was occupied by the Funj. Other African societies were scattered throughout central and southern Africa. All those developments, however, were arrested by the arrival of Europeans.

Impact of the Europeans

The first European nation to become seriously interested in sub-Saharan Africa was Portugal. Prince Henry the Navigator sent Portuguese sailors to explore the west coast of Africa in the early 1400s. Their expeditions brought them as far south as Sierra Leone. Subsequent Portuguese expeditions led to the discovery of an all-sea travel route to the Far East by sailing around the Cape. Soon, the Dutch, the French, and the British followed the Portuguese in establishing trade routes and settlements serving as supply stations for ships traveling to the Far East. The presence of the European nations disrupted age-old African social patterns and traditional powers.

Before the arrival of Europeans, Arab slave traders dealt in the profitable business of buying and selling human beings. Under the Europeans, the African slave trade became the most lucrative business in supplying cheap labor for plantations in the newly discovered lands of South, Central, and North America and the Caribbean. The first African slaves arrived in Haiti in 1502. African tribes and kingdoms waged wars against each other to take captives and sell them to British, Dutch, French, and Portuguese agents. The king of Dahomey, for instance, sent his armies against neighboring tribes each year to capture slaves. By the mid-1800s, most European nations considered slave trafficking an illegal enterprise. In the meantime, millions of Africans were sold, the effects of which are still felt in Africa, Europe, and the Americas.

During all those years, Europeans made little effort to explore the interior of Africa. They lived along the shores of western and southern Africa, while African traders brought them slaves, ivory, gold, and other valuables from the interior. The two most famous African explorers were David Livingstone (1813–1873) and Henry M. Stanley (1841–1904). Livingstone, a Scottish medical missionary, came to Africa in 1841 and lived there for several long periods, during which he explored the interior. In 1869, Stanley, who was then a reporter for the New York Herald, was sent to search for Livingstone, who had not been heard from for over five years. When they finally met, Stanley greeted Livingstone with the now famous words, "Dr. Livingstone, I presume?"

Others followed suit. European governments, private companies, scientific institutions, and missionary societies all entered the race of exploring inland Africa. The European advance spurred national rivalries among British, French, German, and Belgian powers. In 1884–1885, the major European powers held a conference in Berlin to decide territorial rights in equatorial Africa. The decision of the conference stipulated that any nation had the right to claim any African territory it could occupy and develop. Consequently, most of Africa, with the exception of Ethiopia, the Union of South Africa (comprising four British colonies), and Egypt, was under colonial rule from 1900 until the end of World War II in 1945.

The massive advance of European civilization into Africa had two far-reaching effects: (1) the disappearance of many, though not all, African tribes and (2) the modification of traditional African patterns of life as a compromise required for life in a European society. After World War II, resistance to such compromises developed as Africans increasingly demanded self-rule. European powers soon found themselves caught between pro- and anti-independence movements. Before long, the majority of Africans were chanting the slogan "Africa for Africans." One by one, African societies gained their freedom from colonial rulers. But the struggle for independence is by no means over, especially in South Africa, where colonial heritage is still a haunting problem.

Christian and Muslim Intrusion

Undoubtedly, African religion was most affected by its contact with Christianity and Islam, although the interaction of those religions did not mean a total abandonment of African religious traditions. Christianity reached Egypt, Ethiopia, Sudan, and northern Africa within the first five centuries of its history, but it suffered serious setbacks when Islam conquered and occupied northern Africa immediately after its inception in the seventh century CE. From then on, Islam's expansion in other parts of Africa was relatively slow until the colonial period, when it once again spread south of the Sahara, establishing various important centers both inland and along the entire coast of Africa. During the colonial period, European Christians also were active in spreading their form of Christianity.

The relationship of colonial Christians to the peoples of Africa was based on the assumption that Africans were savages with an inferior culture who needed the Christian faith and European civilization before they could take their place proudly with the Western world. The two most effective means to achieve that end were conversion and education. Consequently, the Christian scriptures were translated into hundreds of vernacular languages, and modern institutions of learning were established in virtually all of Africa.

By contrast, cultured Muslims held a certain degree of disdain for the masses of African tribes, and Islamic scriptures remained untranslatable in principle. True, the steps to become a Muslim were easier than those necessary for Christian conversion and baptism. Moreover, Muslim converts had more freedom to achieve religious status or leadership roles than their Christian counterparts, who had to acquiesce to the demanding requirements of ordination and strong moral discipline. Islam was able to accommodate readily to a wide range of African practices, such as polygamy, certain forms of magic and divination, and traditional male dominance. Yet at certain points Islam rejected African traditions, particularly the representation of divinities by images and the secret societies that challenged the prerogatives of the Islamic *umma,* or unitary community.

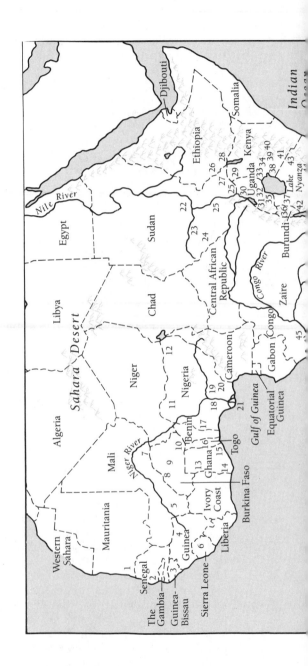

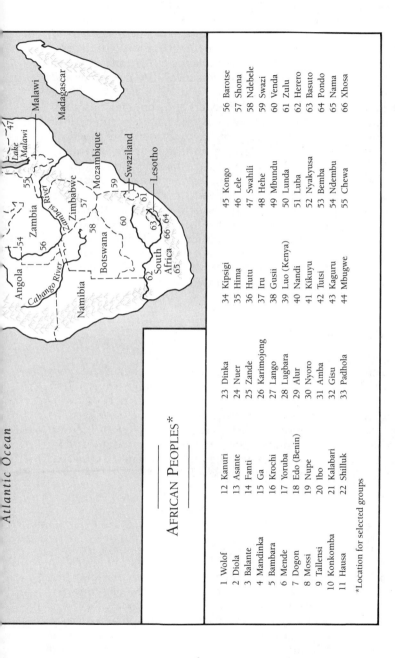

Atlantic Ocean

AFRICAN PEOPLES*

1 Wolof
2 Diola
3 Balante
4 Mandinka
5 Bambara
6 Mende
7 Dogon
8 Mossi
9 Tallensi
10 Konkomba
11 Hausa

12 Kanuri
13 Asante
14 Fanti
15 Ga
16 Krochi
17 Yoruba
18 Edo (Benin)
19 Nupe
20 Ibo
21 Kalabari
22 Shilluk

23 Dinka
24 Nuer
25 Zande
26 Karimojong
27 Lango
28 Lugbara
29 Alur
30 Nyoro
31 Amba
32 Gisu
33 Padhola

34 Kipsigi
35 Hima
36 Hutu
37 Iru
38 Gusii
39 Luo (Kenya)
40 Nandi
41 Kikuyu
42 Tutsi
43 Kaguru
44 Mbugwe

45 Kongo
46 Lele
47 Swahili
48 Hehe
49 Mbundu
50 Lunda
51 Luba
52 Nyakyusa
53 Bemba
54 Ndembu
55 Chewa

56 Barotse
57 Shona
58 Ndebele
59 Swazi
60 Venda
61 Zulu
62 Herero
63 Basuto
64 Pondo
65 Nama
66 Xhosa

*Location for selected groups

In spite of those restrictive features, both Christianity and Islam took root and expanded in sub-Saharan Africa. Today, the two religions are the dominant faiths of the continent. But the most dynamic modern phenomenon has been the emergence of a wide range of new religious movements that draw on local African religious traditions and one or both of the introduced faiths. The new movements represent the creative attempts of African peoples to adapt religion to African conditions and needs by synthesizing in varying degrees all available religious and cultural resources.

Syncretism involving African, Christian, and Muslim religious traditions has resulted in thousands of new movements among hundreds of African peoples. Some movements are more concerned with practical, relevant social issues than with African traditions or Christian and Muslim orthodoxies. Others tend to emphasize the indigenous religious tradition but also have adopted important features from one or both of the other faiths. A few groups have added to their traditional spirit-possession cults the Muslim *jinn* (spirits) and claim that that spirit power is present in human embodiment rather than in a cultic object. Others endeavor to minimize African traditions by adopting Christian or Muslim features in a reshaped form. For instance, the movement founded by Hamallah in 1925 regarded Nioro, Mali, as a holy city and more important than Mecca or Jerusalem; Yakouba Sylla, who in the 1930s claimed to have received a new revelation from Fatima, the daughter of Muhammad, rejected the authority of the Qur'an and the centrality of Islamic prayer and made fasting optional; the God's Kingdom Society has replaced the festivity of Christmas with the Jewish Feast of Tabernacles.

Some syncretistic attempts are flexible in matters of belief and practice. They usually lack the elements inherent in an established tradition or the characteristics of an organized institution. Essentially, such movements do not represent anti-Western protests. Rather, they seek positive spiritual goals. Most of those new movements offer religious identity and status based on what they consider to be African values. Today, such religious movements are increasing and represent a distinctive part of African religion that cannot be ignored.

AFRICAN TRADITIONAL RELIGIONS

The conversion of African peoples to Christianity, Islam, or the new movements has in no way eclipsed African traditional religions. In terms of the entire population of Africa, the proportion of followers of African traditional religions has declined since the beginning of the twentieth century. But in specific areas of Africa today, there is a resurgence of traditional religions. Thousands of self-contained tribes, with their distinct languages and cultures, live on the continent of Africa and constantly shift from territory to territory. The size and complexity of these scattered tribes create an enormous problem in identifying common beliefs and practices. Nonetheless, an analysis of concepts and practices shared by African tribes is offered here, after a brief description of two African tribes: the Dinka and the Yoruba. These two examples suffice for grasping the general in terms of the particular.

The Dinka Religion

The Dinka are a tribal group, numbering nearly 4 million people, who speak different dialects of a common language and live in the southern Sudan region. Their way of life is simple, rural, and centers on cattle herding. Some of the Dinka grow crops of grain and vegetables. Others are poor, have no cattle, do not cultivate, and depend on hunting and fishing for subsistence.

The Dinka believe in superhuman forces in the world, called *Jok* or *Nhialic,* that transcend ordinary human ability. They are powerful and unseen and affect human lives for good or ill. Some Dinka tribes believe that their "first" ancestor was one such power. Other tribes use the word *Nhialic* to identify the greatest of those powers. In that context, *Nhialic* is referred to as creator, father, and bestower of rain. Prayers and sacrifices are offered to both *Nhialic* and *Jok.*

Clan divinities form part of the pantheon of occult powers. They are associated with a great number of symbols that represent birds, insects, animals, trees, rivers, and forests. Clan divinities are treated with great respect. For instance, a portion of whatever hunters and gatherers take for themselves they return as sacrificial offerings that are left for the animals or thrown into rivers, since those are the totems or personifications of different clan divinities.

Other Dinka divinities have general rather than specific tribal associations and are known by name although they are not endowed with human forms. They operate as natural but invisible and immaterial agents of unusual and unexplainable events, such as dreams, sickness, and sudden rain or thunder.

Dinkas believe that every individual has a *tiep,* a ghost, shadow, or spirit. At death, the individual's *tiep* escapes from the body but then hovers or lingers near the corpse at the place of burial. Survivors offer sacrifices to the *tiep* of relatives who have died recently as propitiatory gestures to safeguard the living against any possible disaffection from the lingering *tiep* of the dead. In time, each *tiep's* presence or influence fades and weakens so that, with the passage of several generations, ancient *tieps* may be safely ignored.

Among other rituals and ceremonies, prayers and sacrifices play a major role among the Dinka. Animal sacrifices are offered to divine powers as well as to the dead. For instance, life and health are thought of as gifts attributable to *Nhialic* and *Jok.* In return, gifts of prayer and sacrifice to them form part of regular rather than seasonal or sporadic observances, such as votive offerings in thanksgiving for recovery from illness, relief from famine, and success in hunting.

Those who lead the prayers are known as *spear masters.* It is their function to intone prayer phrases, often with spear in hand and sometimes thrusting it toward the sacrificial offering to emphasize a particular phrase. Observers and participants repeat the prayer phrases in chorus, usually with more fervor than is generally characteristic of worship in a temple, church, or mosque. The pattern of invocation and response, especially on occasions of particular significance or crisis, may continue for several hours and may induce in the spear master a condition of deep ecstasy.

The vitality and well-being of the Dinka tribe depend on the prayer leaders or spear masters. They preside over all affairs of life, including petitions made to divine powers. They settle quarrels, plead for rain, make peace between enemies, and ask protection for their tribe and herds. They are the most important men in the tribe. The office of spear master is hereditary. Sometimes, however, an individual may be recognized as being possessed by a divine power. The signs of such possession are trembling fits followed by a trance. In that state, the possessed is capable of answering questions and solving problems.

The Dinka build small shrines to "house" the *tieps* of important people. The shrines are nothing more than clay mounds where relatives can place their offerings. Slightly more elaborate sanctuaries resembling small cattle barns shelter divine powers. They also house sacred spears and other objects of ritual and veneration.

The term *myth* has been denigrated by its association with the supernatural and merely fanciful. It also refers to an allegory or a traditional narrative embodying ideas on natural and social phenomena, including topics of a sacred or religious nature. The Dinka have an interesting myth about the origin of the human condition. In the beginning, the sky, domain of the divine, and the earth, home of mortals, were joined by a rope that made a concept like death meaningless because humans could climb up and down at will. The divinity granted one grain of millet per day to the first human couple to satisfy their needs until, one day, the woman decided to plant the grain of millet and, in raising her hoe, struck the divinity. Offended, the divinity retaliated by sending a small blue bird to sever the rope that gave humans access to the sky. Ever since, humans have had to labor for food; have become subject to famine, sickness, and death; and are denied free access to the divinity.

According to another myth, *Nhialic* created the first people and placed them in a world of darkness. When *Aruu* (Dawn), one of the ancestors, asked *Nhialic* to make an opening in the world so people could see, *Nhialic* refused. *Aruu* then split the world in two with an axe, dividing the sky and the earth to allow light (dawn) to appear.[1]

Those stories are just two of the many Dinka myths. Another myth rationalizes human dependence on fire, especially for cooking. Another myth illustrates the life-supporting role of rivers. Yet another explains the origin of the priestly function of the spear masters. All Dinka myths represent expressions of their ethos or life-style. The universe, for the Dinka people, contains an intermixture of benign and dangerous elements or powers. Those powers must be properly and respectfully treated to maintain a consistent equilibrium between tribal society and the entire cosmos.

The Yoruba Religion

Unlike the pastoralist society of the Dinka, the Yoruba are a highly urbanized society organized around large city-state kingdoms, numbering between twelve and fifteen million people. They occupy portions of southwestern Nigeria and the neighboring areas of Dahomey and Togo, in western Africa.

Yoruba religion is centered on the worship of a variety of *orisha* (divinities), each having its own priests, shrines, cultic functions, and a special section in town. At the head of the extensive *orisha* pantheon is *Olorun* (whose name means "Lord Owner of the Sky"), the supreme being in Yoruba religion, who is regarded as having partly transcendent and partly immanent features.

Olorun is said to have created the world by delegating the task to one of his sons, Obatala. One version relates how Olorun gave Obatala the necessary supplies, some dry soil, and a five-toed hen to scratch and spread the soil over the primordial waters covering the earth. After that performance, Obatala fashioned human beings from clay. Another version, however, has Oduduwa, Olorun's younger son, being entrusted to complete the task, because Obatala's drunkenness while performing the work of creation resulted in misshapen people. Oduduwa fashioned people, built a town, and became its first king. Whatever the political implications behind the two versions, Olorun clearly retains his supreme position. In fact, Olorun is rewarded as the supreme determiner of human destiny. Every individual's guardian soul receives a destiny and a fixed span of life from Olorun. If a person has led a good life, Olorun will consider that person worthy of reincarnation. If, however, the person has led an evil life, Olorun will consign him or her to a hot place of punishment and destruction.

The numerous *orisha* worshiped in Yoruba religion differ from region to region and from group to group. Generally, however, a person worships the *orisha* of his or her father. The desire for a close association with *orisha* at times verges on personal identification with them. If an individual encounters some misfortune, it is time to change one's devotion to another *orisha*. Thus, to the Yoruba devotee, the *orisha* symbolize certain unconscious aspects of the self and also act as guardian spirits.

The most popular and widely accepted *orisha* is Ogun, the divinity of war, hunting, iron, and steel. Dogs, who help in hunting and war, are uniquely appropriate to be sacrificed to Ogun. The ritual of sacrifice is an annual festival celebrated by the entire people of a town or, more often, by family compounds. The feast consists of several phases. First, the most appropriate date to celebrate the ritual is determined by divinatory acts. Next, the officiating family heads prepare themselves by abstaining from cursing, fighting, eating certain foods, and sexual intercourse. Then, the men go on a hunting expedition to gather fresh game. In the evening, an all-night vigil is kept near Ogun's shrine, which consists of a simple stone column set before a tree. Throughout the night, family members chant songs in honor of Ogun and consume quantities of beer and palm wine. The ceremony of sacrifices begins on the day following the vigil, with offerings made to Ogun, offerings of kola nuts, snails, pigeons, palm oil, and dogs. Following the immolation and consecration of the victims, participants share the consecrated flesh of the dogs, and a general carnival atmosphere prevails, particularly if the festival involves a whole town.

The offerings are appropriate mediating symbols that control Ogun's relations with his people. Conceived in that way, rituals of sacrifice have special power to evoke the spirits and channel them according to the wishes of the worshiper. Other rituals consist of mythic celebrations, such as the reenactment of the battle between Oduduwa and Obatala. In fact, feasts play a significant role in Yoruba religion. The annual feast of male ancestors consists of a masked stately procession; the feast of mothers celebrates female powers; and the feast of kings and ritual functionaries deals with dialectical relations.

BASIC COMMON VIEWS

African religious concepts and practices differ from tribe to tribe, but several basic patterns are common to most of them. Many Africans believe that the essence of life lies in the perception that the chief god, lesser gods, ancestors, spirits, sky, earth, vegetation, water, climate, animals, and persons all form an integral part and are inextricably bound to the rhythms and patterns of the universe.

Chief God

The concept of a chief god or supreme being as creator, preserver, and sustainer of the universe is self-evident to most Africans. The chief god, called by a hundred different names that vary from tribe to tribe, is conceived of as self-existent, eternal, maker of the world, master of human destiny, omnipotent, omnipresent, kind, just, good, father, mother, and friend.

Several questions puzzle Western observers. Is the chief god a personal being, an impersonal spirit, a sort of creative energy, or an abstract idea? Does the chief god exist apart from the universe or pervade it? Is the chief god indifferent to or actively involved in human affairs? The answers to those questions differ from group to group. To the Bantu and the Sudanese, for instance, the chief god Mulungu is both a personal being and an impersonal spirit. As such, Mulungu is ruler, judge, omnipotent, and omnipresent, whose voice is heard in thunder and whose power appears in lightning. Similarly, to the Dogon, the chief god Amma created the heavens and the earth and then united himself with the earth to produce a series of mortal twins. In other instances, such as with the Shona and the Kimbu, the chief god is clearly and exclusively personalized as a creator and life giver. Thus, sometimes the chief god is spoken of personally, often with a wife and family, and sometimes the chief god is associated with nature, represented by sun, rain, lightning, mountains, rivers, and so on.

Other Gods, Ancestors, and Spirits

In addition to a chief god, many Africans believe in the existence of lesser gods, ancestor spirits, nature spirits, various powers, and impersonal forces. The lesser divinities, who derive their power from the chief god, govern all human activities and natural phenomena. Sometimes they act directly as messengers of the chief god; sometimes they appear as personifications of natural phenomena, such as wind, rain, thunder, and death; and sometimes they manifest themselves in an object or place, such as a rock, a tree, or a lake. No matter how they appear, many Africans regard the lesser spirits and forces as the most immediate link between themselves and the chief god. Although generally beneficent, the lesser gods also can be dangerous, causing harm and damage. Consequently, most Africans attach great importance to the lesser divinities and try to live in peace with them.

The belief in spirits and powers is so widespread throughout Africa that it often is difficult to distinguish their role and function. Generally, however, Africans recognize different levels of spirits. Totemic spirits are invoked as the guardians of clans and lineages. Territorial spirits (i.e., ancestor spirits of chiefs or eminent personalities) are invoked on behalf of larger social groupings. Ancestor spirits, who are the most important members of a community, offer protection to living relatives. Hence, each group, each family, each individual maintains a special relationship with ancestors. Much of traditional morality, therefore, is based on pleasing the ancestor spirits and living in harmony with them. The method of contact with ancestor spirits varies from tribe to tribe but generally involves the use of libation, prayers, sacrifices, and offerings.

There also are gods created in the form of various disembodied spirits, and still other spirits are enshrined in nature. Storm spirits are most popular in areas where tropical tornadoes, torrential rains, lightning, and thunderbolts cause severe damage. Water spirits are revered by fishermen and those dwelling close to rivers or lakes. Earth spirits include mountains, hills, forests, trees, and rocks. Hunters, soldiers, and rainmakers, among others, call on earth spirits by placing their offerings at the foot of a hill, tree, or stone.

Many African peoples claim to see, hear, or be possessed by spirits, often for purposes of divination. Some societies perform masquerades both to renew human contact with the spirits and to maintain a friendly relationship between the spiritual and material worlds. The two worlds are inseparable and represent a dynamic, unified universe. Any evil or disorder, either among humans or in the material world, commonly is traced to those who possess special powers to bring harm secretly. Consequently, people appeal to those various sources of power for help. Many houses and villages have images or symbols of guardian divinities, whose powers are turned against intruders and in favor of the householders.

Mythical Views

African myths are extremely popular and are told at all levels of society. They include animal fables, creation stories, heroic feats, divine intrigues, folk tales, and countless numbers of legends. Collections of such myths have been made from various parts of Africa, but there are still peoples whose mythology is hardly known. The collected myths throw light on the religious dimension of African peoples. Most African peoples have their own version of creation. The Dogon, for instance, believe that the chief god created the sun and the African moon like pots, the sun with red copper rings and the moon with white copper rings. Next, he created the stars and the earth, the stars from pellets of clay that were flung into space and the earth from a lump of clay. Next, the union of the chief god and the earth resulted in a series of twins, four males and four females, who were the ancestors of the tribe.

Another creation account is found among the Luyia of Kenya. They believe that the chief god created his own dwelling place in heaven all by himself but then required the help of two assistants to place the pillars that support heaven. Next, he created the moon and its younger brother, the sun. Because the moon was bigger and brighter than the sun, jealousy stirred the sun to wrestle with the moon, and the moon easily defeated the sun. A second round of wrestling, however, resulted in the victory of the sun. The moon was thrown down and splashed with dirt. At that point, the chief god intervened and determined their boundaries: the sun was to shine brightly during the day, and the moon was to glow through its muddy face at night.

Other myths depict the withdrawal of the chief god from earth after completing his work of creation. Such myths describe how in ancient times the chief god lived on earth among human beings but eventually was forced to leave the world because of some human misdeed. The Mende, for instance, believe that the chief god quietly left this world while people slept, because they bothered him with their requests. A more common theme, however, depicts the departure of the chief god from this world by means of a rope or a spider's web hanging from heaven to earth.

A number of myths related to the origin of human beings suggest that humankind was lowered from the sky to the earth as husband and wife. Other myths tell that men and women emerged out of the ground, out of a tree, or out of a reed bed. The Zulu and Thonga, for instance, believe that the first man and woman burst out of the explosion of the reed. The Ashanti hold the view that several men and women, a dog, and a leopard emerged together from the earth at night. According to a Pygmy story, the first man and woman came out of a tree when the chameleon split the tree with an axe because it heard a noise within the tree. Other myths tell that the chief god pulled the first man and woman out of the marshes or waters.

A number of other myths deal with the origin of death. One myth explains death as the result of sleep. The story goes that primordial ancestors were told to stay awake until the chief god came back from a trip. But the ancestors were so overcome by sleep that they failed to receive from the chief god their reward of immortality. Another myth suggests that at one time human beings lived together with the chief god in the same village in heaven. But the human beings quarreled so much with each other that the chief god finally exiled them in disgust to a place below, where they experienced hunger, sickness, and death. Long-

African Zulu chief with his wives, in their ceremonial dresses, in front of his *kraal* (village compound).
Courtesy of South African Tourism Board, Toronto.

ing for their earlier heavenly place, they quickly built a tower, whose top reached heaven. Overtaken with joy over their accomplishment, they beat their drums and played their flutes so loudly that the noise angered the chief god, who quickly flattened the tower.

Many African myths depict the original state of human beings as one of childlike ignorance, happiness, immortality, and eternal bliss. The loss of that original state of bliss differs in detail from one group to another. According to some myths, human beings disobeyed one or another divine law; according to others, a mischievous divine creature interfered. In some myths, people pestered the chief god until he withdrew from them; in others, the loss of the original state was a consequence of unforeseen circumstances. No matter how the stories depict the original state and present condition of African peoples, they all attempt to establish a divine-human link, which in turn provides a framework for self-identity.

Society and Morality

African people are conscious of themselves in terms of kinship and relationships. That means each individual is inextricably bound to three interrelated entities:

- A group, community, or society, including its social, economic, religious, and political obligations
- The universe, with all its rhythms and patterns, and its animate and inanimate objects
- The chief god, his divine assistants, ancestors, and all other spirits, who provide the immediate context in which life must be lived.

In addition, each person is believed to possess two components: the material body, inherited from one's parents, and the animating principle, received from either the chief god or some other divine being. The harmony and interdependence of those two components define one's personality and character. Hence, individual qualities, facial character, tone of voice, and physical stature all belong to an individual and cannot be acquired by another person. Any physical abnormality suggests that the person is possessed by the spirit of disease. Children born with such bodily marks are burdened with protective charms, neglected for fear of bad luck, or exposed to die.

A person's happiness or misery usually is attributed to the activity of the chief god or to any one of the lesser divinities, powers, or forces. People believe that illness and death do not happen naturally but because of the maleficence of some person or power. The wicked person may be a witch or a sorcerer who lives among wild beasts and acts by

African Bantu (Swazi) tribe en route to the queen's *kraal* (homestead) to celebrate a special ceremony.
Courtesy of South African Tourism Board, Toronto.

night, plotting against a person or a group. By contrast, the person who knows how to harness and use power for the happiness of a person or for the benefit of a group is greatly respected.

Moral virtues and offenses naturally vary from place to place and group to group, but their presence is always recognized. The ethical teachings and moral responsibilities of most African traditional religions are not codified, since there is no writing. Proper and improper human behavior are delineated in the customs, laws, taboos, and traditions of each African people. Custom regulates what ought not to be done. Stealing, lying, disrespecting elders, adultery, murder, causing deliberate injury to persons or property, and practicing witchcraft, among others, are considered great social offenses. African traditional religions generally are silent about rewards and punishments in eternity. Rather, society rewards the good person and punishes the evildoer. If an offender is not detected immediately by the community, the chief god, the ancestor spirit, or some other divine power sooner or later will punish that person by means of a misfortune.

The primacy of society over the individual is so important that any offense against the laws, customs, and rules that govern a particular society is considered to diminish the value of that society. Ethics and morality, therefore, are conceived in terms of kinship or relationships. And it is precisely that sense of kinship that guides an individual's action and generates a wide range of social expectations.

RELIGIOUS ACTIVITIES

African religion is a communal affair, and certain individuals within the community are responsible for the religious activities of the group or community. Those individuals include kings, royal personages, chiefs, rulers, priests, priestesses, prophetic figures, spiritual intermediaries, diviners, elders, holy men and women, shamans, shamanesses, keepers of sacred places, musicians, drummers, and so on. Some religious leaders inherit their role by virtue of birth, some require long training before a formal commissioning is publicly declared, and some are self-made specialists who claim to have received divine power, knowledge, or insight to assist an individual or a group in times of crisis. Regardless of the role they play, those individuals are highly respected within the community, because the community relies on them to perform important rituals.

Sacrifice

The most important ritual among African religious practices is sacrifice, which may be in the form of offering libations, foodstuffs, first fruits, first portions of harvested grain, nonedible goods, and living animals such as cows, goats, sheep, or fowl. Sacrifices are made for various purposes, either individually or communally. Some sacrifices are preventive in character and serve to avert dangers or misfortunes that threaten a person, a family, or the whole community. Others are expiatory in nature and are intended to remove guilt or offense. Still others are periodic offerings made to ancestors at their graves. Special occasions, such as an annual festival, call for a great sacrifice offered to honor and propitiate the chief god, his divine assistants, ancestors, and other spirits.

Prayer

Many Africans offer prayers daily to the guardian spirit or other deities enshrined in the home or hut. In many families, the oldest person, male or female, performs daily devotions on behalf of the rest of the family, while the other members stand in devotional respect or join in a simple prayer. Naturally, the words of the prayer vary, but generally petitions are made for the health and welfare of the family. A simple offering of a libation and a tiny portion of some foodstuff customarily is placed in front of the shrine.

Rites of Passage

To African peoples, practically every element of life, from birth to final entry into the ancestral community after death, has a religious aspect marked with a specific ritual. Four stages in the life of an individual represent significant transitional moments that require appropriate ritual acts: birth, initiation, marriage, and death.

Birth ceremonies vary from group to group, but almost all African peoples observe the happy occasion by naming the child, introducing the child to relatives and neighbors, and offering sacrifices and prayers to the ancestors for the cleansing of the mother and child from birth impurities.

Initiation rites usually are elaborate, lasting from a few days to more than two years. They often are performed in seclusion with the aim of introducing the youth into adult membership. In some societies, initiates submit to physical hardships and emotional strains, symbolizing their transition from the childhood condition to the stage of adult responsibility. Widely practiced are the rites of circumcision for boys and *clitoridectomy* (incision of the clitoris) for girls. The whole purpose of the initiation rite is to ensure that boys and girls receive basic knowledge of tribal history, social duties, and ancestral customs before they assume their proper role in society.

Marriage is a festive communal event involving the entire extended family—the bride and the groom, their families, clans, ancestors, and the unborn. Customs vary from group to group, but generally speaking, the ritual associated with marriage includes the preparation and arrangement of the ceremony to cement family alliances and to sustain the sanctity of life. With few exceptions, everyone is expected to get married, whether the marriage partners choose each other or are matched by parents or relatives. Failure to do so constitutes an offense against society. The concept of renunciation or asceticism is foreign to African peoples. Rather, marriage and procreation are the proper duties of a person; the more children one has, the greater the blessings both in this life and hereafter. Consequently, polygamy is accepted and

African Xhosa women prepare ochre and paint it on children's faces.
Courtesy of South African Tourism Board, Toronto.

respected in most societies. In cases of sterility or barrenness, custom dictates the following options: if the wife is barren, the husband marries another woman; if the husband is sterile, the wife produces children through the brother of her husband; and in a few cases, divorce is permitted. In some societies, if a man dies before being married, his parents or close relatives arrange for his marriage in absentia, so that children born on his behalf may perform the necessary ancestral rites.

Death is considered to provide the passage from this world to the world of spirits and the company of departed ancestors. Thus, funeral rites are observed carefully so as not to offend the departed. The rites vary from society to society and last from several months to several years. The corpse may be kept for a while in a special hut before it is buried in a grave. Some societies bury the dead with foodstuffs, personal belongings, weapons, and money to ensure the sustenance and safety of the departed during the journey to the next world. In most cases, a shrine near the household or village of the departed acts as a contact point between the living and the "living dead."

Occultism

Another important category of religious activity in African traditional religions is occultism. At the popular level, that involves either manipulating or counteracting the forces or powers of evil. Witches, sorcerers, diviners, and medicine men, among others, render an important service by providing a protective or retaliatory course of action. Seeking omens, consulting magicians, and appealing to diviners to discover or influence the will of the spirits is, of course, common practice among most Africans. Symbolism and ritual are common to occult activity. Objects that are ordinary in a daily situation may be endowed with magical significance. Similarly, the forces symbolized in rituals frequently function as external representations of the supernatural or spiritual world.

The art of magic, as practiced in most African traditional religions, is always for the attainment of practical aims or specific goals. In case of failure, stronger magic is used, or a substitute magic is called on to offset the countermagic of enemies. The techniques of attaining such goals are diverse and vary not only in form but also in motivation and significance. Some persons, for instance, wear protective amulets, whose efficacy has proved to protect against evil powers and influences. Some groups impose various restrictions and prohibitions not so much to please deities but to protect themselves from the dangers and harms of evil influences and hostile spirits. Among pastoral and agricultural peoples, magical acts are performed in the belief that departed spirits are able to grant or withhold fertility to the soil. Imitative magic (also referred to as mimetic or sympathetic magic) is employed for numerous purposes, for example, banishing evil and misfortune, such as sickness, guilt, and uncleanness; casting or averting curses or spells; and gaining victory in war.

Incredible as the alleged phenomenon may appear to modern, scientifically oriented people, most Africans sincerely believe that certain individuals have the power to evoke and communicate with the "living dead" or other spirits. These possessors of extrasensory powers claim to be able to act on the course of events and obtain any required information. Their art, commonly known as *divination,* is popular, and their message varies from discovering the past to revealing future events or interpreting dreams. Because they are in constant contact with spirits, they respond to seekers of guidance and information either by direct intuition or through spirit-possessed trances.

Sacred Sites and Objects

Natural objects and places are focal points for African peoples to interact with the world of the spirits and deities. Trees, caves, springs, ponds, stones, hills, and mountain peaks are regarded as possessed by spirits or as the abodes of spirits and deities. Such spots acquire a sacred character and are recognized as sites of worship. Each region has its sacred sites, which are used for saying prayers, making vows, offering sacrifices, or holding ceremonial meetings.

Sacred objects include, among other things, drums, masks, headdresses, amulets, hunting trophies, divination objects such as rainmaking stones, fires, carvings, certain animals, colors, and numbers. Masks and body painting often reflect ritual possession. Certain colors have a potent effect for certain groups, so that during certain ceremonies only animals bearing these colors are offered for sacrifice. Among other

South African Bevenda maidens performing Domba Dance. Other maidens, in the center, beat the drums.

Courtesy of South African Tourism Board, Toronto.

groups, the number nine is so significant that certain ceremonies require the use of nine items. Many taboos are associated with such objects, the misuse of which entails misfortune, even death.

Sacred sites and objects thus represent the presence of a spirit or a deity. The deep affinity with natural objects and places reflects not a form of nature worship but the African understanding of the inseparable link between the visible and the invisible worlds.

STUDY QUESTIONS

1. What do we know about the beginnings of Africa?
2. When did the first Europeans arrive in Africa and what far reaching effects did they have?
3. Analyze the effects of Christianity on African religion.
4. Discuss the role of Islam among African tribes.
5. Who are the Dinka and what beliefs do they maintain?
6. Describe some of the more important rituals and ceremonies of the Dinka.

7. Recount the Dinka myth on the origin of human beings.

8. Who is the supreme being of the Yoruba and what characteristics are attributed to him?

9. Consider why Ogun is the most popular divinity among the Yoruba.

10. Analyze the concept of *chief god* among most African tribes.

11. What beliefs are connected with lesser gods, ancestors, and spirits?

12. Describe some creation stories that are popular among Africans.

13. Recount a number of myths related to the origin of human beings.

14. How is morality understood in African societies?

15. Describe the rites of passage observed by most Africans.

16. Discuss the art of magic as practiced in most African traditional religions.

17. Explain the meaning of sacred sites and objects.

Suggested Reading

Dinka Religion

Deng, Francis Mading. *Dinka Cosmology.* London: Ithaca Press, 1980.

————. *The Dinka of the Sudan.* Prospect Heights, Ill.: Waveland, 1984.

Lienhardt, R. Godfrey. *Divinity and Experience—The Religion of the Dinka.* Oxford: Clarendon Press, 1970.

Makec, John Wuol. *The Customary Law of the Dinka People of Sudan: African Traditional Law in Comparison with Aspects of Western and Islamic Laws.* London: Afroworld, 1988.

Yoruba Religion

Courtlander, H. *Tales of Yoruba Gods and Heroes.* New York: Crown, 1973.

Eades, Jeremy Seymour. *The Yoruba Today.* Cambridge: Cambridge University Press, 1980.

Hallgren, Roland. *The Vital Force. A Study of àse in the Traditional and Neo-Traditional Culture of the Yoruba People.* Vol. 10 of *Lund Studies in African and Asian Religions.* Lund, Sweden: University of Lund, 1995.

Simpson, George Eaton. *Yoruba Religion and Medicine in Ibadan.* Ibadan, Nigeria: Ibadan University Press, 1980.

Staewen, Christoph. *Ifa, African Gods Speak: The Oracle of the Yoruba in Nigeria.* Hamburg: Lit Verlag, 1996.

African Traditions

Ephirim-Donkor, Anthony. *African Spirituality: On Becoming Ancestors.* Trenton, N.J.: Africa World Press, 1997.

Geschiere, Peter. *The Modernity of Witchcraft: Politics and the Occult in Postcolonial Africa.* Charlottesville, Va.: University Press of Virginia, 1997.

Kramer, Fritz. *The Red Fez: Art and Spirit Possession in Africa.* London and New York: Verso, 1993.

Lawson, E. Thomas. *Religions of Africa: Traditions in Transformation.* San Francisco: Harper & Row, 1984.

Mbiti, John S. *African Religions and Philosophy,* 2nd ed. Oxford: Heineman International, 1990.

Somi, Malidoma Patrice. *Of Water and the Spirit: Ritual, Magic, and Initiation in the Life of an African Shaman.* New York: Putnam, 1994.

Note

1. Both myths appear in R. G. Lienhardt, *Divinity and Experience: The Religion of the Dinka* (Oxford: Clarendon Press, 1961), pp. 33–35.

18 American Indian Traditions

American Indians (also referred to as Natives, Native Americans, and Amerindians) live in various parts of Canada, the United States, and Central and South America. Their existence on the American continents is estimated to date from as early as 40,000 to 20,000 BCE. Some groups, such as the Sioux, the Crow, and the Comanche, were primarily nomadic, hunting societies; others, such as the Hopi and the Algonquin, developed advanced agricultural societies. The societies spoke different languages and evolved different ways of life. Even groups, or nations, living in close proximity to each other differed significantly in linguistic dialects, beliefs, and ceremonies.

Because of their contact with white, Western cultures, few American Indians today live as their ancestors did. Many tribes have been virtually annihilated, either by European expansion since the sixteenth century or through internation warfare. Contact with Christianity over four centuries resulted in bloody conflict with settlers and pioneers, in defeat when resistance provoked military intervention, and in survival in restricted areas in North America and on reservations in various locations all over the continent. Inevitably, those events brought irremediable changes, although a few American Indian nations were able to retain certain aspects of their ancient life-styles and religious traditions.

ANCIENT CIVILIZATIONS

Recent excavations conducted by Mexican archeologists indicate that about 10,000 to 12,000 years ago nomadic hunters and food gatherers wandered in the valley of Mexico (the region around present-day Mexico City). It is not known precisely when the earliest settlements were

American Indian Traditions

BCE

c. 30,000 Migration of humans from northeast Asia to the Americas
c. 10,000 Evidence of hunters and food gatherers in Mexico
c. 1500 Earliest evidence of settlements in Mexico
c. 800s Olmecs settle on southeastern coast of Mexican Gulf

CE

c. 200 Toltec monuments discovered in Teotihuacán
c. 300 Rise of Mayan civilization in Peru; lasted till 900s
c. 1200s Aztecs occupy valley of Mexico and surrounding areas
1200 Incas build Cuzco in the Andes Mountains
1325 Aztecs settle at Tenochtitlán, the site of modern Mexico, which becomes the capital of an aggressive military campaign
1492 Christopher Columbus lands in what is now the Bahamas
1519 Hernando Cortés and his Spanish troops invade the Aztec capital, Tenochtitlán
1521 Hernando Cortés, with the aid of thousands of Indian allies, conquers the Aztec empire
1532 Francisco Pizarro finds the Incas
1541 Francisco Vasquez Coronado, Spanish explorer, meets Zuni Indians
1562 *Auto-da-fé* in Yucatán. Thousands of Mayan artifacts and books are burned, while 4500 Mayans are tortured and a further 158 killed during interrogation
1598 Franciscan missionaries bring Christianity to Zuni Indians
1607 English settlers in Jamestown, Virginia, encounter Powhatan Indians. Sporadic clashes between the two peoples
1620 Pilgrim Fathers come ashore at Cape Cod and move on to establish a settlement they name Plymouth
1637 British colonists kill almost the entire Pequot tribe in Connecticut
1675 Metacom, an Algonquin chief, leads the bloodiest Indian war against non-Indian settlers in New England's history
1801 Indian rebellion in Nayarit, Mexico
1827 Cherokees describe themselves as "one nation under God" and adopt a constitution based on that of the United States
1838–1839 "Trail of Tears." United States government troops force 16,000 Cherokees to march on foot from Georgia to the Indian Territories, now Oklahoma. Nearly one quarter of the Cherokees die from cold and starvation
1862 Great Sioux Uprising in Minnesota. Santee warriors kill hundreds of white settlers

(continues)

1886   Wowoka, a Paiute from Nevada, inaugurates a pantribal movement
       called "the Ghost Dance"
1890   United States cavalry and support troops massacre 200 Sioux Indians at
       Wounded Knee, South Dakota, to put an end to "the Ghost Dance"
1969   Brazilian government agencies accused of waging biological warfare
       against Indians
1984   The Inuvialuit obtain control of 35,000 square miles of mineral-rich
       territory in northern Canada from the Canadian government and set
       up their own oil-producing company
1988   Brazil's new constitution recognizes the existence of collective rights,
       Indians' social organizations, and their practices, religions, languages,
       and beliefs.
1991   Colombia's new constitution sets out the most comprehensive set of
       rights enjoyed by indigenous peoples anywhere in the Americas
1993   United Nations Year of Indigenous Peoples. The United Nations Work-
       ing Group on Indigenous Populations prepares a draft for a Universal
       Declaration on Indigenous Rights
1995   Beginning of the United Nations Decade of Indigenous Peoples

established in the valley of Mexico, but radiocarbon techniques reveal dates between 1500 and 900 BCE.

Among the early civilizations in present-day Mexico and surrounding areas were those of the Olmec, Toltec, Mayan, and Aztec peoples. Archeological discoveries include ceremonial centers, erected carved monoliths and altars, clay statuettes and vases, mural paintings and bas-reliefs, statues of deities, and a devised system of writing, that combined ideograms, pictography, and phonetic symbols.

The Olmecs lived on the southern coast of the Mexican Gulf sometime between the ninth and fourth century BCE. They left behind a good deal of fine sculpture of images that appear to be related to deities, carefully oriented temple mounds, and stone stela with elaborate pictorial compositions. There are also huge stone heads that apparently represent stellar beings. Beyond that, we have little knowledge about the nature of religion among the Olmecs.

The Toltecs worshiped earth, water, and astral deities. Archeologists have discovered in Teotihuacán (in central Mexico) monuments that date from 200 to 700 CE. The site, which is teeming with small pyramids and buildings, is dominated by two huge pyramids, popularly known as the Pyramid of the Sun and the Pyramid of the Moon.

The Mayans

Mayan civilization was at its height between 300 and 900 CE. Little is known of the formative period (starting perhaps as early as 1200 BCE) or just when it assumed its distinctive role and character. What is

Gigantic figures that once supported the roof of the temple of Quetzalcoatl (ket-säl-kwat-əl), lord of life, death, and the wind. The Toltecs who built them considered themselves to be the descendants of Quetzalcoatl. In the fifteenth century CE, Aztec chiefs married the Toltec princesses in order to inherit the divine right to rule.
Courtesy of Mexican Government Tourism Office, Toronto.

known is that the Mayan civilization spread over what is now Mexico, Guatemala, Honduras, and Belize. The Mayans developed the highest civilization in the so-called New World before the arrival of the Spaniards, who conquered the area in the years 1520–1545, leaving the entire region in an uninhabitable condition.

During the classic period (c. 350–800 CE), Mayan cities were composed of many pyramidlike structures. Impressive flights of steps led to the temples and palaces situated on top of the pyramids. People also lived in scattered settlements over the surrounding countryside. All important events, such as religious ceremonies and judicial proceedings, took place in the cities.

Some time in the ninth and tenth centuries CE, the cities, or centers, were abandoned. No conclusive evidence is available to explain that shift, although several conjectures have been offered. One hypothesis is that the peasants revolted and overthrew (or massacred) the ruling theocratic class. Other hypotheses hinge on natural causes: soil exhaustion or pestilence. Whatever the reason, the area was invaded by native "foreigners" who ruled for a brief period of time (c. 1000–1200). Then followed a period of stability (c. 1200–1450), during which the power of control passed from the priesthood to the warrior chiefs. Soon, however, warfare between petty chiefs led to independent chiefdoms (c. 1450–1545). The disunited period accelerated a cultural decline and helped the Spanish, who easily won allies among discontented Mayans.

Although the Spaniards ended the chaotic situation brought about by the warring states, they also put an end to what is considered to be the most brilliant pre-Columbian civilization.

Four main sources provide valuable knowledge of Mayan religion: (1) archeological remains, such as temples, tombs, sculpture, pottery, and other artifacts; (2) three books written in Mayan hieroglyphics (possibly copies of early originals), although modern scholars still are unable to decipher most of the inscriptions; (3) several books written by European-instructed Indians in native languages transliterated into Latin that provide historical chronicles mixed with mythology, divination, and prophecy; and (4) accounts of Mayan life and history written in Spanish by conquerors and priests. To those sources can be added the observations recorded by modern anthropologists about the few existing Mayan people who have resisted conversion to Christianity.

Mayans believed that before the existence of the present world, several worlds had been successively created and destroyed. Humans were made first from earth, but because they possessed no minds, they were destroyed. Next, humans were made of wood, but lack of intelligence and absence of souls made them ungrateful to the deities, and they were drowned in a flood (or, according to another version, devoured by demons). Finally, humans were made of maize gruel and survived to become the ancestors of the Mayans.

According to the Mayans, humanity and the universe were, in the beginning, in darkness. The deities created the sun (god) and the moon (goddess), both of whom at first inhabited this world. However, as a result of the moon's sexual license, they were both taken up to the sky. As a punishment for the moon's infidelity, the sun pulled out one of her eyes; hence, lunar light is less bright than solar light.

Mayan deities were thought of as being simultaneously one and four: the one-and-four gods who sustained the sky, the one-and-four deities assigned to each direction of the universe, and the one-and-four rain gods. Then there were the sun god and his wife, the moon goddess; the young maize god; the snake god; the feathered serpent; the nine gods of darkness, who ruled the nine subterranean worlds; and Itzamna, the lord of heavens, a benevolent god. To those deities must be added divinized stars and planets and the gods of the months, the days, and the numerals.

The Mayans believed that their dead descended to the nine underworlds. There is no evidence of belief in a paradise. As to the universe, the Mayans believed it was doomed to come to a sudden end, just as the previous worlds had ended. But a new world would be created, so the eternal succession of cycles would remain unbroken. The Mayans believed time to be divine and worshiped it. Time periods were considered as gods, and priest astronomers viewed time as a succession of cycles, with no beginning and no end.

Religion was woven into the entire social and political fabric of Mayan culture. Prayers and sacrifices were used to placate the deities. Sacrifices were made of animals, birds, fish, insects, food, drink, incense, gold, jade, and human blood drawn from the tongue, ears, arms, legs, and genitals. Prayers, fasting, sacrifices, dancing, and drawing blood from one's body often preceded important ceremonies. To those practices

Temple of Kukulkan (also known as El Castillo) in Chichen Itza, Mexico. The pyramid
structure is seventy-five feet high, and the Temple of Kukulkan, situated on top of the
pyramid, is another fifteen feet high. The number of steps on the four sides, plus the
summit platform, add up to 365, the number of days in a year. During the fall and
spring equinox, the afternoon sun creates the image, in light and shade, of a serpent
descending the northwest stairway. The Mayans considered it the descent of Kukulkan.
Courtesy of Mexican Government Tourism Office, Toronto.

were added human sacrifices. The Mayans killed the victims by arrows,
beheading, or, more commonly, splitting the breast to remove the heart.
As with the Aztecs, most victims were males.

Specialized priests dominated all of Mayan life, especially as sun worship and human sacrifice gained more and more importance. The priests
acted as state administrators, architects, scholars, and astronomers. In
fact, an extraordinary refinement of mathematical and astronomical
knowledge, inextricably mixed with mythological concepts, is deemed
one of the most brilliant achievements of the Mayan priesthood.

Some priests used hallucinatory drugs to induce prophetic and
divinatory messages. Others made use of magical formulas or medicinal herbs in their roles as sorcerers and occult practitioners. Witchcraft
was widespread, and because of their occult knowledge, priests were
thought to inflict as well as heal diseases and to determine favorable
and unfavorable days for undertakings. Even when the nobility acquired increased power in the postclassical period, the priesthood remained the most influential group in Mayan society until the Spanish
conquest.

The Aztecs

The Aztecs were one of a number of small nomadic peoples that moved southward from the present-day western United States, troubling the civilized people of central Mexico, most notably, the Toltecs. Shortly before 1200, the Aztecs occupied the valley of Mexico and its surrounding areas. Then, as they became more numerous and warlike, they formed allies with other powerful groups, conquered much of central Mexico, and expanded their territory into a large empire that included most of central and southern Mexico. Much of Aztec culture was borrowed from the people of the region that they conquered.

The capital of the Aztec Empire was Tenochtitlán (modern-day Mexico City), which had an estimated population of 100,000. Thousands of artisans worked to build and maintain numerous flat-topped pyramids, temples, and palaces. In 1519, Cortés and his Spanish troops invaded the Aztec capital; within two years, they had conquered the Aztec Empire with the aid of thousands of Indian allies. The Spanish troops leveled the ceremonial center in Tenochtitlán and converted the buildings for public use. Aztec religion is known through a large number of primary and secondary sources, usually divided into five groups: (1) archeological materials, which include clay statuettes and vases, mural paintings and bas-reliefs, and statues of deities; (2) painted Aztec works (known as codices) on deerskins or agave-fiber paper, done by priests who used a combination of ideograms, pictography, and phonetic symbols; (3) Aztec works written in Latin script by European-instructed native Indians, who used ancient pictographic manuscripts as their basis; (4) early accounts of the *conquistadores* (conquerors), notably the letters sent by Hernando Cortés to his emperor, Charles V; and (5) accounts of Roman Catholic missionaries, who described the observances of Aztec life from a Christian cultural perspective. (The letters from Cortés to Charles V are treated with utmost caution by modern scholars, because of the deep hostility they harbor against the Aztecs.)

Religion was a central element of Aztec life. Many deities, rites, and myths were inherited from the earlier inhabitants of the Mexican plateau. In fact, the Aztec religion was a synthesis that combined many features from different cultures. The Aztecs shared with the Mayans the belief that the world had been created five times and destroyed four times by floods, earthquakes, hurricanes, and jaguars. The present creation, they believed, was to be destroyed by fire.

The Aztecs also believed in thirteen heavens and nine underworlds, all arranged in layers. In the highest heaven resided the deities (male and female) of creation. In the lowest underworld resided the deities (male and female) of death. Those who died went to the underworld, except for warriors, traveling merchants, women who died in childbirth, and those who were offered as sacrifices — they all went to be with the sun god.

The inhabitants of central and southern Mexico worshiped numerous deities for centuries before the arrival of the Aztecs, who adopted the deities. The concept of a supreme divine couple took the form of Mother Earth and Father Sun. There were also the deities of rain, fertility,

Stone sculpture at San Agustin, Colombia. Note the elaborate headdress, the feline teeth, and the wide nostrils. The feline cult is an ancient element in American Indian culture. The jaguar personifies fertility as well as an ambivalent force capable of good and evil.
Courtesy of E. Neglia.

crops, plants, running waters, drunkenness, and so on. The Aztecs did bring with them the cult of their tribal warrior sun god, Huitzilopochtli. In fact, the Aztecs thought of themselves as the "people of the sun." Consequently, they considered it their duty to wage war to provide the sun god with nourishment. As a result, human sacrifice became the most important feature of Aztec religion. The very survival and welfare of the people depended on the human offerings to the sun god, a notion that later was extended to all sorts of deities.

The practice of human sacrifice was not unique to the Aztecs — the Toltecs also performed this ritual — but the sheer number of sacrifices the Aztecs performed was singular. Most of the victims were either slaves or prisoners of war, although in some cases small children (five or six years old) and women were chosen. The Aztecs fought many wars to get a supply of prisoners to sacrifice. The priests forced the victim backward onto a sacrificial stone, opened the breast with a stroke of a flint knife, and tore out the heart to be sacrificially burned. Some ceremonies required decapitation, drowning, or burning. The practice reached incredible extremes: according to Aztec sources, some 20,000 prisoners were sacrificed at the dedication of the great pyramid and temple of Tenochtitlán.

Other offerings to the deities consisted of blood drawn from various parts of the body (the tongue or ears), birds, animals, produce, and incense. The priests who presided over human sacrificial rites were ranked in categories. A special category of priests interpreted magical formulas to predict the future. Others were in charge of ritual, and yet others were in charge of education. Each deity had his or her own group of priests and priestesses. Priests of high rank were members of the electoral body; although they did not intervene directly in affairs of state, they certainly designated rulers and greatly influenced their policies.

Witchcraft and sorcery were widespread among the Aztecs. Sorcerers were believed to possess the power to transform themselves into animals, such as owls and dogs. Moreover, sorcerers could cause great harm by practicing magic. They also could prepare love potions and poisonous drinks.

The Spanish conquest and mass conversion to Christianity did not prevent the Aztecs from retaining some of their magical rites and religious beliefs, which have survived to the present. Many descendants of the Aztecs still live in small villages around Mexico City, speak their ancestral language, and often combine their Christian faith with ancient traditions to form a distinctive style of Mexican Catholicism.

MODERN AMERICAN INDIANS

Recent developments among modern American Indians indicate considerable changes in terms of religious belief and practice. In 1886, Wowoka, a Paiute from Nevada, inaugurated a pantribal movement called the Ghost Dance. That movement spread rapidly across the United States, because it promised deliverance from the oppression of the white people and the return of the dead and the buffalo simply through the ritual of dancing for periods of up to five days without stopping. In 1890, the United States cavalry and support troops surrounded a large group of American Indians at Wounded Knee and slaughtered unarmed men, women, and children. That tragedy, along with further suppression by the United States government, put an end to the Ghost Dance movement. Instead, new religious movements emerged that combined old tribal traditions with certain features of Christianity. The Native American church, the members of which were once known as Peyotists because of their belief in peyote as a sacramental food, is one such interesting movement whose membership is growing in both the United States and Canada.

Today, American Indians of one or more nations drive long distances to be together for a day or a week, to greet old friends, and to eat and dance together. Such events, known as *powwows*, commonly occur throughout the summer months and provide a good opportunity to renew national identification. For American Indians, religion is not something nurtured by books, doctrines, scholars, or monks. Rather, it is an aspect of human activity that is linked to the orderly system of the universe.

Unfortunately, certain constraints are involved in the study of modern Native American cultures. First, American Indians kept no written records. Much of the information that survives derives from oral traditions passed from generation to generation. Second, anyone who does not belong to the nation is considered an outsider. That means a certain amount of information is withheld, so that even the most scholarly study or close observation is ultimately doomed to be somewhat restricted or deficient. Third, many members are never fully initiated into a particular rite, for various reasons, one of which is the constraint imposed by long, involved ceremonies. Hence, it is difficult, if not impossible, to obtain any clear definition of doctrine or of religious systems. Finally, American Indians have developed diverse religious traditions involving the beliefs and practices of particular nations in particular geographical locations.

In spite of those points of contrast, the beliefs of Native Americans are distinguished by some common characteristics. For instance, they all seem to share a belief in the existence of a high god or vital force, along with lesser gods and spirits. They all hold to the idea that certain individuals possess sacred power and therefore can act as intermediaries between humans and the deities. In ceremonies associated with ritual and initiation, they all engage in certain traditional rites designed to perpetuate the smooth operation of the natural order, including human society, and they all believe that by repeating stories and by storytelling they literally keep the world alive. What follows is a summary of the rituals and traditions of a few surviving groups of Native Americans, illustrating both the characteristics they share and their points of contrast.

BASIC COMMON VIEWS

Primary Force or High God

American Indians of North America believe in the existence of a variety of natural and supernatural forces, at the center of which is a primary force or high god. For the Sioux nation, that primary holy force is *wakan;* for the Algonquin, it is *orenda;* for other nations, it is a mystery that never can be fully comprehended. Life, for American Indians, revolves around a holy force that holds all things together. The basic goal in life, then, is to be in harmony with all natural and supernatural powers. In fact, the key to success in hunting or war, as well as in the maintenance of good health, high fertility, and bountiful crops, is behavior calculated to maintain harmony between human beings and the powers that populate the environment. In contrast, disharmony leads to individual and communal disaster, ill health, and the ruin of crops.

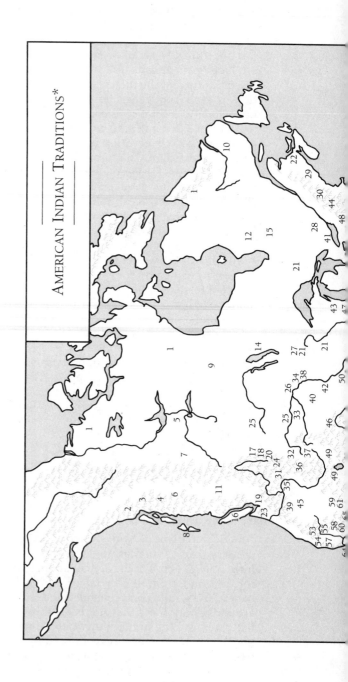

AMERICAN INDIAN TRADITIONS*

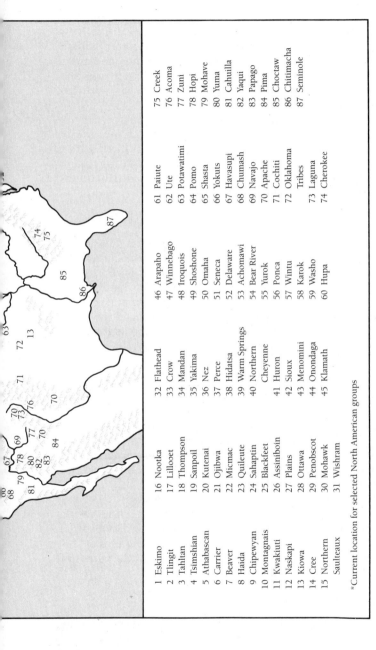

1 Eskimo
2 Tlingit
3 Tahltan
4 Tsimshian
5 Athabascan
6 Carrier
7 Beaver
8 Haida
9 Chipewyan
10 Montagnais
11 Kwakiutl
12 Naskapi
13 Kiowa
14 Cree
15 Northern Saulteaux
16 Nootka
17 Lillooet
18 Thompson
19 Sanpoil
20 Kutenai
21 Ojibwa
22 Micmac
23 Quileute
24 Sahaptin
25 Blackfeet
26 Assiniboin
27 Plains
28 Ottawa
29 Penobscot
30 Mohawk
31 Wishram

32 Flathead
33 Crow
34 Mandan
35 Yakima
36 Nez
37 Perce
38 Hidatsa
39 Warm Springs
40 Northern Cheyenne
41 Huron
42 Sioux
43 Menomini
44 Onondaga
45 Klamath
46 Arapaho
47 Winnebago
48 Iroquois
49 Shoshone
50 Omaha
51 Seneca
52 Delaware
53 Achomawi
54 Bear River
55 Yurok
56 Ponca
57 Wintu
58 Karok
59 Washo
60 Hupa

61 Paiute
62 Ute
63 Potawatimi
64 Pomo
65 Shasta
66 Yokuts
67 Havasupi
68 Chumash
69 Navajo
70 Apache
71 Cochiti
72 Oklahoma Tribes
73 Laguna
74 Cherokee
75 Creek
76 Acoma
77 Zuni
78 Hopi
79 Mohave
80 Yuma
81 Cahuilla
82 Yaqui
83 Papago
84 Pima
85 Choctaw
86 Chitimacha
87 Seminole

*Current location for selected North American groups

The ways in which the primary force is recognized in rituals and ceremonies vary from group to group. By and large, American Indians believe that the aid of the high god may be propitiated by ritual action. Alternatively, the pleasure or displeasure of the high god—for that matter, of all the other powers—is communicated through special messengers, or shamans. For instance, the shamans among the Zuni of New Mexico (a subgroup of the Pueblo nation of the southwestern United States) are believed to possess special powers that enable them to predict future events, explain unusual experiences, and deal with religious and sociopolitical affairs, including the nation's relationships with the United States government.

Some Native American nations associate the supreme power with the sky or the sun, an animal or a bird, or a particular creator spirit. Thus, the Maidu of California believe that a turtle collaborated with a heavenly spirit to bring the earth up out of the water. The Yavelmani Yokuts of California have a slightly different version, in which a duck and an eagle replace the turtle and the heavenly spirit.

The Trickster

Then there is the culture hero, whose function is to socialize the tribe. In contrast to that figure is the antihero, often called the trickster, whose dualistic role sets him aside from all others. The trickster is considered to be the founder of convention and, at the same time, its chief defier. He brings order and disorder; he is shrewd yet stupid; he makes jokes and mocks jokers. He has an insatiable appetite, an enlarged intestine, an incontinent bladder, and an enormous, uncontrolled penis that travels on its own for fun and adventure.

Protective and Evil Spirits

Despite seeming disparities among regions, the majority of American Indians believe in the active role of both protective and evil spirits. Among the protective spirits are mythical creatures such as thunderbirds, as well as mountains, rivers, minerals, flint, and arrowheads. Opposing the protective spirits are giant monsters, water serpents, tiny creatures that haunt woods and ponds, and the spirits of the dead that come to inflict pain, sorrow, or death.

All supernatural beings and protective and evil spirits possess ambivalent powers. In general, creator gods and protective spirits reside on mountaintops or in celestial worlds, while monsters and evil spirits inhabit the depths of the sea or underground worlds. The universe is regarded as a series of worlds set one above the other, at the center of which is the world inhabited by human beings.

Cosmic Sectors

The series of ascending worlds (or cosmic sectors) is thought to be linked and to be characterized by six points of space or direction: north, south, east, west, zenith (top), and nadir (bottom). Each cosmic sector is, in turn, associated with a sacred mountain, animal, plant, and color.

For instance, several Pueblo societies think of north as yellow, south as red, east as white, west as blue, the zenith as multicolored, and the nadir as black.

All such views can in no way be considered abstract inferences or philosophical conclusions; rather, they provide the substance of song, dance, and storytelling, that is, of mythical and ceremonial matters. Such views express the particular ways in which American Indians understand their relationship to each other and to the world in which they live. Hence, an instinctive reverence for supernatural powers, spirits, land, nature, creatures, and human beings—both living and departed—is strikingly evident in their ancestral traditions.

Creation Myths

Creation myths, that is, myths associated with the beginnings of the universe, are a common feature of American Indian traditions. In these imaginative stories, no distinctions are made among gods, spirits, the universe, nature, animals, and human beings. On the contrary, the stories imply a close mystical relationship binding each element. The creation story of the Osage nation of Oklahoma illustrates that quite clearly.[1]

Once, the Osage Indians lived in the sky, way beyond. Wanting to know their origin—the source from which they had come into existence— they went to the sun, who told them that they were his children. Then they wandered about until they came to the moon. She told them that she had given birth to them and that the sun was their father. Moreover, she told them that they were to leave their present abode and go and settle on earth.

When they came to the earth, they found it covered with water. So they wept, because no one would answer them, nor could they return to their former place. Floating in midair, they sought help from a god but found none. The animals were with them, too, and of all these the finest and most stately was the elk, who inspired them with confidence. So they appealed to the elk for help.

He dropped into the water and began to sink; but then he called to the winds, who came blowing from all quarters and lifted up the water like a mist. First, rocks were exposed and people moved from rock to rock, but there was nothing to eat. Soon, however, the water subsided and the soft earth was exposed. So overjoyed was the elk that he rolled over and over on the soft earth until all his loose hair clung to the soil. From that hair sprang grass, trees, corn, beans, potatoes, and wild turnips.

Although American Indians have several types of creation stories, the two most common themes are creation emerging out of chaos and creation resulting from a conflict between good and evil forces. The creation account of the Osage is representative of the first type. An example of the second type can be seen in the story of the Seneca nation.[2] According to that story, the earth emerged from the fall of the bride of the Sky Chief from heaven. After first landing on the back of a turtle,

American Indian drummers from Curve Lake reservation performing the powwow celebration of a sacred tradition: mimicking the solemn rhythm of creation.
Courtesy of Wolf Arnold.

she was impregnated by the wind and finally gave birth to twins, who created whatever exists today. One twin caused the good things to come into being, such as the sun, moon, stars, fruit, vegetables, and domestic animals. The other twin created all evil things and creatures of darkness on earth, such as snakes, monsters, owls, worms, flies, bats, and carnivorous animals. No matter how hard the evil twin tried, he was unable to overcome the good created by his twin. Consequently, there is more good than evil in the present world.

The imaginative language and the graphic imagery of the creation stories establish bonds between present and past, among nature, humans, creatures, and divine beings, and between the natural and supernatural forces that cause things to come into existence. To ensure a harmonious relationship among spirits, humans, animals, trees, rivers, birds, and the earth, American Indians developed intriguing religious songs, dances, and ceremonies.

Social and Moral Values

In keeping with their belief in maintaining equilibrium between themselves and nature, the moral principles of American Indians represent a harmonious, patterned system that promotes social equilibrium, community well-being, and an orderly universe. There is no concept of individual sin and salvation. Rather, the good of the group is always more important than the interests of the individual. As a result, there are specific rules for appropriate and inappropriate behavior. Any person who violates the rules or acts irresponsibly is brought before the tribal council and judged. Commonly, it is assumed that the offender is sick, insane, or possessed; seldom is anyone found guilty. A medicine man then performs a ritual to heal the sickness of the offender and thereby ensure the stability of the group. If the ritual fails, alternative measures may include banishment or death either at the hand of a tribal elder or through starvation, freezing, or animal attack.

Rules governing the conduct of members within a society deal with a wide range of matters, including property belonging to the group, sexual abuses, behavior toward relatives and other members of the society, lying, stealing, fighting, gambling, laziness, drinking of alcohol, and killing. Naturally, the enforcement of appropriate behavior varies from nation to nation and from region to region.

Most American Indians believe they have several souls, which may live on after death. The notion of reincarnation seems to be a common belief, although the conception of what that continuing existence is like varies. Some nations, such as the Pueblo, believe that the dead either join a *kachina* (masked dancer) or become rain clouds. Others, such as the Hopi (a Pueblo subgroup), believe that the soul leaves the body at death to travel to the next world, where an earthlike existence awaits.

CEREMONIALS

Traditionally, Native Americans express their close, mystical unity with all forms of existence in a variety of ways, including visual representations, songs, dances, games, and ceremonies. Visual representations of gods, spirits, animals, birds, fish, and humans are widespread and diverse. Some groups, such as the Nootka and Tlingit nations of the Pacific coast of Canada, use totem poles to produce naturalistic images of animals or human beings, historical or mythical. Others, such as the Pueblo, express the unity among all forms of existence in their artistic, geometric pottery designs. Still others express the coherence of the physical and spiritual world in costumes, paintings, craftsmanship, textiles, weaving, and decorated weapons.

Sacred Pipe

Of all the symbols used to express the oneness of all existence among some American Indians of North America, the sacred pipe is accorded the highest place of honor. No artifact is more endowed with mystery and reverence among some tribes than is the ceremonial pipe, whose role in all ceremonies cannot be overemphasized. It is used for numerous purposes, including the ratification of contracts and treaties, the reception of important guests, the declaring of war and peace, invocation of the spirits for a safe journey, and all activities that require the bond of sincerity and brotherhood.

The origin of the ceremonial pipe among Native Americans is as mysterious as its role and function. Among the Sioux, it is believed that in ancient times two hunters met a woman who said that she was sent from the high god to deliver the sacred pipe to their village as a gift to be used in all future ceremonies. The Pawnee claim to have received the sacred pipe as a gift directly from the sun. Whatever the explanation of the origin of the sacred pipe, its importance is enormous. It is made in different shapes and sizes, with distinct, elaborate decorations of human figures, animals, birds, beads, and feathers. Almost every activity is bound with the ritual of the ceremonial pipe.

Masked Costume

Next in importance among symbols is the masked costume worn by performers who assume various roles in sacred dancing ceremonies. Elaborate preparations ensure that every color and part of the costume, every gesture and every utterance of the performer are faultless. Some dancing ceremonies are performed by shamans in private, for the purpose of healing individual members of the tribe. Other dancing ceremonies are public displays designed to taunt supernatural forces into granting a request. In the event of failure, recourse is made to a sequence of magical rites until all avenues have been exhausted.

Rites and Ceremonies

Many of the rituals and ceremonies of American Indians are associated with the celebration or recognition of stages in the cycle of human life: as birth, puberty, marriage, old age, and death. Other rites and ceremonies have to do with activities such as hunting, fishing, rainmaking, planting, harvesting, and healing. American Indians believe that through their songs, dances, and ceremonies, it is possible to join with the forces of nature to produce rain and good crops. Corn, beans, and other vegetables are as much the gifts of Mother Earth as are human lives. Naturally, specific rituals used in connection with planting and harvesting vary greatly from one nation to another and from region to region. The rituals range from singing simple songs (a characteristic of the Papago of Arizona) to the elaborate ceremonies of the Pueblo. No matter how simple or complex the ritual is, the goal is the same: to promote the sustenance and welfare of the nation.

Medicine Man

Some chants, prayers, and dances are the perquisites of specialists, who are equipped to confer added benefits, including fertility and healing. Traditionally, the American Indian medicine man is expected to perform a wider variety of services than is the modern medical doctor. In addition to his knowledge of medicine, he is expected to communicate with gods and to perform religious ceremonies; accordingly, his role combines the functions of healer, shaman, and priest. Medicine, magic, and religion are combined in treating illness. Prophecy, clairvoyance,

American Indian dancers from Curve Lake reservation preparing to dance in a circle, searching the ground for the footprints of their ancestors in order to follow their ways.
Courtesy of Wolf Arnold.

spiritualism, demonology, herbs, roots, pollen, leaves, and religious practices all harmoniously blend for the curing of both physical and mental illness. Many such ceremonies deal with the evil forces that have invaded the body of a patient. Only the medicine man possesses the power to exorcise the evil forces that consume body and mind with sickness and to restore individuals as productive members of society through appropriate rituals.

Vision Quest

Another important ritual among most Native Americans is the vision quest, the seeking of a vision from a guiding spirit. Traditionally, no national undertaking, such as war or hunting, was begun without invoking or soliciting a vision. Today, the vision quest serves several purposes, including preparing brave warriors, healing sick relatives, asking favors from gods, and offering thanksgiving to spirits and forces.

All young males (and females, in some nations) are expected to submit to the vision quest ritual, which determines their role and status among their people, their place in hunting and war parties, and their assigned duties in performing religious functions. A young person whose vision quest fails is barred from participating in various roles and is often considered a marginal tribal member. Although a shaman serves as a spiritual guide and conducts certain secondary rites connected with the vision quest, the onus is on the postulant, or candidate, to complete six rituals, as follows:

- Preparation and withdrawal from other members of the nation for a brief period of fasting
- Taking a steam bath to exclude all worldly thoughts
- Ascending the most commanding summit or hilltop
- Stripping down to moccasins and breechcloth
- Standing erect and motionless for several days
- Cutting off the little finger or offering strips of flesh from the arm as a sign of sincerity

To qualify, the candidate's vision should include a glimpse of a tutelary animal, a promise for the tribe, a token (which is valued as the holder's most prized possession), and a song (which is reserved for important occasions only). If additional visions occur in the future, the individual may accumulate a "medicine bundle" for treating or healing illness.

Regardless of differences in beliefs and practices held by American Indians in North America, they seem to be less concerned with life in the hereafter than they are in a good life here and now. To know the spirits intimately, to enjoy the gifts of Mother Earth, and to have many children are for American Indians far more important than a future heaven. Happiness and success in this existence far outweigh the promise of bliss beyond the grave.

STUDY QUESTIONS

1. What have recent excavations in the valley of Mexico revealed?
2. Give a brief description of the history of the Mayans.
3. What is known about Mayan beliefs?
4. Describe some of the Mayan rituals, particularly those performed by the priests.
5. Give a brief description of the history of the Aztecs.
6. Describe the religious practices of the Aztecs.
7. Analyze the difficulties involved in the study of modern American Indians.
8. Discuss the belief in a "primary force" among American Indians.
9. What are the role and the function of the trickster?
10. Explain the American Indian belief in spirits.
11. Why are ceremonials so significant among American Indians?
12. Relate some of the more important creation myths.

13. State the rules that govern the conduct of members in an American Indian society.

14. Discuss the importance of the sacred pipe.

15. How are medicine, magic, and religion all combined?

16. Describe a vision quest.

Suggested Reading

Mayan Religion

Benson, Elizabeth P. *The Maya World.* New York: Crowell, 1977.

Thompson, John Eric Sidney. *Maya History and Religion.* Norman, Okla.: University of Oklahoma Press, 1972.

Aztec Religion

Caso, Alfonso. *The Aztecs: People of the Sun.* Norman, Okla.: University of Oklahoma Press, 1970.

Soustelle, Jacques. *The Daily Life of the Aztecs.* London: Weidenfeld & Nicolson, 1961.

Modern American Indians

Burland, Cottie Arthur. *North American Indian Mythology.* New York: Peter Bedrick Books, 1985.

Coffer, William E. *Spirits of the Sacred Mountain: Creation Stories of the American Indians.* New York: Van Nostrand Reinhold, 1978.

Donovan, Kathleen M. *Feminist Readings of Native American Literature: Coming to Voice.* Tucson: University of Arizona Press, 1998.

Gill, Sam D. *Native American Religions.* Belmont, Calif.: Wadsworth, 1982.

Hultkrantz, Ake. *Native Religions of North America.* Hagerstown, Md.: Torch Publishing, 1988.

Markman, Roberta, and Peter Markman. *The Flayed God: The Mesoamerican Mythological Tradition.* San Francisco: HarperSan-Francisco, 1992.

Paper, Jordan. *Offering Smoke, The Sacred Pipe and Native American Religion.* Moscow, Idaho: University of Idaho Press, 1988.

Radin, Paul. *The Trickster: A Study in American Indian Mythology.* New York: Schocken Books, 1972.

Sayer, John William. *Ghost Dancing the Law: The Wounded Knee Trials.* Cambridge: Harvard University Press, 1997.

Warrior, Robert Allen. *Tribal Secrets: Recovering American Indian Intellectual Traditions.* Minneapolis: University of Minnesota Press, 1994.

Notes

1. Adapted from F. La Flesche, *The Osage Tribe: The Rite of Vigil,* Thirty-ninth annual report of the Bureau of American Ethnology (Washington, D.C.: 1925), pp. 123–24.

2. Recounted in W. E. Coffer, *Spirits of the Sacred Mountain: Creation Stories of the American Indians* (New York: Van Nostrand Reinhold, 1978), p. 85.

19 Baha'i

The Baha'i faith originated in Iran in 1844 and is one of the more recent religions that seek converts throughout the world. Its appeal is due largely to its progressive features, particularly in the areas of reason, science, education, global community, and international languages and government. It denounces prejudices against race, sex, and religion. Its openness to the truth found in all religions, its vision of one world at peace under one government, and its teachings of disarmament have all contributed to its successful spread.

Although the Baha'is are not a large group, they are found throughout the world. The World Centre, the international headquarters of the faith, is situated in Haifa, Israel. Unlike in other religious organizations, Baha'i institutions are social rather than ecclesiastical. Their Spiritual Assemblies, both local and national, are responsible for upholding the teachings, conducting the meetings, stimulating active service, and promoting the welfare of the Baha'i cause.

The word *Baha'i* derives from the title by which the founder of the faith is known: Baha'u'llah, meaning "Glory of God." A Baha'i is one who accepts Baha'u'llah as Lord, knows his teachings, and obeys his precepts. A Baha'i's sole object in life is to love God—and to love God means to love everything and everybody, for all are of God. This love transcends sect, nation, class, and race.

THE ORIGIN AND DEVELOPMENT OF BAHA'I

Islamic Roots

Shi'ite Muslims, particularly in Iran, have always claimed that there are twelve legitimate descendants, or *imams,* of 'Ali, the son-in-law and successor of the Prophet Muhammad (see Chapter 15). The twelve *imams*

Baha'i

CE

1817 Birth of Baha'u'llah (d. 1892)

1819 Birth of The Bab (d. 1850)

1844 Birth of Abdul Baha (d. 1921)

1850 Execution of The Bab

1863 Baha'u'llah assumes leadership of group

1873 *Kitab-i-Aqdas* completed by Baha'u'llah

1892 Leadership of group assumed by Abdul Baha

1896 Birth of Shoghi Effendi (d. 1957)

1909 Remains of Baha'u'llah placed in the shrine on Mount Carmel in Haifa, Israel

are often referred to as *babs* (gates), because they are believed to function as the gates by which believers gain access to the true faith. Shi'ites have always believed that one day the twelfth *imam*, who disappeared in mysterious and unexplained circumstances during the ninth century, would reappear as the Messiah.

The Bab

In 1844, a Persian Shi'ite Muslim named 'Ali Muhammad (1819–1850) declared that he was the long-awaited twelfth *imam* and assumed the title of *bab*. Gathering around him a group of disciples, who called themselves Bab'is, The Bab launched a movement for religious and social reform. Within a short time, the movement had gained so much momentum that both religious and political forces in Iran took drastic counteraction. The Bab was publicly executed on July 9, 1850, and many of his followers were eliminated through either imprisonment or execution. Before The Bab died, however, he foretold the appearance of a leader greater than he to carry on the work of establishing a universal religion. Thus, his remaining disciples were sustained by the hope that all was not lost.

Baha'u'llah

Among the group of survivors was a man called Mirza Hussain Ali (1817–1892), the eldest son of the minister of state, who, by virtue of his family connections, was spared the fate of many of his companions. He had abandoned his family name and assumed the title *Baha'u'llah* (Glory of God).

In 1852, an event occurred that affected the future course of the movement. One of The Bab's followers attempted to assassinate the Iranian shah, an act that provoked further persecution against the Bab'is. Baha'u'llah was imprisoned and later exiled to Baghdad, then under the jurisdiction of the Turkish government. During that period, which lasted approximately ten years, a number of significant developments occurred.

First, Baha'u'llah made his place of residence in Baghdad a center of learning that attracted many students from near and far and the many Bab'is gradually formed a community in exile. Second, Baha'u'llah wrote several books, including *Hidden Words, Seven Valleys* and *The Book of Certitude,* aimed at encouraging and guiding his followers. Third, it was revealed to Baha'u'llah that he was the long-awaited leader predicted by The Bab. Fourth, when the authorities in Baghdad sought to suppress The Bab's movement, Baha'u'llah was ordered into even more distant exile—Istanbul.

While the caravan was being prepared for the long journey, Baha'u'llah and his dedicated followers encamped for twelve days (April 21–May 2, 1863) in the garden of Ridvan, just outside Baghdad. When all had assembled, Baha'u'llah made an unexpected announcement: the one whose coming had been foretold by their master, The Bab, was none other than he, Baha'u'llah. All those who recognized him as the Chosen of God, the Promised One of all the prophets, were to follow him. Except for a few who remained unconvinced, the company of Bab'is recognized him as the fulfillment of the prophecy and from that day called themselves Baha'is.

The caravan of displaced Baha'is paused in Istanbul for only a few months before being forced to move on to Adrianople, in European Turkey. During his four and a half years in Adrianople, Baha'u'llah resumed his teaching and gathered a large following. He wrote letters to numerous religious leaders, rulers, and kings, including the pope and the president of the United States. To all, he announced his mission and called on them to promote the unity of humankind and the establishment of the true, universal religion.

His energetic proselytizing, however, stimulated further opposition, which resulted in the banishment of Baha'u'llah and his followers to Acre, in Palestine, then a Turkish enclave to which criminals were exiled. A few years later the restrictions that had at first been imposed on the small religious colony were relaxed, and shortly afterward Baha'u'llah and his group moved to Bahji, on the slopes of Mount Carmel, in Israel. His mission, however, terminated with his death on May 29, 1892, at the age of seventy-five. Today, a shrine dedicated to his memory stands on Mount Carmel.

Abdul Baha

Baha'u'llah left a will in which he appointed his eldest son, Abbas Effendi (1844–1921), as his successor. In assuming leadership of the movement, Abbas Effendi changed his name to Abdul Baha ("Servant of Baha," or "Servant of Glory"). He had shared persecutions, exiles, and imprisonment with his father, and now as leader he carried on his father's program of writing. In 1908, when he was freed by the Turkish authorities, he undertook extensive teaching tours in Europe, the United States, and Canada. He preached and taught the faith of the

The Shrine of The Bab on Mount Carmel in Haifa, Israel. The site was selected by
Baha'u'llah before his death in 1892, and his remains were placed there in 1909.
Courtesy of Israel Government Tourist Office, Ministry of Tourism, Toronto.

Baha'i and established numerous Assemblies in various nations. On
his return to Palestine he wrote *The Divine Plan,* a work that invoked all
Baha'is to spread Baha'u'llah's message — the unification of humankind
through the medium of Baha'i — to the four corners of the world. He
died on November 28, 1921, at the age of seventy-seven, leaving a will
that directed his grandson, Shoghi Effendi (1896–1957), to assume leadership of the Baha'i faith.

Shoghi Effendi

Shoghi Effendi ("the Guardian") was the last in the direct line of succession from Baha'u'llah. He continued the work of establishing local and
national Assemblies in various parts of the world until his death on
November 2, 1957. Two important innovations were made under his
guidance: the structure that governs matters of administration and the
Universal House of Justice, which is the supreme legislative body governing the affairs of the Baha'i faith at the international level.

Pioneers

Today, there are neither paid missionaries nor professional clergy in
the Baha'i religion. All the work of teaching and spreading the faith
is done by volunteer teachers known as pioneers. Normally, application for membership is made to the local spiritual Assembly and is
open to all who accept the tenets of the Baha'i faith, recognize the
five stations of prophethood (The Bab, Baha'u'llah, Abdul Baha, Shoghi
Effendi, and the Universal House of Justice), and accept the Baha'i
scriptures (known as the Tablets of God) and the administrative order.
In matters of financial support, contributions are accepted only from

Baha'is and are wholly voluntary; personal solicitation is strictly forbidden.

The Baha'i faith has followers on every continent in the world. Much of the work demands sacrifices from individual believers, who leave their homes, their careers, and their comforts to spread the Baha'i faith.

SACRED WRITINGS

The written works of The Bab, Baha'u'llah, Abdul Baha, and Shoghi Effendi, which make up the sacred literature of the Baha'is, are considered to be inspired yet human, poetic yet practical. The writings of The Bab consist mainly of commentaries, expositions, exhortations, and prayers. Those of Baha'u'llah are more comprehensive in range and deal with every phase of human life: individual and social, material and spiritual. His work also includes interpretations of ancient and modern scriptures of other religions, as well as prophetic pronouncements, all written in either Persian or Arabic.

Book of the Covenant

One of the unique features of the Baha'i faith is the *Book of the Covenant,* in which Baha'u'llah provides, in clear and unambiguous terms, an authorized interpretation of what he is saying. In that book, Baha'u'llah vested full powers over the interpretation of his writings and over the direction of the Baha'i faith in his eldest son, Abdul Baha. In the same way, when Abdul Baha appointed his eldest grandson, Shoghi Effendi, as his successor, he stipulated in his will that Shoghi Effendi should be the sole interpreter of the writings and the guardian of the faith. Since Shoghi Effendi's death, no individual can claim special authority for interpreting the sacred writings of the Baha'i.

The Kitab-i-Aqdas and the Kitab-i-Iqan

Among the hundreds of writings of Baha'u'llah, two books are regarded as especially important by Baha'is: the Kitab-i-Aqdas (Most Holy Book) and the Kitab-i-Iqan (Book of Certitude). The former deals with Baha'i laws and institutions, and the latter consists of revelatory concepts. Baha'is consider both books to be no less divinely inspired than the sacred writings of other religions.

BAHA'I TEACHINGS

A global awareness animates the Baha'i faith. Like all other modern religious groups, Baha'i assimilates beliefs and practices from other previous faiths, Eastern and Western, extant and extinct. In addition, it adumbrates elements of modern science. The integration of religious and scientific ideas on a global scale has been its magnetic appeal to masses in the modern era.

God's Chosen Prophets

The basic teaching of the Baha'i faith can be summed up in nine words: the oneness of God and the unity of humanity. God is one, even though people call him by different names. In essence, God is unknowable, but he has made known his truth according to the requirements of an advancing civilization through his chosen prophets, or messengers, in nearly every era. The prophets are considered by the Baha'is to be "manifestations of God." Included in that group are Abraham, Moses, Zoroaster, Krishna, Buddha, Jesus, Muhammad, and Baha'u'llah. The religions that evolved out of the manifestations of God were the product of two factors: interpretations influenced by human limitations and varying degrees of revealed truth.

On the basis of those assumptions, Baha'is affirm that Baha'u'llah, for the first time in religious history, took the necessary step to ensure the unity of his followers for all time: he appointed his eldest son, Abdul Baha, as his successor and decreed that Abdul Baha was divinely authorized to interpret his teachings. In a thousand or more years, another manifestation of God may appear; but until then, the words of Baha'u'llah, Abdul Baha, and "the Guardian," Shoghi Effendi, along with the decisions of the Universal House of Justice, constitute the authorities to which all believers must turn. No Baha'i may found a sect based on any supposed divine revelation or particular interpretation. That teaching is expressed explicitly in the Kitab-i-Aqdas:

> Whoso layeth claim to a Revelation direct from God, ere the expiration of a full thousand years, such a man is assuredly a lying imposter. We pray God that He may graciously assist him to retract and repudiate such claim. Should he repent, God will, no doubt, forgive him. If, however, he persisteth in his error, God will, assuredly, send down one who will deal mercilessly with him. Terrible, indeed, is God in punishing! Whosoever interpreteth this verse otherwise than its obvious meaning is deprived of the Spirit of God and His mercy which encompasseth all created things. Fear God, and follow not your idle fancies.[1]

Baha'i Principles

Abdul Baha, as the authorized interpreter of the Baha'i faith, summarized its teachings in a set of principles. Twelve of the most important of those principles can be summarized as follows:

- *Humanity.* All the people of the world are created by God and are therefore members of one human family. Because God is just, kind, and merciful to all members of the human race, each individual should follow God's example in dealing with others.
- *Truth.* Truth is one and does not admit of multiple divisions. Each individual must seek the truth independently, forsaking imitations and traditions.
- *Religions.* The universal message of all religions is the same: peace and goodwill. It is in the interest of humanity that all religious systems dispel animosity, bigotry, and hatred and promote love, accord, and spiritual brotherhood.

Baha'i house of worship in Sydney, Australia. While each house of worship differs from the others in general design, they all have the unifying architectural feature of nine sides — nine being the largest single digit, symbolizing oneness and unity.
Courtesy of Baha'i Community of Canada.

- *Religion and science.* Humanity is endowed with intelligence and reason to test the validity of ideas. If religious beliefs and opinions fly in the face of scientific evidence, they are little more than superstitions and unfounded assumptions.
- *Sex.* Differences that distinguish one sex from the other are not peculiar to humans; those differences are common to all living things and do not favor one sex over the other. Therefore, the equality of men and women must be universally acknowledged.

- *Prejudice.* Prejudice destroys human well-being and happiness; therefore, humanity must actively work to abolish all forms of prejudice—religious, racial, class, and national.

- *Peace.* The establishment of a permanent and universal peace through world government will be achieved in this century (i.e., twentieth).

- *Education.* Because education is essential to humanity, there should be one universal standard of training and teaching. The universal curriculum should also establish a global code of ethics.

- *Economy.* Happiness, prosperity, and the stability of humanity depend on economic equality. Society, therefore, must adjust the balance of the global economy in favor of the majority instead of the few.

- *Human rights.* God's dominion is characterized by justice and equity without distinction or preference, so a uniform standard of human rights must be universally recognized and adopted.

- *Language.* One of the great factors in the unification of human beings is language. Therefore, a specially appointed committee should select an auxiliary language that will be universally adopted as a medium of international communication.

- *Work.* Any work performed in a spirit of service is considered to be an act of worship.

Day of Judgment

Aside from those fundamental teachings, Baha'is believe that the Day of Judgment is determined as much by events in the present as in the future. In that sense, every day is a Day of Judgment. Every individual is being tested or judged now by the advent of the revelation of God. In addition, each individual is called after death to account for his or her actions. By rejecting the oneness or unity of humankind, civilization is destroying itself—in itself the Day of Judgment. However, Baha'is affirm, on the basis of Baha'u'llah's sayings, that humanity and the physical earth will survive as a new, universal civilization eventually emerges.

After death, the soul continues to evolve into different states and conditions. The so-called spiritual body that a soul inhabits when the physical body dies is thought of as comprising the moral qualities and spiritual perceptions developed during one's lifetime. Heaven and hell are not places but conditions of the soul, which is in a continual and eternal state of evolution. When the soul is near God and his purposes, that is heaven. When the soul is distant from God, that is hell. In other words, according to the Baha'i faith, heaven represents a state of perfection, and hell of imperfection; heaven is the fulfillment of harmony with God's will and one's fellow beings, and hell is the absence of such harmony. The joys of heaven are spiritual, and the sorrows of hell consist of the absence of those joys. Baha'is reject any belief in the objective existence of the forces of evil. Just as darkness is simply the absence of light, so evil is explained as the absence of divine qualities at any particular level of existence.

BAHA'I OBSERVANCES

Worship

The Baha'i faith has no rituals, no professional priesthood, and no monastic orders. A respected individual in the community who is well educated in the Baha'i faith conducts the regular meetings for united worship. The meetings consist of prayers, selected readings from the writings of Baha'u'llah and Abdul Baha and the scriptures of the other world religions, and, occasionally, questions and answers. Mutual service and spiritual fellowship are the factors that bring adherents together for worship.

The basic unit of worship is the local spiritual Assembly. In every city, town, or district where there are nine or more adult Baha'is, a nine-member administrative body is elected annually, on April 21, to govern the affairs of the particular community. The second level of Baha'i administration is the national spiritual Assembly. That, too, is a nine-member body and is elected annually by delegates attending a national convention. The third and highest level of Baha'i administration is the Universal House of Justice, made up of nine members elected once every five years at a convention.

Baha'is meet in the homes of members or in other buildings—they do not have local houses of worship. They have constructed several magnificent temples around the world, however. All the temples are constructed according to Baha'u'llah's instructions. Each is located in a large garden adorned with fountains, trees, and flowers and is surrounded by a number of accessory buildings devoted to educational, charitable, and social purposes. All the temples are nine-sided, and all are covered with domes. The number nine is significant to Baha'is, because, as the largest single-digit numeral, it represents the universal unity that Baha'is seek.

Devotional Acts

Few obligations regulate the lives of the Baha'is. One duty is to pray. Numerous passages in the Kitab-i-Aqdas prescribe that duty. Here are a few selections:

> We have enjoined obligatory prayer upon you with nine rak'ahs (prostrations), to be offered at noon and in the morning and the evening unto God. He hath exempted from this [duty] those who are weak from illness or age, as a bounty from His presence. Save in the Prayer for the Dead, the practice of congregational prayer hath been annulled. God hath exempted women who are in their course from obligatory prayer and fasting. Let them, instead, after performance of their ablutions, give praise unto God, repeating ninety-five times between the noon of one

day and the next "Glorified be God, the Lord of Splendour and Beauty."[2]

Although the recitation (or chanting) of prayer is enjoined on every Baha'i, prayer is not confined to the use of prescribed forms, important as those are. Baha'is believe that one's whole life can be a prayer and that work devoted to the glory of God and the good of one's neighbor is also prayer.

Another obligation is to fast. The month of 'Ala (the nineteenth month in the Baha'i calendar) is appointed for fasting. During the entire nineteen days of the month, both food and drink are forbidden from sunrise to sunset. All Baha'is, except children, invalids, travelers, pregnant women, and the sick, are enjoined to keep the fast, as this passage from the Kitab-i-Aqdas indicates quite clearly:

> O people of the world! We have enjoined upon you fasting during a brief period, and at its close have designated for you Naw-Ruz (New Year) as a feast. The traveller, the ailing, those who are with child or giving suck, are not bound by the Fast; they have been exempted by God as a token of His grace.[3]

A third obligation relates to marriage. Monogamy is the rule, and a couple may marry only after the consent of their parents. In the matter of divorce, a couple is bound not only by Baha'i teaching, but also by the laws of the country of residence. According to Baha'i teaching, divorce is permitted after a year's separation and only if, during that period, the couple is not able to restore a harmonious relationship.

Finally, Baha'i parents are under a religious obligation to educate their children. The use of narcotics and intoxicants of any kind, except for medicinal purposes, is strictly prohibited.

Ceremonies and Festivals

Baha'i followers observe a number of festivals based primarily on important historical events and religious anniversaries. The following are some of the more important ceremonies.

The birth of The Bab is celebrated annually on October 20, the day The Bab was born in Shiraz, Iran, in 1819. Baha'is honor him as the forerunner of Baha'u'llah and the herald of a new era.

The Bab revealed his mission to his first disciple, Mulla Husayn, in 1844. The anniversary of that declaration is commemorated annually on May 23. It was The Bab who also inaugurated the Baha'i calendar, which dates from the year of his declaration (1844).

The anniversary of The Bab's martyrdom is commemorated on July 9 at noon, with readings and prayers from Baha'i scriptures. The Bab was martyred by a firing squad in the barracks square of Tabriz, Iran, at noon on July 9, 1850.

The birth of Baha'u'llah (Mirza Hussain Ali) is celebrated annually on November 12, to commemorate the day he was born in Teheran, Iran, in 1817.

The most important festival in the Baha'i faith is the Feast of Ridvan (known as the Lord of Feasts), which extends over a period of twelve days, from April 21 to May 2. It commemorates the period in 1863 during which Baha'u'llah declared his mission in the garden of Ridvan, just outside Baghdad. The first of Ridvan (April 21) is also the day on which every town, district, or village elects nine representatives to the local Assemblies.

The ascension of Baha'u'llah is commemorated on May 29, the day that Baha'u'llah died in 1892, in Akko, Palestine, where he had lived in exile. His burial place in Bahji, just outside Akko, is considered the holiest shrine of the Baha'i world. The Covenant of Baha'u'llah, in which he declared the appointment of his eldest son, Abdul Baha, as the authorized interpreter of his teachings, is celebrated annually on November 26.

The ascension of Abdul Baha (Abbas Effendi) is commemorated annually on November 28, the day he died in 1921 at the age of seventy-seven.

The Nineteen-Day Feast assumed a special importance after the death of Abdul Baha. It is observed on the first day of each of the nineteen Baha'i months.

The Feast of *Naw Ruz* (New Year) is celebrated on March 21 and immediately follows nineteen days of fasting. It is celebrated by picnics or festal gatherings at which music, the chanting of verses, and short addresses suitable to the occasion are contributed by those present.

An interesting item to note is that Baha'is date their calendar from 1844, the year in which The Bab announced his mission. The Baha'i New Year is astronomically fixed, commencing at the spring equinox, or about March 21. Moreover, the Baha'i calendar is solar and consists of nineteen months of nineteen days each, with the addition of "intercalary days" (four days in ordinary years and five days in leap years) between the last two months to achieve a total of 365 days.

STUDY QUESTIONS

1. Describe the Islamic roots of The Bab.

2. What are the significant events in the life of Baha'u'llah?

3. Did Baha'u'llah displace The Bab? Discuss.

4. What do we know about Abdul Baha?

5. Who was "the Guardian" and what did he achieve?

6. Describe the work performed by pioneers.

7. List the Baha'i writings that are considered to be inspired.

8. Analyze the Baha'i concept of "chosen prophets."

9. Discuss the twelve basic Baha'i principles.

10. How do Baha'i conceive the Day of Judgment?

11. Describe the Baha'i meetings of worship.

12. Give a brief description of the obligations that regulate the lives of Baha'is.

13. Describe some of the more important Baha'i festivals.

Suggested Reading

Badiee, Julie. *An Earthly Paradise: Baha'i Houses of Worship around the World.* Oxford: G. Ronald, 1992.

Baha'u'llah. *The Kitab-i-Aqdas. The Most Holy Book.* London: Baha'i Publishing House, 1993.

Esslemont, John E. *Baha'u'llah and the New Era.* Wilmette, Ill.: Baha'i Books, 1976.

Hatcher, William S. *The Baha'i Faith: The Emerging Global Religion.* San Francisco: Harper & Row, 1985.

Hofman, David. *Baha'u'llah, The Prince of Peace: A Portrait.* Oxford: G. Ronald, 1992.

Lee, A. A., ed. *Circle of Unity: Baha'i Approaches to Current Social Issues.* Los Angeles: Kalimat Press, 1984.

Martin, J. Douglas, and William S. Hatcher. *The Baha'i Faith: The Emerging Global Religion.* New York: Harper & Row, 1985.

Miller, William McElwee. *The Baha'i Faith: Its History and Teachings.* Pasadena, Calif.: Carey Library, 1974.

Smith, Peter. *The Babi and Baha'i Religions: From Messianic Shi'ism to a World Religion.* New York: Cambridge University Press, 1987.

Notes

1. Baha'u'llah, *The Kitab-i-Aqdas* (London: Baha'i Publishing Trust, 1993), p. 32.

2. Ibid., pp. 21–24.

3. Ibid., pp. 24–25.

20 Religions: A Comparison

We are witnessing the beginning of the end of the age of cultural and religious isolation. Previously isolated one from another by distance, culture, and language, we are becoming increasingly aware of each other's customs and ways of thinking. A constant stream of journals, books, films, documentaries, and conferences keeps us current on news and events from around the world. Similarly, the scientific and technological achievements of this century, as much as they have altered the pattern of everyday living, have had no effect more profound or far reaching than the development of global awareness.

That global awareness, fed by the development of extensive trade, economic interdependence, efficient transportation, and rapid means of communication, inevitably is creating a climate conducive to a full understanding of what is meant by human solidarity. The words of Socrates, "I am neither an Athenian nor a Greek, but a citizen of the world," are echoed today with increasing conviction by a growing number of enlightened citizens of a true world community.

The independent histories and religious traditions of nations and civilizations, past and present, are being forged into something new: an integrated world history. Consequently, ancient views and traditional beliefs are seriously being questioned. All over the world, many people are discarding the traditional answers proposed by religions to questions centered on the meaning of existence, because they feel that the answers no longer address the increasing complexities of modern society.

The scientific and technological achievements that have radically altered the patterns of human life also are affecting moral and religious values. We have been so successful in breaking the bonds of gravity — not merely yearning for the moon but grasping it — that we can look at the universe and our position in it from a new perspective. Progress in explaining natural cause and effect has modified the fear and awe of supernatural phenomena. Medical advances have allowed us to explain healing without reference to taboos and magical rites. Hence, religious beliefs are being questioned or actually discarded as inadequate and obsolete. In addition, people are examining their own, personal faith and comparing it with various religions as alternative ways of interpreting life.

At no time since the Greco-Roman period have ordinary people been more attracted to the fusion of religious ideas and practices from East and West than they are now. Evidence of a departure from traditional religious hegemonies can be seen from the sheer volume of literature relating to interreligious encounters; from the active participation in dialogue of both lay and clerical members of different and sometimes divergent religious faiths and persuasions; from the worldwide phenomenon of experimentation with alternative religions by people raised in traditional faiths confirmed and affirmed by a particular culture; and, most significantly, from the proliferation of modern religious groups.

Modern religious groups have been profoundly affected by the vaulting achievements of science and technology and their concomitant global integration. They have assimilated beliefs and practices from other faiths — Eastern and Western, extant and extinct. Never before have we witnessed the integration of religious ideas and practices on such a global scale.

Of course, all religious movements have appropriated elements from other cultures. Judaism, for instance, reflects the influences of ancient Mesopotamian, Egyptian, Canaanite, and Persian religions. Similarly, Christianity retains, in addition to Judaic characteristics, vestiges of ancient Greek, Roman, and native Mediterranean religions. Islam, Buddhism, and Jainism mirror their ancient and primordial roots. All those accretions are relatively ancient. The sixteenth century, the Age of Discovery, was a watershed of sorts between geographic isolation and the global village.

Before the sixteenth century, characteristics assimilated or incorporated by neophyte religious systems in particular could be attributed to the influence exerted by local or contiguous cultures. Geographic isolation confirmed, reinforced, and perpetuated the natural inclination of people to think of themselves as special.

The Age of Discovery did not change that way of thinking, but it initiated a process that worked gradually like yeast in a stodgy leaven of hardened misconceptions. In the last thirty years, there has been an unprecedented acceleration of that process: an explosive fermentation, as people rise from cultural isolation to global integration. One consequence has been the proliferation of modern religious movements that draw inspiration for their interpretations from many disparate religious, political, social, philosophical, psychological, and scientific systems.

A global awareness animates most, if not all, modern religious groups, which tend to be highly syncretistic. They have been able to reconcile, within the framework of their individual systems, modern scientific knowledge and ideas and practices from religions around the world. Their emergence since the nineteenth century has provoked the interest of sociologists, historians, and comparative historians of religion, among others.

UNITY OR DIVERSITY

The recent fusion of religious ideas and practices from around the world has contributed to the idea that the goals of all religions are similar and that they all have a common essence.[1] In other words, all religions are simply different paths to the same ultimate goal or destination. Is that assumption correct or unfounded?

It is often said that no matter when or how we developed, from the time we became human our irresistible urge to worship has created, and still creates, endless forms of religious behavior. Indeed, so powerful is that force within us that it has produced a mosaic of beliefs, attitudes, and practices. Yet there is a unity in that rich diversity.

Surrounded and often threatened by seldom understood forces, human beings have always sought to penetrate the mystery of life. Neither time nor place has changed religious needs: to bear the sorrows of life, we need strength; to face the daily battle for survival, we need protection; in the hour of conflict, we need assurance; in the hour of grief, we need comfort. To soothe the pangs of conscience, we need a faith; to face the dangers of life, we need a conviction; to break the grip of fear and loneliness, we need sustaining courage.

Finding a way to live peacefully in spite of forces that tend toward destructive conflict is only one aspect of the search. Another is the eternal quest for a purpose in our existence. Both are legitimate goals: to look for ways of avoiding or escaping dangers that threaten our life, on the one hand, and to look for inspiration or a profound motivation to justify our existence, on the other. Those two goals are inseparable and together represent the ultimate goal of all religions; they will remain so to the end of time.

Those who advocate that position maintain that all religions have identical goals and, therefore, are relative ways of reaching ultimate truth. As a result, all religious traditions are considered as simply different paths to the same ultimate goal or destination.[2]

That view seems to have been imported from the East. The Bengaliborn Brahmin, Gangadhar Chatterji (1836–1886), popularly known by his title, Sri Ramakrishna, set out to try all other religious ways of experiencing the Divine Mother. In a twelve-year period he practiced Shaktism, Jainism, Buddhism, Islam, and Christianity. He concluded that the diverse religions, including the several traditions of Hinduism, were different paths to the same spiritual goal.[3]

The subsequent establishment of Ramakrishna Mission centers in various parts of Europe and America and the influence of the philosopher-statesman Sarvepalli Radhakrishnan greatly contributed to that all-inclusive view of religion. An articulate spokesman of modern Hinduism, Radhakrishnan proclaimed that the essential truth of all religions is the same: "The different religious traditions are governed by the same spirit, and work for the redemption of both man and universe. Cosmic salvation is the aim of all religions. The different names we give to the Supreme apply to the one Supreme."[4]

Such assertions are, without doubt, worthy of consideration, but they leave unresolved a number of problematic issues. On what basis can one admit that the diverse religious traditions are simply different ways to the same ultimate destination? Is the end, or goal, of all religions similar? How correct or unfounded is the assertion that all religions are simply different paths to the same ultimate goal or destination?

Recently a number of scholars explored those questions and expressed their misgivings. For instance, Pujjiah Narada Maha Thera, chief priest of the Vajirarama Temple of Theravada Buddhism in Colombo, Sri Lanka, states: "[Buddhism] does not assert that all religions lead to the same goal, and that all faiths are different interpretations of one supreme Truth."[5] Similarly, R. C. Zaehner states: "The basic principles of Eastern and Western, which in practice means Indian and Semitic, thought are, I will not say irreconcilably opposed: they are simply not starting from the same premises."[6] And G. Rupp declares that "the frequently advanced if somewhat facile assertion that the various religious perspectives and correlative practices are simply different paths or ways to the same ultimate destination . . . is, I think, inadequate because it does not do justice to the situation of pluralism even within a single tradition. Hence a more accurate aphorism would be: each of the various religious traditions includes different approaches leading to different goals."[7]

The difficulty of the all-inclusive view is clearly evident. First, it is based on the supposition that different religions offer different answers to the same questions. Wilfrid Cantwell Smith argues that different religions offer different answers because they raise different questions.[8] Second, and more important, the all-inclusive view paves the way for compromising the fundamental and valuable differences among various religious traditions. The point that is argued is that different religions (and sectarian branches within them) satisfy different people for different reasons. And that is precisely why each religion is essentially a distinct religion: each religion emphasizes a different path and a different goal.[9] A few general remarks may be in order to illustrate significant differences in the ultimate goals and the paths that lead to those goals in the different religions.

COMPARISON OF PATHS

Obeying the Torah is the path of Judaism that leads to blessings in this life and a favorable portion in the world to come. *Believing* in the plan of redemption in Christ as provided by God is the path of Christianity that leads to salvation and eternal life. *Submitting* to the will of God is the path of Islam that leads to eternal pleasures in paradise.

A cursory comparison of those so-called "Western" religions indicates the immense gulf that separates them from each other. Not only does each religion have a distinctive ultimate path and a distinctive ultimate destination but also a distinctive conception of God and humanity. Let us analyze this.

The Torah means the "whole Torah," which consists of a dual divine revelation: the written part that was handed down at Mount Sinai and the oral part that was "preserved by the scriptural heroes, passed on by prophets in the obscure past, finally and most openly handed down to the rabbis who created the Palestinian and Babylonian Talmuds."[10] Rabbinic Judaism holds that just as rabbis on earth study and live by the Torah, so do God and the angels in heaven. As a matter of fact, God prays in the rabbinic mode, dons phylacteries, carries out his acts of compassion according to Judaic ethics, and governs the world according to the rules of the Torah.[11] One rabbinic exegesis of the creation story is that God was guided by the Torah in creating the world.[12] Hence, he who embodies the teachings of the Torah not only conforms to God's will but to God's way.

In that sense, humanity is divided into two groups: those who are bound to live by the Torah and those who are not bound by the Covenant. It is expected, therefore, of every pious Jew to discharge as many of the six hundred and thirteen commandments of the Torah as are applicable to that individual; for the non-Jew, the requirement is to at least conform to the "seven commandments ordained upon the sons of Noah."[13] Thus, the values that shape Judaism — in fact, its organizing principle of reality — is the divine covenant, the Torah.

To speak of the divine covenant brings up in Islam the question of living according to divine will, the will of God. In fact, the term *Islam* is closely associated with that cardinal idea. The Arabic term *salama,* from which *Islam* is derived, has two meanings: peace and submission. Therefore, those who through free choice submit themselves to God's will gain peace. The order and regularity of the world of nature indicate its subservience to God's will. But the difference between the regularity of the natural order and humanity is choice. A stone has no choice but to fall. A tree has no choice but to grow. Only a person can accept or refuse to submit to God's will. Moreover, a person's choice is conscious and active, whereas that of nature is passive or servile. Hence, humanity can be divided into two groups: those who have surrendered to God's will (i.e., Muslims) and those who have rejected conformity to the divine will (i.e., non-Muslims).

To speak of surrendering to divine will brings up in Christianity the issue of faith in God. "Faith is the assurance of things hoped for, the conviction of things not seen" (Hebrews 11:1). Faith is the assent to whatever God reveals as true, simply because God has revealed it. In other words, the act of faith is based on the absolute reliability of the revealing authority. The experience of "being a Christian" begins in the very commitment of faith. One believes, because God says so. It is by faith, then, that a person accepts God's revelation. The content of divine revelation can be seen in nature, in Christ, and in the Church that is the mystical Body of Christ. The Incarnation — that is, God becoming man by the union of a divine and a human nature in the person of Christ — is the mystery that lies at the heart of Christian faith. Christ is, therefore, in every sense God as well as man. That is the mystery of the Incarnation: the unity of a dual nature in one person, Christ.

Similarly, the Trinity is the mystery of the unity in three persons: God, Christ, and the Holy Spirit. Christ, the second person, is God's Son incarnate, while the Holy Spirit, the third person of the Trinity, is the Spirit of Love. One God, three persons. A mystery infinitely unfathomable to the human mind.

The Incarnation reveals the supreme love of God in the redemption of humankind. Because Adam, the first man, sinned, all humanity is tainted with what is known in Christianity as original sin. Adam's disobedience merited for the human race the miseries that accompany a fallen nature as well as eternal punishment. The human race was incapable of redeeming itself from that state; it needed a "new Adam." And there is where God's love to act on behalf of humanity is seen. In the dispensation of divine providence, Christ, the God-man, came to buy humanity back from sin and to restore it to its destiny. Faith in Christ, therefore, means faith in the plan of redemption in Christ as provided by God. Hence, humanity is divided into two groups: those who have accepted by faith God's salvation in Christ and those who have not.

As one can see, the differences among these three religions in their view of God, of humanity, and of the required path for the acquisition of happiness are striking. Moreover, the view of a triune God in Christianity is considered by Judaism and Islam to be highly offensive and scandalous.[14] Muslims usually interpret Christ's "sonship" in the physical sense and look on it with a feeling akin to horror.[15] Judaism, too, does not accept the divinity of Jesus as the "only begotten" son of God.

Again, the doctrine of original sin is absolutely repudiated in Islam. Hereditary depravity and "natural sinfulness" are emphatically denied. A Muslim cannot conceive how the Almighty Creator of the universe, the All-good, the All-wise, could create a world to be tainted by humanity's sin. Similarly, Judaism differs from Christianity on the doctrine of original sin. Judaism does not interpret the story of Adam and Eve as reflecting humanity's fall from grace. Unlike Christianity, Judaism makes no attempt to derive from the Garden of Eden allegory any lessons or rules about the nature of human beings.

COMPARISON OF GOALS

While Judaism, Christianity, and Islam do share a broad common heritage, there are some deep-rooted sensitive areas that need to be explored. Furthermore, there is the question of the ultimate goals. A "portion in the world to come," "salvation and eternal life," and "eternal pleasure in paradise," are the respective goals of Judaism, Christianity, and Islam. An extraordinary similarity seems to leap out at first glance. But, sooner or later, one realizes that the similarity is simply in terminology. Just as the words *God, Messiah, humanity,* and *sin* are common terms that denote different suppositions in different religious traditions, so also do the terms *salvation, eternal life,* and *world to come.*

Judaism has always been more concerned with this world than the next and has always concentrated its religious efforts toward building an ideal world for the living. One rabbinic conception is that had Israel not sinned (by disobeying the Torah), the end would have come at the time of the conquest of Palestine and "the sacred community would have lived in eternal peace under divine law."[16] Another view is that "the rule of the pagans depends upon the sin of Israel. If Israel would constitute a full and complete replication of 'Torah' . . . then pagan rule would come to an end."[17] "If all Israel," says another rabbinic theory, "would properly keep a single Sabbath, the Messianic age would be ushered in."[18] Thus, the Judaic notion of the "world to come" is inextricably bound up with the restoration of Israel to the land, the reconstruction of the Temple and of the holy city of Jerusalem, and the inauguration of the Messianic age that would end the rule of pagans over the "people of God" and restore peace and justice.

The Judaic anticipation of the future is quite different from Christianity's anticipation of "the last things" and the Islamic concept of the "Day of Judgment." For Christianity, Christ will come again triumphant at the end of the world as judge of all human beings and all angels. The second coming and the general judgment will manifest the mercy and the justice of God. In fact, Christ's second coming will be preceded by the universal preaching of the Gospel, the conversion of the Jews, the great apostasy with the coming of the anti-Christ, and cataclysmic events and extraordinary disturbances of nature (see Matthew 24:14; Romans 11:25, 2 Thessalonians 2:3–4; Matthew 24:29). Moreover, there will be a general resurrection of the dead, followed by the Last Judgment, which will determine the eternal destiny of each person in heaven or hell. Finally, the eternal "kingdom of God" will be established by the creation of a new heaven and a new earth.

In Islam, the so-called end of the world (al-akhirah), which will come suddenly and cataclysmically, is not the beginning of the establishment of the kingdom of God, but a Day of Judgment. Islam regards that realization of Judgment as taking place in this world. The final objective of Islam, therefore, is not extrinsic to this world but in it and of it. Paradise and hell are not "places and/or regimes beyond space-time but moral principles whose reality is so vividly grasped by the Islamic consciousness as to give them the appearance of a space-time beyond space-time."[19]

EAST-WEST COMPARISON

Our inquiry so far has been restricted to the Western religions. An attempt to compare the Eastern religions, either one with another or Eastern with Western, will yield the same result. For instance, a person's ultimate destination in Hinduism is the realization of the identity of Brahman-Atman, the One and the All. The highest bliss, says Hinduism, is the realization that the individual self (Atman) is the Universal Self (Brahman). The Ultimate—the One, Brahman—is all that exists, including human beings. There is no hierarchy of God, humans, and universe;

there is no Creator above and creatures below; no duality; only One. To attain the ultimate goal of bliss, Hinduism, unlike the Western religions, does not prescribe an exclusive path. Through the centuries, it developed numerous paths and various systems, all designed to capitalize on the nature, temperament, interests, and aptitudes of the individual. Hinduism, therefore, recommends different paths for different people. To speak of people, however, is to speak of human beings, and here there is a radical difference between Hinduism and the Western religions in the concept of the nature of human beings.

The doctrine of *karma-samsara* is one of the distinctive features of Hinduism. *Karma-samsara* operates like a law of nature. There is no judge to whom one must account for one's actions on earth. There is no judgment to be pronounced, as in Christianity or Islam, that justifies a person's eternal damnation or bliss. According to Hinduism, one's destiny is not determined by God, as in most Western religions, but by the eternal twin law of *karma-samsara*. Seen from a Hindu perspective, the theory of eternal retribution, so common in Judaism, Zoroastrianism, Christianity, and Islam, reveals not only a total disproportion between cause and effect but also an inconsistency with God's love for his created beings. One's life on earth, therefore, is not terminated by one existence but is an inevitable consequence of *karma-samsara*. As such, a person's suffering, pain, sickness, and all sorts of ill fortune are not regarded as originating from God or Satan, as in some Western religions, but as the result of one's evil *karma* in past existences. Hence, the eternal law of *karma-samsara* and the theory of Brahman-Atman certainly are foreign to Judaism, Zoroastrianism, Christianity, and Islam.

Similarly, various distinctive elements, related to the concept of God and human beings, can be pointed out not only between Buddhism and the Western religions but also between Buddhism and Hinduism. It is unnecessary to belabor the point, except to indicate, as an instance, the doctrine of *anatta* (no self), which, although it is a fundamental feature in Buddhism, is nevertheless diametrically opposed to the central concept of self (or soul) in Hinduism and in most of the Western religions. Hinduism affirms that the self *(atman)* is eternal, immortal (which Christianity and Islam also maintain), and moving from one perishable form to another (which Western religions do not maintain). Buddhism, however, flatly denies the idea of a self separate from the body, let alone the immortality of the self.

These few general remarks clearly illustrate an important factor: the profound differences in the paths and the ultimate goals in the various religious traditions. Captivated by the ideal of relativity of all religious traditions, many scholars either have glossed over the characteristic features that distinguish religions from each other or simply have emphasized the presence of common elements in all the various religious traditions. As we have seen, adopting the view that the diverse religious traditions are simply different ways to the same ultimate destination is highly problematic. In the first place, it is based on an unfounded supposition. In the second place, it paves the way for compromising the fundamental and valuable differences among various religious traditions. And in the third place, that view prohibits the exploration of deep-rooted differences and how those differences can be negotiated and resolved to meet the challenge of religious pluralism in an emerging world culture.

STUDY QUESTIONS

1. What are the advantages and disadvantages of global awareness?
2. Which of the modern religious groups tends to be highly syncretistic? Present your arguments in an academic fashion.
3. Discuss the aims and goals of world religions. Are they similar or different?
4. Does it matter which path a person chooses to arrive at the final purpose of life?
5. Is belief in a god or gods a necessary element of religion?
6. Does religion enlarge or compress our intellectual capacity?
7. It is commonly assumed that truth is one. What arguments are presented for and against that assumption?

Suggested Reading

Burch, G. B. *Alternative Goals in Religion*. Montreal: McGill-Queen's University Press, 1972.

Choquette, Diane. *New Religious Movements in the United States and Canada: A Critical Assessment and Annotated Bibliography*. Westport, Conn.: Greenwood Press, 1985.

Galanter, Marc. *Cults: Faith, Healing, and Coercion*. London and New York: Oxford University Press, 1989.

Neville, Robert C. *Behind the Masks of God: An Essay Toward Comparative Theology*. Albany, N.Y.: SUNY Press, 1991.

Reynolds, Frank E., and David Tracy (eds.). *Religion and Practical Reason: New Essays in the Comparative Philosophy of Religions*. Albany, N.Y.: SUNY Press, 1994.

Richardson, E. Allen. *East Comes West: Asian Religions and Cultures in North America*. New York: Pilgrim Press, 1985.

Saliba, John A. *Understanding New Religious Movements*. Grand Rapids, Mich.: W. B. Eerdmans, 1996.

Schuon, Frithjof. *The Transcendent Unity of Religions*, rev. ed. New York: Harper & Row, 1975.

Smart, Ninian, and B. Srinivasa Murthy (eds.). *East-West Encounters in Philosophy and Religion*. Long Beach, Calif.: Long Beach Publications, 1996.

Notes

1. The following discussion is condensed from S. A. Nigosian, "Dialoguing for Differences," *Al-Mushir* 21/1 (1979):4–10.

2. So considered, for instance, by F. Schuon, *The Transcendent Unity of Religions* (New York: Harper and Row, 1975).

3. Sri Ramakrishna, *The Gospel of Ramakrishna* (New York: The Vedanta Society, 1907); idem., *Teachings of Sri Ramakrishna* (Almora: Advaita Ashrama, 1934).

4. S. Radhakrishna, *Religion in a Changing World* (London: Allen and Unwin, 1967), p 129.

5. P. N. M. Thera, "Buddhism," in M. Jung, S. Nikilananda, and H. W. Schneider, eds., *Relations among Religions Today* (Leiden: E. J. Brill, 1963), p. 31.

6. R. C. Zaehner, *Foolishness to the Greeks: An Inaugural Lecture Delivered before the University of Oxford on 2 November 1953* (Oxford: Oxford University Press, 1953), p. 17. Cf. also R. C. Zaehner, *Concordant Discord: The Interdependence of Faiths* (Oxford: Oxford University Press, 1970), pp. 7–9, 19–24.

7. G. Rupp, "Religious Pluralism in the Context of an Emerging World Culture," *HTR* 2 (April 1974), p. 217.

8. W. C. Smith, "Some Similarities and Differences between Christianity and Islam: An Essay in Comparative Religion," in J. Kritzeck and R. Bayly, eds., *The World of Islam. Studies in Honour of Philip K. Hitti* (London: Macmillan, 1960), p. 49.

9. This point is also stressed in G. B. Burch, *Alternative Goals in Religion: Love, Freedom, Truth* (Montreal: McGill-Queen's University Press, 1972).

10. J. Neusner, *Between Time and Eternity: The Essentials of Judaism* (Belmont, Calif.: Dickenson, 1975), p. 36.

11. Ibid., p. 37.

12. Genesis Rabbah 1:1.

13. These seven commandments, which the ancient rabbis conceived as binding on all humanity, are to refrain from idolatry, incest and adultery, bloodshed, the profanation of God's name, injustice and lawlessness, robbery, and inhumane conduct.

14. On this, see for instance, A. Ali, "Islam and Christianity," in R. Eastman, ed., *The Ways of Religion* (San Francisco: Canfield Press, 1975), pp. 467–475; K. Cragg, *The Call of the Minaret* (New York: Oxford University Press, 1956), pp. 304–318; W. Herberg, "Judaism and Christianity: Their Unity and Difference," *The Journal of Bible and Religion* 21/2 (1953): 67–78; M. N. Kertzer, *What Is a Jew?* (New York: Macmillan, 1972), pp. 172–179.

15. Qur'an 19.91–94.

16. J. Neusner, *Between Time and Eternity*, p. 38.

17. Ibid., p. 38.

18. Ibid., p. 38.

19. I. R. al Faruqi, "Islam," in Wing-tsit Chan, et al., *The Great Asian Religions* (New York: Macmillan, 1969), p. 312.

Glossary

acolyte One who waits on a person; an attendant.

agni Fire, the household hearth, or ritual fire; written with uppercase A, it refers to the Vedic god of fire.

agnostic A person who believes that the existence of a God or of a spiritual world is unknown or unknowable.

ahimsa Indian term meaning noninjury or nonviolence.

ajiva One of the two eternal realities in Jain dualism, identified with matter, or lifeless things.

Allah Arabic term for God.

Amitabha The Buddha of Infinite Light, regarded as the incarnation of infinite compassion and the object of worship in the Buddhist Pure Land school. The Chinese term is *O-mi-to,* while the Japanese term is *Amida.*

anatta Buddhist term for no self, that is, no permanent ego or soul that makes a person.

anicca Impermanence, change, transformation; a characteristic of existence, according to Buddhists.

animism The belief that every object, like every human being, harbors an individual spirit or soul.

anthropomorphic Personifying; treating an animal or a thing as though it were human.

apocalyptic Pertaining to a supposed revelation or vision about events or things to come.

Apocrypha The "hidden" books; a collection of fourteen books, the authority of which is disputed for inclusion in the Christian Bible.

Aranyakas The Forest Books, which are Vedic speculations about sacrifice.

arhat The ideal person in Theravada Buddhism who has attained the goal of no-rebirth, or liberation.

ascetic One who lives a life of contemplation and rigorous self-denial for religious purposes.

asha-vant In Zoroastrianism, a truth follower.

ashrama One of the four stages of Hindu life: (1) student, (2) householder, (3) forest dweller, or (4) renouncer or wanderer.

Atash Zoroastrian word for fire.

atheist A person who disbelieves in the existence of God.

atman The individual self, soul, essence, or nature of a person. Written with uppercase A, it refers to the Hindu Supreme Self.

aum Expanded form of *om*, a mystic syllable.

avatar Hindu term for incarnation of a deity in human or animal form.

avidya Indian term for ignorance, especially about the self and the universe.

bab Arabic term meaning *gate* and, by implication, *forerunner.* The Baha'i use the title *The Bab* in reference to their founder, 'Ali Muhammad.

Bar Mitzvah Jewish religious ceremony for boys who are ready to assume religious duties.

Bat Mitzvah Jewish religious ceremony for girls who are ready to assume religious duties.

bhakti Devotion to a deity; in Hinduism, one of the paths to liberation *(bhakti-marga)*.

bodhi Knowledge, enlightenment.

bodhisattva The ideal person in Mahayana Buddhism who has attained enlightenment but who, moved by compassion to aid humanity, delays indefinitely the final step to *nirvana* or Buddhahood; such a person is regarded as a savior.

Brahman The nondual, self-existent, supreme soul; the Ultimate or Absolute Reality of Hinduism.

Brahmanas Supplements to the Vedas that describe ritual observances, sacrifices, and their mystical meanings.

brahmin The priestly caste, the highest ranked of the four Hindu castes.

Buddha A title meaning "Awakened One" or "Enlightened One." There have been past Buddhas and there will be others in the future; the historical figure Siddhartha Gautama is one of the Buddhas, though he is often referred to simply as Buddha.

butsudan A Buddhist shelf, altar, or shrine.

caliph Arabic term meaning successor; a title given to the successors of Muhammad.

canon Officially accredited group of writings accepted as scripture or of divine authority.

caste The stratification of Indian society into a hierarchy of distinct groups.

celibacy Unmarried or single state, marked by abstinence from sexual intercourse.

centaurs In Greek mythology, demonic spirits inhabiting bodies that were half-human and half-horse, representing the nature spirit of wood and wilderness.

Ch'an Chinese term meaning meditation; introduced by Bodhidharma in the sixth century, the Ch'an sect developed into a school that emphasizes meditation as a means of liberation. The Japanese equivalent is Zen.

chandala An outcast, or "untouchable," in Hindu society.

charismatic Gifted; possessed of divine powers or talents.

chiao Taoist term meaning relativity; everything that is relative to time and place.

chrismation Eastern Orthodox sacrament, involving the rite of applying consecrated oil or chrism.

chun-tzu The superior man; the ideal or noble man in Confucianism.

circumambulate To walk around in a circular fashion.

clan A social unit smaller than the tribe but larger than the family, usually claiming descent from a common ancestor.

clitoridectomy Incision of the clitoris; practiced among various African and Asian societies.

cosmogony A theory or account of the origin of the universe.

cosmology A theory or body of doctrines concerning the origin and structure of the natural order of the universe.

Covenant A contract or bond made between God and the Jewish people, pledging mutual rights and duties.

cult Religious worship, devotion, or homage to a deity, person, or thing.

daevas Demons, evil spirits, or malevolent gods.

dakhma The Zoroastrian Tower of Silence, where corpses are exposed to the sun and vultures.

dar-al-harb Arabic term meaning "zone of war."

dar-al-Islam Arabic term meaning "zone of Islam."

dar-as-sulh Arabic term meaning "zone of peace."

deva Vedic divine being; a god.

dharma In Hinduism, law; one's religious and social duty. In Buddhism, cosmic truth; the teaching of the religion concerning ultimate order of things.

dhikr (zikr) Arabic term meaning remembrance.

dhimmi Non-Muslims living under Islam and protected by it.

diaspora Greek term meaning dispersion throughout the world, applied to the Jewish people after the downfall of the kingdom of Judah.

divination The art of interpreting dreams, revealing future events, discovering the past, or obtaining any required information.

dreg-vant A Zoroastrian follower of evil or falsehood.

dualism The theory that recognizes two independent principles, such as good and evil, mind and matter.

dukkha Buddhist term for human suffering, dissatisfaction, anxiety, frustration, and misery.

episcopate Position or office of bishop.

eschatological Pertaining to the last things or final age.

eschatology Any system of doctrines concerning last, or final, matters such as death, the judgment, or future state.

esoteric Secret, private, select.

Eucharist Holy Communion; the Lord's Supper. One of the sacraments performed by all Christian churches.

exorcism The process of trying to cast out evil spirits thought to have possession of a person.

fetishism The belief in or worship of an object regarded, with a feeling of awe, as having mysterious powers residing in it.

flamen Roman priest assigned to a particular god and whose duty was to light the altar fires.

fu Taoist term meaning return or reversal; the invariable law of nature; the process by which all things are ordained to return to their original state.

gahambar Zoroastrian seasonal festivals or celebrations.

geisha A woman trained in the Japanese art of hospitality, entertainment, and friendship.

genius The guardian deity or ancestral spirit of a person or family.

ghee Melted or liquid butter that has been clarified.

gurdwara The name for a Sikh temple.

guru A Hindu or Sikh spiritual teacher or instructor.

Hadith The title given to the collection of Islamic traditions, especially the sayings and actions of the Prophet Muhammad.

Hajj Title given to a Muslim pilgrim who has traveled to Mecca, which every Muslim is obliged to do at least once in a lifetime.

halakah The guiding law of Jewish life; a collection of legal materials in the Midrash.

hamestagan In Zoroastrianism, an intermediate place between heaven and hell.

haoma A plant whose juice is used in Zoroastrian ritual. The Hindu equivalent is *soma*.

hara-kiri In Shinto, the act of honorable self-execution or ritual suicide by ripping open the abdomen with a knife.

haruspex Roman diviner consulted for important matters.

heresy Religious opinion contrary to established dogma.

hierophant In Greek mystery religions, a revealer of sacred mysteries and esoteric principles.

hijrah Arabic term meaning flight; (in Latin, *hegira*) the flight of Muhammad and his disciples from Mecca to Medina on September 24, 622.

honden Main altar, sanctuary, or hall in Shinto shrine.

hua Taoist term meaning transformation; an eternal or infinite process of change involving ceaseless mutations with no absolute end.

Iblis Distortion of the Greek word *diabolos;* Islamic term for devil or Satan.

ijma' Consensus of scholars reflecting their unanimous opinion.

imam The title for a religious leader in Islam who directly represents God on earth.

Injil Arabic term meaning gospel.

Jataka Pali term meaning "Birth Tales"; a collection of 550 stories about Buddha.

jati Hindu term meaning birth and used in reference to the caste system.

jen Virtue, compassion, human-heartedness, love; a cardinal virtue in Confucianism.

jihad Arabic term meaning "holy war."

jinn The rebellious angels in Islam; genies, evil spirits.

jiva One of the two eternal realities in Jain dualism, identified with soul, or living things.

jnana Knowledge; in Hinduism, one of the paths to liberation (*jnana-marga*).

Jok In Dinka belief, the invisible, superhuman forces in the world that transcend ordinary human ability and affect human lives for good or evil.

Ka'ba The rectangular or cube-like temple in Mecca; the center of Islamic pilgrimage.

kachina A masked dancer, one of the most important features of Pueblo ritual.

kami In Shinto, any being, object, or natural phenomenon believed to possess a mysterious power or spirit.

karma Action; moral law of cause and effect; in Hinduism, one of the paths to liberation (*karma-marga*).

koan The technical term in Ch'an or Zen Buddhism for a riddle, a phrase, or a word of nonsensical language that cannot be understood by reason or by intellect; it is used as an exercise for breaking the limitations of reason and thought.

kshatriya The second caste in Hindu society, which protects and promotes the material welfare of society.

kuei Malevolent spirits in early Chinese religion.

kusti The Zoroastrian sacred thread given at the time of initiation.

Lamaism A term or title used for some members of the Tibetan order of Buddhism.

li Proper conduct exemplified by the criterion of reciprocity; a code of behavior followed by Confucians.

lingam A representation of the erect penis among Hindus as the male creative force of the universe.

mandala Symbolic diagrams, charts, or circles, used especially as aids in mystical and magical rites by Buddhist esoteric sects.

mantra A magical formula based on the power of sound; used by Hindu and Buddhist esoteric sects.

Mara In Buddhism, the personification of evil who tempted Siddhartha.

marga Hindu term meaning way or path.

menorah A candelabrum used in Jewish worship. The nine-branched menorah is used during Hanukkah; the seven-branched one is used in synagogue services.

Midrash The Jewish collection of literary works containing scriptural expositions and interpretations of both legal and nonlegal matters.

moksha In Hinduism, release or liberation from the cycle of existence.

monasticism Organized asceticism as practiced by orders of monks and nuns.

monist A person who accepts the view that one single principle or reality exists.

monotheist A person who accepts the view that one God exists.

mosque The Muslim place or building of prayer.

mudra Ritual gestures of the hands and fingers used symbolically and magically, especially in Buddhist esoteric sects.

mystae Initiates, particularly in mystery religions.

Nhialic In Dinka belief, the unseen, powerful forces that affect human lives for good or evil.

nirvana Extinction; the state achieved by Buddhists, releasing the individual from the cycle of existence; the state of perfect bliss.

numen In Roman religion, a supernatural quality or presiding spirit (pl., *numina*).

occultism The art of manipulating or counteracting against malevolent spirits, forces, or powers.

Olorun The supreme deity ("Lord Owner of the Sky") in Yoruba religion.

on In Shinto, the obligation individuals have to their benefactors and the gratitude that expresses it.

oracle A person, a shrine, or an authoritative or wise answer.

orenda Algonquin high god or holy force that holds all things together.

orisha Divinities in Yoruba religion believed to control the relation between heaven and earth.

pantheist A person who believes that all laws, forces, and existing phenomena in the universe are the manifestations of God; one who believes that God is everything and everything is God.

Parsee (Parsi) Name given to followers of the Zoroastrian faith.

patriarch Father and ruler of family or tribe, especially Abraham, Isaac, and Jacob; title of bishop in early and Eastern churches.

polytheist A person who believes that numerous supernatural beings, usually endowed with anthropomorphic (humanlike) characteristics, govern various aspects of the natural world.

powwow Gathering of Native Americans to perform old ceremonies and participate in ancestral traditions.

proselyte A convert to some group, party, or religion.

prostration Lying flat on the ground at a shrine or before a person as a token of humility or submission.

puja In Hinduism, actions prescribed for the worship of a deity by offering food, flowers, music, lights, and adoration.

Purusha Hindu term meaning "cosmic Man."

Qur'an The name of the Islamic scripture.

rabbi A teacher or spiritual leader of a Jewish congregation.

rajah Indian term for a prince, chieftain, or tribal head.

Ramadan The ninth month of the Islamic calendar, during which Muslims fast to commemorate the revelation that came to Muhammad.

rasul'ullah Arabic term meaning messenger or prophet of God; title applied to Muhammad.

rishi Hindu term for a seer or holy sage.

sacerdos Roman priest who officiated at sacrificial rites.

sacrament A rite ordained or accepted by a Christian church through which divine grace is sought and conferred. The Eastern Orthodox and Roman Catholic churches administer seven sacraments: Baptism, Chrismation/Confirmation, Penance/Confession, Eucharist/Holy Communion, Matrimony, Holy Orders and Holy Unction/Euchelaion. Many Protestant groups consider only two sacraments: Baptism and Holy Communion.

sadhu A Hindu ascetic or holy man.

saisei-itchi In Shinto, the principle by which religious and political dimensions of life are integrated or essentially one.

sake Japanese alcoholic beverage made from rice.

samadhi The deepest state of trance or yoga self-possession.

samsara Rebirth; reincarnation; the cycle of successive existences.

samurai A member of the military class or leading family in Japan.

sangha The name given to the monastic order founded by Buddha; Buddhist community of monks and nuns.

sannyasin A Hindu renunciate and spiritual seeker (i.e., a homeless mendicant) who has entered on the fourth stage of life.

sati (suttee) Hindu practice of burning alive a widow on her husband's funeral pyre.

satori Enlightenment; in Buddhism, a technical term to describe a state of consciousness beyond the realm of differentiation.

seilenoi In Greek mythology, demonic spirits distinguished by the head, torso, and arms of a man atop the hindquarters (legs, tails, and testicles) of a horse. Roman counterpart: satyrs.

shahada The Muslim proclamation or recitation of witness: "There is no other god but God, and Muhammad is the Prophet of God."

shaikh A Sufi master who initiates novices into the practice of *dhikr*.

Shaitan Arabic term for Satan.

shakti Hindu term for active, creative feminine power extrapolated into a cosmic principle.

shari'ah Islamic divine law or regulations.

shekinah In Judaism, divine presence; the manifestation of God's presence.

Shema The Jewish prayer or proclamation of God's unity, based on Deuteronomy 6:4–9.

shen Beneficent spirits in early Chinese religion.

shu The Confucian virtue of reciprocity.

shruti The eternal, sacred knowledge of Hindus, revealed to the *rishis* and transmitted orally by *brahmins* from generation to generation.

skandhas In Buddhism, the five impermanent elements that form a person: body, feelings, perceptions, dispositions, and consciousness.

smriti The body of remembered sacred tradition in Hinduism as distinguished from *shruti*, or revelation.

sopherim Jewish scribes and expounders of Jewish laws.

spear-master A Dinka prayer leader, often with spear in hand, sometimes thrusting toward the sacrificial offering; the most important person in the Dinka tribe who presides over all affairs of life.

sudra The fourth caste in Hindu society, the only duty of which is to serve the three upper castes.

sudreh A sacred shirt worn by Zoroastrians from the time of their initiation.

sunna Arabic term meaning tradition. Written with uppercase S, it refers to Muslim law based, according to tradition, on the teachings and practices of Muhammad and observed by orthodox Muslims; it is supplementary to the Qur'an.

sunyata Emptiness; according to Buddhist theory, the true nature of all things.

sura Arabic term for chapter.

synagogue A building used by a Jewish congregation as a house of worship and religious instruction.

syncretism The blending or combining of differing religious traditions.

tablet In Chinese religion, a piece of wood, stone, or metal with an inscription, and used as a memorial wall panel.

taboo Originally, a Polynesian word used to designate something forbidden; one should avoid what is proscribed because of its dangerous or sacred character.

Tad Ekam Hindu term for That One; the First Principle, which is indescribable, uncharacterizable, and without qualities or attributes.

Talmud The collection of commentaries, traditions, and precedents that supplements Jewish scriptures.

tanha Selfish craving for sentient existence from which Buddhists seek release.

Tantrism (Tantricism) The belief in the search for spiritual power and ultimate release from the cycle of rebirth by the repetition of *mantras* and other esoteric rites.

Tao The metaphysical cosmic force behind all phenomena; a code of behavior (way or path of moral rightness).

Tathagata A title of the Buddha, translated as "he who has discovered the truth," used by the Buddha and later by his followers.

tat tvam asi A Hindu expression or formula that means "That art Thou." It refers to humans and the universe as being part of and one with the Absolute.

taurobolium Roman baptismal font in the form of a pit into which initiates of the Cybele mystery cult stood to undergo their initiatory rites.

te A general term for Confucian virtue, truth, or power.

theism A belief in the existence of God (or gods) and in a spiritual world.

theocracy Government or state in which God is considered to rule.

T'ien The ancient Chinese deity whose name meant the sky or heaven; in Confucianism, the Mandate of Heaven.

tiep In Dinka belief, an individual's ghost, shadow, or spirit.

Tirthankara In Jainism, the line of succession pre- and post-Mahavira.

Tripitaka The Triple Canon or Three Baskets, referring to the Pali canon of Buddha's discourses as accepted by the Theravada schools.

'ulama Divines; theologians; teachers of Islam.

umma A term applied to the Islamic community.

Uniate Designation for Eastern churches in communion with Rome but retaining certain distinctive Eastern Orthodox customs and institutions, such as baptism by immersion, marriage of clergy.

Upanishads A class of philosophical treaties (108 in number) attached to the Aranyakas portion of Hindu scriptures.

vaisya The third caste in Hindu society, the duty of which is to contribute to the economic well-being of society.

varna Hindu term for caste or social-class system.

Vedas The four works that constitute the Hindu scriptures: Atharva-Veda, Sama-Veda, Yajur-Veda, and the Rig-Veda. Attached to the Vedas are the Brahmanas and the Upanishads.

wakan The Sioux high god or holy force that holds all things together.

wu-wei Taoist term meaning nonaction; the natural course of things.

yang In Chinese religion, the male, bright, positive force in the universe.

yi Righteousness; a cardinal virtue of Confucianism.

yin In Chinese religion, the female, dark, negative force in the universe.

yoga A system of disciplinary exercises and meditation directed toward identification or union with Brahman.

yoni A representation of the vagina among Hindus as the female creative force of the universe.

Zamzam The name of the well next to the Ka'ba temple in Mecca, where Hagar and Ishmael are said to have stopped for water.

zazen Sitting in meditation; part of Ch'an or Zen Buddhist training.

Zen See Ch'an.

Index

Abdul Baha, 401–2, 403, 404, 407, 409
Abraham, 235, 237–38, 267, 312, 314, 328, 335, 337, 338, 404
Absolute Being, 33, 34, 138, 180
Absolute Reality
  Hinduism, 29, 32, 34, 44
  Buddhism, 89, 90
Adi Granth. *See* scriptures, Sikhism
ahimsa, 59, 60, 61
Ahmadiya. *See* groups, Islam
Ahriman, 223–24, 225, 227, 233
Ahura Mazda, 217, 218, 219, 220, 222–23, 224, 225, 227, 232, 233. *See also* God, Zoroastrianism
Amaterasu. *See* God, Shinto
Amritsar, 347
Analects. *See* scriptures, Confucianism
anatta, 82, 418
ancestors, 4, 15, 289
  African, 366–67, 368, 370, 371, 372, 373, 376
  American Indian, 378, 382
  Buddhism, 98
  Dinka, 363, 364
  Hinduism, 36, 37, 51, 52
  Judaism, 238, 250
  Mesopotamian, 182

  Shinto, 138, 139, 144, 146, 151, 155, 158, 159
  Taoism and Confucianism, 104, 108, 109–10, 111, 120, 129, 131, 133, 134
  Yoruba, 366
angels, 217, 223, 227, 245, 246, 253, 274, 304, 312, 314, 327, 329, 333, 334, 335, 337, 415, 417
Anglican. *See* groups, Christianity
anicca, 82, 85
Apocrypha, 299
Aranyaka. *See* scriptures, Hinduism
Articles of Faith, 333–35
Aryan, 20–21, 23, 29, 44, 55, 216
ascetic (asceticism)
  African, 372
  Buddhism, 70, 71, 72, 82, 98
  Christianity, 282, 284
  Greek, 197
  Hinduism, 20, 25, 26, 28, 30, 34
  Islam, 326
  Jainism, 59, 60, 61, 62, 64, 66, 67
  Judaism, 273
  Shinto, 154
  Sikhism, 344, 353
  Zoroastrianism, 225
Ashkenazim. *See* groups, in Judaism
ashrama, 25–26, 55

Ashur, 181
Asoka, 69, 74–75, 98
Atman, 32–34, 36, 37, 38, 41, 49,
        56, 417, 418
Aton, 167–70
Augustine, 5, 283
avatar, 29, 45
Avesta. *See* scriptures,
        Zoroastrianism
awareness, 7, 39, 70, 90

Bab, 400, 401, 402, 403, 408, 409
Baha'u'llah, 8, 400–401, 402, 403,
        404, 406, 407, 408, 409
Bhagavad-Gita. *See* scriptures,
        Hinduism
Bhakti Marga, 42–46
Bible. *See* scriptures
Bodhidharma, 90
bodhisattva, 91, 92, 97
Brahma, 44–46
Brahman, 32–34, 36, 37, 38, 40, 41,
        51, 56, 417, 418
Brahmana. *See* scriptures,
        Hinduism
Brahman-Atman. *See* God,
        Hinduism
brahmin. *See* priest, Hinduism
Buddha, 8, 45, 68–74, 79, 80, 86,
        88, 89, 94, 97, 101nn.1, 2,
        3, 146, 282, 404

Caliph, 315–18, 341
    Abu Bakr, 315, 326
    'Ali, 315, 317, 318, 325, 326, 340,
        341
    Mu'awiyah, 317, 318
    'Umar, 315, 317
    'Uthman, 317, 325, 327
caliphate
    'Abbasid, 318–19
    abolishment of, 322–23
    Mongol, 46, 319–20
    Mughal, 46, 320–22
    Ottoman, 320
    rival caliphates, 318
    Umayyad, 318
Canaanites, 237, 238, 240, 256

caste, 22, 23–24, 25, 28, 36, 37, 47,
        48, 49, 51, 52, 55, 59, 60,
        62, 68, 72, 349, 353
Ch'an (Zen). *See* groups,
        Buddhism
Christ. *See* Jesus Christ
Chuang Tzu, 112, 115–16, 118, 119,
        134
circumcision, 247, 262, 273, 340,
        372
clitoridectomy, 372
Code of Manu. *See* scriptures,
        Hinduism
comparison of religions, 411–21
Confucius, 8, 102, 104, 106, 111,
        112, 119–22, 123, 124, 125,
        127, 128–31, 134
consciousness, 3, 7, 27, 39, 42, 47,
        60, 64, 71, 81, 84, 293
Conservative Judaism. *See*
        groups, Judaism
Constantine, 213, 281
cosmic reality, 32, 52
covenant, 235, 239, 240, 261, 262,
        298, 415
    book of, 403, 409
cow, 50–51, 52, 54, 213, 229, 240
creed, 9, 120, 282
    Buddhism, 94–95
    Christianity, 284, 300–302
    Islam, 336
    Shinto, 144, 150
crusades, 288–89, 307, 319

Dalai Lama, 78
deity (deities). *See* God
demon (demoness)
    African, 356, 359, 367, 374
    American Indian, 382, 395
    Buddhism, 71
    Greek, 190, 193–94, 200
    Hinduism, 20, 25, 28, 54
    Jainism, 64
    Judaism, 242, 245, 246, 253
    Mesopotamian, 183,
    Taoism and Confucianism, 107,
        116
    Zoroastrianism, 218, 227

Dhammapada. *See* scripture, Buddhism
dharma, 21, 22, 72, 81, 94, 96, 98, 99
dialogue, 76, 80, 296–97, 412
Digambara. *See* groups, Jainism
divination
    American Indian, 382
    Hinduism, 49
    Mayan, 383
    Mesopotamian, 183–84
    Roman, 205
    Shinto, 142, 146, 152
    Taoism and Confucianism, 103, 108, 111, 118
doctrine. *See* teachings
dreams, 4, 68, 76, 108, 194, 218, 363, 374
dualism, 40, 64, 219, 220, 224, 225, 230, 233, 246
dukkha, 81–82, 84, 85

Eastern Orthodox. *See* groups, Christianity
ecumenism, 294
emancipation, 37, 39, 44, 56, 250, 297
emperor worship, 108–109, 139, 141, 147, 148, 149, 150, 151, 206–207, 214, 270
enlightenment, 43, 68, 71–72, 86, 94, 291–93, 307
Epics. *See* scriptures, Hinduism
Essene. *See* groups, Judaism
ethics, 3, 6, 7, 293
    African, 371,
    Baha'i, 406
    Buddhism, 87
    Greek, 192
    Hinduism, 28, 37, 39
    Jainism, 64
    Judaism, 242, 245, 253, 415
    Shinto, 138, 139, 140, 144, 146, 150, 152, 157
    Taoism and Confucianism, 102, 104, 120, 126, 131
    Zoroastrianism, 220, 227
exile, 242–43, 244, 250, 251, 252, 256, 257, 267, 289

festivals, 7
    Baha'i, 408–409
    Buddhism, 97–99
    Christianity, 303, 304–307
    Egyptian, 173
    Greek, 197–99
    Hinduism, 52–55
    Islam, 340–41
    Judaism, 240, 244, 265, 266–67, 275
    Mesopotamian, 184
    Roman, 204, 209, 210, 213–14
    Shinto, 138, 142, 146, 149, 159–160, 161
    Sikhism, 354
    Taoism and Confucianism, 131, 132–134
    Yoruba, 365–66
    Zoroastrianism, 232–33
Five Classics, 110–11
flood, 181–82
Frazer, James G., 4
Freud, Sigmund, 4

Gandhi, Indira, 25
Gandhi, Mahatma, 47, 48, 51, 56, 349
Gautama, Siddhartha. *See* Buddha
ghosts, 4, 110, 133, 301, 363, 386
Gilgamesh, 182, 185
gnosticism, 281–82
God (goddess, deity), 2, 4, 5, 6, 15
    African, 366–70, 371, 372, 376
    American Indian, 387–90, 391, 393, 394, 395
    Aztec, 384, 385, 386
    Baha'i, 399, 400, 401, 402, 404, 406, 407, 408
    Buddhism, 71, 76, 80–81, 85, 90
    Christianity, 270, 272, 273, 274, 275, 276–77, 278, 280, 289, 296, 298, 300, 301, 302, 304, 307, 414, 415, 416, 417
    Dinka, 363
    Egyptian, 164, 165–71, 172, 173, 174

God (goddess, deity) *(continued)*
  Greek, 187–89, 190, 191, 192,
     193, 194, 195, 196, 197,
     199, 200
  Hinduism, 20, 24, 25, 28, 29–30,
     31, 32–34, 36, 37, 38, 40,
     41, 42, 44, 45, 47, 49, 50,
     51, 52, 54, 418
  Islam, 310, 311, 312, 313, 315,
     322, 323, 326, 327, 328,
     329, 330, 332, 333–34, 335,
     336, 338, 339, 415
  Jainism, 59, 60, 64, 66
  Judaism, 235, 237, 238, 239, 240,
     242, 243, 244, 245, 246,
     247, 248, 252, 253, 258–60,
     261, 263, 264, 266, 267,
     415, 417
  Mayan, 382
  Mesopotamian, 178, 180–81,
     182, 183, 184, 185
  Roman, 203, 204, 205, 206, 207,
     208, 209, 210, 211, 212,
     213, 214, 247
  Shinto, 137, 138, 140, 141, 142,
     143, 145, 146, 148, 149,
     150, 151, 152, 153, 154,
     155, 156
  Sikhism, 344, 346, 350–52, 254
  Taoism and Confucianism, 102,
     106, 107, 108, 116, 131,
     132, 134
  Yoruba, 365
  Zoroastrianism, 212, 217, 218,
     219, 220, 222–23, 224, 225,
     227, 232, 233
groups
  American Indian, 378, 383, 384,
     386, 387, 388, 392, 393
  Buddhism, 86–92, 146, 154
  Christianity, 283–88, 290–91,
     302–307
  Hinduism, 37–42, 44–47, 49
  Islam, 325–27
  Jainism, 62
  Judaism, 248, 249, 250, 252–54,
     257, 261, 262, 264, 265,
     266, 267, 272

  Shinto, 148–57
  Sikhism, 352–53
  Taoism, 113–15
  Zoroastrianism, 232
gurdwara, 344, 345, 349, 350, 353,
    354
guru, 25, 344, 345, 346, 347–48,
    349, 350, 351, 352, 353,
    354, 355
Guru Granth Sahib. *See* scriptures,
    Sikhism

Hadith, 330–31
Hammurabi, 178–79
Hasidic. *See* groups, Judaism
heaven, 204, 205, 211, 282
  African, 366, 368, 369
  American Indian, 390, 391,
    396
  Aztec, 384
  Baha'i, 406
  Buddhism, 81, 88, 89
  Christianity, 273, 274, 275, 277,
    280, 301, 302, 417
  Egyptian, 165, 169, 170–71
  Hinduism, 25, 31, 32, 35, 42
  Islam, 327, 328, 333, 334, 341
  Judaism, 239, 245, 246, 253, 259,
    415
  Mayan, 382
  Mesopotamian, 184
  Roman, 210, 212
  Sikhism, 351
  Taoism and Confucianism, 106,
    107, 108, 110, 113, 116, 117,
    118, 120, 131, 132, 134
  Zoroastrianism, 220, 222, 223,
    224, 226, 227
heavenly masters, 113–14
hell
  Baha'i, 406
  Buddhism, 88, 89
  Christianity, 301, 417
  Egyptian, 170–71
  Hinduism, 35, 42
  Islam, 329, 334, 335, 341, 417
  Judaism, 253
  Roman, 212

Sikhism, 351
Zoroastrianism, 220, 222, 224, 226, 227
heroes, 58, 111, 138, 158, 182, 190, 193–94, 200, 221, 415
hijrah (hegira), 313
history, 1, 2, 4, 6, 7
    African, 356–62
    American Indian, 380, 386–87
    Aztec, 380, 384–86
    Baha'i, 399–403
    Buddhism, 74–79
    Christianity, 270–72, 281–98
    Confucianism, 104–106, 119–20, 122–27
    Egyptian, 163–64
    Greek, 186–87
    Hinduism, 20–22, 46–49
    Islam, 315–23
    Jainism, 58
    Judaism, 237–52
    Mayan, 380–83
    Mesopotamian, 177–79
    of religion, 1, 2, 4, 6, 7
    Roman, 202
    Shinto, 141–51
    Sikhism, 347–49
    Taoism, 104–106, 112–15
    Zoroastrianism, 216, 220–21
Holy Spirit, 42, 245, 275, 301, 303
holy war, 288, 339–40
Homer, 188–89, 190, 192, 199
Horus. See Isis

imam, 326, 336, 341
immortality, 200, 210, 212, 220, 227, 232, 270, 280, 418
incarnation, 301–302, 393, 415, 416
inquisition, 289, 307, 319
Ismaili. See groups, Islam
Isis, 165, 167, 170, 171, 173, 174, 199, 210–11, 214, 270

Jataka. See scriptures, Buddhism
Jesus Christ, 8, 47, 209, 210, 218, 270, 272–79, 280, 282, 298, 300, 301, 302, 303, 304,
305, 307, 312, 327, 328, 329, 333, 335, 404, 414, 416, 417
jihad. See holy war
Jnana Marga, 37–42, 43
Jordan, Louis Henry, 1
judgment
    Baha'i, 406–7, 409
    Christianity, 273, 292
    Hinduism, 35
    Islam, 330, 334–35
    Judaism, 242, 246
    Roman, 210, 212
    Sikhism, 352
    Taoism, 117
    Zoroastrianism, 35, 226, 227, 228

ka'ba, 312, 314, 337, 338, 339
Kabir, 46, 346
Kali, 30, 44, 47, 54
kami, 137–38, 139, 140, 141, 142, 143, 146, 147, 150, 152, 154, 155, 157, 159, 160, 161
karma, 23, 24, 25, 34–36, 37, 38, 43, 56, 60, 64, 65, 66, 418
Karma Marga, 37, 43
khalsa, 348, 349, 353, 354
Kharijii. See groups, Islam
koan, 90, 91
Krishna, 28, 29, 42, 45, 47, 52, 54, 404
K'ung-Fu-Tzu. See Confucius

Lalita Vistara. See scriptures, Buddhism
Lao Tzu, 8, 106, 112–13, 114, 115, 124, 134
Law, 7, 281, 408, 418
    Baha'i, 403
    Buddhism, 81, 85, 94
    Egyptian, 164, 167
    Hinduism, 21, 22, 24, 28, 35, 37, 48
    Islam, 311, 323, 325, 328, 330–32
    Jainism, 62

Law (continued)
  Judaism, 244, 254, 256, 257, 258,
      264, 278, 280, 417
  Mesopotamian, 180
  Roman, 204, 205
  Taoism and Confucianism, 108,
      118, 129, 130
  Zoroastrianism, 222, 224
liberation
  Buddhism, 72, 85, 86, 87, 88, 89
  Hinduism, 26, 28, 29, 36–46, 56
  Jainism, 60, 62, 65–66, 67
  Sikhism, 352
Luther, Martin, 290–91, 299, 304

Madhva, 40–42, 56
Madhyamika. See groups,
      Buddhism
magi, 218, 304
magic, 290, 412
  African, 359, 373–74, 376
  American Indian, 394, 397
  Aztec, 386
  Buddhism, 91, 94
  Egyptian, 170, 173, 175
  Greek, 192
  Hinduism, 20, 27, 39, 40, 49
  Judaism, 242, 253
  Mayan, 383
  Mesopotamian, 183
  Prehistoric, 12, 14–16
  Roman, 204, 205–206, 213, 214
  Shinto, 137, 142, 143, 156, 158
  Taoism and Confucianism, 108,
      116
  Zoroastrianism, 218
Mahabharata. See scriptures,
      Hinduism
Mahavira, 8, 58–61, 62, 63, 66, 67
Mahavastu. See scriptures,
      Buddhism
Mahayana. See groups,
      Buddhism
Mani, 282–83
mantra, 30, 39, 51, 54, 91
mara, 71
Marduk, 181, 184
Marx, Karl, 4, 293

Mary, the Virgin, 210, 273, 289,
      301, 304, 328, 329, 334
Mencius, 122, 128
Meng Tzu. See Mencius
messiah, 113, 228, 247, 248, 261,
      270, 272, 273, 277, 289,
      329, 334, 400, 416. See also
      savior
messianic (concept), 113, 114, 245,
      248, 251, 252, 253, 261,
      272, 417
Midrash, 257–58, 268
missionary, 46–47, 75, 92, 147, 151,
      153, 154, 280, 288, 291,
      297, 300, 358, 384, 402
moksha. See liberation
monastic (monasticism), 72, 86, 87,
      92–93, 100, 168, 272, 283,
      407
monk, 70, 72, 74, 76, 77, 78, 79, 84,
      86, 87, 88, 89, 92–93, 94,
      273, 284, 290, 353, 387
monotheism, 20, 24, 314
morals, 3, 6, 7, 411
  African, 367, 369–71, 376
  American Indian, 392–93
  Baha'i, 406
  Buddhism, 76, 98
  Greek, 190
  Hinduism, 20, 23, 28, 29, 36
  Islam, 313, 314, 328, 331, 417
  Jainism, 61, 62, 64, 66
  Judaism, 242, 257, 258, 260
  Shinto, 140, 144, 152
  Taoism and Confucianism, 118,
      119, 120, 123, 124, 125,
      129, 130, 131
  Zoroastrianism, 223, 225, 226
Moses, 8, 235, 238–40, 244, 256,
      257, 264, 267, 298, 312,
      328, 329, 335, 404
mosque, 7, 251, 327, 336, 337, 364
Muhammad, 8, 310, 311–15, 317,
      318, 322, 325, 326, 327,
      329, 330, 333, 335, 336,
      337, 338, 340, 341, 362,
      399, 404
Muharram, 340, 341

Müller, Friedrich Max, 1, 4
mystery religions, 188, 192,
        195–97, 200, 208, 209, 213,
        214, 270, 280
mystic (mystical, mysticism), 3
    American Indian, 391, 393
    Buddhism, 70, 91, 92
    Christianity, 415
    gnosticism, 281
    Hinduism, 20, 33, 39, 47
    Islam, 326–27
    Judaism, 252, 253
    Roman, 212
    Taoism and Confucianism, 111,
        112, 115, 124
myth (mythology, mythical) 4, 5,
        281, 292, 382
    African, 367–69
    American Indian, 390, 391–92,
        393, 396
    Aztec, 384
    definition of, 364
    Dinka, 364
    Egyptian, 171–72, 210
    Greek, 189–90, 192, 193, 195,
        196, 199, 208
    Hinduism, 28, 30, 50, 52, 53,
        211
    Mayan, 383
    Mesopotamian, 181–82
    Roman, 203, 208, 211
    Shinto, 146, 149, 151
    Yoruba, 365–66
    Zoroastrianism, 211, 218, 222

Nagarjuna, 88, 100
Nanak, 8, 46, 345–46, 347, 349, 350,
        352, 354, 355
new year
    Baha'i, 408, 409
    Hinduism, 53–54
    Judaism, 265
    Mesopotamian, 184, 185
    Roman, 204
    Shinto, 159
    Taoism and Confucianism, 131,
        133–34
    Zoroastrianism, 232–33

nirvana, 76, 80, 82, 83–86, 87, 88,
        91, 97, 98
numina, 203–204
nuns, 66, 73, 77, 79, 93–94, 96, 284,
        289
Nyaya system, 38

observances, 7, 18, 104, 110, 114
    African, 371–75
    American Indian, 393–96
    Aztec, 384, 385, 386
    Baha'i, 407–409
    Buddhism, 92–99
    Christianity, 303–307
    Egyptian, 172–74
    Hinduism, 20, 25, 26, 27, 32,
        49–55
    Islam, 340–341
    Jainism, 66
    Judaism, 262–67
    Mayan, 382–83
    Mesopotamian, 182–84
    Shinto, 158–60
    Sikhism, 353–54
    Taoism and Confucianism, 114,
        131–34
    Zoroastrianism, 228–32
occultism, 7
    African, 373–74
    Aztec, 386
    Buddhism, 91
    Dinka, 363
    Egyptian, 173–74
    Greek, 188
    Hinduism, 30, 49–50
    Islam, 327
    Judaism, 240, 242, 243, 252
    Mayan, 383
    Mesopotamian, 182, 183
    Shinto, 142, 143, 152, 154, 155,
        156
    Taoism and Confucianism, 106,
        114
oracles, 156, 184, 187, 188, 192,
        194–95, 200, 205, 208, 242,
        258
Oriental Orthodox. See groups,
        Christianity

Orthodox Judaism. *See* groups,
    Judaism
Osiris. *See* Isis

Patanjali, 39
patriarchates, 284
Paul, 279–80
persecution
    of American Indians, 386
    of Aztecs, 384, 386
    of Baha'i, 400–401
    of Buddhism, 76–78, 146, 148
    of Christianity, 147, 280, 281,
        284, 313–14
    of Confucianism, 123–26
    of heretics, 289, 318
    of Hinduism, 46, 321, 322
    of Judaism, 249, 253, 289–90,
        313–14
    of Manicheism, 282–83, 318–19
    of Mayans, 381
    of pagans, 313–14, 318, 339
    of Romans, 210–11, 212–13
    of Sikhism, 322, 344, 347–48,
        353
    of Taoism, 113
pharaoh, 163, 164, 165, 167, 170,
        172, 173, 174, 237, 238
Pharisee. *See* groups, Judaism
pilgrim (pilgrimage)
    Buddhism, 76, 96
    Hinduism, 50, 52, 56
    Islam, 314, 319, 324, 327, 336,
        337–39, 341, 342
    Sikhism, 346, 347
    Shinto, 152, 158
    Taoism and Confucianism, 110
Pillars of Islam, 336–39
Plato, 191–92, 197, 200, 208
pope, 147, 284, 288, 290, 303
    Leo I, 283
    Urban II, 288
powwow, 386–87
prehistoric
    artwork, 15–17
    bear skulls, 12–14
    civilization, 11
    corpses, 14–15

human skulls, 11–12, 14, 16
    religion, 11–18
    stone structures, 17–18
    tombs, 17–18
priest, priestess
    African, 371
    American Indian, 394
    Aztec, 384, 385, 386
    Baha'i, 407
    Buddhism, 78, 102, 414
    Christianity, 289, 290, 298, 303
    Dinka, 364
    Egyptian, 166, 168, 170, 172
    Greek, 194
    Hinduism, 23, 24, 26, 27, 30, 31,
        34, 52, 68, 70, 71, 72
    Islam, 331
    Jainism, 58, 59, 60
    Judaism, 244, 247, 256, 264.
        See also rabbi
    Mayan, 381, 382, 383, 396
    Mesopotamian, 184
    Roman, 204, 205, 208, 209, 213,
        214
    Shinto, 139, 143, 144, 145, 146,
        148, 149, 150, 153, 154,
        157, 158, 159
    Sikhism, 349
    Taoism and Confucianism, 112,
        114, 116
    Yoruba, 365
    Zoroastrianism, 217, 218, 219,
        222, 228, 229, 231, 232
prophet, 274, 282, 301, 328, 329,
        333, 401
    African, 371
    Baha'i, 402, 404, 409
    Islam, 310, 311, 312, 313, 315,
        317, 318, 322, 325, 326,
        330, 331, 335, 336, 338,
        339, 340, 341, 399
    Judaism, 242, 244, 246, 252, 256,
        257, 264, 267, 415
    Zoroastrianism, 218, 221
Protestant. *See* groups,
        Christianity
Puranas. *See* scriptures,
        Hinduism

Pure Land. *See* groups, Buddhism
Purva-Mimansa, 40
pyramid, 164, 170, 172–73, 175,
    380, 381, 384, 386

Qur'an. *See* scriptures, Islam

rabbi, 243, 244, 249, 252, 253, 257,
    264, 273, 415, 417
Radhakrishnan, 47, 49
Ramadan, 336–37, 341
Ramakrishna, 47, 55
Ramanuja, 40–42
Ramayana. *See* scriptures,
    Hinduism
reality, 7, 195, 292, 417
    Buddhism, 80, 81, 82, 89, 90
    Christianity, 276
    Hinduism, 27, 29, 30, 32, 33, 34,
        37, 38, 40, 41, 42, 44, 52
    Jainism, 58, 60, 64
    Shinto, 154,
    Taoism and Confucianism, 118
rebirth
    African, 365
    American Indian, 393
    Buddhism, 71, 76, 81, 83, 84, 85,
        87, 89, 91, 94
    Greek, 197
    Hinduism, 23, 26, 28, 29, 34–36,
        37, 38, 39, 40, 41, 42, 52,
        56, 418
    Jainism, 60, 65–66
    Sikhism, 352, 355
    Taoism, 113
Reconstructionist. *See* groups,
    Judaism
reformation, 290–91, 304, 307
Reform Judaism. *See* groups,
    Judaism
reincarnation. *See* rebirth
Religion
    approaches and goals of, 7–9
    comparison of, 1–2
    definitions of, 5–7
    etymology of, 5
    history of, 4, 7
    origin of, 4–5, 11

phenomenology of, 3
philosophy of, 3
psychology of, 3, 4
science of, 1
sociology of, 3
study of, 1–4
religious encounters, 46–47,
    143–48, 199, 207–13,
    244–49, 259–62
religious pluralism, 294–97
Remus, 202
resurrection, 7, 270, 274, 417
    of Attis, 209, 270
    of Christ, 209, 274–75, 279, 280,
        301, 302
    in Islam, 329, 334, 341
    in Judaism, 245, 246, 248
    of Marduk, 184
    of Osiris, 167, 173, 210, 270
    in Zoroastrianism, 226, 227,
        246
revelation, 3, 7, 47, 49, 70, 113, 114,
    153, 156, 217, 238, 245,
    252, 253, 260, 283, 293,
    300, 312–13, 327, 330, 335,
    344, 346, 352, 362, 404,
    406, 415
rishis. *See* seers
Roman Catholic. *See* groups,
    Christianity
Romulus, 202

Sacraments, 303–304
Sacred pipe, 393–94, 396
sacrifice, 6, 14, 281, 302, 312, 403
    African, 367, 371–72, 374
    Aztec, 385, 386
    Buddhism, 92
    Dinka, 363,
    Egyptian, 172, 173
    Greek, 197, 199
    Hinduism, 23, 27, 28, 30, 31, 32,
        33, 37, 47
    Islam, 339, 340
    Jainism, 58
    Judaism, 240, 242, 244
    Mayan, 382, 383
    Mesopotamian, 182, 183, 184

sacrifice *(continued)*
  Roman, 203, 205, 209, 212, 213, 214, 247
  Taoism and Confucianism, 107, 108, 109, 110, 111, 124, 125, 131, 132
  Yoruba, 365, 366
  Zoroastrianism, 218, 228
Sadducee. *See* groups, Judaism
sages, 28, 34, 69, 70, 115, 123, 131, 257
saints, 253, 283, 301, 303, 304, 327, 353
salvation, 85, 86, 89, 232, 276, 291, 301
samsara. *See* rebirth, Hinduism
sangha, 72–73, 74, 94
Sankara, 40–42
Sankhya system, 38
Sargon, 177, 178
satan, 223–24, 227, 245, 246, 274, 328, 335
sati (satee), 25
savior, 88, 226, 234, 270, 272, 280. *See also* messiah
scriptures
  Baha'i, 403
  Buddhism, 80
  Chinese, 110–11
  Christianity, 298–300, 335
  Confucianism, 121, 124, 127–28
  Hinduism, 20, 24, 27–28, 29, 33, 35, 36, 37, 38, 39, 40, 41, 42–44, 47, 51, 55
  Islam, 327–30, 346, 362
  Jainism, 60, 63–64, 66
  Judaism, 235, 244, 247, 254–58, 259, 260, 261, 264, 266, 267, 274, 278, 280, 329, 335, 414, 415, 417
  Shinto, 140–41, 146, 151, 152, 153, 154, 161
  Sikhism, 344, 347, 348, 349–50, 351, 352, 353, 354, 355
  Taoism, 112, 113, 115–16, 134
  Zoroastrianism, 221–22
Sectarian Shinto. *See* groups, Shinto

seers, 27, 31, 32, 51
Sephardim. *See* groups, Judaism
Shari'a, 311, 323, 331–32
Shi'ite. *See* groups, Islam
Shiva, 30, 44–45, 50, 52, 54
Shoghi Effendi, 402
shrine, 5, 7, 281, 356
  African, 372, 373
  Baha'i, 401, 409
  Buddhism, 76, 77, 94, 98
  Dinka, 364
  Egyptian, 172
  Greek, 187, 194, 200
  Hinduism, 50, 52
  Islam, 327, 337, 338, 341
  Jainism, 62
  Judaism, 240
  Roman, 206, 213
  Shinto, 142, 143, 145, 146, 147, 148, 149, 150, 152, 153, 155, 158, 159, 160, 161
  Taoism and Confucianism, 109, 132, 133
  Yoruba, 365
Shrine Shinto. *See* groups, Shinto
Shruti. *See* scriptures, Hinduism
sin, 170, 222, 228, 230, 246, 259, 266, 278–79, 280, 301, 302, 303, 307, 392, 416, 417
skandhas, 81, 84
slave (slavery), 237, 238, 313, 317, 358, 385
Smriti. *See* scriptures, Hinduism
Socrates, 191, 192
soul, 4, 282
  American Indian, 393
  Baha'i, 406
  Buddhism, 80, 81, 82
  Greek, 192
  Hinduism, 33, 34, 35, 36, 37, 42, 418
  Jainism, 60, 64, 65, 66
  Judaism, 253, 263
  Mayan, 382
  prehistoric, 17
  Roman, 212
  Sikhism, 352

Shinto, 152, 159
Taoism and Confucianism, 118, 130, 133
Yoruba, 365
Zoroastrianism, 220, 226, 227
Spencer, Herbert L., 4
spirits, 4, 282
    African, 362, 366, 367, 370, 371, 372, 373, 374, 375, 376
    American Indian, 387, 390, 391, 392, 393, 395, 396
    Buddhism, 94, 98
    Dinka, 363
    Egyptian, 172
    Greek, 192, 193
    Hinduism, 49, 52
    Judaism, 246, 259
    Mesopotamian, 183
    prehistoric, 17
    Roman, 204, 206
    Sikhism, 352, 354
    Shinto, 137, 138, 143, 146, 150, 153, 154, 156, 157
    Taoism and Confucianism, 102, 106–107, 108, 109, 110, 116, 131, 133
    Yoruba, 365, 366
    Zoroastrianism, 219, 224, 225
State Shinto. See groups, Shinto
Stonehenge, 18
Sufi. See groups, Islam
Sunni. See groups, Islam
Svetambara. See groups, Jainism
synagogue, 243, 254, 261, 262, 264, 265, 266, 267, 274, 289

Talmud, 257–58, 268
tanha, 81, 82, 84, 85, 89
tantrism
    Buddhism, 77, 88, 91–92, 100
    Hinduism, 39–40
tao, 6, 104, 112, 114, 115, 116–17, 118, 119, 131
Tao Te Ching. See scriptures, Taoism
teachings, 6
    African, 366–71

American Indian, 387–92
    Aztec, 384–86
    Baha'i, 403–407
    Buddhism, 80–86, 417–19
    Christianity, 275–80, 300–303, 414–19
    Confucianism, 128–31
    Dinka, 363–64
    Egyptian, 164–71
    Greek, 190–92
    Hinduism, 29–46, 417–19
    Islam, 333–35, 414–19
    Jainism, 64–66
    Judaism, 258–61, 414–19
    Manicheism, 382–83
    Mayan, 380–83
    Sikhism, 350–52
    Shinto, 137–40, 145, 149, 150, 151
    Taoism, 116–19
    Yoruba, 365–66
    Zoroastrianism, 218–20, 222–28
temple, 5, 7, 281, 364, 380
    Aztec, 384, 386
    Buddhism, 75, 76, 77, 78, 79, 90, 94, 98, 145, 146, 148, 158, 414
    Egyptian, 168, 172–73, 237
    Greek, 188, 196, 197
    Hinduism, 20, 23, 30, 42, 46, 50, 51
    Jainism, 62, 66
    Judaism, 240, 243–44, 247, 248, 250, 251, 266, 272, 273, 417
    Mayan, 381, 382
    Mesopotamian, 180, 182, 184
    Roman, 204, 205, 206, 208, 209, 210, 211
    Sikhism, 344, 349, 350
    Taoism and Confucianism, 102, 109, 112, 120, 123, 124, 131, 132, 133
    Zoroastrianism, 228
Theravada. See groups, Buddhism
Tibetan Buddhism, 78, 80, 86, 91, 92
T'ien-t'ai (Tendai). See groups, Buddhism

Tirthankara, 58, 62, 66
Torah. *See* scriptures, Judaism
trickster, 390, 396
trimurti, 44–46
trinity, 301, 333, 334, 416
Tripitaka. *See* scriptures,
        Buddhism
truth, 3, 7, 192, 283, 288, 292, 296,
        326, 344, 399, 404, 413,
        414, 419
    Buddhism, 70, 71, 72, 81–82, 84,
        85, 88, 89, 92, 99, 100
    Egyptian, 166, 170, 171
    Hinduism, 20, 30–31, 32, 34, 37,
        40, 48
    Jainism, 61
    Roman, 211
    Sikhism, 346, 352
    Taoism and Confucianism, 118
    Zoroastrianism, 217, 219, 220,
        224, 225
Tylor, Edward B., 4

umma, 311, 315, 320, 331, 359
Uniate. *See* groups, Christianity
Universal House of Justice, 402,
        404, 407
Upanishads. *See* scriptures,
        Hinduism

Vaisheshika system, 38
varna. *See* caste
Vedanta, 27, 40–42
Vedas. *See* scriptures, Hinduism
Vishnu, 29, 42, 44–45, 52, 54
vision quest, 395–96, 397

Vivekananda, 47, 55

women, 293
    in African, 368, 371
    in American Indian, 386
    in Aztec, 384, 385
    in Baha'i, 405, 407, 408
    in Buddhism, 73, 93–94, 100
    in Christianity, 297–98, 307
    in Egyptian, 171, 173
    in Greek, 194, 196, 197, 199
    in Hinduism, 24–25, 28, 44, 48,
        50, 55
    in Islam, 323–25
    in Jainism, 61, 62
    in Judaism, 254, 259, 262,
        264–65, 268
    in Mesopotamian, 183
    in Roman, 213, 214
    in Shinto, 157
    in Sikhism, 346, 347, 353
    in Taoism and Confucianism,
        126, 127, 131, 134

yin-yang, 107
yoga, 38–40, 51, 56, 58, 70, 91
Yoga Sutras. *See* scriptures,
        Hinduism

Zarathustra. *See* Zoroaster
Zealots. *See* groups, Judaism
Zen, 88, 89–91, 100, 146
ziggurat, 184, 185
Zionism, 250, 261. *See also* groups,
        Judaism
Zoroaster, 8, 216–20, 282, 404